SPURS

ABOUT THE AUTHOR

Born in North London, Graham Betts attended his first game at White Hart Lane in 1965 and has seldom been absent since, family commitments notwithstanding. Aside from a number of football books he has also written extensively on music, an industry he has worked in for the last twenty or so years. He lives in Aston Clinton in Buckinghamshire with his wife and two children.

SPURS

DAY-TO-DAY LIFE AT WHITE HART LANE

GRAHAM BETTS

MAINSTREAM
PUBLISHING
EDINBURGH AND LONDON

First published in Great Britain in 1998 by
MAINSTREAM PUBLISHING COMPANY (EDINBURGH) LTD
7 Albany Street
Edinburgh EH1 3UG

ISBN 1 84018 040 4

A catalogue record for this book is available from the British Library

Typeset in Times
Printed and bound in Great Britain by Butler and Tanner Ltd, Frome

Spurs are one of the most famous names in the world of club football, with a string of honours and achievements to match their reputation – the first British club to win a major European trophy, the only non-League side to have won the FA Cup since the formation of the Football League, the first side this century to have won the double; the list is almost endless.

Of course, it is usual in history books to start at the beginning and finish at the end, but this is much more than a history book, for in many instances it allows the reader to follow on a day-to-day basis some of the more intriguing stories of the club's history; their resignation from the Southern League and eventual acceptance in the Football League, the stories behind the double of 1960-61, brief biographies of key players and characters who have passed through the doors of White Hart Lane, and much, much more.

This is a book that can be delved into at almost any date and find facts and feats, trials and tribulations and other items of trivia along the way. No doubt the next hundred years or so will be as interesting and as varied as the previous century at White Hart Lane.

I am indebted to a number of people who have helped out, in one way or another, along the way. I would therefore like to thank Barry and Dyl Charles, Brian Watts, Keith Greenhalf, Fred Dowry, Mark Hammond, Julie and Martin Willis, John Goodman, John Betambeau and especially Bob Goodwin, who has written many excellent books about our club and has a rare, very rare talent for bringing that history to life. Also to Richard Lerman who, despite his allegiance to a side from another part of North London, believed in the project right from the start and offered encouragement throughout. Special thanks also to Bill Campbell and his team at Mainstream.

I would also like to thank my family, Caroline, Jo and Steven, who will now be able to get around the house without having to step over assorted books and programmes.

The photographs in this book have been supplied by Wellard Huxley Promotions, Bob Bond and John Allen (proprietor of *The Football Card Collector* magazine).

JANUARY 1ST

1898	Rushden	A	United League	2-5
1910	Blackburn Rovers	A	First Division	0-2
1913	Everton	A	First Division	2-1
1914	Bolton Wanderers	A	First Division	0-3
1915	Everton	A	First Division	1-1
1916	Fulham	A	London Combination [1st competition]	2-0
1921	Bolton Wanderers	A	First Division	0-1
1923	Everton	A	First Division	1-3
1924	Manchester City	A	First Division	0-1
1925	Bury	A	First Division	2-5
1929	Middlesbrough	A	Second Division	0-3
1934	Blackburn Rovers	A	First Division	0-1
1935	Blackburn Rovers	A	First Division	0-2
1938	Coventry City	A	Second Division	1-2
1944	West Ham United	H	Football League South	1-0
1949	Lincoln City	H	Second Division	1-2
1955	Sunderland	A	First Division	1-1
1966	Everton	H	First Division	2-2
1972	Crystal Palace	A	First Division	1-1
1974	Leeds United	A	First Division	1-1
1977	West Ham United	H	First Division	2-1
1983	West Ham United	A	First Division	0-3
1985	Arsenal	A	First Division	2-1

At the turn of the New Year both North London clubs harboured hopes they might be able to lift the League title, with Spurs going into the game as League leaders, closely followed by a chasing pack that included Everton, Liverpool, Manchester United and Arsenal. It was Spurs' away form that had enabled them to mount a serious challenge, and goals from Mark Falco and Garth Crooks ensured they came away from Highbury with all the points. Indeed, they were not to lose another away game all season in the League, but wretched home form, coupled with Everton's blistering finish, snatched the title away from White Hart Lane.

1986	Arsenal	A	First Division	0-0

Although there were no goals during the game, the main talking point was to be Graham Roberts's challenge on Charlie Nicholas; Nicholas literally ended up in the crowd although he was not seriously hurt.

1987	Charlton Athletic	A	First Division	2-0
1988	Watford	H	First Division	2-1
1990	Coventry City	A	First Division	0-0
1991	Manchester United	H	First Division	1-2

Paul Gascoigne was sent off for the third time in his career. More importantly, he became the first player to be dismissed during a live televised League match.

1992	Coventry City	A	First Division	2-1
1994	Coventry City	H	FA Premier League	1-2
1996	Manchester United	H	FA Premier League	4-1

Misfortune hit the League leaders United before the start, with Peter Schmeichel injuring himself during the warm-up. As such he was little more than a passenger during the first half; on a another day and fully fit he might have got to either of the goals that he conceded. But Spurs had begun in lively fashion, hitting the post and the bar before finally scoring. Although Cole equalised almost immediately, Spurs were not to be denied. United took Schmeichel off at half-time, but his replacement could do little to stop a further two goals in the second half. It was the first time United had conceded as many as four goals since the Premiership was established.

JANUARY 2ND

1886	St Martin's	H	Friendly	3-0
1892	Uxbridge	H	Friendly	3-0
1899	Chatham	A	Thames & Medway League	0-5
1904	Fulham	H	Southern League	1-0
1905	Fulham	H	Western League	0-5
1909	Leeds City	H	Second Division	3-0
1915	Chelsea	A	First Division	1-1
1926	Arsenal	H	First Division	1-1

1928	Arsenal	A	First Division	1-1
1932	Wolverhampton Wanderers	H	Second Division	3-3
1937	Norwich City	A	Second Division	3-2
1943	Southampton	A	Football League South	1-2
1954	Middlesbrough	A	First Division	0-3
1960	Birmingham City	A	First Division	1-0
1965	Birmingham City	A	First Division	0-1
1971	Sheffield Wednesday	H	FA Cup 3rd Round	4-1
1978	Sheffield United	A	Second Division	2-2
1982	Arsenal	H	FA Cup 3rd Round	1-0

This was only the second time Spurs and Arsenal had been paired in the FA Cup, a remarkable run considering both clubs were almost 100 years old! Spurs, the FA Cup holders, won with one of the softest goals of Garth Crooks's career; a miss-hit shot rolled along the ground and appeared to be easy meat for Arsenal's ex-Spurs goalkeeper Pat Jennings. Unfortunately, he dived right over the ball and it ended up in the net. Jennings said after the match that the shot had been so weak he could have thrown his cap at it and saved it! The day was disaster all round for Jennings, for later in the game he tore a muscle and was carried off the field on a stretcher.

1984	Watford	H	First Division	2-3
1988	Chelsea	A	First Division	0-0
1989	Arsenal	A	First Division	0-2
1993	Marlow	A	FA Cup 3rd Round	5-1

Although Marlow's name was drawn out of the hat first it was agreed to switch the tie to White Hart Lane. Although this reduced Marlow's chances of causing an upset, they did get a healthy slice of the receipts produced by a crowd of 26,636 in compensation.

| 1995 | Arsenal | H | FA Premier League | 1-0 |

JANUARY 3RD

| 1885 | Hadley | A | Friendly | Score unknown |

Until Spurs joined the Southern Alliance in 1892 and then the Southern League in 1896, their fixtures were almost entirely friendlies, apart from the various cup competitions. Whilst the results of these cup competitions are relatively easy to trace with one or two exceptions, those from their friendly matches are somewhat more elusive. It has to be remembered that in their early days Spurs, in keeping with just about every other club, were little more than a Saturday afternoon/Sunday morning side, little realising that historians would be interested in their activities and scores in the years to come. Therefore, there are quite a few matches for which the final scores are unknown.

1903	Wellingborough	A	Southern League	2-0
1911	Manchester City	A	First Division	1-2
1914	Derby County	A	First Division	0-4
1920	Stockport County	A	Second Division	2-1
1925	Notts County	H	First Division	1-1
1931	Wolverhampton Wanderers	H	Second Division	1-0
1942	Queens Park Rangers	A	London War League	0-1
1948	Sheffield Wednesday	A	Second Division	0-1
1953	Newcastle United	H	First Division	3-2

On the same day Peter Taylor was born in Rochford in Essex. Although Peter was turned down by Spurs as a youngster he soon got fixed up with Southend and after two years was snapped up by Crystal Palace in October 1973. Whilst at Palace he developed into a winger of true potential, so much so that he became one of the few players to have been capped by England whilst playing in the Third Division. As such it was not long before bigger clubs starting enquiring about his availability, and in September 1976 a fee of £400,000 brought him to White Hart Lane. Unfortunately his career at Spurs did not really take off, for although he was a regular in the side during his first season, the arrival of Ricky Villa and then a series of injuries limited his opportunities. In November 1980 he was sold to Orient for £150,000 and subsequently drifted into the non-League game. He is currently part of Glenn Hoddle's backroom staff for England.

1970	Bradford City	A	FA Cup 3rd Round	2-2
1976	Stoke City	H	FA Cup 3rd Round	1-1
1981	Queens Park Rangers	A	FA Cup 3rd Round	0-0

Ever since the season had started there had been the belief that this might be Spurs' year in one or the other of the three competitions open to them. Whilst their League form had been inconsistent and their League Cup had come to an end the previous month at West Ham, the FA Cup had always been a competition Spurs excelled in. The run towards Wembley started at the home of Queens Park Rangers, then in the Second Division, but who acquitted themselves well against their opponents from the higher division. A goalless draw might not have been an auspicious start, but remaining in the cup was paramount.

| 1983 | Everton | H | First Division | 2-1 |
| 1994 | Sheffield Wednesday | A | FA Premier League | 0-1 |

JANUARY 4TH

1890	Foxes	H	Friendly	1-1
1896	Reading	H	Friendly	2-1
1902	Reading	H	Southern League	4-2
1908	West Ham United	H	Southern League	3-2
1913	Blackburn Rovers	H	First Division	0-1
1919	Brentford	H	London Combination	1-1
1930	Barnsley	A	Second Division	0-2
1936	Newcastle United	A	Second Division	4-1
1941	Clapton Orient	H	London War Cup Section B	3-0
1947	West Bromwich Albion	H	Second Division	2-0
1958	Leicester City	H	FA Cup 3rd Round	4-0

For the second consecutive season Spurs met Leicester City in the FA Cup 3rd round. Following last year's 2-0 victory, Spurs won this tie 4-0 thanks to goals from Terry Medwin, Bobby Smith (2) and Alfie Stokes. Three years later Spurs met Leicester in the FA Cup again, although this battle was at Wembley in the final and with Spurs on the brink of lifting the double.

1962 Peter Southey born in Parsons Green. Although Peter made only one appearance for the League side, his tragic death is remembered on each anniversary by the club, and rightly so, for Peter was an exceptionally talented young player for whom great things were predicted. He joined the club in July 1978 as an apprentice and was upgraded in October the same year. He made his debut for the club in a pre-season friendly in August 1979 and his League debut the following month but was then diagnosed as having leukaemia. After a lengthy and brave battle Peter died on 28th December 1983.

1964	Chelsea	H	FA Cup 3rd Round	1-1
1969	Walsall	A	FA Cup 3rd Round	1-0
1975	Nottingham Forest	A	FA Cup 3rd Round	1-1
1986	Oxford United	A	FA Cup 3rd Round	1-1
1987	Arsenal	H	First Division	1-2

This was the 100th League meeting between the two North London rivals, with the honours in the previous 99 clashes even. That alone ensured interest from outside the normal confines of North London, and thus the game was chosen for live transmission on television. The two sides did much to try and dilute the normal tension whenever they met, appearing on the cover of the programme side by side and producing a magazine which gave details of all the previous League clashes. As it was, Arsenal went home with the points, with Spurs' consolation goal being scored by Mitchell Thomas. The two were also destined to meet a further three times in the Littlewoods Cup semi-final, with Arsenal finishing triumphant in this as well.

JANUARY 5TH

1895	London Welsh	A	FA Amateur Cup Divisional Final Replay	3-3
1903	New Brompton	H	Southern League	3-1
1907	Bristol Rovers	H	Southern League	4-0
1918	Brentford	A	London Combination	3-2
1924	Birmingham	A	First Division	2-3
1929	Southampton	H	Second Division	3-2
1935	Huddersfield Town	H	First Division	0-0
1946	Brentford	H	FA Cup 3rd Round 1st Leg	2-2

With League football still to resume following the end of the Second World War, the FA decreed, for the first and only time, that FA Cup ties would be decided over two legs. Whilst this may have ultimately mattered little to Spurs (they drew the first leg and lost the second) it has thrown up one or two trivia items; Charlton became one of the few teams to have lost a match and still reach the final, which they did this season.

1952	Bolton Wanderers	A	First Division	1-1
1955	Gateshead	A	FA Cup 3rd Round	2-0
1957	Leicester City	H	FA Cup 3rd Round	2-0
1972	Chelsea	H	League Cup Semi-Final 2nd Leg	2-2

Although Chelsea had won the first leg with a late goal, Spurs were confident of overturning the deficit and winning through to Wembley, even if extra time was required. And so they should have done, for with some five minutes or so left to play, the score was 2-1 on the night and 3-3 on aggregate. Chelsea were awarded a free-kick out near the touchline; there was no immediate danger, although a low cross was fired into the Spurs penalty area. Cyril Knowles, guarding the near post, had the ball covered and could have chosen to kick the ball with either foot into the crowd for safety. Somehow, he changed his mind over which foot to use whilst the ball was in mid-flight and missed it altogether. Jennings, unable to see the ball until it was too late, could not prevent it going into the net to bring Chelsea level on the night and into the final.

1974	Leicester City	A	FA Cup 3rd Round	0-1
1980	Manchester United	H	FA Cup 3rd Round	1-1
1985	Charlton Athletic	H	FA Cup 3rd Round	1-1
1991	Blackpool	A	FA Cup 3rd Round	1-0

It would have been no surprise if this match had been postponed or abandoned – freak weather conditions in Blackpool had already closed the Magic Mile (an area of amusement arcades along the sea front) and made playing football very difficult. Just when everyone appeared to have settled for a replay, Paul Stewart (an ex-Blackpool player) scored the only goal of the game.

| 1992 | Aston Villa | A | FA Cup 3rd Round | 0-0 |
| 1997 | Manchester United | A | FA Cup 3rd Round | 0-2 |

Irrespective of where either team lay in the League, there was still a magic about a United and Spurs cup tie, and the reaction that greeted their pairing in the third round when the draw was made meant that this would be another such special occasion and the game was selected for live television transmission. As it was Spurs were decimated by injuries, but United were in such sparkling form that even a full-strength opposition would have found it difficult to live with the rampant Reds. Goals from Cole and Cantona ensured passage into the fourth round for United and elimination for Spurs.

| 1998 | Fulham | H | FA Cup 3rd Round | 3-1 |

JANUARY 6TH

| 1883 | Latymer | A | Friendly | 1-8 |

This was only the second match Hotspur FC played and thus includes the very first goal ever scored by the club; sadly, history does not recall the name of that scorer. Latymer were to become the club's chief rivals over the next few years, in much the same way that Arsenal have assumed that mantle during the 20th century. On the same day Ernie Coquet was born in Durston-on-Tyne. Ernie joined Spurs in March 1908 after impressing with Sunderland and Reading, missed only one game for Spurs in their first season in the Football League and went on to make 109 appearances for the first team. Strong competition from the likes of Tom Collins, Bert Elkin and Fred Wilkes for the full-back spots in 1910-11 season curtailed Coquet's first-team opportunities and in May 1911 he left Spurs for Burslem Port Vale, finally finishing his playing career with Fulham in 1919. He died in Gateshead on October 26th 1946.

1897	Maidenhead	H	FA Cup 2nd Qualifying Round	6-0
1900	Queens Park Rangers	A	Southern League	0-0
1902	Millwall Athletic	A	London League	1-1
1906	Watford	A	Southern League	0-0
1912	West Bromwich Albion	A	First Division	0-0

After 67 minutes of play fog descended on the pitch, leaving the referee with little option but to take the two sides off the field. Despite a lengthy wait the fog refused to lift and the match was then abandoned. The game was replayed in March with Spurs losing 2-0.

1917	Clapton Orient	A	London Combination	2-1
1922	Middlesbrough	H	First Division	2-0
1934	Aston Villa	A	First Division	5-1

1943 Terry Venables was born in Bethnal Green. The only man to have been capped by England at every possible level (schoolboy, youth, amateur, Under-23 and full), Venables made his name with Chelsea who he joined as a junior straight from school. He made his League debut in 1959 and won a League Cup winners' medal in 1965 before joining Tottenham in May 1966. The following season he won an FA Cup winners' medal with Spurs (against Chelsea) although never really settled at the club and left to join Queens Park Rangers in June 1969. After five years with Rangers he moved on to Crystal Palace, but after only 14 appearances was persuaded by manager Malcolm Allison to move on to the coaching side. As coach and later manager Venables found his true vocation, producing a side that was acclaimed 'Team of the Eighties', although following his departure to Queens Park Rangers his former side suffered relegation. He built a side at Rangers good enough to reach the 1982 FA Cup final (lost to Spurs after a replay) and win the Second Division championship the following season. In 1984 QPR qualified for the UEFA Cup, but before Venables could attempt an assault on this competition he accepted an offer to become manager of Spanish giants Barcelona. They won the Spanish title in Venables' first season as manager (their first Spanish title in 11 years) and the following season reached the final of the European Cup, losing on penalties to Steaua Bucharest. After a bad start to the 1987–88 season Barcelona dismissed Venables, but at the same time Spurs had parted company with David Pleat and Venables took over at White Hart Lane. In 1991, against a backdrop of financial problems and threatened bankruptcy, Venables led Spurs to the FA Cup final, where they beat Nottingham Forest 2-1. During the summer he and colleague Alan Sugar completed the takeover of Tottenham, although the pair fell out spectacularly in 1993, with Venables being dismissed from his position as managing director. For the next six months Venables spent his time between courts and television panels until in January 1994 he accepted the offer he'd always yearned for; that of England manager. Aside from his football activities over the years, Venables is an accomplished writer (his Hazell series was filmed for television) and singer. He held the England position until the end of the 1996 European Championships in England, guiding the host country to the semi-finals where they were beaten in a penalty shoot-out by Germany, and then returned to domestic football in the capacity of chairman of Portsmouth. By the end of the year he was also appointed manager of the Australian national side, although in 1998 he became manager of Crystal Palace for a second time.

1945	Southampton	H	Football League South	4-0
1951	Huddersfield Town	A	FA Cup 3rd Round	0-2
1962	Birmingham City	A	FA Cup 3rd Round	3-3
1973	Leeds United	A	First Division	1-2
1990	Southampton	H	FA Cup 3rd Round	1-3
1996	Hereford United	A	FA Cup 3rd Round	1-1

JANUARY 7TH

1888	St Bride's	H	Friendly	3-2
1899	Royal Artillery	H	Southern League	1-0
1905	Watford	H	Southern League	2-0
1911	Bristol City	H	First Division	3-2
1922	Brentford	A	FA Cup 1st Round	2-0
1928	Newcastle United	H	First Division	5-2
1933	Stoke City	H	Second Division	3-2
1939	Watford	H	FA Cup 3rd Round	7-1
1950	Stoke City	A	FA Cup 3rd Round	1-0
1956	Boston United	H	FA Cup 3rd Round	4-0
1961	Charlton Athletic	H	FA Cup 3rd Round	3-2

Whilst Spurs were runaway leaders of the First Division, the other half of the elusive 'double' required as much luck as skill. Although Charlton were little more than a mid-table Second Division side, the players knew better than to treat them too lightly; Bill Nicholson would never have stood for it. Spurs got off to a dream start, with Les Allen latching on to Danny Blanchflower's through ball after six minutes and putting them ahead. The same two players linked up on the half-hour and Allen put Spurs further ahead, but rather than then try to kill the game off, Spurs began to ease off, allowing Charlton a glimmer of hope when Leary scored. Blanchflower responded in kind, crossing for Terry Dyson to put Spurs 3-1 in the lead three minutes later. The game should have been finished by half-time, but thirty seconds after the restart Charlton scored again and then piled on attack after attack to try and force a replay. Although he was unable to create another goal chance, Blanchflower was at his best during the second half, individually coaxing his team-mates to get their minds on the game and slowing the pace down to frustrate the visitors.

1967	Arsenal	A	First Division	2-0
1970	Bradford City	H	FA Cup 3rd Round Replay	5-0
1978	Bolton Wanderers	H	FA Cup 3rd Round	2-2
1981	Queens Park Rangers	H	FA Cup 3rd Round Replay	3-1
1984	Fulham	A	FA Cup 3rd Round	0-0

Midway through the game Spurs goalkeeper Ray Clemence suffered a bad injury and defender Graham Roberts was forced to take over. He performed heroically for the rest of the game as Fulham threw just about everything into attack, searching for the goal that would surely finish Spurs off. But the defence held firm, ensuring a replay at White Hart Lane. The injury to Clemence was sufficiently serious enough to curtail his season; although he returned to full fitness, the form of replacement Tony Parks was such that he held on to his place until the end of the season, including the UEFA Cup final.

| 1989 | Bradford City | A | FA Cup 3rd Round | 0-1 |
| 1995 | Altrincham | H | FA Cup 3rd Round | 3-0 |

This was a tie few Spurs supporters thought they would be seeing at the start of the season when their team were hammered with a 12-point deduction from the League and banned from the FA Cup following an investigation into illegal payments to players. After appeals and arbitration Spurs had only been re-admitted into the competition in December, so this was a moment to savour, and not only for Spurs, for when the draw had been made Altrincham had announced that should the Spurs ban be upheld, Altrincham would sue the FA for compensation, irrespective of the fact they would be guaranteed a place in the fourth round! Goals from Teddy Sheringham, Stuart Nethercott and Ronnie Rosenthal ensured Spurs' passage into the next round, although Altrincham had been unlucky not to have got back into contention when they had a goal disallowed whilst the score was still poised at 2-0.

JANUARY 8TH

1881   Joe Walton born in Lunes. He began his career with Preston North End as a 17-year-old before switching to Spurs in May 1903. Despite five years' experience at Deepdale he took time to settle at Spurs and it was not until his second season at White Hart Lane that he established himself as a regular member of the team, at outside-right, making 218 appearances over the next six years. Once established he began to attract the attention of international selectors, but despite playing in three trial matches could not graduate into the full England team. In April 1909 he was offered the maximum permissible wage to remain at Spurs but chose instead to join Sheffield United. After two years at Sheffield he moved on to Stalybridge Celtic.

1898	Rushden	H	United League	3-1
1900	Southampton	H	Southern District Combination	3-2
1910	Everton	H	First Division	3-0
1916	Clapton Orient	H	London Combination [1st competition]	1-1

Three hours before kick off Orient had only four players certain of turning up, although they did manage to start with a full complement of 11. These included a number who were making their debuts for the club and others playing out of position, but they did extremely well to hold Spurs to a 1-1 draw. Spurs' goal was scored by Ted Bassett.

1921	Bristol Rovers	H	FA Cup 1st Round	6-2
1927	West Ham United	A	FA Cup 3rd Round	2-3
1938	Blackburn Rovers	H	FA Cup 3rd Round	3-2
1944	Brentford	H	Football League South	1-0

1945   Phil Beal born in Godstone, Surrey. Whilst there were bigger stars and more extrovert performers at White Hart Lane, there surely was no more consistent or reliable player in a white shirt than Phil Beal. Signed by Spurs as an amateur player in 1960 he joined the professional ranks in January 1962 and made his League debut at Aston Villa in September 1963. The break-up of the 'double' side allowed Phil to establish himself in the first team and he was destined to remain Spurs' long-term full-back until a broken arm interrupted his career during the 1966-67 season. As well as robbing him of a place in the Spurs line-up that won the FA Cup that year, Phil found stiff opposition from incumbent Joe Kinnear when he recovered from injury. The change in tactics from 2-3-5 to four in a defensive line gave Phil the perfect opportunity to excel as a central defender. By the time he left Spurs in 1975 he had collected winners' medals in the League Cup (1971 and 1973) and UEFA Cup (1972) as well as a runners-up medal in the UEFA Cup in 1974. Awarded a testimonial in 1973, the guarantees given to visitors Bayern Munich meant he ended up losing money on what should have been his big night. After making 330 League appearances for Spurs (scoring only one goal; in 1969 against QPR) he joined Brighton for one season before heading across the Atlantic. He finished his playing career after a few games for Crewe in the 1979-80 season.

1949	Arsenal	A	FA Cup 3rd Round	0-3
1964	Chelsea	A	FA Cup 3rd Round Replay	0-2
1966	Chelsea	A	First Division	1-2
1972	Manchester City	H	First Division	1-1
1975	Nottingham Forest	H	FA Cup 3rd Round Replay	0-1
1977	Cardiff City	A	FA Cup 3rd Round	0-1
1983	Southampton	H	FA Cup 3rd Round	1-0
1986	Oxford United	H	FA Cup 3rd Round Replay	2-1 [aet]
1992	Norwich City	H	Rumbelows Cup 5th Round	2-1
1994	Peterborough United	A	FA Cup 3rd Round	1-1

A late equaliser by Jason Dozell, with barely minutes left, was all that stood between Spurs and another humiliation in the FA Cup. Peterborough were well worth their draw, perhaps even should have won, but whilst they gained most of the plaudits after the game, Spurs were just relieved to have survived.

JANUARY 9TH

1886	Dalston Rovers	A	Friendly	Won but score unknown
1892	Queens Park Rangers	H	Friendly	1-2
1897	Swindon Town	A	Southern League	0-1

1899	Chatham	H	Thames & Medway League	0-4
1904	Millwall	A	Southern League	1-0
1905	West Ham United	H	Southern Charity Cup Semi-Final	10-0

This was the first time Spurs had reached double figures in a competitive match. Vivian Woodward led the scoring, grabbing five of the goals, with Sandy Tait scoring from the penalty spot and John Brearley and Charlie O'Hagan getting two apiece.

1909	Barnsley	A	Second Division	1-1
1915	Sunderland	H	FA Cup 1st Round	2-1
1926	West Ham United	H	FA Cup 3rd Round	5-0
1932	Sheffield Wednesday	H	FA Cup 3rd Round	2-2
1937	Newcastle United	H	Second Division	0-1
1943	Aldershot	A	Football League South	3-1
1954	Leeds United	A	FA Cup 3rd Round	3-3

1959 John Kirwan died. Born in Wicklow, Ireland in 1878, he began his career with Southport but was soon being lured by the bigger clubs. He finally chose to join Everton, where he was seen as a ready made replacement for the Spurs-bound John Cameron. Twelve months later, with Cameron appointed manager/secretary at Spurs, Kirwan was persuaded to join the White Hart Lane outfit, one of Cameron's first signings. He joined at exactly the right time, for in his debut season Spurs won the Southern League championship and the following season the FA Cup, with Kirwan, playing outside-left, proving to be an exemplary goal-maker and astute goal-taker. He also had an opportunist's eye – when the final whistle blew at the end of the FA Cup final replay, Kirwan grabbed the match ball and kept it as a souvenir until his death! He remained at Spurs until 1905, during which time he won 12 caps for Ireland, before surprisingly electing to join the newly-formed Chelsea, along with David Copeland. He spent three seasons at Stamford Bridge before heading north to Clyde, finishing his playing career with Leyton Orient and then turning to coaching.

1960	Newport County	A	FA Cup 3rd Round	4-0
1965	Torquay United	A	FA Cup 3rd Round	3-3
1971	Leeds United	A	First Division	2-1
1980	Manchester United	A	FA Cup 3rd Round Replay	1-0 [aet]

Spurs and Manchester United had been involved in titanic FA Cup struggles before and since, but this battle had been one of the best. The two had fought out a 1-1 draw on the Saturday and it looked to all intents and purposes as though a third match would be required in order to separate them. Then, in pretty much the very last minute of extra time, Ossie Ardiles collected the ball from Ricky Villa and hooked in a shot to win the game.

1988	Oldham Athletic	A	FA Cup 3rd Round	4-2
1993	Manchester United	A	FA Premier League	1-4

JANUARY 10TH

1885	Abbey	A	Friendly	1-1

Although the game finished all-square at 1-1, both goals were disputed by the opposition. Spurs were also only able to field nine players during the match.

1889	Civil Engineers	H	Middlesex Senior Cup 1st Round	0-0
1897	Kettering Town	A	United League	2-4
1903	Bristol Rovers	H	Southern League	3-0
1914	Leicester Fosse	A	FA Cup 1st Round	5-5

1918 Les Bennett born in Wood Green. A local lad, he graduated through Spurs juniors and the Northfleet nursery before being signed in May 1939. His career was therefore shortened before it even began, although he did guest for a number of clubs during the Second World War. At the end of hostilities he returned to Spurs and made his League debut at the age of 28 in August 1946 against Birmingham City. In the next eight years he recorded 273 appearances in the League side, scoring 104 goals during which Spurs won the Second Division and First Division titles in successive seasons, 1949-50 and 1950-51. By 1954 Spurs had a younger man in mind to fill the inside-forward slot and Les was allowed to join West Ham United. After one season at West Ham he drifted into the non-League game with Romford and Clacton Town, where he served as manager. He later worked on the security staff of a local university.

1920	Bristol Rovers	A	FA Cup 1st Round	4-1
1925	Northampton Town	H	FA Cup 1st Round	3-0
1931	Preston North End	H	FA Cup 3rd Round	3-1
1942	Reading	H	London War League	2-1
1946	Brentford	A	FA Cup 3rd Round 2nd Leg	0-2

After a 2-2 draw in the first leg, Brentford won 4-2 on aggregate in the only season the FA Cup has been decided by home and away legs.

1948	Bolton Wanderers	A	FA Cup 3rd Round	2-0 [aet]
1953	Tranmere Rovers	A	FA Cup 3rd Round	1-1
1959	West Ham United	H	FA Cup 3rd Round	2-0
1962	Birmingham City	H	FA Cup 3rd Round Replay	4-2
1970	Derby County	H	First Division	2-1

Jimmy Greaves scored his last competitive goal for Spurs, for by the end of the month he had been dropped from the team following the cup defeat by Crystal Palace. Spurs' other goal was grabbed by Roger Morgan.

1976	Derby County	A	First Division	3-2
1978	Bolton Wanderers	A	FA Cup 3rd Round Replay	1-2 [aet]
1979	Altrincham	H	FA Cup 3rd Round	1-1
1981	Birmingham City	H	First Division	1-0
1987	Scunthorpe United	H	FA Cup 3rd Round	3-2
1998	Manchester United	A	FA Premier League	0-2

JANUARY 11TH

| 1890 | Romford | A | Friendly | 0-0 |

The game was halted after only 40 minutes.

1896	Millwall Athletic	H	Friendly	1-1
1897	Chatham	A	Friendly	1-2
1902	Southampton	A	Western League	1-5
1904	Brentford	H	London League	2-1
1908	Everton	A	FA Cup 1st Round	0-1
1913	Blackpool	H	FA Cup 1st Round	1-1
1919	West Ham United	A	London Combination	0-2
1930	Manchester City	H	FA Cup 3rd Round	2-2
1936	Southend United	H	FA Cup 3rd Round	4-4
1941	Clapton Orient	A	London War Cup Section B	9-1
1947	Stoke City	H	FA Cup 3rd Round	2-2
1958	Burnley	A	First Division	0-2
1964	Blackburn Rovers	H	First Division	4-1
1969	Stoke City	A	First Division	1-1
1975	Newcastle United	A	First Division	5-2
1977	Queens Park Rangers	A	First Division	1-2
1984	Fulham	H	FA Cup 3rd Round Replay	2-0

With Ray Clemence still injured following the first clash the previous Saturday, reserve goalkeeper Tony Parks was given the chance to establish himself in the side. He was rarely troubled, but much of the following controversy concerned the rather robust tackling of the Spurs defenders. Goals from Graham Roberts, the hero on Saturday, and Steve Archibald gave Spurs passage into the fifth round.

| 1986 | Nottingham Forest | H | First Division | 0-3 |
| 1992 | Chelsea | A | First Division | 0-2 |

JANUARY 12TH

1884	Woodgrange	A	Friendly	0-1
1901	Swindon Town	A	Southern League	1-1
1903	Brentford	H	London League	1-0
1907	Hull City	H	FA Cup 1st Round	0-0
1918	Arsenal	H-Highbury		
			London Combination	4-1
1924	Crystal Palace	A	FA Cup 1st Round	0-2

Palace were little more than a side still struggling to come to terms with the Second Division and this should have been a formality for Spurs. Unfortunately, they were unable to play their normal game, being continually knocked off their stride by the more direct Palace, and the loss of Arthur Grimsdell through injury took much of the fight out of Spurs, allowing Palace to emerge 2-0 victors.

1929	Reading	A	FA Cup 3rd Round	0-2
1935	Manchester City	H	FA Cup 3rd Round	1-0
1946	Luton Town	A	Football League South	1-3
1952	Scunthorpe United	A	FA Cup 3rd Round	3-0
1953	Tranmere Rovers	H	FA Cup 3rd Round Replay	9-1
1957	Wolverhampton Wanderers	A	First Division	0-3
1974	Sheffield United	A	First Division	2-2
1980	Manchester City	A	First Division	1-1

1985	Queens Park Rangers	A	First Division	2-2
1991	Arsenal	H	First Division	0-0
1994	Aston Villa	H	Coca-Cola Cup 5th Round	1-2
1997	Manchester United	H	FA Premier League	1-2

JANUARY 13TH

1894	3rd Grenadier Guards	H	Middlesex Senior Cup 1st Round	1-1
1900	Chatham	H	Southern League	2-1
1906	Burnley	H	FA Cup 1st Round	2-0
1912	West Bromwich Albion	A	FA Cup 1st Round	0-3
1917	Fulham	H-Homerton		
			London Combination	1-0
1923	Worksop Town	H	FA Cup 1st Round	0-0

Spurs were widely expected to beat their opponents from the Midland League, but frost, sleet and rain had produced patches of ice on parts of the ground, and under such conditions Spurs' normal style of football was difficult to reproduce. Worksop, to their credit, took to the conditions perfectly and held on to register a scoreline that shocked the football world. Immediately after the game the Worksop officials spoke to their Tottenham counterparts; although Worksop now had the right to the stage the replay, they would be more than happy if this was to take place at White Hart Lane, to which Spurs readily agreed.

1932	Sheffield Wednesday	A	FA Cup 3rd Round Replay	1-3
1934	Everton	H	FA Cup 3rd Round	3-0
1940	Charlton Athletic	A	Football League South Group A	5-1
1945	Charlton Athletic	A	Football League South	2-1
1951	Manchester United	A	First Division	1-2
1954	Leeds United	H	FA Cup 3rd Round Replay	1-0
1962	Cardiff City	A	First Division	1-1
1973	Margate	A	FA Cup 3rd Round	6-0
1979	Bristol City	A	First Division	0-0
1990	Manchester City	H	First Division	1-1
1996	Manchester City	H	FA Premier League	1-0

JANUARY 14TH

1888	Bowes Park	A	Friendly	2-2
1893	Erith	A	Southern Alliance	1-2
1899	Gravesend United	A	Southern League	2-4
1901	CW Brown's XI	H	Jack Oliver Benefit	4-2
1903	Reading	A	Southern Charity Cup 1st Round Replay	2-3
1911	Millwall	H	FA Cup 1st Round	2-1
1922	Preston North End	A	First Division	2-1
1928	Bristol City	A	FA Cup 3rd Round	2-1
1933	Oldham Athletic	A	FA Cup 3rd Round	6-0
1939	Nottingham Forest	H	Second Division	4-1
1950	Leeds United	A	Second Division	0-3
1956	Arsenal	A	First Division	1-0
1967	Manchester United	A	First Division	0-1

1968 Ruel Fox born in Ipswich. Ruel began his career as an apprentice with Norwich City, signing full professional forms in January 1986 and made his debut later the same year. In February 1994 he was transferred to Newcastle United for £2.25 million, although he was in and out of the side. He was signed by Spurs for £4.2 million in October 1995 and impressed with his tricky wing play and ability to score crucial goals.

1976	Newcastle United	H	League Cup Semi-Final 1st Leg	1-0
1978	Notts County	A	Second Division	3-3
1984	Ipswich Town	H	First Division	2-0
1986	Liverpool	H	Screen Sports Super Cup Group A	0-2
1992	Aston Villa	H	FA Cup 3rd Round Replay	0-1
1995	West Ham United	A	FA Premier League	2-1

JANUARY 15TH

1887	Park	H	East End Cup 2nd Round	2-0
1898	Northfleet	H	Southern League	4-0
1902	Reading	A	Western League	1-1

1910	Plymouth Argyle	A	FA Cup 1st Round	1-1
1914	Leicester Fosse	H	FA Cup 1st Round Replay	2-0
1916	Watford	A	London Combination [1st competition]	1-0
1921	Arsenal	H	First Division	2-1
1923	Worksop Town	H	FA Cup 1st Round Replay	9-0

In the two days since their goalless draw, a thaw had removed the last patches of ice and softened the pitch; ideal conditions for Spurs to go about their usual business. They made no mistake the second time around, and goals from Seed, Lindsay (four), Handley (three) and Dimmock ensured passage into the next round and a home tie with Manchester United.

1927	Everton	A	First Division	2-1
1930	Manchester City	A	FA Cup 3rd Round Replay	1-4

Spurs crashed out of the cup at the first hurdle and by a scoreline that would have indicated a comfortable victory for City. The reality was somewhat different, for City's three winning goals were all scored in the closing minutes and it was only woeful finishing on the part of Spurs that prevented this becoming an away win. Spurs had much of the early exchanges and it was against the run of the play when City took the lead through Toseland. Spurs equalised early in the second half and continued to take the game to their opponents, although all of the chances created by the midfield were spurned by the attack. City regained the lead with a lucky effort, with Marshall's shot being deflected into the net by Herod. As Spurs pressed in search of a second equaliser, City grabbed two further goals to put the tie beyond Spurs' reach.

1936	Southend United	A	FA Cup 3rd Round Replay	2-1
1938	Nottingham Forest	H	Second Division	3-0
1944	Southampton	A	Football League South	3-2
1947	Stoke City	A	FA Cup 3rd Round Replay	0-1
1949	Chesterfield	A	Second Division	0-1
1955	Arsenal	H	First Division	0-1
1966	Newcastle United	H	First Division	2-2
1972	Carlisle United	H	FA Cup 3rd Round	1-1
1983	Luton Town	A	First Division	1-1
1989	Nottingham Forest	H	First Division	1-2
1994	Manchester United	H	FA Premier League	0-1

JANUARY 16TH

1886	Woodgrange	A	Friendly	0-3
1889	Windsor Phoenix	A	Friendly	1-2
1897	Luton Town	A	FA Cup 3rd Qualifying Round	0-3
1899	Sheppey United	H	Thames & Medway League	3-0
1904	Queens Park Rangers	H	Southern League	2-2
1909	Manchester City	A	FA Cup 1st Round	4-3

This was one of Spurs' best performances in the cup since they had won the competition in 1901. Although City were in the First Division and Spurs were in their inaugural season of League football, confidence was high at White Hart Lane that a draw could be achieved. Although Spurs soon found themselves 2-0 behind, a gritty performance ensued and goals from Morris from the penalty spot, Minter (two) and Bobby Steel won the day.

1913	Blackpool	H	FA Cup 1st Round Replay	6-1

Despite having been held at home 1-1 by Blackpool in the first match, the replay took place at White Hart Lane as Blackpool sold the home rights (then permissible by the FA) to the replay. Spurs made sure the second time around, with 16,926 in attendance.

1915	Bradford City	H	First Division	0-0
1926	Manchester City	A	First Division	0-0
1932	Bradford Park Avenue	A	Second Division	1-2
1937	Portsmouth	A	FA Cup 3rd Round	5-0
1943	Millwall	A	Football League South	3-0
1954	West Bromwich Albion	H	First Division	0-1
1960	Arsenal	H	First Division	3-0
1961	Manchester United	A	First Division	0-2
1963	Burnley	H	FA Cup 3rd Round	0-3

Spurs met Burnley for the third consecutive season in the FA Cup, having beaten them at the semi-final stage in 1961 and in the final the following season. By virtue of their 3-0 win, Burnley inflicted Spurs' first FA Cup defeat since 1960.

1965	West Ham United	H	First Division	3-2
1971	Southampton	H	First Division	1-3

| 1979 | Altrincham | A | FA Cup 3rd Round Replay | 3-0 |

Such was the interest generated by Altrincham's draw at White Hart Lane that the non-League club switched the game to Manchester City's Maine Road ground for the replay. Spurs made sure the second time around winning 3-0.

1988	Coventry City	H	First Division	2-2
1991	Chelsea	A	Rumbelows Cup 5th Round	0-0
1993	Sheffield Wednesday	H	FA Premier League	0-2

JANUARY 17TH

1885	Grange Park	A	Friendly	0-1
1900	Portsmouth	A	Southern District Combination	0-0
1903	Northampton Town	A	Southern League	1-3
1907	Hull City	A	FA Cup 1st Round Replay	0-0 [aet]

Ten minutes into extra-time, with the score still at 0-0, bad light forced the match to be abandoned. The FA ordered the result to stand, leaving the two clubs to sort out the venue for the second replay between themselves. It was jointly decided to hold the match at White Hart Lane.

1914	Oldham Athletic	H	First Division	3-1
1920	Stockport County	H	Second Division	2-0
1925	Everton	A	First Division	0-1
1931	Bradford Park Avenue	A	Second Division	1-4
1940	Southend United	H	Football League South Group A	2-4
1942	Brighton & Hove Albion	A	London War League	2-5
1948	Cardiff City	H	Second Division	2-1
1953	Burnley	A	First Division	2-3
1959	Newcastle United	A	First Division	2-1
1968	Sheffield Wednesday	A	First Division	2-1
1970	Sunderland	A	First Division	1-2
1976	Manchester United	H	First Division	1-1
1981	Arsenal	H	First Division	2-0
1989	AS Monaco	H	Friendly	1-3
1990	Nottingham Forest	A	Littlewoods Cup 5th Round	2-2
1996	Hereford United	H	FA Cup 3rd Round Replay	5-1
1998	West Ham United	H	FA Premier League	1-0

Jurgen Klinsmann scored his first goal for Spurs since his return to the club in this League match.

JANUARY 18TH

1890	Old St Stephen's	A	Middlesex Senior Cup 1st Round	4-2
1896	Ilford	H	Friendly	2-1
1902	Bristol Rovers	H	Southern League	1-0
1904	West Ham United	H	London League	2-0
1908	New Brompton	A	Southern League	2-1
1913	Derby County	A	First Division	0-5
1919	Clapton Orient	H	London Combination	2-4
1930	Blackpool	H	Second Division	6-1
1936	Sheffield United	H	Second Division	1-1
1941	Millwall	A	London War Cup Section B	3-1
1947	Newcastle United	A	Second Division	0-1
1958	Preston North End	H	First Division	3-3
1964	Blackpool	A	First Division	2-0
1965	Torquay United	H	FA Cup 3rd Round Replay	5-1
1969	Leeds United	H	First Division	0-0
1972	Carlisle United	A	FA Cup 3rd Round Replay	3-1
1975	Sheffield United	H	First Division	1-3
1982	Nottingham Forest	H	League Cup 5th Round	1-0

A mis-hit shot by Ossie Ardiles proved to be the only goal of the game, but Spurs had opportunities to have put the tie beyond the reach of Forest. Glenn Hoddle had a penalty saved by Peter Shilton, but the referee ordered it to be retaken as Forest defenders had been encroaching into the area. Hoddle made no mistake the second time around, but Mark Falco was now adjudged to have encroached, necessitating a third attempt. This was also saved by Peter Shilton, who thereafter performed heroics to keep his side in the game.

| 1986 | Manchester City | H | First Division | 0-2 |
| 1992 | Southampton | H | First Division | 1-2 |

JANUARY 19TH

1879   Herbert Chapman born in Kiveton Park, Sheffield. One of the greatest names in English football, it is often said Chapman was determined to become a successful manager of Arsenal because he had not been a successful player at Spurs! True or not, it certainly lends the Chapman story a degree of romanticism. He joined Spurs from Notts County for £70 in 1905 after playing for numerous clubs around the country, but despite being an almost ever-present in the first team during his first season was relegated to the reserves and subsequently left in 1907 to rejoin Northampton. If his career as a player was nondescript, then the same could not be said for his prowess as a manager. His first appointment was as player-manager of Northampton Town in April 1907, the season the club finished bottom of the Southern League. Two years later, with Chapman having retired from playing in order to concentrate fully on managerial matters, they were champions. In May 1912 he was appointed manager of Leeds City, then facing re-election to the Football League. Whilst he was not quite able to repeat the Midas touch, his time as manager was not unnoticed – in 1919 the club were summoned before the Football League to answer charges of financial irregularities, charges that referred to payments made to players during the war years. Leeds refused to allow inspection of their books, with the result that the Football League threw them out and suspended all of the officials, including Chapman, from the game. In September 1920 the suspension was lifted and Chapman returned to football with Huddersfield Town as secretary after a spell as an engineer. In February 1921 he was appointed assistant manager and then later the same month manager. The following year Chapman guided Huddersfield to their first major honour, the FA Cup. The following season they finished third in the First Division before embarking on a domination never previously experienced within the Football League, winning the title for three consecutive seasons (the first time such a feat had been achieved). However, Chapman had left Huddersfield (who he felt were unable to sustain long-term success owing to low population and therefore low crowds) in May 1925 to become manager at Arsenal. His impact at Highbury was equally impressive, both on and off the pitch. Within two years Arsenal were making their first appearance at Wembley, losing 1-0 to Cardiff City in the FA Cup final. They returned in 1930 to win their first honour, the FA Cup, against Huddersfield Town. The following season they won their first League title, added another FA Cup victory in 1932, and were on their way to the second of three consecutive titles at the time Chapman died. Aside from his trophy wins, Chapman is remembered for, amongst other things, getting London Transport to rename Gillespie Road Tube Station to Arsenal and trying to introduce numbers to players' shirts. He died on January 6th 1934.

1884	Grafton	A	Friendly	1-0
1889	Civil Engineers	A	Middlesex Senior Cup 1st Round Replay	1-4
1894	London Welsh	N	FA Amateur Cup Divisional Final 2nd Replay	4-2

The second replay was held at The Spotted Dog ground where goals from Jull, Welham, Payne and Hunter finally overcame The London Welsh.

1898	Southampton	A	United League	2-2
1901	Watford	H	Southern League	7-0
1907	Swindon Town	H	Southern League	3-0
1910	Plymouth Argyle	H	FA Cup 1st Round Replay	7-1
1918	West Ham United	A	London Combination	2-2
1924	Newcastle United	H	First Division	2-0
1929	Wolverhampton Wanderers	A	Second Division	2-4
1935	Wolverhampton Wanderers	A	First Division	2-6
1946	Luton Town	H	Football League South	2-3
1952	Stoke City	H	First Division	2-0
1957	Aston Villa	H	First Division	3-0
1963	Blackpool	H	First Division	2-0
1974	Coventry City	H	First Division	2-1
1980	Brighton & Hove Albion	A	First Division	2-0
1983	Burnley	H	Milk Cup 5th Round	1-4

Burnley were propping up the Second Division table when the draw for the Milk Cup fifth round had been made and should have presented Spurs with a relatively comfortable passage into the semi-finals, especially as they managed to avoid Liverpool, Manchester United and Arsenal. To make matters worse, Burnley parted company with their manager on the morning of the game! Despite this Burnley absorbed all Spurs could throw at them, took advantage of two own goals (both scored by Graham Roberts) and took their place in the semi-finals.

| 1994 | Peterborough United | H | FA Cup 3rd Round Replay | 1-1 [aet – won 5-4 on penalties] |
| 1997 | Nottingham Forest | A | FA Premier League | 1-2 |

JANUARY 20TH

1894	3rd Grenadier Guards	H	Middlesex Senior Cup 1st Round Replay	0-2
1900	Reading	A	Southern League	1-0
1906	Brighton & Hove Albion	H	Southern League	3-1
1907	Plymouth Argyle	H	Southern League	0-1
1912	Sunderland	H	First Division	0-0
1917	Queens Park Rangers	A	London Combination	1-1

1920   Alf Ramsey born in Dagenham, Essex. A grocer's lad, he was spotted by Portsmouth and signed as an amateur in 1940. With the Second World War in full swing, however, he never got to play for Portsmouth, being snapped up by their great rivals Southampton whilst playing against them for the Army. He therefore signed as an amateur to Southampton in 1943 and was upgraded to professional level the following year. He won his first England cap in 1948 (against Switzerland) and the following year signed for Spurs for a then record fee for a full-back of £21,000. A member of the 'push and run' side that won the Second and First Division championships in consecutive seasons, Ramsey won a total of 32 England caps (including one in the infamous 1-0 defeat against the USA in the 1950 World Cup – 'Did you play?' asked an inquisitive journalist a few years later. 'Yes,' replied Ramsey, 'and I was the only bloody one who did!') before retiring to become part-time manager of Elton Manor. He was appointed full-time manager of Ipswich Town in 1955, steering the club from the Third Division South (champions in 1957), through the Second Division (champions in 1961) and into the First Division for the first time in their history. Astonishingly, Ramsey then led them to the League title in 1962, ostensibly because no one had played Ipswich before and didn't know what to expect and because Ramsey was the master tactician, able to take little more than average players and fashion them into an effective working unit. His achievements at Portman Road did not go unnoticed and he was appointed England manager in October 1962. His 'wingless wonders' won the World Cup at Wembley in 1966 and might have retained the title in Mexico in 1970 with a little more luck. England's reign as World Champions was perhaps ended as much by the substitution of Bobby Charlton too early into the quarter-final against West Germany as by the mysterious illness which kept Gordon Banks out of the side. Sir Alf (he was knighted following the 1966 World Cup win) turned his attentions to the 1974 World Cup in West Germany and came close to qualifying, drawing at Wembley against Poland when they needed to win, with the Polish goalkeeper performing heroics. The Football Association relieved him of the manager's position in May 1974. His next involvement with football came in January 1976, when he became a director of Birmingham City, subsequently taking over the reigns as caretaker manager between September 1977 and March 1978.

1923	Oldham Athletic	A	First Division	3-0
1934	Leicester City	H	First Division	0-1
1940	Clapton Orient	H	Football League South Group A	2-3
1945	Crystal Palace	H	Football League South	3-1
1951	Wolverhampton Wanderers	H	First Division	2-1
1962	Manchester United	H	First Division	2-2

1965   Colin Calderwood born in Glasgow. Colin began his career as an apprentice with Mansfield Town in 1981, upgrading to the professional ranks in March 1982. After 100 League appearances for Mansfield he was sold to Swindon Town in June 1985 for £30,000, going on to make 330 appearances for the Robins. His former manager at Swindon Ossie Ardiles swooped to buy Colin in July 1993 for £1.25 million, slotting him into a defensive role. Although he struggled at first, in part due to the exposure all the defence were coming under, through Ardiles' attack-minded formation, his career began to blossom when Gerry Francis reversed the tactics, and Colin was subsequently capped for Scotland.

1968	Arsenal	H	First Division	1-0
1973	Ipswich Town	H	First Division	0-1
1979	Leeds United	H	First Division	1-2
1987	Linfield	A	Friendly	3-2

This match was a testimonial for Roy Coyle and Spurs' goals were scored by Clive Allen (penalty), Danny Thomas and an own goal.

1990	Arsenal	A	First Division	0-1
1991	Derby County	A	First Division	1-0

With media speculation that Derby chairman Robert Maxwell wished to sell his shareholding in the club and buy into Spurs, coupled with the presence of live television cameras, Derby fans took the opportunity to let Maxwell know how they felt about him. The planned pitch invasion however, did not take place.

JANUARY 21ST

1888	Old St Paul's	A	Friendly	2-1
1893	Slough	A	Southern Alliance	3-3
1899	Brighton United	A	Southern League	1-0

On the same day Andrew Thompson was born in Newcastle-under-Lyme. Andy spent 11 seasons with Spurs but took almost five of those years trying to break into the first team. He still managed to rack up 153 League appearances for Spurs and was considered a vital squad member, so much so that Spurs frequently turned down transfer enquiries from other clubs. It was the emergence of Willie Davies and Taffy O'Callaghan that finally limited his first-team opportunities and persuaded manager Percy Smith that Thompson could leave, with Andy joining Norwich City in November 1931. After spells with Chester and Clapton Orient as a player Thompson joined Spurs Northfleet nursery on the coaching side. He then had a spell at Stamford Bridge before rejoining Spurs, initially on the coaching side but later fulfilling several other backroom jobs. He died in East London on January 1st 1970.

1905	West Ham United	H	Southern League	1-0

This match was also staged as a joint benefit for David Copeland and John Kirwan and drew a crowd of 14,000 to White Hart Lane. Kirwan scored the only goal of the game.

1907	Hull City	H	FA Cup 1st Round 2nd Replay	1-0
1911	Newcastle United	A	First Division	1-1
1922	West Bromwich Albion	A	First Division	0-3
1928	Huddersfield Town	A	First Division	2-4
1933	Manchester United	A	Second Division	1-2

On the same day Tony Marchi was born in Edmonton. Tony joined Spurs as an amateur in 1948 and made his debut in the reserves when aged only 15 before being upgraded to professional status in 1950. That same year he made his League debut, in the Second Division against Grimsby, and over the next four seasons established himself as the regular left-half, finally displacing Ron Burgess. He seemed set to give Spurs great service over the ensuing years until in 1957 Lanerossi paid Spurs £42,000 to take him to Italy, his father's home country. Marchi's performances in Italy were such that he was widely tipped to pick up full Italian honours, but a lone appearance in the England B team against Scotland in February 1957 ensured he was ineligible for Italy. After one season with Lanerossi he moved on to Torino, spending one season there before indicating he wished to return home to England. Although Arsenal were known to be keen to sign him Spurs had first option and signed him for £20,000 in 1959. By this time most of the 'double' team were in place and Marchi could not break back into the first team, although he remained an important squad member. In May 1963 he replaced the injured Dave Mackay in the line-up for the European Cup-Winners' Cup final in Rotterdam and won his only major honour. In June 1965 he left Spurs to become player-manager at Cambridge City and then spent a year in charge at Northampton Town.

1934	John Hollowbread born in Enfield. John joined Spurs as an amateur in 1950 and was upgraded to the professional ranks in 1952. The continued form of Ted Ditchburn in the Spurs goal limited John's chances of first-team action, but his eventual retirement presented John with a chance to establish himself. Unfortunately, although he played one season as first choice, the subsequent arrival of Bill Brown pushed John down the order and he was sold to Southampton for £3,000.

1939	West Ham United	A	FA Cup 4th Round	3-3
1950	Bury	A	Second Division	2-1
1953	Preston North End	H	First Division	4-4
1956	Everton	H	First Division	1-1
1961	Arsenal	H	First Division	4-2

1963 Tony Parks born in Hackney, London. One dramatic save from Icelandic international Arnor Gudjohnsen on May 23rd 1984 ensured Tony Parks a permanent place in Spurs' history – the occasion was the second leg of the UEFA Cup final between Spurs and Anderlecht and a penalty shoot-out. With Spurs 4-3 ahead, Parks guessed the right way to dive and tipped Gudjohnsen's shot away to win the cup for Spurs. Nothing before or after quite matched that moment in Parks' career. He had only come into the side when Ray Clemence was injured and although Parks held his place during the 1983-84 season, Clemence was back in time for the following season. When Clemence finally retired in October 1987 Parks had the perfect opportunity for an extended run but failed to impress new manager Terry Venables, who bought Bobby Mimms from Everton. After loan spells with Oxford United and Gillingham, Tony was transferred to Brentford in July 1988. He then played for numerous clubs in the Football League before trying his hand in Scotland.

1967	Burnley	H	First Division	2-0
1976	Newcastle United	A	League Cup Semi-Final 2nd Leg	1-3

Newcastle United won 4-3 on aggregate and went into the final to face Manchester City.

1978	Cardiff City	H	First Division	2-1

1984	Everton	A	First Division	1-2
1989	Middlesbrough	A	First Division	2-2
1996	Aston Villa	A	FA Premier League	1-2

JANUARY 22ND

1887	Foxes	A	Friendly	2-1
1898	Wolverton	H	Southern League	7-1
1910	Manchester United	A	First Division	0-5
1916	Millwall	H	London Combination [1st competition]	2-2
1921	Arsenal	A	First Division	2-3
1927	Blackburn Rovers	H	First Division	1-1
1938	New Brighton	A	FA Cup 4th Round	0-0

There had been considerable speculation that New Brighton might move the tie from their own ground to White Hart Lane and take a share in bigger receipts, although the Spurs board made no move to suggest such a thing to their New Brighton counterparts. As it was, Spurs were distinctly unhappy at having to play on an uneven playing surface that also sloped and more than glad to emerge still in the cup at the end. A crowd of 13,039 was in attendance.

1944	Aldershot	A	Football League South	1-0
1949	West Bromwich Albion	H	Second Division	2-0
1955	Sheffield Wednesday	H	First Division	7-2
1966	Middlesbrough	H	FA Cup 3rd Round	4-0
1972	Newcastle United	A	First Division	1-3
1977	Ipswich Town	H	First Division	1-0
1983	Sunderland	H	First Division	1-1
1994	Swindon Town	A	FA Premier League	1-2

JANUARY 23RD

1892	Westminster Criterion	H	Friendly	2-2
1897	Aston Villa	H	Friendly	2-2
1899	Reading	H	United League	1-1
1904	Plymouth Argyle	A	Southern League	3-1
1909	Bolton Wanderers	A	Second Division	1-0
1915	Burnley	A	First Division	1-3
1923				

Harry Clarke born in Woodford in Essex. Signed by Arthur Rowe from Welsh side Lovells Athletic in March 1949, centre-half Harry was slotted straight into the first team and became an integral member of the side that won the Second Division and First Division titles in consecutive seasons. He also won an England cap in 1954 and finished his playing career in 1957, subsequently joining the coaching staff and working with the juniors.

1926	Everton	H	First Division	1-1
1932	Manchester United	H	Second Division	4-1
1937	Bradford Park Avenue	A	Second Division	2-3
1943	Reading	H	Football League South	2-2
1954	Liverpool	A	First Division	2-2
1960	Manchester United	H	First Division	2-1
1965	West Bromwich Albion	A	First Division	0-2
1971	Carlisle United	A	FA Cup 4th Round	3-2
1982	Leeds United	H	FA Cup 4th Round	1-0
1985	Charlton Athletic	A	FA Cup 3rd Round Replay	2-1
1988	Newcastle United	A	First Division	0-2
1991	Chelsea	H	Rumbelows Cup 5th Round Replay	0-3

JANUARY 24TH

| 1885 | Victoria Wanderers | H | Friendly | 4-0 |

The game was halted after only 60 minutes.

1891	Barnes	A	London Senior Cup 1st Round	1-0
1903	Watford	A	Southern League	1-1
1914	Manchester City	A	First Division	1-2
1920	Huddersfield Town	H	Second Division	2-0
1925	Sunderland	H	First Division	1-0
1931	West Bromwich Albion	A	FA Cup 4th Round	0-1
1948	West Bromwich Albion	H	FA Cup 4th Round	3-1
1959	Newport County	H	FA Cup 4th Round	4-1

| 1970 | Crystal Palace | H | FA Cup 4th Round | 0-0 |
| 1975 | Watford | A | Friendly | 3-2 |

With both Spurs and Watford having been eliminated from the FA Cup (the fourth round was due to take place the following day) the two sides organised a friendly Friday night match at Vicarage Road which Spurs won 3-2 thanks to goals from Neil McNab, Alfie Conn and John Duncan.

1976	Stoke City	A	FA Cup 3rd Round Replay	1-2
1981	Hull City	H	FA Cup 4th Round	2-0
1987	Aston Villa	H	First Division	3-0
1990	Nottingham Forest	H	Littlewoods Cup 5th Round Replay	2-3
1993	Norwich City	A	FA Cup 4th Round	2-0
1998	Barnsley	H	FA Cup 4th Round	1-1

JANUARY 25TH

1896	Notts County	H	Friendly	1-5
1902	Southampton	H	FA Cup 1st Round	1-1
1908	Swindon Town	H	Southern League	1-0

1911 Andy Duncan born in Renton in Dumbartonshire. Andy joined Spurs in March 1935 from Hull City, Spurs paying £6,000 for the inside-forward who had already scored 16 goals for Hull that season. Although Spurs were relegated at the end of the season, Andy appeared relatively regularly over the next four seasons, scoring 22 goals in 93 League appearances and was not seriously threatened until the arrival of Ronnie Dix. He made his last appearance for the club in a war-time fixture in 1942 and signed for Chelmsford City at the end of the war. He died in Southall on 10th October 1983.

1913	Sunderland	H	First Division	1-2
1919	Chelsea	H-Highbury		
			London Combination	1-1
1930	Bury	A	Second Division	1-2
1936	Huddersfield Town	H	FA Cup 4th Round	1-0
1940	Arsenal	H	Football League South Group A	0-1
1941	Millwall	H	London War Cup Section B	4-0
1947	Arsenal	H	Friendly	2-0
1958	Sheffield United	H	FA Cup 4th Round	0-3
1964	Aston Villa	H	First Division	3-1

1967 David Ginola born in Gossin in France. After playing for Paris St Germain, Toulon, Racing Paris and Brest he was signed by Newcastle United for £2.5 million in July 1995, immediately proving himself an exceptionally talented winger with a superb eye for goal. The change in management at Newcastle resulted in his appearances becoming less consistent and during the close season of 1997 he asked for a transfer. Despite rumours of interest from Barcelona and Marseilles, he signed for Spurs for £2 million. He soon endeared himself to the Spurs crowd, and his consistently high-standard performances were often the only highlights of an extremely depressing season.

| 1969 | Wolverhampton Wanderers | H | FA Cup 4th Round | 2-1 |
| 1986 | Notts County | A | FA Cup 4th Round | 1-1 |

But for a last minute save from Ray Clemence, Spurs might have suffered the indignity of defeat, for they had been largely unimpressive throughout. Clive Allen scored Spurs' lone goal.

| 1992 | Oldham Athletic | H | First Division | 0-0 |
| 1995 | Aston Villa | A | FA Premier League | 0-1 |

JANUARY 26TH

1884	Albion	H	Friendly	0-1
1895	London Welsh	H	London Senior Cup 1st Round	5-0
1901	Bristol Rovers	H	Southern League	4-0
1907	Norwich City	A	Southern League	0-5
1918	Fulham	H-Highbury		
			London Combination	0-1

1919 Bill Nicholson born in Scarborough. He began his playing career with Spurs' nursery side Northfleet before signing professional forms with Spurs in August 1938. He made his debut for the club in October 1938. Like many of his generation his best playing days were lost to the Second World War but, on the resumption of League action, he was a stalwart of the Spurs side that won the Second and First Divisions in the consecutive seasons of 1949-50 and 1950-51. Upon his retirement as a player in 1955 he was appointed coach at Spurs and held this position until October 1958, when he accepted an offer to take over as manager from Jimmy Anderson. During his 16 years in charge Spurs won the League and FA Cup double in 1961, the first side this century to accomplish the feat, the FA Cup in 1962 and 1967, the European Cup-Winners' Cup in 1963, and were the first British side to win a major European honour, the League Cup in 1971 and 1973 and the UEFA Cup in 1972. It had been Nicholson's intention to step down as manager following the UEFA Cup final in 1974, which Spurs lost against a backdrop of crowd violence, but the following season found him still holding the reins. After four matches of the new season, all of which were lost, and in dispute with a number of his players, Nicholson announced his retirement, to take effect as soon as Spurs had appointed a replacement. With no alternative role within the club, Nicholson spent some 18 months at West Ham United as scout, until in July 1976 he accepted an invitation from Keith Burkinshaw to return to White Hart Lane as consultant. He continued in this role until 1991, when he was made club president. He made but one appearance for England, scoring with his first touch of the game against Portugal, unfortunate that Billy Wright made the wing-half position his own for almost all of the forties and fifties. He was awarded the OBE for his services to football in 1975.

1924	Newcastle United	A	First Division	2-2
1929	Notts County	H	Second Division	3-0
1931	Stoke City	H	Second Division	3-0
1935	Newcastle United	H	FA Cup 4th Round	2-0
1938	New Brighton	H	FA Cup 4th Round Replay	5-2

On a surface much more suited to Spurs' style of play they made no mistake this time around against New Brighton, with goals from Morrison (two), Gibbons (two) and Lyman setting up a fifth round tie at Chesterfield.

1946	Coventry City	H	Football League South	2-0
1952	Manchester United	A	First Division	0-2
1957	Chelsea	H	FA Cup 4th Round	4-0
1963	Arsenal	H	Friendly	3-1

The winter of 1963 was one of the worst on record, totally decimating the League programme. Spurs played only two competitive matches in January, one League match and an FA Cup tie, and only one further League match in February. In desperation they hastily organised a friendly match against local rivals Arsenal, with a one hour match between the two club's reserve sides kicking off proceedings. Spurs won both encounters 3-1, with Jimmy Greaves (two) and Cliff Jones scoring in the first-team battle. A crowd of over 19,000 attended the main match.

| 1980 | Swindon Town | A | FA Cup 4th Round | 0-0 |
| 1990 | Plymouth Argyle | A | Friendly | 3-0 |

This match was a testimonial for Geoff Crudgington with Spurs' goals being scored by Gary Mabbutt, Paul Gascoigne and an own goal.

| 1991 | Oxford United | H | FA Cup 4th Round | 4-2 |

A match which Paul Gascoigne won almost single-handedly. Not only did he score two goals, one a particularly brilliant dribble along the goal-line, but he created the other two for Gary Lineker and Gary Mabbutt.

JANUARY 27TH

1894	Chesham	H	Wolverton & District Charity Cup 1st Round	2-2
1898	Gravesend United	H	Friendly	1-2
1900	Preston North End	A	FA Cup 1st Round	0-1
1906	West Ham United	A	Southern League	1-0
1912	Blackburn Rovers	A	First Division	0-0
1917	West Ham United	H-Homerton		
			London Combination	0-0
1923	Oldham Athletic	H	First Division	3-0
1934	West Ham United	H	FA Cup 4th Round	4-1

West Ham took the lead through Watson early on in the game although Spurs soon equalised thanks to Willie Evans. In the second half Spurs moved up a gear, and two goals from George Hunt and another from Evans gave them a 4-1 victory.

1945	Chelsea	A	Football League South	2-1
1947	Swansea Town	H	Second Division	3-1
1951	Cardiff City	A	Friendly	3-2
1962	Plymouth Argyle	A	FA Cup 4th Round	5-1
1968	Manchester United	A	FA Cup 3rd Round	2-2
1973	Crystal Palace	A	First Division	0-0
1975	Enfield	A	Friendly	2-1
1982	Middlesbrough	H	First Division	1-0
1985	Liverpool	A	FA Cup 4th Round	0-1

Spurs and Liverpool were destined to meet four times during the season, with Spurs winning three of the clashes, including a historic victory at Anfield in the League, and Liverpool one, the FA Cup tie.

Spurs took the game to Liverpool and were perhaps unlucky to be denied a penalty after Perryman was hauled down, but Liverpool held on to win the game with the only goal of the match.

1987	West Ham United	A	Littlewoods Cup 5th Round	1-1
1993	Ipswich Town	H	FA Premier League	0-2
1996	Wolverhampton Wanderers	H	FA Cup 4th Round	1-1

JANUARY 28TH

1893	Casuals	H	London Senior Cup 4th Round	0-1
1897	Chatham	H	Friendly	2-2
1899	Newton Heath	H	FA Cup 1st Round	1-1
1903	Millwall Athletic	A	Western League	1-1
1905	Reading	A	Southern League	2-3
1911	Oldham Athletic	H	First Division	1-1

At half-time fog descended on the pitch and forced the referee to call a halt to proceedings. When the match was replayed in March, Spurs won 2-0.

1922	Watford	H	FA Cup 2nd Round	1-0
1928	Oldham Athletic	H	FA Cup 4th Round	3-0
1933	Luton Town	A	FA Cup 4th Round	0-2
1939	West Bromwich Albion	H	Second Division	2-2

The gathering war clouds over Europe prompted a half-time parade designed to enlist volunteers to the local Air Raid Personnel units.

1950	Sunderland	H	FA Cup 4th Round	5-1
1956	Middlesbrough	H	FA Cup 4th Round	3-1
1961	Crewe Alexandra	H	FA Cup 4th Round	5-1
1967	Millwall	A	FA Cup 3rd Round	0-0
1970	Crystal Palace	A	FA Cup 4th Round Replay	0-1

Manager Bill Nicholson was furious with the team after they had slipped out of the FA Cup in this replay with local rivals Crystal Palace. For the next game he made wholesale changes to the side, dropping Jimmy Greaves, Alan Gilzean from the front line and full-backs Joe Kinnear and Cyril Knowles. Whilst Gilzean, Kinnear and Knowles were later to return and form part of the successful side of the early 1970s, Jimmy Greaves did not, being sold to West Ham in part of the deal that brough Martin Peters to White Hart Lane. This was, therefore, Jimmy's last competitive appearance for Spurs.

| 1984 | Norwich City | H | FA Cup 4th Round | 0-0 |

JANUARY 29TH

1898	Chatham	A	Southern League	2-4
1902	Southampton	A	FA Cup 1st Round Replay	2-2
1906	Queens Park Rangers	H	Western League	1-2
1910	Bradford City	H	First Division	0-0

The Spurs line-up included Danny Steel, Spurs' regular centre-half, his brother Bobby, the regular inside-forward, and their other brother Alex, who made his only appearance for the first team. This is therefore the only occasion on which as many as three brothers all played for the first team in a League match.

| 1921 | Bradford City | H | FA Cup 2nd Round | 4-0 |

Spurs' hero on the day was Jimmy Seed, who scored a hat-trick (two of the goals were scored in 30 seconds!), with Banks getting the other. A crowd of 39,048 produced gate receipts of £3,339.

1927	Huddersfield Town	A	First Division	0-2
1938	Luton Town	H	Second Division	3-0
1944	Brighton & Hove Albion	A	Football League South	2-0
1949	Middlesbrough	H	Friendly	4-1
1955	Port Vale	H	FA Cup 4th Round	4-2
1966	Blackburn Rovers	H	First Division	4-0
1969	Queens Park Rangers	H	First Division	3-2
1972	Leeds United	H	First Division	1-0
1978				

Former England international Jimmy Greaves, one of the greatest goalscorers of his generation, announced in a newspaper article that he had a serious drink problem and often spent periods in hospital to 'dry out'.

1983	West Bromwich Albion	H	FA Cup 4th Round	2-1
1986	Notts County	H	FA Cup 4th Round Replay	5-0
1994	Ipswich Town	A	FA Cup 4th Round	0-3
1995	Sunderland	A	FA Cup 4th Round	4-1
1997	Blackburn Rovers	H	FA Premier League	2-1

JANUARY 30TH

1892	Old St Luke's	H	Friendly	3-1
1897	Wellingborough	A	United League	2-2
1904	Reading	H	Southern League	7-4
1909	Hull City	H	Second Division	0-0
1915	Norwich City	A	FA Cup 2nd Round	2-3
1922	West Bromwich Albion	H	First Division	2-0
1926	Manchester United	H	FA Cup 4th Round	2-2
1932	Barnsley	A	Second Division	2-3
1935	Chelsea	H	First Division	1-3
1937	Plymouth Argyle	H	FA Cup 4th Round	1-0
1939	West Ham United	H	FA Cup 4th Round Replay	1-1 [aet]

The match report according to the *Daily Mail* read 'One good goal to the Hotspur, and one that in my judgement was definitely bad to West Ham, left the cup tie between the two London rivals still undecided. West Ham badly missed their chance when Macaulay failed to score from a penalty, driving the ball almost straight at the goalkeeper.' How strange that the current style seems to be shooting straight at the goalkeeper in the hope he's moved out of the way!

1943	Portsmouth	H	Football League South	5-2
1954	Manchester City	A	FA Cup 4th Round	1-0
1960	Crewe Alexandra	A	FA Cup 4th Round	2-2

With Spurs having frequently stumbled over lower opposition in the cup in recent seasons there were many in the 20,000 crowd convinced that Crewe could pull off a shock. They nearly did too, with only the post saving Spurs' blushes near the end with the home side still pressing for a winner.

1965	Ipswich Town	H	FA Cup 4th Round	5-0
1971	Everton	H	First Division	2-1
1980	Swindon Town	H	FA Cup 4th Round Replay	2-1
1982	Everton	A	First Division	1-1
1988	Port Vale	A	FA Cup 4th Round	1-2
1993	Crystal Palace	A	FA Premier League	3-1

JANUARY 31ST

1885	St Martin's	H	Friendly	1-0
1891	Millwall Athletic	A	London Senior Cup 2nd Round	1-5
1903	Brentford	A	Southern League	1-1
1914	Manchester City	A	FA Cup 2nd Round	1-2
1920	West Stanley	H	FA Cup 2nd Round	4-0
1925	Bolton Wanderers	H	FA Cup 2nd Round	1-1
1931	Millwall	A	Second Division	3-2
1934	Arsenal	A	First Division	3-1
1942	Crystal Palace	A	London War League	2-2

The Spurs line-up for this fixture included Wilf Mannion who played under an assumed name. This was not because he was not registered with the club – after all, many clubs, Aldershot in particular, were using players as 'guests' – but in order to confuse the Germans. If German spies had seen that Wilf Mannion was playing for Spurs, they would have known that his battalion was in London and therefore informed German High Command! For this reason, tracking down the exact line-ups of virtually every club in the country during the war years is extremely difficult.

1948	Bradford Park Avenue	A	Second Division	2-0
1953	Preston North End	A	FA Cup 4th Round	2-2
1959	Arsenal	H	First Division	1-4

Len Julians of Arsenal became the first player to be dismissed from an Arsenal v Spurs match after a tangle with Maurice Norman. That was the only thing to go wrong for Arsenal as they won 4-1.

1968	Manchester United	H	FA Cup 3rd Round Replay	1-0 [aet]
1970	Southampton	H	First Division	0-1
1976	Ipswich Town	A	First Division	2-1
1981	Brighton & Hove Albion	A	First Division	2-0
1987	Crystal Palace	H	FA Cup 4th Round	4-0
1998	Derby County	A	FA Premier League	1-2

FEBRUARY 1ST

1890	Robin Hood	H	Friendly	1-0
1896	Stoke City	A	FA Cup 1st Round	0-5

This was the first competitive match Spurs played as a professional club, with the players earning between 15 and 25 shillings a week for the privilege.

1899	Newton Heath	A	FA Cup 1st Round Replay	5-3
1902	Northampton Town	H	Southern League	1-0
1913	Reading	A	FA Cup 2nd Round	0-1
1919	Arsenal	A	London Combination	3-2

1927   Billy Minter was officially appointed manager of Spurs in succession to Peter McWilliam, although he did not take up the post until 27th February. Minter had joined the club in 1908 as a player, serving the club in that capacity until 1920 when he was appointed trainer under manager Peter McWilliam. Following McWilliam's resignation in February 1927 Minter was elevated to the post of manager, with the outgoing custodian spending almost a month training the new one in preparation for the job. Unfortunately, Minter was not the success the club had hoped for and his two years in charge were brought to an end when illness, initiated by the stresses of the job, were considered sufficient for him to be relieved of his position in November 1929. He subsequently became assistant-secretary at Spurs, a position he held until his death in May 1940.

1930	Chelsea	H	Second Division	3-3
1933	Bury	H	Second Division	2-1
1936	Port Vale	A	Second Division	5-1
1941	West Ham United	H	London War Cup Section B	1-2
1947	Manchester City	A	Second Division	0-1
1958	Sheffield Wednesday	A	First Division	0-2
1964	Chelsea	H	First Division	1-2
1967	Millwall	H	FA Cup 3rd Round Replay	1-0
1969	Sunderland	A	First Division	0-0
1975	Everton	A	First Division	0-1
1984	Norwich City	A	FA Cup 4th Round Replay	1-2
1986	Everton	A	First Division	0-1
1992	Manchester City	A	First Division	0-1
1997	Chelsea	H	FA Premier League	1-2

FEBRUARY 2ND

| 1884 | Clarence | A | Friendly | 1-0 |
| 1898 | Luton Town | H | United League | 2-2 |

The Luton Town players were attacked by the crowd at this game with the result that after an investigation Northumberland Park was suspended for one match. Although the incident took place during a United League match, the suspension resulted in a Southern League match being played elsewhere!

| 1907 | Blackburn Rovers | H | FA Cup 2nd Round | 1-1 |
| 1918 | Queens Park Rangers | A | London Combination | 7-2 |

1920   Arthur Willis born in Northumberland. Arthur was working as a miner and playing non-League football when he was offered contracts with Barnsley, Sunderland and Spurs, deciding on signing as an amateur with Spurs in 1938. He was farmed out to the club's nursery sides and then upgraded to the professional ranks in January 1944. He finally broke into the first team in place of Charlie Withers as left full-back in the last two games of the 1949-50 season and kept his place the following season as Spurs lifted the First Division title for the first time. In October 1951 he was capped by England, but as he was similar in style to Withers, both he and Arthur tended to alternate the left-back position with the result Arthur could not add to his England tally. He was released in September 1954 and joined Swansea Town, later becoming coach at the club. He died in Haverfordwest on 7th November 1987.

1928   Tommy Harmer born in Hackney. One of the most gifted players to have played for Spurs, Tommy joined the club as an amateur in 1945 and signed professional forms in August 1948. Unfortunately, his small frame (he was 5' 6" tall and weighed under 9 stone) often counted against him in the hustle and bustle of League football, and he was therefore overlooked by Arthur Rowe when he assembled the push-and-run side, and Bill Nicholson when he put together the 'double' team. In between, Tommy, known affectionately as 'Harmer The Charmer', made 205 appearances in the League and 17 in the FA Cup, although he missed out on the 1956 semi-final clash with Manchester City because Jimmy Anderson wanted a bigger man on the field. In October 1960 he was allowed to leave the club and signed with Watford, although he was back in the capital by September 1962 when he joined Chelsea, eventually becoming coach at Stamford Bridge until released in June 1967.

1929	Millwall	A	Second Division	1-5
1935	Aston Villa	A	First Division	0-1
1938	Newcastle United	A	Second Division	0-1

| 1939 | West Ham United | N | FA Cup 4th Round 2nd Replay | 1-2 |

After draws at Upton Park and White Hart Lane Spurs and West Ham faced each other for the third time at Highbury. Spurs had been decimated by injuries but still managed to take the lead through Morrison, but he was later injured and spent the rest of the game little more than a passenger. Spurs' hopes were further dented when Albert Hall suffered an injury leaving the team with only nine fit men. West Ham equalised to force extra time and then made their two additional players count, scoring the winner in Spurs' last cup-tie before the war.

1946	Aston Villa	A	Football League South	1-5
1952	Newcastle United	H	FA Cup 4th Round	0-3
1957	Luton Town	A	First Division	3-1
1963	Portsmouth	A	Friendly	3-2
1974	Manchester City	A	First Division	0-0
1980	Southampton	H	First Division	0-0
1981	Jersey Select XI	A	Friendly	5-0
1985	Luton Town	A	First Division	2-2
1987	West Ham United	H	Littlewoods Cup 5th Round Replay	5-0
1991	Leeds United	H	First Division	0-0

FEBRUARY 3RD

1894	City Ramblers	H	Friendly	0-0
1900	Sheppey United	A	Southern League	4-1
1902	Southampton	N	FA Cup 1st Round 2nd Replay	1-2

Spurs' defence of the cup won the previous season ended at the first hurdle, but it took three games before Southampton were finally able to progress. The FA had ordered the second replay to be held at Reading, but when the teams arrived at the ground, they found the area covered in snow and a heavy storm in progress. There seemed little likelihood of the game proceeding, but an army of unemployed men was set to work clearing the pitch. A lawn tennis marker was borrowed and a blue compound made which would enable the lines to stand out against the snow. The storm eased sufficiently for the match to be started, but play had to be halted every so often so that the lines could be remarked. Under such circumstances Spurs slid out of the cup.

1906	Reading	H	FA Cup 2nd Round	3-2
1917	Southampton	H-Highbury		
			London Combination	3-1
1921	Bradford Park Avenue	H	First Division	2-0
1923	Manchester United	H	FA Cup 2nd Round	4-0
1926	Manchester United	A	FA Cup 4th Round Replay	0-2
1934	Liverpool	A	First Division	1-3
1937	Barnsley	H	Second Division	3-0
1945	Queens Park Rangers	H	League South Cup Group 3	1-1
1951	Sunderland	A	First Division	0-0
1960	Crewe Alexandra	H	FA Cup 4th Round Replay	13-2

According to legend, the train carrying the Crewe Alexandra team arrived at London's Euston Station at platform 2 and departed after the game from platform 13. A fanciful notion, but Crewe were probably too shellshocked after the game to have noticed what platform they were on! Spurs piled into a 10-1 lead by half-time and only eased up in the second half. The goals were scored by Bobby Smith, who got four, Les Allen (five), Cliff Jones (three, of which one was a penalty) and Tommy Harmer. The Crewe goalkeeper announced after the game that he had feared conceding eight goals and still couldn't work out where the other five had come from!

1962	Wolverhampton Wanderers	A	First Division	1-3
1968	Manchester United	H	First Division	1-2
1973	Derby County	A	FA Cup 4th Round	1-1
1979	Manchester City	H	First Division	0-3
1982	West Bromwich Albion	A	League Cup Semi-Final 1st Leg	0-0

Both Tony Galvin of Spurs and Martin Jol of West Bromwich were sent off in a game that also saw seven players booked. Galvin's dismissal was especially harsh for he seemed to wave his arm in an attempt to extricate himself as he was being impeded as he ran down the wing. The referee misconstrued the gesture and sent both men off the field.

| 1996 | Liverpool | A | FA Premier League | 0-0 |

FEBRUARY 4TH

| 1888 | Royal Arsenal | A | Friendly | 2-6 |
| 1893 | Slough | H | Southern Alliance | 5-2 |

1905	Middlesbrough	A	FA Cup 1st Round	1-1
1911	Blackburn Rovers	A	FA Cup 2nd Round	0-0
1922	Manchester City	A	First Division	3-3
1925	Bolton Wanderers	A	FA Cup 2nd Round Replay	1-0

Bolton were renowned cup fighters throughout the 1920s winning the cup on no fewer than three occasions during the decade (including the first final held at Wembley), and when Spurs had been held at home few gave much hope for their chances in the replay. They defended exceptionally well throughout, especially after Bill Lane had given them the lead early on in the second half. The general consensus was that Bill Hinton was Spurs' man of the match, and the goalkeeper certainly pulled off a string of saves to ensure the cup victory. When the team arrived back at Euston after the game an enthusiastic crowd gathered to cheer them home.

1928	Manchester United	H	First Division	4-0
1933	Grimsby Town	H	Second Division	4-3
1939	Norwich City	A	Second Division	2-1
1950	Leicester City	H	Second Division	0-2
1953	Preston North End	H	FA Cup 4th Round Replay	1-0
1956	Newcastle United	A	First Division	2-1
1961	Leicester City	H	First Division	2-3

This was the first home defeat Spurs suffered in their double season and according to legend Leicester claimed after the game that Spurs would not win a thing that season. Although Spurs were below par during the game they were still some considerable way ahead of the chasing pack in the League.

1967	Nottingham Forest	A	First Division	1-1
1978	Fulham	A	Second Division	1-1
1984	Nottingham Forest	A	First Division	2-2
1990	Norwich City	H	First Division	4-0
1998	Barnsley	A	FA Cup 4th Round Replay	1-3

FEBRUARY 5TH

1887	Park	H	Friendly	4-1
1898	Swindon Town	A	Southern League	0-3
1910	Chelsea	A	FA Cup 2nd Round	1-0
1911				

Ralph Ward born in Oadby in Leicestershire. Ralph began his professional career with Bradford Park Avenue in 1929 and was transferred to Spurs in 1936 after impressing in an FA Cup tie between the two sides. He immediately slotted into the team at full-back and was only briefly troubled for the position by the arrival of Bert Sproston in 1938. Bert of course left four months after his arrival and Ralph continued to put in solid and reliable performances up to and throughout the Second World War. When the war ended and Ralph realised his playing career was coming to an end he took up the position of assistant golf professional at Bush Hill Golf Club, subsequently applying to Spurs to be released from his contract. This they did and he subsequently signed for Crewe Alexandra and played for them for three years. He returned to Gresty Road in 1953 as manager, holding the post until 1955.

1916	West Ham United	A	London Combination [2nd competition]	0-2
1920	Bradford Park Avenue	A	First Division	1-1
1927	Sunderland	H	First Division	0-2
1936	Manchester United	H	Second Division	0-0
1938	Barnsley	A	Second Division	1-1
1944	Reading	H	Football League South	2-2
1949	Bury	A	Second Division	1-1
1955	Portsmouth	A	First Division	3-0
1960				

Micky Hazard born in Sunderland. Although Micky represented Sunderland Schools as a youth, he was signed by Spurs as an apprentice in July 1976 and later upgraded to the professional ranks in February 1978. An exceptionally talented midfield player, his style of play was similar to that of Glenn Hoddle, and whenever Glenn was out of the side through injury, Micky would step into the gap. Unfortunately, it was considered the two players were too similar to fit successfully into the same side and Micky was sold to Chelsea in 1985 for £310,000, later playing for Portsmouth and Swindon before returning to White Hart Lane in 1994. Whilst he had lost a bit of pace all of his silky skills were still in evidence, although a back injury that failed to clear up prompted him to announce his retirement.

1966	Blackpool	A	First Division	0-0
1972	Rotherham United	H	FA Cup 4th Round	2-0
1977	Middlesbrough	A	First Division	0-2
1983	Manchester City	A	First Division	2-2
1986	Everton	H	Screen Sport Super Cup Semi-Final 1st Leg	0-0

1989	Manchester United	A	First Division	0-1
1994	Sheffield Wednesday	H	FA Premier League	1-3
1995	Blackburn Rovers	H	FA Premier League	3-1

FEBRUARY 6TH

1886	Edmonton Independent	H	Friendly	4-1
1892	St Albans	A	Friendly	1-2
1897	3rd Grenadier Guards	H	Friendly	9-3
1899	Grays United	H	Thames & Medway League	2-1
1904	Everton	A	FA Cup 1st Round	2-1
1909	Fulham	H	FA Cup 2nd Round	1-0
1926	Sunderland	H	First Division	0-2
1928	Bolton Wanderers	H	First Division	1-2
1932	Nottingham Forest	A	Second Division	3-1
1937	Sheffield United	A	Second Division	2-3
1943	Chelsea	A	Football League South	1-0
1951	Combined Liege XI	Liege	Friendly	4-1
1954	Newcastle United	H	First Division	3-0
1960	Preston North End	A	First Division	1-1
1965	Manchester United	H	First Division	1-0
1971	Manchester United	A	First Division	1-2
1974	Birmingham City	H	First Division	4-2
1982	Wolverhampton Wanderers	H	First Division	6-1

Shortly before kick off Sir Stanley Rous, the former president of FIFA, officially opened the new West Stand. The carnival atmosphere of the day was continued during the game with Spurs beating a Wolves side languishing near the bottom of the table. Ricky Villa grabbed a hat-trick and there were single strikes from Mark Falco, Garth Crooks and a Glenn Hoddle penalty.

FEBRUARY 7TH

1872   Stanley Briggs born in Stamford Hill, North London. Stanley joined Spurs from the Tottenham club in 1892 and his early career therefore pre-dates Spurs' entry into the Southern League, although he did make appearances in the Southern Alliance in the 1892-93 season. As an amateur he was also free to play for whoever he wished and he made two appearances for Woolwich Arsenal in the Football League! Stanley's amateur status eventually curtailed his Spurs career (he even refused to attend the meeting at which Spurs adopted professionalism in 1895), for although he continued his association with Spurs until 1898 his appearances were sporadic to say the least, playing only seven games for the club in the Southern League. He was rightly regarded one of the most famous players in London at the time and might have gone on to play for the full England side had he become a professional player. At the end of his playing career he emigrated to Canada where he died in September 1935.

| 1885 | Fillebrook | H | Friendly | 3-0 |

Only ten Spurs players turned up for the match but they were still able to win.

1891	Orion Gymnasium	H	Middlesex Senior Cup	7-1
1903	West Bromwich Albion	H	FA Cup 1st Round	0-0
1907	Blackburn Rovers	A	FA Cup 2nd Round Replay	1-1 [aet]
1914	Manchester United	H	First Division	2-1
1920	Blackpool	A	Second Division	1-0
1925	Preston North End	H	First Division	2-0
1931	Oldham Athletic	A	Second Division	4-0

1935   Cliff Jones born in Swansea. Signed by Swansea Town in May 1952 this fast and tricky winger played alongside his brother Bryn and went on to play for his country, winning his first cap in 1954. He was transferred to Spurs for £35,000, then a record for a winger, in 1958, but he more than repaid that fee over the next ten years. As well as setting up many chances for others, Cliff also scored an extremely high rate himself, netting 135 goals in 314 League games. Whilst at Spurs he helped the club win the 1961 double, the FA Cup in 1962 and the European Cup-Winners' Cup in 1963, and although he collected a third FA Cup medal in 1967 he was a non-playing substitute. He was given a cut-price transfer to Fulham in October 1968, costing the Cottagers £5,000. He later finished his playing career in non-League circles, although he continued to make the occasional appearance in ex-Spurs sides.

1948	Leicester City	H	FA Cup 5th Round	5-2
1953	Arsenal	A	First Division	0-4
1959	Manchester United	H	First Division	1-3

1961   Danny Blanchflower caused a sensation on live television. Confronted by Eammon Andrews and presented with the famous red book of *This Is Your Life*, Blanchflower called 'Oh no it isn't' and ran off, refusing to appear on the programme. He was the first celebrity to refuse to appear on the programme (as a result of this, the programme would never again be shown 'live' but instead was pre-recorded for transmission). Asked later why he refused to appear, Blanchflower said 'It was for personal reasons, and if I told you what they were they wouldn't be personal anymore.'

1970	Wolverhampton Wanderers	A	First Division	2-2
1973	Derby County	H	FA Cup 3rd Round Replay	3-5 [aet]

Spurs were 3-1 ahead with less than ten minutes left to play when Derby striker Roger Davies took over, forcing the game into extra time and continuing to run the Spurs' defence ragged as Derby won 5-3.

1976	West Ham United	H	First Division	1-1
1981	Leeds United	H	First Division	1-1
1993	Southampton	H	FA Premier League	4-2

All four Spurs goals came in a spell of four minutes 44 seconds, midway through the second half. Southampton had led at one stage!

1996	Wolverhampton Wanderers	A	FA Cup 4th Round Replay	2-0
1998	Blackburn Rovers	A	FA Premier League	3-0

FEBRUARY 8TH

1890	Vulcan	H	Friendly	2-1
1894	London Hospital	H	Friendly	1-1
1896	Royal Scots Greys	H	Friendly	2-1

1899 Less than a year after taking over as manager at Spurs, Frank Brettell handed in his resignation, to take effect on April 1st. Brettell resigned because he had been offered substantially more money to take over at Portsmouth, and as Spurs found a new manager before April 1st, Brettell was allowed to leave on February 17th.

1902	Watford	A	Southern League	3-0
1908	Luton Town	H	Southern League	1-2
1913	Middlesbrough	H	First Division	5-3
1919	Crystal Palace	H-Highbury		
			London Combination	4-2
1930	Nottingham Forest	A	Second Division	0-0
1936	Fulham	H	Second Division	2-2

1934 Dave Dunmore born in Whitehaven. He began his League career with York City and was spotted by Spurs manager Arthur Rowe at a time when he was looking to rebuild the push-and-run side, joining Spurs for £10,500 in February 1954. National Service meant his early career at White Hart Lane was blighted, and by the time he returned Len Duquemin and Bobby Smith stood in front of his first-team chances and he was transferred to West Ham as part of the deal that brought John Smith to Spurs in 1960. He later played for Leyton Orient before returning to York City.

1941	West Ham United	A	London War Cup Section B	2-3
1958	Manchester City	H	First Division	5-1
1964	West Ham United	A	First Division	0-4
1975	Stoke City	H	First Division	0-2
1984	Sunderland	H	First Division	3-0
1986	Coventry City	H	First Division	0-1
1987	Arsenal	A	Littlewoods Cup Semi-Final 1st Leg	1-0

A single strike from Clive Allen, his tenth in the competition that season, was enough to give Spurs a single-goal lead to take back to White Hart Lane.

FEBRUARY 9TH

1875 Tom Morris born in Grantham. After impressing with Grantham Rovers and Gainsborough Trinity there were plenty of clubs keen to acquire the talents of half-back Tom, and he chose to join Spurs in 1899, making his debut for the club in a Southern League match in September of that year. Thereafter he was almost ever-present until his retirement as a player in 1912 – he played in the first match at White Hart Lane, throughout the cup run of 1901 and was still playing when the club played their first Football League match in 1908. Upon retiring as a player Tom joined the Spurs groundstaff and remained with the club until his death in April 1942.

1884	Albion	A	Friendly	3-0

The game was halted after 50 minutes, Jack Jull having scored a hat-trick. This is certainly the first recorded hat-trick scored by a Spurs player, but it may well be that the feat was achieved on October 6th 1883 when Spurs defeated Brownlow Rovers 9-0; sadly the scorers are not known.

1898	Sussex	A	Friendly	2-1
1901	Preston North End	H	FA Cup 1st Round	1-1

The first round of the FA Cup had been delayed owing to the death of Queen Victoria and Spurs began the game as though they were still in mourning – they were a goal behind before half an hour had elapsed but thereafter put Preston under constant pressure, with Peter McBride in the visitors' goal stopping almost everything that was thrown at him, in particular from Sandy Brown, who had an unhappy and nervous afternoon. With barely eight minutes of the game left, Kirwan raced clear of the defence and centred where Brown was waiting to throw himself at the ball and finally get one past McBride. Despite clawing themselves back into the game, Spurs were not given much hope for the replay, set for Deepdale on February 13th.

1905	Middlesbrough	H	FA Cup 1st Round Replay	1-0
1907	Crystal Palace	A	Southern League	1-0
1911	Blackburn Rovers	H	FA Cup 2nd Round Replay	0-2
1918	Millwall	H-Homerton		
			London Combination	4-2
1924	West Ham United	A	First Division	0-0
1929	Port Vale	H	Second Division	4-2
1935	Derby County	H	First Division	2-2
1946	Arsenal	A	Football League South	1-1
1952	Arsenal	H	First Division	1-2

With King George VI having died during the week a minute's silence was observed at this and every other game played on the day, whilst the players all wore black armbands in memory of the monarch. Once play started Arsenal settled quicker, taking the lead after only five minutes through Roper, but Spurs were level on 12 minutes thanks to Sonny Walters. Arsenal's winner was scored early in the second half by Forbes.

1957	Sunderland	H	First Division	5-2
1980	West Bromwich Albion	A	First Division	1-2
1992	Nottingham Forest	A	Rumbelows Cup Semi-Final 1st Leg	1-1

FEBRUARY 10TH

1894	Polytechnic	H	Friendly	5-0
1896	Luton Town	A	Friendly	0-9
1897	Gravesend	A	Friendly	3-1
1900	Brighton United	A	Southern League	3-0
1902	Queens Park Rangers	H	London League	1-5
1906	Queens Park Rangers	A	Southern League	0-0
1912	Bury	A	First Division	1-2
1917	Crystal Palace	A	London Combination	1-0
1923	Blackburn Rovers	A	First Division	0-1

1926 Danny Blanchflower born in Belfast. He began his professional career with Glentoran and was transferred to Barnsley in 1949 for £6,500 and six months later won the first of his 56 caps for Northern Ireland. Aston Villa paid £15,000 for his signature in 1951 and three years later he was bought as replacement for Bill Nicholson for Spurs for £30,000. With the push-and-run side all ageing together Blanchflower was unknowingly the first of the great double side to arrive at the club. His stylish midfield play was one of the keys to the double winning side of 1961, a team that then went on to retain the FA Cup and, in 1963, lift the European Cup-Winners' Cup. Troubled by knee injury for some time Blanchflower retired in 1964 and immediately launched into a career in journalism, broken only by spells in charge at Chelsea in 1978 and as Northern Ireland's manager. Footballer of the Year in both 1958 and 1961, he died in 1993.

1934	Chelsea	H	First Division	2-1
1940	West Ham United	A	Football League South Group C	0-2
1945	West Ham United	A	League South Cup Group 3	0-1
1962	Nottingham Forest	H	First Division	4-2
1968	Sunderland	A	First Division	1-0
1973	Manchester City	H	First Division	2-3
1979	Coventry City	A	First Division	3-1
1982	West Bromwich Albion	H	League Cup Semi-Final 2nd Leg	1-0

With the first leg having finished goalless, a single strike by Micky Hazard was enough to give Spurs a place in the final, where they would face Liverpool.

1986	Jersey Select XI	A	Friendly	7-0
1990	Chelsea	A	First Division	2-1
1993	Everton	A	FA Premier League	2-1

FEBRUARY 11TH

1890	Clapton	H	Middlesex Senior Cup 2nd Round	2-4
1893	Polytechnic	H	Southern Alliance	2-2
1899	Sunderland	H	FA Cup 2nd Round	2-1
1903	West Bromwich Albion	A	FA Cup 1st Round Replay	2-0
1905	Northampton Town	A	Southern League	3-0
1907	Blackburn Rovers	N	FA Cup 2nd Round 2nd Replay	2-1
1911	Preston North End	A	First Division	0-2
1922	Manchester City	H	First Division	3-1
1928	Everton	A	First Division	5-3
1933	Oldham Athletic	A	Second Division	5-1
1939	Luton Town	H	Second Division	0-1
1950	Everton	A	FA Cup 5th Round	0-1
1956	Birmingham City	H	First Division	0-1
1961	Aston Villa	A	First Division	2-1
1967	Fulham	H	First Division	4-2

1974 Nick Barmby born in Hull. Nick signed with Spurs as a trainee in 1991 and was soon established as an integral part of the team, linking up exceptionally well with Teddy Sheringham as the team reached the FA Cup semi-final in 1993. The arrival of Jurgen Klinsmann threatened that partnership and Nick expressed his wish to return to the North, finally joining Middlesbrough for £5.25 million in August 1995. A little over a year later a £5.75 million fee took him to Goodison Park and Everton. Having broken into the England set-up whilst at Spurs, he has since suffered from considerable competition for places.

1978	Blackpool	H	Second Division	2-2
1984	Leicester City	A	First Division	3-2
1989	Charlton Athletic	H	First Division	1-1
1995	Chelsea	A	FA Premier League	1-1

FEBRUARY 12TH

1887	Fillebrook	H	Friendly	3-0
1898	Sheffield United	H	Friendly	1-1
1906	Fulham	H	Southern League	0-1
1908	Crystal Palace	A	Southern League	2-0

On the same day that Spurs were winning at Crystal Palace, there was a meeting of the Southern League. Spurs were represented by club director Morton Cadman and he had an important resolution, designed to win back for the Southern League the support and popularity it was rapidly losing to the Football League. Despite Cadman's eloquent presentation, the resolution failed to find even a seconder amongst the other clubs. Incensed at the snub, Cadman hurried back to White Hart Lane to confer with chairman Charles Roberts. When Charles Roberts heard of the goings on he decided enough was enough; the Southern League was too narrow-minded in its thinking and Spurs would therefore have to leave such company and apply for membership of the Football League. This was not merely the whim of Roberts alone either, for the rest of the board were of one mind and had been waiting for a decision along these lines for some time. The Tottenham board were therefore unanimous; they would be leaving the Southern League at the end of the current season and the Southern League management committee would be informed as soon as was possible.

1910	Bristol City	H	First Division	3-2
1916	Croydon City	H	London Combination [2nd competition]	2-0
1921	Manchester City	H	First Division	2-0
1927	West Bromwich Albion	A	First Division	0-5
1938	Chesterfield	A	FA Cup 5th Round	2-2
1944	Luton Town	H	Football League South	8-1
1949	Nottingham Forest	H	Second Division	2-1
1955	Blackpool	H	First Division	3-2
1966	Burnley	H	FA Cup 4th Round	4-3
1969	Aston Villa	H	FA Cup 5th Round	3-2
1972	Nottingham Forest	A	First Division	1-0
1977	Manchester United	H	First Division	1-3
1979	Wrexham	H	FA Cup 4th Round	3-3
1983	Swansea City	H	First Division	1-0
1994	Blackburn Rovers	H	FA Premier League	0-2
1996	West Ham United	H	FA Premier League	0-1

FEBRUARY 13TH

1886	Grange Park 2nd XI	H	Friendly	0-3
1892	Clapton	A	Friendly	2-0
1897	Northfleet	H	Friendly	5-0
1897	Northfleet	H	Southern League	0-2
1901	Preston North End	A	FA Cup 1st Round Replay	4-2

A large number of Spurs fans made the day-return journey from London to be present at Preston for the FA Cup 1st round replay. Spurs showed two changes from the side that drew the first match, with Hughes replacing the injured McNaught at centre-half and Jack Jones returning to the side in place of Stormont, as well as resuming his role as captain. Freed from the demands of playing in front of their own expectant crowd, Spurs settled quickly and effectively killed the game off as a contest before half-time, with John Cameron (the player-manager) and Sandy Brown scoring in quick succession. In the second half Brown completed his hat-trick and two Preston goals, from Becton and Pratt were little more than consolation. Spurs' reward for knocking out Preston was one of the toughest ties of the second round – at home to the cup-holders Bury.

1904	Bristol Rovers	H	Southern League	5-1
1909	Blackpool	H	Second Division	4-1
1911	Middlesbrough	H	First Division	6-2
1915	Middlesbrough	A	First Division	5-7
1926	Blackburn Rovers	A	First Division	2-4
1932	Chesterfield	H	Second Division	3-3
1937	Burnley	H	Second Division	3-0
1943	Arsenal	A	Football League South	0-1
1954	Manchester United	A	First Division	0-2
1960	Leicester City	H	First Division	1-2
1965	Fulham	A	First Division	1-4
1971	Nottingham Forest	H	FA Cup 5th Round	2-1
1982	Aston Villa	H	FA Cup 5th Round	1-0
1988	Oxford United	A	First Division	0-0

FEBRUARY 14TH

1885	Latymer	H	Friendly	0-0

The game was halted after only 75 minutes.

1891	Clapton	H	Middlesex Senior Cup 2nd Round	Lost

Although Spurs lost this cup tie with Clapton, there is no record of the final score.

1896	Royal Ordnance	A	Friendly	1-2
1899	Reading	A	Southern League	0-2
1903	West Ham United	A	Southern League	0-1

Although he was not yet a regular in the Spurs side, Vivian Woodward made his debut for the full England side on this day, helping them to a 4-0 win over Ireland at Wolverhampton. He was therefore the first player to be capped by England whilst on Spurs' books.

1914	Bradford City	A	First Division	1-2
1920	Blackpool	H	Second Division	2-2
1923	Blackburn Rovers	H	First Division	2-0
1925	Burnley	A	First Division	4-1
1931	Nottingham Forest	A	Second Division	2-2
1942	Clapton Orient	A	London War League	3-2
1948	Doncaster Rovers	A	Second Division	1-1
1953	Halifax Town	A	FA Cup 5th Round	3-0

With Halifax having already disposed of First Division sides Cardiff and Stoke in previous rounds local cup fever had reached boiling point by the time of the match, although the pitch was still covered in snow. Watched by the Mayors of Halifax and Brighouse and 34,000 others, Spurs made their class tell in the end thanks to two goals from Les Bennett and one from Len Duquemin.

1959	Norwich City	H	FA Cup 5th Round	1-1
1962	Dukla Prague	A	European Cup 2nd Round 1st Leg	0-1
1970	Leeds United	H	First Division	1-1
1976	Queens Park Rangers	H	First Division	0-3
1981	Coventry City	H	FA Cup 5th Round	3-1
1987	Southampton	H	First Division	2-0
1993	Wimbledon	H	FA Cup 5th Round	3-2
1998	Leicester City	H	FA Premier League	1-1

FEBRUARY 15TH

1897	Southampton St Mary's	A	Friendly	0-2
1898	St Barnard's	H	Friendly	4-0
1899	Southampton	A	United League	1-2
1902	West Ham United	H	Southern League	1-2
1904	Queens Park Rangers	A	London League	3-0
1908	Brighton & Hove Albion	A	Southern League	0-2
1913	Notts County	A	First Division	1-0
1919	Queens Park Rangers	A	London Combination	1-7
1930	Oldham Athletic	H	Second Division	2-1
1936	Bradford Park Avenue	A	FA Cup 5th Round	0-0
1941	Bournemouth & Boscombe Athletic	H	Football League War Cup 1st Round	4-1
1958	Nottingham Forest	A	First Division	2-1
1964	Sheffield United	H	First Division	0-0
1969	Queens Park Rangers	A	First Division	1-1
1975	Coventry City	A	First Division	1-1
1988	AS Monaco	H	Friendly	0-4

A match arranged as part of the deal that had taken Spurs favourite Glenn Hoddle to Monaco at the end of the 1986-87 season saw Spurs field pretty much an experimental side in this friendly, but Hoddle still ran the show throughout.

1994	Athletico Madrid	A	Friendly	2-1
1997	Arsenal	H	FA Premier League	0-0

FEBRUARY 16TH

1884	Hanover United 2nd XI	H	Friendly	1-2

The game was halted ten minutes early.

1900 William Davies born in Glamorgan. Willie was already a Welsh international when he joined Spurs from Notts County in 1930, having previously played for Swansea Town and Cardiff City. Upon signing for Spurs this fast winger missed only four of the next 105 League and cup ties, but the subsequent emergence of John McCormick thereafter limited his first-team appearances and he returned to Swansea in September 1933. He died in Llandiello on 6th August 1953.

1901	West Ham United	A	Southern League	4-1
1903	West Ham United	H	Western League	1-0
1907	Brentford	H	Southern League	2-1
1918	Crystal Palace	H-Highbury	London Combination	8-0
1920	Huddersfield Town	H	Second Division	2-0
1924	Cardiff City	H	First Division	1-1
1935	Bolton Wanderers	H	FA Cup 5th Round	1-1
1938	Chesterfield	H	FA Cup 5th Round Replay	2-1
1946	Arsenal	H	Football League South	2-0
1952	Manchester City	A	First Division	1-1
1957	Bournemouth & Boscombe Athletic	A	FA Cup 5th Round	1-3

Bournemouth were managed at the time by former player Freddie Cox but Spurs should still have progressed at the expense of their Third Division rivals. Spurs never really got going in the match and so thoughts of trip to Wembley would have to be put aside for another year.

1974	Arsenal	A	First Division	1-0
1980	Birmingham City	H	FA Cup 5th Round	3-1
1991	Portsmouth	A	FA Cup 5th Round	2-1

The undoubted star of the show was Paul Gascoigne, who was turning the 1991 FA Cup into a personal crusade. He got both goals this day after Spurs had fallen behind; one with his head and then a superb run through the middle of the field to fire home the winner.

1992	Crystal Palace	H	First Division	0-1

FEBRUARY 17TH

1894	Highland Light Infantry	H	Friendly	2-2

1899 Immediately after receiving Frank Brettell's resignation as manager of Spurs the board of directors had advertised the vacancy and had received a huge number of applications. Almost all of these were irrelevant for the club already had the man they wanted on the staff – player John Cameron. Although he had only joined the club as a player in 1898 and was still in his early 20s, he had clearly impressed as soon as he arrived at the club. He was therefore persuaded by the board to assume the role of player-manager, a position he accepted on this date. The move was an unqualified success, for by 1900 the team were Southern League champions and the following year won the FA Cup, still the only time a non-League club has won the premier cup competition since the Football League started in 1888.

1900	Bedminster	H	Southern League	5-2
1902	Millwall Athletic	A	Western League	3-1
1906	Bristol Rovers	H	Southern League	2-2

1908 Spurs informed the Southern League of their intention to resign membership at the end of the current season. Whether the Southern League were informed of the full reasons behind Tottenham's resignation is a matter of some debate, but Spurs felt that the conservative attitude of the League towards many aspects of the game, in particular towards professional clubs, was intolerable. In recent years the likes of Chelsea and Clapton Orient had applied to join and been rejected, only to be welcomed by the Football League. If they did but know it, the Southern League was under considerable threat, for Fulham had left and joined the Football League in 1907; the Southern League was in danger of becoming obsolete. Quite what reaction Spurs expected when they made their decision public we do not know, but within days Queens Park Rangers (who were on their way to winning the championship) and Bradford Park Avenue announced they would be following suit. In the face of such wholesale resignations, the Southern League called an extraordinary general meeting for March 23rd.

1912	Middlesbrough	H	First Division	2-1
1917	Portsmouth	A	London Combination	4-2
1923	Bolton Wanderers	H	First Division	0-1
1934	Aston Villa	H	FA Cup 5th Round	0-1
1936	Bradford Park Avenue	H	FA Cup 5th Round Replay	2-1
1940	Charlton Athletic	H	Football League South Group C	2-0
1945	Aldershot	H	League South Cup Group 3	6-1
1951	Aston Villa	H	First Division	3-2
1953	Burnley	A	First Division	2-3
1962	West Bromwich Albion	A	FA Cup 5th Round	4-2
1968	Preston North End	H	FA Cup 4th Round	3-1
1971	West Bromwich Albion	H	First Division	2-2
1973	Coventry City	A	First Division	1-0
1981	Manchester United	A	First Division	0-0
1982	Aston Villa	A	First Division	1-1

FEBRUARY 18TH

1888	Olympic	A	Friendly	5-1
1893	London Welsh	H	Friendly	2-2
1899	Bristol City	H	Southern League	3-2
1901	Reading	H	Western League	3-2
1905	Newcastle United	H	FA Cup 2nd Round	1-1
1911	Notts County	H	First Division	3-0
1922	Manchester City	H	FA Cup 3rd Round	2-1
1928	Leicester City	A	FA Cup 5th Round	3-0

1931 John Ryden born in Alexandria, Dumbarton. Having begun his career with various Scottish junior sides John signed as a part-time player with Alloa Athletic and subsequently turned full-time with English club Accrington Stanley in 1954. In November 1955 he was transferred to Spurs for £12,000, making his debut at half-back the following April. Although John briefly took over as captain when Tony Marchi was transferred to Italy, he never quite managed to command a regular place in the side, and the subsequent arrival of Jim Iley and Dave Mackay put him well down the list. He was transferred to Watford in June 1961 and later played non-League football for a number of clubs before retiring.

1933	Preston North End	H	Second Division	1-1
1939	Fulham	A	Second Division	0-1
1947	Burnley	A	Second Division	0-0
1950	Bradford Park Avenue	A	Second Division	3-1
1956	Doncaster Rovers	A	FA Cup 5th Round	2-0
1959	Norwich City	A	FA Cup 5th Round Replay	0-1

Norwich City were the surprise package of the 1958-59 FA Cup, eventually going out at the semi-final stage to Luton. Among the scalps they claimed along the way were Spurs, beating them in a replay after the two sides had drawn at White Hart Lane the previous Saturday.

1961	Aston Villa	A	FA Cup 5th Round	2-0
1967	Portsmouth	H	FA Cup 4th Round	3-1
1975	Birmingham City	A	First Division	0-1
1995	Southampton	H	FA Cup 5th Round	1-1

FEBRUARY 19TH

| 1887 | St Luke's | H | East End Cup 3rd Round | 2-1 |
| 1898 | Northfleet | A | Southern League | 3-1 |

John L. Jones was missing from the Spurs line-up as he was in Llandudno representing Wales in their international match against Ireland. The Irish won 1-0.

1906	Millwall	A	Western League	1-1
1910	Swindon Town	A	FA Cup 3rd Round	2-3
1916	Fulham	A	London Combination [2nd competition]	1-3
1921	Southend United	A	FA Cup 3rd Round	4-1

Just as Spurs had required a piece of good fortune on their way to the 1901 FA Cup final, so they were the recipients of luck on their way to the trophy in 1921. A goal down after only 15 minutes Spurs had battled back and equalised through Cantrell, but shortly before half-time Southend were awarded a penalty. Just as Fairclough prepared to take it, the referee noticed the ball was not on the spot and replaced it himself. Fairclough then advanced in order to reposition the ball more to his liking but found the referee refusing him permission to touch it. After a brief argument, won by the referee, Fairclough took the kick and promptly shot wide. In the second half Spurs did not allow Southend any respite and scored three goals to march into the next round.

1927	Bury	H	First Division	1-0
1938	Manchester United	A	Second Division	1-0
1944	Millwall	A	League South Cup Section 2	1-0
1949	West Ham United	H	Second Division	1-1
1955	York City	A	FA Cup 5th Round	1-3

It had been 22 years since Spurs were last beaten by a team from a lower division in the FA Cup, but this 3-1 defeat at Bootham Crescent did much more than end that run; Arthur Rowe suffered a second nervous breakdown after the result and never returned to White Hart Lane as manager.

1966	Fulham	H	First Division	4-3
1972	Stoke City	H	First Division	2-0
1977	Leeds United	A	First Division	1-2
1983	Everton	A	FA Cup 5th Round	0-2

Defeat by Everton finally ended Spurs' great FA Cup run; 18 matches unbeaten which had seen them lift the trophy on two consecutive seasons. There was little joy for Everton, however, for they were beaten by Manchester United in the following round.

| 1988 | West Bromwich Albion | A | Friendly | 1-4 |

This match was a benefit for Mick Brown with Spurs' goal being scored by Paul Walsh.

| 1996 | Nottingham Forest | A | FA Cup 5th Round | 0-0 |

Snow had begun falling even as the teams were warming up, and by the time the game kicked off, a full scale blizzard was in progress. After 15 minutes, at which point the lines were disappearing and the referee could not see both goals, the match was abandoned.

FEBRUARY 20TH

1886	South Hackney	H	Friendly	8-0
1892	City Ramblers	H	Friendly	Score unknown
1897	New Brompton	A	Southern League	1-2
1899	Rushden	A	United League	1-2
1904	Aston Villa	H	FA Cup 2nd Round	0-1

A crowd of 32,000 packed into White Hart Lane for Spurs' FA Cup second round tie against Aston Villa, confident that once again this might be Spurs' year. The club installed extra benches around the pitch perimeter to accommodate the influx, and at half-time, with Villa leading 1-0, the crowd from here swarmed on to the pitch to stretch their legs, joined soon after by others from the terraces. When the players tried to return to the field for the second half the crowd refused to return to their places, leaving the referee with little option but to abandon the tie. It has often been stated that this was the first occasion in which a crowd had invaded the pitch in an attempt to get a cup-tie abandoned, but this was not the case – having left their vantage points most of the crowd were unable to return, hence the abandonment. Indeed, when word got around the ground that the game had been abandoned, a demonstration took place in front of the main stand and threats were made of wholesale destruction if the game was not resumed. It took the police to clear the pitch and ensure there was no riot.

| 1909 | Burnley | H | FA Cup 2nd Round | 0-0 |

1915	Notts County	H	First Division	2-0
1926	Bury	H	First Division	4-2
1932	Burnley	A	Second Division	0-2
1935	Bolton Wanderers	A	FA Cup 5th Round Replay	1-1
1937	Everton	A	FA Cup 5th Round	1-1

1940 Jimmy Greaves born in East Ham. Perhaps the most prolific goalscorer of his and any other era, Greaves was a schoolboy phenomenon, scoring over 100 goals in a single season for Chelsea Juniors and a first-team regular by the time he was 17, scoring on his debut against Spurs. Thereafter Greaves scored on every debut match; for England Youth, England Under-23, England full, AC Milan (who he joined in 1960 for £80,000), Spurs (who paid £99,999 to bring him back home to England) and West Ham (joining in 1970). In all he scored 357 League goals, all of which were scored in the First Division, and 44 goals for England (he is England's third top goalscorer behind Bobby Charlton and Gary Lineker, although Greaves played only 57 matches), but it was Alf Ramsey's decision to leave him out of the 1966 World Cup final for which he is probably best remembered – a bout of hepatitis the season before the World Cup robbed him of a yard or two of pace and contributed to his grabbing only 15 League goals that season, his worst tally ever. After retiring as a player (although he made a brief comeback with non-League Barnet in the seventies) he slipped into a well-publicised alcoholic state before emerging with a successful career in journalism and broadcasting, forming a partnership with former Liverpool and Scotland striker Ian St John.

1943	Luton Town	H	Football League South	4-1
1946	Aston Villa	H	Football League South	3-0
1954	Hull City	A	FA Cup 5th Round	1-1
1957	Chelsea	H	First Division	3-4
1960	Blackburn Rovers	H	FA Cup 5th Round	1-3
1963	Chelsea	A	FA Cup 5th Round	0-1
1965	Chelsea	A	FA Cup 5th Round	0-1
1971	Newcastle United	A	First Division	0-1
1982	Manchester City	H	First Division	2-0
1993	Leeds United	H	FA Premier League	4-0

FEBRUARY 21ST

1885	St Peter's	H	Friendly	1-1
1891	Vulcan	H	Friendly	6-0
1903	Bristol City	H	FA Cup 2nd Round	1-0
1920	West Ham United	H	FA Cup 3rd Round	3-0
1925	Blackburn Rovers	H	FA Cup 3rd Round	2-2
1931	Bury	A	Second Division	0-2
1934	Sunderland	A	First Division	0-6
1942	Portsmouth	H	London War League	1-1
1948	Southampton	H	Second Division	0-0

With the two clubs due to meet at The Dell the following week in the FA Cup 6th round, this was never going to be anything more than a hesitant dress rehearsal. Spurs were without Ronnie Burgess, severely injured in the previous week's match against Doncaster Rovers, and felt the absence throughout. At the end of 90 minutes of dour action, both sides knew little about each other that they didn't already know. The cup tie was to be an altogether different proposition.

1953	Preston North End	H	First Division	4-4
1959	Portsmouth	H	First Division	4-4
1962	Aston Villa	A	First Division	0-0
1970	Stoke City	H	First Division	1-0
1976	Stoke City	A	First Division	2-1
1979	Wrexham	A	FA Cup 4th Round Replay	3-2 [aet]
1981	Leicester City	H	First Division	1-2
1984	Notts County	A	First Division	0-0
1987	Newcastle United	H	FA Cup 5th Round	1-0
1989	Norwich City	H	First Division	2-1
1990	Aston Villa	H	First Division	0-2
1998	Sheffield Wednesday	A	FA Premier League	0-1

FEBRUARY 22ND

1896	Clapton	H	Friendly	4-0
1902	Wellingborough	H	Southern League	3-0
1904	Swindon Town	H	Southern League	1-0

On the same day Spurs officials had to attend a FA Council meeting to give an account of the activities two days previously which had seen a pitch invasion cause the abandonment of the FA Cup tie against Aston Villa. The official minute of the meeting stated 'That the match should be replayed on the Aston Villa ground on Thursday, February 25th, and in the event of there being a drawn game it must be played at Stoke two days later. The Tottenham Hotspur Club was ordered to pay to the Football Association £350 out of their share of the gate receipts, the amount to be distributed by the Association among London charities.'

| 1905 | Newcastle United | A | FA Cup 2nd Round Replay | 0-4 |

1910   George Hunt born in Barnsley. After trials for Barnsley, Sheffield United and Port Vale George was signed by Chesterfield and quickly established himself as a proven goalscorer, earning the nickname 'The Chesterfield Tough'. He soon attracted interest from bigger clubs, and although Herbert Chapman was known to be keen chose to join Spurs in June 1930. Initially introduced as a replacement for the injured Ted Harper, George soon started scoring goals with regularity, netting 125 in the League in just 185 games. In October 1937 he did join Arsenal, replacing Ted Drake, but stayed only six months before moving on to Bolton. He played for a number of clubs during the Second World War and retired as a player in May 1948 to become coach at Burnden Park, a position he held until September 1968.

1913	Sheffield United	H	First Division	1-0
1919	Fulham	H-Homerton		
			London Combination	0-2
1930	Wolverhampton Wanderers	H	Second Division	4-2

1933   Bobby Smith born in Lingdale in North Yorkshire. Bobby joined Chelsea as an amateur in 1948 and was upgraded to the professional ranks in May 1950. He made his debut at the age of 17 and hit 30 goals in 86 games for the first team, but he was seldom a regular for the centre-forward slot, that honour being held by Roy Bentley. In December 1955 Spurs paid £16,000 to take him to White Hart Lane where the club were engaged in a desperate battle against relegation. It was largely his goals that enabled them to build a side good enough to win the double in 1961, retain the FA Cup and then become the first British side to win a major European trophy, but that only tells part of the story about Bobby Smith. Although only 5' 10" he used every ounce of his 12 stone 11 pounds weight to intimidate opponents, not only for his own benefit but also to create space and chances for his team-mates. He was also extremely skilful and able to forge good goalscoring opportunities purely by his positional sense. Smith, along with Les Allen and Jimmy Greaves, made Spurs the most feared forward line during the early 1960s, and was also rewarded with a total of 15 caps, scoring 13 goals for England. In May 1964 he was transferred to Brighton for £5,000 and scored 18 goals to help them win the Fourth Division championship in his only season with the club, for he was sacked before the following season owing to some newspaper comments. He then drifted into the non-League game before retiring.

| 1936 | Bradford Park Avenue | A | Second Division | 5-2 |
| 1937 | Everton | H | FA Cup 5th Round Replay | 4-3 |

Those fortunate enough to have either played in or attended this game claim it was the most exciting match ever seen at White Hart Lane. Everton powered into a seemingly unassailable 3-1 lead and then appeared to have the chance to put matters beyond doubt when Gillick was fouled in the area and the referee awarded a penalty with just seven minutes left of normal time. Then his attention was drawn to the linesman, who had been waving frantically whilst Everton mounted their attack. It was pointed out that Everton's move had begun with a foul throw and that play should have been halted earlier. Although the proper decision would have been to carry on as though the foul throw had not occurred and award the penalty, the referee reversed his decision and gave Spurs a throw-in. Soon after Spurs reduced the deficit to 3-2 thanks to a goal from Jack Morrison. With barely four minutes left on the clock, Joe Meek equalised with a fine solo goal. And then, with the referee looking at his watch and everyone contemplating extra time, Morrison got a winner that had seemed impossible seven minutes earlier.

| 1941 | Bournemouth & | | | |
| | Boscombe Athletic | A | Football League War Cup 1st Round | 6-1 |

1949   John Duncan born in Dundee. John was the first signing made by manager Terry Neill, joining Spurs in October 1974 for £150,000. He scored 12 goals during his season with the club, vital goals which helped Spurs stave off the threat of relegation that year. Indeed, but for a serious back injury which caused him to miss almost the entire 1976-77 season, Spurs might have avoided relegation, for John's average of a goal every two games was an exceptional rate in an era when scoring became harder. He was leading scorer when the club won promotion back into the First Division in 1977-78, but in September 1978 he was sold to Derby County. He moved on to Scunthorpe United, becoming manager in 1981. He later managed Hartlepool, Chesterfield and Ipswich Town.

| 1958 | Arsenal | A | First Division | 4-4 |

1961	Wolverhampton Wanderers	H	First Division	1-1
1964	Arsenal	H	First Division	3-1
1969	Wolverhampton Wanderers	H	First Division	1-1
1975	Leicester City	H	First Division	0-3
1978	Luton Town	A	Second Division	4-1
1983	Jersey Select XI	A	Friendly	8-3
1986	Sheffield Wednesday	A	First Division	2-1
1992	Arsenal	H	First Division	1-1

FEBRUARY 23RD

| 1884 | Grange Park | H | Friendly | 1-0 |

The game was halted after 60 minutes, Robert Buckle having scored the only goal of the game.

| 1895 | Beeston | H | FA Amateur Cup 1st Round | 2-0 |
| 1901 | Bury | H | FA Cup 2nd Round | 2-1 |

A crowd of 20,250 gathered at White Hart Lane to see Spurs, the flower of the south, take on the pride of Lancashire, FA Cup-holders Bury. Just as they had done against Preston, Spurs started nervously, perhaps showing too much respect for their opponents and allowing Bury to take the lead inside two minutes. Despite constant pressure from Bury for the next half hour, Spurs managed to recover their composure and get back into the game, equalising through Sandy Brown just before half-time. The second half went more Spurs' way, although they had only one further goal to show for their efforts; once again Sandy Brown was the scorer to register his sixth of the competition thus far. This success put Spurs through to the quarter-final stage for only the second time in their history (the previous occasion being 1899).

1903	Bristol Rovers	A	Western League	0-2
1907	Notts County	A	FA Cup 3rd Round	0-4
1914	Burnley	H	First Division	2-0
1918	Chelsea	A	London Combination	0-3
1921	West Bromwich Albion	A	First Division	1-3
1929	Bradford Park Avenue	H	Second Division	3-2
1935	Sunderland	H	First Division	1-1
1938	Stockport County	H	Second Division	2-0
1946	Charlton Athletic	H	Football League South	2-1
1952	Preston North End	H	First Division	1-0
1963	Arsenal	A	First Division	3-2
1965	Arsenal	A	First Division	1-3
1974	Ipswich Town	H	First Division	1-1
1980	Derby County	A	First Division	1-2
1985	West Bromwich Albion	A	First Division	1-0
1988	Manchester United	H	First Division	1-1
1991	Wimbledon	A	First Division	1-5

FEBRUARY 24TH

| 1894 | Chesham | A | Wolverton & District Charity Cup 1st Round Replay | 3-1 |
| 1900 | Bristol Rovers | A | Southern League | 2-2 |

On the same day John Kirwan was in Llandudno representing Ireland in their international match against Wales, the first Spurs player to represent Ireland whilst on the club's books. The Welsh won 2-0.

| 1906 | Birmingham | H | FA Cup 3rd Round | 1-1 |
| 1909 | Burnley | A | FA Cup 2nd Round Replay | 1-3 |

Defeat by Burnley did not go down well at Spurs. According to the board of directors 'The replay on Wednesday made us feel rather sore – physically and mentally. Burnley offended much more than in the first meeting against the properties of the game, and the wonder is that we have not several cripples. Fouls were constantly being given against them, but something more than that might have been done to enforce the observance of the laws. As the home team played it was not surprising that they won, although more steadiness in front of goal on the part of our forwards might have brought a better result. The district of Burnley was excited over the result, and there was a record gate (30,000). With £1,386 taken on Saturday, and £1,248 on Wednesday, the cloud of defeat certainly had a golden lining.'

1912	Notts County	A	First Division	2-2
1917	Crystal Palace	H-Highbury		
			London Combination	4-1
1923	Cardiff City	A	FA Cup 3rd Round	3-2

1934	Portsmouth	H	First Division	0-0
1937	Southampton	A	Second Division	0-1
1940	Chelsea	A	Football League South Group C	2-0
1945	Queens Park Rangers	A	League South Cup Group 3	0-1
1951	Burnley	A	First Division	0-2
1954	Hull City	H	FA Cup 5th Round Replay	2-0
1962	Bolton Wanderers	H	First Division	2-2
1973	Everton	H	First Division	3-0
1976	Everton	A	First Division	0-1
1979	Birmingham City	A	First Division	0-1
1990	Derby County	A	First Division	1-2
1996	Sheffield Wednesday	H	FA Premier League	1-0
1997	West Ham United	A	FA Premier League	3-4

FEBRUARY 25TH

| 1893 | Upton Park | H | Southern Alliance | 1-0 |

1895 Bob MacDonald born in Inverness. Spotted by Spurs whilst playing amateur football for Inverness Caledonians, Bob was persuaded to come south and signed in August 1919, just as League football was about to resume. Initially used as a right-back, he took his chance in the first team so well that when Tommy Clay returned after injury, Bob was switched to half-back and retained his place for the rest of the season and collected an FA Cup winners' medal. He was released in April 1927 and after an unsuccessful trial with Hearts joined Clapton Orient, remaining with the club for two years. He died in April 1971.

| 1897 | Woolwich Arsenal | H | United League | 2-2 |
| 1899 | Stoke | A | FA Cup 3rd Round | 1-4 |

This was Spurs' tenth game in the FA Cup that season, having required six games in the qualifying rounds and four in the competition proper before going out to Stoke. Spurs' only goal was scored by Tom Bradshaw.

| 1904 | Aston Villa | A | FA Cup 2nd Round Replay | 1-0 |

This match was the FA-ordered replay following a pitch invasion by Spurs fans at the original match on February 20th. A crowd of 30,000 saw Jack Jones score the only goal to ensure Spurs' passage into the next round.

1905	Brentford	A	Southern League	0-0
1911	Aston Villa	A	First Division	0-4
1920	Bristol City	A	Second Division	2-1
1922	Everton	H	First Division	2-0
1928	Blackburn Rovers	A	First Division	1-2
1935	Bolton Wanderers	N	FA Cup 5th Round 2nd Replay	0-2

The second replay was held at Villa Park and Spurs, already without George Hunt, Willie Hall, Willie Evans and Tom Evans lost 2-0.

1939	Blackburn Rovers	H	Second Division	4-3
1950	Southampton	H	Second Division	4-0
1956	Chelsea	H	First Division	4-0
1961	Manchester City	A	First Division	1-0
1967	Manchester City	H	First Division	1-1
1978	Orient	H	Second Division	1-1
1984	Birmingham City	H	First Division	0-1
1987	Leicester City	H	First Division	5-0
1989	Southampton	A	First Division	2-0
1995	Wimbledon	H	FA Premier League	1-2

FEBRUARY 26TH

| 1898 | Reading | H | Southern League | 1-1 |

As Northumberland Park was under suspension owing to incidents during a United League match with Luton Town, this fixture was played at Millwall.

1906	Brentford	A	Western League	1-0
1910	Middlesbrough	A	First Division	3-4
1916	Luton Town	H	London Combination [2nd competition]	7-4
1921	West Bromwich Albion	H	First Division	1-0
1925	Blackburn Rovers	A	FA Cup 3rd Round Replay	1-3
1927	Birmingham	A	First Division	0-1

Manager Peter McWilliam had joined Spurs in 1913 and had proved to be one of the finest appointments made by the club, winning the Second Division championship and the FA Cup in consecutive seasons and then finishing second in the First Division, the highest placing achieved by a southern club up to that point. His achievements with Spurs did not go unnoticed by other clubs, and in 1926 Middlesbrough, then top of the Second Division, offered him £1,500 to become their manager. McWilliam relayed Middlesbrough's offer to the board at Spurs, stating that he would be more than happy to stay at White Hart Lane for £1,000, an increase of only £150 on what he was already receiving. To their lasting shame, the Spurs board did not match this request, and in December 1926 accepted his resignation from the position of manager of Spurs, a post he officially left on February 26th 1927, to be replaced by Billy Minter. In May 1938 McWilliam was re-appointed manager at Spurs, but the Second World War effectively ended his second spell with the club.

1938	Fulham	H	Second Division	1-1
1944	Portsmouth	H	League South Cup Section 2	1-0
1949	Blackburn Rovers	A	Second Division	1-1
1962	Dukla Prague	H	European Cup 2nd Round 2nd Leg	4-1

Although Spurs had lost the first leg 1-0, a 4-1 win in the home leg was sufficient to give them a 4-2 aggregate victory and a place in the semi-final against Benfica.

1968	Sheffield United	A	First Division	2-3
1972	Everton	A	FA Cup 5th Round	2-0
1975	Red Star Belgrade	A	Friendly	1-0
1977	Newcastle United	A	First Division	0-2
1983	Norwich City	H	First Division	0-0

FEBRUARY 27TH

| 1886 | Silesia College | H | Friendly | 1-2 |
| 1892 | Grenadier Guards | H | Friendly | 9-0 |

1895 Billy Cook born in Evenwood in County Durham. By the time he joined Spurs in June 1929 Billy had already won an impressive collection of medals; an FA Amateur Cup-winners' medal with Bishop Auckland and three League titles with Huddersfield. He switched to Aston Villa in 1927 and remained with them for two years before coming to White Hart Lane. Although he was over 34 when he joined Spurs, he made 63 appearances over the next two seasons before being released in 1931, subsequently spending a season with Brentford.

1897	Loughborough	H	United League	1-2
1899	Kettering Town	A	United League	1-0
1901	Swindon Town	H	Western League	5-0
1904	Portsmouth	H	Western League	1-1
1905	Millwall	H	Western League	4-1
1909	Glossop North End	H	Second Division	3-3
1915	Aston Villa	A	First Division	1-3
1926	Manchester United	H	First Division	0-1
1932	Notts County	H	Second Division	2-0
1937	Swansea Town	H	Second Division	3-1
1943	Watford	A	Football League South	3-0
1954	Arsenal	A	First Division	3-0
1960	Blackburn Rovers	A	First Division	4-1
1965	Leeds United	H	First Division	0-0
1971	Aston Villa	Wembley	League Cup Final	2-0

After the disappointment of 1969, when defeat at Highbury and a draw at White Hart Lane had denied Spurs a place in the League Cup final at Wembley, Spurs made it all the way this year. Not that there was any doubt Spurs would make it, for after all, didn't the year end in 'one'? Although their opponents were Aston Villa, languishing in the Third Division, there was no complacency on Spurs' part – in 1969 Spurs' despair at missing the final was no doubt tempered by seeing their greatest rivals suffer one of the biggest Wembley shocks of all time in losing 3-1 to Third Division Swindon. Despite Villa's lowly League placing there were more than a few experienced heads in the team. Not for the first or last time, the final did not live up to expectations. Two goals from Martin Chivers inside the last 12 minutes won the cup for Spurs, but there was a more telling contribution from Steve Perryman which ensured victory – 'Lochhead appeared to foul Collins and poked the ball towards our goal. Everyone had stopped, expecting a foul, but for some reason, perhaps because I just couldn't stop running, I kept going and slid after it and kicked it out. As it turned out, the whistle didn't go, so if I hadn't played on, it would have counted.' Having defended resolutely for near on 80 minutes, the chances are that had Villa taken the lead they would have held on to spring the third major League Cup final surprise inside six years. But they didn't and Spurs took the trophy and, more importantly for Bill Nicholson, ensured the team's presence in Europe for the following season.

1980	Coventry City	H	First Division	4-3
1982	Stoke City	A	First Division	2-0
1988	Sheffield Wednesday	A	First Division	3-0
1993	Queens Park Rangers	H	FA Premier League	3-2
1994	Chelsea	A	FA Premier League	3-4

FEBRUARY 28TH

| 1885 | Bedford Rovers | A | Friendly | 1-1 |

1889 Charlie Rance born in Bow in East London. As an amateur player Charlie was originally linked with Clapton and was a member of the side that won the FA Amateur Cup in 1907. He also came close to winning an amateur cap for England, for he was selected for the match against Denmark in May 1910 but the game was postponed owing to the death of King Edward VII. By the time the amateur side played their next game, Charlie had joined the professional game with Spurs. A reliable defender, Charlie made over 100 appearances for the League side, but of course the First World War cut across his career. He made 130 appearances for Spurs in the London Football Combination. By the time the war ended Charlie had one further season with Spurs, playing his part in the Second Division title win of 1919-20. He signed for Derby County in March 1921 and later returned to the capital with QPR in September 1922. Although Charlie scored a total of 14 goals for Spurs during his time with the club, only one of these was in the League and even then it didn't count; the game against Notts County in October 1912 was abandoned owing to fog! Charlie died in Chichester on 29th December 1966.

1891	Old St Stephen's	H	Friendly	3-0
1898	Chesham	A	Friendly	4-2
1906	Birmingham	A	FA Cup 3rd Round Replay	0-2 [aet]
1914	Blackburn Rovers	A	First Division	1-1
1920	Bristol City	H	Second Division	2-0
1925	Arsenal	H	First Division	2-0
1940	Crystal Palace	A	Football League South Group A	1-1
1942	Chelsea	H	London War League	2-0
1948	Southampton	A	FA Cup 6th Round	1-0

Such was the interest generated in this cup-tie, and with Southampton unable to supply sufficient tickets to the Spurs fans who wished to see the game, Tottenham made arrangements for bulletins to be made every 15 minutes at the reserve match at home to Portsmouth! Les Bennett scored the goal that took Spurs into the semi-final.

1953	Birmingham City	A	FA Cup 6th Round	1-1
1959	Everton	A	First Division	1-2
1970	Newcastle United	A	First Division	2-1
1976	Leicester City	H	First Division	1-1
1979	Oldham Athletic	A	FA Cup 5th Round	1-0
1981	Sunderland	A	First Division	1-1
1996	Nottingham Forest	A	FA Cup 5th Round	2-2

FEBRUARY 29TH

1896	Burslem Port Vale	H	Friendly	4-0
1904	Plymouth Argyle	H	Western League	5-1
1908	Bradford Park Avenue	A	Southern League	2-1
1936	Sheffield United	A	FA Cup 6th Round	1-3

While the first team were sliding out of the FA Cup at Sheffield, a far more telling contribution to the history of Tottenham Hotspur FC was taking place at White Hart Lane. Chief scout Ben Ives settled down in his office to write to the parents of one lad who had been recommended by a Mr Jones, organiser of a local team in Scarborough. Although the young lad was only 17 years of age and his experience of football had been limited to turn outs for Scarborough Working Men's Club and Scarborough Young Liberals, Ives had either heard or seen enough of the player's abilities to invite him down to London for a month's trial. 'You need not fear about him as at present we have about 20 boys his age and we get them good lodgings with personal friends of mine . . . The boys seems very bright and I am sure he will get on (here) and in any case I trust you realise that he must have a far greater chance of making headway in London than elsewhere.' Having also enclosed instructions for either Mr Jones to put the lad on a night train from York to London or bring him down himself, Bert Ives signed the letter and put it in the despatch tray. It was addressed to a Mr and Mrs Nicholson, parents of Bill. With the exception of an 18-month spell during which time he was scout for West Ham United, Bill Nicholson has been a Tottenham servant (if not *the* Tottenham servant) ever since – 62 years as player, coach, manager, consultant and president.

| 1964 | Birmingham City | A | First Division | 2-1 |

MARCH 1ST

1888   Fanny Walden born in Wellingborough. After impressing for the local side Fanny was signed by Northampton Town in 1909 and scored a hat-trick on his debut, even though he had been selected at centre-forward and stood only 5' 2" tall! Despite his lack of height he displayed intricate ball skills and was subsequently switched out on to the right wing, being selected for the Southern League in that position in a match against the Football League. When Northampton manager Herbert Chapman moved on to Leeds City he made enquiries about buying Fanny, but by then Northampton had already accepted a record bid of £1,700 from Spurs, and Fanny came to White Hart Lane in April 1913. An instant crowd favourite his progress continued unchecked and he won the first of his two England caps in April 1914. The outbreak of the First World War interrupted his career, although it did allow Herbert Chapman to get an opportunity of seeing Fanny in a Leeds City shirt, for Fanny enlisted during the war and guested on a number of occasions for the club managed by his previous boss. When League football resumed Fanny was a permanent fixture within the Spurs side, helping the club win the Second Division title in 1919-20 and reach the FA Cup final the following year, although Fanny had to miss the final owing to injury. He remained with Spurs until 1926 when he returned to Northampton Town, retiring the following year and subsequently coaching. He was also a more than useful cricketer who represented Northamptonshire in tandem with his football career and later became an umpire, attaining Test-match level. He died in Northampton on 3rd May 1949.

Year	Opponent		Competition	Score
1890	Swindon Town	A	Friendly	1-2
1902	Corinthians	H	Dewar Shield	5-2

The Dewar Shield (also known as the Sheriff of London Charity Shield) was something of a forerunner to the FA Charity Shield. The shield had been instigated by the Corinthians, whose strict observance of their amateur status prevented them from entering into any competition. They did, however, advocate a match between themselves and the leading club of the day, which happened to be Spurs, with the proceeds being distributed to charity. When the Corinthians withdrew the shield in 1908, the FA stepped in with one of their own.

1913	Aston Villa	A	First Division	0-1

1914   George Forman born in Walthamstow. He began his career as an amateur with Leyton and Walthamstow before signing professional with West Ham in 1938. It was whilst guesting for Spurs during the Second World War that he first came to the attention of the club, and when the war ended his was the first transfer effected, signing in February 1946. He impressed early on, but the subsequent emergence of Len Duquemin restricted George's first-team opportunities and he was released in April 1949. He died in Waltham Forest on 19th June 1969.

1919	Brentford	A	London Combination	1-4
1924	Sheffield United	H	First Division	1-2
1930	Bradford City	A	Second Division	2-0
1939	Newcastle United	A	Second Division	0-1
1941	Northampton Town	H	Football League War Cup 2nd Round 1st Leg	4-0
1947	Sheffield Wednesday	A	Second Division	1-5
1952	Derby County	H	First Division	5-0
1958	Partick Thistle	H	Friendly	4-1
1960	Burnley	A	First Division	0-2
1968	West Bromwich Albion	H	First Division	0-0
1969	Manchester City	A	FA Cup 6th Round	0-1
1972	Everton	A	First Division	1-1
1975	Derby County	A	First Division	1-3
1980	Leeds United	H	First Division	2-1
1987	Arsenal	H	Littlewoods Cup Semi-Final 2nd Leg	1-2

Spurs had won the first leg 1-0 thanks to Clive Allen's goal, and it was the same player who scored first at White Hart Lane seemingly to put Spurs into an unassailable lead. The announcer at Spurs obviously thought so, for at half-time details of how the tickets for Wembley were to be distributed were given out over the tannoy! Whether this fired Arsenal still further is not known, but they emerged in the second half prepared to fight every inch of the way and equalised on the day and then on aggregate with barely minutes left. Extra time also failed to separate the two teams, and so the two managers tossed a coin to decide home advantage – David Pleat won and so the replay would take place at White Hart Lane.

1988	Derby County	H	First Division	0-0
1989	Aston Villa	H	First Division	2-0
1992	Nottingham Forest	H	Rumbelows Cup Semi-Final 2nd Leg	1-2

The game was delayed by almost an hour following bomb scares in and around the ground. With the score from the first leg having finished all-square, Forest's 2-1 win enabled them to advance to Wembley where they would face Manchester United.

| 1995 | Southampton | A | FA Cup 5th Round Replay | 6-2 [aet] |

By half-time Spurs were 2-0 down and seemingly heading for a cup exit, but Gerry Francis introduced substitute Ronnie Rosenthal and told him to go and win the game for him. Ronnie took him at his word, scoring twice to take the tie into extra time. When he completed his hat-trick shortly into the first half of extra time, Southampton all but collapsed, and three later goals gave the final scoreline an unbelievable air.

| 1997 | Nottingham Forest | H | FA Premier League | 0-1 |

MARCH 2ND

| 1889 | Windsor Pheonix | A | Friendly | 1-2 |
| 1895 | Old Westminsters | A | London Senior Cup 2nd Round | 3-3 |

1898 Charles Roberts called a meeting of the club at the Red Lion public house on Tottenham High Road. Roberts had been approached by the club to look at ways of fund raising and at the meeting Roberts suggested the club should consider turning themselves into a limited company, with the flotation of 8,000 shares at £1 each. The proposal was accepted by the meeting and a new board of directors appointed, with John Oliver elected chairman and Charles Roberts, Bobby Buckle (one of the club's original founders), Jack Thompson (another of the original members) and Ralph Bullock duly elected. Despite the enthusiasm the share issue generated amongst those present at the meeting, the public did not share similar confidence, for 12 months later only 296 applications for shares had been received, accounting for only 1,558 of the 8,000 shares. Oliver resigned later in the year and was replaced as chairman by Charles Roberts, a position he would hold until his death in July 1943, and a Mr J. Hawley was co-opted to the board.

1901	New Brompton	H	Southern League	2-1
1903	Millwall Athletic	A	London League	3-0
1907	Leyton	H	Southern League	0-0
1912	Preston North End	A	First Division	1-0
1918	Brentford	H-Highbury		
			London Combination	3-0
1929	Grimsby Town	A	Second Division	0-2
1940	Southampton	H	Football League South Group C	4-1
1946	Chelsea	H	Friendly	4-2
1955	Arsenal	H	Friendly	1-4
1957	Leeds United	A	First Division	1-1
1959	Wolverhampton Wanderers	A	First Division	1-1
1963	West Bromwich Albion	H	First Division	2-1
1974	Queens Park Rangers	A	First Division	1-3
1985	Stoke City	A	First Division	1-0
1986	Liverpool	H	First Division	1-2

Steve Perryman made his 654th and final League appearance for Spurs, this figure including the abandoned game against Everton in 1969. Steve also made two further appearances as a substitute in League matches and appeared in 69 FA Cup ties, 66 League Cup ties, 63 European matches (plus once as a substitute) and 162 other matches (plus five as a substitute), a grand total of 1014 full appearances and eight as substitute.

1991	Chelsea	H	First Division	1-1
1993	Sheffield United	A	FA Premier League	0-6
1994	Aston Villa	H	FA Premier League	1-1
1996	Southampton	H	FA Premier League	1-0

MARCH 3RD

1894	Uxbridge	H	Friendly	1-1
1900	Portsmouth	A	Southern League	0-1
1906	Portsmouth	H	Western League	1-1
1917	Luton Town	H-Homerton		
			London Combination	3-2
1923	Manchester City	H	First Division	3-1
1926	Huddersfield Town	A	First Division	1-2
1928	Huddersfield Town	A	FA Cup 6th Round	1-6

Spurs' progress to the 6th round of the cup had been such that there was genuine hope that this might be the year the club made it to Wembley, but against Huddersfield it all went tragically wrong. After the game the players complained bitterly that their preparation for the game had been poor, for the long walks on the snow covered fields during the week before had not been beneficial; indeed, all of the players went into the game with heavy colds!

1934	Everton	H	First Division	3-0
1945	West Ham United	H	League South Cup Section 3	4-0
1951	Chelsea	H	First Division	2-1
1954	Bolton Wanderers	H	First Division	3-2
1956	West Ham United	H	FA Cup 6th Round	3-3

West Ham had the better of the opening exchanges and were soon seemingly headed for the semi-final, leading 3-1 with barely minutes to go. Near the end Len Duquemin reduced the deficit to a single goal, but the equaliser still wouldn't come. Captain Danny Blanchflower, having spotted that the presence of Harry Clarke and Maurice Norman in the West Ham area had frightened their opponents, now ordered both men to join the attack. In the dying moments, Maurice played a part in getting the ball to George Robb who slammed home an equaliser and set up a replay at Upton Park. After the game Danny was hailed as a hero for having made the switch, although he modestly pointed out that desperate times sometimes called for desperate measures. It was when he tried a similar tactic in another game Spurs were losing and which didn't come off that he was criticised by both the media and his manager!

1962	Manchester City	A	First Division	2-6

1972   Darren Anderton born in Southampton. He joined Portsmouth as a trainee in 1990 and quickly graduated through the ranks. He was an integral part of the side that reached the FA Cup semi-finals in 1992, putting in some outstanding performances that soon alerted the bigger clubs to his potential, and in June 1992 he was signed by Spurs for a fee of £1.75 million. Although he took a while to settle in at the club, when he found his form and consistency England honours beckoned and he currently holds 22 caps for the full side. A series of niggling injuries have limited his appearances over the last few seasons, but on his day he is an outstanding and influential player.

1973	Norwich City	Wembley	League Cup Final	1-0

Wembley has played host to some memorable games – this sadly wasn't one of them – for which most of the blame must lie with Norwich. If their defensive display had succeeded in winning the cup then there would have been those from the Norfolk area who would have claimed the end justified the means. The Football League had decided before the game that in the event of a draw there would be no extra time; the general consensus among the media was that Coates's goal was enough to save us from the tedium of a replay. Ralph Coates was about the only man to have anything by which to remember this game, aside that is John Pratt, who was injured after only 25 minutes and substituted by Coates. The goal came as a result of a long throw by Chivers which was headed on by Peters, Gilzean helping it on its way and Mike England swinging a foot at it and missing. The ball reached Coates and a cross-shot hit the back of the net. Once again, Spurs secured a place in Europe and maintained an unbeaten run at Wembley.

1979	Derby County	H	First Division	2-0
1982	Eintracht Frankfurt	H	European Cup-Winners' Cup 3rd Round 1st Leg	2-0
1984	Stoke City	H	First Division	1-0
1990	Crystal Palace	H	First Division	0-1

Andy Polston's appearance as a substitute made him and his brother John, who had been on from the start, the first pair of brothers to have appeared in the same League match for Spurs since Bobby and Danny Steel in 1912.

MARCH 4TH

1893	Windsor & Eton	H	Southern Alliance	5-2
1896	Gravesend	A	Friendly	1-1
1897	Rushden	H	United League	5-1
1899	Millwall Athletic	A	United League	1-2
1905	Queens Park Rangers	H	Southern League	5-1
1907	Queens Park Rangers	H	Southern Charity Cup Semi-Final	4-0
1911	Liverpool	H	First Division	1-0

1912   Les Howe born in Tottenham. Initially associated with the club as a schoolboy Les was signed as a professional in August 1930 and got an extended run in the team in October 1932. Perhaps most comfortable at right-half Les played in every position for Spurs, even taking over in goal in an emergency. He remained with the club throughout the Second World War and then suffered an injury that eventually finished his career in September 1945, although he did not officially leave the club until April 1947 when given a free transfer.

1916	Arsenal	A	London Combination [2nd competition]	3-0
1922	Cardiff City	A	FA Cup 4th Round	1-1
1933	Southampton	A	Second Division	1-1

1936	Nottingham Forest	H	Second Division	1-1
1939	West Ham United	A	Second Division	2-0
1944	Aldershot	A	League South Cup Section 2	1-2
1950	Coventry City	A	Second Division	1-0
1953	Birmingham City	H	FA Cup 6th Round Replay	2-2 [aet]
1961	Sunderland	A	FA Cup 6th Round	1-1

This is one of the matches that Danny Blanchflower described as one of the most memorable of the 'double' season, mainly because of the atmosphere generated by the crowd. Certainly, the Roker Park crowd had been known for their volume over the years, and with the team in the Second Division they were desperate for any sort of success. Cliff Jones gave Spurs the lead and set in motion almost constant Sunderland attacks, with the home side forcing four consecutive corners. Finally the ball was driven home for an equaliser, the signal for a minor pitch invasion as the Sunderland fans worked off their emotions. For any other side, such a sight might well have preceded a collapse, but captain Danny Blanchflower used the opportunity to go round to each member of his side and lift them mentally. As a result, Sunderland rarely threatened to score any more, although neither did Spurs.

1967	Aston Villa	A	First Division	3-3
1972	Manchester United	H	First Division	2-0
1978	Oldham Athletic	A	Second Division	1-1
1986	Everton	H	FA Cup 5th Round	1-2
1987	Arsenal	H	Littlewoods Cup Semi-Final Replay	1-2

The Littlewoods Cup semi-final clash between Spurs and Arsenal had enthralled the nation, with the two legs being unable to separate the sides on aggregate. After David Pleat won the toss for the right to stage the replay, there were those who felt that the initiative had passed to Spurs, and certainly as the home side they did more of the attacking. Clive Allen gave Spurs the lead with his 12th goal of the competition that season (a record for the League Cup, in its many guises, that has yet to be broken), but Arsenal kept chipping away at their opponents. Their winner was scored in the final minute or so of normal time, the only time they had been ahead in the three games, but it was enough to earn them the right to meet Liverpool in the final. For Spurs, there was still the FA Cup with which to try and compensate.

| 1989 | Bordeaux | H | Friendly | 1-2 |
| 1992 | Feyenoord | A | European Cup-Winners' Cup 3rd Round 1st Leg | 0-1 |

An uncustomary slip by Paul Allen was enough to allow Feyenoord in for the only goal of a dour and uninspiring game. The Feyenoord defence, marshalled by former Spurs player Johnny Metgod playing at sweeper, allowed Gary Lineker and his strike force few chances at levelling the score, with Feyenoord more than happy at having prevented Spurs from scoring a vital away goal.

| 1995 | Nottingham Forest | A | FA Premier League | 2-2 |
| 1997 | Sunderland | A | FA Premier League | 4-0 |

Inconsistent form had seen Spurs slipping down the table and there was the possibility that the club might have been sucked into the relegation dog fight. It was much the same story for Sunderland, whose bright opening to the season back in August had been replaced by a lack of goals and the inability to string two consecutive wins together. This was a night that belonged to Steffan Iversen, whose three goals banished any thoughts of relegation at Spurs, even if they added to the problems at Roker Park. Spurs' other goal was scored by Allan Neilsen.

| 1998 | Leeds United | A | FA Premier League | 0-1 |

MARCH 5TH

1887	Edmonton Association	A	Friendly	3-1
1898	Gravesend United	A	Southern League	2-1
1904	Sheffield Wednesday	H	FA Cup 3rd Round	1-1
1906	New Brompton	A	Southern League	0-1
1910	Preston North End	H	First Division	2-1
1921	Aston Villa	H	FA Cup 4th Round	1-0

Spurs had met Aston Villa at exactly the same stage in the competition the previous year and had lost by the only goal of the game. A crowd of 51,991 paid receipts of £6,992 to watch another enthralling tie. Spurs won rather more convincingly than the 1-0 scoreline suggests but had only one goal to show for their efforts. Villa defender Frank Barson clattered into Jimmy Cantrell after only 25 minutes, causing the Spurs player such injuries that his effectiveness was reduced for the rest of the game. But Villa suffered their own misfortune later when Thompson was hurt and had to move from full-back to outside-right, with Ducat dropping back to cover. The only goal came after Jimmy Dimmock had eluded a tackle on the wing, sent over a cross towards Jimmy Seed who in turn had turned the ball to Jimmy Banks to crash in an unstoppable drive. That was in the first half, and although both ends were threatened in the second 45 minute spell, there were no further goals.

1927	Sheffield United	A	First Division	3-3
1928	Cardiff City	H	First Division	1-0
1932	Plymouth Argyle	A	Second Division	1-4
1938	Sunderland	H	FA Cup 6th Round	0-1

A record crowd of 75,038 packed into White Hart Lane to watch this FA Cup sixth round clash. Although Sunderland ultimately won by a single goal, there was considerable controversy surrounding a Spurs effort that was disallowed. Colin Lyman fired in a shot that had beaten the goalkeeper and Jack Gibbons rushed in to make sure the ball was over line, although he handled the ball. The referee signalled for a goal but was then urged to consult with his linesman, who was signalling on the line. He was of the opinion that Gibbons had handled the ball before it had crossed the line, even though the referee had been nearer the incident. The goal was therefore disallowed and Sunderland later scored the only one that mattered.

1949	Cardiff City	H	Second Division	0-1
1955	Manchester City	H	First Division	2-2
1960	Sheffield Wednesday	H	First Division	4-1
1963	Slovan Bratislava	A	European Cup-Winners' Cup 2nd Round 1st Leg	0-2

Manager Bill Nicholson had been furious after the first leg, accusing his team of being sloppy and half-asleep during their 2-0 defeat.

1966	Preston North End	A	FA Cup 5th Round	1-2
1977	Norwich City	A	First Division	3-1
1983	Notts County	A	First Division	0-3
1994	Sheffield United	H	FA Premier League	2-2

MARCH 6TH

1886	Ilford	H	Friendly	6-1
1897	Northfleet	A	Southern League	0-2
1901	Reading	A	Western League	1-1
1905	Bristol Rovers	A	Western League	1-2
1909	Stockport County	A	Second Division	3-1
1920	Aston Villa	H	FA Cup 4th Round	0-1

A crowd of over 51,000 packed into White Hart Lane for the quarter-final clash with Aston Villa, and whilst the majority would have been disappointed with the final score, even the manner of the goal, the entertainment and effort throughout was of the highest order by both sides. The Villa goal had more than an element of luck; Tommy Clay had plenty of opportunities to clear the ball from the Spurs penalty area but somehow contrived to slice it backwards into his own net. Although there was never any blame aimed in his direction (he was generally regarded as being one of the best Spurs players on the day), he would remember the incident for the rest of his career. The following year Banks played even better as Spurs overcame Villa by the same scoreline at the same stage, and the watching England selectors at this game obviously felt the incident was a rare error, for they picked him for his first England cap two days later. Villa, meanwhile, went on to win the cup.

1926	Liverpool	A	First Division	0-0
1935	Arsenal	H	First Division	0-6
1937	Preston North End	H	FA Cup 6th Round	1-3
1943	Chelsea	H	League Cup	2-0
1948	Plymouth Argyle	A	Second Division	1-1
1954	Cardiff City	H	First Division	0-1
1971	Liverpool	A	FA Cup 6th Round	0-0
1974	1.FC Cologne	A	UEFA Cup 4th Round 1st Leg	2-1
1976	Norwich City	A	First Division	1-3
1982	Chelsea	A	FA Cup 6th Round	3-2
1985	Real Madrid	H	UEFA Cup 4th Round 1st Leg	0-1

Ever since Spurs first entered European competition back in 1961 there was one record they guarded above all else; no European side had come to White Hart Lane and won. Although Real Madrid were a pale shadow of the great side of the late 1950s, there was still a magical quality about their name that ensured a packed White Hart Lane. The only goal of the match came from a Real breakaway, with Ray Clemence palming out a cross, only for the ball to strike Steve Perryman on the knee and cannon into the net! It was a bizarre way to lose the unbeaten record, but such was Spurs' away form they still had hope for the return leg in Madrid in a fortnight's time.

1988	Arsenal	A	First Division	1-2

MARCH 7TH

1885	Marlborough Rovers	A	Friendly	1-0
1891	1st Scots Guards	H	Friendly	Score unknown

1892   Bert Smith born in Higham in Kent. Bert began his career with Huddersfield Town, signing in 1913, although during the First World War he made a number of guest appearances for Spurs, usually in his normal inside-forward role, but later as half-back. When the war finished Spurs manager Peter McWilliam contacted Huddersfield Town and arranged the transfer of Town's reserve inside-forward Smith and converted him into Spurs' first-team half-back! Indeed, so successful was the conversion that Bert was a regular in the side for the next eight years, winning a Second Division championship medal in 1919-20 and an FA Cup winners' medal the following season. He was also capped for England against Scotland in April 1921, a match that saw no fewer than four Spurs players line up for England (the other three being Grimsdell, Dimmock and Bliss). Bert finished his career at Spurs in 1930, went on to coach Northfleet and then worked in Switzerland. He died in Biggleswade in September 1939.

1896	1st Scots Guards	H	Friendly	8-0
1903	Aston Villa	H	FA Cup 3rd Round	2-3
1904	Queens Park Rangers	H	London League	1-3
1908	Millwall	H	Southern League	1-2

1912   Fred Sargent born in Islington. Spotted by Spurs whilst playing for Tufnell Park Fred was signed in August 1934 and made his debut in September the same year. He was in and out of the first team until September 1937 when injury to John McCormick gave Fred an extended run at outside-right that was brought to an end by the Second World War. A broken leg sustained at Chelsea in February 1940 effectively ended any chance he might resume his League career when the war ended, and when he returned to White Hart Lane in May 1946 his contract was cancelled and he moved on to Chelmsford City. He died only two years later, on 22nd August 1948.

1914	Preston North End	H	First Division	1-0

1922   Peter Murphy born in Hartlepool. Initially linked to Birmingham as an amateur Peter signed professional forms with Coventry City and after finishing the 1949-50 season as top goalscorer was signed by Spurs for £18,500 to strengthen the side that had just won promotion into the First Division. He played enough games in 1950-51 to qualify for a championship medal but was unable to command a regular place in the side and was transferred to Birmingham City for £20,000 in January 1952. He remained at City for the next eight years, helping them to the Second Division title in 1955 and the FA Cup final the following year, when he was involved in the incident that left the Manchester City goalkeeper with a broken neck. He retired in 1960 and later served Coventry City on the coaching staff. He died on 7th April 1975.

1925	Aston Villa	A	First Division	1-0
1931	Charlton Athletic	A	Second Division	0-1
1936	Bury	A	Second Division	1-1
1942	Charlton Athletic	H	London War League	2-0
1953	Blackpool	A	First Division	0-2
1959	Leicester City	H	First Division	6-0
1964	Everton	H	First Division	2-4
1972	Unizale Textile Arad	A	UEFA Cup 4th Round 1st Leg	2-0
1973	Vitoria Setubal	H	UEFA Cup 4th Round 1st Leg	1-0
1981	Exeter City	H	FA Cup 6th Round	2-0
1984	FK Austria Vienna	H	UEFA Cup 4th Round 1st Leg	2-0
1987	Queens Park Rangers	H	First Division	1-0
1992	Leeds United	H	First Division	1-3
1993	Manchester City	A	FA Cup 6th Round	4-2

Spurs beat Manchester City 4-2 in the FA Cup quarter-final at Maine Road in a match that was held up for 13 minutes following a pitch invasion by City supporters. City took the lead but goals from Nayim and Sedgeley put Spurs ahead before half-time. In the second half Spurs took command with two further goals, Nayim completing his hat-trick, and finishing the game as a contest. Spurs continued to press and Andy Turner had the ball in the net, although this was disallowed for offside. Terry Phelan collected the goalkeeper's free-kick and ran the entire length of the pitch to score for City, which seemed to be the signal for hundreds of fans to pour out of the new Umbro Stand (opened that day) and on to the pitch. They were joined by countless others from the Kippax and the referee quickly took the teams off the field (although Eric Thorstvedt was attacked as he made his way to the dressing-room). The police arrived on horseback to restore order – although they spent more time watching the Spurs fans, the vast majority of whom remained in their places patiently awaiting the match to restart – and after 13 minutes the two teams returned to play out the final few moments. Even then that wasn't the end of the action, for Spurs were awarded a penalty with barely minutes left. According to legend, City goalkeeper Tony Coton advised Teddy Sheringham to blast it over the bar, 'if you've any sense'; Sheringham complied! Whilst the Spurs fans were held in the ground after the final whistle, the news came through of the draw for the semi-final – Arsenal at Wembley.

MARCH 8TH

Year	Opponent	Venue	Competition	Score
1884	Hanover United 2nd XI	A	Friendly	2-0
1890	Unity	H	Friendly	3-1
1899	Gravesend United	A	Thames & Medway League	3-0
1902	Swindon Town	H	Southern League	7-1
1909	Chesterfield	A	Second Division	3-1
1913	Liverpool	H	First Division	1-0
1919	West Ham United	H-Homerton		
			London Combination	0-1
1924	Sheffield United	A	First Division	2-6
1930	Swansea Town	H	Second Division	3-0
1941	Northampton Town	A	Football League War Cup 2nd Round 2nd Leg	3-1

Having already won the first leg at home 4-0, Spurs won 7-1 on aggregate and moved on to the 3rd round to face Cardiff City.

Year	Opponent	Venue	Competition	Score
1947	Fulham	H	Second Division	1-1
1952	Aston Villa	A	First Division	3-0
1956	West Ham United	A	FA Cup 6th Round Replay	2-1

Having escaped by the skin of their teeth in the first meeting between the two sides Spurs made sure the second time around, goals from Tommy Harmer and Len Duquemin putting them into their third FA Cup semi-final since the Second World War where they would face Manchester City.

Year	Opponent	Venue	Competition	Score
1958	Leeds United	A	First Division	2-1
1961	Sunderland	H	FA Cup 6th Round Replay	5-0

If the sound of the Sunderland crowd had been a daunting prospect for Spurs, then surely the reverse was true at White Hart Lane. With a crowd of 64,797 almost to a man willing Spurs to victory, they were seldom troubled by their Second Division opponents. Goals from Dave Mackay, Bobby Smith, Les Allen and two from Terry Dyson saw Spurs home with plenty to spare.

Year	Opponent	Venue	Competition	Score
1966	Arsenal	A	First Division	1-1
1969	Everton	H	First Division	1-1
1980	Liverpool	H	FA Cup 6th Round	0-1
1986	West Bromwich Albion	H	First Division	5-0
1995	Ipswich Town	H	FA Premier League	3-0

MARCH 9TH

Year	Opponent	Venue	Competition	Score
1889	Royal Arsenal	H	Friendly	0-1
1895	Old Westminsters	H	London Senior Cup 2nd Round Replay	4-5
1896	Royal Ordnance	A	Friendly	1-3
1897	Eastbourne	A	Friendly	1-0
1898	Tunbridge Wells	A	Friendly	5-0
1901	Bristol Rovers	A	Southern League	0-1
1903	Brentford	A	Western League	0-0
1907	Portsmouth	A	Southern League	1-3
1914				

Colin Lyman born in Northampton. Colin joined Northampton Town after failing to impress either West Bromwich Albion and Southend United, but made the grade with the Cobblers. He was transferred to Spurs in June 1937 and went straight into the first team as a winger, although the outbreak of the Second World War cut across his career and in May 1946 he was allowed to sign for Port Vale. He later played for Nottingham Forest and Notts County before switching to the non-League game.

Year	Opponent	Venue	Competition	Score
1918	Arsenal	A	London Combination	1-4
1921	Manchester City	A	First Division	0-2
1922	Cardiff City	H	FA Cup 4th Round Replay	2-1
1925	Leeds United	H	First Division	2-1
1929	Stoke City	H	Second Division	1-0
1935	Portsmouth	A	First Division	1-1
1938	Plymouth Argyle	A	Second Division	2-2
1940	Brentford	H	Football League South Group C	1-1
1946	Fulham	A	Football League South	1-1
1953	Birmingham City	N	FA Cup 6th Round 2nd Replay	1-0

1955	Racing Club de Paris	H	Friendly	6-0
1957	West Bromwich Albion	A	First Division	1-1
1963	Manchester United	A	First Division	2-0
1968	Liverpool	H	FA Cup 5th Round	1-1
1977	Liverpool	H	First Division	1-0
1982	Brighton & Hove Albion	A	First Division	3-1
1988	Everton	H	First Division	2-1
1996	Nottingham Forest	H	FA Cup 5th Round Replay	1-1 [lost 3-1 on penalties]

1996 Spurs met Nottingham Forest for the third time in their enthralling fifth round clash and once again there was little to choose between the two. After 120 minutes had still failed to separate them, a penalty shoot out followed.

MARCH 10TH

1894	Smethwick	N	Wolverton & District Charity Cup Semi-Final	0-1
1900	Thames Ironworks	A	Southern League	0-0
1902	West Ham United	A	Western League	1-1
1904	Sheffield Wednesday	A	FA Cup 3rd Round Replay	0-2
1906	Swindon Town	A	Southern League	0-2
1915	Liverpool	H	First Division	1-1
1917	Southampton	A	London Combination	4-2

1919 The First World War had brought an end to the Football League after the 1914-15 season; on this day the League met to announce the resumption of a different battle, that for League points in September. It was also announced that the Football League was to be extended by two clubs. On all previous occasions that this had occurred, the two teams who had occupied the bottom places in the First Division had been automatically re-elected to retain their position together with the promotion of the top two teams in the Second Division. This season bucked that trend. At the Football League meeting that decided the composition of the First Division for the following season it was announced there were exonerating reasons for automatically re-electing the club which had finished in 19th place in the First Division in 1914-15, which were Chelsea. The reason given, correctly enough, was that it had been proven that the match between Manchester United and Liverpool on April 2nd had been fixed and that had such a fix not taken place then Chelsea would most likely have finished higher up the table. Football League President John McKenna of Liverpool made his position clear; Chelsea should automatically retain First Division status without the matter going to a vote. In the light of such considerations the Spurs chairman, Charles Roberts, must have allowed himself a huge sigh of relief, for although his team had finished bottom of the First Division, a position they would still have retained even if their Manchester rivals had lost against Liverpool, the very fact that a match had been declared to have been squared must surely safeguard the Tottenham position? John McKenna's next address must have knocked Charles Roberts off his feet; there were exonerating reasons why Arsenal, who had finished the season before the pause in fifth place in the Second Division, should be allowed to replace Spurs in the First Division. First and foremost, Arsenal had been a member of the Football League for far longer than Tottenham! This was true; Arsenal had been admitted to League membership in 1893; Spurs in 1908, but League positions never had and never have been decided on seniority. Besides, in that final League season the Second Division had been headed by Grimsby Town (who were admitted to League membership in 1892, a full 12 months before Arsenal), with their attendant 'bridesmaids' Preston North End, founder members in 1888. And if seniority were reason enough for deciding the composition of the First Division, then Wolverhampton Wanderers, also founder members in 1888 and the fourth placed club in the 1914-15 League table would surely hold precedence over Arsenal? Whatever the logic (or lack of it) the meeting quickly picked up on the thread of John McKenna's motive; Arsenal must be elected to the First Division, even if it was at the expense of Spurs. And so it happened; when the voting slips were counted, Arsenal had received 18 'ayes', Spurs 8, Barnsley (who finished the 1914-15 season in third place in the Second Division, two above Arsenal) 5, Wolves 4, Nottingham Forest 3, Birmingham 2 and Hull 1. All of which suggested that had Charles Roberts and the Tottenham delegation had prior notice of the bombshell (and evidence suggests that they may well have known of Arsenal's move, for there was considerable speculation to this effect in the local press; if this is true, then Roberts ignored it out of hand and at his peril) that was to be landed in their direction they might have been able to persuade the other combatants to withdraw from the fray and throw their lot in with Spurs. The official record of the vote is unusually terse: 'The League was extended to 44 clubs. Chelsea was elected to the First Division without going to the vote. For the other vacancy Arsenal was elected with 18 votes. Tottenham Hotspur 8, Barnsley 5, Wolverhampton Wanderers 4, Nottingham Forest 3, Birmingham 2 and Hull City 1, were not elected.' If Tottenham had reason to despair of their North London rivals before (given the circumstances of Arsenal's arrival in the vicinity), they now had enough to despise them; North London's intense rivalry was well and truly cast.

1923	Derby County	H	FA Cup 4th Round	0-1
1928	Derby County	H	First Division	1-2
1934	Middlesbrough	A	First Division	1-1
1937	Bradford City	A	Second Division	2-2
1945	Aldershot	A	League South Cup Section 3	2-0
1951	Stoke City	A	First Division	0-0
1956	Portsmouth	H	First Division	1-1

1958 Garth Crooks born in Stoke-on-Trent. Signed by Stoke City in 1976 he was signed by Spurs manager Keith Burkinshaw in the summer of 1980 along with Steve Archibald, and the two immediately formed an effective partnership. Garth, who cost Spurs £650,000, had an excellent eye for goal and scored many fine ones during his time with the club, including two in the FA Cup semi-final replay and one in the final replay in 1981. He also helped the club to the FA Cup final the following year, scoring in the semi-final against Leicester. The later arrival of Alan Brazil and the form of Mark Falco saw first-team opportunities limited and in 1983 he went on loan to Manchester United, later joining West Bromwich Albion for £100,000 in 1985. He later played for Middlesbrough and Charlton before injury forced him to retire in 1990. He then became a television and radio presenter.

1962	Aston Villa	H	FA Cup 6th Round	2-0
1965	Chelsea	A	First Division	1-3
1971	Nottingham Forest	H	First Division	0-1
1973	Norwich City	H	First Division	3-0
1979	Manchester United	H	FA Cup 6th Round	1-1
1984	Liverpool	A	First Division	1-3
1990	Charlton Athletic	H	First Division	3-0
1991	Notts County	H	FA Cup 6th Round	2-1
1993	Aston Villa	A	FA Premier League	0-0

MARCH 11TH

1893	Queens Park Rangers	H	Friendly	1-0
1899	Woolwich Arsenal	A	United League	1-2
1901	Southampton	A	Western League	1-1
1905	Millwall	A	Southern League	2-0
1911	Bury	A	First Division	1-2
1916	Queens Park Rangers	H	London Combination [2nd competition]	0-0
1922	Sunderland	H	First Division	1-0
1933	Millwall	H	Second Division	2-1
1939	Manchester City	H	Second Division	2-3
1944	Millwall	H	League South Cup Section 2	1-0
1950	Luton Town	H	Second Division	0-0
1961	Cardiff City	A	First Division	2-3

One week before they were due to play in the FA Cup semi-final, Spurs lost a League match they should have won. Although the game was switched to Saturday evening to avoid clashing with a rugby international, there was no doubting what the big sporting event of the day was, as 45,463 packed into Ninian Park to see the team all of football was talking about. Spurs twice took the lead, through Les Allen and Terry Dyson, but each time allowed Cardiff to get back into the game. When they took the lead for the first and last time, pandemonium broke out, and at the end of the game thousands invaded the pitch to hail their heroes. Although Spurs should have won, the general feeling in the dressing-room was they were due a defeat and would rather it had been a League match than the forthcoming FA Cup semi-final.

1967	Bristol City	H	FA Cup 5th Round	2-0
1970	Everton	H	First Division	0-1
1972	Derby County	H	First Division	0-1
1978	Charlton Athletic	H	Second Division	2-1
1980	Nottingham Forest	A	First Division	0-4
1981	Stoke City	H	First Division	2-2
1989	Derby County	A	First Division	1-1
1992	Luton Town	A	First Division	0-0
1995	Liverpool	A	FA Cup 6th Round	2-1

Spurs' reward for their late comeback at Southampton was a sixth round clash at Anfield with Liverpool. Whilst Anfield was not perhaps the daunting prospect it had been during the '60s and '70s, it was still quite the hardest tie Spurs could have faced at this stage in the competition, and Liverpool had been beaten only once at home in the League that season. When Robbie Fowler fired the home team into the lead after 38 minutes it might have appeared that things were going according to

Liverpool's script, but Teddy Sheringham's delightful side-footed shot on the stroke of half-time brought Spurs level. Spurs had much the better of the second half, and as time ticked away there was the unlikely sight of a Liverpool side hanging on for dear life to ensure a replay. With two minutes left Sheringham returned the compliment to Klinsmann (it had been the German who had set up Sheringham's equaliser) by putting him clear in the Liverpool area and as Grobbelaar advanced, Klinsmann flicked the ball past him for the winner. It was a remarkable win, one which was fully appreciated by the 7,000 or so travelling fans. Stunned as they were, the Liverpool fans also gave Spurs a generous and well-deserved standing ovation at the end.

MARCH 12TH

1892	Casuals	H	Friendly	3-1
1898	Millwall Athletic	H	United League	3-2
1900	Bristol City	H	Southern District Combination	2-0
1904	Brentford	H	Southern League	1-1
1910	Notts County	A	First Division	0-3

This was a match Spurs could ill afford to lose, for the victory over Preston the previous week had given the club hope that they might avoid relegation back into the Second Division after only one season in the top flight. As it was this defeat started something of a bad run for Spurs and only two victories between now and the middle of April made their League position very precarious.

1921	Everton	H	First Division	2-0
1927	Derby County	H	First Division	3-2
1932	Bristol City	H	Second Division	2-1
1938	Chesterfield	H	Second Division	2-0
1949	Queens Park Rangers	A	Second Division	0-0
1953	Derby County	H	First Division	5-2
1955	Preston North End	A	First Division	0-1
1958	Bolton Wanderers	H	First Division	4-1
1960	Nottingham Forest	A	First Division	3-1
1966	Liverpool	A	First Division	0-1
1968	Liverpool	A	FA Cup 5th Round Replay	1-2
1977	West Bromwich Albion	H	First Division	0-2
1983	Coventry City	A	First Division	1-1
1985	Manchester United	H	First Division	1-2
1988	Norwich City	H	First Division	1-3

MARCH 13TH

1886	Rutland	H	Friendly	5-0
1897	Luton Town	H	United League	1-2
1899	New Brompton	A	Southern League	1-1
1907				

Having won the Southern League championship in his first season and the FA Cup in his second, anything less was always going to be viewed as failure by player-manager John Cameron. As the need to get results and success increased, Cameron had taken steps to try and improve the situation, playing less and less in order to concentrate on coaching more, and in 1906 the club had brought in Arthur Turner as secretary in order to further lighten the load on John Cameron. Unfortunately, this did little to improve results and so Cameron handed his resignation to the board on this date, citing 'differences with the directorate' as his reason.

1909	West Bromwich Albion	H	Second Division	1-3
1912	West Bromwich Albion	A	First Division	0-2
1915	Bradford Park Avenue	A	First Division	1-5
1920	West Ham United	A	Second Division	1-2
1926	Leicester City	H	First Division	1-3
1937	Aston Villa	H	Second Division	2-2
1943	Reading	A	League Cup	1-1
1948	Blackpool	Villa Park	FA Cup Semi-Final	1-3 [aet]

Spurs' first appearance in the FA Cup semi-final since 1922 was to end in despair, but not before they thought they were home and dry. Although Blackpool could boast the talents of a holy trinity in Matthews, Mortensen and Johnston, Spurs had their own match winners, and in the early stages it was the Spurs men who rose to the occasion. Len Duquemin gave Spurs the lead midway through the second half, and with the defence repelling everything that Blackpool could throw at them, Wembley beckoned. There were barely four minutes left when Mortensen took a pass from Matthews and headed towards the goal-line, running fully 30 yards and leaving some four defenders in his trail. With everyone expecting a cross he chose to shoot and watched the ball elude Ted Ditchburn from an impossible angle. It was, to say the least, an unbelievable goal, but given the circumstances and the event, it had to be one worth trying. Spurs heads dropped almost immediately, having seen their dreams dashed so near to the end, and extra time was little more than a formality. Two further goals from Stan Mortensen took Blackpool through to Wembley at Spurs' expense. The cup defeat had a devastating effect on Spurs, for they won only two more League matches and saw their promotion hopes disappear too.

1954	West Bromwich Albion	A	FA Cup 6th Round	0-3
1957	Arsenal	H	First Division	1-3
1965	Blackpool	H	First Division	4-1
1971	Chelsea	H	First Division	2-1

On the same day Allan Nielsen was born in Esbjerg in Denmark. Allan began his career with his local club before being spotted by German club Bayern Munich in 1989. He later played for OB Odense and FC Copenhagen before signing for Brondby in 1995. A year later he was signed by Spurs for £1.65 million and immediately imposed himself in midfield. He has won 20 caps for Denamrk.

| 1976 | Aston Villa | H | First Division | 5-2 |
| 1982 | Liverpool | Wembley | League Cup Final | 1-3 [aet] |

Just before the final the Football League announced they had concluded a sponsorship agreement with the Milk Marketing Board and that the League Cup would henceforth be known as the Milk Cup. This meant that the winners of today's match would collect two trophies from the Royal Box – the old (League Cup) and the new (Milk Cup). For much of the game it looked as though it would be Spurs collecting the silverware, for Steve Archibald latched on to a lofted pass from Glenn Hoddle, took advantage of a mix-up between Grobbelaar and Thompson and put Spurs ahead in the 11th minute. Although Liverpool pressed for much of the rest of the game, the Spurs defence appeared to be holding up well. Four minutes from the end Spurs worked another opening for Archibald, but with the Liverpool goal at his mercy he elected to wait for the ball to reach his favoured foot and in that split second the chance had gone. Barely a minute later the action swung back to the Spurs goalmouth and a momentary lapse of concentration allowed a cross from McDermott to reach Ronnie Whelan and he put the equaliser home. The goal knocked Spurs off their stride and fired up Liverpool; there was only ever going to be one winner in extra time and ten minutes from time Whelan knocked in his second of the game. A final effort from Ian Rush ensured both trophies were going to Anfield rather than White Hart Lane. This was Spurs' first defeat in a domestic cup final (at the ninth attempt) and their first defeat at Wembley (also at the ninth attempt), although there was still plenty to play for in this centenary season.

MARCH 14TH

1885	Victoria Wanderers	A	Friendly	Score unknown
1896	Uxbridge	H	Friendly	4-0
1903	Kettering Town	H	Southern League	4-0
1904	Millwall	A	London League	2-3
1908	Brentford	A	Southern League	0-3
1910	Sheffield Wednesday	A	First Division	1-1
1914	Sunderland	A	First Division	0-2
1923	Manchester City	A	First Division	0-3
1925	Huddersfield Town	H	First Division	1-2
1931	Bradford City	H	Second Division	3-1
1936	West Ham United	H	Second Division	1-3
1942	West Ham United	A	London War League	3-2
1953	Chelsea	H	First Division	2-3
1955	Hibernian	A	Friendly	1-1
1959	Leeds United	A	First Division	1-3
1962	Ipswich Town	H	First Division	1-3

The story of the 1961-62 season, Europe aside, basically boiled down to this one match. Had Spurs won 3-1 instead of losing by that score, they would have retained the title on goal average. Of course, football is seldom that simple, but the facts were these; Ispwich had taken the First Division by storm, with manager Alf Ramsey realising his team's strengths and weaknesses and adopting a formation that compensated for them. Although Bill Nicholson realised Ramsey's game plan, the players were not happy to change their style in order to accommodate anybody else's, believing that Ipswich should worry about Spurs more than they should worry about Ipswich. The result was that Ipswich won the title by three points from Burnley and four from Spurs, thereby denying both the chance of a double. Had Spurs won this game, an unprecedented double double would have been theirs.

| 1963 | Slovan Bratislava | H | European Cup-Winners' Cup 2nd Round 2nd Leg | 6-0 |

Just as they had done a year previously in the European Cup tie against Gornik, the crowd played a significant part in helping Spurs overturn a first leg defeat into an aggregate victory. Goals from Mackay, White, Smith, Jones and Greaves (2) enabled Spurs to advance into the semi-finals 6-2 on aggregate.

1970	Everton	A	First Division	2-3
1973	Stoke City	A	First Division	1-1
1979	Manchester United	A	FA Cup 6th Round Replay	0-2
1981	Ipswich	A	First Division	0-3
1992	Sheffield Wednesday	H	First Division	0-2
1998	Liverpool	H	FA Premier League	3-3

During the week Jurgen Klinsmann had openly criticised manager Christian Gross's tactics, claiming he had received too few crosses and passes from David Ginola, which in turn was contributing to the team's inability to score goals. The need, therefore, for all concerned to put their differences behind them and grind out a result in the battle against relegation was paramount. They nearly did it too, with Ginola supplying an inch-perfect cross for Klinsmann to head Spurs into the lead, only for Liverpool to equalise. Then Ginola scored a remarkable goal with a bending shot, only for Liverpool to equalise. With ten minutes left and with Neilsen having just hit the bar, Vega swept Spurs into the lead for a third time. Neilsen hit the post again before Liverpool equalised for the third and final time, with barely a minute or so left on the clock. It was one point, rather than three, but a happier dressing-room at the end of an arduous week.

MARCH 15TH

1884	Latymer	A	Friendly	2-0
1890	Edmonton	H	Friendly	1-4
1897	Kettering Town	A	United League	1-1

With the Kettering team reduced to ten men following one of their number suffering a broken leg, the match was abandoned and replayed on April 17th.

1902	Brentford	A	Southern League	1-2
1911	Manchester United	A	First Division	2-3
1913	Bolton Wanderers	A	First Division	0-2
1915	Manchester City	H	First Division	2-2
1919	Clapton Orient	A	London Combination	2-1
1922	Everton	A	First Division	0-0
1924	Aston Villa	A	First Division	0-0
1930	Cardiff City	A	Second Division	0-1
1941	Millwall	A (but played at WHL)	Football League South	0-1
1948	Barnsley	H	Second Division	0-3
1952	Sunderland	H	First Division	2-0
1958	Sunderland	H	First Division	0-1
1975	Middlesbrough	A	First Division	0-3
1980	Crystal Palace	H	First Division	0-0
1986	Birmingham City	A	First Division	2-1
1987	Wimbledon	A	FA Cup 6th Round	2-0

1991 Italian club Lazio confirmed they had made a world record bid of £8.5 million for Paul Gascoigne and were given first option on the player by Spurs. Although Gascoigne eventually moved to Lazio in 1992, the final figure was almost halved – after a career-threatening injury had put Gascoigne out of the game for a year, he moved on for £4.8 million.

| 1995 | Manchester United | A | FA Premier League | 0-0 |
| 1997 | Leeds United | H | FA Premier League | 1-0 |

MARCH 16TH

| 1889 | Edmonton | H | Friendly | 1-1 |
| 1895 | Old Carthusians | H | FA Amateur Cup 2nd Round | 0-5 |

Spurs contested their last ever match in the FA Amateur Cup, being beaten 5-0 by Old Carthusians before a crowd of 5,000 at Northumberland Park. The Old Carthusians were one of the strongest teams of the day, able to boast no fewer than five England internationals in their line-up and one of only two clubs to have won both the FA and FA Amateur Cups. Although Spurs entered the competition the following season (and were drawn against Chesham) they adopted professionalism before the match could be played and were obliged to withdraw.

1896	Woolwich Arsenal	A	Friendly	3-1
1899	Thames Ironworks	A	Thames & Medway League	1-2
1901	Reading	H	Southern League	1-0

1903	Queens Park Rangers	A	London League	0-1
1907	New Brompton	H	Southern League	2-0
1912	Liverpool	A	First Division	2-1

Spurs won at Anfield with Ernie Numan and Thomas Mason scoring in the 2-1 victory. They would have had no way of knowing at the time, but this was the start of one of the longest runs in football – it took 73 years to the very day before another Spurs side could claim both points at Anfield. A crowd of 15,000 were in attendance.

1918	West Ham United	H-Highbury		
			London Combination	0-5
1929	Clapton Orient	A	Second Division	3-2
1931	Everton	H	Second Division	1-0
1935	Manchester City	H	First Division	0-0
1940	Portsmouth	A	Football League South Group C	2-1
1946	Fulham	H	Football League South	1-3
1957	Portsmouth	H	First Division	2-0
1963	Ipswich Town	A	First Division	4-2
1968	Nottingham Forest	A	First Division	0-0
1971	Liverpool	H	FA Cup 6th Round Replay	0-1
1974	Norwich City	H	First Division	0-0
1976	Wolverhampton Wanderers	A	First Division	1-0
1985	Liverpool	A	First Division	1-0

Having lost at home to Manchester United during the week and not won at Anfield for 73 years, there were few who gave Spurs much chance of finally ending the run at Liverpool. But, for the first time in many a year, Spurs were an altogether better side away from home and took the game to Liverpool right from the start. In the 70th minute Mark Falco charged down a Liverpool clearance, the referee ignoring calls for handball and the ball found its way to Micky Hazard. Grobbelaar could only parry his snap shot and Garth Crooks was on hand to knock the ball home and thus end one of the longest runs in football. After each previous attempt at winning at Anfield had ended in failure, the media delighted in reminding the Spurs faithful that the Titanic was afloat the last time they won. As the fans made their way out of Anfield today, one commented 'The skipper of the QE2 must be nervous!'

| 1991 | Aston Villa | A | First Division | 2-3 |

Aston Villa's captain David Platt grabbed a hat-trick to become the first player to score as many as three goals against Spurs since 1981, when David Cross scored all four in West Ham's win on September 2nd.

| 1996 | Blackburn Rovers | H | FA Premier League | 2-3 |

MARCH 17TH

1888	St Bride's	A	Friendly	3-0
1902	Portsmouth	H	Western League	0-0
1906	Millwall	H	Southern League	3-1
1917	Clapton Orient	H-Highbury		
			London Combination	5-2
1923	Stoke	A	First Division	0-0
1928	West Ham United	A	First Division	1-1
1934	West Bromwich Albion	H	First Division	2-1
1951	West Bromwich Albion	H	First Division	5-0
1954	Manchester City	A	First Division	1-4

Ted Ditchburn appeared in goal for Spurs for the 247th consecutive League match, a club record. The last match he had missed was against Nottingham Forest on 12th April 1948, the only game of that season he didn't play in! He also missed only one game in the first League season after the war, meaning he had missed only two of Spurs' 331 League games since the war.

| 1956 | Manchester City | Villa Park | FA Cup Semi-Final | 0-1 |

Spurs' third post-war FA Cup semi-final at Villa Park ended in the same way as the previous two, but there are still those convinced that Spurs were denied an equaliser, either from a goal or the penalty that should have been awarded. The Spurs manager had already sprung a surprise in dropping Tommy Harmer, a player who had been largely responsible for getting the club through in the first place, reasoning that Harmer's small frame would be easily knocked off the ball by the robust City defenders. The result was Spurs struggled to get into their stride and fell behind to a Bobby Johnstone header. With 20 minutes to go and Spurs still struggling, captain Danny Blanchflower made one or two changes, pushing Maurice Norman up front and pulling Johnny Brooks back, a ploy that had worked in the sixth round match against West Ham. Then he sent Brooks back up front, for with only minutes to go, what had they to lose? With barely minutes on the clock George Robb broke through and was confronted with an open goal. Just as he was pulling his foot back to shoot, City keeper Bert Trautmann grabbed hold of his legs. Both the referee and linesman missed the incident and so Spurs slid out of the cup. The atmosphere in the dressing-room after the game was a mixture of pain, anger and despair. Jimmy Anderson was furious with Blanchflower for having changed the team around, although Danny had only tried to win the game.

1962	Burnley	A	First Division	2-2
1979	Norwich City	H	First Division	0-0
1982	Eintracht Frankfurt	A	European Cup-Winners' Cup 3rd Round 2nd Leg	1-2

Just four days previously Spurs' quest for an unprecedented four trophies had come to an end with defeat in the League Cup final against Liverpool at Wembley. There were still three left, however; the FA Cup, the League title and the European Cup-Winners' Cup, but after some 20 minutes or so the latter of these looked in jeopardy as well, with Spurs 2-0 lead from the first leg having evaporated thanks to some sloppy defending. Then Glenn Hoddle came to the rescue, shooting from long range and a slight deflection taking the ball past the goalkeeper. A 2-1 defeat on the night left Spurs 3-2 ahead on aggregate and into the semi-finals for the first time since 1963. Waiting for them were the butchers of Barcelona.

| 1984 | West Bromwich Albion | H | First Division | 1-0 |
| 1990 | Queens Park Rangers | A | First Division | 1-3 |

MARCH 18TH

1899	New Brompton	H	Southern League	3-0
1901	Queens Park Rangers	A	Western League	1-1
1905	Brighton & Hove Albion	H	Southern League	1-1
1911	Sheffield United	H	First Division	2-1
1916	Croydon City	A	London Combination [2nd competition]	3-3
1922	Huddersfield Town	H	First Division	1-0
1925	Cardiff City	A	First Division	2-0
1933	Port Vale	A	Second Division	1-1
1939	Bradford Park Avenue	A	Second Division	0-0
1944	Portsmouth	A	League South Cup Section 2	2-1
1950	Barnsley	A	Second Division	0-2
1961	Burnley	Villa Park	FA Cup Semi-Final	3-0

As respective captains Danny Blanchflower and Jimmy McIlroy lined up before venturing out on to the field, they engaged in a little light-hearted banter designed to win a psychological advantage over the other. 'We've got the lucky dressing-room [Spurs were in the home team's dressing-room] and you never win at Villa Park,' stated Danny. 'We've not been here in our own jerseys yet,' retorted McIlroy, referring to the usual colour clash between Aston Villa and Burnley. 'We've never lost against those jerseys here,' responded Danny, by way of pointing out Spurs hadn't lost at Villa Park in the League since the war. Danny then went on the attack. 'Where did you stay last night?' 'Droitwich' came the reply. 'Poor sods, we stayed there before our 1956 semi-final here and lost.' If Danny's comments had been intended to unsettle McIlroy and his team-mates then they failed in the opening exchanges of the game, for Burnley settled considerably quicker than Spurs. Indeed, it was Spurs' defence who were busiest in the opening half hour. Then luck, which had been conspicuous by its absence in 1948, 1953 and 1956, fell on Spurs' side. Jimmy Adamson attempted to intercept a pass from Les Allen but was beaten as much by the wind as by the pace of the ball and Bobby Smith latched on to it to fire Spurs into a lead they barely deserved. Spurs should have had a penalty just before the half-time break when Angus punched out a Dyson header after goalkeeper Blacklaw had been beaten, but the referee didn't spot the infringement and waved play on. Burnley began the second half pressing for an equaliser and thought they had it when Robson headed home after two minutes, but this was disallowed by the referee, who thought Robson had climbed on Maurice Norman when jumping for the ball. Then it was Spurs' turn to benefit from an unsighted handball, Ron Henry handling on the goalline. The boos from the Burnley fans had barely subsided when Spurs increased their lead, Bobby Smith volleying from just inside the area, and with that goal any chance Burnley might have had went. Cliff Jones added a third right on the stroke of full-time to complete the scoring, but the game had been over as a contest some time earlier. Spurs were at last at Wembley.

1967	Chelsea	H	First Division	1-1
1969	Ipswich Town	H	First Division	2-2
1972	Leeds United	A	FA Cup 6th Round	1-2
1978	Bristol City	A	Second Division	3-2
1989	Coventry City	A	First Division	1-1
1992	Feyenoord	H	European Cup-Winners' Cup 3rd Round 2nd Leg	0-0

An unfortunate slip by Paul Allen in the first leg had allowed Feyenoord to score the only goal of the game. And whilst previous encounters with the Dutch club, at least on the field, had been open and attacking, this was little more than stalemate. Feyenoord were a pale shadow of their former selves, and having gained an advantage were determined to hold on to it. Spurs tried all night but could find no way through a solid defence, slipping out of the competition 1-0 on aggregate.

| 1995 | Leicester City | H | FA Premier League | 1-0 |

MARCH 19TH

| 1887 | London Caledonians | N | Friendly | 0-2 |

Spurs had battled their way through to the semi-finals of the East End Cup and were due to play London Caledonians at North Greenwich. However, when both teams saw the state of the pitch, they agreed to postpone the semi-final until the following week and played a friendly instead.

1896	Royal Ordnance	H	Friendly	2-2
1898	Sheppey United	H	Southern League	4-0
1900	Bristol Rovers	H	Southern League	5-1

This was the replay of the match abandoned on October 21st owing to fog – Spurs took more of the chances they created against Rovers this time around.

1903	West Ham United	A	Western League	0-0
1904	West Ham United	A	Southern League	2-0
1906	Bristol Rovers	A	Western League	0-0
1910	Newcastle United	H	First Division	0-4
1921	Preston North End	Hillsborough		
			FA Cup Semi-Final	2-1

Spurs kept the same line-up that had beaten Aston Villa in the previous round, meaning Hunter kept his place in goal. A crowd of 44,648 paid receipts of £4,495 for the privilege of attending the game and were treated to a titanic struggle between Spurs and Preston. In truth Spurs should have won rather more convincingly than the scoreline suggests but were denied possibly two penalties that might have been given on another day, in a contest not so vital. As it was, two goals from Bert Bliss put Spurs in the driving seat, and Preston's lone reply was a late consolation. Spurs also had a goal disallowed; although Banks had fired home, the referee brought play back to give Spurs a free-kick for a foul on Seed!

1927	Bolton Wanderers	A	First Division	2-2
1928	Portsmouth	H	First Division	0-3
1932	Swansea Town	A	Second Division	1-1
1938	Swansea Town	A	Second Division	2-3
1949	Luton Town	H	Second Division	2-1
1955	Sheffield United	H	First Division	5-0
1957	Combined Antwerp XI	Antwerp	Friendly	2-1
1960	Fulham	H	First Division	1-1
1966	Aston Villa	H	First Division	5-5

On the same day Andy Sinton was born in Newcastle. Andy began his career with Cambridge United, signing as an apprentice in 1982 and upgrading to the professional ranks the following year. A fee of £25,000 took him to Brentford in 1985, but he made his reputation with QPR whom he joined in 1989 for £350,000. Capped whilst at Loftus Road he was sold to Sheffield Wednesday for £2.75 million in 1993, but struggled to command a regular place in the side. He returned to the capital with Spurs in 1996 for £1.5 million and soon rediscovered his form, returning to the fringes of the England squad.

1977	Birmingham City	A	First Division	2-1
1983	Watford	A	First Division	1-0
1986	Everton	A	Screen Sport Super Cup Semi-Final 2nd Leg	1-3 [aet]

The competition introduced to give those clubs who would have qualified for Europe some tangible reward for their efforts had coughed and spluttered its way towards its conclusion, unloved and largely ignored by the players and spectators alike. Not even the prospect of a final appearance (although quite where was anyone's guess) could lift the gloomy atmosphere, and although Mark Falco scored first to give Spurs the lead, an Everton equaliser and two further goals in extra time ensured they would meet Liverpool in the final by virtue of a 3-1 aggregate win.

1988	Wimbledon	A	First Division	0-3
1994	Ipswich Town	H	FA Premier League	1-1
1997	Leicester City	A	FA Premier League	1-1

MARCH 20TH

1886	Upton Excelsior	H	Friendly	Won but score unknown
1897	Reading	H	Southern League	4-4
1899	Royal Engineers	H	Thames & Medway League	1-2

1905	Queens Park Rangers	A	Western League	1-1
1909	Birmingham	H	Second Division	3-3
1915	Oldham Athletic	H	First Division	1-0
1920	Rotherham County	H	Second Division	2-0
1926	West Ham United	A	First Division	1-3
1937	Chesterfield	A	Second Division	3-1
1943	Millwall	H	League Cup	5-0
1948	Brentford	A	Second Division	0-2
1954	Sunderland	H	First Division	0-3
1965	Sunderland	A	First Division	1-2
1971	Burnley	A	First Division	0-0
1974	1.FC Cologne	H	UEFA Cup 4th Round 2nd Leg	3-0

Having already established a 2-1 lead in the first leg, Spurs were in no mood to let the tie slip. Goals from Martin Chivers, Martin Peters and Ralph Coates ensured a 5-1 aggregate victory and passage into the semi-final, where a team from the other side of the Berlin Wall lay in wait.

1976	Burnley	A	First Division	2-1
1982	Southampton	H	First Division	3-2
1985	Real Madrid	A	UEFA Cup 4th Round 2nd Leg	0-0

Although Spurs started the match one goal behind on aggregate there was genuine hope that they might still progress, for their away form throughout the season had been exceptional; the previous weekend they had won at Anfield for the first time in over 70 years. By comparison, Real Madrid's Bernabeau Stadium held no fears and Spurs went on the attack from the off. Whilst the Real Madrid of old had made their name with exhilarating attack, their modern counterparts were quite happy to sit back and absorb the pressure and then hope for a breakaway or two to settle the matter. Spurs launched wave after wave of attacks, even when down to ten men (Steve Perryman was sent off for a late challenge) and looked to have squared the tie with a Mark Falco header in the second half. Although Real Madrid did not appeal for an offside or a foul, the referee disallowed the goal and Spurs' hold on the UEFA Cup won the previous season was loosened. Just as it had some 23 years previously, a trip to the Iberian Peninsula had ended in heartache.

| 1993 | Chelsea | A | FA Premier League | 1-1 |
| 1996 | Bolton Wanderers | A | FA Premier League | 3-2 |

MARCH 21ST

1885	Remington	A	Friendly	Score unknown
1895	Old Carthusians	A	London Charity Cup 2nd Round	0-3
1896	Manchester Regiment	H	Friendly	8-0
1903	Luton Town	A	Southern League	0-3
1904	West Ham United	A	London League	1-0
1906	Plymouth Argyle	A	Western League	0-0
1908	Bristol Rovers	H	Southern League	1-2
1913	West Bromwich Albion	H	First Division	3-1
1914	Newcastle United	H	First Division	0-0
1925	Blackburn Rovers	A	First Division	1-1
1931	Swansea Town	A	Second Division	2-1
1936	Swansea Town	A	Second Division	1-1
1942	Reading	A	London War Cup	2-1
1953	Blackpool	Villa Park	FA Cup Semi-Final	1-2

By the time of the 1953 FA Cup semi-final, Arthur Rowe's 'push and run' side was already beginning to belong in the past, for other teams had worked out how to nullify their threat and they were no longer as effective in the League. The FA Cup was to have been a fitting parting shot for the side, but a defensive slip in the last minute wrecked all of Rowe's plans. Blackpool had taken the lead through Perry in the first half, although Spurs were more than a match for their opponents. In the second half they fashioned an equaliser, Bennett setting up Duquemin, and the rest of the half was almost all Spurs. As the game moved into its final minutes, all minds began to think ahead to extra time. Then Eddie Baily was penalised for handball and stood arguing with the referee. Blackpool took the kick quickly, setting Perry free on the wing, although Alf Ramsey was equally quick to intercept. He turned to play the ball back to Ted Ditchburn but he slipped, knocking the ball only a few feet towards the goalkeeper. In an instant Mudie pounced on the ball and knocked it home past the helpless Ditchburn for a late, late winner. There was barely time to kick off before the whistle blew for the last time, ending Spurs' hopes.

| 1956 | Bolton Wanderers | A | First Division | 2-3 |
| 1959 | Manchester City | H | First Division | 3-1 |

| 1962 | Benfica | A | European Cup Semi-Final 1st Leg | 1-3 |

Having reached the European Cup semi-final Spurs were given the hardest tie of all – Benfica, the reigning European champions. Real Mardid, past their peak, or Standard Liege, relatively unknown would have been preferable, but Spurs were drawn against Benfica. There was a slight advantage; Benfica were drawn out first, so Spurs would know exactly what they had to do to reach the final by the time the home leg came around. Manager Bill Nicholson prepared himself well, going to see Benfica play in Nuremberg and also watching Real Madrid beat Juventus. His view was that if Spurs got past Benfica they could also beat Real Madrid. Nicholson had also learnt from previous rounds about how to play away from home in Europe – Tony Marchi was invariably drafted in as an extra defender, but this was also the first match for which Jimmy Greaves had been eligible. All managers say that no matter how well they prepare themselves and their team, there is nothing they can do for the players once the team cross the white line. This was undoubtedly true in Lisbon, for despite all the planning, scheming and contingencies, everything fell apart in Lisbon. Within 20 minutes Benfica were two ahead, Aguas and Augusto taking advantage of Spurs' defensive frailties. In between these two goals Spurs thought they had equalised when Jimmy Greaves was adjudged offside after putting the ball in the net (although Greaves claimed after the game that he had beaten the full-back before scoring). At half-time Benfica indulged in a piece of blatant gamesmanship – Spurs arrived back on the field for the second half but were kept waiting by Benfica, who finally deigned to return after an 18-minute break. In the 54th minute Spurs finally reduced the deficit, Bobby Smith heading in a Danny Blanchflower cross. They might have equalised too, for Smith, Greaves, White and Jones all went close with chances. However, it was Benfica who got one that mattered, Augusto heading his second after 19 minutes of second-half action. That might have been the end of the scoring but it was not the end of the drama, for in the last minute of the game Jimmy Greaves unselfishly crossed when he might have shot and found Bobby Smith who did the rest. The referee signalled the goal, but then noticed the linesman flagging and disallowed the goal without further consultation. After the game Jimmy Greaves was adamant the goal was a good one, claiming he had been ahead of Smith when he crossed and that there were two defenders stood on the line when Smith scored. Bill Nicholson was more concerned with his defence, furious about two goals that were given away rather than the goal that slipped away. As good as his defence were, it was to be another linesman who stole the headlines in the second leg.

1964	Manchester United	H	First Division	2-3
1970	Coventry City	H	First Division	1-2
1972	Unizale Textile Arad	H	UEFA Cup 4th Round 2nd Leg	1-1

Spurs' 2-0 win in Rumania in the first leg was sufficient to ensure passage into the semi-finals, but it was a largely unimpressive performance in the second leg. Whilst the draw gave Spurs a 3-1 aggregate win, they failed to impress in front of their own fans.

| 1973 | Vitoria Setubal | A | UEFA Cup 4th Round 2nd Leg | 1-2 |

Spurs went into the second leg with the slenderest of leads from the first leg, a 1-0 home win thanks to a goal from Martin Peters. As important as that goal was, it was the strike by Martin Chivers that was to prove vital, for it enabled Spurs to progress at the expense of their Portuguese opponents by virtue of an away goal win.

| 1981 | Aston Villa | H | First Division | 2-0 |
| 1984 | FK Austria Vienna | A | UEFA Cup 4th Round 2nd Leg | 2-2 |

The Austrian side had been incensed by Spurs' 2-0 home win, claiming that both Graham Roberts and Paul Miller should have been dismissed for some extremely robust tackling. Whilst the majority of the tackles put in by Roberts and Miller had been hard, they were for the most part fair. Chasing a two goal deficit Austria Vienna were forced to take the game to Spurs in the second leg, leaving gaps at the back that Spurs were only too happy to exploit. Goals from Alan Brazil and Ossie Ardiles gave Spurs a 4-2 aggregate win and a semi-final clash with Hajduk Split.

| 1990 | Liverpool | H | First Division | 1-0 |
| 1992 | Liverpool | A | First Division | 1-2 |

MARCH 22ND

| 1884 | Remington | H | Friendly | 2-0 |

The game was halted after 80 minutes with Spurs leading thanks to goals from Jull and Watson.

1897	Gravesend	H	Friendly	3-2
1899	Grays United	A	Thames & Medway League	0-1
1902	Kettering Town	H	Southern League	4-0
1908	Millwall	N	London FA Charity Cup Semi-Final	0-2
1915	George Ludford born in Barnet. George joined the Spurs groundstaff upon leaving school in 1931 and was signed as a professional player in May 1936. Unable to shift Johnny Morrison from the first team prior to the Second World War, George made the most of the chances that came his way during the

conflict, even if it meant changing position. When his playing career finished in 1954 he joined the coaching staff, later moving to Enfield as manager.

1919	Chelsea	A	London Combination	2-1
1920	West Ham United	H	Second Division	2-0
1930	Preston North End	H	Second Division	1-0
1940	Millwall	H	Football League South Group C	1-2
1941	Cardiff City	H	Football League War Cup 3rd Round 1st Leg	3-3
1947	Luton Town	H	Second Division	2-1
1952	Wolverhampton Wanderers	A	First Division	1-1
1958	Luton Town	A	First Division	0-0
1961	Newcastle United	H	First Division	1-2

With Spurs having booked their place in the FA Cup final thoughts could turn once again to winning the League. They were facing a Newcastle side third from bottom in the table and therefore equally desperate for points. The first half was all Spurs, with the Newcastle goalkeeper being forced to make some 20 or so saves as United battled to stay in the game. He was beaten only once, Les Allen converting a Cliff Jones cross, and Danny Blanchflower missed a penalty, but it appeared as though matters would be put right in the second half. They weren't, for desperation began to creep into Spurs' game and Newcastle, from being on the ropes in the first half, were allowed back into contention. Ivor Allchurch equalised just after the hour, and 13 minutes from the end Albert Scanlon grabbed an unlikely winner.

1967	Everton	A	First Division	1-0
1969	Chelsea	H	First Division	1-0
1975	Liverpool	H	First Division	0-2
1978	Stoke City	H	Second Division	3-1
1980	Bolton Wanderers	A	First Division	1-2
1986	Newcastle United	A	First Division	2-2
1987	Liverpool	H	First Division	1-0
1989	Nottingham Forest	A	First Division	2-1
1995	Liverpool	H	FA Premier League	0-0
1997	Derby County	A	FA Premier League	2-4

MARCH 23RD

1894	2nd Scots Guards	H	Friendly	3-1

On the same day Arthur Grimsdell was born in Watford. Arthur began his career as a centre-forward when he signed with Watford in 1909, although they soon converted him to his more usual half-back position. He was subsequently signed by Spurs whilst still only 18 and played his initial games for the club at centre-half, although when manager Peter McWilliam was appointed he soon realised Arthur's true abilities lay as a half-back. He might well have earned international honours during his early Spurs career, but the outbreak of the First World War meant he had to wait considerably longer. Upon returning to Spurs after the war in 1919 he was made captain and guided the club to the Second Division title and FA Cup in consecutive seasons. In October 1925 the club were top of the First Division but lost their inspirational captain to a broken leg, and it is a measure of his influence that Spurs effectively struggled for the 18 months or so it took him to recover. When he returned he was not the player he had been before and he was released, subsequently serving Clapton Orient as player, secretary and manager. He later served both Orient and Watford as a director. He died in Watford on 12th March 1973.

1895	London Caledonians	H	Friendly	5-1

One of Spurs' goals was scored by James Collins, the only goal he scored for the club. He had joined Spurs in January 1895, making his debut in the London Senior Cup match against London Welsh the same month. Just as he was on the verge of establishing himself in the side he was suspended for six weeks, and was later imprisoned for two months for assaulting the landlord of a public house. He was released at the end of that season!

1901	Reading	A	FA Cup 3rd Round	1-1

Of the eight sides left in the FA Cup, six were Football League sides – Middlesbrough, West Bromwich Albion, Small Heath (Birmingham City), Aston Villa, Wolverhampton Wanderers and Sheffield United – and two were from the Southern League – Reading and Spurs. Spurs' first slice of good fortune came with the draw; they faced Reading away from home. Although Reading were known as a hard-tackling team, they were little more than a modest Southern League outfit, standing ninth in that Division on the day of the game. That said, Spurs made surprisingly heavy weather of the tie, falling behind (as they had done in each previous tie) in the first half to a 20-yard shot from Evans, which John Kirwan equalised in the second half. Two minutes from the end of the match there came an incident that was talked about for many years – a speculative shot dropped over Spurs keeper

Clawley's head and was destined to go in for a goal when Sandy Tait dashed back and punched the ball away. There were quite possibly only two people inside Elm Park who were not convinced it was a penalty; the referee and the nearest linesman. Indeed, they did not see the incident at all! Thus reprieved, Spurs lived to fight another day.

| 1903 | Millwall Athletic | H | London League | 1-0 |
| 1907 | Plymouth Argyle | A | Southern League | 0-0 |

1908 The Southern League held its EGM to discuss the proposed resignations of Tottenham, Queens Park Rangers and Bradford Park Avenue. In reality it was less a meeting than an opportunity for the other clubs to make various verbal attacks on three clubs who had the temerity to make their intentions public. The Southern League did not see it that way: Millwall (who had been a prime motivating force behind the formation of the Southern League and would therefore have been the most vociferous in its support) proposed that the action of announcing their intention to resign whilst still members of the Southern League was objectionable. Northampton Town seconded the motion and it was put to the vote; all bar Spurs and QPR who voted against and Bradford, who abstained, voted in favour of the resolution. Millwall then proposed calling for the three clubs to resign from the Southern League on April 30th. Once again Spurs and QPR voted against and Bradford abstained, but the resolution was passed. The Southern League's rules were also amended so that the League now had the power to expel any rebel club. A further meeting of the Southern League was set for May 27th; this was perhaps indicative of how petty the Southern League had become, for the Football League meeting to discuss and vote on the applications for membership from the three clubs was set for the same day!

1912	Aston Villa	H	First Division	2-1
1918	Fulham	A	London Combination	3-0
1919	West Ham United	H	Victory Cup 1st Round	3-1
1929	Swansea Town	H	Second Division	1-1
1935	Middlesbrough	A	First Division	1-3
1940	Fulham	A	Football League South Group C	3-2
1946	Plymouth Argyle	H	Football League South	2-0
1951	Fulham	A	First Division	1-0

1954 Paul Price born in St Albans. After signing with Luton Town as a professional in July 1971, Paul's career was twice interrupted by a broken leg, but when he recovered he showed himself to be a stylish defender and won the first of his caps for Wales in 1980. He had also helped Luton into the First Division and was bought by Spurs for £250,000 in June 1981. Although he was unable to dislodge the usual pairing of Paul Miller and Graham Roberts permanently from the central defence, he did feature in the side that won the FA Cup in 1982, with Roberts being switched to midfield. At the end of the 1983-84 season he was given a free transfer and went to play in America, later returning to play for Swansea City and Peterborough United and a number of non-League clubs.

1957	Newcastle United	A	First Division	2-2
1963	Leicester City	A	First Division	2-2
1968	Stoke City	H	First Division	3-0
1971	Ipswich Town	A	First Division	2-1
1974	Manchester United	A	First Division	1-0
1976	Brighton & Hove Albion	A	Joe Kinnear Testimonial	6-1

Brighton played host to a testimonial match for former Spurs player Joe Kinnear, with Micky Stead, John Pratt, Keith Osgood, Gerry Armstrong, Martin Chivers and Chris Jones scoring for Spurs.

1977	Derby County	H	First Division	0-0
1982	Birmingham City	A	First Division	0-0
1983	Aston Villa	H	First Division	2-0
1985	Southampton	H	First Division	5-1
1991	Queens Park Rangers	H	First Division	0-0

MARCH 24TH

1894	Slough	H	Friendly	2-0
1898	Loughborough	H	United League	5-0
1900	New Brompton	H	Southern League	1-0
1902	Millwall Athletic	H	London League	1-1
1906	Luton Town	A	Southern League	0-2
1913	West Bromwich Albion	A	First Division	1-4
1917	West Ham United	A	London Combination	0-3
1923	Stoke	H	First Division	3-1

1926 Eddie Gibbins born in Shoreditch, London. Although Eddie was signed as a player to the club for eight years, he made only one League appearance for the first team. In fact, he played more FA Cup ties, appearing in three! He had made his debut for the club in a friendly against Millwall in 1944 and then had to wait nine years before making his debut in a senior match! He subsequently moved on to the club's coaching staff at the end of the 1953-54 season.

1928	Aston Villa	H	First Division	2-1
1934	Newcastle United	A	First Division	3-1
1945	Brentford	A	Football League South	2-0
1951	Portsmouth	A	First Division	1-1
1956	Manchester City	H	First Division	2-1
1962	Everton	H	First Division	3-1
1969	Arsenal	A	First Division	0-1
1973	Manchester United	H	First Division	1-1
1979	Aston Villa	A	First Division	3-2
1984	Coventry City	A	First Division	4-2
1993	Manchester City	H	FA Premier League	3-1
1996	Manchester United	A	FA Premier League	0-1

MARCH 25TH

1893	Old St Stephen's	H	Southern Alliance	1-2
1899	Brighton United	H	Southern League	1-3
1905	Luton Town	H	Southern League	1-0
1907	Luton Town	H	Southern League	1-2
1910	Sunderland	H	First Division	5-1
1916	Fulham	H	London Combination [2nd competition]	4-0

Although the London Combination might have lacked the passion of the Football League, that did not stop the players giving their all and the media reporting the game as normal. This game was reported as being a farce, with fouls, hackings and fights punctuating the action throughout. Jimmy Banks was sent off, along with Fulham's Grossart, after they had squared up to each other following a challenge by the Spurs players, and after Fulham had lost a second player through injury Spurs took command, finally winning 4-0 thanks to goals from Harry Lloyd (two), Bert Bliss and Bobby Steel.

1921	Liverpool	A	First Division	1-1
1922	Preston North End	Hillsborough		
			FA Cup Semi-Final	1-2

Spurs and Preston met in the FA Cup semi-final stage for the second consecutive season. Spurs, the cup holders, were widely held as favourites and played throughout the first half in a manner which reflected their popularity. Jimmy Seed scored his third cup goal of the season to fire Spurs into the lead and Preston appeared beaten when half time arrived. It was later rumoured that the Preston players drank champagne at half time (contemporary reports certainly indicated that they played in a much more lively fashion in the second half) and they eventually equalised. Spurs were then the victims of a bizarre refereeing decision; Bert Bliss fired in a shot that was destined to end up in the net with the goalkeeper well beaten, but just as the ball was entering the net the referee blew his whistle because of a Preston player down further up the field. The goal was disallowed (the referee claimed to have blown before the ball crossed the line) so that the injured player could receive attention, although it transpired he wasn't injured at all! The incident deflated Spurs and that allowed Preston to grab the winner. If Spurs were aggrieved in the semi-final, then it was Preston's turn in the final; a penalty was awarded to Huddersfield for a foul that was committed outside the area.

1926	Newcastle United	H	First Division	1-0
1932	Stoke City	H	Second Division	3-3
1933	Lincoln City	H	Second Division	3-2
1939	Swansea Town	H	Second Division	3-0
1940	Millwall	A	Football League South Group C	1-1
1944	Aldershot	H	League South Cup Section 2	2-0
1950	West Ham United	H	Second Division	4-1

On the same day Terry Yorath was born in Cardiff. Signed by Leeds United to professional forms in 1967, Terry was often on the fringes of the great Leeds side of the late 1960s and early 1970s, although he was substitute in the 1973 FA Cup final and appeared in both the European Cup-Winners' Cup and European Cup finals of 1973 and 1975 respectively, collecting losers' medals in all three. In 1974 he was a member of the side that won the League, but by 1976 was considered surplus to requirements and sold to Coventry City. In August 1979, with Spurs looking for considerably more bite in the midfield, he was signed for £275,000 and performed heroically for a season. He was injured shortly after and upon his return found the role had been handed to Graham Roberts, with the result that Terry was allowed to head off to Canada. He returned in December 1982 to Bradford City, eventually becoming assistant manager. He officially retired as a player with Bradford in 1985 and then in October 1986 accepted the manager's job at Swansea, later playing one League match owing to an injury crisis at the club. He was appointed part-time manager of Wales in July 1988, resigned from Swansea in order to take up the vacant managerial chair at Bradford in February 1989 and was then involved in an amazing legal wrangle that was only resolved when he bought out his own contract. Even that was not the end of his troubles, for in March 1990 he was re-appointed manager at Swansea, a post he held for one year before leaving, although there were arguments over whether he resigned or was sacked. He then became full-time manager of Wales until being replaced by Bobby Gould.

1953	Manchester United	A	First Division	2-3
1961	Fulham	A	First Division	0-0
1967	Leicester City	A	First Division	1-0
1972	Sheffield United	H	First Division	2-0
1978	Mansfield Town	A	Second Division	3-3
1987	Newcastle United	A	First Division	1-1

MARCH 26TH

1887	London Caledonians	H	East End Cup Semi-Final	1-0

The result of this game is somewhat misleading, for whilst Spurs were due to play London Caledonians (believing the game to have been arranged at the end of the previous week's friendly) the opposition failed to turn up. Spurs, however, took to the field, kicked off, scored and then claimed the match (perhaps it is as well Spurs won the toss and elected to kick off!), although a replay was subsequently ordered.

1892	Luton Town	A	Friendly	1-3
1894	New Brompton	A	Friendly	3-3
1896	Woolwich Arsenal	H	Friendly	1-3
1898	Sunderland	H	Friendly	0-2
1903	Brentford	H	Western League	4-0
1904	Swindon Town	A	Southern League	0-0
1906	West Ham United	H	Western League	1-0
1910	Liverpool	A	First Division	0-2
1911				

Johnny Morrison born in Belvedere in Kent. Signed by Spurs as an amateur in August 1931 he was upgraded to full professional rank in July 1933. At the time Spurs had a number of fine centre-forwards, including George Hunt, Ted Harper and Johnny himself, and it is perhaps surprising that Spurs were unable to win any major honours in the decade before the outbreak of the Second World War. In truth, whilst Johnny was able to rattle in 90 goals in just 134 League appearances, and both Hunt and Harper also scored a healthy number, they were seldom in the side at the same time. The war cut across Johnny's career to such an extent that he played one final game in December 1945 and then announced his retirement. He died in Devon on 13th September 1984.

| 1916 | | | | |

Bill Edrich born in Lingwood. Bill was an outstanding all-round sportsman and played cricket for England as well as professional football. Having been on the books of Norwich City as an amateur he moved to London in order to qualify for Middlesex as a cricketer, but was spotted by Spurs and signed in August 1935. Although he made an immediate impression at Spurs, cricket was still his first choice and in 1937 he asked to be released from his contract in order to go on tour with England. Spurs agreed on the understanding he would return, but when he did he announced his retirement from football. Although he later played non-League football and guested for a couple of League sides during the war, he is better remembered as a cricketer, scoring 86 centuries during his career. He died in Chilton in Buckinghamshire on 23rd April 1986.

| 1921 | Sunderland | A | First Division | 1-0 |

Injuries had deprived Spurs of both their normal goalkeepers Alex Hunter and Bill Jacques and so Tom Clay, more usually found at full-back, was forced to take over for this one game. He kept a clean sheet.

1927	Aston Villa	H	First Division	0-1
1932	Bury	H	Second Division	0-0
1937	Bury	A	Second Division	3-5
1938	Norwich City	H	Second Division	4-0
1940	Millwall	A	Second Division	0-0
1949	Bradford Park Avenue	A	Second Division	1-1
1951	Fulham	H	First Division	2-1
1952	FC Austria	Brussels	Friendly	2-2
1955	Cardiff City	A	First Division	2-1
1960	Bolton Wanderers	A	First Division	1-2
1966	Sunderland	A	First Division	0-2
1977	Everton	A	First Division	0-4
1983	Northerners	Jersey	Friendly	6-1

| 1984 | Wimbledon | A | Friendly | 5-0 |

This match was a testimonial for Dave Bassett with Spurs' goals being scored by Micky Hazard, Mark Falco (two) and Garth Crooks (two).

1988	Nottingham Forest	H	First Division	1-1
1989	Liverpool	H	First Division	1-2
1994	Everton	A	FA Premier League	1-0

MARCH 27TH

1886	Enfield Lock	H	Friendly	7-0
1897	New Brompton	H	Southern League	2-0
1899	Rushden	H	United League	0-0
1901	Bristol City	A	Western League	1-4

As the club were playing an FA Cup replay the following day, the reserve side turned out for this fixture.

1905	West Ham United	A	Western League	1-1
1909	Gainsborough Trinity	H	Second Division	1-1
1911	Oldham Athletic	H	First Division	2-0
1915	Manchester United	H	First Division	1-1
1920	Rotherham County	A	Second Division	1-1
1922	Huddersfield Town	A	First Division	1-1
1937	Nottingham Forest	H	Second Division	2-1
1943	Chelsea	A	League Cup	2-0
1948	Leicester City	H	Second Division	0-0
1954	Chelsea	A	First Division	0-1
1958	Rotterdam Select XI	A	Friendly	4-1
1959	Aston Villa	H	First Division	3-2
1963	Leyton Orient	H	First Division	2-0
1964	Liverpool	H	First Division	1-3
1965	Wolverhampton Wanderers	H	First Division	7-4
1967	Everton	A	First Division	2-0
1970	Nottingham Forest	H	First Division	4-1
1976	Sheffield United	H	First Division	5-0
1978	Millwall	H	Second Division	3-3
1982	West Bromwich Albion	A	First Division	0-1

MARCH 28TH

| 1884 | Jabez Darnell born in Potton, Bedfordshire. Jabez joined Spurs from Northampton Town in 1905 and |

over the next 15 years made over 300 appearances for the first team, appearing in the Western League, Southern League and Football League. The outbreak of the First World War saw many of the Spurs players enlist for service, with the result that Jabez was pressed back into playing service even though his best playing days were behind him. When League football resumed in 1919, Jabez retired and became assistant trainer at White Hart Lane, a position he held until his retirement in 1946. He died in Edmonton in December 1950.

1885	St Martin's	A	Friendly	Score unknown
1896	London Caledonians	A	Friendly	5-0
1898	Southampton	H	United League	7-0
1901	Reading	H	FA Cup 3rd Round Replay	3-0

There was a growing feeling that this might be Spurs' year. Were they not fortunate to have survived a penalty scare two minutes from the end of the first match with Reading; had they not already put out two of Lancashire's finest teams, and had not Johnson, the Spurs trainer, promised John Cameron that he would get them to the Palace? Spurs began well, continued well and finished well in the replay against Reading. They scored five times in all, although two of these efforts were disallowed. The chief reason for their confidence was the improved form of Sandy Brown, who rediscovered the goalscoring habit just when it was most needed. He scored twice on this day (taking his tally to eight) and could have had as many as four more. Another goal from David Copeland completed the scoring and earned Spurs' passage into the semi-final. The directors of their opponents, West Bromwich Albion, were present at this replay and approached their counterparts on the Spurs board to suggest that Villa Park be a suitable choice of venue (this was a time when such matters were arranged between the clubs concerned with the FA's approval), even though this ground is only three miles from the Hawthorns, where West Bromwich play. Such considerations were not part of the Tottenham board's thinking; with the match to be played on Easter Monday and at a venue that could hold a large crowd, thereby ensuring Spurs a healthy proportion of the match receipts, they agreed.

1902	Southampton	H	Southern League	2-2
1903	Reading	H	Southern League	2-0
1904	Brentford	A	Western League	2-1
1908	Leyton	A	Southern League	5-2
1910	Blackburn Rovers	H	First Division	4-0

Billy Minter became the first Spurs player to score a Football League hat-trick with three in this match, Spurs' other goal being scored by Percy Humphreys. Minter later served Spurs as manager, trainer and assistant secretary and remained with the club until 1940.

1914	Everton	A	First Division	1-1
1921	Liverpool	H	First Division	1-0
1925	West Ham United	H	First Division	1-1
1928	Sunderland	A	First Division	0-0
1931	West Bromwich Albion	H	Second Division	2-2
1932	Stoke City	A	Second Division	2-2
1935	Leicester City	A	First Division	0-6
1936	Southampton	H	Second Division	8-0
1942	Watford	H	London War Cup	5-2
1953	Portsmouth	H	First Division	3-3
1959	Bolton Wanderers	A	First Division	1-4
1964	Fulham	A	First Division	1-1
1970	West Bromwich Albion	A	First Division	1-1
1972	Huddersfield Town	A	First Division	1-1
1975	Wolverhampton Wanderers	H	First Division	3-0
1979	Southampton	H	First Division	0-0
1981	Coventry City	A	First Division	1-0
1987	Luton Town	A	First Division	1-3
1988	Manchester United	H	Danny Thomas Benefit	2-3

After a brave but vain battle, Danny Thomas's career had been ended by a robust tackle in a League match with QPR the previous year. A popular player at White Hart Lane the pinnacle of his career had been the 1984 UEFA Cup win. Among the guest players who turned out for Spurs this evening were former heroes Graham Roberts and Steve Archibald, and Liverpool duo John Barnes and Kenny Dalglish. Archibald and Steve Hodge scored for Spurs.

1989	Luton Town	A	First Division	3-1
1992	Coventry City	H	First Division	4-3
1993	Crystal Palace	A	Friendly	3-3

This match was a testimonial for Malcolm Allison with Spurs' goals being scored by Nayim, Neil Ruddock and Nick Barmby.

1998	Crystal Palace	A	FA Premier League	3-1

MARCH 29TH

1868	David Black born in Irvine, Ayrshire. After playing for Grimsby Town, Middlesbrough, Wolves and Burnley he was signed by Spurs in May 1897 as a replacement for Richard McElhaney. Despite only staying at Spurs for one year he became a very popular player among the faithful at Northumberland Park, who delighted in his tricky wing play. He also weighed in with a fair number of goals too, scoring eight in the Southern League and six in the Western League during his only season. He moved on to Woolwich Arsenal and finished his career back in Scotland with Clyde, retiring in 1900.

1897	Southampton St Mary's	A	Southern League	1-1
1902	Luton Town	A	Southern League	0-0
1905	Southampton	H	Western League	1-1
1907	Southampton	H	Southern League	2-0
1913	Newcastle United	A	First Division	0-3
1918	Clapton Orient	A	London Combination	3-2
1919	Arsenal	H-Highbury		
			London Combination	0-1
1924	Liverpool	A	First Division	0-1
1929	Preston North End	A	Second Division	2-2
1930	Bristol City	A	Second Division	0-1
1937	Bury	H	Second Division	2-0
1941	Cardiff City	A	Football League War Cup 3rd Round 2nd Leg	3-2
1947	Plymouth Argyle	A	Second Division	4-3
1948	Millwall	H	Second Division	3-2
1958	Aston Villa	H	First Division	6-2

1969	Burnley	A	First Division	2-2
1975	Queens Park Rangers	A	First Division	1-0
1980	Liverpool	H	First Division	2-0
1982	Arsenal	H	First Division	2-2

Alan Sunderland of Arsenal grabbed both of their goals, whilst Spurs' goals came from Steve Archibald and Chris Hughton. Both Hughton and Sunderland would have preferred to forget the game however, for five minutes from the end they were sent off in the first ever double dismissal since the fixture began.

| 1986 | Arsenal | H | First Division | 1-0 |

MARCH 30TH

| 1895 | City Ramblers | H | Friendly | 2-0 |

On the same day Charlie Wilson was born in Atherstone, Derbyshire. Although Charlie was signed to Coventry City he had not played for the club when he made a number of guest appearances for Spurs and, being impressed with his performances at centre-forward, was promptly transferred to White Hart Lane in May 1919. Although he scored a hat-trick in his League debut he was initially signed as cover to Jimmy Cantrell, although Charlie did help secure the Second Division title that season. When Cantrell left Charlie was widely expected to make the centre-forward slot his own, but competition from Alex Lindsay meant that when Huddersfield enquired about signing him he was allowed to leave. Charlie helped Huddersfield win consecutive League titles in 1924 and 1925, finishing top scorer in both seasons, but the following year, as Huddersfield completed the first hat-trick of League titles, Charlie was allowed to sign for Stoke City. There he won a Third Division North championship medal and finally finished his career with non-League Stafford Rangers having scored a total of 194 League goals for his three League clubs.

| 1901 | Queens Park Rangers | H | Southern League | 4-1 |
| 1903 | Queens Park Rangers | H | London League | 3-0 |

Spurs won the London League, four points ahead of West Ham United. Finishing top was a fitting position, for this was the last time Spurs fielded the first team in this competition; from next season it became a reserve team league.

1907	Brighton & Hove Albion	H	Southern League	3-0
1912	Newcastle United	A	First Division	0-2
1918	Queens Park Rangers	H-Homerton		
			London Combination	1-2
1923	Preston North End	H	First Division	1-1
1929	Nottingham Forest	A	Second Division	2-2
1934	Stoke City	H	First Division	0-0
1935	West Bromwich Albion	H	First Division	0-1
1940	Arsenal	H	Football League South Group C	1-1
1946	Plymouth Argyle	A	Football League South	1-0
1955	FC Servette	H	Friendly	5-1
1956	Preston North End	H	First Division	0-4
1957	Sheffield Wednesday	H	First Division	1-1
1959	Aston Villa	A	First Division	1-1
1962	Gary Stevens born in Hillingdon.			

Gary Stevens born in Hillingdon. Gary began his professional career with Brighton, signing for them in October 1979. He quickly established himself as a reliable performer, able to switch effortlessly between defence and midfield, was an integral part of the side that reached the 1983 FA Cup final and scored one of their goals in the 2-2 draw. Although they lost the replay Spurs had seen enough to offer £350,000 for the utility player and he joined in June 1983. At the end of his first season at Spurs he helped them win the UEFA Cup. As a utility player he was seldom played in the same position for any considerable length of time, and was capped for England in October 1984. A serious knee injury in March 1985 (which coincided with Spurs relinquishing their title aspirations) kept him out of the side for six months. He fought back to full fitness, collecting a further six caps and went to Mexico in the World Cup, but then suffered another serious injury in November 1986. Thereafter he suffered a string of injuries and was loaned to Portsmouth in January 1990, with the move becoming permanent in March for a fee of £250,000. He retired as a player in 1992, still troubled by injuries, and became a media commentator and presenter.

1963	Burnley	H	First Division	1-1
1964	Liverpool	A	First Division	1-3
1968	Burnley	H	First Division	5-0
1970	Sheffield Wednesday	A	First Division	1-0

1974	Everton	H	First Division	0-2
1985	Aston Villa	H	First Division	0-2
1991	Coventry City	H	First Division	2-2
1996	Coventry City	H	FA Premier League	3-1

MARCH 31ST

1894	Polytechnic	H	Friendly	0-0
1899	Southampton	H	Southern League	0-1
1900	Gravesend United	A	Southern League	6-2
1902	Portsmouth	A	Southern League	0-1
1906	Northampton Town	A	Southern League	0-0
1913	Manchester United	H	First Division	1-1
1917	Portsmouth	H-Highbury		
			London Combination	10-0
1923	Sunderland	A	First Division	0-2
1928	Sheffield United	A	First Division	1-2
1934	Leeds United	H	First Division	5-1
1945	Aldershot	A	Football League South	2-1
1951	Everton	H	First Division	3-0
1956	Sunderland	A	First Division	2-3
1961	Chelsea	H	First Division	4-2
1962	Manchester United	Hillsborough		
			FA Cup Semi-Final	3-1

Although Spurs had won in the semi-final the previous year at Villa Park, they still regarded Hillsborough as a lucky ground for them. They were facing a United side at something of a transitional stage; the side that had been decimated by Munich had yet to be effectively rebuilt. The end result was a comparatively easy semi-final success for Spurs, with goals from Terry Medwin, Jimmy Greaves and Cliff Jones against one from David Herd.

1972	Coventry City	H	First Division	1-0
1973	Liverpool	A	First Division	1-1
1979	Middlesbrough	A	First Division	0-1
1984	Wolverhampton Wanderers	H	First Division	1-0
1986	West Ham United	A	First Division	1-2
1990	Sheffield Wednesday	A	First Division	4-2

APRIL 1ST

1893	City Ramblers	H	Friendly	1-0
1897	Wolverton	H	Southern League	2-0

On the same day Charlie Walters was born in Sandford-on-Thames. First spotted whilst playing as an amateur with Oxford City, Charlie signed amateur forms with Spurs in December 1919 and full professional forms the following April. Soon after he made his League debut at centre-half and eventually replaced Charlie Rance so effectively Walters retained his place to the end of the season and collected an FA Cup winners' medal. Charlie held the position for the next two seasons as well before competition from Harry Skitt prompted a move to Fulham in October 1926. He finished his career with Mansfield Town and died in Bath on 13th May 1971.

1899	Gravesend United	H	Southern League	3-0
1904	Southampton	H	Southern League	2-1
1905	Swindon Town	A	Southern League	1-2
1907	Millwall	A	Southern League	0-2
1911	Sunderland	H	First Division	1-1
1916	Luton Town	A	London Combination [2nd competition]	2-1
1918	Clapton Orient	H-Homerton		
			London Combination	5-2
1922	Birmingham	A	First Division	3-0
1929	Preston North End	H	Second Division	1-1
1933	Chesterfield	A	Second Division	1-1
1939	Chesterfield	A	Second Division	1-3
1944	Charlton Athletic	N	League South Cup Section 2 Semi-Final	0-3

Spurs' hopes of a double (they were to win the Football League South) came to an end with a defeat at Stamford Bridge in front of a crowd of 35,000.

1950	Queens Park Rangers	A	Second Division	2-0
1961	Preston North End	H	First Division	5-0

1967	Liverpool	H	First Division	2-1
1972	West Ham United	A	First Division	0-2
1978	Burnley	A	Second Division	1-2
1989	West Ham United	H	First Division	3-0
1991	Luton Town	A	First Division	0-0
1992	West Ham United	H	First Division	3-0

APRIL 2ND

1875 David Copeland born in Ayr. David joined Spurs from Walsall in May 1899 and quickly established an exceptional understanding with John Kirwan, helping the club to the Southern League title in 1900 and the FA Cup the following season. He remained at Spurs until 1905 when he and Kirwan switched across London to sign for the newly formed Chelsea Football Club. A broken leg sustained at the beginning of the 1906-07 season effectively ended his playing career, although he did later make two appearances for Glossop. He died from heart failure on 16th November 1931.

1888	Clapton	A	Friendly	1-6
1898	New Brompton	H	Southern League	3-1
1900	Thames Ironworks	A	Tom Bradshaw Benefit	3-0

Tom, who had played for Spurs for some 18 months before signing with Thames Ironworks, had died the previous Christmas Day at the age of only 26. Spurs sent their complete first team for this match to raise funds for his dependants.

1904	Luton Town	H	Southern League	1-1
1907	Spurs 1901 XI v Team of South	H	S Mountford Benefit	1-4
1910	Aston Villa	H	First Division	1-1
1915	Newcastle United	H	First Division	0-0

Although Spurs grabbed a point in their desperate battle against relegation, the focal point of this day was the activities taking place in Manchester, where Manchester United beat Liverpool 2-0. Whilst the result was something of a surprise (United were battling relegation, Liverpool had settled for mid-table respectability) the match was one of the most bizarre in League history – the crowd booed the players for their lack of effort throughout. A couple of days after the game, a letter in *Athletic News* suggested that the football authorities might care to take a closer look at the game and in particular the final result. The letter was almost certainly from a disgruntled bookmaker, for there had been a rush of bets shortly before the game on United to win by two goals to nil. The FA did indeed look into the circumstances surrounding this match and announced some time later that the match had been fixed by arrangement between players from both sides. Life bans to those involved were handed out, although all but one were subsequently lifted after the First World War in recognition of war service. The one exception was Enoch West, who took the FA (and *Athletic News*) to court in an attempt to clear his name and failed, and whose ban was not lifted until 1945. The relevance of this match, however, to Spurs' history is that despite their findings the FA allowed the result to stand, thereby enabling Manchester United to finish the season one place above the relegation trapdoor, occupied by Chelsea and Spurs. When League football resumed in 1919, reference was made to the Manchester United and Liverpool match to justify keeping Chelsea in the First Division – Arsenal's underhand dealings ensured they took the other vacancy.

1920	Wolverhampton Wanderers	H	Second Division	4-2
1921	Sunderland	H	First Division	0-0
1923	Preston North End	A	First Division	0-2
1926	West Bromwich Albion	H	First Division	3-2
1927	Cardiff City	A	First Division	2-1
1932	Port Vale	A	Second Division	3-1
1934	Stoke City	A	First Division	0-2
1938	West Ham United	A	Second Division	3-1
1949	Southampton	H	Second Division	0-1
1952	Huddersfield Town	H	First Division	1-0

One of the most controversial goals in League history was scored at White Hart Lane during the last minute of the match between Spurs and Huddersfield Town. Eddie Baily of Spurs took a corner kick that hit the referee in the back. The ball rebounded back to Baily who centred for Duquemin to score. Immediately the Huddersfield team surrounded the referee to claim, rightly, that the goal should be disallowed because Baily had played the ball twice. The referee consulted his linesman but allowed the goal to stand; Spurs won 1-0. But that was not the end of the matter. Huddersfield's chairman immediately announced that the club would be appealing to the Football League to have the game replayed. The request was turned down by the Football League, the League Management Committee and a Board of Appeal set up by the FA. It will have been of little comfort to Huddersfield (who were relegated at the end of the season!) but the matter was relatively simple: the referee's decision is final on questions of fact; it can be changed if he erred on a question of law: as the referee believed another player had played the ball, then the fact he was incorrect was irrelevant.

1955	Chelsea	H	First Division	2-4
1956	Preston North End	A	First Division	3-3
1960	Luton Town	H	First Division	1-1
1966	Nottingham Forest	H	First Division	2-3

On the same day, fittingly enough (given that Spurs would later buy the player from Nottingham Forest), Teddy Sheringham was born in Highams Park. Snapped up by Millwall in 1984 as a youngster and having spent a brief loan spell at Aldershot, Teddy developed into one of the best goalscorers outside of the top flight, scoring 93 goals in just over 200 League appearances. That form earned him a £2 million transfer to Nottingham Forest in July 1991, but a little over a year later he was surprisingly allowed to leave, this time costing Spurs £2.1 million. At White Hart Lane he proved more than capable of linking with whoever happened to be in the team at the time, forming an exceptional partnership with Nick Barmby, then Jurgen Klinsmann and finally Chris Armstrong during his time with the club. His club form dictated a chance at international level, and whilst he was not blessed with blistering pace, his cool head, good ball control and ability to bring other players into the game meant he was to prove as invaluable to his international managers as he was at club level. In the summer of 1997 he announced he wished to leave Spurs, and although the club initially held out for a £6 million fee, he was allowed to join Manchester United for a cut price £3.5 million.

1969	Newcastle United	H	First Division	0-1
1977	Coventry City	A	First Division	1-1
1980	Ipswich Town	H	First Division	0-2
1983	Brighton & Hove Albion	A	First Division	1-2
1988	Portsmouth	H	First Division	0-1
1994	Norwich City	A	FA Premier League	2-1
1995	Southampton	A	FA Premier League	3-4

APRIL 3RD

1887   Fred Webster born in Sheffield. Fred began his career with perennial strugglers Gainsborough Trinity, developing into one of the best players they had on their books following his arrival in 1906. In April 1911 he was transferred to Spurs, where competition for places was considerably keener, but once Fred had broken into the team on a regular basis he proved an extremely capable full-back. Injury in October 1914 prompted him to enlist in the forces and therefore not be available during the war years, and upon his return to Spurs in 1919 it was realised he was past his best and allowed to sign for Brentford. A year later he returned to Gainsborough Trinity to finish his career.

1896	Reading	A	Friendly	3-2
1897	Millwall Athletic	H	United League	1-3
1899	Swindon Town	H	Southern League	1-1
1901	Gravesend United	A	Southern League	1-2
1905	Brentford	A	Western League	0-2
1909	Grimsby Town	A	Second Division	2-1
1915	Bolton Wanderers	H	First Division	4-2
1920	Stoke	H	Second Division	2-0
1926	Bolton Wanderers	A	First Division	1-1
1931	Cardiff City	H	Second Division	2-2
1937	Plymouth Argyle	A	Second Division	2-2
1943	Reading	H	League Cup	1-2

Some months previously Les Bennett had guested for Distillery, whose line-up also included the Manchester United captain Jack Rowley. Bennett suggested that should Rowley find himself in London during the war years he should contact Spurs with a view to guesting for them. This he did, and this day made his debut in Spurs colours in this League Cup match against Reading. Although Rowley did not score on this occasion, he did finish the next season as top scorer as Spurs won the Football League South. Indeed, Rowley's form when guesting for Spurs (he made 20 League appearances) was such that he was subsequently capped for England in the war-time international against Wales in May 1944. After the war he returned to Manchester United and led them to the FA Cup in 1948 and the League championship in 1952 before embarking on a managerial career.

1948	Leeds United	A	Second Division	3-1
1953	Stoke City	H	First Division	1-0
1954	Blackpool	H	First Division	2-2
1961	Chelsea	A	First Division	3-2
1965	Aston Villa	A	First Division	0-1
1971	Coventry City	A	First Division	0-0

1972	Ipswich Town	A	First Division	1-2
1973	Chelsea	A	First Division	1-0
1974	Chelsea	H	First Division	1-2
1976	Arsenal	A	First Division	2-0
1979	Wolverhampton Wanderers	A	First Division	2-3
1982	Leicester City	Villa Park	FA Cup Semi-Final	2-0

A few weeks previously, it had been announced that Ossie Ardiles would be going back home on April 4th in order to begin preparations for Argentina's defence of the World Cup in Spain. As it turned out it meant his last appearance of the season in a Spurs shirt would be in the FA Cup semi-final, although Argentina manager Cesar Menotti implied that he would give serious consideration to letting Ardiles return to England to play in the FA Cup final, if Spurs got that far. This was in recognition of the help Keith Burkinshaw had given Menotti, releasing Ardiles and Villa whenever either player had been needed for international duty. The day before the semi-final, against Leicester City and scheduled for Villa Park, Argentina had grown tired of waiting for a diplomatic solution to the question of sovereignty of the Falkland Islands and staged an invasion. This ensured Ardiles was continually booed by Leicester fans whenever he went anywhere near the ball. The political intrigue was certainly more interesting than the first 45 minutes of action at Villa Park, with both sides hesitant, perhaps because of what was at stake. Spurs finally began to wear down their Second Division opponents in the second half, with Ardiles marking his last appearance for Spurs for a considerable time with a telling contribution. In the 56th minute he came short for Glenn Hoddle's quickly taken corner and put in a low cross which Garth Crooks volleyed home from six yards to put Spurs ahead. A short while later, Leicester were unfortunate to lose Tommy Williams, carried off on a stretcher after an innocuous collision with Tony Galvin had resulted in a hairline fracture of the shin. Leicester's ten men (including a youthful Gary Lineker leading the attack) battled on gamely, but in the 76th minute delivered a sucker punch from which there was no coming back. Tony Galvin was again involved, this time sending in a cross that went begging. Full-back Ian Wilson collected the ball 20 yards from his goal and had a number of options; he chose to pass the ball back to keeper Mark Wallington, but instead of simply rolling the ball along the ground, got his toe under it and sent it perfectly over the keeper's head for the second decisive goal. It ensured Spurs would be back at Wembley for the tenth time in their history. They ultimately did so without Ardiles; the collapsing political crisis with Argentina and Ardiles' own comments on the situation once he returned to Buenos Aires guaranteeing that. Indeed, there were many who thought this might have been Ardiles' last ever game for Spurs.

1985	Everton	H	First Division	1-2
1990	Brighton 1983	A	Friendly	3-0

This match was a testimonial for Graham Moseley with Spurs' goals being scored by Paul Gascoigne (two) and Paul Stewart.

APRIL 4TH

1885	Mars	H	Friendly	Score unknown
1890	Dreadnought	H	Friendly	0-1
1896	Oswaldtwistle Rovers	H	Friendly	4-0
1899	Brighton United	H	United League	3-0
1902				

Cyril Spiers born in Whitton, Birmingham. Cyril joined Aston Villa in 1920 and although he took a while to establish himself as the first choice goalkeeper, made over 100 appearances for the first team before being released in 1927 after being injured. He underwent an experimental operation during the close season and when recovered asked Spurs for a trial. Although the trial was to have lasted a month, he showed enough ability after two games to be offered a full contract and went straight into the side after regular keeper Jock Britton had been injured in a road accident. Cyril went on to give Spurs exceptional service during his time with the club, being released in May 1933 and signing for Wolves, subsequently becoming assistant manager. He later served Cardiff City, Norwich City, Crystal Palace and Exeter City as manager and also scouted for Leicester. He died on 21st May 1967.

1903	Reading	A	Southern League	0-0
1904	Portsmouth	A	Southern League	0-1
1908	Reading	H	Southern League	2-0
1914	Liverpool	H	First Division	0-0

Missing from the Spurs line-up for this match was Fanny Walden, who was at Hampden Park winning his first cap for England against Scotland. Scotland won the match 3-1, whilst Fanny had to wait almost eight years before collecting his second cap, against Wales in 1922.

1925	Sheffield United	A	First Division	0-2
1931	Port Vale	A	Second Division	0-3
1936	Blackpool	A	Second Division	4-2
1942	Reading	H	London War Cup Group 3	2-1

1947	Nottingham Forest	H	Second Division	2-0
1953	Bolton Wanderers	A	First Division	3-2
1958	West Bromwich Albion	H	First Division	0-0
1959	Luton Town	H	First Division	3-0
1964	Ipswich Town	H	First Division	6-3
1969	Coventry City	H	First Division	2-0
1970	Chelsea	A	First Division	0-1
1981	Everton	H	First Division	2-2
1983	Arsenal	H	First Division	5-0
1987	Norwich City	H	First Division	3-0
1988	Queens Park Rangers	A	First Division	0-2
1989	Charlton Athletic	A	Friendly	3-4

This match was a testimonial for Steve Gritt with Spurs' goals being scored by Paul Walsh and Paul Stewart (two).

| 1992 | Aston Villa | H | First Division | 2-5 |

Spurs were ahead 2-0 at one stage and then collapsed defensively to suffer their biggest home defeat in many a year.

| 1993 | Arsenal | | Wembley | FA Cup Semi-Final | 0-1 |

The first hundred years of Spurs' history produced only two FA Cup ties with Arsenal; in 1949 and 1982. Now they met each other twice in three seasons and both times at the semi-final stage. Once again the FA decreed that Spurs and Arsenal should meet at Wembley, whilst the other semi-final (between Sheffield rivals United and Wednesday) was originally scheduled for Elland Road, Leeds. After protests from both clubs about Elland Road, Manchester United's Old Trafford was suggested. This too was unacceptable to Sheffield; they wanted parity with London. So it was that Wembley began hosting FA Cup semi-final weekends, with Sheffield battling it out the previous day (Wednesday winning 2-1) and North London taking its turn this day. Spurs had much the better of the opening exchanges and were unfortunate to be denied a penalty; Andy Linighan bringing Darren Anderton's run to a halt with a scything tackle inside the penalty area. The referee saw no foul; he awarded Spurs a corner, although Linighan had clearly made no contact with the ball and if it was not a penalty, then the correct decision should surely have been a goal-kick to Arsenal. The only goal of the game came from Arsenal captain Tony Adams, who headed home a corner at the far post. Although Spurs attacked furiously thereafter they could find no way through and Arsenal held on to earn the right to face Sheffield Wednesday in the final. Arsenal lost Lee Dixon three minutes from full-time, sent off for tripping Justin Edinburgh.

| 1994 | West Ham United | H | FA Premier League | 1-4 |
| 1998 | Everton | H | FA Premier League | 1-1 |

APRIL 5TH

| 1869 | William Almond born in Blackburn, Lanchasire. He began his career with the local Witton club, switching to Blackburn Rovers in 1888 when the Football League began. He spent four seasons with Rovers, although he missed out on their FA Cup final appearances in 1890 and 1891, switching to Accrington in 1892. He then spent a year with both Middlesbrough and Millwall Athletic before signing for Spurs in time for the 1895-96 season, making his debut in the London Charity Cup. When Spurs adopted professionalism he remained an amateur, enabling him also to appear for Clapton and Millwall during his two years with Spurs. When released by Spurs in 1897 he returned to Millwall and later turned out for a number of amateur clubs in London. |

1890	Uxbridge	A	Friendly	2-2
1897	Rushden	N	Wellingborough Charity Cup Semi-Final	2-1
1901	Southampton	H	Southern League	1-0

On the same day Sandy Brown was representing Scotland in their international match against England at Ibrox Park. As the crowd strained to follow the action a temporary stand collapsed and 25 people fell to their deaths, with another 500 injured. Although the game was completed as the authorities feared a riot if it was abandoned, the game was later declared void. Despite this, Sandy was the first Spurs player to have represented Scotland whilst on the club's books.

1902	New Brompton	A	Southern League	0-0
1904	New Brompton	H	Southern League	1-0
1905	Plymouth Argyle	A	Southern League	1-2
1912	Manchester City	A	First Division	1-2
1913	Oldham Athletic	H	First Division	1-0
1919	Crystal Palace	A	London Combination	2-2
1920	Wolverhampton Wanderers	A	Second Division	3-1
1922	Sunderland	A	First Division	0-2

1924	Liverpool	H	First Division	1-1
1926	West Bromwich Albion	A	First Division	0-1
1930	Notts County	H	Second Division	2-0
1941	Arsenal	A	Football League War Cup 4th Round 1st Leg	1-2
1947	Leicester City	H	Second Division	2-1

1952 Alfie Conn born in Kirkcaldy, Fife. Signed by Glasgow Rangers in 1968 Alfie later became the last player to be signed by Bill Nicholson for Spurs, coming to White Hart Lane in June 1974 for £140,000. He became an instant crowd favourite, with supreme talent and flair lifting the morale of the team and the fans in the battle against relegation. Unfortunately, a succession of injuries restricted the number of first-team appearances, and in 1977 he went on loan to Celtic, with the move becoming permanent once he had proved his fitness. He later played in the United States and on loan for Hearts and Motherwell before retiring in 1984. As well as being one of the few players to have played for both Glasgow giants, he was the first man to win Scottish FA Cup winners' medals for both – at Rangers he was a member of the team that beat Celtic in 1973 and a member of the Celtic team which beat Rangers in 1977! He also won a Scottish League Cup winners' medal and European Cup-Winners' Cup medal with Rangers, and two League titles with Celtic.

1954	Hibernian	H	Friendly	3-2
1958	Everton	A	First Division	4-3
1962	Benfica	H	European Cup Semi-Final 2nd Leg	2-1

In the end, a two goal deficit against the reigning European champions proved just beyond Tottenham's reach, but they went close. So close that it was relief that gripped Benfica when the final whistle went, elation came later. Spurs were given a veritable mountain to climb right from the kick-off and pushed forward in search of the goals needed. Inevitably, gaps were left at the back which Jose Aguas punished with the opening goal on 15 minutes. Spurs appealed for offside, but unlike Lisbon, fortune was not to favour the home side; the goal stood. Spurs now needed three goals to level. The first seemed to have arrived on 23 minutes, when Jimmy Greaves moved on to a pass from Bobby Smith and slid it past the despairing dive of Costa Pereira in the Benfica goal. The 65,000 crowd greeted the goal with wild applause, the referee turned back towards the centre circle and then the figure of Hensen, the Danish linesman, came into view, stood erectly on the touchline with his flag pointed upwards. The two officials consulted for a brief moment and then the goal was ruled offside. Since this was the moment that Spurs' chance of forcing extra time disappeared, it is worth dwelling on the decision for a moment or two. Firstly, no Benfica player had appealed for an offside decision. Secondly, Jimmy Greaves had moved between two Benfica players to collect Smith's pass. Thirdly, and most importantly, photographs of the incident showed the linesman vainly trying to catch up with the action, already raising his flag to indicate offside; but how could he have known? The goal may not have counted, but Spurs never let their heads drop, with the following hour's football an almost non-stop barrage on the Benfica goal. The breakthrough finally came in the 35th minute, Bobby Smith driving home a John White pass. Half-time came and went and Spurs maintained the initiative, battling the clock and Benfica in equal measure. Two minutes after the break John White was fouled; penalty to Spurs. If all around him was madness then Danny Blanchflower appeared the calmest man on the field, sending Pereira the wrong way with the spot kick. The deficit was down to one goal. It did not come, despite Spurs hitting the bar and spurning a couple of chances that on another day against different opposition they would have gleefully taken. When the final whistle went Spurs players warmly embraced the opposition. The match had been hard, mostly fair, but in the moment of their greatest agony, Spurs retained their sportsmanship. After the game manager Bill Nicholson said, 'My men played too quickly. They were too hurried. Their enthusiasm ran away with them. They lacked a little control, and one or two players did not quite do what we had hoped. If we kept our heads the result might have been different. Losing that first goal was vital, but we had our chances.' On the same day Richard Gough was born in Stockholm, Sweden. Richard signed for Charlton Athletic when he was 16 but returned home to South Africa after only seven months because of homesickness. A year later he made another attempt at becoming a professional footballer, signing for Dundee United and playing a major part in the side that won the 1983 Scottish League and reached the finals of both domestic cups. Such form earned interest from many other clubs, and both Spurs and Glasgow Rangers were in the hunt to sign him in 1986. Spurs ultimately won because Dundee United refused to sell him to their rivals in Glasgow, and Richard headed south for a fee of £700,000. He spent a little over a year at Spurs, being made captain and helping the club to the 1987 FA Cup final, but his family's inability to settle in the south led to him asking for a transfer. This was duly granted and he signed for Rangers for £1.5 million in October 1987.

| 1972 | AC Milan | H | UEFA Cup Semi-Final 1st Leg | 2-1 |

The morning before the big UEFA Cup showdown with AC Milan, Spurs manager Bill Nicholson recalled Alan Mullery from his loan spell with Fulham. If the circumstances surrounding the original loan and its abrupt ending seem intriguing now, they were little short of sensational at the time. Alan

Mullery had complained for much of the season of a pelvic strain, one which restricted his ability to run, turn and perform the movements that are second nature to a professional footballer. All the king's medical experts and all the king's men had failed to find the root of the problem; rest was diagnosed as the only known cure. So Alan Mullery had rested and the problem had taken its time to correct itself. By the time it had, Bill Nicholson had a settled side that was advancing on three fronts – the UEFA Cup, the League Cup and the FA Cup. True to the manager's adage, Nicholson did not want to disrupt his team by bringing Alan Mullery back into the side and he was loaned out to a Fulham team battling in the lower regions of the Second Division. Fulham's rivals were less than happy at the expected impact an England international was to have but they need not have worried; Fulham were capable of losing to anyone regardless of who was in their team! Meanwhile, things did not go quite as expected for Spurs; Easter again took its toll, not only mentally but physically as well; the club were due to play Friday, Saturday, Monday and then the UEFA Cup semi-final on Wednesday. The League would not allow the postponement of any matches, which left Nicholson shuffling his side to keep at least 11 players fit and refreshed enough for the challenge of AC Milan. When John Pratt broke his nose over the Easter holiday, Nicholson ran out of permutations and Mullery was brought back. And not just as a player, but re-installed as captain as well. As it turned out Alan Mullery was the right player to bring back for the right occasion, for never were his undoubted leadership qualities needed as much as they were tonight. AC Milan were so concerned with stopping Spurs playing that most, if not all, of the Spurs players who had survived a tough Easter ended up with some injury or another after this evening. Spurs won, but AC Milan were the team celebrating at the end, reasoning that the goal they scored would be worth double should they record a single goal win in Milan – single goal wins being the norm in Italian football! Their one goal this night had been scored by Benetti, who was described in the match programme as keeping pet canaries as a hobby. After his 25th minute strike, it might as well have been sick parrots as far as Spurs were concerned. Once again, as countless Spurs teams before and after, Tottenham raised their game after the hammer blow, finally levelling after Alan Gilzean and Martin Peters had combined to lay the ball to Steve Perryman in the 33rd minute. His 20-yard shot snaked along the ground and into the net. With half an hour to go, the Spanish referee finally lost patience with some of the Italian tackling and dismissed Sogliano. Spurs took advantage of the extra man and it was Steve Perryman again who shot from roughly the same distance to give Spurs the slenderest of advantages for the second leg.

1975	Luton Town	H	First Division	2-1
1980	Wolverhampton Wanderers	A	First Division	2-1
1986	Leicester City	A	First Division	4-1
1997	Wimbledon	H	FA Premier League	1-0

APRIL 6TH

1895	Casuals	H	Friendly	1-2
1896	Middlesbrough	H	Friendly	5-0
1901	Bristol City	H	Southern League	1-0
1907	Reading	A	Southern League	0-2
1908	Portsmouth	H	Southern League	2-3
1912	Sheffield United	H	First Division	1-1
1915	West Bromwich Albion	A	First Division	2-3
1917	Arsenal	H-Homerton	London Combination	0-0
1918	Millwall	A	London Combination	1-0
1928	Sheffield Wednesday	H	First Division	1-3
1929	Bristol City	H	Second Division	1-1
1931	Cardiff City	A	Second Division	0-0
1935	Sheffield Wednesday	A	First Division	0-4

1938 Manager Jack Tresadern handed in his resignation, although no official announcement was made until April 9th. Tresadern had proved unpopular with both the players and supporters, and with results not going his way, his was always likely to be a short managerial reign. His contract was due to expire on June 20th, and with it unlikely to be renewed, he made a successful last-minute application to take over the vacant managerial chair at Plymouth Argyle.

1940	West Ham United	H	Football League South Group C	2-6
1942	Watford	A	London War Cup Group 3	0-0
1946	Portsmouth	A	Football League South	1-0

1949 Sandy Tait died in Croydon. Born in Ayrshire in 1873, Sandy initially worked as a pitboy, leading the ponies down the mines and playing football in his spare time. He turned professional with Motherwell in 1892 and subsequently signed for Preston North End. He was snapped up by Spurs in May 1899, the perfect full-back for the side John Cameron was assembling, and had already earned the nickname

'Terrible Tait' in recognition of the ferocity of his tackle. A member of the side that won the Southern League championship and FA Cup in successive seasons, Sandy remained with Spurs until May 1908 when he joined Leyton, initially as a player and then as manager. He later became a coach, including a spell with the famous amateur side Corinthians.

1953	Stoke City	A	First Division	0-2
1957	Manchester United	A	First Division	0-0
1968	Southampton	H	First Division	6-1
1974	Wolverhampton Wanderers	A	First Division	1-1
1985	West Ham United	A	First Division	1-1
1986	Rangers	A	Friendly	2-0
1991	Southampton	H	First Division	2-0
1996	Nottingham Forest	A	FA Premier League	1-2

APRIL 7TH

1879 Alexander Brown born in Glenbuck, Ayrshire. Sandy Brown is assured an eternal place not only in Spurs' history but in football history as well; in 1901 he scored in every round of the FA Cup, the first player to achieve such a feat, and netted a total of 15 goals in the competition, also a record and which has been seldom troubled since. Of course, it was for his cup goals that Sandy is best remembered at Spurs and with good reason; he played for the club for only two years and he disappeared from the Spurs scene as mysteriously as he arrived. He joined the club from Portsmouth in May 1900, was Spurs' top goalscorer in the Southern League in each of his two seasons with the club and then rejoined Portsmouth in May 1902. The closest he came to achieving international honours whilst at Spurs was when he was picked to play for Scotland against England in April 1902, but as one of the stands at Ibrox collapsed midway through the match the game was later declared void. His career never shone as brightly as it did after his time at Spurs, and one can but still wonder why the club allowed such a prodigious goalscorer to move on so quickly.

1890	Maidenhead	A	Friendly	3-2
1894	Old St Stephen's	H	Friendly	1-1
1896	Swindon Town	H	Friendly	2-3
1900	Swindon Town	H	Southern League	3-0
1906	Brentford	H	Southern League	4-1
1917	Crystal Palace	A	London Combination	3-0
1923	Sunderland	H	First Division	0-1
1924	Cardiff City	A	First Division	1-2
1928	Arsenal	H	First Division	2-0
1934	Derby County	A	First Division	3-4
1939	Plymouth Argyle	H	Second Division	1-0
1947	Nottingham Forest	A	Second Division	1-1
1948	Luton Town	H	Second Division	0-2
1950	Hull City	H	Second Division	0-0
1951	Newcastle United	A	First Division	1-0
1956	Aston Villa	H	First Division	4-3
1958	West Bromwich Albion	A	First Division	2-0
1962	Sheffield Wednesday	H	First Division	4-0
1969	West Bromwich Albion	A	First Division	3-4
1971	Derby County	H	First Division	2-1
1973	Southampton	H	First Division	1-2
1979	Middlesbrough	H	First Division	1-2
1980	Arsenal	H	First Division	1-2
1982	Barcelona	H	European Cup-Winners' Cup Semi-Final 1st Leg	1-1

This was Spurs' second semi-final within a week; Leicester City at Villa Park in the FA Cup on Saturday, at home to Barcelona in the European Cup-Winners' Cup on the Wednesday. The contrast between the two games could not have been greater either, for Barcelona arrived in London with a reputation for being a fine attacking side and left with one of a different sort. It was not that Barcelona set out to stop Spurs play, they just set out to stop Spurs full stop. It did not matter whether the player they were detailed against had the ball or not, whether he was moving upfield or back, Barcelona used every trick in the book, together with one or two that have yet to make it, in an effort to put Spurs off their stride. Long before the referee brought this sorry excuse for a match to its conclusion the crowd were chanting 'animals, animals' at the Barcelona team. They either didn't understand or care about the jibes; they had achieved the draw they set out for and with a priceless away goal to boot. Barcelona's spoiling tactics worked during the first half, the Dutch referee's reluctance to take any decisive action against the Spaniards as frustrating to Spurs as the Barcelona defence. It took just over ten minutes of second half action, if you could call it that, for the referee's patience finally to reach breaking point and his hand reach for a red card, Estella being dismissed for a wild lunge at Tony Galvin. With extra space suddenly available we at last had a goal, although it was Barcelona who scored it, Antonio Olmo letting fly from 40 yards with a shot that lacked pace and conviction but which somehow squirmed out of Ray Clemence's fingers and dropped into the net. The tempo raised itself after that freak goal, Spurs in desperate search of an equaliser, Barcelona even more determined to hold out. Spurs finally found a way through five minutes from the end, Hoddle's free-kick sailing in towards the far post and Graham Roberts slotting home from close range. After the game Spurs manager Keith Burkinshaw observed, 'If we play in Spain like Barcelona did there will be a revolution. And I fear it will be worse out there. We will go out there to win it fairly.' Even Barcelona manager Udo Lattek said, 'I don't think teams like Spurs and Barcelona should do things like that to each other.'

1984	Sunderland	A	First Division	1-1
1987	Sheffield Wednesday	A	First Division	1-0
1990	Nottingham Forest	A	First Division	3-1
1992	Notts County	A	First Division	2-0

APRIL 8TH

1893	Upton Park	A	Southern Alliance	4-1
1897	Southampton St Mary's	H	Southern League	2-2
1898	Woolwich Arsenal	H	United League	0-0

At a public meeting held the previous month the club had decided to turn themselves into a limited company, and with a healthy crowd anticipated at this fixture with Arsenal, copies of the prospectus for Tottenham Hotspur Football and Athletic Company Limited were handed out to spectators. These also offered an allowance of 2s 6d which would be deducted from the price of a season ticket, which normally cost 15s a season.

| 1899 | Chatham | A | Southern League | 0-1 |
| 1901 | West Bromwich Albion | Villa Park | FA Cup Semi-Final | 4-0 |

West Bromwich Albion began the FA Cup semi-final as the undoubted favourites; they ended it soundly beaten. According to the *Sporting Life*, such was Spurs' team play it was impossible to pick any one out from the side as being deserving of special praise. That did not stop them then lauding Sandy Brown who scored all four of the goals by which Spurs put paid to their opponents. This took Brown's tally to 12 and carried on his record of having scored in every round (although not in every match, for he had not scored in the first game with Reading). Although Spurs were through to the FA Cup final at Crystal Palace they would not know who their opponents were to be for a good few days yet; Aston Villa and Sheffield United drew 2-2 at Nottingham and it was only after a replay at Derby, which ended 3-0 in favour of the Sheffield club that Spurs knew just who they would face.

1905	New Brompton	H	Southern League	2-0
1907	West Ham United	H	Western League	4-0
1911	Woolwich Arsenal	A	First Division	0-2
1912	Manchester City	H	First Division	0-2
1916	Arsenal	H	London Combination [2nd competition]	3-2
1922	Birmingham	H	First Division	2-1
1933	Bradford City	H	Second Division	1-1
1939	Tranmere Rovers	H	Second Division	3-1
1944	Chelsea	A	Football League South	1-1
1950	Preston North End	H	Second Division	3-2
1959	Burnley	H	First Division	2-2
1961	Birmingham City	H	First Division	3-2
1963	Sheffield Wednesday	A	First Division	1-3
1966	West Ham United	H	First Division	1-4
1967	Birmingham City	A	FA Cup 6th Round	0-0

Although the game finished goalless, much of the discussion afterwards concerned an incident in which Pat Jennings dropped a Fenton cross on the line, with Birmingham claiming it had gone beyond the line for a goal. The referee did not agree and Spurs lived to fight another day.

1972	West Bromwich Albion	A	First Division	1-1
1978	Bolton Wanderers	H	Second Division	1-0
1985	Guernsey FA XI	A	Friendly	5-0
1996	Middlesbrough	H	FA Premier League	1-1

APRIL 9TH

| 1898 | Chatham | H | Southern League | 2-1 |
| 1902 | Swindon Town | A | Western League | 1-0 |

1904	New Brompton	A	Southern League	1-0
1906	Woolwich Arsenal	H	Southern Charity Cup Semi-Final	0-0
1909	Clapton Orient	H	Second Division	0-1
1910	Sheffield United	A	First Division	1-1
1912	Manchester United	H	First Division	1-1
1917	Arsenal	A	London Combination	2-3

On the same day Ron Burgess was born in Cwm, South Wales. Ron began his playing career as a forward but was converted to half-back in an emergency and was such a success in this new position his career never looked back. Signed by Spurs in May 1936 as an amateur he was upgraded to the professional ranks in August 1938. He made his debut in February 1939 against Norwich and ended his career at Spurs in 1954 with 301 appearances to his credit; like many of of his generation his figure would have been considerably higher but for the Second World War. He was an integral part of the 'push and run' team of the late 40s-early 50s and won 32 caps for Wales between 1946 and 1952, as well as making appearances in numerous war-time internationals. At the end of his Spurs career he became player-coach at Swansea, later being elevated to player-manager and was later manager at Watford, where he signed Pat Jennings. He finished his involvement with professional football with a spell scouting for Luton.

1921	Bradford City	A	First Division	0-1
1927	Burnley	H	First Division	4-1
1932	Millwall	H	Second Division	1-0
1938	Bradford Park Avenue	H	Second Division	2-1

Immediately after the game the Spurs board announced the name of the new manager to replace Jack Tresadern; Peter McWilliam, who was returning to the club where he had enjoyed considerable success between 1913 and 1917. McWilliam, who since leaving Spurs in 1927 had been manager at Middlesbrough and more lately Arsenal's North-East scout, rejoined the club on May 16th and began making a number of changes to the way the club was run, including the promotion of a number of juniors from the club's Northfleet nursery in order that Spurs might develop their own players. Unfortunately, the Second World War brought football to a halt, and by the time the war ended he felt he was too old for the rigours of football management and retired.

1949	Barnsley	A	Second Division	1-4
1955	Everton	A	First Division	0-1
1959	Everton	A	First Division	1-2
1962	Sheffield United	H	First Division	3-3
1965	Liverpool	H	First Division	3-0
1966	Sheffield Wednesday	A	First Division	1-1
1977	Queens Park Rangers	H	First Division	3-0
1983	Nottingham Forest	A	First Division	2-2
1993	Norwich City	H	FA Premier League	5-1
1994	Coventry City	A	FA Premier League	0-1
1995	Everton	Elland Road		
			FA Cup Semi-Final	1-4

Elland Road at 1 p.m. was not a popular choice among many supporters. The venue was chosen by the FA, the timing by police, but neither made much sense. The reasoning behind the kick off time was that it would prevent fans from spending the morning and early afternoon drinking and prevent any trouble, but there was no history of ill-feeling between the two sets of supporters (the folly of this decision was revealed later the same day at the other semi-final, which pitted Manchester United against Crystal Palace. Palace had been the opponents when Eric Cantona had been sent off and launched an attack on a fan in the crowd, and it was undoubtedly this ill-feeling that was partly to blame for the trouble that flared outside a public house in Walsall that left one dead and five seriously injured). As it was Everton shook off the early cobwebs first, firing into a two-goal lead. In truth, changes imposed by injuries to key players had played their part, but Spurs looked little like the side that had beaten the other half of Merseyside in the previous round. Although Klinsmann scored from the penalty spot, two late goals from Amokachi completed Spurs' misery. Having believed ever since their reinstatement into the competition that this was to be their year, the defeat and its manner was hard to take.

1997	Sheffield Wednesday	A	FA Premier League	1-2

APRIL 10TH

1886	Park	H	Friendly	8-0
1897	Luton Town	A	United League	1-2
1899	New Brompton	A	Thames & Medway League	4-5
1903	Southampton	H	Southern League	2-1

| 1909 | Fulham | H | Second Division | 1-0 |
| 1914 | Bolton Wanderers | H | First Division | 3-0 |

The only known occasion on which the Spurs goalkeeper, in this particular case 'Tiny' Joyce, has scored in a League match. Although Joyce was renowned for his ability to punt the ball further upfield than almost any other goalkeeper, this was the first and only time he managed to score. Joyce's goal set Spurs on the road to a 3-0 victory. On the same day Jack Gibbons was born in Fulham. Initially signed by Spurs as an amateur in July 1937 (he retained his amateur status throughout his career) Jack proved to be an exceptional goalscorer and grabbed 18 in 33 first-team appearances during his first season with the club. He then elected to sign for Brentford, but returned to Spurs in August 1939. Although he guested for the club regularly during the war, when League football resumed he announced he was moving to the North and signed for Bradford Park Avenue, later returning to London and becoming manager of Brentford in 1949, a position he held until 1952.

1915	Blackburn Rovers	A	First Division	1-4
1917	Portsmouth	H-Highbury		
			London Combination	2-1

Ernie Williamson had been Arsenal's regular goalkeeper before the war but made one appearance for Spurs, turning out in goal to help out Spurs in a crisis. Spurs had known all week that they were unlikely to have a regular goalkeeper, with Jacques probably unavailable, and had informed Williamson he might be needed. On the day of the game Jacques did not appear and Williamson was asked to play,, although no Spurs director could be found until ten minutes before kick off. By this time no Arsenal director could be found either, so Spurs took a chance that Arsenal would not object to Williamson taking part in the match. Ernie Williamson played a large part in Spurs winning the game 2-1, although the sequel was that Arsenal did find out and did object, lodging a complaint with the London Combination. Spurs were subsequently found guilty of playing a player from another club without permission and fined five guineas.

| 1920 | Stoke | A | Second Division | 3-1 |
| 1923 | | | | |

Sid Tickeridge born in Stepney. Associated with the club whilst a schoolboy Sid was signed to the groundstaff in 1937 and sent to the Northfleet nursery. During the war he played for Spurs, Aldershot, Fulham and Millwall and at the end of the war signed professional forms with Spurs in April 1946. He was a regular full-back in the side from 1947, but lost his place following the subsequent arrival of Alf Ramsey. He was transferred to Chelsea in 1951 and later played for Brentford before injury called a halt to his career.

1925	Birmingham	H	First Division	0-1
1926	Notts County	H	First Division	4-0
1928	Sheffield Wednesday	A	First Division	2-4
1936	Charlton Athletic	H	Second Division	1-1
1937	Coventry City	H	Second Division	3-1
1939	Plymouth Argyle	A	Second Division	1-0
1940	Fulham	H	Football League South Group C	3-1
1943	Millwall	A	League Cup	1-0
1948	Fulham	H	Second Division	0-2
1950	Hull City	A	Second Division	0-1
1954	Huddersfield Town	A	First Division	5-2

Spurs were 2-0 up after only 54 seconds, the best performance in the League's history. After that there was no coming back for Huddersfield and Spurs ran out 5-2 victors.

| 1971 | Ipswich Town | H | First Division | 2-0 |
| 1973 | Liverpool | A | UEFA Cup Semi-Final 1st Leg | 0-1 |

One of the major appeals of European football, apart form the opportunity to stock up on the duty frees, is the chance to play against different styles and formations. No matter how often you have the opposition watched prior to your match, there is always a sense of stepping into the unknown. That could not be said this night. Spurs and Liverpool had already met each other four times this season; twice in the League and twice in the League Cup. Whilst Liverpool had won the League battles on points (winning at White Hart Lane 2-1 and drawing 1-1 at Anfield), Spurs had proven what cup fighters they were with a 1-1 draw at Anfield and a 3-1 replay win at White Hart Lane. There was little therefore that one club did not know about the other; two tense and tight matches were expected in the UEFA Cup semi-finals. The first leg was undoubtedly tight, the only goal being little more than a freak as a Spurs clearance cannoned off Alec Lindsay's shin and careered into the net. It was possibly the only way Pat Jennings was going to be beaten all evening and much the same could be said for the custodian of the other goal, Ray Clemence. Liverpool did most of the attacking, although that is not to imply that Spurs set out their stall to defend, merely the way things turned out as Liverpool tried ever harder for the cushion of a second goal. Spurs held firm, just, and might have equalised through Martin Chivers or Ralph Coates. Bill Nicholson took his two forwards off with five minutes to go, bringing on the fresh Ray Evans and Jimmy Pearce to try to stem the Liverpool tide. After the match he said 'I had hoped for a goal because away goals are so important in these competitions. But it is always hard at Liverpool and I suppose that in the circumstances I have to be happy with this result.'

| 1974 | 1.FC Lokomotiv Leipzig | A | UEFA Cup Semi-Final 1st Leg | 2-1 |

If attack really is the best form of defence, then there are any number of coaches operative in European football who have yet to be made fully aware of the adage. All too often, teams travel to away legs with little intention of doing anything other than stopping the opposition scoring, content to soak up the pressure and perhaps score a vital away goal on a breakaway. Bill Nicholson scored the first surprise of the evening, selecting winger Jimmy Neighbour in place of injured striker Chris McGrath. Then he sent his team out to take the game to the East Germans, catching them by surprise not once but twice in the early exchanges, before they had a chance to settle fully. By the time they had, the damage had been done. Martin Peters gave Spurs the lead after only 15 minutes, half-volleying the ball left footed into the corner of the net. Ten minutes later Ralph Coates added a second, converting a chance that Martin Chivers had swung at but missed. There might have been a third; Martin Chivers heading against the post with the keeper well beaten. Quite what was said in the Lokomotiv dressing-room at half-time is unknown, but it transformed the Germans in the second half, who piled on the pressure in a desperate search for goals. They got just one, virtually on the hour, when World Cup striker Lowe headed in at the near post. Spurs stood firm after that, surviving one or two shocks, holding on to a lead that almost certainly guaranteed their presence in the following month's final.

1976	Leeds United	H	First Division	0-0
1979	Arsenal	A	First Division	0-1
1982	Ipswich Town	H	First Division	1-0
1991	Norwich City	A	First Division	1-2

Paul Gascoigne made a surprise turn out barely four weeks after entering hospital for a hernia operation. The object of the exercise was to test how fit he was, especially with the FA Cup semi-final against Arsenal looming on the horizon. Gascoigne, made captain for the evening, passed with flying colours.

APRIL 11TH

| 1885 | Grove | A | Friendly | Score unknown |
| 1896 | Aston Villa | H | Friendly | 1-3 |

Spurs had only recently adopted professionalism and as they were still not members of any formal league, arranged a series of prestigious friendlies to keep the paying customers satisfied. When Aston Villa, one of the most famous clubs in the land and League Champions, arrived at Northumberland Park for this fixture, they were unhappy with the changing facilities and instead hired the local public house, The Northumberland Arms.

1898	Swindon Town	H	Southern League	2-0
1903	New Brompton	A	Southern League	0-3
1904	Fulham	A	London League	5-1
1905	Brentford	H	Western League	0-0
1908	Watford	A	Southern League	2-2
1914	West Bromwich Albion	A	First Division	1-1
1921	Clapton Orient	N	London FA Charity Cup Semi-Final	1-2
1923	Bolton Wanderers	A	First Division	2-0
1925	Newcastle United	H	First Division	3-0
1931	Plymouth Argyle	H	Second Division	1-1
1936	Leicester City	H	Second Division	1-1
1942	Charlton Athletic	H	London War Cup Group 3	0-3
1953	Aston Villa	H	First Division	1-1
1955	Huddersfield Town	H	First Division	1-1
1959	Birmingham City	A	First Division	1-5
1977	Arsenal	A	First Division	0-1
1981	Wolverhampton Wanderers	Hillsborough	FA Cup Semi-Final	2-2 [aet]

Hillsborough, along with Villa Park, had been an automatic choice as venue for FA Cup semi-finals for many years and would continue hosting them until the end of the decade, when disaster during the Liverpool and Nottingham Forest match changed the face of British football for ever. There were signs during the match between Spurs and Wolves, however, that things weren't quite right. On the insistence of South Yorkshire Police, Spurs fans were allocated the Leppings Lane End and Wolves the Kop End. This was despite the fact that Spurs had the larger support and that such an arrangement involved supporters 'crossing' each other in order to get to their allocated ends. As this was Spurs' first FA Cup semi-final since 1967 (which had also been staged at Hillsborough) demand for tickets was great, so much so that there was a severe crush inside the Leppings Lane end before the match. Police and officials on duty at this end took the decision to move a considerable number of Spurs fans up to the Kop End, where there was ample room, thereby avoiding the disastrous scenes that were to halt the 1989 semi-final. Spurs found plenty of room on the pitch as well, carving out an opening for Steve Archibald after only four minutes for him to register his 25th goal of the season. Wolves equalised only minutes later. A patched-up Andy Gray, regarded by Spurs as the main danger man of the Wolves side, nodded down for Ken Hibbitt to send home a low shot. Spurs reclaimed the lead before half-time following the first controversial incident of the afternoon. Ossie Ardiles was scampering towards the Wolves penalty area when his run was brought to a halt by George Berry's tackle, which sent the Spurs man flying into the area. Spurs appealed for a penalty, Wolves insisted the challenge was fair. Referee Clive Thomas, no stranger to controversial incidents, awarded a free-kick just outside the box. The sake of a few inches was to reap benefits for Spurs. Glenn Hoddle, who would have taken the penalty had it been awarded, had recalled on the morning of the match that the last spot kick he had missed was against Paul Bradshaw. With the Wolves wall lined up between him and the goal, he was unable to see the whites of Bradshaw's eyes, but he did see enough of the goal to send the ball into the top corner. The second half never looked likely to match the first for drama until the very last minute. Wolves were still desperately seeking the equaliser and throwing virtually everyone into attack, Spurs equally determined to stop them and pulling everyone back. With time running out came the second and most decisive incident. Glenn Hoddle went in to tackle Ken Hibbitt and appeared to win the ball fairly, although the Wolves player tumbled inside the penalty area. Whether Clive Thomas was unsighted is uncertain, but as Hibbitt hit the deck he was pointing to the spot to indicate a penalty to Wolves. Spurs, and in particular Archibald and Ardiles, were furious and argued at length that the challenge had been a fair one. Indeed, television replays shown after the game did show the tackle to have been fair and that it was unlikely Hoddle had even touched Hibbitt whilst making it. But Thomas had made his decision, and Willie Carr struck home the equaliser. The incident drained both sides, with the result that extra time was little more than going through the motions. After the game, both sides returned to the Hibbitt and Hoddle clash. Most tellingly, Ken Hibbitt claimed that it was natural to fall in the area when tackled, and his manager John Barnwell added that teams had to do what they had to do, especially in the closing minutes of a semi-final they were losing. Spurs fans never forgave nor forgot, booing Ken Hibbitt whenever he went anywhere near a ball whenever he was on an opposing side.

1984	Hajduk Split	A	UEFA Cup Semi-Final 1st Leg	1-2

But for a manic ten-minute spell in the second half, Spurs' confidence at reaching their third UEFA Cup final might have been greater, for having prised the lead from their Yugoslavian hosts Spurs then conceded two goals to give Split hope for the second leg. Mark Falco scored the goal that gave Spurs the better chance of reaching the final and he was involved in both the beginning and end of the action. His cross into the penalty area was needlessly handled by Ivan Gudelj, and Falco it was who took the penalty. It wasn't a particularly good one, almost straight at the keeper, but in the tricky conditions Aoran Simovic was unable to hold it cleanly. The ball came straight back to Falco, who saw his second shot blocked. As the ball headed away from the goal Split could have been forgiven for thinking the danger had passed, but Tony Galvin reacted quickly enough to send a low hard cross directly into the goalmouth. From barely a yard out, Falco made no mistake with his third attempt, the first goal Split had conceded at home in the competition this season. Spurs might, perhaps should have held on to the lead, but in the 67th minute struggled to clear from a corner and Gudelj atoned for his earlier mistake and fired in a shot that was helped on its way past Tony Parks by a deflection. Ten minutes later Gudelj was again involved, nodding on a left wing corner for Dusran Pesic to head home. Despite the defeat, Spurs were confident they could overcome Split and reach the final. Outgoing manager Keith Burkinshaw said, 'When Split come to White Hart Lane they will find out what noise is all about.'

1987	Watford	Villa Park	FA Cup Semi-Final	4-1
1992	Queens Park Rangers	A	First Division	2-1
1995	Manchester City	H	FA Premier League	2-1
1998	Chelsea	A	FA Premier League	0-2

APRIL 12TH

1895	Liverpool Casuals	H	Friendly	6-0
1898	Lincoln City	H	Friendly	2-1
1902	Luton Town	H	Southern League	0-0
1909	Clapton Orient	A	Second Division	0-0
1913	Chelsea	A	First Division	0-1

1919	Queens Park Rangers	H-Highbury		
			London Combination	2-3
1924	Everton	H	First Division	2-5
1930	Reading	A	Second Division	0-3
1941	Arsenal	H	Football League War Cup 4th Round 2nd Leg	1-1

With Arsenal having won the first leg 2-1, this draw saw them progress into the next round with an aggregate victory of 3-2.

1947	Chesterfield	A	Second Division	0-0
1948	Nottingham Forest	H	Second Division	0-3
1952	Portsmouth	H	First Division	3-1
1955	Huddersfield Town	A	First Division	0-1
1958	Manchester United	H	First Division	1-0
1963	Liverpool	A	First Division	2-5

1964 Chris Fairclough born in Nottingham. He joined Nottingham Forest as a youngster and worked his way through the ranks to become a professional in October 1981, making his debut in a League Cup tie that December. Once he broke into the side on a regular basis he was confirmed as a solid and reliable performer at the heart of the defence, and when his Forest contract was allowed to expire in 1987 had his pick of clubs to join, preferring to come to Spurs, with a tribunal setting the fee at £375,000. An ever present in the 1987-88 season, he was injured in November 1988 and struggled to reclaim his place in the side, being loaned out to Leeds United with a view to the deal becoming permanent at the end of the season, and with the fee set at £500,000. He won a First Division title medal in 1991-92 and was sold to Bolton in 1995 for a further £500,000.

| 1967 | Birmingham City | H | FA Cup 6th Round Replay | 6-0 |

Having been more than fortunate to have survived in the first match, Spurs made sure there was to be no repeat in the replay. An early goal from Terry Venables set them up for a good evening's work, scoring twice early on, and Alan Gilzean converted one of many crosses from Jimmy Robertson before the break. For once they didn't ease up in the second half either, with further goals from Jimmy Greaves (two) and Frank Saul completing the scoring.

1968	Leeds United	H	First Division	2-1
1969	Nottingham Forest	A	First Division	2-0
1971	Blackpool	A	First Division	0-0
1975	Burnley	A	First Division	2-3
1977	Bristol City	A	First Division	0-1
1980	Manchester United	A	First Division	1-4
1982	Arsenal	A	First Division	3-1
1986	Luton Town	A	First Division	1-1
1989	Sheffield Wednesday	H	First Division	0-0
1993	Nottingham Forest	A	FA Premier League	1-2
1997	Everton	A	FA Premier League	0-1

APRIL 13TH

1872 John Cameron born in Ayr. John would be assured a place in Spurs' history if we were to consider only his exploits as a player, but add to that his dual role of manager and he remains one of the most important signings ever made by the club. He began his career with Ayr Parkhouse before being signed by Queens Park, the noted Scottish amateur side. He then transferred to Everton, still an amateur, coupling his playing duties with work in the Cunard office. This was not popular with his team-mates, who felt that as an amateur he was not as committed to the game as they were and in 1896 he was finally persuaded to sign professional forms. In 1897 Frank Brettell signed the inside-forward for Spurs and was rewarded when Cameron finished his first season at Spurs as top goalscorer. In February 1899 Brettell accepted the vacant manager's position at Portsmouth and Cameron was elevated to player-manager-secretary, the only occasion in the club's history when the three roles have been combined. Cameron proved the ideal man for the job, guiding the team on and off the field to the Southern League championship in 1900 and then, one year later, the FA Cup against Sheffield United. Indeed, Cameron scored Spurs' equaliser in the 3-1 win at Bolton. Although he was still playing regularly the following season, he thereafter began to concentrate more on the administrative and managerial duties, although in 1906 he successfully applied to be reinstated as an amateur player. In March 1907 he sensationally resigned as manager of Spurs, claiming 'differences with the directorate' as his reason. After a short spell in journalism he returned to coaching and was working in Germany at the time the First World War broke, spending the four year duration interned by the Germans. After the war he became manager at Ayr for a short time before returning once again to sports journalism. He died in Glasgow on April 20th 1935.

1889	Orion Gymnasium	H	Friendly	6-1
1895	2nd Scots Guards	H	Friendly	1-1
1897	Kettering Town	A	United League	2-5
1899	Dartford	H	Thames & Medway League	9-0
1900	Southampton	H	Southern League	2-0

A crowd of 15,000 (the second highest of the season, after 18,000 attended the game with Gravesend United) turned out to see this game between the two strongest sides in the Southern League – Spurs led the League, but Southampton, having reached the FA Cup final (where they subsequently lost eight days later 0-4 to Bury) had had other considerations during the season.

1901	Millwall Athletic	H	Western League	1-0
1903	Portsmouth	A	Southern League	0-2
1904	Brighton & Hove Albion	A	Southern League	2-1
1906	Southampton	H	Southern League	1-1
1907	Watford	H	Southern League	0-0
1912	Oldham Athletic	A	First Division	1-2
1914	Middlesbrough	A	First Division	0-6

This was Spurs' heaviest defeat of a season that had begun brightly with three straight victories and then tailed away remarkably. From March to the end of the season, Spurs won only two games and were perilously close to be being relegated, finishing only four points above the trap door at the end of the season.

1918	Chelsea	A	London Combination Subsidiary	1-1
1929	Barnsley	A	Second Division	1-4
1935	Birmingham City	H	First Division	1-1
1936	Charlton Athletic	A	Second Division	1-2
1940	Charlton Athletic	A	Football League South Group C	4-2
1946	Portsmouth	H	Football League South	2-0
1957	Birmingham City	H	First Division	5-1
1963	Fulham	H	First Division	1-1
1964	Sheffield Wednesday	A	First Division	0-2
1968	Chelsea	A	First Division	0-2
1970	Manchester United	H	First Division	2-1
1974	Southampton	H	First Division	3-1
1985	Leicester City	A	First Division	2-1
1998	Coventry City	H	FA Premier League	1-1

APRIL 14TH

1894	Ilford	H	Friendly	0-1
1900	Bristol City	A	Southern League	0-3
1902	Queens Park Rangers	A	London League	2-1
1903	Millwall Athletic	H	Southern League	2-0
1906	Norwich City	A	Southern League	1-4
1917	Luton Town	A	London Combination	4-5
1922	Oldham Athletic	H	First Division	3-1
1923	Birmingham	A	First Division	1-2
1928	Burnley	A	First Division	2-2
1933	Plymouth Argyle	H	Second Division	0-0
1934	Manchester City	H	First Division	5-1
1941	Reading	H	London War Cup Section B	2-2
1945	Millwall	H	Football League South	4-0
1951	Huddersfield Town	H	First Division	0-2

On the same day Milija Aleksic was born in Newcastle-Under-Lyme. Having failed to make the grade at Port Vale Milija Aleksic could have been forgiven for thinking his chance at the big time had passed him by. After being released by the Potteries club he drifted into the non-League game, turning out in goal for Stafford Rangers. His performances as Rangers won the 1972 FA Trophy brought renewed attention from League clubs and he accepted an offer to join Plymouth in 1973. After three years with Plymouth, during which time he had been loaned out to Oxford and Ipswich, he was loaned and then signed by Luton Town. In 1978 Spurs, having released Pat Jennings at the end of the previous season, were looking for cover for Barry Daines and signed Aleksic for £100,000. Although his first-team appearances were extremely limited, he was fortunate enough to step into the breach in the FA Cup semi-final against Wolves and then hold on to the position for the final against Manchester City. With Spurs signing Ray Clemence in the summer of 1981, Aleksic went back into the reserves and at the end of the 1981-82 season allowed to leave, heading for South Africa with a 'rebel' tour and later coaching.

1952	Preston North End	A	First Division	1-1
1956	Blackpool	A	First Division	2-0
1958	Hibernian	H	Friendly	4-0
1973	Arsenal	A	First Division	1-1
1979	Queens Park Rangers	H	First Division	1-1
1982	Sunderland	H	First Division	2-2
1984	Luton Town	H	First Division	2-1
1990	Coventry City	H	First Division	3-2
1991	Arsenal	Wembley	FA Cup Semi-Final	3-1

Tottenham Hotspur and Arsenal met in the FA Cup semi-final at Wembley, the first time Wembley had hosted an FA Cup match other than the final. As it was the semi-final, the FA ruled that the match should not have the ceremony normally associated with the final – the teams were led out by mascots rather than the managers. Paul Gascoigne fired Spurs into an early lead with a free-kick described by manager Terry Venables as being one of the best goals ever seen at Wembley – 20 yards from goal, Gascoigne bent the ball over the wall and out of reach of Seaman in the Arsenal goal. A few minutes later Gary Lineker prodded home a second and Spurs appeared to be coasting. Just before half-time Alan Smith headed home and for the first 20 minutes of the second half Spurs were under severe pressure as Arsenal sought the equaliser. Gascoigne left the action after an hour, with a rapturous roar from the Spurs fans ringing in his ears, and Gary Lineker grabbed a third goal to settle the scoring and ensure Spurs would return to Wembley to face Nottingham Forest in the final. With all of the financial problems Spurs had off the field put to the back of the mind for a few moments at least, there were wonderful scenes as the final whistle blew; Gascoigne's rapport with the fans being an undoubted highlight.

1992	Sheffield United	A	First Division	0-2
1995	Crystal Palace	A	FA Premier League	1-1

APRIL 15TH

1893	Smethwick	N	Wolverton & District Charity Cup	0-2
1895	Southampton St Mary's	A	Friendly	0-0
1896	Swindon Town	A	Friendly	2-0
1899	Bedminster	A	Southern League	0-1
1901	Queens Park Rangers	H	Western League	2-2
1905	Wellingborough	A	Southern League	1-0
1911	Bradford City	H	First Division	2-0
1916	Queens Park Rangers	A	London Combination [2nd competition]	3-1
1922	Arsenal	H	First Division	2-0
1927	West Ham United	H	First Division	1-3
1929	Hull City	A	Second Division	1-1
1933	Swansea Town	A	Second Division	2-0
1938	Sheffield United	H	Second Division	1-2
1939	Millwall	A	Second Division	0-2
1949	Brentford	H	Second Division	2-0
1950	Sheffield United	A	Second Division	1-2
1960	Chelsea	A	First Division	3-1
1963	Liverpool	H	First Division	7-2

Spurs exacted ample revenge for their 5-2 defeat at Anfield three days earlier with a 7-2 hammering at White Hart Lane. Jimmy Greaves led the scoring with four, including one a penalty, with Cliff Jones adding two and Frank Saul the other. At the end of the season Greaves had racked up 37 League strikes, a Spurs record for a season by one player, beating Ted Harper's record set in 1930-31.

1967	Sheffield Wednesday	H	First Division	2-1
1972	Chelsea	H	First Division	3-0
1974	Chelsea	A	First Division	0-0
1978	Brighton & Hove Albion	A	Second Division	1-3
1980	Crystal Palace	A	Friendly	3-2

This match was a testimonial for Martin Hinshelwood and Spurs goals were scored by Don McAllister, Gerry Armstrong and Peter Taylor.

1981	Wolverhampton Wanderers	Highbury	FA Cup Semi-Final Replay	3-0

The injustice of the final minute of normal time in the first meeting had fired Spurs up. The venue for the replay, Highbury, meant there were considerably more of their fans inside than those of Wolves. Just before the kick-off, Spurs received the final psychological advantage – Andy Gray had failed a fitness test and Spurs' main worry would not be playing. In the face of such adversity, Wolves were faced with an uphill struggle, even more so when Garth Crooks gave Spurs an early lead with a header in front of the North Bank, where Spurs fans were packed. Wolves tore back, mounting a number of challenges, but could come no closer than the woodwork in their search for an equaliser. A few moments before half-time, Garth Crooks sealed victory with a lightning burst of pace to latch on to Glenn Hoddle's through ball and finished with aplomb. The celebrations were already well under way when Ricky Villa added a third, unleashing a shot with the minimum of effort but the maximum of power from outside the area. Hundreds of fans poured on to the pitch at the final whistle, acclaiming not only Spurs' progress to the final but also the performance and manner in which it was accomplished – some were of the opinion it was the best performance seen by the home side at Highbury all season!

| 1987 | Manchester City | A | First Division | 1-1 |
| 1988 | Hull City | A | Friendly | 1-2 |

This match was a testimonial for Jeff Radcliffe and Spurs' goal was scored by Paul Walsh.

| 1989 | Wimbledon | A | First Division | 2-1 |
| 1996 | Arsenal | A | FA Premier League | 0-0 |

APRIL 16TH

| 1887 | London Caledonians | H | East End Cup Semi-Final | 0-1 |

After two false starts, Spurs and London Caledonians played their East End cup semi-final. Unfortunately for Spurs, Caledonians won by the only goal of the game when the greasy ball shot through the legs of goalkeeper J Anderson.

1888 Billy Minter born in Woolwich. Having failed to make a name for himself when signed to Norwich City and Woolwich Arsenal, Billy's career took off when he signed with Reading, and after finishing top scorer for two seasons was transferred to Spurs in 1908. After helping the club win promotion in its first season as a League club, Billy was then top scorer for the next three seasons. Following the outbreak of the First World War Billy enlisted and was thus unavailable for the club for the duration of the war, but he returned and played a major part in the club walking away with the Second Division title in 1919-20. He then announced his retirement as a player and moved on to the coaching staff. Appointed trainer in June 1920 he was offered the manager's job in February 1927 following the resignation of Peter McWilliam, but Spurs' relegation at the end of his first full season in charge and their inability to bounce back immediately took its toll and he suffered from ill-health. He tendered his resignation in November 1929, although it had not been asked for, and such was the esteem with which he was held at the club he was immediately appointed assistant secretary. He held this job until his death on 21st May 1940.

1895	Bristol South End	A	Friendly	7-0
1897	Nottingham Forest	H	Friendly	1-1
1898	Millwall Athletic	A	Southern League	1-3
1900	Sheppey United	H	Southern League	3-0

By virtue of this win Spurs ensured they would finish the season as Southern League Champions for the first and only time in their history, despite losing six points they had in the bag following the withdrawals of both Brighton United and Cowes.

1904	Kettering Town	H	Southern League	5-1
1906	Portsmouth	A	Southern League	0-1
1910	Woolwich Arsenal	H	First Division	1-1
1921	Bradford City	H	First Division	2-0

With the FA Cup final a week away Spurs played like a team with one eye on a greater prize than two League points, with tackles that might have involved an element of risk being avoided. Jimmy Seed and Jimmy Cantrell were rested in order to ensure their full fitness for Wolves the following Saturday and it was also confirmed that Fanny Walden had still not recovered and would therefore not be playing at Stamford Bridge. Despite all this, Spurs still had a little too much for Bradford City, with Charlie Wilson scoring both goals and giving perhaps his best ever performance in a Spurs shirt.

1927	Newcastle United	A	First Division	2-3
1932	Bradford City	A	Second Division	0-2
1938	Aston Villa	A	Second Division	0-2
1949	Grimsby Town	H	Second Division	5-2
1953	West Ham United	A	Friendly	1-2
1954	Preston North End	A	First Division	1-2
1955	Burnley	H	First Division	0-3
1960	Manchester City	H	First Division	0-1
1965	Blackburn Rovers	H	First Division	5-2
1966	Northampton Town	H	First Division	1-1
1977	Sunderland	H	First Division	1-1
1979	Southampton	A	First Division	3-3
1983	Ipswich Town	H	First Division	3-1
1986	Birmingham City	H	First Division	2-0
1990	Millwall	A	First Division	1-0

APRIL 17TH

1886	Hermitage	H	Friendly	3-0
1897	Kettering Town	H	United League	1-1
1899	Wellingborough	A	United League	1-3
1900	Woolwich Arsenal	H	Southern District Combination	4-2
1901	Portsmouth	A	Western League	0-1
1905	Portsmouth	H	Western League	0-1
1906	Norwich City	H	Southern League	3-0
1908	Southampton	H	Southern League	3-0
1909	Burnley	A	Second Division	2-1
1911	Everton	H	First Division	0-1
1915	Sheffield United	H	First Division	1-1
1920	Grimsby Town	H	Second Division	3-1
1922	Oldham Athletic	A	First Division	0-1
1926	Aston Villa	A	First Division	0-3
1933	Plymouth Argyle	A	Second Division	2-2
1937	Doncaster Rovers	A	Second Division	1-1
1946	Charlton Athletic	A	Football League South	0-1
1948	Coventry City	A	Second Division	1-1
1954	Sheffield United	H	First Division	2-1
1961	Sheffield Wednesday	H	First Division	2-1

Ten years previously, almost to the day, Spurs had clinched their first ever League title by beating Sheffield Wednesday at home. A full decade later, Sheffield Wednesday again stood in front of Spurs as they pursued not only the title but the first half of a momentous double. Ten years previously, Wednesday had stood in front of Spurs knowing they would be relegated into the Second Division at the end of the season. A full decade later they stood considerably taller; not only were they currently second in the table and therefore Spurs' closest rivals for the trophy, but it was at Wednesday that Spurs had suffered their first defeat of the season. That alone required revenge, but the opportunity to get one hand on the League title (the other hand being reserved for the FA Cup) gave this match an edge that possibly only Arsenal's completion of the League title, yet another decade away, has ever given a League match at White Hart Lane. A crowd of 61,205 (one of the highest of the season) crammed into the ground to witness history being made. It was not a match for the faint hearted, especially when Don Megson gave Wednesday the lead after half an hour, hitting home after his free-kick had rebounded off the Spurs' defensive wall. The action was fast and furious throughout; fast because the same prize was available to both sides, furious enough to see Dave Mackay and Peter Johnson booked, three Wednesday players lectured, goalkeeper Ron Springett charging into a post and having to leave the field for treatment only to return four minutes later, Keith Ellis get knocked out and Cliff Jones require stitches in his knee. Wednesday held their lead, indeed might have increased it when Ellis hit the post in the 42nd minute, but their attacking activity was restricted to breakaways; Spurs were on the charge. A minute later Spurs drew level; Bobby Smith collected a Terry Dyson back-header, flicked the ball over Peter Swan and ran around the player to smash it past Springett. A couple of minutes later Maurice Norman headed on a free-kick and Les Allen was on hand to volley the ball into the net for the winner. The second half was something of an anti-climax, but the reaction that greeted the final whistle was anything but – 5,000 of the crowd swarmed on to the pitch, chanting over and over 'We want Danny' whilst the remaining 56,000 sang much the same tune from the terraces. Danny duly obliged after some ten minutes, appearing in the director's box with the rest of the team of the season. Leicester City therefore became the final barrier between Spurs and the double – the same Leicester that had been the first side to win at White Hart Lane this season!

1962	Fulham	A	First Division	1-1
1965	Sheffield Wednesday	A	First Division	0-1
1968	Leeds United	A	First Division	0-1
1971	Liverpool	A	First Division	0-0
1976	Birmingham City	A	First Division	1-3
1982	Manchester United	A	First Division	0-2
1985	Arsenal	H	First Division	0-2
1991	Crystal Palace	H	First Division	0-1
1993	Oldham Athletic	H	FA Premier League	4-1
1994	Leeds United	A	FA Premier League	0-2
1995	Norwich City	H	FA Premier League	1-0

APRIL 18TH

1896	Southampton St Mary's	A	Friendly	1-4
1898	Reading	A	Friendly	3-3
1904	West Ham United	A	Western League	1-0

1907   Following the shock resignation of John Cameron in March 1907, Spurs had advertised for a new manager and subsequently appointed Fred Kirkham. Kirkham had made his name as a referee, officiating at the 1902 and 1906 FA Cup finals and numerous internationals. Five days prior to his appointment he had refereed the Southern League match between Spurs and Watford at White Hart Lane. His appointment was not made official until April 22nd, at which time it was revealed he had been given a five year contract worth £350 per annum.

1908	Norwich City	H	Southern League	3-0
1914	Aston Villa	H	First Division	0-2
1919	Millwall	H-Homerton		
			London Combination	2-2
1925	Liverpool	A	First Division	0-1
1927	West Ham United	A	First Division	2-1
1930	West Bromwich Albion	H	Second Division	0-2
1931	Bristol City	A	Second Division	1-2
1936	Norwich City	A	Second Division	0-1
1938	Sheffield United	A	Second Division	0-1
1942	Charlton Athletic	A	London War Cup Group 3	0-4
1949	Brentford	A	Second Division	1-1
1953	Sunderland	A	First Division	1-1
1956	Wolverhampton Wanderers	A	First Division	1-5

On the same day Chris Jones was born in Jersey. Signed as an apprentice in May 1971 he was upgraded to the professional ranks in 1973 and made his League debut in August 1974. An abundance of strikers throughout his time with the club restricted first-team opportunities, although by the time he left in 1982 he had amassed 149 League games, scoring 37 goals. He joined Manchester City in 1982, later playing for Crystal Palace, Charlton Athletic and Orient before going returning home to Jersey in order to manage St Peters.

1959	West Bromwich Albion	H	First Division	5-0
1960	Chelsea	H	First Division	0-1

Two defeats in two days, both at home, effectively ended Spurs' chance of winning the title. As the club had entered the final straight, the title was a three-horse race between Spurs, defending champions Wolves and Burnley, with Spurs holding a slight advantage. But defeat against Manchester City and then Chelsea allowed Wolves to glimpse a third consecutive title. Although Spurs were able to deny them this and the double by winning at Molineaux the following week, the defeats against City and Chelsea were perhaps an indication that Spurs weren't yet ready to become champions. Meanwhile, thousands of miles away in Nigeria, John Chiedozie was born in Owerri. His family emigrated to England when he was 12 and John was soon being courted by a number of London clubs, finally signing for Leyton Orient in 1976. In 1981 he joined Notts County and made over 100 appearances for them before they were relegated into the Second Division. A fee of £375,000 took him to Spurs in August 1984 and a series of fine performances on the wing won over the fans, but niggling injuries limited his appearances. He was given a free transfer in 1988 and later played for Derby, Notts County and Chesterfield before dropping into the non-League game.

1964	Bolton Wanderers	H	First Division	1-0
1973	Derby County	H	First Division	1-0
1981	Norwich	H	First Division	2-3
1984	Aston Villa	H	First Division	2-1
1987	Charlton Athletic	H	First Division	1-0
1992	Wimbledon	H	First Division	3-2
1998	Barnsley	A	FA Premier League	1-1

With both clubs battling against relegation this was a vital match at Oakwell, scene of Spurs' dismissal in the FA Cup. That night had seen Stephen Clemence sent off for allegedly diving; today it was Ramon Vega's turn to see the red card following a professional foul on Ashley Ward. Barnsley had taken the lead in the first half, but Spurs had chances to have got back on level terms before the break, including a miss from Jurgen Klinsmann when it looked easier to score. That prompted a tactical switch at half-time, with Chris Armstrong linking up front with Les Ferdinand for the second half, although Spurs' equaliser came from Colin Calderwood, alone in the box to redirect a shot from Allan Nielsen. Towards the end David Ginola had a chance to win the game for Spurs but shot at the goalkeeper, although the point Spurs gained was enough to maintain the two point advantage they held over Barnsley with only three games left to play.

APRIL 19TH

1874   John Eggett born in Wisbech, Norfolk. Having failed to make the grade at both Woolwich Arsenal and West Ham, John was signed by Spurs in May 1904 and made his debut in goal in October the same year. He was almost ever present thereafter until injury forced the club to sign Matt Reilly as replacement. When John recovered he was unable to reclaim the number one jersey and was released in April 1907, joining Croydon Common. He died in Doncaster in 1943.

1897	Wellingborough	H	United League	1-1
1913	Woolwich Arsenal	H	First Division	1-1
1919	Fulham	N	Victory Cup Semi-Final	0-2
1924	Everton	A	First Division	2-4
1930	Charlton Athletic	H	Second Division	3-0
1935	Blackburn Rovers	H	First Division	1-0
1941	Reading	A	London War Cup Section B	2-2
1946	Nottingham Forest	H	Football League South	3-2
1947	Millwall	H	Second Division	2-1
1952	Liverpool	A	First Division	1-1
1954	Preston North End	H	First Division	2-6
1957	Charlton Athletic	A	First Division	1-1
1958	Leicester City	A	First Division	3-1
1965	Blackburn Rovers	A	First Division	1-3
1969	West Ham United	H	First Division	1-0
1972	AC Milan	A	UEFA Cup Semi-Final 2nd Leg	1-1

Spurs made it to the second European final in their history with one of their most accomplished and assured performances. Once again Alan Mullery led by example, just as he had done in the first leg. Buoyed by his recall to the England squad (less than three weeks previously he was helping Fulham in a Second Division relegation battle with Orient – has there ever been such a remarkable elevation for a player?) it was he who scored the goal that ensured Spurs' place in the UEFA Cup final. Bill Nicholson had demanded and prayed his men would score an early goal, one which would silence the crowd and unsettle the opposition; his prayers were answered in the seventh minute. Martin Chivers had a shot blocked, the ball found its way to Steve Perryman, the goalscoring hero of the first leg and he in turn found his captain 20 yards from goal. Alan Mullery made up his mind to shoot and the ball was quickly curving its way into the top corner of the net. That goal was worth at least double in psychological terms, for its cancelled Milan's goal scored at White Hart Lane and meant the Italians needed to score twice to force extra time, three times to win the tie. And Spurs were in no mood to let them accomplish either. Although Mike England headed against his own bar, Spurs contained Milan so effectively that the only clear shot at goal Milan were given came from the penalty spot. And even the awarding of the penalty was a harsh decision; Phil Beal making a clean tackle but then seeing Bignon dive over his feet. The crowd pressurised the referee into making the award, which Rivera converted. There were 20 minutes left, but Spurs held on and put themselves into the final, where they would face Wolves in a two-legged affair.

1975	Chelsea	H	First Division	2-0
1976	Coventry City	H	First Division	4-1
1980	Everton	H	First Division	3-0
1983	Bristol Rovers	A	Friendly	3-2

This match was a centenary celebration for Rovers, with Spurs' goals being scored by Gary O'Reilly, Steve Perryman and Garth Crooks.

| 1986 | Manchester United | H | First Division | 0-0 |
| 1997 | Aston Villa | A | FA Premier League | 1-1 |

APRIL 20TH

1886   The club held its first annual dinner, at the Milford Tavern in Park Lane (the Tottenham variety, not the West End!) with 40 members and friends in attendance. The evening was chaired by club president John Ripsher, with J H Thompson the vice-chair. Aside from the singing of many songs (led by a Mr F.C. Hobbs) loyal toasts were proposed to the armed forces, the president of the club, the vice-presidents and the visitors. The final toast of the evening was given to Mr Reeves, the host of the Milford Tavern, who was informed by John Ripsher that though this was the first annual dinner of the club, it would not be the last.

1897	Blackburn Rovers	H	Friendly	1-2
1901	Sheffield United	Crystal Palace		
			FA Cup Final	2-2

When Spurs lined up at 3.30 p.m. for the kick-off at Crystal Palace, the FA Cup was not yet 30 years old and the Tottenham club not yet 20. Since professionalism was legalised, no amateur club had won the FA Cup. Since the formation of the Football League, no non-League side had won the FA Cup. Although the FA Cup final was invariably played in London (with three exceptions; the 1886 replay, 1893 and 1894), no London-based club had won the FA Cup since 1882, the very year of Spurs' formation. So the Spurs side that lined up at Crystal Palace carried with them more than just the hopes of the Tottenham district; the whole of London, if not a goodly proportion of the south, were willing them to victory. They turned out in force to see them attempt it too; a world record crowd of 114,815 had converged on the Crystal Palace. So great was the attendance the Spurs team had difficulty entering the ground; they could not get anywhere near the player's gate, so director Ralph Bullock took them round to the official entrance. Here they were told they did not have the right tickets and so could not enter, although Bullock managed to convince the gateman that without the team there would be no match, world record crowd or not! Spurs made it out on to the pitch and lined up against Sheffield United. Although United had struggled in the First Division during the season (they finished 14th out of 18 clubs) they had a good pedigree and a good team and were favourites to win the cup – they had been League champions in 1898, won the FA Cup the following year and in their line-up could boast the likes of William 'Fatty' Foulke, who filled the goal (in every sense!), Tom Morren, Ernest 'Nudger' Needham and Fred Priest. By comparison, only Sandy Brown of the Spurs team had any kind of reputation and that was based purely on his cup exploits that season. The game kicked off and not for the first time it was the opposition that settled first and took the lead; Priest firing home past Clawley from 20 yards. Within 13 minutes Spurs were level, Brown heading home a cross from Kirwan. It was all-square at half-time. Five minutes after the restart came the third goal of the game – Jones began the move and pushed the ball forward to Kirwan who in turn slipped it inside to Brown. As Brown moved upfield he was joined by Cameron and the two played a neat interchange to wrong-foot the United defence: Brown was now through with only Foulke to beat. He steadied himself before shooting and in an instant the ball hit the underside of the bar and settled into the net. On the banks of the Crystal Palace pandemonium reigned – hats were thrown into the air, handkerchiefs were waved and the cheering didn't seem as though it would stop. Spurs were ahead and more than holding their own. But if luck had been on their side at Reading, it would now conspire against them at the Palace – a shot from Lipsham was parried none too convincingly by Clawley and ball dropped behind the keeper and was on its way to the goal. Clawley scrambled back at much the same time as Bennett rushed in and got a touch which bounced off Clawley and behind the goal-line. Bennett threw his hands up to appeal for a corner, Clawley his for a goal-kick, but as they turned to the referee in joint protest, Mr A Kingscott was signalling a goal! He refused to consult with his linesman, who was indicating a corner, and so one of the earliest contentious goals had been awarded. The incident knocked Spurs for six, and the remaining minutes were played out in an air of unreality. United might have won the game, or rather Spurs might have lost it, but at 5.12 p.m., with there being no provision for extra time, the final whistle was blown. The players shook hands and trooped off to the dressing-rooms, the United and Spurs' directors made for the pavilion where an FA Council meeting was to decide the venue for the replay. It had been originally decided to host the replay at Goodison Park (where the 1894 final had been played) but the council meeting read out a letter of protest from Liverpool FC, who were due to meet Nottingham Forest at Anfield Road on the same day, stating that their 'gate' would be adversely affected by the replay. It was therefore decided that the replay would take place one week hence at Burnden Park, the home of Bolton Wanderers FC.

1904	Plymouth Argyle	A	Western League	0-0
1907	Northampton Town	A	Southern League	0-2
1908	Plymouth Argyle	A	Southern League	0-1
1910	Bury	A	First Division	1-3
1912	Bolton Wanderers	H	First Division	1-0
1918	Chelsea	H-Highbury		
			London Combination Subsidiary	0-1

1928   Johnny Gavin born in Limerick, Eire. After impressing for Limerick Johnny was signed by Norwich City in 1948 and went to make over 200 appearances for the Carrow Road club before switching to Spurs in 1954. An Eire international by the time he arrived at Spurs he went on to win two further caps whilst with the club. A little over a year after arriving at Spurs Johnny was on his way back to Norwich, for when Spurs wanted to sign Maurice Norman from the Canaries, Norwich would only do business if Johnny Gavin was included as part of the deal. After more than 100 appearances for Norwich he moved on to Crystal Palace and finished his career with Cambridge City.

1929	Chelsea	H	Second Division	4-1
1935	Stoke City	H	First Division	1-4
1936	Burnley	A	Second Division	0-0
1940	Crystal Palace	A	League Cup 1st Round 1st Leg	1-4
1946	Newport County	A	Football League South	4-1
1953	Reading	A	Friendly	4-0

This was a testimonial for Alan Wicks and Spurs' goals were scored by Len Duquemin (two), Eddie Baily and Sid McClellan.

1957	Cardiff City	A	First Division	3-0
1962	Blackburn Rovers	H	First Division	4-1

Spurs' third goal was scored by Jimmy Greaves, the ninth consecutive League match he had scored in and a new Spurs record. The run had begun with the match against Bolton on February 24th. Although Jimmy failed to score in the next match, at home to West Bromwich Albion, he scored in each of the last three games of the season and the opening game of the next!

1963	Everton	A	First Division	0-1
1968	Coventry City	H	First Division	4-2
1974	Stoke City	A	First Division	0-1
1977	Aston Villa	A	First Division	1-2
1981	Southampton	A	First Division	1-1
1985	Ipswich Town	H	First Division	2-3
1987	West Ham United	A	First Division	1-2
1991	Sheffield United	A	First Division	2-2
1992	Oldham Athletic	A	First Division	0-1
1993	Middlesbrough	A	FA Premier League	0-3

APRIL 21ST

1894	Crouch End	A	Friendly	2-2
1902	West Ham United	H	London League	2-2
1905	Southampton	H	Southern League	1-2
1906	Plymouth Argyle	H	Southern League	0-1
1916	Crystal Palace	H	London Combination [2nd competition]	3-1
1917	Southampton	H-Homerton		
			London Combination	4-0
1919	Millwall	A	London Combination	4-2
1923	Birmingham	H	First Division	2-0
1924	Manchester City	H	First Division	4-1
1928	Bury	H	First Division	1-4
1930	West Bromwich Albion	A	Second Division	3-4
1934	Birmingham City	A	First Division	0-2
1937	Nottingham Forest	A	Second Division	0-3
1945	Clapton Orient	H	Football League South	4-0
1951	Middlesbrough	A	First Division	1-1
1956	Huddersfield Town	H	First Division	1-2
1962	West Bromwich Albion	H	First Division	1-2
1964	Burnley	A	First Division	2-7
1973	Leicester City	H	First Division	1-1
1976	North Herts XI	Stevenage	Friendly	1-2

This match was a testimonial for Roy Dingwall with Spurs' goal being scored by Gerry Armstrong.

1979	Manchester United	H	First Division	1-1
1982	Barcelona	A	European Cup-Winners' Cup Semi-Final 2nd Leg	0-1

A little over a month previously, Spurs were chasing a unique and historic grand slam of trophies – the League title, the League Cup, FA Cup and European Cup-Winners' Cup. The League Cup was the first to go by the wayside, with Spurs beaten by Liverpool in the final. Then the League slipped by, Spurs having too many games to cram into too little time to mount an effective and sustained challenge. Tonight the European Cup-Winners' Cup disappeared. Barcelona began this second leg tie in much the same manner they had performed throughout the first, kicking anything and anybody in a white shirt. Steve Perryman, Glenn Hoddle and Garth Crooks were all chopped down the first time they touched the ball. Midway through the first half the lights cut out around half the stadium, plunging much of the pitch into darkness, although there was precious little action to witness when they had been on full power. After a five minute delay the game resumed in much the same manner as previously. The only goal of the game came in the second half, Danish international Allan Simonsen capitalising on Paul Price's failure to control the ball and nipping in to poke the ball past Ray Clemence. Spurs pushed forward in search of the equaliser, but the strain of a long and exhausting season took its toll and Spurs never quite worked out how to get round or through the Barcelona defence. With the final of the European Cup-Winners' Cup being played in Barcelona's Nou Camp stadium it would take a very brave or foolish man to bet against them lifting the trophy against Standard Liege. For Spurs, their chance at the Cup-Winners' Cup again would come if they managed to beat QPR.

1984	Arsenal	A	First Division	2-3
1990	Manchester United	H	First Division	2-1

APRIL 22ND

1893	London Welsh	H	Friendly	4-1
1896	Gravesend	A	Friendly	1-1
1897	Everton	H	Friendly	2-1
1899	Millwall Athletic	H	Southern League	3-1
1901	Bristol Rovers	A	Western League	0-4
1903	Swindon Town	A	Southern League	0-2
1905	Southampton	A	Western League	0-1
1907	Millwall	A	Western League	0-0
1911	Blackburn Rovers	A	First Division	0-3
1916	Crystal Palace	A	London Combination [2nd competition]	0-4
1922	Arsenal	A	First Division	0-1
1924	West Ham United	H	First Division	0-1
1933	Fulham	H	Second Division	0-0
1939	Bury	H	Second Division	4-3
1944	Arsenal	A	Football League South	3-3
1946	Nottingham Forest	A	Football League South	2-0
1950	Grimsby Town	H	Second Division	1-2

Spurs were so far ahead of the pack in the Second Division that the title had been won with three games still to play and with the last two games both lost. The Football League chose this occasion on which to present the cup and medals for winning the Second Division title, with League president Mr Arthur Drewry (coincidentally connected with Grimsby) handing over the silverware to Spurs captain Ronnie Burgess. That was all Grimsby handed out this afternoon, for they were to win and stretch Spurs' number of consecutive losses to three.

1957	Charlton Athletic	H	First Division	6-2
1961	Burnley	A	First Division	2-4
1967	Southampton	A	First Division	1-0
1969	Southampton	H	First Division	2-1
1972	Southampton	A	First Division	0-0
1978	Sunderland	H	Second Division	2-3

As the season entered the home stretch, the three promotion places were between four teams: Bolton, Southampton, Spurs and Brighton. Spurs' defeat at Brighton the previous week had closed the gap at the top and put Spurs most at risk of missing out, for of their last eight games in the season they won only two, and three defeats meant they only managed to claim the third spot on goal difference. This particular defeat was one they could ill afford to suffer, but a nervous performance allowed Sunderland, in the top half of the table but well behind the leading pack, to return home with both points.

1986	Chelmsford City	A	Friendly	8-2

This match was a testimonial for Colin Johnson with Spurs' goals being scored by Mark Falco (five), Clive Allen (two) and John Chiedozie.

1987	Wimbledon	A	First Division	2-2
1989	Everton	H	First Division	2-1

APRIL 23RD

1887	Enfield Lock	H	Friendly	7-1
1898	Wellingborough	A	United League	2-2
1902	Woolwich Arsenal	A	Southern Charity Cup Semi-Final	0-0

Spurs had been due to play West Bromwich Albion in the quarter-final of the competition but their opponents had failed to appear, giving Spurs a walkover into the semi-final where they faced Woolwich Arsenal. Although Spurs beat Arsenal after a replay, the final was held over to the next season.

1904	Southampton	A	Western League	0-1
1910	Bolton Wanderers	A	First Division	2-0
1921	Wolverhampton Wanderers	Stamford Bridge		
			FA Cup Final	1-0

According to legend, Spurs manager Peter McWilliam allowed himself a wry smile when he woke up this morning and peered out his window – a light drizzle was falling which would make the pitch ideal for his team of favourites in the cup final against Wolves. The first of the crowd had arrived at Stamford Bridge (Crystal Palace, the final venue from 1895 until 1914, was requisitioned by the Army during the war and had not been restored to its former glory, with Stamford Bridge being judged the only suitable venue within the capital) at 2.00am; the gates opened at 10.30am to relieve the crush and closed again, with 72,805 spectators inside, at 2.55pm (although one newspaper report suggested that the ground had been fuller on previous occasions). The majority of the crowd, who paid contemporary record receipts of £13,414 4s 7d, were following Spurs, although no doubt their Second Division opponents were favoured by the neutrals. Just as the gates were closed King George V, accompanied by the Duke of York (and future King George VI), walked across the touch-line to greet the teams. And then a violent thunderstorm swept across the ground, turning the pitch into little more than a mudheap. No doubt the smile was wiped from Peter McWilliam's face, for no team could hope to play stylish football on this surface, and so it proved. Both Spurs and Wolves struggled to overcome the treacherous surface and attempt to carry the ball, only to find it had held in the mud. The first half contained little football of any note; it was more a lottery as the players tried to keep their footing. In all probability the second half might have ended much the same way and the two clubs have to try again on another day but for one piece of audacity by Jimmy Dimmock. He collected the ball on the left-wing from Bert Bliss and moved upfield in much the same manner as the previous 54 minutes. He drew Gregory, tricked and rounded him and continued his advance on the Wolverhampton goal. Another defender, Woodward, moved out to counter the threat, although there were plenty of Dimmock's colleagues in support and calling for the ball. Dimmock attempted to play the ball through the legs of his adversary; Woodward was quick enough to close his legs and see the ball strike his thigh, but not quick enough to stop Dimmock retrieving the ball from the mud and set off towards goal. He cut in and from 15 yards shot left-footed towards the far corner of the net. Just in front of the diving George in the Wolves goal the ball skidded off a greasy patch and passed underneath the outstretched hands to slip just inside the far post. Spurs were ahead and were troubled but once during the remaining 35 minutes or so; Brooks had the ball only ten yards from goal, was unmarked but appeared to lose concentration for the briefest of moments, allowing Charles Walters to fling himself in front of the ball just as Brooks shot. Minutes later the final whistle blew and Spurs had won the cup for a second time. Captain Arthur Grimsdell collected the trophy from the King, posed for one or two photographs outside the ground and then caught a train to his home in Watford. The rest of his team-mates were driven by open charabanc back to Tottenham, with trainer Billy Minter clutching the famous trophy, adorned by the ribbons first placed on the FA Cup in 1901. It was not a great victory; the weather had ensured that, but it did mean that Spurs were still the only southern club to have lifted the FA Cup since the amateur's held sway in the 1870s and early 1880s.

1927	Leeds United	H	First Division	4-1
1932	Leeds United	H	Second Division	3-1
1938	Southampton	H	Second Division	5-0
1949	Nottingham Forest	A	Second Division	2-2
1951	Hibernian	A	Friendly	0-0
1952	Hibernian	H	Friendly	1-2
1955	Leicester City	A	First Division	0-2
1956	Cardiff City	A	First Division	0-0
1960	Wolverhampton Wanderers	A	First Division	3-1

By the time Spurs arrived at Molineux for the penultimate game of the season, their chances of winning the League had virtually gone. From being firmly in the driving seat just before Easter they had taken a back seat – two home defeats had seen to that. The momentum therefore passed to Wolves – the reigning League champions, on the verge of lifting the title for the third successive season and, more importantly, within sight of the double. At 3 o'clock they stood at the top of the table, three points clear of Spurs and four points ahead of Burnley. If they beat Spurs, then only Chelsea stood between them and history. They might not have to go that far, for if they beat Spurs and Burnley got anything less than maximum points from their remaining games then the title would remain at Molineux. Under such circumstances, this match is perhaps one of the most vital Spurs have ever played, outside cup finals and their own title-winning efforts. Perhaps Spurs realised that the title had gone and thus were a far more relaxed outfit than that which had been beaten twice inside 48 hours and relinquished their chances. Danny Blanchflower held his team talk out on the pitch and Spurs put in one of their finest performances, taking the lead within two minutes through Bobby Smith. Although Peter Broadbent equalised, Spurs were in the mood to deny Wolves their prize; goals from Dave Mackay and Cliff Jones saw to that. The aftermath to this particular match is both interesting and worth recording – Wolves won their final match at Stamford Bridge, beating Chelsea 5-1. But, just as expectedly, Burnley won their final games as well, clinching the title with a 2-1 win at Manchester City – it was the first time they had headed the League all season! Wolves never quite recovered from being pipped at the post, for although they won the FA Cup that season (rather easily – 3-0 against Blackburn) they have won neither League nor cup since. Wolves therefore missed out on performing the first double since 1897 – 12 months later the feat was to be achieved, but by Spurs.

1962	Blackburn Rovers	A	First Division	1-0
1966	Stoke City	A	First Division	1-0
1977	Stoke City	A	First Division	0-0
1980	Wolverhampton Wanderers	H	First Division	2-2
1983	West Bromwich Albion	A	First Division	1-0
1988	Liverpool	A	First Division	0-1
1990	Valerengens IF	Oslo	Friendly	1-1
1993	Real Zaragoza	A	Friendly	0-2
1994	Southampton	H	FA Premier League	3-0

APRIL 24TH

1897	Loughborough	A	United League	2-3
1899	Wellingborough	H	United League	5-2
1900	Woolwich Arsenal	A	Southern District Combination	1-2

Although Arsenal had yet to supplant themselves in Highbury there was still an intense rivalry between the two clubs, exemplified by this clash. One week ago Spurs beat Arsenal 4-2 at home; at Plumstead Arsenal went all out for revenge. A bad-tempered match was abandoned after 75 minutes owing to bad language with the result allowed to stand 2-1 in Arsenal's favour.

1905	Portsmouth	A	Southern League	2-3
1909	Bradford Park Avenue	A	Second Division	3-0
1915	Sunderland	A	First Division	0-5

Spurs began their First Division career with a match at Roker Park with Sunderland; they ended their first sojourn in the top flight at the same venue. A 5-0 win for Sunderland ensured Spurs finished bottom of the First Division, one point behind Chelsea and two behind Manchester United, although Manchester United's position was achieved by virtue of a fixed match. This was also the last League match before football effectively shut down for the duration of the First World War; both Spurs' position and the Manchester United débâcle were to become prominent when the Football League resumed in 1919.

| 1920 | Grimsby Town | A | Second Division | 0-2 |

This was the only occasion all season Spurs failed to score in an away League match, and their 21 games produced a record of 13 wins, four draws and four defeats.

1926	Burnley	H	First Division	0-2
1933	Burnley	A	Second Division	1-1
1937	Fulham	H	Second Division	1-1
1940	Arsenal	A (but played at WHL)	Football League South Group C	4-2
1948	Newcastle United	H	Second Division	1-1
1950	Chelmsford City	A	Friendly	4-1

This was a testimonial for Les Pyle and Spurs' goals were scored by Les Bennett (three) and Len Duquemin.

1954	Wolverhampton Wanderers	A	First Division	0-2
1958	Canto Do Rio	H	Friendly	4-1
1963	OFK Belgrade	A	European Cup-Winners' Cup Semi-Final 1st Leg	2-1

Jimmy Greaves became the first Spurs player to be sent off in over 39 years when he was dismissed in the 55th minute. He was generally considered unlucky, for if anyone should have been sent off it was perhaps his partner up front Bobby Smith. On the 25th minute Smith was bundled over and a free-kick awarded. As Spurs prepared to take the kick the Belgrade right half was observed writhing on the ground, the cue for a posse of players to surround Bobby Smith, pushing and jostling him until the referee raced over to calm matters down. Although the referee consulted with his linesman, nothing untoward had been observed and no further action was taken. When the free-kick was finally allowed to proceed, Tony Marchi flicked the ball forward to Bobby Smith, who in turn tapped it on for John White to volley home for the first goal. Belgrade equalised nine minutes before the interval, Popov firing home a penalty. There had been speculation that Spurs might try to defend this first leg tie – nothing could have been further from the truth, especially in the second half. It was after a Spurs attack had broken down that the Jimmy Greaves incident occurred; with most eyes following the ball upfield Greaves and Krivokuca squared up to each other, the referee adjudging Greaves guilty of retaliation and sending him off. Rather than buckle under Belgrade assault after losing Greaves and got ample revenge when Terry Dyson shot home the winner 20 minutes from time. Spurs were cheered by a 60,000 partisan crowd as they left the field; Belgrade received little more than hoots of derision. After the match Jimmy Greaves explained, 'The back had been kicking me all across the park and as he was running away after the last kick, I turned and clipped him. I was wrong, but it was in the heat of the moment.' As Greaves had made his long walk back to the dressing-room the first man to offer a consoling word had been Cecil Poynton, whose comforting 'Don't let it worry you, Jim' was not only well intentioned, for Cecil, sitting tonight on the trainers bench had been the last Spurs player to receive his marching orders 39 years previously!

| 1965 | Leicester City | H | First Division | 6-2 |

The last occasion on which Spurs had gone through an entire season unbeaten at home was confirmed with this 6-2 win over Leicester City. Of the 21 League matches played at White Hart Lane this season, 18 were won and three were drawn, the best record in the division. By comparison, Spurs had the worst away record in the division; only one win and four draws being the reason why Spurs could finish no higher than sixth in the First Division at the end of the season. Spurs had twice previously gone through an entire season without losing at home; 1919-20 and 1932-33.

| 1971 | Crystal Palace | H | First Division | 2-0 |
| 1974 | 1.FC Lokomotiv Leipzig | H | UEFA Cup Semi-Final 2nd Leg | 2-0 |

The outcome was never seriously in doubt; a 2-1 win in Leipzig had all but ensured Spurs would progress to their second European final in three seasons and their third in all, but there was still plenty play for. Spurs had not lost any of the nine previous matches played in the competition this season, scoring 27 goals and conceding only seven. That parity needed to be maintained. And so it was, Spurs scoring two goals without a German reply to win the tie 4-1 on aggregate. Both goals came in the second half, the first through Chris McGrath, restored after missing the first leg through injury, in the 55th minute. Martin Chivers set the seal on another 'glory-glory night' with a low left foot shot four minutes from the end. Once again Spurs had raised their game, much as they had throughout the European campaign, to a level definitely not attainable during ordinary League matches. Victory over Lokomotiv therefore set Spurs up for a two-legged final against Feyenoord. Spurs had beaten Feyenoord on their way to the European Cup semi-finals in 1961 – this Feyenoord side would be a different type of animal altogether.

| 1976 | Newcastle United | H | First Division | 0-3 |
| 1979 | Queens Park Rangers | A | Friendly | 3-1 |

This match was a testimonial for Ian Gillard and Spurs' goals were scored by Ricky Villa, who grabbed a hat-trick.

1982	Notts County	H	First Division	3-1
1991	Everton	H	First Division	3-3
1997	Middlesbrough	H	FA Premier League	1-0

APRIL 25TH

1895	London Caledonians	H	Friendly	2-0
1896	Wellingborough	H	Friendly	3-0
1898	Aston Villa	H	Friendly	2-3
1901	Luton Town	H	Southern League	3-2
1903	Kettering Town	A	Southern League	0-1
1904	Northampton Town	A	Southern League	1-0
1906	Southampton	A	Western League	0-1
1914	Sheffield Wednesday	A	First Division	0-2
1921	Huddersfield Town	A	First Division	0-2
1925	Nottingham Forest	A	First Division	0-1
1931	Barnsley	H	Second Division	4-2

Ted Harper scored twice to take his tally for the season to 36, a new Spurs record. Ted had been injured in the League clash at Swansea in March and was forced to miss six matches, and finished the season having appeared in only 30 games. His record, which would undoubtedly have been higher had he not missed 12 games, stood for 32 years until Jimmy Greaves broke it in 1962-63.

1936	Doncaster Rovers	H	Second Division	3-1
1942	Brentford	H	London War League	2-1
1949	Hibernian	H	Friendly	2-5
1953	Wolverhampton Wanderers	H	First Division	3-2
1959	Preston North End	A	First Division	2-2
1964	Leicester City	A	First Division	1-0
1965	Alistair Dick born in Stirling. Although Ally later became the youngest player to have played for Spurs in the Football League when making his debut in 1982 at the age of 16 years and 301 days, he never fulfilled his potential and was allowed to leave in 1986, signing with Ajax of Amsterdam. After trials and brief spells with Derby, Southampton, Wimbledon and Brighton, he returned to Ajax in 1990. He later had a trial with Sheffield Wednesday.

| 1966 | West Ham United | A | First Division | 0-2 |
| 1973 | Liverpool | H | UEFA Cup Semi-Final 2nd Leg | 2-1 |

Bill Nicholson's words after the first leg at Anfield came back to haunt him tonight. For although

Spurs won, thanks to two goals from Martin Peters in a marvellous match that was a credit to English football, Liverpool's goal was enough to ensure they progressed to the final by virtue of the away goal counting double. And doubles were the order of the day at Anfield – this win kept them on target for placing the UEFA Cup alongside the League championship trophy in the Anfield boardroom. Spurs really needed to cancel out Liverpool's 1-0 lead from the first leg relatively early to have a realistic chance of keeping their hold on the UEFA Cup, for then Liverpool would have been forced out into the open themselves. As it was, Spurs did not find a way through until just after the half-time break, Alan Gilzean flicking on a Martin Chivers long throw and Martin Peters coming stealing in to head home from close range. Spurs continued to press thereafter for a second goal, leaving gaps of their own in defence. Mike England was caught upfield when an Emlyn Hughes' clearance sailed over his head. Kevin Keegan latched on to the ball and sent a low cross into the goalmouth where Steve Heighway was waiting to side foot home. That left Spurs once again chasing two goals to win; they managed only one, again through Martin Peters, in the 71st minute. Spurs could have little argument over the manner of their exit, especially as they themselves had progressed from the previous round by virtue of a similar set of results. And so it proved; Spurs fans had cheered both teams on to the pitch before the start and cheered Liverpool off at the end. The stakes might have been high, but so was the sportsmanship.

| 1981 | Liverpool | H | First Division | 1-1 |
| 1984 | Hajduk Split | H | UEFA Cup Semi-Final 2nd Leg | 1-0 |

Ever since Keith Burkinshaw announced his intention to retire as Spurs manager at the end of the season, the players had been driven by the desire to give the departing manager the best possible leaving present – the UEFA Cup. This single goal victory over Split ensured they would at least contest the final against Anderlecht. The only goal again came as a result of a needless handball offence committed by Split. This time the culprit was Nikica Cukrov, yet on this occasion the offence took place outside the penalty area. The defensive wall appeared to have covered all the angles, blocked all of the openings for a shot, but Micky Hazard managed to bend the ball around the wall and inside the post after only six minutes. In the celebrations that immediately followed he lost one of his contact lenses and had to leave the field for a few minutes to have a replacement installed. With Spurs now ahead and through if the score remained the same, by virtue of the away goal, Split were forced to abandon any plans they had of sitting back on their lead and took the game to Spurs. To their credit, this they did, forcing one of the most nail-biting moments in White Hart Lane's long and colourful history. A Split free-kick was lost in flight by goalkeeper Tony Parks; when the ball arrived in front of him he could not hold it, parrying it instead on to the crossbar. He groped at the ball as it ran along the bar for what seemed like eternity, groped again as it fell to the floor and finally managed to dive on the ball just before an attacker could benefit. Nothing Spurs produced quite matched that moment for drama, but the general consensus was that if Spurs could survive a scare like that they could survive anything. And so it proved. Going through on away goals may not be the ideal way of progressing, but just try telling that to the Spurs players at the final whistle.

1987	Oxford United	H	First Division	3-1
1992	Everton	H	First Division	3-3
1998	Newcastle United	H	FA Premier League	2-0

APRIL 26TH

1897	London Caledonians	A	Friendly	1-1
1899	Millwall Athletic	H	United League	1-3
1900	Millwall Athletic	A	Southern District Combination	0-0

With Spurs having already won the Southern League there was a strong possibility the double might be achieved, for Spurs went into this game with a faint hope of catching League leaders Millwall in the Southern District Combination, but only if they were to beat them. A 0-0 draw ensured Millwall won the League.

| 1902 | Brentford | H | Southern League | 3-0 |
| 1912 | | | | |

Jimmy McCormick born in Rotherham. Signed by Spurs in March 1933 from Chesterfield after injuries had robbed Spurs of Taffy O'Callaghan and Les Howe, Jimmy held his place for the rest of the season and played an integral part in the side that finished the following year third in the First Division. An injury sustained during the 1937-38 season effectively ended his playing career at Spurs, although he remained with the club until November 1945 when he signed for Fulham. He later played for Lincoln City, and Crystal Palace before turning to coaching and was manager of York City between May 1953 and September 1954. He was killed following a road accident in Spain on 3rd January 1968.

| 1913 | Bradford City | A | First Division | 1-3 |
| 1920 | Birmingham | H | Second Division | 0-0 |

This was the only occasion all season Spurs failed to find the net during a home game, with their 21 games having produced a record of 19 wins and two draws and 60 goals scored and 11 conceded. Spurs also failed to score in only one away; two days previously at Grimsby.

1924	Burnley	A	First Division	2-2
1930	Hull City	A	Second Division	0-2
1941	Aldershot	A	Football League South	3-2

1946   Ralph Coates born in Hetton-le-Hole, County Durham. Having been passed over as a youngster Ralph took a job at the Eppleton Colliery and was subsequently spotted by Burnley whilst playing for the Colliery Welfare side. Signed as an amateur in October 1961 he was elevated to the professional ranks in June 1963, making his debut in December 1964. By this time Burnley's great side of the late 1950s and early 1960s had all but broken up, and Ralph's spell at Turf Moor was one of almost constant battling against relegation. A £190,000 move to Spurs followed in May 1971, and he was an important member of the team that won the UEFA Cup at the end of his first season at White Hart Lane. Although he was on the bench for the following season's League Cup final against Norwich, an injury to John Pratt gave Ralph an early opportunity to make a name for himself, and he scored the only goal of the game. Ralph remained with Spurs until 1978 when he went to play in Australia, later returning to England and signing with Leyton Orient. After finishing his playing career Ralph became the manager of a leisure complex.

1947	Bradford Park Avenue	A	Second Division	1-2
1952	Blackpool	H	First Division	2-0
1958	Blackpool	H	First Division	2-1
1961	Nottingham Forest	H	First Division	1-0

1970   Dean Austin born in Hemel Hempstead, London. He began his career with non-League St Albans City before signing with Southend United in 1990 for a fee of £12,000. Just over two years later he joined Spurs for £375,000, linking up again with former team-mate Justin Edinburgh. Heavy competition for places and a number of injuries made it difficult for him to break into the first team with any regularity and he joined Crystal Palace on a free transfer in 1998.

1975	Arsenal	A	First Division	0-1
1978	Hull City	H	Second Division	1-0
1980	Aston Villa	A	First Division	0-1
1986	Queens Park Rangers	A	First Division	5-2
1988	Crystal Palace	A	Friendly	3-3

This match was a testimonial for Jim Cannon and Spurs' goals were scored by Steve Hodge, Paul Walsh and Nico Claesen.

APRIL 27TH

1897	Brimsdown	A	Friendly	2-0
1901	Gravesend	H	Southern League	5-0

The Southern League refused to allow Spurs to postpone this match (or any of the other two games played the same week), even though the club were playing in the FA Cup final on the same day! Not surprisingly, Spurs fielded a reserve 11 for this fixture (as they did in the other two games against Portsmouth and Luton), although none of the 5,000 crowd were much concerned with activities on the pitch at White Hart Lane; their thoughts were on the progress at Burnden Park.

1901   Sheffield United   Burnden Park
                                     FA Cup Final Replay   3-1

Bolton was not the ideal choice for hosting the FA Cup final replay. The railway station was undergoing extensive alterations at the time and would therefore not be able to cope with the anticipated heavy volume of passengers that a cup final brings. Perhaps that is why the Lancashire and Yorkshire Railway decided not to offer cheap-day return tickets – the end result was that from playing in front of a world record crowd one week ago, Spurs played the replay in front of the lowest cup final crowd since 1890, and the lowest crowd this century. Tales have been told of the Bolton pie salesmen losing a fortune on the game, having to throw away countless wares because the expected exodus from London and Sheffield never materialised. The Bolton club did their best, decorating the stands with banners and bunting, but only 20,470 paid admission on the gate (although Bolton season-ticket holders probably pushed the final figure to up around the 30,000 mark). On a cold, windy and showery day, Spurs again found themselves a goal behind, Fred Priest scoring five minutes before the interval (and therefore becoming the first man to score as many as two goals in a cup final and still finish on the losing side, a record that was not equalled until Mick Jones of Leeds United in 1970). But Spurs were not unduly worried, for the goal had come against the run of play. They carried on the second half in much the same fashion and took the game to United, getting their reward in the 55th minute with an equaliser from John Cameron. Still the pressure was applied; Needham miskicked a clearance and Smith was on hand to put Spurs ahead. Seven minutes from the end, after three successive corners, Brown settled the matter with a back-header that won Spurs the cup and Brown a place in history – he had become the first man to score in every round of the competition and, with 15 goals, is still the highest goalscorer in a single season in the FA Cup. Spurs supporters who had made it to Bolton swarmed on to the pitch and rushed to the front of the main stand to see Lord Kinnaird, President of the FA (and captain of the last southern side to lift the trophy) present the cup to Spurs' captain Jack Jones. That was only the start of the celebrations, for on the train journey back to London a Tottenham bricklayer begged club chairman Charles Roberts to allow him to hold the cup for a second and before anyone realised what he was doing he had filled it with champagne! Even Lord Kinnaird, a teetotaller, drank from the cup to toast Spurs' success. The train steamed into South Tottenham at 1.00 a.m. the following morning. A crowd had been waiting for three hours to greet them and as the train came into sight the band played 'See The Conquering Hero Comes'. Two 'broughams' (short closed four-wheeled one-horse or electric carriages) were waiting to take the team back to their headquarters, pulled all the way by the crowd who cheered each and every time Jones held the cup aloft. It was dawn before the crowd dispersed and allowed the players to make their weary way home; each with a medal and for one the added memento of the match ball. It was not Jack Jones who had that honour (it has become cup final tradition that the ball used in the match goes to the winning captain) but John Kirwan, who guarded the ball for the rest of his life more fervently than he ever did his medal!

| 1904 | Bristol Rovers | A | Western League | 4-2 |

Spurs finished the season champions of the Western League, four points ahead of closest rivals Southampton. This was despite a defeat at the hands of Southampton four days previously, for Spurs had already built up a considerable lead in the League and with a record of played 18, won 11, drawn 3 and lost only 2 were unlikely to be troubled at the top of the table.

| 1905 | Reading | | Craven Cottage | |
| | | | Southern Charity Cup Final | 0-0 |

The final was played at Fulham's Craven Cottage ground and although it ended goalless there was no replay held.

1907	Queens Park Rangers	H	Southern League	2-0
1912	Bradford City	A	First Division	0-3
1918	Fulham	A	London Combination Subsidiary	0-3
1921	Everton	A	First Division	0-0
1929	Blackpool	A	Second Division	2-2
1935	Liverpool	H	First Division	5-1
1940	Crystal Palace	H	League Cup 1st Round 2nd Leg	2-1
1945				

Martin Chivers born in Southampton. He was signed by the local club in 1962 and quickly established himself as an exceptional striker, partnering Ron Davies in the side that won promotion to the First Division in 1967. After scoring 97 goals in 175 League appearances for the Saints he was signed by Spurs for £125,000, with Frank Saul making the opposite journey. His Spurs career got off to a blistering start, as he scored on his debut and then grabbed two in the cup tie against Manchester United, but a serious injury sustained in September 1968 ended his season. When he returned he struggled for form and confidence and was dropped, but the subsequent sale of Jimmy Greaves and the arrival of play maker Martin Peters coincided with a return to form, and it was his goals more than anything else that enabled Spurs to win the 1971 League Cup (he scored both goals in the final) and 1972 UEFA Cup (both goals again in the first leg of the final), as well as the 1973 League Cup. After 268 League appearances for Spurs and 118 goals, he was sold to Servette in Switzerland for £80,000, later returning to England and Norwich City and Brighton. He retired from playing in 1982 to run a hotel and restaurant business in Hertfordshire. He won 24 caps for England whilst with Spurs, scoring 13 goals.

1946	Newport County	H	Football League South	1-0
1955	West Bromwich Albion	A	First Division	2-1
1957	Blackpool	H	First Division	2-1
1963	Bolton Wanderers	H	First Division	4-1

Spurs' second goal, scored by Jimmy Greaves, enabled him to draw level with Ted Harper for the record of most goals scored in the League in a single season; 36. Greaves now had four games in which to beat the record.

1965	Anderlecht	A	Friendly	2-4
1968	Newcastle United	A	First Division	3-1
1974	Leicester City	H	First Division	1-0
1976	Toronto Metros-Croatia	Toronto	Friendly	1-0
1985	Chelsea	A	First Division	1-1
1993	Internazionale	H	Fiorucci Cup	0-0
1993	Real Madrid	H	Fiorucci Cup	0-1

The matches against Internazionale and Real Madrid were of 45 minutes duration each, with the two foreign visitors also playing each other in a final game. Spurs lost to Internazionale 6-5 on penalties and therefore finished bottom of the group of three.

| 1996 | Chelsea | H | FA Premier League | 1-1 |

APRIL 28TH

1888   Daniel Tull born in Folkestone. Although Daniel played only ten League games for Spurs, having joined the club from Clapton, he is widely believed to have been the first coloured player to have represented Spurs and is also quite possibly the first coloured man to have played in the Football League. Indeed, he was known by his nickname of 'Darkie' Tull, and after his Spurs career didn't quite work out joined Northampton Town. He was killed in action on 25th March 1918.

1893   Jimmy Banks born in Wigan. Jimmy signed for Spurs in December 1913 but was not able to break into the first team until the outbreak of the First World War, for although he enlisted in the forces he was based in London and therefore available for selection most weeks. Although signed as an inside-forward, his best spell at the club came when he was switched to outside-right, reverting back to his more familiar position at the end of the war. The arrival of Jimmy Seed saw Jimmy Banks relegated to the reserves, but an injury to Fanny Walden meant manager Peter McWilliam tried Banks at outside-right again, with the result Jimmy held his place for the 1921 cup-winning team. He left Spurs for Norwich City in 1923 and finished his playing career with Luton Town, then becoming a coach. He died in London on 25th August 1942.

| 1898 | Woolwich Arsenal | A | Friendly | 0-3 |
| 1900 | New Brompton | A | Southern League | 2-1 |

The final match of Spurs' championship season. Of the 28 matches played (a further three were expunged from the records), Spurs won 20, drew four and lost four, scoring 67 goals and conceding only 26. They finished three points ahead of runners-up Portsmouth.

| 1906 | Woolwich Arsenal | A | Southern Charity Cup Semi-Final Replay | 0-5 |
| 1909 | Derby County | A | Second Division | 1-1 |

Spurs' first ever season in the Football League drew to a close with the club on the verge of promotion to the First Division at the first attempt. There were three clubs battling for two promotion places; West Bromwich Albion, Bolton and Spurs. Purely by coincidence, all three had to play Derby County in the final week of the season! West Bromwich turned up at the Baseball Ground on April 26th with 51 points in the bag and returned with the same number; they were beaten 2-1. This day it was Spurs' turn; a goal by Bobby Steel was enough to give Spurs a point and ensured promotion, but if Bolton failed to win at home on April 30th, then Spurs would go up as champions. As it happened, Bolton won 1-0 and took the title. When the mathematics were finished it revealed how close Spurs had come to missing out; if they had drawn 2-2 at Derby, West Bromwich would have sneaked into second place.

1917	Clapton Orient	A	London Combination	8-0
1923	Huddersfield Town	A	First Division	0-1
1928	Liverpool	A	First Division	0-2
1934	Sheffield Wednesday	H	First Division	4-3
1945	Fulham	A	Football League South	4-2
1951	Sheffield Wednesday	H	First Division	1-0

The previous season it was only Spurs' unassailable lead in the Second Division that had carried them through April, a month in which they won only two out of seven games. There were those who, as this season had progressed, were sure that Spurs would falter in April, if they made it that far. Spurs had stuck resolutely to their task through the late summer, autumn and winter. It was as spring approached that the nerves began to get tight – would history repeat itself? For whilst Spurs could afford to let slip a dozen or so points in the run-in to the Second Division title, even a couple of points here and there in the First Division could see Manchester United, runners-up on three occasions since League football resumed four seasons ago, go one better and claim the title. Spurs had lost against Manchester United on January 13th and then embarked on a run that brought 20 points out of a possible 28. April had not seen them collapse – true, they had lost at home to Huddersfield, but victory over Newcastle and a point gained against another North East club, Middlesbrough, had taken Spurs to the very brink – victory over Sheffield Wednesday today and Manchester United could not catch them; they would be confirmed as champions. Given then the historic nature of the match it was surprising that only 46,645 came to see the last hurdle. Their opponents had accompanied them at the end of the previous season out of the Second Division; they were due an immediate return. Despite this Wednesday were never going to make things easy for Spurs, especially after Len Duquemin had put Spurs ahead. Whilst Wednesday were never likely to equalise or deny Spurs their first title, there were anxious glances at watches throughout the second half until the referee called a halt to proceedings. Spurs were champions! At the same time, they equalled a feat only previously accomplished by Liverpool and Everton – champions of the Second Division and First Division in

Cigarette cards depicting the 1901 FA Cup success: (from top) player-manager John Cameron, a team photograph and the cup. The cup is shown with the ribbons attached, the first time a club had done this

TOP: A handbill advertising the 1901 FA Cup final between Spurs and Sheffield United at Crystal Palace which was drawn 2–2, Spurs winning the replay 3–1 at Burnden Park, Bolton
BOTTOM: Cigarette cards from the late 1920s depicting Spurs' FA Cup-winning sides of 1901 and 1921

TOP: A caricature of Danny Blanchflower, captain of the 1961
double-winning side
BOTTOM: A cheque from 1923, made payable to the then
secretary Arthur Turner

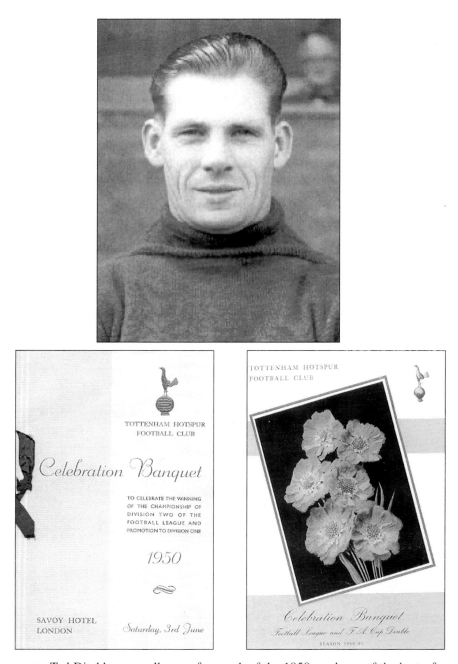

TOP: Ted Ditchburn, goalkeeper for much of the 1950s and one of the best of all time in that position
BOTTOM LEFT: The celebration banquet for the 1950 Second Division championship at the Savoy Hotel
BOTTOM RIGHT: The menu from the 1961 celebration banquet at the Savoy Hotel

CLOCKWISE FROM TOP LEFT: Picture cards of Dave Mackay and Bobby Smith,
two key players from the 1961 double-winning side, and Jimmy Greaves,
Spurs' record goalscorer with 220 League goals between 1961 and 1970

THE FOOTBALL ASSOCIATION CHALLENGE CUP COMPETITION

FINAL TIE

LEICESTER CITY

v

TOTTENHAM HOTSPUR

SATURDAY, MAY 6th, 1961   KICK-OFF 3 p.m.

EMPIRE STADIUM

WEMBLEY

OFFICIAL PROGRAMME - ONE SHILLING

TOTTENHAM HOTSPUR
FOOTBALL AND ATHLETIC
COMPANY LIMITED

SATURDAY, APRIL 29th, 1961   PRICE TWOPENCE

A Message from the Chairman

My co-Directors join me to-day, at the end of this unforgettable season, in congratulating our players on their success in winning the Championship of the League. They have indeed written another memorable page in the history of the Club, and by the high skill and excellence of their play they have delighted countless followers of the game both at Tottenham and on the grounds of other clubs. Looking back over the season we have many memories of the dramatic quality of their football, which has received so many tributes from supporters. Congratulations also to our Manager, Mr. W. Nicholson, who has been such an inspiring personality in this happy season, his second in the capacity of Manager, and incidentally his 25th season with the Club. This is a proud day for him, and for all associated with the Club, and may Tottenham Hotspur continue to win new fame in the future. That is the wish of us all.

At the conclusion of to-day's game the League trophy and medals will be presented by a member of the League Management Committee.

FRED J. BEARMAN

The Football League
Div. I Championship Cup

Souvenir Programme

ABOVE: The programme for the 1961 FA Cup final between Spurs and Leicester City, which Spurs won 2–0 to complete the first double this century

RIGHT: Spurs completed the first half of the double with the presentation of the League trophy in 1961

ABOVE: Captain Danny Blanchflower is chaired after Spurs beat Leicester City in the FA Cup final in 1961

RIGHT: A ticket stub from the final

WEST STANDING ENCLOSURE

ENTER AT **G** TURNSTILES
(See plan & conditions on back)
ENTRANCE 66

EMPIRE STADIUM, WEMBLEY
The Football Association
Cup Competition

FINAL TIE

SATURDAY, MAY 6th, 1961
KICK-OFF 3 p.m.

Price 3/6

Chairman,
Wembley Stadium Limited

THIS PORTION TO BE RETAINED
This ticket is issued on the condition that
it is not re-sold for more than its face value.

FINALE EUROPACUP VOOR BEKERWINNAARS

Officieel
Programma

Stadion
Feijenoord

Woensdag
15 mei 1963

Prijs
50 cent

ATLETICO
MADRID
BEKERHOUDER

1/-

TOTTENHAM
HOTSPUR

Cognac
HENNESSY
„Le plus grand stock de cognac du monde"

ABOVE: The programme for the 1963
European Cup-Winners' Cup final
in Rotterdam between Spurs and
Atletico Madrid, which
Spurs won 5–1

RIGHT: Pat Jennings, Spurs' ever-
reliable goalkeeper between 1964
and 1977 and Spurs' most capped
player with 74 appearances for
Northern Ireland

successive seasons, Liverpool's feat being achieved in 1905-07 and Everton's in 1930-32. Spurs had one match left to play and the trophy would be handed over in that final match – at home to Liverpool!

1954	Austrian State XI	Vienna	Friendly	0-2
1956	Sheffield United	H	First Division	3-1
1962	Birmingham City	A	First Division	3-2
1964	Coventry City	A	Friendly	6-5
1971	Huddersfield Town	H	First Division	1-1
1973	Newcastle United	H	First Division	3-2
1975	Leeds United	H	First Division	4-2
1979	Ipswich Town	A	First Division	1-2
1982	Birmingham City	H	First Division	1-0
1984	Queens Park Rangers	A	First Division	1-2
1990	Wimbledon	A	First Division	0-1

APRIL 29TH

| 1897 | Wellingborough | A | Wellingborough Charity Cup Final | 0-2 |
| 1899 | Woolwich Arsenal | H | United League | 3-2 |

A record gate for the Northumberland Park ground was set with the visit of Woolwich Arsenal – nearly 14,000 were believed to have crammed into a ground that could only accommodate half that number in any comfort. Dozens of people climbed on to the roof of the refreshments bar in an effort to get a better view of the game, and as this proved incapable of supporting their weight, it collapsed and caused numerous injuries. Spurs won 3-2 in the United League match, but it was as a result of the crush that the club began to look around for another venue, finally settling on what has now become their world famous home – White Hart Lane.

| 1901 | Luton Town | A | Southern League | 4-2 |

It ended as of no real consequence, but the 1901 final at Crystal Palace was the first to have been filmed and the film-makers were obviously aware of the controversy over United's second goal, for they rushed out the prints for everyone to see and make up their own minds. The film, screened on this night in London for the first time, proved the referee was wrong – the ball had not crossed the line for a goal but for a corner!

| 1902 | Woolwich Arsenal | H | Southern Charity Cup Semi-Final | 2-1 |

This was the replay to a match drawn at Arsenal six days previously. As there was insufficient time to stage the final at the end of the season, it was held over until the following season.

1905	Bristol Rovers	H	Southern League	1-0
1907	Southampton	H	Southern Charity Cup Final	2-0
1912	Woolwich Arsenal	Park Royal Ground		
			Daily Telegraph Titanic Fund	0-3

A crowd of 5,000 attended this match to raise funds for the dependants of the *RMS Titanic* which had sunk earlier in the month whilst on route from Southampton to New York.

1916	West Ham United	H	London Combination [2nd competition]	1-1
1922	Blackburn Rovers	H	First Division	2-1
1933	West Ham United	A	Second Division	0-1
1939	Sheffield Wednesday	A	Second Division	0-1
1944	Clapton Orient	H	Football League South	1-0
1950	Swansea Town	A	Second Division	0-1
1955	Newcastle United	H	First Division	2-1
1957	Burnley	A	First Division	0-1
1961	West Bromwich Albion	H	First Division	1-2
1965	Coventry City	A	Friendly	3-0
1967	Nottingham Forest	Hillsborough		
			FA Cup Semi-Final	2-1

Whoever Spurs faced in the FA Cup semi-final it was going to be a difficult match – Chelsea, who had reached the semi-final stage for the third consecutive season and would therefore be trying just that bit harder to go one stage further; Leeds United, who had just begun the decade of dominance; or Nottingham Forest, who were currently lying second in the table and pushing Manchester United hard for the title, thereby harbouring hopes and dreams of emulating Spurs' feat of 1961 – the double. Spurs were eventually paired with Forest, on paper the hardest tie of the three possible, but Spurs had two things working to their advantage – Forest's key player, Joe Baker, had been injured in the quarter-final clash with Everton and would be unable to play in this tie, and Jimmy Greaves. There must have been a love/hate relationship between Jimmy Greaves and Nottingham Forest, for he scored more of his goals against Forest than any other club. If Forest paid any extra attention to Greaves because of his affinity then it did not work; after half an hour and against the run of play,

Alan Gilzean headed a long clearance by Mike England sideways to Greaves. As the ball bounced by his left foot, Greaves suddenly twisted and caught it on the half-volley, sending the ball along the ground for 25 yards until it hit the inside of the post and ended up in the net. Forest attacked frantically thereafter, but Frank Saul put the game beyond reach with a quarter of an hour left, robbing Terry Hennessey of the ball and hitting it on the run into the net. Forest got a consolation goal from Hennessey himself, but could not equalise as time ran out. Spurs had therefore made it to the FA Cup final for the third time in seven years.

1968	Liverpool	A	First Division	1-1
1969	Leicester City	A	First Division	0-1
1972	Leicester City	H	First Division	4-3
1978	Southampton	A	Second Division	0-0

Momentous occasions in any club's history are usually recollected by the memory of a goal or two scored – any of the three goals Spurs scored against Sheffield Wednesday which clinched two League titles, any of the three against Wolves in 1960 which denied them their double. This match joined the growing list of momentous occasions in Spurs' history, despite the lack of goals. For as Southampton and Spurs took to the field at The Dell, both needed only one point more from their season's endeavours to secure promotion to the First Division. It did not matter that Spurs were the top scorers in the Second Division, having rattled in 83 during the season, or that Southampton were second highest scorers with 70 – one more point would be sufficient to send them both up at Brighton's expense. Herbert Chapman at Arsenal had been perhaps the first to voice publicly the observation that teams take to the field with one point; assuming they do not concede a goal they should be more than capable of walking off ninety minutes later with that point still intact. So when the result of this match was broadcast around the country it brought a cynical comment or two, especially from the Goldstone Ground, where Brighton beat Blackpool 2-1. If the game was goalless then it certainly wasn't incident free – Southampton might, indeed could have taken both points with a number of chances that fell to Tony Funnell, all of them spurned. The point apiece was enough to carry Southampton into second place, Spurs into third in the Second Division and give them both automatic promotion back to the First Division.

1980	Crystal Palace	H	Terry Naylor Testimonial	0-2
1985	Bristol Rovers	A	Friendly	6-2
1989	Millwall	A	First Division	5-0
1995	Arsenal	A	FA Premier League	1-1

APRIL 30TH

1896	Woolwich Arsenal	H	Friendly	3-2
1898	Bolton Wanderers	H	Friendly	2-2
1900	Southampton	A	Southern District Combination	4-1

Although Southampton were one of the strongest sides of the day, they had lost the FA Cup at Crystal Palace the previous week and were in a somewhat dejected state for this game. Indeed, only 1,000 people turned out to watch the game, a figure that would have been considerably higher had the trophy been won and the cup on display.

1901	Kettering Town	A	Southern League	1-1
1904	Wellingborough	A	Southern League	3-3
1910	Chelsea	H	First Division	2-1

In the final match of the season, Spurs faced Chelsea at White Hart Lane. Before the kick-off, Spurs held 30 points to Chelsea's 29; defeat for either club would send them down into the Second Division with Bolton Wanderers. A crowd of 35,000 saw Spurs scrape home 2-1 and thus avoid an immediate return to the division they left barely 12 months ago.

| 1921 | Huddersfield Town | H | First Division | 1-0 |

Following the club's win in the FA Cup the previous week, the trophy was carried around the ground by groundsman John Over prior to the game kicking off. Over is worthy of a special mention, for some 40 years previously he had laid the pitch at Kennington Oval for the first Test Match between England and Australia and had joined Spurs from Edmonton Cricket Club. It was claimed that he protected the pitch at White Hart Lane with a vengeance, allowing no one on it during the week and even having his doubts about letting 20 men run around on it on a Saturday! When he died the honour of becoming head groundsman passed on to his son Will.

1927	Liverpool	A	First Division	0-1
1932	Oldham Athletic	A	Second Division	2-1
1938	Blackburn Rovers	A	Second Division	1-2
1949	Fulham	H	Second Division	1-1
1951	Chelmsford City	A	Friendly	7-3

This was a testimonial for George Foreman and Spurs' goals were scored by Les Bennett, Sid McClellan (four) and Peter Murphy (two).

1952	Chelsea	A	First Division	2-0
1953	Charlton Athletic	A	First Division	2-3
1960	Blackpool	H	First Division	4-1
1962	Leicester City	A	First Division	3-2
1966	Burnley	H	First Division	0-1
1973	Wolverhampton Wanderers	H	First Division	2-2
1977	Aston Villa	H	First Division	3-1
1979	West Ham United	H	Steve Perryman Testimonial	2-2
1981	Wolverhampton Wanderers	A	First Division	0-1
1983	Liverpool	H	First Division	2-0
1994	Wimbledon	A	FA Premier League	1-2

MAY 1ST

| 1913 | Red Star Amical | Paris | Friendly | 2-1 |
| 1920 | Birmingham | A | Second Division | 1-0 |

Spurs finished the season with a record of 32 wins, six draws and only four defeats, for a tally of 70 points, a record for the division. Not surprisingly, they finished as champions, six points ahead of Huddersfield and 14 in front of Birmingham in third place.

1926	Leeds United	A	First Division	1-4
1937	Leicester City	A	Second Division	1-4
1948	Birmingham City	A	Second Division	0-0
1950	Hibernian	H	Friendly	0-1
1963	OFK Belgrade	H	European Cup-Winners' Cup Semi-Final 2nd Leg	3-1

Spurs completed the job begun in Belgrade a week previously and marched into the European Cup-Winners' Cup final. Already 2-1 from the first leg, a match in which Jimmy Greaves was sent off (and therefore missed this night's match through suspension), it seemed as though it would be a cakewalk into the Rotterdam final. This was anything but, despite the flattering scoreline. Spurs' heroes were almost all defenders on this occasion, having to be constantly on their toes to repel attack after attack as OFK tried to fight their way back into contention. Dave Mackay, moved further up front in place of the banished Greaves, eased the tension and pressure with the first goal of the night after 23 minutes. Six minutes later, however, OFK equalised through Skoblar and that set up a storming 15-minute spell for the Yugoslavian club when they did everything but score. Cliff Jones restored Spurs' lead just before half-time, applying the finishing touch to a great move by Danny Blanchflower, John White and Dave Mackay. Early in the second half, Bobby Smith scored the best goal of the night, diving full length to head home John White's cross. For the rest of the match OFK, perhaps sensing the game was up and lost, did little more than body check and niggle their opponents. Cliff Jones was involved in an altercation with several Yugoslavs, and Terry Dyson was three times admonished by the referee for over-zealous tackles. If the manner of their victory this night was not entirely deserving of the ultimate honour, then their efforts in the previous matches *en route* certainly were. Spurs were in the final on merit.

1971	Manchester City	A	First Division	1-0
1976	Fijian Select XI	Lautoka	Friendly	4-0
1982	Coventry City	A	First Division	0-0
1986	Inter Milan	H	Ossie Ardiles Benefit	2-1

Ever since his arrival at White Hart Lane, Ossie Ardiles had been a popular player with the fans, and so many wished to pay tribute to him that the kick off to his benefit match was delayed in order to allow everyone into the ground. Whilst Ardiles had been struggling with injury for much of the season and made little more than a token appearance in the game, the crowd were equally drawn by the appearance of another Argentinian; Diego Maradona. He wore the number ten shirt for Spurs, which Glenn Hoddle thoughtfully vacated, and the pair linked incredibly well to turn on a performance for the fans. Goals from Mark Falco and Clive Allen enabled Spurs to win 2-1.

| 1990 | Northern Ireland XI | H | Danny Blanchflower Benefit | 2-1 |

When it was revealed former Spurs captain Danny Blanchflower had hit lean times financially, the club set about organising a testimonial match for one of their favourite sons. It was a night when the old, in Danny Blanchflower, came face to face with the new, in the shape of Paul Gascoigne. Gascoigne did not disappoint either, running through his entire repertoire of tricks to delight the crowd, and scoring the most outrageous penalty ever seen at White Hart Lane, shaping up to kick the ball with one foot and then striking it with the other cross-legged! Danny Blanchflower must have purred with delight at Gascoigne's abilities.

| 1993 | Wimbledon | H | FA Premier League | 1-1 |

MAY 2ND

1884	Danny Steel born in Newmilns, Ayrshire. Danny joined Spurs in May 1906 and managed to replace Walter Bull so effectively in the club's first season in the League that the club were able to sell Bull. Indeed, for Spurs' first four seasons of Football League action Danny and his brother Bobby formed the cornerstone of the side. Danny was released by the club in 1912 and signed for Third Lanark, later returning to London to play for Clapton Orient. He died in London on 29th April 1931.			
1921	Middlesbrough	A	First Division	0-1
1925	Manchester City	A	First Division	0-1
1931	Burnley	A	Second Division	0-1
1934	Corinthians	H	Dewar Shield	7-4
1936	Barnsley	A	Second Division	0-0
1942	Fulham	H	London War League	7-1
1960	Crystal Palace	A	Friendly	2-2
1970	Arsenal	H	First Division	1-0

This match was originally scheduled for 15th April but subsequently postponed owing to Arsenal's involvement in the Fairs Cup. It had originally been planned by the Football League to have the season ending earlier than usual to help Sir Alf Ramsey with his preparation for the World Cup in Mexico, but with bad weather having caused havoc throughout the season it still ended in May, although Spurs had played their last game on 13th April! The only goal of the game was scored by Alan Gilzean.

1973	Sheffield United	A	First Division	2-3
1981	West Bromwich Albion	A	First Division	2-4
1987	Nottingham Forest	A	First Division	0-2
1988	Charlton Athletic	A	First Division	1-1
1992	Manchester United	A	First Division	1-3

Gary Lineker made his farewell appearance in a Spurs shirt, for he had previously announced he was retiring from English League football at the end of this season and taking up an offer to play in Japan when the J League came into operation later in the year. He was given a rapturous farewell by supporters of both teams even though he was unable to sign off with a goal.

1996	Leeds United	A	FA Premier League	3-1

With the European Championships due to take place in England during the summer, Darren Anderton faced a race against time to prove himself match fit for selection for the England squad. The two goals he scored against Leeds, coupled with his overall contribution, would not have done his chances any harm.

1998	Wimbledon	A	FA Premier League	6-2

With Bolton beating already relegated Crystal Palace 5-2 it was imperative that Spurs gained all three points in this clash with Wimbledon. Although Spurs took an early lead through Les Ferdinand, Wimbledon fought back to take the lead after two goals from Peter Fear, with Jurgen Klinsmann levelling the score before half-time. The game swung early in the second half with the dismissal of Ben Thatcher following a two-footed lunge at Allan Nielsen, with Klinsmann scoring a further three goals inside five minutes and setting up a final goal for Moussa Saib. Tottenham's safety was assured some 24 hours later with Arsenal's 4-0 win over Everton, but Spurs had effectively made themselves safe with a commanding second half performance at Selhurst Park.

MAY 3RD

1914	Hanover FC	Hanover	Friendly	6-3
1924	Burnley	H	First Division	1-0
1930	Stoke City	A	Second Division	0-1
1941	Arsenal	H	London War Cup Section B	3-3
1947	Bury	A	Second Division	2-1
1952	Racing Club de Paris	A	Friendly	2-1
1966	WKS Legia	Warsaw	Friendly	0-2
1967	Sunderland	H	First Division	1-0
1971	Arsenal	H	First Division	0-1

This was probably the most important League match ever played at White Hart Lane, for Arsenal were battling towards the double of League title and FA Cup, the honour that Spurs had achieved ten years previously. By the time of the match, the situation had become clear; Arsenal needed a win or a goalless draw to lift the title, a Spurs win or scoring draw would give the title to Leeds United. If Leeds' manager Don Revie could have asked for anyone to come up against Arsenal on their final match he would have chosen Spurs, for as the last team to have won the double they would be keen to protect their feat. Alan Mullery set his mind at ease, for as he told the press Spurs were having a good season of their own and still stood a chance of claiming third spot in the First Division. The crowds began gathering for the Monday night match soon after noon; by 5 p.m. the entire area around the ground was awash with people. Although just over 50,000 managed to shoehorn their way into White Hart Lane, an estimated 200,000, probably more, had tried to gain admission! Indeed, so great was the crush that Steve Perryman was forced to abandon his car whilst still a mile away from the ground and battle his way into the dressing-room. Just as expected, Spurs tore into Arsenal from the off desperate to prevent their nearest rivals lifting the title. They nearly succeeded too, with the Arsenal goal surviving a number of near misses. So too did the Spurs goal; the action was equally shared. Then, four minutes from the end, Arsenal scored after Armstrong sent over a cross which Ray Kennedy headed home. This merely intensified Spurs' efforts, for an equaliser would hand the title back to Leeds. After the longest four minutes of Arsenal goalkeeper Bob Wilson's life, the final whistle blew to signal their title. As disappointed as they were at seeing their rivals lift the crown, Spurs were magnanimous enough to send champagne into the Arsenal dressing-room, a gesture for which Bertie Mee later paid tribute.

| 1972 | Wolverhampton Wanderers | A | UEFA Cup Final 1st Leg | 2-1 |

While Spurs were finding success in France, Rumania and Italy, English counterparts Wolverhampton Wanderers were engaged on an equally impressive surge towards the UEFA Cup final. The end result was that two British sides contested a European final for the first time since European competition began in 1955. The two clubs clashed in the first leg at Molineux; perhaps familiarity bred contempt for both sides started nervously, only too aware of each other's strengths and weaknesses. The game effectively hinged on two pieces of opportunism from Martin Chivers. His first was a powerful header from a free-kick that was expected to give Spurs a little breathing space, but within two minutes Wolves were level following their own free-kick success which caught the Spurs defence napping. The goal that settled the game was one worthy of any final; Chivers collected the ball out by the touchline and shrugged off one challenge, took a couple of strides towards goal and then let fly with a shot that simply crashed into the net from fully 30 yards.

1976	Auckland FA XI	Auckland	Friendly	5-3
1978	Truro City	A	Friendly	8-2
1980	Bristol City	H	First Division	0-0
1982	Liverpool	H	First Division	2-2
1983	Southampton	A	First Division	2-1
1986	Aston Villa	H	First Division	4-2
1995	Newcastle United	A	FA Premier League	3-3
1997	Liverpool	A	FA Premier League	1-2

MAY 4TH

| 1901 | At the King's Hall at the Holborn Restaurant Spurs held an official dinner in celebration of winning |

the English Cup. The cup itself was placed at the head of the table, where Mrs Morton Cadman, wife of the vice-chairman of the club, tied blue and white ribbons to the handles, a tradition that has since been repeated at each and every cup final. When 20 years later Spurs again won the FA Cup, Mrs Cadman brought out the same ribbons, carefully preserved, and used them again. It was said that the Cadman family kept the ribbons for decades, waiting for Spurs to win the trophy a third time.

1905	Homen Wart Club	Vienna	Friendly	6-0
1913	Red Star Amical	Paris	Friendly	9-0
1918	Fulham	H-Upton Park		
			London Combination Subsidiary	2-3
1929	West Bromwich Albion	H	Second Division	2-0
1931	Arsenal	N	London FA Charity Cup Final	1-2
1935	Leeds United	A	First Division	3-4
1940	Brentford	A	Football League South Group C	3-2
1946	Coventry City	A	Football League South	1-0
1953	Arsenal	A	Friendly	2-0
1963	Sheffield United	H	First Division	4-2

Spurs' third goal was scored by Jimmy Greaves and took his tally of goals for the season to 37 in the League, a new record. He had drawn level with Ted Harper's tally of 36, achieved in the 1930-31 season, the previous week, and although he was not to score any further goals in League football this season, his record has been seriously threatened only once, when Clive Allen grabbed 33 in season 1986-87.

1968	Manchester City	H	First Division	1-3
1985	Coventry City	H	First Division	4-2
1988	Luton Town	H	First Division	2-1
1991	Nottingham Forest	H	First Division	1-1

With barely two weeks to go before the two sides met in the FA Cup final, neither manager was likely to show his hand too early. A draw was always going to be the most likely outcome for this match.

MAY 5TH

1910   Fred Channell born in Edmonton. Having been associated with Spurs since he left school he joined the groundstaff in 1928, signing professional forms in 1930 and making his debut in October 1933. A stylish full-back he was considered a great prospect by the club, so much so that they were able to let Bill Felton go. International honours were also predicted for Fred, and he played in two trial matches. Unfortunately, he was badly injured in a match against West Ham and retired at the age of 26 only two years later. He subsequently became a publican and died in Colchester on 6th August 1976.

Year	Opponent	Venue	Competition	Score
1923	Huddersfield Town	H	First Division	0-0
1945	Luton Town	H	Football League South	1-0
1951	Liverpool	H	First Division	3-1
1952	Ipswich Town	A	Ipswich Hospital Charity Cup	2-2
1954	Eintracht Frankfurt	Brunswick	Friendly	0-1
1955	Charlton Athletic	A	First Division	2-1
1962	Burnley	Wembley	FA Cup Final	3-1

With Ipswich having won the League title and Benfica ending Spurs' involvement in the European Cup, the FA Cup remained the last trophy able to provide Spurs with some tangible reward for their season. Burnley would not be easy opposition, for they had finished second in the League (behind Ipswich and ahead of Spurs), but they were destined to finish runners-up in both the League and Cup. Spurs got off to the best possible start, taking the lead through Jimmy Greaves. Although Burnley equalised Spurs moved up a gear, and goals from Bobby Smith (who had scored in the previous year's final) and Danny Blanchflower from the penalty spot ensured the cup remained at White Hart Lane. It was the first time the cup had been retained since 1952 when Newcastle had won, but for Spurs the additional icing on the cake was the qualification for Europe, albeit in the European Cup-Winners' Cup.

Year	Opponent	Venue	Competition	Score
1971	Stoke City	A	First Division	1-0
1976	Wellington FA XI	Wellington	Friendly	3-2
1978	Orient	A	Friendly	3-1

This match was a joint testimonial for Orient players Peter Angell and Brian Blower with Spurs' goals being scored by Chris Jones, John Duncan and Peter Taylor.

Year	Opponent	Venue	Competition	Score
1979	Everton	H	First Division	1-1
1980	Bournemouth & Boscombe Athletic	A	Friendly	2-1

This match was a testimonial for Keith Miller with both Spurs' goals being scored by Terry Gibson.

Year	Opponent	Venue	Competition	Score
1982	Swansea City	H	First Division	2-1
1984	Norwich City	H	First Division	2-0
1986	Southampton	H	First Division	5-3
1990	Southampton	H	First Division	2-1
1992	Cardiff City	A	Friendly	2-0

This match was a testimonial for Harry Parsons with Spurs' goals being scored by Andy Gray and John Hendry.

Year	Opponent	Venue	Competition	Score
1993	Blackburn Rovers	H	FA Premier League	1-2
1994	Oldham Athletic	A	FA Premier League	2-0

Although never seriously in danger of being relegated, Spurs had been gradually sucked into the relegation dogfight. Oldham's plight was desperate; they needed all the points on offer, whilst Spurs could guarantee their safety with a win. As it was goals from Vinny Samways and David Howells gave Spurs the victory and Premiership football for another season.

Year	Opponent	Venue	Competition	Score
1996	Newcastle United	A	FA Premier League	1-1

MAY 6TH

Year	Opponent	Venue	Competition	Score
1914	1st Club of Nuremburg	Nuremburg	Friendly	1-1
1922	Blackburn Rovers	A	First Division	1-1
1928	Olympic A Team	Amsterdam	Friendly	5-2
1929	Millwall	N	London FA Charity Cup Final	5-1
1933	Notts County	H	Second Division	3-1
1939	Sheffield United	A	Second Division	1-6
1944	Watford	A	Football League South	1-1
1950	Sheffield Wednesday	A	Second Division	0-0

1953   Graeme Souness born in Edinburgh. Graeme Souness is probably one of the greatest players Spurs missed out on, for although he made one brief appearance as a substitute in a UEFA Cup tie in 1971, a combination of homesickness and perceived competition for places in the Spurs midfield led to him demanding a transfer, walking out on the club at one point and being reluctantly sold to Middlesbrough for £32,000 in January 1973. That he would go on to help Middlesbrough to the Second Division title in his first full season, win his first cap in October 1974 and then go on to help Liverpool dominate the game both domestically and in Europe during his six years at Anfield was never in doubt. He later played in Italy for Sampdoria and returned home to Scotland in 1986 to become player-manager at Rangers. He then returned to Liverpool as manager, but despite guiding them to the FA Cup in 1992 was not viewed as successful. He has since managed in Turkey, Italy, at Southampton and is currently manager of Benfica.

| 1961 | Leicester City | Wembley | FA Cup Final | 2-0 |

Having already secured the League Championship, Tottenham Hotspur faced Leicester City chasing the first FA Cup and League double this century. Spurs were in a relaxed mood as they strode out on to the Wembley turf, and Danny Blanchflower was probably calmer than most. As the teams were being presented to the various dignitaries before the game, one happened to ask why it was that the Leicester players had their names on their tracksuits whilst those of Spurs didn't. 'That's because we know each other,' remarked the Irishman. Indeed Spurs did know one another, for these 11 players had taken the club to the very summit during the season and would not be denied at the very end. The two main talking points after the game concerned the injury to Chalmers which had weakened Leicester, and the manner of Spurs' win. Since Spurs had been christened the team of the season the punters expected them to perform like it in every game, but as Spurs had found out during the 42 League matches, the opposition had frequently raised their game whenever they played Spurs. The loss of Chalmers following an awkward but not malicious challenge from Les Allen was unfortunate, but ultimately it probably fired Leicester up more than Spurs. Gradually Leicester tired and Spurs began to take control, and after Cliff Jones had had a goal disallowed for offside Bobby Smith fired them into the lead. Shortly before the end Terry Dyson put the matter beyond doubt with a header and Spurs thus became the first side to win the coveted double since 1897.

1967	Liverpool	A	First Division	0-0
1985	Newcastle United	A	First Division	3-2
1988	Barnet	A	Friendly	2-1

This match was a testimonial for Kevin Millett with Spurs' goals being scored by Chris Waddle (penalty) and Paul Walsh.

| 1995 | Queens Park Rangers | A | FA Premier League | 1-2 |

MAY 7TH

1905	Everton	Vienna	Friendly	0-2
1911	North German Combined XI	Hamburg	Friendly	4-1
1921	Middlesbrough	H	First Division	2-2
1927	Arsenal	H	First Division	0-4
1932	Preston North End	A	Second Division	0-2
1937				

Eddie Clayton born in Bethnal Green, London. Inside forward Eddie joined the club as an amateur in 1955 and was elevated to the professional ranks in December 1957, making his League debut the following year against Everton and scoring twice. However, first-team opportunities were extremely limited and in ten years with the club he made only 88 full appearances in the League side, scoring 20 goals. In March 1968 he moved on to Southend United and then into non-League football, appearing for Margate in their FA Cup tie against Spurs in 1973. He finished his playing career with Aylesbury.

1938	Sheffield Wednesday	H	Second Division	1-2
1946	FA XI	H	Willie Hall Benefit	4-1
1949	Plymouth Argyle	A	Second Division	5-0
1951	FC Austria	H	Festival of Britain	0-1
1966	West Bromwich Albion	A	First Division	1-2
1977	Manchester City	A	First Division	0-5

Spurs journeyed to Manchester City needing a miracle if they were to survive in the First Division for another season. Their cause was not helped by City's own desperation for points, for they were battling with Liverpool for the title. In the end form told, with City running out easy 5-0 winners and Spurs' relegation to the Second Division confirmed after an absence of 27 years. Immediately after the game the Spurs board announced that manager Keith Burkinshaw's position was safe and that he would remain in charge to try and lift the club back into the top flight at the first attempt.

1980	Hertford Town	A	Friendly	4-0
1983	Birmingham City	A	First Division	0-2
1984	Southampton	A	First Division	0-5

Spurs put out pretty much a reserve side for this Easter Monday fixture, for two days later they were due to play Anderlecht in the first leg of the UEFA Cup final in Brussels. Indeed, of the 11 players who took to the field against Southampton, only Paul Miller would play in the final. Spurs had originally asked for the game to be postponed and had been turned down, and when the Football League saw the team sheet for the Spurs side, announced they would be charging Spurs with fielding an under-strength side.

| 1994 | Queens Park Rangers | H | FA Premier League | 1-2 |

MAY 8TH

1934   Maurice Norman born in Mulbarton, Norfolk. Maurice joined Norwich City in September 1952 and made his debut in February 1955, and after only 35 games for the Canaries was the subject of a bid from Spurs to take him to White Hart Lane. He was wanted to replace Alf Ramsey at full-back, and with winger Johnny Gavin returning to Carrow Road as part of the deal, Maurice became a Spurs player in November 1955. An injury sustained in September 1956 kept him out of the side for half a dozen games, and upon recovering he found Peter Baker had taken the full-back slot. Maurice was therefore moved to the centre-half position, a role he took to immediately. A member of the double-winning side in 1961, the FA Cup-winning team in 1962 and the European Cup-Winners' Cup victors' team the following season, Maurice also won 23 caps for England, collecting his first in 1962 against Peru. His career came to an end following a horrific broken leg sustained in a friendly match against a Hungarian Select XI in 1965, and despite a number of operations he never played again, retiring in the summer of 1967.

1948	Jersey	A	Friendly	3-0
1950	Norwich City	A	Norwich Hospital Charity Cup	2-2
1954	SV Hamburg	Hamburg	Friendly	2-2

1955   Keith Osgood born in Isleworth. Signed by Spurs as an apprentice in June 1971 he was upgraded to the professional ranks 12 months later. He made his debut in May 1974 but didn't really command a regular place in the defence until March 1975. When his form deserted him in December 1977 and he was dropped from the team, he asked for a transfer and was duly sold to Coventry City for £125,000. He later played for Derby County, Orient and Cambridge United as well as a number of non-League sides.

1974	Liverpool	H	First Division	1-1
1978	Aleppo FC	Aleppo	Friendly	1-0
1979	Bolton Wanderers	A	First Division	3-1
1982	Leeds United	H	First Division	2-1
1985	Arsenal	A	Pat Jennings Testimonial	3-2

Pat Jennings had already been the recipient of a testimonial match whilst playing for Spurs; this had taken place in 1976 against Arsenal. Now, he was granted a similar match by Arsenal against Spurs! The score finished exactly the same too.

| 1992 | Hull City XI | A | Friendly | 6-2 |

This match was a testimonial for Garreth Roberts with Spurs' goals being scored by Vinny Samways, John Hendry (two), Nick Barmby (two) and Andy Turner.

| 1993 | Liverpool | A | FA Premier League | 2-6 |

MAY 9TH

1914	Bayern Munich	Munich	Friendly	6-0
1925	Basel Old Boys	A	Friendly	3-0
1928	Den Haag	The Hague	Friendly	6-2
1949	Cornwall County XI	Penzance	Friendly	2-0
1966	Blackburn Rovers	A	First Division	1-0
1967	West Ham United	A	First Division	2-0

1968   Neil Ruddock born in Battersea. Having been linked with both Charlton Athletic and Millwall as a youngster Neil was signed by Spurs for £50,000 in March 1986 without having played for the first team. After making a few appearances in the Spurs first team he was transferred back to Millwall for £300,000 in June 1988, his White Hart Lane career seemingly at an end. In February 1989 he was sold to Southampton for £250,000 and began to recapture the form that had brought him to Spurs in the first place, showing fine defensive abilities that enabled Southampton to avoid relegation. Although it had been Terry Venables who had sold Neil back to Millwall in the first place, he now wrote out a cheque for £750,000 in May 1992 to bring him to Spurs for a second time. A year later, Venables' sacking prompted Neil to demand a transfer and he was duly sold to Liverpool for £2.5 million. His inability to command a regular place at Anfield fuelled speculation that he might one day return to White Hart Lane for a third time, although he subsequently signed for West Ham in 1998.

1976	Victoria	Victoria	Friendly	3-1
1981	Manchester City	Wembley	FA Cup Final	1-1 [aet]

The FA Cup final has always been the premier event in the domestic football calendar; the fact that this was the 100th such cup final ensured additional interest from around the world. The pageantry started early, with 31 cup-winning captains being introduced to the crowd before the two teams arrived. Once again the event fell flat, with Manchester City hustling and bustling in midfield and knocking Spurs well out of their stride. Crooks and Archibald were little more than observers up front, starved of the service that had made them one of the most lethal pairings in the Football League. City took the lead after half-an-hour; Tommy Hutchinson superbly heading home at the near post. That looked to have settled the matter and with just over ten minutes left manager Keith Burkinshaw took off the ineffective Ricky Villa and brought on Gary Brooke. With ten minutes to go the other Argentinian, Ardiles, set off on a run across the field directly in front of the City penalty area, a run that was halted by an over-enthusiastic tackle. Among Spurs' armoury was a well-rehearsed free-kick that involved Ardiles, Hoddle and Perryman, with Hoddle curling the ball this way or that, hopefully into the goal. City seemed to have the situation covered; the wall was well-stationed, until the most vital moment, when Tommy Hutchinson left the end of the wall and deflected a shot that Corrigan had seemed to have covered. The ball struck Hutchinson on the shoulder and shot off towards the unguarded far corner of the goal. Ricky Villa may not have seen this, for since being substituted he had walked a lonely trek towards the dressing-rooms; the roar of the crowd made him go to where he should have been, alongside his manager on the Spurs bench. Tommy Hutchinson meanwhile had become the first player since 1946 to score for both sides in an FA Cup final, and with no further score in extra-time Wembley could await its first ever FA Cup final replay.

1984	RSC Anderlecht	A	UEFA Cup Final 1st Leg	1-1

The night before the game a young Spurs fan was shot to death in a bar in the city centre of Brussels. This had raised fears of a backlash and further violence as upwards of 8,000 Spurs fans were expected to travel over for the game, but a healthy police presence in the city, coupled with self restraint shown by the supporters, allowed the game to pass without any repetition of the trouble that had accompanied Spurs' last appearance on the continent for a European final. Anderlecht were worthy opponents for Spurs, for they were the holders of the cup (interestingly, no club had managed successfully to defend the UEFA Cup or the European Cup-Winners' Cup since the competitions were introduced) and had overcome a 2-0 deficit in the semi-final first leg against Nottingham Forest to earn their place in the final (although years later it was revealed they had bribed the referee in the second leg and had been awarded a highly dubious penalty to enable them to triumph 3-0). Despite Anderlecht's strengths, it was Spurs who started brighter and carried the game to their opponents. Mark Falco went close once or twice, Graham Roberts and Paul Miller looked solid in central defence and Micky Hazard was at his creative best in midfield. Early in the second half Spurs got a vital goal when Paul Miller rose to meet a corner and powerfully headed Spurs into the lead. Even though this prompted Anderlecht to go on the attack, Spurs looked more than capable of weathering the storm. The only setback was an unfortunate booking for Steve Perryman that would mean his suspension for the second leg. Then, three minutes before the final whistle, Tony Parks made his only error of the night and mishandled the ball a few feet from the goaline. An Anderlecht foot poked the ball home for an equaliser, but the away goal scored left Spurs very much in the driving seat and Tony Parks would redeem himself in the second leg.

1986	Brentford	A	Friendly	3-4

This match was a testimonial for Danis Salman with Spurs' goals being scored by John Chiedozie and Clive Allen (two).

1987	Watford	A	First Division	0-1
1995	Coventry City	H	FA Premier League	1-3

MAY 10TH

1905	Vienna Athletic Club	Vienna	Friendly	4-1
1914	Furth FC	Furth	Friendly	2-2
1919	Fulham	H	National War Fund	2-2
1925	Zurich Young Fellows	A	Friendly	2-0
1941	Crystal Palace	H	Football League South	1-1
1947	Southampton	A	Second Division	0-1

1955	Johnny Gavin became the first Spurs player to be capped by Eire when selected for the match against Holland in Rotterdam. Eire won 4-1.

1957	The Spurs team gathered at Euston Station for the boat train to Liverpool. Later that afternoon they boarded the *Empress of England* for the seven day voyage to Montreal for their forthcoming tour of Canada.

1978	Syrian Police	Damascus	Friendly	4-0

1982	West Ham United	A	First Division	2-2
1988	Euskadi	Bilbao	Friendly	0-4
1998	Southampton	H	FA Premier League	1~1

Jurgen Klinsmann said farewell to Spurs for the second time, signing off with a terrific drive home from the edge of the penalty area to equalise after Matt Le Tissier had given Southampton the lead. Also making their farewells were Gary Mabbutt and David Howells, both of whom had been given free transfers. Gary Mabbutt came on for the final ten minutes to a tremendous reception from the crowd and later undertook a tearful lap of honour around the stadium he had graced for 16 years. David Howells was not part of the squad for the game, but the reception afforded him was just as warming, with both players being given a silver salver by Alan Sugar thanking them for their efforts on behalf of Spurs over the years.

MAY 11TH

1929	Sliema Wanderers	A	Friendly	7-1
1933	Channel Islands	Guernsey	Friendly	6-0
1940	Portsmouth	H	Football League South Group C	4-1
1948	Guernsey	A	Friendly	7-0
1952	Crittals Athletic	Braintree	Friendly	8-1
1953	Hibernian	N	Coronation Cup Semi-Final	1-1 [aet]

Spurs were involved in a four-team tournament also featuring Celtic and Arsenal who were playing at Hampden Park on the same day. A crowd of 43,000 saw Spurs and Hibernian draw 1-1 after extra time, with Spurs' goal being scored by Sonny Walters. A replay at Hampden Park was hastily arranged for the following day.

1955	FC Austria	Vienna	Friendly	2-6
1963	Manchester City	A	First Division	0-1
1968	Wolverhampton Wanderers	A	First Division	1-2
1972	Arsenal	A	First Division	2-0
1974	Newcastle United	A	First Division	2-0
1979	Gillingham	A	Friendly	3-2

This match was a testimonial for Graham Knight and Spurs' goals were scored by Mark Falco, Glenn Hoddle and Ricky Villa.

1980	Rapid/FC Austria XI	Vienna	Friendly	0-3
1981	West Ham United	H	Barry Daines Testimonial	2-3
1983	Manchester United	H	First Division	2-0
1985	Watford	H	First Division	1-5
1987	Everton	A	First Division	0-1

This match was played only five days before Spurs were due to play Coventry City in the FA Cup final at Wembley. The top three positions in the League were already established; Everton were champions, Liverpool runners-up and Spurs third. These positions would not be affected irrespective of the result. So Spurs rested a number of the players who had got them to the FA Cup final and were later fined £10,000 for so doing!

1991	Liverpool	A	First Division	0-2
1993	Arsenal	A	FA Premier League	3-1
1997	Coventry City	H	FA Premier League	1-2

White Hart Lane has played host to many memorable and vital matches, usually with some significance to Spurs. This match was different, for Coventry were once again battling against relegation and needing a miracle to survive. Not only did they have to win, they also had to pray that Sunderland and Middlesbrough lost to enable them to escape the trapdoor. Coventry took a 2-0 lead and heard that results elsewhere were going in their favour, although a late Spurs goal set up a nail-biting final ten minutes.

MAY 12TH

1905	Buda Pesth Thorna	Budapest	Friendly	7-1
1912	Hull City	Brussels	Friendly	0-2
1929	Valetta United	A	Friendly	2-1
1932	Guernsey	A	Friendly	2-1
1947	Norwich City	A	Norwich Hospital Charity Cup	2-0
1951	Borussia Dortmund	H	Festival of Britain	2-1
1953	Hibernian	N	Coronation Cup Semi-Final Replay	1-2
1969	Sheffield Wednesday	A	First Division	0-0
1976	Northern New South Wales	Newcastle		
			Friendly	5-1

1978	Arsenal	H	John Pratt Testimonial	3-5
1982	Nottingham Forest	A	First Division	0-2
1984	Manchester United	H	First Division	1-1
1986	West Ham United	A	Friendly	1-5

This match was a benefit for Gerhardt Ampofo with Spurs' goal being scored by Clive Allen.

1994 The FA formally charged Spurs with misconduct concerning alleged irregular payments to a number of players. The charges, which related to payments made to players between 1985 and 1989, had come to light following the Alan Sugar and Terry Venables court case, and Spurs had voluntarily handed over a number of documents which purported to show these payments had been made.

MAY 13TH

1911	Preussen	Berlin	Friendly	7-0
1914	Milan	Milan	Friendly	5-0
1928	All Holland	Almelo	Friendly	3-0
1933	Guernsey	A	Friendly	8-0
1967	Sheffield United	H	First Division	2-0
1970	Valetta United	A	Friendly	3-0
1980	Gais/Sturm Select XI	Graz	Friendly	0-2

1986 Peter Shreeve was sacked as manager of Spurs after two seasons in charge. Although the side enjoyed a flirtation with the League title in his first season in charge, bad home form and a long injury list finally proved insurmountable, with Everton winning the League and Liverpool pushing Spurs into third position. Much was expected during 1985-86, but a bad start and even worse middle of the season left the club with nothing to play for from March, although they rallied considerably during the final few weeks. There then followed considerable speculation that Shreeve's spell was to be ended, culminating in this day's announcement. Shreeve's assistant, former Spurs player John Pratt, was also dismissed.

1989	Queens Park Rangers	A	First Division	0-1

MAY 14TH

1875 Bob Clements born in Greenwich, London. Bob, known as 'Topsy' joined Spurs in March 1895 and made his debut appearance in the FA Cup tie against Luton Town in October that year. Spurs' adoption of professionalism put his position in jeopardy, and following the arrival of Bob Stormont he decided to move on at the end of the 1897-98 season, subsequently signing with Chatham. When they folded in 1900 he moved on to Grays United.

1905	Testgyakorborora	Budapest	Friendly	12-1
1911	Hertha FC	Berlin	Friendly	4-1
1921	Fulham	Camberley		
			Friendly	4-0

This match was played on behalf on the RMC (Sandhurst) War Memorial Fund with the then Prince of Wales (and later Edward VIII and Duke of Windsor) kicking off. Each player was presented with a gold medal at the end as a souvenir.

1950	Hanover Arminia	Hanover	Friendly	3-0
1977	Leicester City	H	First Division	2-0
1979	West Bromwich Albion	H	First Division	1-0
1981	Manchester City	Wembley	FA Cup Final Replay	3-2

If Tommy Hutchinson had gone from hero to villain on Saturday then it was Ricky Villa's turn tonight, except his was the opposite journey. There were those who felt he should be left out of the side for the replay, partly because he had been so ineffective on Saturday (not that he was alone) and because his original walk towards the dressing-rooms had been construed as a snub to his manager. But Burkinshaw restored him to the side and was rewarded for his faith when Villa put Spurs ahead after only six minutes; Ardiles tried a shot that hit his colleague Archibald, who in turn shot towards goal. Corrigan could only parry the ball and in an instant Villa had appeared to slam the ball home from six yards. It did not take City long to get even, Steve Mackenzie volleying home the kind of goal that would have been on everyone's lips were it not for the drama that was to unfold later. There was no further score until early in the second half. Dave Bennett chased a long ball into the Spurs' penalty area and was brought down by a combined tackle from Chris Hughton and Paul Miller and the referee had little hesitation in awarding a penalty. Kevin Reeves put City ahead from the penalty spot. For the next ten minutes or so Spurs lost their way and their heads before settling and beginning to play the kind of football that had taken the team to Wembley in the first place. A corner was cleared only as far as Hoddle, who lofted the ball back into the danger area. Archibald seemed to have sufficient time to take stock of the situation, but Crooks nipped in and poked home the equaliser. There were 14 minutes left on the clock when Galvin chased down the left flank, checked and played the ball inside to Ricky Villa. He was still some way from goal but set off on a run that seemed sure to end in a safe pass for much of the next few moments. As Villa entered the Ciy penalty area, Caton and then Ranson appeared to block his path to goal. A twist here, a dummy there took him past these two and more; Reid had also lost track of the ball. Villa was now in front of goal and Corrigan advancing off his line, but a quick shot saw the ball slip under him and register a goal that would be remembered for ever and a day. As a goal it would stand comparison with any; as a goal with which to win the 100th FA Cup final, it entered folklore. Spurs survived one or two close calls, none more so than when substitute Tueart went very close with a ground shot, and hung on to win their first major trophy since 1973's League Cup. By the time captain Steve Perryman walked up the famous Wembley steps to pick up the cup from Princess Michael of Kent, people were beginning to talk about 'that' goal. They have yet to stop.

1983	Stoke City	H	First Division	4-1
1985	Sheffield Wednesday	H	First Division	2-0
1993	Enfield	A	Eddie Baily Testimonial	5-1

A day of high drama, the like of which had never been seen at Tottenham before. An emergency board meeting was called by chairman Alan Sugar and Terry Venables was sacked as chief executive of the club. Venables then went to the High Court and won a ruling reinstating him for ten days until a further hearing could be held. In the evening the club were playing a friendly testimonial match at Enfield for former Spurs player and coach Eddie Baily, and the day's activities ensured a higher attendance than might otherwise have been expected. The fans and one or two of the players (most notably Neil Ruddock) used the occasion to show their support for Venables.

| 1995 | Leeds United | H | FA Premier League | 1-1 |

MAY 15TH

| 1920 | West Bromwich Albion | H | FA Charity Shield | 0-2 |

Spurs, the Second Division champions, took on their First Division counterparts in the FA Charity Shield, their first appearance in the Shield. Although this has since become the traditional curtain-raiser to the season with a sell-out crowd at Wembley, a crowd of 3,000 turned out at White Hart Lane to see West Bromwich Albion win 2-0.

1953	Heart of Midlothian	A	Friendly	0-2
1955	FC Kinizsi	Budapest	Friendly	1-4
1961	Feyenoord	A	Friendly	2-1
1963	Athletico Madrid	Rotterdam		
			European Cup-Winners' Cup Final	5-1

It has always been claimed that Bill Nicholson was a worried man before Spurs went out to face Athletico Madrid in the Cup-Winners' Cup final in Rotterdam. Worried enough to have built the Athletico side up to almost super-human levels in his pre-match team talk. Worried enough to wish the Gods had been kinder and given him Dave Mackay for one of the most vital matches in the club's history. Certainly, Spurs' preparations for the final could hardly have been much rougher. The dreadful winter of 1963 had caused a fixture pile-up for every club in the country, but for Spurs, tasting success in European competition, the problem was further compounded. It might have been expected that the League season would have been over by the time of this final; Spurs still had two matches to play. Dave Mackay was still suffering from a stomach injury and was therefore ruled out of this match, a major blow for Nicholson and Spurs, for Mackay had been inspirational throughout the long slog across Europe, but Tony Marchi was a ready, willing and able replacement. Danny Blanchflower had also been suffering. He had been crocked in the second leg against Rangers and was still not fully fit, so Nicholson and Blanchflower discussed the alternatives. 'It's a simple choice – either me on one leg or John Smith on two,' was Blanchflower's version of events. In the end Nicholson chose Danny, and his captain did him proud. He set about lifting his side's spirits after Nicholson's team talk. So what if Athletico had a fast winger called Jones (which they did); Spurs' version was so fast he could catch pigeons. Spurs' centre-half was bigger and uglier than his counterpart, and Bobby Smith frightened his own side, so what kind of impact would he have on the opposition? After that Spurs took to the field confident that they could beat anyone, and so it proved. An early goal by Jimmy Greaves settled Spurs' nerves, and a later addition by John White seemingly put the match beyond Athletico's grasp. But they were not holders of the trophy for nothing and they simply tore into Spurs, especially after the break. The Spurs goal survived a number of scares and the defence looked to have held firm when Ron Henry punched out a goalbound shot. Unfortunately, Henry was playing full-back rather than goalkeeper, and Collar reduced the deficit from the resulting penalty! But just as Athletico had taken the initiative, so Spurs shifted up a gear. Terry Dyson, who was playing the match of his life, sent in a deep cross that the Athletico keeper lost in the night air and allowed to sail over him for a third Spurs goal (although Terry would later try to claim that he had spotted the keeper move off his line and tried a shot!) Jimmy Greaves then added a fourth with a goal similar to his first, and Terry Dyson rounded the scoring off with a magnificent drive. When the final whistle blew captain Danny Blanchflower collected the cup, Britain's first such success in Europe, and was chaired around the field by his team. As the players made their way towards the dressing-room, Bobby Smith turned to Terry Dyson and told him, 'You'd better retire now, you'll never play that good again.' It had been one of those nights.

1966	Sarpsborg	A	Friendly	3-0
1968	Panathinaikos	Athens	Friendly	2-2
1969	West Ham United	Baltimore	Friendly	4-3
1978	FC Hamar	A	Friendly	0-3
1982	Liverpool	A	First Division	1-3
1992	Spurs informed team manager Peter Shreeves that his contract would not be renewed.			

MAY 16TH

1905	Everton	Prague	Friendly	0-1
1912	Bewegungs Spiele	Leipzig	Friendly	3-1
1921	Burnley	H	FA Charity Shield	2-0

With Spurs having just won the FA Cup and Burnley the League, the FA Charity Shield match was played at the end of the season rather than at the beginning of the following one. Goals from Cantrell and Bliss in front of a crowd of 18,000 saw Spurs win the FA Charity Shield for the first time in their history.

1928	Rotterdam	Rotterdam		
			Friendly	3-0
1929	British Army	Malta	Friendly	5-0
1932	Jersey	A	Friendly	9-0
1935	Channel Islands	Guernsey	Friendly	5-0
1951	Racing Club de Paris	A	Friendly	4-2
1970	Sliema Wanderers	A	Friendly	2-1
1976	Australian National XI	Sydney	Friendly	3-2
1979	Kuwait Army XI	A	Friendly	2-1
1987	Coventry City	Wembley	FA Cup Final	2-3 [aet]

By the time Spurs and Coventry faced each other in the FA Cup final, Spurs were firmly established as red-hot favourites. The disappointment of the Littlewoods Cup semi-final defeat by Arsenal had been erased, the team were playing as well now as anyone could remember, and confidence was high. There were coincidences to consider too, for in the 1960s Spurs had won the cup in '61, '62 and '67; here in the 1980s they'd already triumphed in '81 and '82. The team wanted to win the cup for injured full-back Danny Thomas; that had driven them on since the sixth round. The first chinks in the Spurs armour were revealed as the team took off their tracksuit tops before kick-off; half the team had the sponsor's name of Holsten on their shirts, the other half didn't. The claim after the game that the players hadn't noticed was not entirely convincing, unless they were so wound up or nervous before the start. Once again the second minute proved crucial for Clive Allen; in 1982 playing for QPR he had been injured and eventually replaced, this time around he scored a glancing header from Chris Waddle's cross, giving Spurs a dream start. But Coventry refused to be dispirited and responded well, equalising soon after. Again Spurs surged forward, and a tussle between Gary Mabbutt and Brian Kilcline saw the ball hit the back of the net, although quite who got the final touch remained in doubt. At 2-1 ahead Spurs should have consolidated, but their style throughout the season had been attack and be damned, and so it proved to be today. A glorious diving header from Keith Houchen equalised the match for a second time and forced extra time. Then Gary Mabbutt tried to stop a cross coming in from Coventry's right wing and only succeeded in deflecting the ball upwards. This took it over the grasping hands of Ray Clemence and into the net for the winning goal – Spurs were to finish empty-handed after all. If there was some consolation to be gained it was that Spurs had played their part in one of the best finals seen at Wembley for many a year. That would have counted for little to the Spurs players who trooped off the field dejectedly at the end of the game; Coventry had just won the first major honour of their history.

MAY 17TH

1914	Zurich	Zurich	Friendly	6-0
1925	Winterthur	A	Friendly	4-0
1941	Leicester City	A	Football League South	2-1
1947	West Ham United	H	Second Division	0-0
1961	Amsterdam Select XI	Amsterdam		
			Friendly	3-0
1969	Aston Villa	Atlanta	Friendly	2-2

| 1970 | Maltese Select XI | A | Friendly | 0-1 |
| 1972 | Wolverhampton Wanderers | H | UEFA Cup Final 2nd Leg | 1-1 |

Although Spurs were 2-1 up from the first leg they knew enough about their opponents to appreciate that the tie was anything but settled. White Hart Lane's biggest crowd of the season were convinced Spurs would do it, and though they were proved right at the end it was a titanic struggle between the sides. Throughout the early 1970s the one Spurs saviour had been Martin Chivers; if he played well and scored, the team invariably did well. This often put enormous personal pressure on him, and the verbal battles he had with Bill Nicholson and Eddie Baily over this reliance on him are legendary. This was probably the most important game that Spurs played and disproved the theory, for Martin had a largely anonymous evening. His performance in the first leg, when he had fashioned two goals out of almost nothing, had ensured he would be constantly watched this evening, perhaps allowing others to get into the scoring positions he was vacating. So it proved. A free-kick out on the left wing was flighted into the penalty area and Alan Mullery, hero of the semi-final second leg, ghosted in to head the ball home. He took a knock in the process, unable to get up and celebrate with his delirious team-mates, but his goal was a vital one. Although Wolves responded well and equalised on the night, they were unable to find another way through to goal and so ended the evening empty handed. Alan Mullery, on what was to be his last appearance in a Spurs shirt in a competitive match, therefore collected Spurs' second European trophy. Alan was determined to enjoy every last minute of the adulation; while all the other players trooped back to the dressing-room shortly after the presentations, Alan remained outside being cheered around the ground by supporters.

1976	South Australia	Adelaide	Friendly	5-2
1977	Stord FC	A	Friendly	5-0
1978	Kvik Halden	A	Friendly	2-0
1982	Ipswich Town	A	First Division	1-2
1983	Trinidad & Tobago XI	A	Friendly	2-2
1985	Nottingham Forest	H	First Division	1-0
1986				

After much soul searching, Luton Town manager David Pleat agreed to become the new manager of Spurs. The popular Pleat had long been regarded one of the best managers in the game and been responsible for establishing Luton in the First Division with a reputation of playing open attractive football, in keeping with Spurs tradition. As a player Pleat's career began with Nottingham Forest before he was transferred to Luton, then Shrewsbury Town, Exeter City and Peterborough United. He then moved to non-League Nuneaton Borough as player-manager where he stayed three years before returning to Kenilworth Road as coach. He was elevated to manager in 1978.

MAY 18TH

1925	Lausanne	A	Friendly	6-1
1929	Royal Navy	Malta	Friendly	1-0
1933	Jersey	A	Friendly	5-1
1935	Guernsey	A	Friendly	5-0
1940	Southampton	A	Football League South Group C	3-3
1950	Tennis-Borussia	Berlin	Friendly	2-0
1955	FC Vasas	Budapest	Friendly	2-4
1963	Nottingham Forest	A	First Division	1-1
1965	DWS Club	Amsterdam	Friendly	0-1
1978	FC Karlstad	A	Friendly	4-1
1984	West Ham United	A	Friendly	1-4

This match was a testimonial for Patsy Holland with Spurs' goal being scored by Steve Archibald.

| 1991 | Nottingham Forest | Wembley | FA Cup Final | 2-1 [aet] |

The FA Cup final was both a relief and a saviour for Spurs. The run-up to the game had been dominated by matters off the field; the proposed sale of the club by Paul Bobroff and Irving Scholar to Terry Venables and whoever happened to be backing him at the time, the proposed sale of Paul Gascoigne and Gary Lineker to any interested parties (Gascoigne was already the subject of considerable interest from Lazio and they had tentatively agreed an £8 million fee to take the player after the cup final, whilst Lineker was being offered for sale throughout Europe, without the player's knowledge or approval), whether the Midland Bank would pull the plug on the club after over a hundred years of glory, what the future would hold for Terry Venables if they lost, and even if there was a future at all; was this to be Tottenham's swansong? Forest's preparations had been calm by comparison, with most of the country willing them to victory for their enigmatic manager Brian Clough. Clough lived up to his reputation throughout; walking alongside Terry Venables when the teams emerged from the tunnel he grabbed hold of Terry's hand and refused to let go. Venables later said that he spoke to Brian and tried to make him laugh, otherwise the watching millions would have thought the pair were a couple of lovers! Right from the first kick there was something wrong with Spurs; Paul Gascoigne was too fired up, with his mind perhaps wandering towards his impending move to Italy. After only five minutes he kicked out chest high at Garry Parker and was lucky not to be booked; the tackle had warranted a sending off at the very least. In 13 minutes Gascoigne did it again, bringing Gary Charles down just outside the area with another horrific tackle. Whilst Charles merely dusted himself down and picked himself up, Gascoigne rose gingerly to his feet and took his place in the wall being constructed in front of the Spurs goal. Stuart Pearce, possessor of one of the hardest shots in football, was deadly accurate as well, and his shot flew into the net, although Gary Mabbutt, who was pushed out of the way as the ball passed him, might have been able to get in the way. Then Gascoigne collapsed, his final over as he was carried off the field and taken immediately to hospital, Nayim his replacement. Gary Lineker soon responded and had the ball in the net, but this was ruled out for offside. Lineker went through again, this time to be hauled down by goalkeeper Mar Crossley, and took the resulting penalty. It was a good shot, but an equally fine save, for Crossley got his hand to the ball and sent it away for a corner. Half time probably represented the worst moment in Spurs' entire history. Their talisman had gone and the word from the hospital was that he was out for at least six months, possibly for ever, with torn cruciate ligaments. Replays revealed that Lineker's goal had not been offside at all and that the linesman had erred. Everything was conspiring against them. But cometh the hour, cometh the man. Just as he had done in a League match earlier, Paul Stewart grabbed the game by the throat and put in the finest performance of his career in a Spurs shirt. Collecting the ball from Paul Allen, another marvel on the day, he strode towards Forest's goal and stroked home a cross field shot. His influence gave Spurs the initiative and might have settled the game before the end of 90 minutes, but extra time was going to be needed. Venables rushed on to the field to give his men their instructions, telling them that they were going to win. Brian Clough stood on the touchline and chatted to a policeman! Whether Clough could have lit the Forest flame is a matter of debate, but Spurs played through the extra half hour convinced that the cup was theirs. A Nayim corner was headed on towards Gary Mabbutt, but Des Walker would get there first. In trying to head the ball away for another corner, he only succeeded in turning it into his own net. Forest never looked likely or close to forcing an equaliser, and so Spurs held on to claim their eighth FA Cup, a new record. Whether it was to be their swansong was still in doubt, but for the moment there was the little matter of handing Paul Gascoigne's medal over to him – the whole team and their wives went to the hospital to see the distraught player.

MAY 19TH

| 1929 | Floriana | A | Friendly | 2-1 |
| 1957 | Celtic | New York | Friendly | 4-3 |

Spurs' previous tour of North America five years previously had been a success, and the exhibition matches they had played against Manchester United had done much to increase the popularity of football in both Canada and America. Their return visit featured only one match in America, with the remaining eight games being played in Canada, and this match was the first of four clashes against Celtic. A crowd of 12,342 attended the opening game at the Downing Stadium on Randalls Island. Celtic powered into a 2-0 lead through Smith and Tully before Spurs got going, Bobby Smith netting to open their account, although Celtic soon restored their two-goal advantage thanks to Peacock. Spurs' fightback started again through Bobby Smith, and second-half goals from Smith and Dulin gave them victory.

1966	Bermuda Select XI	Hamilton	Friendly	3-2
1968	Anorthosis	Famagusta	Friendly	5-0
1977	Sogndal FC	A	Friendly	6-0

MAY 20TH

1907	Fulham	OsteNd	Friendly	2-1
1911	Wacker FC	Leipzig	Friendly	8-1
1912	Sports Athletic Club	Vienna	Friendly	5-2
1925	La Chaux de Fonds	A	Friendly	8-1
1955	Pecs Dozsa	Pecs	Friendly	1-0

1961 Clive Allen born in Stepney, East London. The son of former Spurs player Les Allen, Clive began his career with Queens Park Rangers despite having trained with Spurs as a schoolboy. He made an immediate impact as a striker with Rangers and at the end of his only full season was transferred to Arsenal in June 1980 for a fee of £1,250,000. Less than two months later and having made only three appearances in friendlies, Clive was on the move again, this time in a swap deal with Kenny Sansom of Crystal Palace. With the Palace manager Terry Venables himself departing two months later Clive found it difficult to settle at Selhurst Park and moved back to Loftus Road and Queens Park Rangers in 1981. In 1982 he was part of the QPR team that reached the FA Cup final against Spurs, although it was a match Clive would like to forget; injured after only two minutes he hobbled on for a further eight minutes until substituted and was forced to miss the replay. He continued to score at a prolific rate and was awarded his first England cap in 1984 shortly before a £700,000 move took him to White Hart Lane. Spurs fans caught the briefest glimpse of Clive Allen in full flight over the next two seasons as a succession of injuries limited his appearances. He was fully recovered in time for the 1986-87 season, scoring a hat-trick on the opening day at Aston Villa. and that was basically the Clive Allen story of the season; goals all the way. He was particularly lethal when playing as a lone striker in front of a five man midfield and rattled in an unprecedented 49 goals in this season as Spurs reached the Littlewoods Cup semi-final and FA Cup final. In the latter competition the second minute again became significant for Clive; he scored the opening goal against Coventry, although the Sky Blues later recovered to win 3-2. It was always going to be impossible for Clive to register similar goalscoring exploits and in March 1988 he was on his way once again, this time a £900,000 fee taking him to Bordeaux. A year later he returned home to join Manchester City, remaining 18 months before he joined another of his father's former clubs Chelsea. He later played for West Ham and Millwall before retiring.

| 1963 | Blackburn Rovers | A | First Division | 0-3 |
| 1967 | Chelsea | Wembley | FA Cup Final | 2-1 |

The first all-London FA Cup final clash pitted the experienced Spurs, winners of the FA Cup on a previous four occasions, against a young Chelsea side that had yet to win the FA Cup and were making their first appearance at Wembley. The two managers could not have been more different either; Bill Nicholson, the master coach who preferred to let his teams do all his talking for him, and Tommy Docherty, seldom lost for words but yet to prove himself as a tactician. The talking before the game turned out to be rather more interesting than the match itself, for Chelsea's inexperience showed and they allowed Spurs to take the game to them almost throughout. This proved their undoing, for after Jimmy Robertson (hitting the rebound after an Alan Mullery shot had been blocked) and Frank Saul (turning well to meet a cross and firing home) had fired Spurs 2-0 ahead there was never any likelihood that Chelsea were going to force their way back. Bobby Tambling's goal, four minutes from the end, was little more than a consolation effort.

| 1983 | ASL Trinidad | A | Friendly | 2-1 |
| 1991 | Manchester United | A | First Division | 1-1 |

Originally scheduled for earlier in the season, this game was delayed because of Manchester United's exploits in Europe. With the permission of the Football League it was agreed to play the match on the Monday night after the FA Cup final, which meant Spurs, having won the cup on the Saturday, visited the ground of the team who had won it the previous year. In fact this was a double celebration, for United had won the European Cup-Winners' Cup the previous Wednesday – both trophies were paraded around the ground by the respective captains – Bryan Robson of United and Gary Mabbutt of Spurs. Despite the carnival atmosphere and a huge crowd of 46,791, the actual game was played with all of the passion of a testimonial.

MAY 21ST

1905	Slavia	Prague	Friendly	8-1
1911	Eintracht FC	Brunswick	Friendly	4-1
1914	St Gallen	St Gallen	Friendly	3-0
1925	Berne	A	Friendly	5-0
1929	Pick of Malta	A	Friendly	5-1
1941	Arsenal	A	London War Cup Section B	3-0
1950	Wacker Club	Berlin	Friendly	5-2
1966	Celtic	Toronto	Friendly	0-1
1974	Feyenoord	H	UEFA Cup Final 1st Leg	2-2

When Spurs took to the field for their first leg clash with Feyenoord they were playing in their ninth major final. All the previous eight had been won, but Feyenoord would be stiff opposition. A good lead was required before the second leg and that was not going to be easy against a side that were on their way to winning their domestic League title. A headed goal from Mike England gave Spurs the lead in the first half, but Feyenoord were level before half-time. Mike England was involved in Spurs' second goal, although whether he got a touch or the ball came off a defender wasn't clear, but the only thing that mattered was that Spurs were ahead again. The lead lasted until four minutes from the end, when a fine move upfield resulted in Feyenoord equalising for a second time. The omens did not look good for the second leg.

| 1995 | Kitchee/Eastern XI | A | Friendly | 7-2 |

MAY 22ND

1952	Toronto & District FA	Toronto	Friendly	7-0
1957	Essex County All Stars	Windsor	Friendly	8-1
1965	Telstar Club	Ukjmuiden	Friendly	3-2

1967 Willie Hall died in Newark, Nottinghamshire. Born in Newark on 12th March 1912 he began his career with Notts County and was an important member of the side that won the Third Division North championship before signing with Spurs in December 1932. Interestingly, Willie made his debut for Spurs against Notts County! The subsequent emergence of Willie Hall as an influential inside-forward compensated somewhat for the loss of George Greenfield, who broke his leg the same month as Willie arrived at White Hart Lane. So convinced were Notts County of Willie's potential they inserted a clause in his transfer contract to Spurs that they would receive an additional £500 when he played for England; he made his debut a year later against France. The Second World War and a serious leg disease forced him to retire from the game in 1944, and he later had the lower part of both legs amputated. He served Clapton Orient as coach and manager but found his disability affected his work and resigned after only two months.

| 1968 | AEL | Limassol | Friendly | 7-1 |
| 1982 | Queens Park Rangers | Wembley | FA Cup Final | 1-1 [aet] |

Even though Spurs started the game as favourites against Second Division QPR (managed by former player and future manager of Spurs, Terry Venables), the long and hard season they had endured had taken a lot out of them. From fighting on four fronts – the League, League Cup, Europe and FA Cup – they were left with one last chance to finish the season with some tangible reward. Ricky Villa, despite being fit and with the memory of his winning goal the previous year still fresh in the mind, wouldn't be playing owing to the continued Falklands Islands crisis, although he was given a rapturous welcome by the Spurs fans as he walked around Wembley to get to his seat. Ardiles wasn't playing either, for he was back home in Argentina preparing for the forthcoming World Cup. Steve Perryman was struggling for fitness, although a couple of late injections would enable him to get through the 120 minutes. The match itself was largely forgettable, Spurs looking as though it was their 65th competitive game of the season. They took the lead in extra time, Glenn Hoddle shooting from just outside the area and the ball taking a slight deflection off Tony Currie to go beyond the grasp of man-of-the-match Peter Hucker in the QPR goal. But QPR fought back and Terry Fenwick, later a Spurs player, headed home the equaliser to become the first full-back to score from open play in an FA Cup final. That was about the only memorable thing all afternoon.

MAY 23RD

| 1914 | Pforzhiem | Pforzhiem | | |
| | | | Friendly | 4-0 |

1954 Gerry Armstrong born in Belfast. He was working as a clerical officer in local government when he first began playing football, signing with a number of local junior clubs before joining Bangor on a part-time basis. He was then spotted by Spurs and signed in November 1975, making his League debut at the beginning of the 1976-77 season. Unfortunately that season was to see Spurs relegated into the Second Division, and for the next three seasons Gerry was one of five strikers competing for a place in the first team. With the arrival of Steve Archibald and Garth Crooks in 1980 Gerry became surplus to requirements at White Hart Lane and moved to Watford for a fee of £250,000 in November 1980. He later played for Real Mallorca, West Bromwich Albion, Chesterfield and Brighton and whilst with Spurs collected 27 of his 63 caps for Northern Ireland.

1976	Western Australia	Perth	Friendly	4-0
1979	Malaysian Select XI	Kuala Lumpar		
			Friendly	4-0
1983	Charlton Athletic	A	Friendly	4-4
1984	RSC Anderlecht	H	UEFA Cup Final 2nd Leg	1-1
				[aet – won 4-3 on penalties]

In the end the players got the trophy they all wanted for their manager, but not before the hardest of fights and by the slenderest of margins on a night packed with drama and emotion. If Spurs thought they had done all of the hard work by drawing the first leg they were mistaken, for Anderlecht were to prove worthy opponents and earn most of the plaudits once the game was over. Even though a goalless draw would have been enough to earn Spurs victory, manager Keith Burkinshaw was shrewd enough to know his side were better going forward and that goals were what was needed to win. And yet it was Anderlecht who scored first, working the ball cleverly up the wing and putting Czerniatynski through on goal. As time ticked towards the end Spurs became more frantic and Burkinshaw sent on Ardiles in order to try and inspire his troops towards one last effort. Ardiles might have grabbed the equaliser too, but perhaps the adrenalin flow was too great and he fired the ball against the bar when it appeared easier to score. With the ball then despatched to the wing Anderlecht could have been excused a short breath of relief, but Micky Hazard fired it straight back into the area, Mark Falco virtually manhandled a defender out of the way and Graham Roberts chested the ball down before firing home from six yards. That set up extra time, but with tired limbs excelling over alert minds, there was no further score after 120 minutes. That set up a penalty shoot out and the final dramatic twist of the evening. Anderlecht went first, Tony Parks dived to his left and tipped the ball away. Roberts stepped up for Spurs' first kick and provided the perfect example to his team-mates by finding the net. So too did Steve Archibald, Mark Falco and Gary Stevens, along with their three respective Anderlecht rivals. By the time Danny Thomas placed the ball on the spot the score was at 4-3 – a goal now and the cup was Spurs'. He shot well too, but Anderlecht's Munaron guessed the right way and kept it out. Thomas clutched his head in his hands and made his way back to the centre circle as the Spurs fans chanted his name. Then Tony Parks took his place in goal to face the last of the scheduled penalties from Arnor Gudjohnsen. Parks had dived to his left for all the previous efforts, this time he decided to go to the right. Which was exactly where Gudjohnsen placed the ball, and with that the cup was won. Whilst most of the players ran on to the pitch to embrace the hero, manager Keith Burkinshaw and Steve Perryman hugged on the touchline and offered their condolences to the Anderlecht management team. Graham Roberts, captain on the night in place of the suspended Perryman, collected the cup, Spurs third in Europe. This finish had been more dramatic than the previous two put together.

| 1985 | Seiko FC | Hong Kong | | |
| | | | Friendly | 4-0 |

MAY 24TH

| 1912 | Woolwich Arsenal | Vienna | Friendly | 0-4 |
| 1914 | Stuttgart | Stuttgart | Friendly | 1-0 |

Whilst the match may have been billed as a friendly, the atmosphere which greeted Spurs was anything but. With war just around the corner, Spurs had had to endure almost continuous anti-English feeling and propaganda whenever they played in Germany, although matches played in Italy and Switzerland on the same tour had passed almost without incident. The same could not be said for their experiences in Germany, for almost anything was allowable whenever Spurs took to the field. Not only did Spurs have to contend with the German opposition, there was a German referee and an increasingly hostile crowd to deal with. Goalkeeper Tiny Joyce was attacked by one spectator who cut his head open with an umbrella, the supposed financial guarantees proved difficult to collect (although chairman Charles Roberts, who spoke fluent German, could usually be relied upon to extract every last Deutschmark from the hosts), and perfectly legitimate goals were disallowed on the whim of the referees. Whilst Spurs managed to return home unbeaten, winning five and drawing two of the seven matches on the tour, the hostility afforded the club was sufficient for Charles Roberts to state upon his return to England 'Never again will Tottenham go to Germany while I am chairman of the club.' They didn't either, finally returning in 1950 after Roberts's death.

1925	Basel	A	Friendly	1-0
1941	Leicester City	H	Football League South	3-0
1950	Borussia Dortmund	Dortmund	Friendly	4-0
1981	Bahrain Select XI	A	Friendly	3-0
1995	Guangzhou	A	Friendly	2-1

MAY 25TH

| 1903 | Spurs signed John Brearley from Everton. Born in Liverpool in 1875 John had already served Notts County, Millwall Athletic and Middlesbrough before signing with Everton in 1902. Spurs player-manager John Cameron signed Brearley effectively to replace himself, leaving Cameron free to concentrate on management. Used as both a centre-forward and half-back, John remained at Spurs for four years, joining Crystal Palace in May 1907 and later Millwall. He did, however, later link up again with John Cameron – when the First World War broke out both players were working in Germany and were subsequently interned at Ruhleben Prison. | | | |

1911	Kickers-Victoria FC	Frankfurt	Friendly	6-0
1940	Chelsea	H	Football League South Group C	3-2
1955	Racing Club de Paris	Paris	Friendly	0-0
1957	Ontario All Stars	Ontario	Friendly	7-0
1960	Juventus	A	Friendly	0-2
1966	Hartford Select XI	Hartford	Friendly	3-0
1968	Cyprus International XI	Nicosia	Friendly	3-0
1993	After a two hour court hearing chairman Alan Sugar and chief executive Terry Venables reached an			

agreement that enabled both men to remain at White Hart Lane until the outcome of their pending legal battle was known.

1994   The FA announced that in the event of Spurs being found guilty of misconduct and being punished by demotion, Sheffield United, who had finished the previous season in 20th place, would replace Spurs in the Premier League.

MAY 26TH

| 1907 | Ostend | Ostend | Friendly | 8-1 |
| 1945 | Fulham | H | Friendly | 2-2 |

1953   Don McAllister born in Radcliffe, Lancashire. After failing a trial with Coventry City Don was signed by Bolton Wanderers in 1968 as an apprentice, joining the professional ranks in June 1970. By 1975 he was widely regarded as one of the best central defenders in the game and Spurs swooped to sign him for a fee of £80,000 in February 1975. He was in and out of the side after arriving at White Hart Lane and even tried switching positions, slotting in at full-back when Cyril Knowles was injured. In August 1981 he was sold to Charlton Athletic and finished his career with Rochdale.

| 1962 | Tel Aviv Select XI | A | Friendly | 2-1 |

1968   Steve Sedgley born in Enfield. Although Steve was a Spurs fan as a boy and played for the club's juniors, he was not offered a contract and subsequently signed for Coventry City in 1986. At the end of his first season with the Sky Blues he collected an FA Cup winners' medal as Coventry beat Spurs, although Steve was a non-playing substitute on that day. In July 1989 Spurs paid £750,000 to bring him home, and got a player equally at home in defence or midfield for their money. He won a second FA Cup winners' medal in 1991 as Spurs beat Forest, having to put in rather more effort than for his first medal! In 1994, having struggled to retain his place in the side, he was transferred to Ipswich Town for £1 million, later joining Wolves.

| 1981 | Kuwait Army XI | A | Friendly | 2-1 |
| 1995 | Singapore Lions | A | Friendly | 1-1 |

MAY 27TH

1879   Ollie Burton born in Derby. He came to Spurs on trial in 1901 as a half-back and impressed enough to have been taken on by the club full-time, making his debut in a friendly match in November 1902. He was later successfully converted to full-back, a position he made his own as the club wound down their career with the Southern League and were elevated into the Football League. The high standard of the First Division, however, made the job much harder and after only five games Ollie was dropped. He died in London on 20th January 1929.

1908   The Southern League AGM was brought forward by half an hour in order that it would clash exactly with that of the Football League! The Southern League meeting's agenda was taken up almost exclusively with the situation relating to Tottenham and QPR (Bradford had formally resigned); it was resolved that both clubs should be excluded from membership of the Southern League and their respective places be given to Coventry City and Southend United. Not that Spurs would have been unduly worried, for they were more concerned with their application for membership of the Football League. Having canvassed for support almost as soon as their resignation from the Southern League had been announced, Spurs were quietly confident that they would be admitted to the Football League. But things didn't go quite the way they had planned, for although Spurs collected the first ten votes that were cast, Grimsby collected 32 votes in all and were re-admitted to the League. Spurs weren't even considered a close second; the voting had gone 32 votes to Grimsby, 23 to Chesterfield (also re-admitted), 20 to Bradford Park Avenue (who might have received fewer votes were it not for the fact that Bradford City had just won the Second Division championship. They nevertheless managed to claim the third vacancy), 18 to Lincoln (who thus left the League for the first time in their history), 14 to Spurs and Boston United one. This left Spurs in utter despair; although the Southern League had unofficially intimated that Spurs would be admitted back, but only to the Second Division, Spurs had determined not to return to the Southern League under any circumstances. Now that they had failed to obtain membership of the Football League they were faced with the very real possibility of having no matches other than cup-ties and friendlies (if they could arrange them – the Southern League clubs would almost certainly have refused invitations to play against such rebels) in the coming season. Things got no better over the next few days either, for whilst QPR backed down to the Southern League and were re-admitted to membership (albeit under the ridiculously punitive conditions that they play their home matches in midweek), an advertisement in the *Athletic News* inviting applications for a proposed Third Division of the Football League went no further. Just when the cloud was at its darkest, the smallest of the sun's rays shone through like a beacon.

1912	Ferencvarosi Torna	Budapest	Friendly	4-1
1950	Royal Beerschot	Antwerp	Friendly	1-2
1959	Torpedo Moscow	Moscow	Friendly	1-0

1967   Paul Gascoigne born in Gateshead. He joined Newcastle United as a junior and made steady progress following his debut in 1985. Local hero Jackie Milburn claimed Gascoigne was the brightest talent he'd ever seen in the game, and in 1988 Spurs paid £2 million for his signature. He remained with Spurs until 1992 – having learned to curb his tendency for pure entertainment and upping his work rate brought about a call-up for England in 1989 and his eventual selection for the 1990 World Cup squad. In Italy he grew in stature as the tournament progressed and ended up being acclaimed throughout the world. Back home he helped Spurs to the 1991 FA Cup final, scoring in virtually every round and then a moment of madness and a rash tackle put him out of the final and the game for nearly a year. When he recovered he was sold to SS Lazio for £5.5 million, later returning to Britain to play for Scottish giants Rangers. In March 1998 he returned to England, signing for Middlesbrough in time to play in their Coca-Cola Cup final against Chelsea.

1971	All Japan XI	Kobe	Friendly	6-0
1979	Indonesia	Yokohama	Japan Cup Group A	6-0
1982	Queens Park Rangers	Wembley	FA Cup Final Replay	1-0

The published crowd figure for this FA Cup final replay was 92,000, Wembley's capacity at that time for a night match, but empty spaces around the ground told a different story. And if those who did attend were hoping for a repeat of the previous year's exhibition, then they were to be sadly disappointed. The match was settled as early as the seventh minute, Graham Roberts surging run from the half way line being brought to an end just inside the penalty area by Tony Currie's outstretched leg and Glenn Hoddle doing the rest from the 12 yard spot. Thereafter QPR probably had the better chances (although Spurs hit the post near the end) as they searched for an equaliser, with John Gregory hitting the bar with a cross and Spurs surviving a number of scares. If the manner of the victory didn't quite match that of the previous year, the relief was probably greater; Spurs had gone into the 1980-81 season hoping to win something, and the 1981-82 season expecting it. It also gave them their seventh FA Cup success, equalling Aston Villa's record, and more importantly a major trophy to place in the boardroom as they entered their centenary season.

1992 Following Peter Shreeves's departure from the club, Spurs announced the new management team; Doug Livermore would be the new first-team coach and Ray Clemence his assistant, with chief executive Terry Venables taking more of an active role in team matters.

MAY 28TH

| 1912 | Olympic Players | Budapest | Friendly | 2-2 |
| 1952 | Saskatchewan FA | Saskatoon | Friendly | 18-1 |

This match was as one-sided as the result suggests, so much so that at half-time, with Spurs already ten ahead, goalkeeper Ted Ditchburn swapped with his opposite number on the Saskatchewan team, Hayes. Ditchburn conceded eight goals in the second half! Leading the way goalscoring-wise was Sid McClellan, who scored nine, with Bennett (three), Duquemin (two) Uphill and Adams (three) getting the rest. Although this is obviously Spurs' biggest ever win, the friendly nature of the match ensures it does not hold a place in the record books.

1969	Fiorentina	Toronto	Friendly	0-3
1981	Bahrain Select XI	A	Friendly	5-3
1987	Millionaros Colombia	Miami	Friendly	0-1

MAY 29TH

1951	Combined Copenhagen XI	Copenhagen	Friendly	4-2
1957	Alberta All Stars	Calgary	Friendly	6-1
1966	Bologna	Jersey City	Friendly	0-1
1968	Apoel	Nicosia	Friendly	3-0
1974	Feyenoord	A	UEFA Cup Final 2nd Leg	0-2

This was to have been Bill Nicholson's swansong for Spurs. If they managed to win the trophy he had every intention of resigning immediately after; going out at the top after giving them so much success was the perfect way to end his managerial career. In the end neither event took place, for against a backdrop of violence among the crowd Spurs lost the first major final of their history. There was no shame in that, for Feyenoord were one of Europe's finest teams and had just won the Dutch League. The shame belonged to the Spurs fans, who were on something of a drunken orgy before, during and after the match. Trouble had begun as some of the groups boarded the ferries to take them over to Holland, had continued in the streets of Rotterdam before the game and threatened to engulf the stadium during it. On the field Spurs were struggling to contain their Dutch opponents, off it the Dutch police were locked in a similar confrontation with Spurs fans. Feyenoord had taken the lead in the first half, although Spurs had their own chances to score and were unlucky when Perryman latched on to a free-kick and poked the ball just wide. Half-time should have been when Bill Nicholson rallied his players, pointed out where they were going wrong, highlighting the things they were doing right and helping them back into the game. He never got the chance, for by now the Spurs fans were rioting to such an extent the Dutch police asked him to make an appeal over the tannoy. Despite his opinion that they were a disgrace to Spurs, England and themselves, they carried on. His team, shorn of a learned voice during the break, went out in the second half and played the same way. Feyenoord scored another goal to confirm their victory by 4-2 on aggregate, but most of the figures printed after the game told a different story – 70 arrests, over 200 injured. What could have been a glorious end to an illustrious career for Bill Nicholson ended in tragedy.

1979	Japan A	Tokyo	Japan Cup Group A	2-0
1984	England XI	H	Keith Burkinshaw Testimonial	2-2
1985	Australia Soccer Federation	Melbourne		
			$200,000 Tournament	0-1

MAY 30TH

1912	Olympic Players	Budapest	Friendly	4-3
1951	Combined Copenhagen XI	Copenhagen		
			Friendly	2-2
1953	Racing Club de Paris	A	Friendly	1-1
1962	Haifa Select XI	A	Friendly	5-0

1964 England played Brazil in Rio, a match in which Alan Mullery had been confidently expected to collect his first England cap. Unfortunately, Alan suffered a muscle spasm whilst shaving on the morning he was due to join the touring party and had to pull out! He did go on to represent England, making his debut in December 1964.

| 1967 | FC Zurich | A | Friendly | 2-0 |

Having undertaken a long and strenuous end-of-season tour to the United Staes, Canada and Mexico the previous season, the club stayed considerably nearer to home for the 1967 tour. Barely ten days after winning the FA Cup against Chelsea, Spurs took to the field to play a friendly against FC Zurich. Despite the obvious attraction of Spurs, dreadful weather on the day of the game was sufficient to deter all but the hardy few from the ground, and only 5,000 witnessed two goals from Jimmy Robertson getting the tour off to a winning start.

| 1983 | Aalesund | Norway | Friendly | 3-2 |

MAY 31ST

1941	Brentford	H	London War Cup Section B Semi-Final	0-2
1951	Combined Copenhagen XI	Copenhagen		
			Friendly	2-0
1952	British Columbia FA	Vancouver		
			Friendly	9-2
1963	NSAFL Invitation XI	Cape Town		
			Friendly	5-1

This was Spurs' first ever tour of South Africa and took place just over two weeks after the European Cup-Winners' Cup victory in Rotterdam. Midway through the first match Terry Medwin, who had not played in that final, broke a leg and was replaced by Terry Dyson. The injury was eventually to bring his playing career to an end, for after a lengthy battle to regain full fitness, he was forced to retire in the summer of 1964 without having played again.

| 1979 | Fiorentina | Nishigaoka | | |
| | | | Japan Cup Group A | 1-1 |

1998 There was both joy and heartbreak for Spurs' players following the announcement of Glenn Hoddle's England squad of 22 for the forthcoming World Cup finals in Spain; in the squad were Sol Campbell, Darren Anderton and Les Ferdinand, out went Ian Walker. Whilst Campbell's inclusion had not been in doubt (he had captained the England side in their last warm-up match before the squad was announced), both Anderton and Ferdinand had faced a race against time to prove themselves fit for the forthcoming tournament, a race both ultimately won. Walker was considered unlucky, his spell out of the Spurs side earlier in the season through injury had allowed Tim Flowers and Nigel Martyn to move up the line behind David Seaman. At the end of the day, however, the squad's chief talking point was the exclusion of former Spurs player Paul Gascoigne, deemed unfit by the manager.

JUNE 1ST

1926 George Robb born in Finsbury Park, London. After playing for Islington Schools and Finchley, George was offered amateur forms by Spurs in 1944. When Spurs did not offer full professional terms he continued playing for Finchley as an amateur and became a schoolmaster until, in December 1951 Spurs again approached him with a view to signing him on amateur forms. He duly signed and made his League debut against Charlton on Christmas Day 1951, scoring once in the 3-0 win. When Les

Medley left the club at the end of 1952-53 George was persuaded to sign full professional forms and went on to give a further seven years service. During this time he won his only England full international cap (he had previously won 11 amateur caps for his country) – he played in the 6-3 home defeat by Hungary! Although he played as a winger he was a more than capable goalscorer, returning 53 goals in only 182 appearances in the League. A serious injury sustained in the 1957-58 season finally ended his playing career in May 1960, upon which he returned to being a schoolmaster.

1957	Celtic	Vancouver		
			Friendly	6-3
1959	Dynamo Kiev	Kiev	Friendly	2-1
1966	Celtic	San Francisco		
			Friendly	1-2
1967	BSC Young Boys	A	Friendly	3-2
1969	Rangers	Toronto	Friendly	4-3
1985	Udinese	Sydney	$200,000 Tournament	0-2

In the three days since Spurs played their first match in this competition, UEFA and FIFA had moved swiftly to isolate English clubs from the rest of the world following the Heysel Stadium disaster, culminating in a ban of English clubs playing anywhere in the world. It was pointed out to both bodies that such a ban would not be possible to implement immediately, for clubs such as Spurs were already contracted to play lucrative and/or prestigious friendlies, but for at least two days the Spurs touring party were ready to return home at a moment's notice should FIFA and UEFA insist. As it turned out, Spurs were allowed to remain in Australia and compete but gave a lacklustre performance, ironically against Italian opposition, going down 2-0 to Udinese in Sydney.

JUNE 2ND

1912	Olympic Players	Vienna	Friendly	0-3

1928   Ron Reynolds born in Haslemere, Hampshire. He began his career with Aldershot, joining the club as a 17-year-old and making his debut in January 1946 in the war-time League fixture with Bournemouth, although it was not an auspicious start; Ron, in goal, had to collect the ball out of the net seven times! However, he was offered professional terms by Aldershot and made over 100 League appearances for them before transferring to Spurs as understudy to Ted Ditchburn. Ditchburn's remarkable consistency and fitness ensured Ron's appearances were limited, but in nearly ten years with the club he did make a total of 86 League appearances. In 1958 he lost his place as first choice reserve to John Hollowbread and in 1960 the one-time England possible was transferred to Southampton for £10,000. Here Ron won a Third Division championship medal in his first season and then suffered a shoulder injury that ended his playing career. After spells scouting for Southampton and Crystal Palace he left the game altogether to concentrate on his insurance business.

1951   Twelve months previously, when Spurs won the Second Division championship, the club celebrated with a banquet at the Savoy for 350 guests. With further success being achieved this season, the First Division title lifted for the first time in the club's history, the club returned to the same venue for a banquet even more memorable. The attendance topped 400; representatives from every League club were present, together with the Marquis of Londonderry, Mr Arthur Drewry (President of the Football League), Sir Stanley Rous (Secretary of the FA) and assorted VIPs, all of whom enjoyed an evening that 'will live in the memory of everybody whose legs were under the hospitable board of the Club. The dinner and wines were first class, the speeches were good, and the cabaret entertainment reached a top note. All went as merrily as a peal of wedding bells, and when it was all over everybody left more than delighted that they had been there to take part in the Club's rejoicings.'

1952	Victoria & District FA	Victoria	Friendly	7-0
1979	San Lorenzo	Tokyo	Japan Cup Semi-Final	3-3
1984	Liverpool	Swaziland		
			Royal Swazi Sun Tournament	2-5
1991	Vasco da Gama	Kobe	Kirin Cup	0-0

JUNE 3RD

1879   Vivian J Woodward born in Kennington, South London. One of the finest players of his or any other age, Vivian Woodward would have shone in any team. That for the best part of his illustrious career that team happened to be Spurs was to the club's distinct advantage. An amateur for his entire career, he began playing with local sides in Clacton and then signed with Chelmsford City. He signed with Spurs in March 1901 but did not become a regular in the side until 1902-03 as he had business commitments and also because he had no wish to let down Chelmsford. He was a regular feature of the Spurs side until 1909 and to him fell the honour of scoring the first goal as a Football League side, in the match against Wolves at White Hart Lane in September 1908. His amateur status saw him make 67 appearances for the England amateur team and he was good enough also to represent the full side on 23 occasions, scoring 28 goals. He was also captain of the United Kingdom teams that won consecutive Olympic titles in 1908 and 1912. He was appointed a director of Spurs in 1908 but the following year announced his retirement from the top level of the game in order to return to playing for Chelmsford. Less than three months later he signed with Chelsea and remained on the playing staff until midway through the First World War. This of course included Chelsea's first appearance in the FA Cup final, and Woodward was given leave by the Army to play in the match against Sheffield United. However, Woodward's principles were such that if he had played, Bob Thomson (who had scored most of the goals that got Chelsea to the final) would have missed out and so Woodward declined Chelsea's offer. He did however become a director of the club in 1922 and served them in this capacity until 1930. Having previously been an architect for most of his professional life he became a gentleman farmer and died in Ealing in January 1954.

1950	Spurs celebrated the winning of the Second Division championship and promotion to the First Division with a banquet at the Savoy Hotel in London. This followed the annual meeting of the Football League and was therefore attended by representatives of nearly all the League clubs. Indeed, over 350 dignitaries, including players and officials, were in attendance at the banquet, together with former Spurs players Jack Kirwan (a survivor of the 1901 cup-winning team) Jimmy Seed and Arthur Grimsdell, with entertainment provided by Janet Hamilton (soprano) and John Hargreaves (tenor), Tommy Cooper and Johnny Lockwood.			
1957	British Columbia All Stars	Vancouver		
		Friendly		0-2
1961	The club celebrated success in the FA Cup and the winning of the League championship with a celebration banquet at the Savoy Hotel.			
1968	Wally Alsford died in Bedford. A graduate of the Spurs nursery at Northfleet, Wally (born in Edmonton in 1911) made his debut in the London FA Charity Cup tie against Chelsea in 1930, although his League debut did not come until two months later, at Reading on December 27th. Although not a regular at any time during the six years he spent with Spurs, he did make a total of 81 League appearances, including being almost a regular in the second half of the 1934-35 season which sadly culminated in Spurs being relegated from the First Division, and winning an England cap in April 1935 against Scotland. In January 1937 Spurs transferred the half-back to Nottingham Forest where, 12 months later, he was found to be suffering from osteomyelitis and told his career was at an end. He retired in May 1938 but made a number of guest appearances for Forest and other clubs during the early months of the Second World War. At the end of the war he became a publican.			
1970	All Japan XI	Tokyo	Friendly	7-2
1992	Spurs signed Portsmouth winger Darren Anderton for a fee of £1.75 million. Darren had caught the eye during Portsmouth's run to the FA Cup semi-final, where they had lost on penalties to Liverpool. As a result, there was stiff competition for his signature, but the chance to work with Terry Venables proved persuasive in the end.			

JUNE 4TH

1952	British Columbia FA	Vancouver		
		Friendly		8-2
1957	Neil McNab born in Greenock, Renfrewshire. Obviously something of a child prodigy for he made his League debut for Morton when aged only 15 and was heralded as 'the new John White'. Bill Nicholson was convinced of his potential for he paid out £40,000 to bring the 16-year-old to White Hart Lane. Because of his age he was only allowed to sign amateur forms and it was thus that he made his debut for Spurs, appearing as a substitute in the game against Chelsea in April 1974. It took until the 1977-78 season, however, before the stylish midfielder could command a regular place in the team and indeed he was an ever present in the side that climbed out of the Second Division at the first attempt that season. The arrival of World Cup stars Ossie Ardiles and Ricky Villa meant someone had to give way in Spurs' midfield and unfortunately it was Neil, and after making his last appearance for Spurs in the 7-0 hammering at Anfield he was transferred to Bolton for £250,000 in February 1980. Subsequent spells at Brighton, Leeds (on loan), Portsmouth (also on loan), Manchester City and Tranmere Rovers saw him enhance his reputation.			
1959	Russian Select XI	Leningrad	Friendly	1-3
1966	Celtic	Vancouver	Friendly	1-1
1979	Dundee United	Tokyo	Japan Cup Final	2-0
1983	Manchester United	Swaziland	Royal Swazi Hotel Tournament	1-2

JUNE 5TH

1909	Everton	Palermo	Friendly	2-2
1957	Manitoba All Stars	Winnipeg	Friendly	12-0
	A crowd of 4,500, an exceptional figure according to the locals, saw Spurs in front and on top right			

from the start. Goals from Alfie Stokes (five), Terry Dyson (three), Micky Dulin (two), Tommy Harmer and Dave Dunmore gave Spurs an easy victory (they were 7-0 ahead at half-time) and at the end of the game each player was given a trophy; a miniature buffalo mounted on a hardwood stand!

| 1963 | NFL Select XI | Durban | Friendly | 5-2 |

1968   Alan Mullery became the first England player to be sent off in an international match when he was dismissed in the European Championship match against Yugoslavia.

| 1985 | Vascoda Gama | Adelaide | $200,000 Tournament | 1-1 |
| 1991 | Thailand | Nagoya | Kirin Cup | 2-1 |

JUNE 6TH

1925   Bill Jacques died in Dartford, Kent. Goalkeeper Bill appeared for Spurs between 1914 and 1923, and was the regular goalkeeper for almost all of this period. Unfortunately, Bill collected an injury in a match with West Bromwich Albion in February 1921 and was unable to reclaim his position once recovered, with the result that Alex Hunter collected an FA Cup winners' medal in April of that year. In addition to making 123 appearances for Spurs in the Football League he turned out for the club on 103 occasions during the four war-time London Combination League seasons. He recovered his first-team place from Hunter in October 1921 and looked set to further his number of appearances for the club until illness forced his retirement in 1923. He died two years later – by the most tragic of coincidences. Spurs' goalkeeper when they won the FA Cup in 1901 (George Clawley) also died comparatively young.

| 1979 | Bermuda Select XI | A | Friendly | 3-1 |

JUNE 7TH

1907   Jimmy Smailes born in South Moor, Yorkshire. Jimmy spent 18 months at White Hart Lane, having joined the club from Huddersfield Town in March 1931. Although he went straight into the Spurs side and held it until early the following season, Willie Evans looked a better prospect and Smailes was relegated into the reserves. He was then sold to Blackpool for £2,000 in December 1932. He played for a further three clubs, finishing his League career with Bradford City at the end of the Second World War.

| 1941 | Fulham | H | Football League South | 2-1 |
| 1947 | Barnsley | H | Second Division | 1-1 |

The only occasion in which Spurs have played a Football League match in June – the season was extended following a particularly harsh winter which decimated the fixtures in February. Spurs had played their last League match on May 17th, had a three-week break and then played this day's game with Barnsley! The novelty of League football in June brought out a 17,000 crowd, and the Football League programme was finally wrapped up the following week.

| 1952 | Alberta FA | Calgary | Friendly | 11-0 |

1964   Paul Stewart born in Manchester. Signed by Blackpool in October 1981 Paul scored 56 goals in 201 appearances for the Seasiders before transferring to Manchester City for £200,000 in 1987. In a little over 12 months Paul found the net with regularity for the City and was then signed by Terry Venables for Spurs' then record fee of £1,700,000, joining at the same time as Paul Gascoigne. A suspension incurred at City prevented him making his Spurs debut until October 1988 when he came on as substitute against Manchester United and promptly missed a penalty. That somehow set the scene for his first two years at Spurs, for as a striker who had thrived on scoring goals he found the going a little tough. Although Gary Lineker arrived to bolster the forward line, it was not until midway through the 1990-91 season that Paul's fortunes changed for the better. Switched to midfield in an emergency in the game with Luton (Spurs had had two players sent off) he took the game by the scruff of the neck and turned in one of the best individual performances seen in a white shirt for many a year, scoring both goals as Spurs came from behind. Thereafter he came to the fore in midfield, scoring Spurs' equalising goal in the 1991 FA Cup final against Nottingham Forest and winning a full England cap in September the same year. By the end of the 1991-92 season Paul's desire to return to his native north had become too great and he was transferred to Liverpool for £2,300,000, subsequently appearing on loan for Crystal Palace and Wolves and later Sunderland.

| 1967 | FC Servette | A | Friendly | 4-1 |
| 1972 | Maccabi Tel Aviv | Tel Aviv | Friendly | 3-2 |

JUNE 8TH

1870   James McNaught born in Dumbarton. After playing in Scotland with Dumbarton and Ireland with Linfield James McNaught came to England to try his luck with Newton Heath (forerunners of the present Manchester United) in the Second Division in 1893. There he made his name as something of a ball-playing centre-half over the next five seasons before transferring to Spurs of the Southern League in 1898. The fact that he gave Spurs exceptional service over the years was recognised by appearances for the Anglo-Scots and an England XI, although he fell just short of collecting a full cap. A member of the team that won the Southern League in 1900 he was unfortunately injured during the FA Cup first round match with Preston the following season and therefore missed out on a medal in the FA Cup-winning side. In an age when one-year contracts were the norm, James McNaught consistent performances for Spurs enabled him to remain at the club for nine years, until in April 1907 he was released and subsequently joined Maidstone. He died in West Ham in 1919.

1957	Celtic	Toronto	Friendly	3-1
1963	South African XI	Johannesburg		
			Friendly	3-1
1966	British Columbia XI	Vancouver		
			Friendly	3-0
1974	Mauritius Select XI	Curepipe	Friendly	5-0

JUNE 9TH

1952	Manitoba FA	Winnipeg	Friendly	5-0
1957	Celtic	Montreal	Friendly	0-2

The fourth and final meeting with Celtic on the tour of North America saw Celtic win for the only time. A crowd of 8,500 saw a goalless first half, with Bobby Smith (who was something of a thorn in the side of Celtic, having scored eight goals in the previous three games) suffering an knock for which he had to be substituted at half-time. Two goals from Mochan in the second half gave Celtic some compensation for their previous efforts.

1971	All Japan XI	Tokyo	Friendly	3-0
1984	Liverpool	Swaziland	Royal Swazi Sun Tournament	1-1
1985	Udinese	Melbourne	$200,000 Tournament 3rd/4th place play-off	4-1
1991	Japan	Tokyo	Kirin Cup	0-4

JUNE 10TH

1909	Uruguay League	Montevideo		
			Friendly	8-0

This was the only match Spurs played in Uruguay on their tour of 1909, the other six matches being played in Argentina. The invitation to tour had originally been offered by the Argentinean FA, who asked both Spurs and Everton if they would play two exhibition matches and a number of local sides in friendlies. Five days after the two English sides had met in Palermo, Spurs crossed the River Plate and met a representative Uruguayan side. Goals from Clark (three), Minter (two), Curtis (two) and McConnor gave Spurs an easy victory.

1981	Trabzonspor	A	Friendly	4-0
1993	The Alan Sugar/Terry Venables saga reached the court, with over 2,500 pages of sworn statements revealing the depth of their acrimonious split.			

JUNE 11TH

1925	Sid McClellan born in Dagenham, London. Signed by Spurs from Chelmsford City Sid took more than a year to make his League debut, finally getting his chance in September 1950. Although Sid was an accomplished goal taker in his own right, the likes of Len Duquemin proved impossible to shift from the first team and in seven years with Spurs Sid made only 68 League appearances. He was released to join Portsmouth in 1956 and finished his League career with Leyton Orient.
1946	Keith Weller born in Islington, London. Keith joined Spurs as an amateur in August 1963 and signed professional forms the following January. He was initially used as little more than cover for established wingers Jimmy Robertson and Cliff Jones, but his inability to obtain regular first-team action prompted a demand for a transfer. Reluctantly, just as they would later do with Graeme Souness, Spurs sold the player, collecting £18,000 from Millwall for his services. At Millwall and, more significantly, Chelsea Keith developed into one of the best midfield players of his era and was later capped for England. He later played for Leicester City and finished his career in North America. He could also show a temperamental side, for during one match for Leicester City in 1974 he went on strike at half-time and refused to appear for the second half!
1983	Manchester United	Swaziland

			Royal Swazi Hotel Tournament	2-0

JUNE 12TH

1945	Pat Jennings born, Newry, County Down. Those who saw the 'push and run' side of the early fifties are convinced that Ted Ditchburn is the greatest goalkeeper to have appeared for Spurs, whilst those who saw Pat Jennings in his prime, which lasted longer than almost any other goalkeeper, are convinced that he was the man. In any case, there is little doubt that Pat Jennings was one of the

most consistent goalkeepers of any age. Having first played Gaelic football (which must surely have accounted for his safe handling of the ball) Pat turned to football with Newry Town and was picked for the Northern Ireland team in a youth tournament at Bognor Regis. There his displays caught the attention of Watford and they paid £6,000 for his signature. Pat spent only one full season with Watford before moving to Spurs in a £27,000 deal in June 1964. Although he made a hesitant start to his Spurs career, alternating the goalkeeping position with Bill Brown, Jennings made the spot his own in 1966-67 and then went on to amass more League appearances for Spurs than any previous player. During his 13-year career at White Hart Lane he picked up winners' medals in the FA Cup (1967), League Cup (1971 and 1973) and UEFA Cup (1974) as well as a runners-up medal in the 1974 UEFA Cup. He was the Footballer of the Year in 1973, awarded the MBE in 1976 and given a testimonial against Arsenal in November the same year. The opponents proved to be somewhat ironic, for at the end of the season, with Spurs finishing bottom of the First Division, manager Keith Burkinshaw decided to place his faith in the up-and-coming Barry Daines and transferred Jennings to Arsenal for a ridiculously low fee of £45,000. Whilst Spurs can never claim to have got the better of their nearest rivals in transfers, the departure of Jennings ranks high on the list of disasters. Pat gave the Gunners eight years sterling service, collected another FA Cup winners' medal (in 1979), two runners-up medals in the same competition (in 1978 and 1980) and a further runners-up medal, this time in the European Cup-Winners' Cup in 1980, despite not conceding a goal in the final (Arsenal being beaten on penalties). Rumours of a long-standing rift between Pat and Spurs were proven unfounded in 1985 when, having been released by Arsenal but needing to keep fit for Northern Ireland's World Cup campaign, he rejoined Spurs and made appearances in numerous friendlies and a Screen Sport Super Cup match. He also had a loan spell with Everton in 1986 (ostensibly as cover for Bobby Mimms as the Goodison Park club made the FA Cup final) and finally bowed out of the game he had graced for so long in the World Cup finals in Mexico. He made 473 League appearances for Spurs (a record since overhauled by Steve Perryman) and had the distinction of scoring in the 1967-68 season – his long-range punt upfield, intended for Alan Gilzean's head, dropped midway between the Spurs forward and the out-rushing Manchester United keeper Alex Stepney and bounced into the net in the FA Charity Shield match! He won a total of 119 caps for Northern Ireland, 75 of which were won whilst at Spurs, making him the most capped Spurs player, and continues to serve Spurs to this day, where he is specialist goalkeeping coach.

1956   Colin Lee born in Torquay, Devon. Colin began his career with Bristol City as a striker but was converted to full-back because of stiff competition for places, being loaned to Hereford and Torquay before signing permanently with the Plainmoor side. He then reverted to striker and it was in this position that he was spotted by Spurs, joining the club in October 1977 for £60,000. He scored four goals on his debut against Bristol Rovers, but this was probably as good as it got for him whilst at White Hart Lane and in January 1980 he was sold to Chelsea for £200,000. Whilst at Stamford Bridge he won a Second Division title medal and the Full Members Cup and he finished his playing career with Brentford.

1966   Mexican National XI   Mexico City
                                            Friendly   1-0

JUNE 13TH

1909   Argentinos   Palermo   Friendly   1-0
        The opposition were confined to players who were born in Argentina and they acquitted themselves exceptionally well, restricting Spurs to a single goal from McConnor. This was McConnor's second goal of the tour, although so far as research indicates, he made only two appearances for Spurs during his career, scoring in both games!

1947   Olympique de Marseilles   A   Friendly   1-2
        This was Spurs' first tour match since they had played in Guernsey in 1935, and their first proper overseas tour since they had visited Malta in 1929. Spurs' only goal was scored by Harry Gilberg.

1974   Mauritius Select XI   Curepipe   Friendly   6-3
1981   Fernabahce   A   Friendly   5-1
1995   Spurs signed a record four-year deal with kit suppliers Pony worth an estimated £10 million.

JUNE 14TH

1952   Manchester United   Toronto   Friendly   5-0
1953   Spurs took on West Essex in a cricket match, winning 159 for 9 wickets against 158! Spurs played a total of 12 cricket matches during the summer, winning eight and seeing one abandoned owing to rain.

1968   Bert Bliss died in Wood Green. Bert, born in Willenhall, Staffordshire, on March 29th, 1890, was spotted by Spurs playing junior football in March 1912 and immediately snapped up, making his League debut in April the same year at home to Manchester City. A diminutive inside-forward, he made up for his lack of inches (he stood only 5' 6" tall) with a knack of finding the net with regularity, hitting 91 goals in only 195 appearances, including netting 21 goals in the 1914-15 campaign that saw Spurs finish bottom of the First Division. Unfortunately, the First World War robbed Bliss of four seasons of League Football, although he did score regularly for the club in the various war-time Leagues. Upon the resumption of League football in 1919, Bert carried on where he left off, netting 31 goals as Spurs romped to the Second Division title. The following season (1920-21) he scored 17 League goals, but from January onwards most minds were concentrated on the FA Cup. He appeared in all six of Spurs' games in the competition, scoring four goals, including both in the 2-1 win over Preston North End in the semi-final. As well as picking up an FA Cup winners' medal, April of 1921 saw Bert collect his only full England cap, against Scotland. His appearances at Spurs became sporadic thereafter and in December 1922 he was transferred to Clapton Orient before finishing his career with Bournemouth.

1971 Ramon Vega born in Olten, Switzerland. Ramon began his career with FC Trimbach and FC Olten but made his reputation as a solid and reliable defender with Grasshopper-Club Zurich, where his manager at one time was Christian Gross. His performances during the Euro '96 Championships in England alerted many European clubs as to his ability, and although he spoke to Spurs at the time joined Cagliari in Italy. A little over six months later Spurs finally got their man, paying £3.75 million to bring him to White Hart Lane in January 1997.

1993 Terry Venables lost his court case against Alan Sugar and was therefore sacked from the club.

1994 The FA inquiry into the charge of misconduct against Spurs began. There were 40 charges of malpractice which were being investigated, involving payments made to 15 players and totalling some £545,000 in all. The enquiry later found the club guilty and imposed a fine of £600,000 (a record), deducted 12 points from their total at the end of the coming season, and announced a 12 month ban from the FA Cup. Spurs were also liable for all the costs of the enquiry. Alan Sugar immediately announced he would appeal against the judgement, stating 'I'm not going to be intimidated by these archaic and barbaric methods . . . a deliberate vendetta against our club and against me personally.'

JUNE 15TH

| 1947 | Toulouse | A | Friendly | 1-2 |
| 1952 | Manchester United | New York | Friendly | 7-1 |

Twenty-four hours earlier Spurs had beaten United 5-0 in an exhibition match in Toronto, even though United were the reigning League champions. The two sides had travelled together for the second fixture in New York, which took place at the Yankee Stadium, more normally used for baseball. Indeed, prior to the start captains Ronnie Burgess and Johnny Carey laid a wreath in front of the memorials to Babe Ruth and Lou Gehrig and the two sides lined up in silent tribute. The British Consul kicked the game off and both sides turned in an exceptional performance, goals from Duquemin (four), Bennett (two) and McLellan leaving Spurs 7-1 winners after Rowley had given United the lead!

| 1966 | America Club of Mexico | Mexico City | | |
| | | | Friendly | 2-0 |

JUNE 16TH

| 1909 | Liga Argentina | Palermo | Friendly | 4-1 |

Argentinos' narrow 1-0 defeat had raised considerable interest in Spurs' tour of Argentina, although there was to be no such shock this time around. Goals from Bull, Minter, Clark and McFarlane were taken, although Spurs created considerably more that they should have finished.

| 1974 | Mauritius Select XI | Curepipe | Friendly | 6-0 |

1983 It was announced that Spurs would be floating on the stock market, the object being the raising of £3.8 million. The prospectus was finally issued in October and the flotation was a success, being over-subscribed three and a half-times.

1998 Spurs' defender Colin Calderwood broke his hand during the World Cup group match against Norway in France and was expected to miss the final group match against Morocco, a match that would be vital to Scotland's hopes of progressing into the next phase of the competition.

JUNE 17TH

1908 Stoke resigned from the Football League. On the face of it, a straightforward decision of little or no relevance to Spurs, but just before the announcement was made public the Stoke chairman contacted his Spurs opposite number, Charles Roberts, and informed him of Stoke's decision. Of course, we have little way of knowing quite what was discussed, but the belief is that Stoke offered to assist Spurs' application to the Football League when the matter came before the vote on June 29th.

| 1966 | Bayern Munich | Detroit | Friendly | 3-0 |

1876   Jock Montgomery born in Chryston, Lanarkshire. Jock is widely believed to have been the very first professional player engaged by Spurs, for he was offered terms in January 1896, barely one month after the club adopted professionalism. He spent two years with Spurs, playing in the Southern League and United League before switching to Notts County in May 1898 and going on to give the Meadow Lane club excellent service for the next 13 years. He then played for Glossop North End and became trainer at Preston North End when his playing career was finished. He died in Edmonton on 6th April 1940.

1952   Quebec FA   Montreal   Friendly   8-0

1998   Allan Neilsen gave Denmark the lead after only 13 minutes in the World Cup group match against South Africa in France. The game ended 1-1, but also saw three players sent off, two from Denmark and one South African, all three having started the game as substitutes.

1909   Everton   Palermo   Friendly   0-4

1935   With Spurs having been relegated to the Second Division and manager Percy Smith resigning shortly before the inevitable, the board were forced to advertise for a new manager during the close season. Their choice was the former West Ham United player Jack Tresadern, who had played in the 1923 FA Cup final at Wembley and had also appeared once for England. Before joining Spurs he had been player-manager at Northampton and more recently manager of Crystal Palace. Unfortunately he was neither successful nor popular, and with rumours circulating in 1938 that the club were trying to bring back Peter McWilliam, he resigned in order to take up the vacant post at Plymouth Argyle.

1947   Olympique de Montpellier   A   Friendly   1-0

1966   Bayern Munich   Chicago   Friendly   1-1

1971   Chris Armstrong born in Newcastle. He began his professional career with Wrexham in 1989 and after impressing at the lower level was signed by Millwall for £50,000 in 1991, switching to Crystal Palace for £1 million a year later. Although Palace suffered an up-and-down existence during his time at Selhurst Park, Chris' ability to find the net was soon spotted by other clubs, and a £4.5 million switch to White Hart Lane followed in 1995.

1993   Ossie Ardiles was named as the new Spurs manager. With a recent court case having upheld Alan Sugar's decision to sack Terry Venables, Alan Sugar had needed very little persuasion to lure Ardiles back to White Hart Lane. Ardiles would announce his backroom staff within a few days, although at this stage it was not known whether Keith Burkinshaw, Ardiles' assistant at West Bromwich Albion, would be joining him.

1909   Rosario   Rosario   Friendly   9-0

1973   Joe Nicholls died in Nottingham. Born in Carlton, Nottinghamshire on March 8th 1905, Joe was spotted by Spurs whilst playing in goal for his regiment, the Grenadier Guards, in an army cup final. When in 1926 it was learnt that he wished to leave the army to pursue football as a career, Spurs jumped to the head of the queue for his signature, beating off other rivals for the 6' 4" giant. He was farmed out to Northfleet, Spurs' nursery, to learn his trade and he made his debut for the club against Liverpool in April 1927. After a lengthy spell as understudy to Cyril Spiers, he became first choice in the 1932-33 season when Spurs finished runners-up in the Second Division. His hey-day was only to last until 1935-36, when lack of form led to the loss of his place to Alan Taylor and at the end of the season he was given a free transfer. He then joined Bristol Rovers.

1947   Saint-Etienne   A   Friendly   2-0
Spurs' third and final match of their French tour saw them win 2-0 at Saint-Etienne thanks to goals from Rundle and Bennett.

1965   Hakoah   Haifa   Friendly   3-1
This was Spurs' first match on tour in Israel, and goals from Jimmy Greaves (two, one from the penalty spot) and Cliff Jones gave them their first victory.

1880   Alex Young born in Slamannan, Stirlingshire. Although he made only five appearances in the Football League for Spurs (in the 1911-12 season) he was undoubtedly a major character in the game at that time. He first came to prominence with Everton, winning an FA Cup winners' medal in 1906 (when he scored the winning goal in the final against Newcastle United) and a runners-up medal the following year. After ten years with Everton and having scored 110 League goals he transferred to

Spurs in June 1911. After a bright opening, scoring on his debut (against Everton!) and hitting two goals in the following game, he failed to find the net in his next three games and was promptly dropped from the team. Rather than battle his way back Young demanded a transfer and was allowed to move back north with Manchester City. After his career ended he emigrated to Australia in 1914, but the following year was charged with the wilful murder of his brother. Evidence was requested from the football authorities in England, who confirmed that during his playing career he had been prone to fits of temporary insanity. In June 1916 he was found guilty of manslaughter and sentenced to three years imprisonment, but was not released at the end of the term on the grounds of 'mental weakness'. It was therefore many years before he was able to return home to Scotland, where he died in 1959.

1915   Bert Sproston born in Elworth, Cheshire. Bert spent only five months at Spurs, making just nine appearances in the League, but he also collected four representative honours during his time at White Hart Lane. By the time he arrived at Spurs in June 1938 for £9,500 from Leeds United he was already an England full-back, and won two further caps and made two appearances for the Football League whilst with Spurs. On 5th November 1938 he was due to have played for Spurs in the match against Manchester City, but having previously complained that he was unable to settle in London was transferred to City the day before the game and therefore played against Spurs. He later served Bolton Wanderers on the coaching staff.

1976   Terry Neill resigned as Spurs manager after a little under two years in charge. He took over from Bill Nicholson in September 1974 with the club bottom of the First Division and avoided relegation in only the final match of the season, beating Leeds United 4-2. During his only full season in charge he led Spurs to mid-table respectability and the semi-finals of the League Cup, where they were beaten by Newcastle United. It was widely reported that Neill and the directors fell out during the club's Australian tour this summer, culminating in Terry Neill resigning as Spurs manager.

1984   Spurs were fined £7,500 by the Football League for fielding a weakened team in the 5-0 defeat by Southampton on May 7th. This match was, however, barely two days before Spurs were due to play Anderlecht in the first leg of the UEFA Cup final in Brussels, and only Paul Miller played at both Southampton and Brussels.

1991   Terry Venables and Alan Sugar's £7.25 million takeover of Spurs was completed, with Venables becoming non-executive managing director and Sugar non-executive chairman.

JUNE 23RD

1909   Spurs were without a match during their tour of Argentina and Uruguay and so took the opportunity of watching two local sides in action. A rather bigger crowd than anticipated turned up to watch as well, with the result there was a minor pitch invasion. Whilst this was nothing new to Spurs, who had seen pitch invasions before, they had not witnessed such a response, for the Argentinean cavalry took to the field and set about the invaders with the flats of their swords! Not surprisingly, order was soon restored and the match was played without further incident.

JUNE 24TH

1909   Alumini   Alumini   Friendly   5-0
Spurs' tour of Argentina and Uruguay had been an unqualified success, with the only defeat being suffered at the hands of fellow tourists Everton in an exhibition match. After the match the touring party boarded a ship to take them home to England, during the course of which a fancy dress contest was held among the passengers. Two players, one dressed as Robinson Crusoe and the other as his Man Friday complete with a parrot were adjudged the winners and allowed to keep the parrot as part of their prize. According to legend, the parrot died on the very day Arsenal took Spurs' place in the First Division in 1919!

1965   Maccabi Tel Aviv   Tel Aviv   Friendly   3-2
The Maccabi side put up a trophy, the John White Cup, for the winners of the match, with Spurs' goals being scored by Alan Mullery, Dave Mackay and Alan Gilzean.

JUNE 25TH

1888   Bobby Steel born in Newmilns, Ayrshire, the youngest of three brothers, all of whom played for Spurs – the other two being Alex and Danny. Bobby proved to be the most consistent of the three, racking up a total of 230 appearances for Spurs in the Football League, making his debut in the very first League match the club played, against Wolves at home in September 1908. He started out as an inside-forward with local Scottish sides before signing with Port Glasgow in 1906. In May 1908 he was transferred to Spurs (although Spurs had to pay a fee to Greenock Morton, who held his registration as a Scottish League player) and was an exceptional performer for the next eight years or so. His talents, which included a fine balance between when to dribble and when to pass, went unnoticed by the Scottish selectors, although he did get picked for the Anglo-Scots against the Home

Scots trial match of 1909. At the end of the First World War he returned to White Hart Lane but, as his best playing days were behind him, was released and took up refereeing in the Southern League. He did however briefly return to active playing, turning out for Gillingham (where his brother Alex was also signed) in 1919. He died on 28th March 1972.

1984   Peter Shreeve was appointed Spurs manager in succession to Keith Burkinshaw. Shreeve began his footballing career with Finchley before being signed by Reading in 1958. Injury brought his playing career to an end in 1966 and he moved into coaching with Charlton Athletic. He joined Spurs in 1974 as youth-team manager, being upgraded to reserve team manager in 1977. In 1980 he was appointed assistant-manager to Keith Burkinshaw. Following Burkinshaw's recent departure the players had made their views known to the board; namely that Peter Shreeve should be given the opportunity of managing the club, which was confirmed on this day.

1995   FC Luzern   H   UEFA Intertoto Cup   0-2
This and the other three games the club played in the competition were not considered first-team matches, and for this reason the club played at Brighton's Goldstone Ground and the reserve side, along with one or two loan players, were selected. This was to have repercussions later.

JUNE 26TH

1875   Ly Burrows born in Ashton-Under-Lyme, Lancashire. Full-back Ly spent four seasons with Spurs, including the one that saw Spurs make their debut in the Southern League. As the Burrows family moved around a lot, Ly made appearances for junior clubs in Glasgow and Sheffield before arriving in London. Whilst playing for Woolwich Polytechnic he was spotted and signed by Woolwich Arsenal but, unable to break into the first team he accepted an invitation to turn out for Spurs in October 1894 in the friendly against 3rd Battalion Grenadier Guards. Whilst there have been very few players who have played for both Arsenal and Spurs, Burrows is the only man to have managed to do both at the same time – he made ten League appearances for Arsenal between 1894 and 1896 whilst playing for Spurs in numerous friendlies and cup competitions in between! He was, however, widely regarded as a 'Spurs man' and when he was selected to play for London Spurs were credited with being his club. In December 1897 the uncompromising full-back announced he was moving to Sheffield for business reasons and although he made a few more appearances for Spurs in the Southern League that season he subsequently joined Sheffield United. He died in Gosforth in August 1952.

1877   John Joyce born in Burton-on-Trent, Staffordshire. Although 6' 0" tall and weighing over 15 stone, John was known as Tiny throughout his playing career. He first came to prominence as goalkeeper with Millwall, having joined the docklands club from Southampton in 1900. He spent two years with Millwall before being transferred to Blackburn Rovers in May 1902, but after only one season returned to Millwall and was first choice for the next six years. In November 1909, with Spurs finding the First Divison something of a struggle he moved to White Hart Lane, took over the number one spot from Fred Boreham and held on to it until the end of the season. Competition from Tom Lunn and then Arthur King saw Joyce in and out of the first team, until the arrival of Bill Jacques effectively ended his Spurs career. However, in April 1914 Joyce became the first (and thus far only) Spurs goalkeeper to score in a League match when his long-range punt evaded the Bolton Wanderers goalkeeper. In early 1916 he returned to Millwall and upon retiring as a player moved on to the coaching staff, becoming assistant trainer (although he made loan appearances in goal for Gillingham in 1919). Joyce continued to serve Millwall in numerous capacities until the Second World War and died in Greenwich in June 1956.

1901   Harry Skitt born in Portobello, Staffordshire. Harry graduated through the Northfleet nursery and signed full forms with Spurs in May 1923, making his debut the following year in November 1924 at home to Aston Villa. Over the next seven years the reliable and solid half-back made a total of 213 appearances in the League side, also being selected to represent the Football League against the Irish League in 1929. As the period he spent at Spurs (1923–31) was one of the most nondescript of the club's history, he had little by the way of domestic honours to show for his time at White Hart Lane. The elevation of Wally Alsford to the first team saw Harry Skitt's openings in the side curtailed and at the end of the 1930-31 season he joined Chester before retiring in 1936 and becoming a publican in his native Staffordshire. He died in Poole, Dorset in March 1976.

1998   Darren Anderton scored England's opening goal in the 2-0 win over Columbia in the World Cup finals in France. The win confirmed England would progress into the knock-out stage of the tournament.

JUNE 27TH

1952   The end of the longest tour Spurs have ever undertaken; having left England on 12th May for Canada and the United States, the Spurs touring party arrived home again aboard the *Empress of Canada*. They had played ten matches on the tour, winning all ten and scoring 85 goals with only 6 conceded in the process.

JUNE 28TH

1941   Bert Middlemiss died in Brixham. Born in Newcastle on December 19th 1888 he began his football career as an amateur with Stalybridge. He transferred to Spurs in November 1907, although Spurs had to pay a fee to Stockport County, who had persuaded Bert to sign professional forms with them in the event that another club wanted his services! Although primarily a winger his speed and ability to cut inside often put him in goalscoring positions and in 248 League appearances he scored 51 goals, a figure only bettered by Vivian Woodward. But for the war Bert would undoubtedly have made more appearances, scored more goals, picked up domestic honours and perhaps gone on to the full England team. As it was, he missed out on all four fronts, although he was selected for England trial matches on four occasions and played for the Football League against the Southern League in 1910. After guesting for Birmingham and Coventry during the war he returned to Spurs for the 1919-20 season, but made only four appearances that term and was released in June and signed for Queens Park Rangers to play in their debut Football League season.

1948   John Pratt born in Hackney, London. Although born locally to Spurs John played for Brentford as a youth player until being recommended to Spurs by Terry Medwin. Signed as an amateur and then professional in November 1965 he had to wait until 1969 before making his first League appearance, turning out against Arsenal in March of that year. Having been switched from centre-half to wing-half, he made sporadic appearances in the first team until the 1972-73 season, during which he also appeared in all of the club's games in winning the League Cup. However, John had little reason to remember the final with fondness; injured early on he was taken off after only 20 minutes and could only watch as substitute Ralph Coates netted the only goal of the game. He also played in the final of the UEFA Cup in 1974, collecting a runners-up medal, and made a total of 331 appearances for the League side (including 24 as substitute). He was rewarded with a testimonial in 1978 against Arsenal and stayed with Spurs for a further two years before going to play in the United States in May 1980. He rejoined Spurs as youth-team coach in 1983 and was upgraded to reserve team coach and then assistant manager under Peter Shreeves until being dismissed in 1986.

1997   Charlie Rundle died in Cornwall. Born in Cornwall on 17th January 1923 Charlie was spotted by Spurs whilst playing for the Navy and signed professional forms in February 1946. After making a number of consecutive appearances in the first team in 1946-47 Charlie found himself in the reserves following the arrival of Len Duquemin, making the occasional appearance thereafter. After a number of injuries he was released in May 1950 and signed with Crystal Palace, later playing in non-League circles.

JUNE 29TH

1908   By the time of the Football League meeting to vote upon their replacement Stoke, (who resigned from the League on June 17th) had decided their original resignation had been too hasty. That meant Stoke would be vying with Spurs (who had failed to obtain League membership on May 27th), Lincoln (who had lost their membership on the same day), Rotherham Town and Southport (both of whom were making their first application). The voting could not have been closer; on the first ballot Spurs and Lincoln tied for first place with 17 votes apiece, with Stoke polling six and both Rotherham and Southport nil. Both latter clubs were therefore obliged to withdraw from the fray. Stoke also withdrew, leaving Spurs and Lincoln to fight it out once again. A second ballot was held; this time Spurs and Lincoln tied at 20 votes each. This left the final decision to the League Management Committee – having been a founder member of the Second Division in 1892 was considered good enough to earn Lincoln three of the committee's votes; having won the FA Cup in 1901, offered the potential of large crowds in London and, presumably, the deal originally concocted with Stoke, earned Spurs five votes and a place in the Football League.

1998   Jurgen Klinsmann scored his 47th goal for Germany, his 11th in the World Cup finals, to bring Germany level in their match against Mexico in the World Cup.

JUNE 30TH

1995   Spurs signed Crystal Palace striker Chris Armstrong for a fee of £4.5 million. Although Chris had achieved notoriety for being banned after testing positive following a drugs test (he later admitted to having smoked cannabis) his goal rate whilst at Palace had been outstanding, and he was widely expected to form a devastating partnership with Teddy Sheringham in the Tottenham attack. The subsequent departure of Sheringham saw Armstrong linking with Les Ferdinand.

JULY 1ST

1995   Rudar Velenje   A   UEFA Intertoto Cup   2-1

This and the other three games the club played in the competition were not considered first-team matches and for this reason the club utilised their reserve team, augmented by a number of loan players. This was also the only victory the club was to record in the competition.

JULY 2ND

1994   Spurs' appeal against the penalties imposed at the FA enquiry the previous month was heard at St Albans. A three-man tribunal represented the FA, whilst chairman Alan Sugar presented Spurs' case himself. The original charge, of misconduct, had been proven and Spurs were handed a 12-point deduction, banned from the FA Cup and given a £600,000 fine. The tribunal now amended this to a six-point deduction and a fine of £1,500,000, with the FA Cup ban still to remain. Alan Sugar announced Spurs would continue to appeal against the penalties that had been imposed.

JULY 3RD

1959   Graham Roberts born in Southampton. A classic case of a late developer as a player, Graham had been on the books of Bournemouth and Portsmouth as an apprentice but broke an ankle just before Portsmouth were to offer professional terms. After he recovered he joined Dorchester Town and then Weymouth. His performances at Weymouth received rave reviews and he was recommended to Bill Nicholson by someone he met on a railway station! Bill Nicholson went to see Graham in action for himself and suitably impressed persuaded Keith Burkinshaw to invest £35,000 for his signature despite opposition from West Bromwich Albion. Graham made his Spurs debut in October 1980, coming on as substitute at Stoke and earning a regular place in the defence from December onwards. By the end of the season the former fitter's mate turned defender had picked up a winners' medal in the FA Cup final (having previously only visited Wembley as a ballboy!). The following season he proved to be something of an all-rounder, slotting in well in midfield and providing some much needed bite to that area of the field. Although he was surprisingly omitted from the side that lost the League Cup final against Liverpool in 1982, he did collect a second FA Cup winners' medal, and it was his surging run from his own half of the field that was ended by Tony Currie's late lunging tackle and earned the penalty in the replay against QPR. In 1983 he collected the first of six full caps for England and the following year was captain on the evening Spurs lifted the UEFA Cup (in place of the suspended Steve Perryman), scoring the late goal which forced extra time and setting the example in the penalty shoot-out. In 1986 manager David Pleat sold him to Rangers where he helped them win the Scottish Premier title and in 1988 the Skol Cup. He fell out with manager Graeme Souness and was transferred to Chelsea and made captain, leading them to the Second Division title in 1989 and then being appointed player-coach. A public row with chairman Ken Bates followed and he was transfer-listed and subsequently sold to West Bromwich Albion in November 1990. He then drifted back into the non-League game, taking over as player-manager of Enfield in August 1992, and is currently in charge at Chesham.

JULY 4TH

1956   Eugene 'Taffy' O'Callaghan died in Fulham, London at the age of 49. Born in Ebbw Vale on October 6th 1906 he was working down the pits and turning out for the local side when he was spotted by Spurs and invited on to the groundstaff in 1925. After spells with the club's nursery outfits Barnet and Northfleet, he signed professional forms in September 1926, making his full debut in February 1927 at Everton. He made such an impact he held his place when Jimmy Seed had recovered from injury and was considered so good a prospect the club could afford to let Seed move to Sheffield Wednesday, ultimately with catastrophic results. Taffy O'Callaghan did indeed provide good service for Spurs over the next eight years, making 252 appearances in the Football League and scoring 92 goals before being allowed to move on to Leicester City in March 1935. After helping Leicester win the Second Division title in his first full season he was transferred to Fulham in October 1937, making his debut for the club against Spurs the same month. He made guest appearances for Aldershot, Brentford and Spurs during the Second World War, and retired as a player during the 1945-46 season. He then moved on to the Fulham coaching staff, a position he held until his death.

JULY 5TH

1982   It was announced that Ossie Ardiles would be joining French club Paris St Germain on loan for a year. In light of the political tension between Argentina and Britain following the recent Falkland Islands crisis it was felt best if the player did not yet return to Britain. Although the deal was initially for one year, he returned to Spurs in December the same year.

JULY 6TH

1993   Ossie Ardiles announced his new management and coaching team at White Hart Lane; former Spurs captain Steve Perryman was appointed assistant manager and Pat Jennings was joining the club as specialist goalkeeping coach, meaning there was no position for Ray Clemence, although Doug Livermore was to remain with club and oversee the scouting.

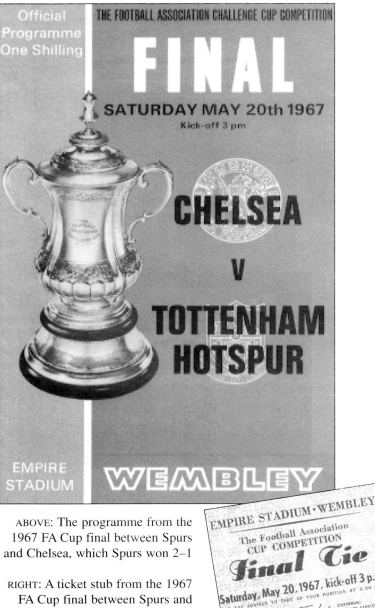

ABOVE: The programme from the 1967 FA Cup final between Spurs and Chelsea, which Spurs won 2–1

RIGHT: A ticket stub from the 1967 FA Cup final between Spurs and Chelsea at Wembley, where it cost ten shillings for a place on the terraces

LEFT: Martin Chivers in full flight. It was his goals that won the 1971 League Cup and the UEFA Cup the following year

BELOW: Ricky Villa scores the winning goal in the 1981 FA Cup final replay

The accounts of the Hotspur Cricket Club in 1882, detailing the club's first expenditure: goalposts costing 2s 6d! A ball was purchased nearly a month later

Paul Gascoigne, who cost Spurs £2 million in 1988

Gary Mabbutt, a Spurs regular between 1982 and 1998 and captain when they won the FA Cup in 1991

ABOVE: German striker Jurgen Klinsmann, who arrived at Spurs in 1994 for one season and returned again in 1997

OPPOSITE PAGE: Spurs' exciting French winger David Ginola, one of the few successes of the 1997–98 season

ABOVE: Spurs and England defender Sol Campbell, one of the stars of the 1998 World Cup in France

RIGHT: Glenn Hoddle and Chris Waddle in unfamiliar pose – promoting their hit record, 'Diamond Lights'

JULY 7TH

1994   Vinny Samways handed in a transfer request to the club. Vinny, who joined Spurs as an apprentice in April 1985, claimed he wanted a fresh challenge, but the recent FA-imposed points deduction and ban from the FA Cup were obviously making the club an unattractive proposition not only for players coming to the club but also those already there.

JULY 8TH

1990   Jurgen Klinsmann, later to join Spurs, helped Germany to a 1-0 win in the World Cup final against Argentina. It was Germany's third victory in the final and also created another record; Franz Beckenbaur became the first man both to captain and manage a country to World Cup success.

JULY 9TH

1883   Tommy Lunn born in Bishop Auckland, County Durham. Tommy began his professional career with Wolves in 1904 and was goalkeeper when they won the FA Cup in 1908. Later the same year he kept goal for Wolves when they played in the very first Football League match staged at White Hart Lane. In April 1910 Spurs, struggling to avoid relegation from the First Division, bought Lunn and he kept a clean sheet on his debut as Spurs won 2-0 at Bolton. In the final game of the season Spurs needed to beat Chelsea to ensure safety at the Pensioners' expense; they won 2-1 and although the goalscorers received much of the acclaim, it was widely accepted that Tommy Lunn's heroics in goal had been the foundation for the success. Tommy remained Spurs' first-choice keeper for the next two seasons until he was replaced by John 'Tiny' Joyce. Although Tommy was brought back for two games early in 1913, he took out a publican's licence which the club claimed was in breach of his contract, suspending him for the rest of the season. When his contract expired he signed for Stockport County, but after just two games a serious leg injury forced his retirement from the game. He died in Edmonton on March 29th 1960 aged 66 years.

1918   William Findlay Weir was killed in action whilst serving in the army in France. Born in Glasgow on April 18th 1889, Findlay made his name with Sheffield Wednesday, signing for the Owls in February 1909 and spending two and a half years with them before his transfer to Spurs. Although he had served Wednesday at centre-half, he was soon moved to half-back at Spurs following the departure of Danny Steel and with Jabez Darnell nearing retirement. He made his debut for Spurs at home to Derby in September 1912 and was a regular for the three remaining seasons before the outbreak of the First World War. One of the first players to enlist he joined the Tottenham Royal Engineers, making a few appearances in the various war-time Leagues until his death.

JULY 10TH

1978   The transfer coup of the decade, if not of all time – Spurs manager Keith Burkinshaw announced the signing of two of Argentina's World Cup-winning squad; Osvaldo Ardiles and Ricardo Villa. Ardiles, who played in the final itself, was signed from the Huracan Club for a fee of £325,000, whilst Villa, who made two substitute appearances during the tournament, cost £375,000 from Racing Club. Both players, 25 years old and midfielders, signed three-year contracts with the club and were due to arrive in London on Sunday.

JULY 11TH

1966   Jimmy Greaves played in England's opening game of the World Cup, a 0-0 draw against Uruguay at Wembley. Although he played in all three of England's group matches, an injury sustained in the final group match against France effectively ended his tournament, for although he was fit for the final, he was not selected by manager Alf Ramsey.

JULY 12TH

1956   Tony Galvin born in Huddersfield, West Yorkshire. Although Tony represented England at schools level a career as a professional seemed to have passed him by and he left school to take a Bachelor of Arts degree in Russian Studies at Hull University. After passing his degree he attended Teacher Training College and made appearances for Goole Town in the Northern Premier League, where he was spotted by Spurs and signed for a £30,000 fee in January 1978. Over the next ten years Tony made the fee look ridiculously low, for after signing as a professional in the summer of 1978 (he had wanted to complete his Teacher Training course) he went on to establish himself as an indispensable member of the team. He made his debut at home to Manchester City in February 1979 and by January 1981 was a regular in the first team, winning an FA Cup winners' medal at the end of that season again against Manchester City. Further honours followed; another FA Cup winners' medal in 1982, a runners-up medal in the League Cup the same year and a winners' medal in the 1984 UEFA Cup. He won his first cap for the Republic of Ireland in September 1982 and went on to represent his country

20 times whilst with Spurs and 30 times in all. After beginning the 1986-87 season as a regular he made fewer and fewer appearances as the season wore on as manager David Pleat exploited the five-man midfield. He was transferred to Sheffield Wednesday for £130,000 in August 1987 but injury restricted his appearances. He then became Swindon manager, Ossie Ardiles' first signing in July 1989, stepping up to assistant manager in February 1991. The Ardiles/Galvin management team then moved to Newcastle United in March 1991 but less than 12 months later was sacked to make way for the arrival of Kevin Keegan. Although Ardiles returned to League management with West Bromwich Albion he chose Keith Burkinshaw as his assistant, leaving Tony Galvin out in the cold. He was awarded a testimonial for Spurs against West Ham in October 1987.

JULY 13TH

1929 Tom Collins died in Edmonton at the age of 47 years. Born in Leven, Fife on April 16th 1882 he began his playing career north of the border with Leven Thistle before joining Hearts in 1903. After a brief loan spell with Bathgate he moved to East Fife in June 1905 and then returned to the Tynecastle club in 1906. This second spell with Hearts made his name and reputation, with Tom being selected for the Scottish League for their match with the Football League in February 1909. In October 1910 he was spotted by Spurs whilst playing for the Scottish League against the Southern League and his move to White Hart Lane was completed by November 1910. He made his League debut in November of that year at Sunderland and went on to amass 115 appearances (scoring 1 goal, against Derby in September 1912 from the penalty spot) in the League before the outset of the First World War. He was one of the earliest players to sign up for active service in the Great War but sadly suffered serious injuries in the trenches that led to him losing both an arm and a leg. In March 1915, therefore, his contract with Spurs was cancelled by mutual consent.

1944 Cyril Knowles born in Fitzwilliam, Yorkshire. Cyril began his career as a winger and had an unsuccessful spell with Manchester United and a trial with Blackpool before being taken on by Middlesbrough who converted him to full-back. He found his true vocation in this position, making his debut in April 1963 and being spotted almost immediately by Spurs manager Bill Nicholson. After just 39 appearances for the Ayresome Park outfit he was transferred to Spurs for £45,000 and almost immediately made the right-back spot his own. After 12 months in the role he was switched to left-back and was one of the most solid and dependable players in the League in this position. He used his previous experience as a winger to good effect, overlapping whenever the opportunity presented itself and seldom being afraid to have a shot at goal. Indeed, on the night Spurs needed to win against Leeds United in 1975 to remain in the First Division, Cyril scored two of the goals! A member of the Spurs teams that won the FA Cup in 1967, the League Cup in 1971 and 1973 and the UEFA Cup in 1984, he picked up four full England caps, unfortunate that England seemed to prefer Terry Cooper in the left-back berth. Spurs and its fans always appreciated Cyril Knowles however, turning the catchphrase 'Nice One Cyril' into a hit record! In 1976 Cyril was forced to retire owing to a serious knee injury sustained in December 1973 and moved into management. Although his career was confined to the football basement, Cyril proved adept at working with limited budgets but unlimited success, taking a succession of clubs to promotion until, in February 1991 he was forced once again to retire, this time owing to a serious brain illness. In June 1991 Hartlepool (where he had been manager) reluctantly announced the cancellation of his contract and in August 1991 he sadly died in Middlesbrough. Both Spurs and Hartlepool staged memorial matches for his dependants and as an opportunity to pay tribute to one of the finest players ever to have graced the football field.

JULY 14TH

1976 Spurs appointed Keith Burkinshaw as manager to replace Terry Neill. After being rejected by Wolves as a youth he played for Denaby United before signing for Liverpool. Although he remained at Anfield for seven years he made only one League appearance, finally moving to Workington in 1957. He ended his career at Workington in 1965, including a spell as player-manager, before finishing his playing career at Scunthorpe United. He then joined Newcastle United as a coach, spending seven years behind the scenes and guiding them to the FA Cup final in 1974. He was sacked in 1975 and almost immediately linked up with Terry Neill at Spurs. Although Neill had recently resigned the Spurs job, Burkinshaw decided to remain at White Hart Lane and applied for the manager's position, which was on this morning confirmed.

JULY 15TH

1997 Ski IL   A   Friendly   2-3

Spurs' first match of their tour of Scandinavia came barely a week after they had reported back for pre-season training and the team could justifiably claim to be a bit rusty. They went down to Ski in front of a crowd of 2,150, with Spurs' goals coming from Ramon Vega and Allan Nielsen.

1920   George Clawley, goalkeeper when Spurs won the FA Cup for the first time in 1901, died in Southampton at the age of only 45. He began his career with Crewe Alexandra and Stoke before joining Southampton St Mary's in 1896, helping the club win the Southern League in 1897 and 1898. He returned to Stoke for a year and was then signed by John Cameron for Spurs in 1899. He made his debut in September of that year, but unfortunately broke his leg a month later and did not reclaim his place until April 1900, too late to register enough appearances for a medal as Spurs won the Southern League that season. He received more than adequate compensation the following year, appearing in all of Spurs' FA Cup ties. He returned to Southampton in 1903 and was their regular keeper when they again won the Southern League in 1904. After retiring in 1907 he became a publican, a position he held up until his death.

1966   Jimmy Seed died in Farnborough, Kent at the age of 71. Born in Blackhill, County Durham on 25th March 1895 and one of the finest players to wear the white shirt of Spurs, Jimmy Seed's main claim to fame was his sensational transfer out of White Hart Lane after he had been unable to reclaim his place after injury. He had been signed by Sunderland in April 1914 but enlisted and suffered from a gas attack during the First World War. When he reported back to Roker Park in 1919 it was felt he would be unable to recover fully from the effects and he was allowed to leave, his playing career seemingly ended. He was snapped up by Mid-Rhondda almost immediately, although Sunderland still held his registration whilst he negotiated a free transfer. The forms came through just before he was spotted by Spurs, who were impressed whilst on a scouting mission to see another player, 'Darkie' Lowdell of Ton Pentre. Seed's transfer to Spurs caused a sensation at the time and Jimmy was soon established in the Spurs side, making his debut against Wolves in April 1920. The following season he was a member of the team that won the FA Cup, scoring five goals along the way. In late 1926 Jimmy suffered a bad ankle injury that kept him out of the side for a considerable time, Taffy O'Callaghan proving a more than adequate replacement. Jimmy was unable to reclaim his place once fully fit, and although the team should have been structured around both Seed and O'Callaghan, manager Billy Minter astonishingly allowed Seed to leave for Sheffield Wednesday, with 'Darkie' Lowdell making the reverse journey and at last joining Spurs. The transfer of Seed was to have catastrophic effects, for at the time Seed joined Wednesday they were bottom of the First Division and seemingly doomed, whilst Spurs were hovering around mid-table. Inspired by Seed Wednesday picked up 17 points in ten games and saved themselves, at the expense of Spurs, who finished bottom! Whilst Spurs languished in the Second Division Seed inspired Sheffield Wednesday to two consecutive championships before retiring as a player in May 1931 and accepting an invitation from Arsenal manager Herbert Chapman to take over the reins at Clapton Orient. Arsenal had designs on making Orient their nursery club, but after the Football League blocked the move Arsenal took all their players out of Orient, leaving Seed with a two-year struggle. He then took over at Charlton, taking the club from the Third to the First Division in consecutive seasons before the Second World War and consecutive FA Cup finals after it, winning in 1947. He was sacked in September 1956, having held the position for 23 years and became adviser and then caretaker-manager at Bristol City. He became manager of Millwall in January 1958, stepping down 18 months later, being appointed to the board in January 1960 and holding the position until his death.

1993   Shelbourne XI   A   Friendly   4-2

1995   Osters IF   H   UEFA Intertoto Cup   1-2

        This and the other three games the club played in the competition were not considered first-team matches and for this reason the club utilised their reserve team, augmented by a number of loan players, and played at Brighton's Goldstone Ground.

JULY 17TH

1924   Len Duquemin born in Cobo, Guernsey. Len was recommended to Spurs by a supporter living on the island and arrived at the club for a trial in December 1945. Offered amateur forms he was loaned out to Chelmsford City and Colchester United until the Football League was ready to resume, signing professional forms with Spurs in September 1946. He made his League debut at centre-forward at home to Sheffield Wednesday in August 1947, scoring in the 5-1 win and thereafter establishing himself as the first choice to lead the attack. A member of the team that won the Second and First Division championships in consecutive seasons, Len stayed with Spurs until November 1958 when competition from the likes of Bobby Smith saw him move out of League football to Bedford Town. During his Spurs career he made 275 League appearances, scoring 114 goals, as well as 33 appearances and 17 goals in the FA Cup, including both of Spurs' strikes in the two unsuccessful semi-finals against Blackpool – 3-1 in 1948 and 2-1 in 1953. After retiring from playing Len became a publican in Cheshunt.

1997   Faaberg IL   A   Friendly   2-0

JULY 18TH

1985 Wycombe Wanderers N Friendly 4-1
Spurs met Wycombe Wanderers, then a non-League side, at the England training camp at Bisham Abbey for this friendly, winning thanks to goals from Danny Thomas, David Leworthy, Chris Waddle and Tony Galvin.

1993 Drogheda United A Friendly 3-1

1997 Fredrikstad FK A Friendly 0-0
David Ginola made his first appearance in a Spurs shirt following his arrival from Newcastle United, coming on as a substitute after 65 minutes when he replaced Ruel Fox.

JULY 19TH

1947 Harry Erentz died in Dundee at the age of 72 years. Born in Dundee on September 17th 1874, Harry began his career with the local Dundee club before joining Oldham Athletic in 1896. After 12 months he was transferred to Newton Heath (the forerunners of the present-day Manchester United) and spent a further year there until his transfer to Spurs. A solid and reliable full-back, he was known as 'Tiger' because of the ferocity of his tackling and was a great favourite with the crowd. After making his Spurs debut in the Southern League against Bedminster in 1898, he was a central figure in the team that won the Southern League in 1900 and the FA Cup the following season. An injury led to him being released by Spurs in May 1904 and he was unable to secure another club until December of that year when he joined Swindon Town. In Match 1905, after only 16 appearances for the Wiltshire club he broke a leg and was forced to retire.

JULY 20TH

1908 Fred Kirkham resigned as manager of Spurs. He had been appointed the previous April with a five-year contract but had proved unpopular with both the players and fans, although whether his previous career as a referee had anything to do with this is unclear! Therefore, when Kirkham announced to the board that he would like to be relieved of the position, a settlement for the remaining balance on his contract was reached and he was allowed to leave the club. The board also decided not to appoint a successor, preferring to deal themselves with the acquisition of new players and team selection. In fact, many of those duties were handled by secretary Arthur Turner, who had joined the club in 1906 in order to lighten the load on John Cameron.

1992 Reading Chase Lodge
           Friendly 3-1
This friendly was played 'behind closed doors' at the club's training ground at Chase Lodge, with Spurs' goals coming from Darren Anderton, John Hendry from the penalty spot and Paul Stewart. The following day they played a similar match under the same circumstances against Gillingham.

JULY 21ST

1964 John White was killed whilst sheltering under a tree during a thunderstorm on Crews Hill Golf Course at Enfield, after the tree was struck by lightning. Born in Musselburgh, Midlothian on April 28th 1937 he began his career in Scottish junior football and was signed by Alloa Athletic in August 1956, moving on to Falkirk in August 1958 for a fee of £3,300. A little over a year later, having already been capped for Scotland, he was the subject of intense interest from Spurs. Nicholson was concerned about White's stamina, despite hearing the likes of Danny Blanchflower, Bill Brown and Dave Mackay praise White's performances for Scotland. This problem was solved when Nicholson made enquiries of White's army officer and learned John was a good cross-country runner. With nothing but praise coming from all quarters, Bill Nicholson moved swiftly to secure John White for Spurs – a £20,000 fee was paid to Falkirk in October 1959 and the player moved to Spurs. As a replacement for Tommy Harmer John White could have been excused had he struggled in higher company, but his ability to ghost into space, deliver telling and killer passes and finish when the need arose soon made him a firm favourite in his own right. A central figure in the side that won the double in 1960-61, retained the cup the following season and then won the European Cup-Winners' Cup in 1963, John White was just as important a player to Scotland, winning a total of 22 full caps. Since his untimely death, White Hart Lane and Hampden Park have seldom been the same. A benefit match for his dependants was staged at White Lane in November 1964, with his brother Tommy guesting for Spurs against a Scotland XI.

1965 Gudni Bergsson born in Reykjavik. Gudni was an amateur with Valur and studying law at Reykjavik when invited to Spurs for a trial in November 1988 and put his legal studies on hold when signing professional forms in February 1989. Although unable to secure a regular place in the side he proved an extremely useful utility player for the club. He returned home to finish his studies and then signed with Bolton in March 1995.

1992	Gillingham		Chase Lodge	
			Friendly	2~0
1997	Rosenborg BK	A	Friendly	0-2

JULY 22ND

1959   Ted Harper died in Blackburn at the age of 57 years. Ted Harper spent two-and-a-half years with Spurs, making only 63 League appearances, but his goalscoring was so prolific that only the great Jimmy Greaves has come anywhere near his goals to games ratio whilst with Spurs. He began his League career with Blackburn Rovers, scoring 43 goals in the 1925-26 season (still a record number of strikes in a single season for the Ewood Park club) and then moved to Sheffield Wednesday in November 1927. In March 1929 Spurs paid £5,000 (a considerable fee for the time and especially for Spurs, who were renowned for refusing to pay stiff prices for players regardless of how good they were) to bring his goalscoring talents to White Hart Lane. He made his debut against Clapton Orient the same month, scoring once in the 3-2 away win. By the end of the season he had scored 11 goals in only 11 appearances. His goalscoring exploits made him an obvious target for some tough opposition tackling and the next season he made only 19 appearances throughout the term, but still managed to score 14 goals. In 1930-31 he managed to avoid injury long enough to make 30 appearances for Spurs, scoring 36 goals, a record number of goals for a season by a Spurs player until Jimmy Greaves netted 37 in 1962-63. Whilst Harper was recovering from injury George Hunt filled in so successfully that Ted was unable to secure a regular place back in the side and was allowed to leave for Preston North End in December 1931. Much to Spurs' regret he showed the goals had not dried up, setting a Preston record of 37 League goals in a season in 1932-33. He finished his playing career back at Blackburn in November 1933, moving on to the coaching side in May 1935 and staying until May 1948. He then went to work for English Electric, a position he held up until his death.

1976   Willie Evans died in Ponders End, London at the age of 63 years. Born in Waunllwyd, near Ebbw Vale on November 7th 1912 he left school and seemed destined for a career down the coal pits until Spurs invited him to join the groundstaff. He began his playing career at inside-forward but was to find greater success as a winger and was loaned out to a number of clubs, all of whom were part of Spurs' nursery set-up. He represented the Spartan League, Middlesex, London FA and the Southern Counties and might have been selected for England at amateur level had he not pointed out he was Welsh! He made his Spurs debut in the final of the London FA Charity Cup in May 1931 and in November the same year made his full League debut, scoring twice against Swansea Town on his 19th birthday. Over the next six seasons he was both goalscorer (he netted 78 goals in 178 appearances) and goal maker, setting up countless chances for the Spurs forward line. First capped for Wales in 1932 he had made six appearances for his country when he sustained a serious knee injury during the match with Aston Villa in 1936, this time on the occasion of his 24th birthday. A cartilage operation did not remedy the knee and after it was learnt a second operation was required, Spurs released him in May 1937. He was immediately snapped up by Fulham, but the second cartilage operation proved as unsuccessful as the first and he announced his retirement from the game in May 1938 at the age of only 25 years and having not made a single appearance for the Craven Cottage club. He did however remain at Fulham in a coaching capacity and later reported on youth football for the *Daily Mirror*.

| 1994 | AFC Bournemouth | A | Friendly | 5-0 |

This match was a testimonial for former Spurs player Richard Cooke with Spurs' goals being scored by Danny Hill, David Howells, Colin Calderwood, Nick Barmby and Darren Casky.

| 1995 | Silkeborg | A | Friendly | 1-3 |
| 1995 | 1FC Cologne | A | UEFA Intertoto Cup | 0-8 |

On the same day as the first team were losing 3-1 on their tour, a reserve side were being beaten 0-8 in the final group match of the Intertoto Cup, and it was this latter competition which was to cause the club considerable problems. UEFA had decided that the UEFA Cup would be extended in 1995-96, with two teams that qualified from the Intertoto Cup given entry to the UEFA Cup 1st Round (indeed it was Cologne who not only qualified in this manner but then went on to reach the later stages of the UEFA Cup, thus vindicating UEFA's decision in their own eyes). In light of this the Premier League applied for three places in the competition, although UEFA's insistence that it should be three Premiership clubs that entered caused problems, simply because none of the Premiership clubs wanted to enter. Then UEFA announced that in the event of no Premiership clubs entering, all English clubs would be banned, so Spurs, Wimbledon and Sheffield Wednesday all agreed to volunteer, subject to certain conditions being met by UEFA, the FA and the Premier League. The conditions were that no home matches would be played at the host ground (as all three would be busy preparing for the forthcoming season), that the clubs would be allowed to play weakened teams which would not include first-team players, and that loan arrangements for other players could be made. All three conditions were agreed both verbally and in writing by the three bodies. Despite this, UEFA subsequently announced that both Spurs and Wimbledon were banned for one season from any

European competition they qualified for within the next five years and that England had lost its 'fair play' place (Sheffield Wednesday escaped because, nearing the end of their group matches and with an outside chance of further progression, they had selected something akin to their first team). This was obviously a farce, for all three clubs had documentary evidence to support their claim that UEFA had known all along under what conditions the clubs had entered the competition. When the matter went to appeal, the ban was reduced to a fine which was then shared by all Premiership clubs. This was still hardly fair, as Alan Sugar pointed out. 'There is still a black mark against our name with UEFA. We entered the Intertoto Cup to protect English football because UEFA threatened to impose punitive measures on all qualifying clubs. We don't see this as any kind of victory. We are simply in the same position as every other club in England – we have the right to qualify for Europe.' He later added in the club's handbook 'We prudently obtained written agreements from the FA, the Premier League and UEFA to participate under certain specific conditions and then we had to go to Appeal to show UEFA that we were only doing what they had already agreed to!'

JULY 23RD

| 1975 | Rot-Weiss Essen | A | Friendly | 1-1 |
| 1987 | Exeter City | A | Friendly | 1-0 |

Johnny Metgod scored his only goal for Spurs in this pre-season friendly at Exeter. Metgod had joined Spurs from Nottingham Forest for £250,000 with a reputation for deadly accuracy with both his passing and shooting. On this early indication he was a valuable asset to the club, but injuries during his only season restricted him to no more than a handful of appearances and at the end of the season he was sold to Feyenoord for £180,000.

| 1989 | Bohemians | A | Friendly | 2-0 |
| 1991 | Sligo Rovers | A | Friendly | 4-0 |

Spurs announced the promotion of chief coach Peter Shreeves to team manager, reporting to Terry Venables. It was the second spell in charge for Shreeves, having previously been manager between 1984 and 1986.

1993	Team Nord Trondelag	A	Friendly	1-0
1995	Halmstads BK	A	Friendly	1-2
1996	Ham-Kam	A	Friendly	2-0
1997	Leyton Orient	A	Friendly	1-0

British fans got their first glimpse of David Ginola playing for Spurs and he did not disappoint in this pre-season friendly, effectively running the entire game. Spurs' only goal was scored by Stephen Clemence, the son of former goalkeeper Ray Clemence.

JULY 24TH

1976	VFL Osnabruck	A	Friendly	3-1
1985	Chesterfield	A	Friendly	4-2
1992	Heart of Midlothian	A	Friendly	2-1

Gary Lineker had retired from the English game at the end of the previous season prior to moving to Japan, leaving Gordon Durie as Spurs' chief striker. Although he scored twice today, including one from the penalty spot, it was obvious that a partner was going to be needed if Spurs were to be serious challengers for the major honours.

| 1995 | IFK Gothenburg | A | Friendly | 2-0 |

JULY 25TH

1886	Alex Steel born in Newmilns, Ayrshire. Alex made only one appearance for Spurs, in a League match against Bradford City in January 1910. However, this match is notable, for the Spurs line-up included his brothers Danny and Bobby, the only time as many as three brothers have appeared in the same first team in a League match.			
1975	Karlsruher SC	A	Friendly	1-2
1987	AFC Bournemouth	A	Friendly	4-4
1989	Cork City	A	Friendly	3-0
1991	Drogheda United	A	Friendly	2-0
1993	Lyn Oslo	A	Friendly	0-0

This match was a testimonial for Tom Sundby.

| 1996 | Odd Grenland | A | Friendly | 1-2 |

JULY 26TH

1988	Vederslav/Danningelanda IF	A	Friendly	4-1
1994	Cambridge United	A	Friendly	3-0
1995	IFK Hassleholm	A	Friendly	1-3

| 1996 | Raufos | A | Friendly | 0-0 |
| 1997 | Swindon Town | A | Friendly | 2-2 |

An obvious attraction of pre-season friendlies are that they are usually played in the late summer with shirt-sleeved crowds basking in the sun. This was different, for a torrential downpour before and during the game turned conditions into a farce and led to the Spurs fans, allocated the open-aired seating, being moved to another part of the ground under cover albeit under protest from the ground officials!

JULY 27TH

1984	St Jordal Blink	A	Friendly	9-0
1985	AFC Bournemouth	A	Friendly	3-0
1991	Shelbourne	A	Friendly	3-1
1993	Team Porsgrunn	A	Friendly	5-4
1994				

Ossie Ardiles announced the capture of Rumanian World Cup star Ilie Dumitrescu. Ilie, who started his career with Steau Bucharest, had already won 44 caps for his country at the time of his transfer (formally signed two days later) and cost Spurs a total of $4.3 million, the Rumanians insisting on payment being made in US dollars.

JULY 28TH

1952 Walter Bull died in Nottingham at the age of 78 years. Born in Nottingham in 1874, Walter signed for Spurs in May 1904 from Notts County (Bull appeared in the first competitive match played at White Hart Lane, starring for County against Spurs) in a move that was considered a major coup for Spurs, for Bull was highly regarded in the football world. He made his debut for Spurs in the Western League match at Millwall in October 1904 and went on to make 23 appearances in this competition, as well as 105 appearances in the Southern League. He was still at Spurs when the club joined the Football League and forced his way back into the first team towards the end of the promotion winning season of 1908-09. He left Spurs for Heanor United in June 1910 and the following April went to coach in Buenos Aires, Argentina. In July 1912 he returned to England and replaced the Leeds City-bound Herbert Chapman as manager of Northampton Town.

1976	Eintracht Frankfurt	A	Friendly	1-4
1980	Southend United	A	Friendly	1-1
1988	Trelleborgs FF	A	Friendly	3-0

JULY 29TH

1972	Bournemouth & Boscombe Athletic	A	Friendly	4-2
1975	Hannover 96	A	Friendly	1-1
1984	Ostersund	A	Friendly	4-0
1992	Brighton & Hove Albion	A	Friendly	1-1
1994	Bristol City	A	Friendly	3-1

Shortly before Spurs took to the field for this pre-season friendly at Bristol, the sensational news came through that club chairman Alan Sugar had completed the transfer of German World Cup star Jurgen Klinsmann. Jurgen, who had starred for Germany during the recent World Cup in America, was joining from French club AS Monaco and cost $3.3 million. The deal was completed on Alan Sugar's yacht and was conducted personally by the player (who mistrusted agents) and the chairman direct.

| 1995 | Sampdoria | Ibrox | Ibrox International Tournament | 0-2 |
| 1997 | Oxford United | A | Friendly | 3-2 |

JULY 30TH

1964 Jurgen Klinsmann born in Goppingen, Germany. After initially playing with TB Gingen, SV Geislingen and Stuttgarter Kickers, Jurgen's career began to blossom following his signing by VFB Stuttgart in 1984. In 1988 he helped Germany win a bronze medal in the Olympic Games and his goalscoring exploits made him a highly prized target for the Italian clubs. He finally signed for Inter Milan in 1989. A member of the German side that won the World Cup in 1990, he helped Inter to the UEFA Cup in 1991 and then moved to AS Monaco in 1992. After two years in the principality and shortly after the 1994 World Cup, he was sensationally signed by Spurs for £2 million. At a time when Spurs had been docked 12 League points and banned from the FA Cup, the club and its fans were in need of a lift; the arrival of Jurgen saw to that. Indeed, his impact upon arriving at the club was similar to that which had greeted Ossie Ardiles when he had arrived in the country some 16 years previously. Jurgen scored on his League debut, formed a devastating partnership with Teddy Sheringham and scored more goals in the season that he had previously managed. When Spurs were re-admitted to the FA Cup later in the season, the stage seemed set for a climactic finale, even more so when Jurgen grabbed the winner in the 6th round at Anfield to knock out Liverpool. Unfortunately, defeat by Everton in the semi-final brought the fairy story to an end, and shortly after Jurgen announced he would be returning home to Germany at the end of the season in order to sign for Bayern Munich. After helping Bayern win the German League in his first season, he was on the move again, this time back to Italy and Sampdoria, but midway through the 1997-98 season and struggling to retain a regular place, a loan deal was put together that saw him return to White Hart Lane for the rest of the season. With Spurs battling against relegation at the time, Jurgen's second coming had much the same effect as his first; lifting the club almost overnight.

1980	Portsmouth	A	Friendly	2-1
1984	Viking	A	Friendly	1-0
1987	Orebo SK	A	Friendly	1-3
1991	Brann	A	Friendly	1-1
1995	Steau Bucharest	Ibrox	Ibrox International Tournament	2-3

JULY 31ST

1960   Jimmy Cantrell died in Bedford at the age of 78 years. Born in Sheepbridge, near Chesterfield on May 7th 1882, he began his professional career with Aston Villa in July 1904 and after four seasons moved on to Notts County. It was with County that Cantrell appeared in a League match at White Hart Lane that was abandoned after 80 minutes after the fog descended. County were leading 3-1 at the time, with Jimmy having scored two of the goals. Six days later Cantrell signed for Spurs, although he did not play when the Spurs v Notts County match was replayed, this time County winning 3-0. More than a useful centre-forward he was virtually a regular in the Spurs team in the seasons leading up to the First World War. When the war broke out he returned to the Midlands and assisted his former Notts County club, his Spurs career seemingly at an end. At the end of the war and at the age of 37 Cantrell returned to Spurs and was still considered good enough to lead the attack in the side that won the Second Division championship of 1919-20, finishing second top goalscorer behind Bert Bliss. More surprisingly, Cantrell held his place the following season as the club won the FA Cup for the second time, appearing in all six games of the cup run and weighing in with two goals. He made his last appearance for Spurs in April 1923 when just weeks short of his 41st birthday, the oldest player to have appeared in the Football League whilst wearing a Spurs shirt. He finished his playing career with Sutton Town, signing in October 1923 and retiring in 1925. He then became a golf professional.

1968	Rangers	H	Friendly	3-1
1976	1.FC Cologne	A	Friendly	1-3
1985	Plymouth Argyle	A	Friendly	0-1
1988	GAIS	A	Friendly	1-1
1993	SS Lazio	H	Makita International Tournament Semi-Final	3-2
1996	Brentford	A	Friendly	3-0

AUGUST 1ST

1987	Lansi Uudenmaan Dist	A	Friendly	7-1
1990	Shelbourne	A	Friendly	3-0
1991	Bryne FK	A	Friendly	0-4
1992	Glenavon	A	Friendly	1-0
1993	Chelsea	H	Makita International Tournament Final	0-4

Spurs were soundly beaten in the final of the tournament they were hosting by the side that has become something of a bogey team for them in recent seasons.

AUGUST 2ND

1969	Heart of Midlothian	A	Friendly	1-1
1972	Aston Villa	A	Friendly	0-0
1979	Gillingham	A	Friendly	1-1
1980	PSV Eindhoven	A	Friendly	2-4
1983	Hertford Town	A	Friendly	2-1
1986	Rangers	H	Paul Miller Testimonial	1-1

Crowd trouble during the game later prompted the Metropolitan Police effectively to ban future 'friendly' matches between London clubs and Rangers. It was not an auspicious start for David Pleat's first game in charge.

1988	Jonkopings Sodra IF	A	Friendly	1-1
1994	Brighton & Hove Albion	A	Friendly	3-0
1995	Derby County	A	Friendly	0-1
1997	Fiorentina	H	David Howells Testimonial	0-2

Home fans were given their first glimpse of new captures David Ginola and Les Ferdinand in this testimonial for David Howells. Unfortunately they were unable to inspire their new club against Italian opposition, for whom former Manchester United winger Andrei Kanchelskis was in sparkling form.

AUGUST 3RD

1952 Osvaldo Ardiles born in Cordoba, Argentina. When Argentina won the World Cup in 1978, there were a number of players who stood out – Mario Kempes for his goalscoring, Ricardo Villa for his ability to come on and provide a bit of meat to the midfield and Osvaldo Ardiles, who skipped around the pitch spraying passes with abandon. When the World Cup finished, the English public switched off their televisions and began to think of the forthcoming domestic season, never dreaming that two of those Argentinians were soon to be among them. In July 1978 Keith Burkinshaw announced he had concluded a £700,000 deal to bring both Ardiles and Villa to White Hart Lane and caught the football world well and truly out. Osvaldo Ardiles was valued at £325,000 in the deal, a ridiculously low fee for a man who has gone on to give Spurs superb service of one kind or another. Ossie (as he quickly became known at Spurs) began his career with a local junior club, Red Star, before being signed as a youth by Cordoba Instituto. In 1975 he moved to Buenos Aires and the Huracan club, winning his first full cap the following year. His subsequent arrival in England had many questioning whether a man of only 5' 6" and less than 10 stone would be able to withstand the rigours of a Football League season, but Ossie was quick to silence the doubters. Once Spurs had sorted out how to accommodate his silky skills with the required steel of players like Graham Roberts *et al*, success followed success. An integral part of the side that won the FA Cup in 1981 (aided by the hit record 'Ossie's Dream', which centred on his long standing wish to play at Wembley) he was the fulcrum of the side that went close on four fronts the following season. After helping Spurs to reach the FA Cup final with a semi-final victory over Leicester, he returned home to Argentina to prepare for the forthcoming World Cup in Spain. Argentina had invaded the Falkland Islands the day before the semi-final and by the time the World Cup came around, Britiain and Argentina were at war. It was agreed that it might be best if Ossie did not return to England immediately after the World Cup and a loan deal was arranged with Paris St Germain. Less than six months later he was back in England and returned to the Spurs side, although he broke his shin after only four games. A lengthy lay-off was followed by sporadic appearances fitted around further injuries, and his extremely brief appearance in his own benefit match, staged in 1986 against Inter Milan and featuring Diego Maradona in the Spurs line-up, seemed to spell the end for Ardiles as a Spurs player. However, the resilient Ardiles was back at the beginning of the following season and producing football that belied his years as Spurs reached the FA Cup final. The arrival of Terry Venables and his rebuilding programme signalled the end of Ardiles as a Spurs player after nearly ten years at White Hart Lane, and he went to Blackburn on loan before signing with QPR. After finishing his playing career in the United States, Ardiles returned to England to take over as manager at Swindon, guiding the club to victory in the First Division play-offs, although they were subsequently relegated following an investigation into financial irregularities. Ossie then moved on to St James's Park to try and revive Newcastle's fortunes, but after a little over a year was sacked. He then spent a year in charge at West Bromwich Albion (with Burkinshaw his assistant!) before accepting an offer from Alan Sugar to come back to his beloved 'Tottingham' as manager in 1993. After barely 16 months in charge he was dismissed, paying the price in particular for a bad 3-0 defeat away to Notts County in the Coca-Cola Cup, the only tangible honour on offer that season, but also suffering because of Spurs dreadful home record during his time in charge.

1957	VfB Stuttgart	A	Friendly	2-2
1968	FK Austria	A	Friendly	2-2
1970	Rangers	A	Friendly	2-0
1974	Heart of Midlothian	A	Friendly	1-1
1975	NAC Breda	A	Friendly	1-0
1982	Scunthorpe United	A	Friendly	5-0
1985	Exeter City	A	Friendly	2-2
1987	IFK/VSK Vasteras Select XI	N	Friendly	4-2
1990	Derry City	A	Friendly	3-0
1992	West Bromwich Albion	A	Friendly	2-0
1996	Reading	A	Friendly	1-0

AUGUST 4TH

1908 George Greenfield born in Hackney. Signed by Spurs from Lea Bridge Gasworks in November 1930 George was considered a bright prospect and a certainty for international honours. Sadly he never got to achieve either, for a broken leg sustained in a League match in 1933 effectively ended his career, although he did manage to return after almost two years. After just five games back in the side, George decided to retire and in February 1935 became a member of the groundstaff at Spurs.

1969	Rangers	A	Friendly	1-0
1976	KSV Baunatal	A	Friendly	2-1
1979	Oxford United	A	Friendly	1-2
1980	Rangers	A	Friendly	1-2
1983	Enfield Town	A	Friendly	4-1
1984	Enfield Town	A	Friendly	7-0

Manager Peter Shreeves was able to field two Argentinean World Cup winners in this match at Enfield; Ossie Ardiles and Mario Kempes. Kempes was on a two-match trial, having recently been playing in Spain with Valencia, and was eager to impress in the hope of securing a contract. Although he flitted around the pitch with similar abandon to that of Ardiles, he was unable to get on to the score sheet which, given the opposition, was a major disappointment. As he did not score in the second 'trial' match, away in Nice, either he was not offered a contract. This match is therefore his only appearance in a Spurs shirt in England. For the record, the man most under threat from the possible signing of Kempes, Garth Crooks, responded well to the challenge – he grabbed four of the goals.

1985	Arsenal	H	Glenn Hoddle Testimonial	1-1
1986	Aldershot	A	Friendly	3-2
1991	Celtic	A	Friendly	0-1

AUGUST 5TH

1948 Ray Clemence born in Skegness, Lincolnshire. Although he was briefly connected with Notts County, making an appearance in their 'A' team, he signed professional forms with Scunthorpe United in August 1965 and made just 50 senior appearances for them before joining Liverpool for £15,000. Signed initially as cover for Tommy Lawrence he took over the first team berth in 1970 and in the next 11 seasons missed just six League games as Liverpool dominated the domestic game. Ray collected five championship medals, three in the European Cup, two UEFA Cup medals and winners' medals in both the FA Cup and League Cup. In the summer of 1981 he was surprisingly sold to Spurs for £300,000, making his debut for the club in the FA Charity Shield against Aston Villa at Wembley. At the end of his first season at Spurs he picked up a further winners' medal in the FA Cup and a runners-up medal in the League Cup, where Spurs were beaten by Liverpool! A bad injury sustained in the FA Cup 3rd round match at Fulham in the 1983-84 season sidelined him for a considerable time and he was unable to reclaim his position when fully fit, which meant he sat on the bench as Spurs won the UEFA Cup that season. He was restored to the first team the following season and held his place as Spurs reached the FA Cup final in 1986-87, losing for the first time at this stage against Coventry. A further serious injury in October effectively ended his playing career, but Ray had passed the 1,000 mark for senior games (only Peter Shilton and Pat Jennings have achieved a similar figure) and been awarded the MBE in the 1987 Birthday Honours List in recognition of his services to football. He won 61 caps for the full England side, a figure that would have been considerably higher had it not been for having to compete with the equally competent Peter Shilton, and on retiring from playing in March 1988 was appointed specialist goalkeeping coach at White Hart Lane. In June 1989 he was upgraded to reserve team coach and made assistant first-team coach, in tandem with Doug Livermore, in May 1992. The arrival of Ossie Ardiles in the summer of 1993 brought Ray's Spurs career to an end and he subsequently took over at Barnet as manager, later resigning to become a part of Glenn Hoddle's England set-up. His son Stephen is currently signed to Spurs.

1964	Glasgow XI	N	Glasgow Charity Cup	2-4
1967	Celtic	N	Friendly	3-3
1978	Aberdeen	A	Friendly	1-3
1980	Dundee United	A	Friendly	1-4
1987	MarstaIK	A	Friendly	5-0
1992	Sunderland	A	Friendly	3-0
1995	Watford	A	Friendly	2-0

AUGUST 6TH

1925 Eddie Baily born in Clapton, East London. Although he signed amateur forms with Spurs during the war he was later reported missing in action and Spurs therefore allowed his registration to lapse. Upon arriving back in England he was persuaded by Chelsea to sign amateur forms, and it was only when he popped into White Hart Lane to collect his boots that the situation became clear. To their credit, Chelsea agreed to tear up his contract and Baily re-signed with Spurs in February 1946, being upgraded to professional status in October the following year. He made his League debut in January 1947 at home to West Bromwich and quickly became a permanent fixture in the first team. It was around his passing skills and vision that 'push and run' centred, bringing player after player into play and carving opening after opening. More than a few fell to Baily himself, all despatched with aplomb. He won a total of nine caps for England and also represented the Rest of the UK and the Football League. In 1956 he moved on to Port Vale for £6,000, but after only nine months moved to

Nottingham Forest and helped them gain promotion to the First Division. He finished his playing career with Leyton Orient and then switched to coaching, returning to White Hart Lane in 1963 as Bill Nicholson's assistant. Nicholson's resignation in 1974 also saw the departure of Eddie Baily and he joined West Ham as chief scout, a position he held until his retirement in 1992. The following year he was honoured with a testimonial at Enfield against Spurs.

1976	FVBadHonnef	A	Friendly	2-0
1982	FC Lausanne	A	Friendly	0-3
1983	Aylesbury United	A	Friendly	4-0

It is of course impossible for any football club to have more than one first team, but Spurs have perhaps come nearest to achieving such a feat – on this day they sent first-team squads to both Brentford and Aylesbury to undertake friendly matches. Manager Keith Burkinshaw chose the match at Aylesbury to view some of the players at his disposal, including Ray Clemence, Gary Mabbutt (who had family in Aylesbury), Paul Miller and Micky Hazard. Although Spurs fielded only five players who might normally be regarded as 'first-team regulars' they still proved more than a match for Aylesbury United.

1983	Brentford	A	Friendly	4-2
1984	Nice	A	Friendly	2-2
1987	Swedish Division 1			
	North Select XI	N	Friendly	0-1
1989	Rangers	A	Friendly	0-1
1993	Brentford	A	Friendly	0-0

This match was a testimonial for Keith Millen.

| 1994 | Watford | A | Friendly | 1-1 |

Not since the celebrated signing of Ardiles and Villa had Spurs attracted such media attention. Once again it was the parade of a major new signing that brought the crowd out in their droves – German World Cup winner Jurgen Klinsmann was making his debut in Spurs colours and, although he did not get on to the score sheet, showed enough touches and made enough runs to convince the watching media and full house that he would settle well and quickly into the English game. Spurs' goal was scored by Teddy Sheringham, still struggling to return to full fitness following his injury sustained at Manchester the previous October. Aside from Klinsmann and Sheringham, the following morning's newspaper headlines were stolen by the stoat that made an appearance on the pitch shortly before kick off and proceeded to run around the pitch in an attempt to evade capture by Watford's hornet-dressed mascot and Spurs goalkeeper Ian Walker!

AUGUST 7TH

1970	FC Cologne	N	Palma de Mallorca Tournament	0-1
1971	Heart of Midlothian	A	Friendly	1-2
1972	Celtic	A	Friendly	0-1
1973				

Freddie Cox died in Bournemouth. Born in Reading on 1st November 1920, Freddie joined Spurs as an amateur in 1936, finally signing professional forms in August 1938. With the Second World War cutting across his best playing years, he was allowed to move to Arsenal in September 1949 for £12,000. Even then White Hart Lane remained a happy hunting ground for him, for he scored five goals in the two semi-finals and replays Arsenal played against Chelsea at Spurs ground. He also played in both finals, collecting a winners' medal in 1950 and a runners-up medal in 1952. He also won a League championship with Arsenal and moved on to West Bromwich Albion as player-coach in July 1953. He was later manager at Bournemouth (his side beat Spurs in the FA Cup in 1957), Portsmouth, Gillingham and Bournemouth again, finally retiring from the game in 1970 in order to concentrate on his newsagents business after more than 40 years in the game. As well as his football medals Freddie was also awarded the Distinguished Flying Cross during the Second World War.

1974	Portsmouth	A	Friendly	2-0
1977	Royale Union	N	Nolia Cup Semi-Final	2-0
1979	Dundee United	A	Friendly	2-3
1988	Dundee United	A	Friendly	1-1

This match was a testimonial for David Narey and Spurs' goal was scored by Paul Walsh.

| 1990 | Brann | A | Friendly | 1-0 |
| 1996 | Southend United | A | Friendly | 3-1 |

AUGUST 8TH

| 1964 | Feyenoord | A | Friendly | 3-4 |
| 1970 | Athletico Madrid | N | Palma de Mallorca Tournament | 0-1 |

Spurs' second consecutive defeat ensured they finished bottom of the four club tournament also featuring FA Cologne.

| 1973 | Ajax Amsterdam | A | Friendly | 1-4 |

This was a testimonial match for Sjaak Swart with Spurs' consolation goal being scored by Martin Peters.

1975	Bristol Rovers	A	Friendly	4-1
1978	Royal Antwerp	A	Friendly	3-1
1979	Aberdeen	A	Friendly	0-2
1980	Swansea City	A	Friendly	0-1
1981	Glentoran	A	Friendly	3-3

Spurs were given a tremendous welcome by both the Glentoran players and fans; the players lined up on either side of the tunnel as a guard of honour to welcome Spurs on to the field, and when the crowd saw that Steve Perryman, who led the team out, had brought the FA Cup with him rapturous applause broke out. Spurs' goals were scored by Ossie Ardiles, Glenn Hoddle from the penalty spot and Mark Falco.

| 1982 | Rangers | A | Friendly | 1-0 |
| 1986 | Brighton & Hove Albion | A | Friendly | 4-0 |

This match was a testimonial for Gerry Ryan with Spurs' goals being scored by Mark Falco (two) and Chris Waddle (two, one from the penalty spot).

| 1989 | Viking | A | Friendly | 5-1 |
| 1992 | Watford | A | Friendly | 1-0 |

AUGUST 9TH

| 1969 | Leeds United | A | First Division | 1-3 |

With the World Cup in Mexico scheduled for the following year, the Football League season started earlier than any season previously, with Spurs' only goal being scored by Jimmy Greaves.

1971	Rangers	A	Friendly	0-1
1982	Portsmouth	A	Friendly	3-1
1990	Viking	A	Friendly	1-1
1993	Peterborough United	A	Friendly	2-1
1994	Shelbourne	A	Friendly	1-0

The only goal of the game was scored by Jurgen Klinsmann, his first strike in a Spurs shirt.

AUGUST 10TH

1901 Cecil Poynton born in Brownhills, Staffordshire. After signing with Spurs in 1922 he went on to give the club over 50 years of service in a variety of capacities – player, trainer and physiotherapist. He made his League debut in December 1923 at home to Birmingham as a half-back, but did not command a regular place in the team until converted to full-back. A bad injury forced him to miss most of the 1925-26 season, although he did appear in the FA Charity Shield for the Professionals against the Amateurs in November 1926. In 1933, having made 152 League appearances for Spurs he was retained as coach for the younger players, but in July 1934 he left the club to become player-manager with Margate. After a brief spell playing for Northmet he returned to Spurs as assistant trainer in January 1946 and took over as trainer on George Hardy's retirement. He became physiotherapist in 1972 and finally announced his retirement in 1975. He died in Edmonton on January 12th 1983.

1968	Arsenal	H	First Division	1-2
1974	Fulham	A	Friendly	1-0
1976	Swindon Town	A	Friendly	1-3
1977	Leicester City	N	Nolia Cup Final	2-1
1978	VVV Venlo	A	Friendly	0-1
1981	Limerick	A	Friendly	6-2
1985	Norwich City	A	Friendly	1-1
1987	Arsenal	H	Chris Hughton Testimonial	3-1
1988	Reading	A	Friendly	1-2

This match was a testimonial for Martin Hicks and Spurs' goal was scored by Paul Gascoigne.

| 1989 | Brann | A | Friendly | 2-0 |
| 1991 | Arsenal | Wembley | FA Charity Shield | 0-0 |

Between them Spurs and Arsenal had amassed 12 League titles and 13 FA Cup victories and competed for the FA Charity Shield on 19 occasions, yet this was the first time they had met for the shield. Perhaps it was too early in the season but the match seldom lived up to its billing, and at the final whistle, with no penalty shoot out, both sides retained the trophy for six months.

| 1992 | Portsmouth | A | Friendly | 2-4 |
| 1996 | Charlton Athletic | A | Friendly | 3-1 |

This match was a testimonial for Colin Walsh with Spurs' goals being scored by Ruel Fox, Andy Sinton and Chris Armstrong.

1997	Manchester United	H	FA Premier League	0-2

The immediate return of Teddy Sheringham in a United shirt was guaranteed to provoke a considerable amount of interest in the game, which was subsequently selected for live transmission on the Sunday. Sheringham had a quiet match by his own standards, for the closest he came to scoring was from the penalty spot, but it struck the post, much to the delight of the Spurs fans. They had little else to cheer, however, as United won 2-0.

AUGUST 11TH

1962	Ipswich Town	A	FA Charity Shield	5-1

Ipswich had been surprise champions the previous season as Alf Ramsey devised a tactical ploy that best utilised the limited resources at his disposal. Ipswich had won both League matches against Spurs 3-1, thus depriving Spurs of an unprecedented second double, largely because Spurs had not adapted their game to nullify the Ipswich threat. This was because the players felt the opposition should worry more about them than vice versa and manager Bill Nicholson conceded the point. But for the Charity Shield match he firmly put his foot down and devised a simple yet extremely effective method of smothering any attacks. The ploy worked to perfection as Spurs ran out easy winners.

1973	Cardiff City	A	Friendly	3-1
1979	Orient	A	Friendly	1-1
1984	Brentford	A	Friendly	3-0
1989	Dinamo Bucharest	N	Friendly	1-3
1990	Sogndal FC	A	Friendly	1-0
1991	AC Messina	N	Nicola Ceravolo Memorial Tournament	0-2

AUGUST 12TH

1961	FA XI	H	FA Charity Shield	3-2

The FA Charity Shield had traditionally been a season curtain-raiser between the League champions and FA Cup winners, but as Spurs had completed the double the season before, an FA XI was selected to provide opposition. Goals from Bobby Smith and Les Allen, who scored twice, ensured the FA Charity Shield would sit in the Spurs boardroom as well.

1967	Manchester United	A	FA Charity Shield	3-3

Whilst Tiny Joyce remains the only goalkeeper to score for Spurs in a League match, Pat Jennings can claim to be the only goalkeeper to score in a match as prestigious as the FA Charity Shield from open play. He had gathered the ball inside his own penalty area and spotted Alan Gilzean virtually unmarked inside the United half. A long-range punt downfield was probably too strong to set Gilzean through, but United keeper Alex Stepney advanced to the edge of his area to try and reduce the effect. The ball bounced in between both Gilzean and Stepney, looped over the keeper's head and promptly hit the back of the net! At this stage of proceedings, this made Jennings Spurs top goalscorer! At the end of the game, with the result a 3-3 draw, both sides retained the trophy for six months.

1972	Coventry City	H	First Division	2-1
1977	Norsjo IF	A	Friendly	3-2
1978	Bohemians	A	Friendly	4-0
1981	Norwich City	A	Friendly	2-2
1983	Brighton & Hove Albion	A	Friendly	0-0
1986	Gillingham	A	Friendly	1-1

This match was a testimonial for Mark Weatherly and Spurs' goal was scored by Mark Falco.

1995	Newcastle United	H	Gary Mabbutt Testimonial	0-2

AUGUST 13TH

1918	Roy White born in Bootle, Lancashire.

But for the Second World War Roy White might have appeared for Spurs in the Football League, but conversely it might be true to say that but for the war he might not have played for Spurs at all. After playing at minor level in Liverpool and at one time being on Everton's books he gave up football for a career in accountancy. He enlisted during the war and was evacuated from Dunkirk although his boat was sunk and he suffered temporary blindness after spending several hours in the water. Whilst recuperating in hospital he met the former Blackburn and Middlesbrough forward Jock McKay who recommended him to Spurs manager Peter McWilliam. Roy left hospital and was assigned to top secret work for the War Office. He popped along to see Spurs play Arsenal and was unexpectedly asked to play; he performed so well against Cliff Bastin that he was asked to sign amateur forms for Spurs. He was then a regular at White Hart Lane for the rest of the war period and at the war's end was asked to sign professional forms for the club. He refused as he wished to return to Liverpool and continue his accountancy course, although he did later sign for Bradford Park Avenue and play for them for five years.

1969	Burnley	H	First Division	4-0

1982	Ajax Amsterdam	A	Amsterdam 707 Tournament 1st Round	2-3
1988	Arsenal	Wembley	Wembley International Tournament	0-4
1989	Athletico Madrid	A	Friendly	0-1
1990	Heart of Midlothian	A	Friendly	1-1
1991	US Catanzaro	A	Nicola Ceravolo Memorial Tournament	1-0
1997	West Ham United	A	FA Premier League	1-2

AUGUST 14TH

1951 John Lacy born in Liverpool. When John joined Spurs during the summer of 1978, his arrival was overshadowed by that of Ossie Ardiles and Ricky Villa. However, John is assured his place in football history, for the £200,000 Spurs had to pay to Fulham for his signature was the first time an independent tribunal had set a transfer fee. He began his career with Fulham in June 1972 and developed into a commanding centre-half, attracting considerable interest from a number of bigger clubs. He arrived at Spurs during a transitional period for the club and was perhaps unfortunate that the emerging talents of Paul Miller restricted his appearances in the first team. After 99 League appearances for Spurs he left to join Crystal Palace in July 1983 and a little over a year later went to play in Norway. He returned to England and played with a number of non-League clubs. The highlight of his career was a runners-up medal in the FA Cup, collected whilst playing for Fulham in 1975.

1954	Lille Olympique	A	Friendly	1-1
1965	Valencia	N	Costa Del Sol Tournament Semi-Final	2-1
1966	Malaga CD	N	Costa Del Sol Tournament Semi-Final	2-1
1971	Wolverhampton Wanderers	A	First Division	2-2
1988	AC Milan	Wembley	Wembley International Tournament	1-2
1993	Newcastle United	A	FA Premier League	1-0

AUGUST 15TH

1920 Les Stevens born in Croydon, London. Les spent almost 12 years associated with Spurs but managed only 54 appearances in the Football League side, the Second World War cutting right across his career. He had joined Spurs an an amateur in May 1937 and was farmed out to the Northfleet nursery club, becoming a professional in January 1940. Although he was a regular during the war years, his League debut had to wait until September 1946 and he remained a regular at outside-left for the rest of the season. Thereafter he lost out to Ernie Jones and was released in February 1949 joining Bradford Park Avenue. He later played for Crystal Palace before playing non-League football.

1953	Aston Villa	H	First Division	1-0
1965	Standard Liege	N	Costa Del Sol Tournament Final	1-0
1966	Benfica	N	Costa Del Sol Tournament Final	2-1
1970	West Ham United	H	First Division	2-2
1982	1.FC Cologne	N	Amsterdam 707 Tournament 3rd/4th place play-off	0-0

Spurs lost 3-1 on penalties after the game had finished goalless, with their only strike from the spot being converted by Steve Archibald.

| 1987 | Coventry City | A | First Division | 1-2 |
| 1992 | Southampton | A | FA Premier League | 0-0 |

AUGUST 16TH

1949 John Gorman born in Winchburgh, West Lothian. Signed by Carlisle from Celtic in 1970, he soon developed into one of the best full-backs in the Second Division, prompting interest from numerous other clubs. He signed for Spurs in November 1976 for £60,000, but was badly injured after only four months and could not play again until August 1978. A further series of injuries effectively ended his career at White Hart Lane and after playing in America he returned to Britain and moved into coaching. He later linked up with Glenn Hoddle at Swindon and is currently assistant to the England manager.

1969	Liverpool	H	First Division	0-2
1972	West Bromwich Albion	A	First Division	1-0
1975	Middlesbrough	H	First Division	1-0
1976	Royal Antwerp	H	Friendly	1-1
1980	Nottingham Forest	H	First Division	2-0
1981	Aberdeen	A	Friendly	1-0

This match was a testimonial for Willie Miller with Spurs' goal being scored by Garry Brooke from the penalty spot.

1983	Celtic	A	Friendly	1-1
1984	Manchester City	A	Friendly	1-0
1988	Chelsea	A	Friendly	0-0

This match was a testimonial for Colin Pates.

| 1993 | Arsenal | H | FA Premier League | 0-1 |

AUGUST 17TH

1934 Ron Henry born in Shoreditch, London. One of the unsung heroes of the double winning side of 1960-61, Ron first signed with Spurs in March 1953 as an amateur, upgrading to professional status in January 1955. He made his debut at centre back at Huddersfield Town in April 1955 but was later converted successfully to full-back. A solid and reliable performer in this position, he was rewarded with an England cap in 1963 against France, Alf Ramsey's first match in charge of England. A 5-1 defeat coupled with the outstanding performances of Ray Wilson meant Ron never won another cap for England, but he did of course collect a League championship, two FA Cup and a European Cup-Winners' Cup winners' medals with Spurs. A cartilage injury and the emergence of Cyril Knowles effectively ended his first-team career at Spurs in the summer of 1965, although he did not retire until May 1969. He then became coach of Spurs juniors, a position he held for many years until leaving to concentrate on his nursery business.

1950 The club held its 52nd Annual General Meeting. The meeting was presided over by club president Lord Morrison and a gross profit of £39,025 8s 2d was announced. After a provision of taxation amounting to £21,243 6s 3d and a further £2,000 set aside for Benefits, a net profit of £15,782 1s 11d was declared. An indication of how successful the club was, both on and off the field, was given in the announcement that the club programme had realised, which sold for 2d a copy and did not carry advertisements, £4,372 18s 5d, which meant the low price could be carried for a further season at least.

1968	Everton	A	First Division	2-0
1974	Ipswich Town	H	First Division	0-1
1983	Dundee United	A	Friendly	1-1

This match was a testimonial for Hamish McAlpine with Spurs' goal being scored by Tony Galvin.

1985	Watford	H	First Division	4-0
1990	West Ham United	H	Ray Clemence Benefit	4-1
1991	Southampton	A	First Division	3-2
1996	Blackburn Rovers	A	FA Premier League	2-0

Midway through the first half captain Gary Mabbutt broke his leg and was therefore ruled out for the rest of the season. Spurs' goals were both scored by Chris Armstrong.

AUGUST 18TH

| 1951 | Middlesbrough | A | First Division | 1-2 |

1952 Ricardo Villa born in Buenos Aires, the capital of Argentina. He began his career with Quilmes, moved to Athletico Tucuman and was then transferred to Racing Club in a deal that made him Argentina's most expensive player. He came to world prominence during the 1978 World Cup in Argentina when he made two substitute appearances during the tournament, providing a calming influence on the under-pressure Argentine side. In the summer of 1978, with Argentina installed as World Champions he and colleague Ossie Ardiles were sensationally tranferred to Spurs in a £700,000 deal, with Villa being valued at £375,000. Although he did not settle in as quickly as Ardiles, Ricky (as he became known) left an indelible mark on the English game; in the 1981 FA Cup semi-final replay against Wolves at Highbury he scored the third Spurs goal with a delightful curling shot from outside the area. This was to prove merely a dress rehearsal for the real thing, for after making little impression in the final, being substituted with Spurs behind, he was restored to the side for the replay. He scored after only seven minutes and then, with the score at 2-2 and time running out, set off on a run that took him past four defenders before slotting the ball home for the Spurs' winner. Instantly hailed as one of the finest goals ever seen at Wembley and a fitting strike with which to win the 100th FA Cup, it seemed as though Villa's career would take off, but the following season he could only make the substitutes bench for the League Cup final against Liverpool and was left out altogether when Spurs again reached the FA Cup final, the political situation with the Falkland Islands making it virtually impossible for Keith Burkinshaw to include him in the team. Ricky remained with Spurs until June 1983 when he joined Fort Lauderdale Strikers and after a spell in Colombia returned to his native Argentina and took up coaching. He did return to Spurs to play in Tony Galvin's testimonial against West Ham in 1987, but the one over-riding memory of the big bearded striker will always be rooted in 1981 – "Ricky Villa. Still Ricky Villa. What a fantastic run. He's scored!"

1956	Preston North End	A	First Division	4-1
1962	Birmingham City	H	First Division	3-0
1971	Newcastle United	H	First Division	0-0
1973	Sunderland	A	Friendly	1-0
1979	Middlesbrough	H	First Division	1-3
1984	Sheffield United	A	Friendly	3-0

AUGUST 19TH

1939	Arsenal	H	Jubilee Trust Fund	0-1
1944	Coventry City	A	Friendly	1-3
1950	Blackpool	H	First Division	1-4

Having stormed through the Second Division the previous season in such wonderful fashion, Spurs fans and players alike were convinced they could carry on where they left off in the First Division. Blackpool brought them back down to earth with a bump, running away with this victory.

1961	Blackpool	A	First Division	2-1
1967	Leicester City	A	First Division	3-2
1969	Burnley	A	First Division	2-0
1970	Leeds United	H	First Division	0-2
1972	Wolverhampton Wanderers	A	First Division	2-3
1978	Nottingham Forest	A	First Division	1-1
1980	Crystal Palace	A	First Division	4-3
1986	PSV Eindhoven	N	Friendly	1-1

This was Spurs' first match in the Juan Gamper Tournament in Barcelona, with the hosts and AC Milan completing the four teams. After the game at the Nou Camp had finished 1-1, Spurs' goal being scored by Mark Falco, there was a penalty shoot out which PSV won 4-3.

1987	Newcastle United	H	First Division	3-1
1989	Luton Town	H	First Division	2-1
1992	Coventry City	H	FA Premier League	0-2
1995	Manchester City	A	FA Premier League	1-1

AUGUST 20TH

1938	Arsenal	A	Jubilee Trust Fund	2-0
1949	Brentford	A	Second Division	4-1
1951	Fulham	H	First Division	1-0
1955	Burnley	H	First Division	0-1
1960	Everton	H	First Division	2-0

Spurs' opening game of the season that was to end with them lifting the coveted double hardly got off to a grand start, for Everton held them at bay for 85 minutes before being hit by two goals in quick succession. Cliff Jones ended the game hobbling up and down the wing after taking a knock that would subsequently keep him out the side for the next six games. Les Allen scored Spurs' first when latching on to a loose ball while Bobby Smith was screaming for a penalty, and Smith himself added a second two minutes later.

1962	Aston Villa	A	First Division	1-2
1966	Leeds United	H	First Division	3-1
1975	Ipswich Town	H	First Division	1-1
1977	Sheffield United	H	Second Division	4-2
1984	Fulham	H	Peter Southey Memorial	3-1
1986	AC Milan	N	Friendly	2-1
1990	Southend United	A	Friendly	4-1
1994	Sheffield Wednesday	A	FA Premier League	4-3

Whilst Jurgen Klinsmann had performed well enough in his two pre-season friendlies with Spurs there was a world of difference between the exertions required in friendlies and those needed for League football, especially in what has long been regarded the toughest League in the world. The additional presence of Rumania's World Cup stars Ilie Dumitrescu, making his Spurs League debut, and Dan Petrescu, similarly appearing for Sheffield Wednesday for the first time, ensured massive interest. Neither side disappointed. The first shock came before the match – Ardiles handed his line-up to the referee and had elected to play with five forwards, a decision that surprised almost everyone, not least Wednesday manager Trevor Francis. The next ninety minutes would reveal whether such a formation, basically relying on little more than all-out attack, was either brave or foolhardy. As it turned out, the decision was vindicated but not before a few mishaps along the way. Teddy Sheringham opened the scoring early in the first half when he was found completely free and unmarked in the Wednesday area, having enough time to place the ball under Pressman. Darren Anderton increased the lead a short while later, playing a one-two with Klinsmann before knocking home. Spurs went to sleep during the early stages of the second half, allowing Wednesday to draw level with goals from Petrescu and a Colin Calderwood own goal, but then powered away again. Nick Barmby broke free and could have used the unmarked Klinsmann but decided to strike home himself. Then came the goal all Spurs fans most wanted to see, Klinsmann rising to head home his first League goal for Spurs. The celebrations were something special too; his supposed reputation as a 'diver' in an attempt to win penalties, was brought to prominence as Klinsmann ran towards the touchline and dived in theatrical style. The move was obviously pre-planned, for six Spurs players ran after the delighted German and did similar dives, including Walker in the Spurs goal, who half the length of the field in order to join in the celebrations! David Hirst scored a third for Wednesday to set up a frantic last few moments, but the next drama saw Klinsmann suffer a facial injury in a clash with Des Walker. Klinsmann was duly carried off the field on a stretcher and had a number of stitches inserted into a nasty face wound, but his contribution to a thrilling and exciting match was recognised by both sets of supporters, who gave him a standing ovation as he left the field.

AUGUST 21ST

1948	Sheffield Wednesday	H	Second Division	3-2
1954	Aston Villa	A	First Division	4-2
1968	West Bromwich Albion	H	First Division	1-1
1971	Huddersfield Town	H	First Division	4-1
1974	Manchester City	A	First Division	0-1
1976	Ipswich Town	A	First Division	1-3
1982	Liverpool	Wembley	FA Charity Shield	0-1

Spurs gave Gary Mabbutt his first senior appearance in the first team in the FA Charity Shield at Wembley, but the real story of the game was a number of tackles that were hardly in keeping with the spirit of the match. This in turn caused tempers to fray, and the sight of Garth Crooks remonstrating with Graeme Souness was indicative of how close the game was to exploding.

1983	West Ham United	H	Bill Nicholson Testimonial	1-1
1985	Oxford United	A	First Division	1-1
1988	West Ham United	A	Friendly	0-2

This match was a testimonial for Alvin Martin.

| 1991 | Sparkasse Stockerau | A | European Cup-Winners' Cup Preliminary Round 1st Leg | 1-0 |

The UEFA enforced ban on English clubs participating in European competition for five years following the Heysel stadium disaster had been lifted in 1990, but one aspect that had not been overturned was the points system in dictating qualification. Because English clubs had not earned any points between 1985 and 1990, Spurs had to play in the preliminary round of the European Cup-Winners' Cup, travelling to Vienna to take on the unknown Sparkasse Stockerau. A single goal from Gordon Durie proved enough to win the game, but the performance was well below par.

| 1993 | Manchester City | H | FA Premier League | 1-0 |
| 1996 | Derby County | H | FA Premier League | 1-1 |

AUGUST 22ND

1914	Arsenal	H	War Relief Fund	1-5
1949	Plymouth Argyle	H	Second Division	4-1
1953	Sheffield Wednesday	A	First Division	1-2
1956	Manchester City	A	First Division	2-2
1959	Newcastle United	A	First Division	5-1
1960	Blackpool	A	First Division	3-1
1964	Sheffield United	H	First Division	2-0
1970	Wolverhampton Wanderers	A	First Division	3-0
1979	Norwich City	A	First Division	0-4
1981	Aston Villa	Wembley	FA Charity Shield	2-2

Although Milija Aleksic had performed more than admirably in the two cup final clashes with Manchester City the previous season, manager Keith Burkinshaw knew that a top-class goalkeeper was needed if the club were to build upon that success. When Liverpool's Ray Clemence became available, therefore, at a cut price £300,000 he was eagerly snapped up and made his debut in the FA Charity Shield against Aston Villa. It was not an auspicious start, for his handling let him down and enabled Aston Villa to draw a match they probably deserved to lose. Both of Spurs' goals were scored by Mark Falco, in the side as Garth Crooks had been undergoing a cartilage operation. Ray Clemence would eventually get the defence sorted out to his satisfaction, whilst Mark Falco would go on scoring goals until a ligament injury halted his progress.

1987	Chelsea	H	First Division	1-0
1989	Everton	A	First Division	1-2
1992	Crystal Palace	H	FA Premier League	2-2

Neil Ruddock became the first Spurs player to be sent off in a Premier League match.

AUGUST 23RD

| 1905 | John Blair born in Neilston, Strathclyde. After impressing for Third Lanark during the 1925-26 season he was snapped up by Spurs and made his League debut in August 1926, scoring in the match against |

Everton. He scored nine goals in his first 11 League appearances until injured, and when he returned could not find the goalscoring touch that had made him so dangerous. The emergence of Taffy O'Callaghan limited his appearances still further and he was allowed to move on to Sheffield United in November 1927. He died in Kilmarnock on 1st January 1972.

1943   Frank Saul born on Canvey Island, Essex. Frank signed as an amateur with Spurs in August 1958 and was appearing for the reserves when he was only 15, later being upgraded to the professional ranks in August 1960. He made his debut the following season, standing in for the injured Bobby Smith and scored three goals in six appearances in the double winning side. However, Spurs propensity for buying big name stars, usually in forward positions meant Frank faced a constant battle to hold a regular place in the side and it was not until 1965-66, when he filled in for the hepatitis-stricken Jimmy Greaves that he got an extended run in the team. Despite this, Frank could always be relied upon to weigh in with vital goals, never more so than in 1966-67 when he scored the winners in both the FA Cup semi-final and final, against Nottingham Forest and Chelsea respectively. In 1968 Spurs negotiated the transfer of Martin Chivers to White Hart Lane from Southampton, with Frank making the opposite journey as a £45,000 part of the £125,000 deal. After two seasons with Southampton he returned to London, firstly with QPR for two seasons and then for five with Millwall, finishing his playing career with Dagenham.

1947	West Bromwich Albion	A	Second Division	0-1
1948	Coventry City	A	Second Division	0-2
1950	Bolton Wanderers	A	First Division	4-1
1952	West Bromwich Albion	H	First Division	3-4
1958	Blackpool	H	First Division	2-3
1961	West Ham United	H	First Division	2-2

On the same day Gary Mabbutt born in Bristol. The son of Ray Mabbutt, a former forward with Bristol Rovers and Newport and brother of Kevin, who played for Crystal Palace, Gary Mabbutt has defied the odds to win limitless honours both inside and outside the game. He signed with Bristol Rovers as a professional in January 1979 and played in every outfield position in his four years at Eastville. He was capped by England at Under-21 level in March 1982 and was snapped up by Spurs for £120,000 in the summer of the same year. With injuries having decimated the Spurs side he made his first senior appearance in the FA Charity Shield at Wembley against Liverpool and quickly settled into the side. In October 1982 he was capped by England at full level, playing at right-back. He won a winners' medal for Spurs playing in the 1984 UEFA Cup (he replaced captain Steve Perryman in the second leg) and was then successfully converted to centre-back by manager David Pleat. He collected a runners-up medal in the 1987 FA Cup final, having the misfortune to score for both sides, but received more than adequate compensation in 1991 when as captain he led the team to victory over Nottingham Forest. He was recalled to the England team for the final qualifying games of the European Championship and won 16 caps. Early in his football career he was diagnosed as suffering from diabetes, but was an inspiration to all other sufferers by continuing to play at the highest level in the game. He was awarded the MBE in 1994 and left Spurs on a free transfer in 1998.

1967	Everton	H	First Division	1-1
1969	Crystal Palace	A	First Division	2-0
1972	Birmingham City	H	First Division	2-0
1975	Liverpool	A	First Division	2-3
1978	Aston Villa	H	First Division	1-4
1980	Brighton & Hove Albion	H	First Division	2-2
1986	Aston Villa	A	First Division	3-0
1995	Aston Villa	H	FA Premier League	0-1
1997	Derby County	H	FA Premier League	1-0

AUGUST 24TH

1873   Tom Bradshaw born in Liverpool. He began his League career with Liverpool, helping them to win the Second Division title in both 1894 and 1896 and then moved to Spurs in May 1898. He was an almost ever present with Spurs during his one season with the club but moved to Thames Ironworks during the summer of 1899. Unfortunately he fell ill during the season and died on Christmas Day 1899, with Spurs later playing Thames Ironworks to raise funds for the dependants of the 26-year-old player.

1900   Matt Forster born in Newburn-on-Tyne. Spotted by Spurs whilst playing for Newburn in the Northern Alliance, Matt came to White Hart Lane as a 19-year-old in October 1919. He made his debut at home to West Bromwich Albion in February 1921 but did not become a regular in the team until midway through the 1922-23 season, replacing full-back Bob McDonald. Over the next six seasons he was to amass 236 appearances for the club at League level, although he did not get on the score sheet. As Matt's time at Spurs was not a particularly successful one for the club, he was overlooked by England, but he did represent the Football League in 1926. In April 1930 he was not retained by the club and so moved to Reading and after three years at Elm Park joined Charlton. He wound down his career in non-League football and after a brief spell scouting for Fulham worked in the fur trade and then for Marconi Electronics. He died in St Albans on October 18th 1976.

1955	Manchester United	A	First Division	2-2
1957	Chelsea	H	First Division	1-1
1963	Stoke City	A	First Division	1-2
1966	Stoke City	A	First Division	0-2
1968	Sheffield Wednesday	H	First Division	1-2
1974	Carlisle United	A	First Division	0-1
1977	Blackburn Rovers	A	First Division	0-0
1985	Ipswich Town	A	First Division	0-1
1991	Chelsea	H	First Division	1-3
1994	Everton	H	FA Premier League	2-1
1996	Everton	H	FA Premier League	1-1

AUGUST 25TH

1923	Preston North End	H	First Division	2-0
1928	Oldham Athletic	H	Second Division	4-1
1934	Everton	H	First Division	1-1
1945	Wolverhampton Wanderers	H	Football League South	1-4
1951	West Bromwich Albion	H	First Division	3-1
1954	Wolverhampton Wanderers	H	First Division	3-2
1956	Leeds United	H	First Division	5-1
1962	West Ham United	A	First Division	6-1

Having been beaten by Aston Villa five days previously in their second match of the season, Spurs bounced back with their biggest away win in many a year. Goals from Terry Medwin, John White, Cliff Jones, Jimmy Greaves (two) and a John Lyall own goal enabled Spurs to swamp West Ham.

1964	Burnley	A	First Division	2-2
1965	Leicester City	H	First Division	4-2
1970	Southampton	A	First Division	0-0
1971	Leeds United	A	First Division	1-1
1973	Coventry City	A	First Division	0-1
1975	West Ham United	A	First Division	0-1
1976	Newcastle United	H	First Division	0-2
1979	Stoke City	A	First Division	1-3
1984	Everton	A	First Division	4-1
1986	Newcastle United	H	First Division	1-1
1990	Manchester City	H	First Division	3-1

The performances of England during the recent World Cup had lifted an entire nation, with two players in particular enjoying adulation on a level never previously experienced. Both players were Spurs players; Gary Lineker, whose goals had taken England to the very brink of the final itself before a penalty shoot-out against Germany ended the dream, and Paul Gascoigne, whose overall contribution had already won widespread acclaim even before he'd burst into tears when he realised he would have to sit out the final, even if England made it, on a suspension. By the time of the opening game of the season, the tears had dried but the memories hadn't and both players received a tremendous reception from all present when they took to the field against Manchester City. Everything went according to plan too, for Lineker grabbed two and Gascoigne one in the 3-1 victory.

1992	Leeds United	A	FA Premier League	0-5
1993	Liverpool	A	FA Premier League	2-1

AUGUST 26TH

1922	Cardiff City	H	First Division	1-1
1933	Sheffield United	A	First Division	0-0
1939	Birmingham City	H	Second Division	1-1
1944	West Ham United	H	Football League South	2-2
1950	Arsenal	A	First Division	2-2
1953	Charlton Athletic	H	First Division	3-1
1959	West Bromwich Albion	H	First Division	2-2
1961	Arsenal	H	First Division	4-3

Terry Dyson scored a hat-trick as Spurs won at Highbury for the second consecutive season. In so doing he became the only Spurs player to have scored three goals against Spurs nearest rivals Arsenal. It was a feat that was to be beyond even the likes of Jimmy Greaves, with Les Allen scoring Spurs other goal.

1967	West Ham United	H	First Division	5-1
1972	Leeds United	H	First Division	0-0
1978	Chelsea	H	First Division	2-2
1985	Everton	H	First Division	0-1
1989	Manchester City	A	First Division	1-1
1995	Liverpool	H	FA Premier League	1-3

AUGUST 27TH

1921	Cardiff City	A	First Division	1-0
1923	Chelsea	A	First Division	1-0
1927	Birmingham	H	First Division	1-0
1928	Middlesbrough	H	Second Division	2-5

Both Spurs and Middlesbrough had been relegated from the First Division at the end of the previous season and obviously harboured hopes that they might make an immediate return to the top flight. Whilst Spurs had won their opening game of the season 4-1 at home to Oldham, Middlesbrough had won 3-2 at Reading. This early meeting between the two sides most likely to lead the chase for promotion was little short of disaster for Spurs as they fell to a 2-5 defeat. At the end of the season Middlesbrough would be promoted as champions, whilst Spurs would finish no higher than tenth.

1932	Charlton Athletic	H	Second Division	4-1
1934	Preston North End	H	First Division	1-2
1938	Southampton	A	Second Division	2-1
1947	Bury	A	Second Division	0-2
1949	Blackburn Rovers	H	Second Division	2-3
1952	Manchester City	A	First Division	1-0
1955	Luton Town	A	First Division	1-2
1958	Chelsea	A	First Division	2-4
1960	Blackburn Rovers	A	First Division	4-1
1965	Blackpool	H	First Division	4-0
1966	Newcastle United	A	First Division	2-0
1969	Chelsea	H	First Division	1-1
1977	Notts County	H	First Division	2-1
1980	Orient	A	League Cup 2nd Round 1st Leg	1-0
1983	Ipswich Town	A	First Division	1-3
1984	Leicester City	H	First Division	2-2

1988 Barely hours before Spurs were due to play Coverntry City in the opening game of the season, the game was postponed! Spurs were in the process of re-developing the East Stand and, although work was not yet complete, assurances had been received during the week leading up to the game that the site would be made safe and a safety certificate issued. Unfortunately, when the officials arrived to carry out the inspection they deemed the site unsuitable and refused to issue the necessary safety certificate. Without this, there was little option but to postpone the game. Spurs were later forced to reimburse Coventry's travelling expenses.

1994	Manchester United	H	FA Premier League	0-1
1997	Aston Villa	H	FA Premier League	3-2

AUGUST 28TH

1873 Tom Pratt born in Fleetwood, Lancashire. After coming to prominence with Grimsby Town and Preston North End Tom signed for Spurs in April 1899, his acquisition being considered something of a coup for the club. Although he scored 25 vital goals in the Southern League (including one in an abandoned match) that ensured Spurs finished the season as champions, he was unable to settle in London and returned to Preston North End, thereby missing out on the FA Cup success of the following season. He later played for Woolwich Arsenal, Fulham and Blackpool before becoming a motor engineer upon his retirement as a player. He died in Fleetwood in August 1935.

1920	Blackburn Rovers	H	First Division	1-2
1926	Everton	H	First Division	2-1
1933	Wolverhampton Wanderers	H	First Division	4-0

The game was to have kicked off in the evening (despite there being no floodlights) but was brought forward to the afternoon as the Grenadier Guards, who Spurs had engaged to entertain the crowd for the coming season, were not available in the evening. Although Spurs won the match convincingly, the change in kick off time had a detrimental effect on the crowd; only 20,953 were in attendance.

1937	Coventry City	H	Second Division	0-0

1943	Crystal Palace	H	Football League South	1-1
1948	Lincoln City	A	Second Division	0-0
1950	Bolton Wanderers	H	First Division	4-2
1954	Sunderland	H	First Division	0-1
1957	Portsmouth	A	First Division	1-5
1961	West Ham United	A	First Division	1-2

1962   Paul Allen born in Aveley, Essex. A dynamic, hard-running midfield player he first came to prominence at West Ham, joining the Hammers in 1978 and being upgraded to professional ranks in August 1979. He made his League debut the following month and in May became the youngest-ever cup final player when he helped West Ham to victory over Arsenal when aged only 17 years and 256 days. He might have gone one better and become the youngest cup final scorer but for a professional foul by Willie Young! In June 1985 a £400,000 deal made him the third member of the Allen clan to play for Spurs (following his uncle Les and cousin Clive) and after two years he had settled well into the team. He picked up a losers' medal in the FA Cup final in 1987 but returned four years later to collect a winners' medal as Spurs beat Nottingham Forest. In 1993 he was surprisingly sold to Southampton and continued to show the kind of determination and skill that had him selected for the England B tour of 1989. He later played for Luton, Stoke, Swindon, Bristol City and Millwall.

1963	Wolverhampton Wanderers	A	First Division	4-1
1968	Manchester United	A	First Division	1-3
1971	Manchester City	A	First Division	0-4
1973	Birmingham City	A	First Division	2-1
1974	Manchester City	H	First Division	1-2
1976	Middlesbrough	H	First Division	0-0
1982	Luton Town	H	First Division	2-2
1990	Sunderland	A	First Division	0-0
1991	Nottingham Forest	A	First Division	3-1
1993	Aston Villa	A	FA Premier League	0-1

AUGUST 29TH

1921	Bolton Wanderers	H	First Division	1-2
1925	Arsenal	A	First Division	1-0

1925   Prior to the start of the season the offside law was changed. Whereas previously an attacker had to have three members of the opposition between him and the ball, now he only required two. Manager Peter McWilliam made no mention of the change in his pre-match tactics, preferring to allow the players to work out the ramifications for themselves. Jimmy Seed obviously did, for he inspired this day's win over Arsenal, although in light of the success Arsenal were to enjoy over the next decade, it could be argued that Herbert Chapman and the tactics that Arsenal adopted were ultimately more successful than those employed by Spurs.

1931	Wolverhampton Wanderers	A	Second Division	0-4
1932	Nottingham Forest	A	Second Division	1-3
1936	West Ham United	A	Second Division	1-2
1938	Sheffield Wednesday	H	Second Division	3-3
1942	Crystal Palace	H	Football League South	1-3

1942   Midway through the game Andy Duncan, who had been the target of some barracking from the crowd throughout, told his colleagues he wasn't going to put up with it any longer and walked off the pitch, leaving Spurs to continue with only ten men! Duncan never made another appearance for the club, although he did remain on the books until the end of the season.

1951	Fulham	A	First Division	2-1
1953	Middlesbrough	H	First Division	4-1
1956	Manchester City	H	First Division	3-2
1959	Birmingham City	H	First Division	0-0
1962	Aston Villa	H	First Division	4-2
1964	Everton	A	First Division	1-4
1967	Everton	A	First Division	1-0
1970	Coventry City	H	First Division	1-0

1974   With Spurs having lost their opening four games in the First Division manager Bill Nicholson announced his resignation from the club. Although the board, players and fans all tried to make him change his mind, Bill was adamant that he needed a rest from the game, although he did agree to remain in charge until a replacement could be found. He had been manager at Spurs for the last 16 years and had guided the club to numerous honours, including the first League and FA Cup double of the century in 1961, the first English club to win a major European trophy, the first side to win the League Cup on more than one occasion and countless others.

1978	Swansea City	A	League Cup 2nd Round	2-2
1979	Manchester United	H	League Cup 2nd Round 1st Leg	2-1
1981	Middlesbrough	A	First Division	3-1
1983	Coventry City	H	First Division	1-1
1987	Watford	A	First Division	1-1

AUGUST 30TH

1919	Coventry City	A	Second Division	5-0
1920	Derby County	A	First Division	2-2
1924	Bolton Wanderers	H	First Division	3-0
1926	Sheffield Wednesday	H	First Division	7-3
1930	Reading	H	Second Division	7-1

Five of Spurs' goals were scored by Ted Harper, the first time any player had scored as many as five goals in a League match. The achievement would not be repeated for another 27 years.

1937	Burnley	H	Second Division	4-0
1941	Watford	H	London War League	5-0
1947	Sheffield Wednesday	H	Second Division	5-1
1948	Coventry City	H	Second Division	4-0
1952	Newcastle United	A	First Division	1-1
1954	Wolverhampton Wanderers	A	First Division	2-4
1958	Blackburn Rovers	A	First Division	0-5

Spurs' third consecutive defeat from the start of the season left them firmly rooted at the bottom of the first table compiled and facing an uphill struggle for the next nine months. Relegation was ultimately avoided, but a final position of 18th, having ended the previous season in 3rd place was a major disappointment for all concerned.

1969	Ipswich Town	H	First Division	3-2
1972	Newcastle United	A	First Division	1-0
1975	Norwich City	H	First Division	2-2
1980	Arsenal	A	First Division	0-2
1986	Manchester City	H	First Division	1-0
1992	Ipswich Town	A	FA Premier League	1-1
1994	Ipswich Town	A	FA Premier League	3-1
1995	West Ham United	A	FA Premier League	1-1
1997	Arsenal	A	FA Premier League	0-0

Although the game finished goalless, Arsenal had far more of the play and should have won convincingly. That they didn't, especially as Spurs had Justin Edinburgh sent off after barely half the game had passed, owed much to some spirited defensive play on the part of Spurs.

AUGUST 31ST

1918	Corporal H Prices XI	A	Friendly	1-1
1925	Sheffield United	A	First Division	3-2
1927	Middlesbrough	A	First Division	1-3
1929	Bradford Park Avenue	A	Second Division	1-2
1931	Preston North End	H	Second Division	4-0
1935	Bradford City	A	Second Division	1-0
1936	Blackpool	A	Second Division	0-0
1939	Newport County	A	Second Division	1-1
1940	West Ham United	H	Football League South	2-3
1946	Birmingham City	H	Second Division	1-2
1949	Plymouth Argyle	A	Second Division	2-3
1955	Manchester United	H	First Division	1-2
1957	Newcastle United	A	First Division	1-3
1960	Blackpool	H	First Division	3-1
1963	Nottingham Forest	H	First Division	4-1

Jimmy Greaves scored a hat-trick in this game, the second time he had scored as many as three goals against Forest. The previous season he had grabbed four in the 9-2 win at White Hart Lane, and he ended his playing career having scored more of his goals against Forest than any other club. It was rumoured they contributed to his benefit match when he finally retired!

1966	Stoke City	H	First Division	2-0
1968	Chelsea	A	First Division	2-2
1974	Derby County	H	First Division	2-0
1976	Middlesbrough	A	League Cup 2nd Round	2-1

| 1977 | Wimbledon | H | League Cup 2nd Round | 4-0 |

This was Wimbledon's first season as a League club, their cup exploits against the likes of Burnley and Leeds United earning them a place in the Football League at the expense of Workington at the Football League AGM during the summer. This was also their first appearance at White Hart Lane for a first class match, with a crowd of 22,807 seeing John Duncan grab a hat-trick and Keith Osgood scoring from the penalty spot.

1982	Ipswich Town	A	First Division	2-1
1985	Manchester City	A	First Division	0-1
1991	Norwich City	A	First Division	1-0

SEPTEMBER 1ST

1898	Gainsborough Trinity	H	Friendly	6-2
1900	Millwall Athletic	H	Southern League	0-3
1901	Heart of Midlothian	H	Friendly	0-0
1903	Woolwich Arsenal	H	London League	0-1
1906	West Ham United	H	Southern League	1-2

On the same day Arthur Rowe was born in Tottenham. Arthur had first linked with Spurs whilst still at school and subsequently signed as an amateur in 1923, being farmed out to the nursery clubs Cheshunt and Northfleet before returning and signing as a professional in May 1929. Although he appeared in the side for a London FA Charity Cup match in 1930 his League debut didn't materialise until the following year, but once he got into the side he was there to stay. With Arthur proving such a solid and reliable centre-half Spurs were able to win promotion back to the First Division and then finish in third place in consecutive seasons. There might have been better things to follow too, but a serious knee injury in 1934 kept him out of the side long enough for the team to slip back into the Second Division. That knee injury seemed to be the start of a series of injuries that put him in and out of the side, and in April 1939 he was made available for free transfer, choosing instead to retire from playing and pursuing a coaching career. He took a position in Hungary, but the sudden outbreak of the Second World War hastened his departure back to England, and he spent much of the war coaching the Army team. At the end of hostilities he accepted the position of manager at Chelmsford City and guided them to the Southern League title at the end of his first season in charge. It wasn't just the success he fashioned that caused others to take an interest either, for with Arthur at the helm Chelmsford were considered one of the most attractive teams in non-League circles. In May 1949 he accepted the one post his career had been building towards; manager of Spurs. Although most of the team that would eventually win the Second and First Division titles in consecutive years was in place (the only major purchase Arthur made was the acquisition of Alf Ramsey from Southampton), it was Arthur who gave them a style that became known simply as 'push and run'. For two seasons the club carried all before it and might have achieved more, for they were runners-up in the First Division in 1951-52 and FA Cup semi-finalists the following year. However, just as some of the Spurs players were reaching the end of their careers so other teams had begun working out how to stop them, and such heights could not be scaled again. Although Arthur toiled long and hard to try and change their fortunes, the effort had a detrimental effect on his health, and after suffering a nervous breakdown in 1954 he was forced to resign. After rest and recuperation he returned to football in 1957, scouting for West Bromwich Albion, later becoming assistant manager at Crystal Palace and then in 1960 taking over at Selhurst Park. He took the club out of the Fourth Division at the end of his first season in charge, but once again found the pressures too great to bear and resigned in December 1962, returning to the backroom staff. He later served both Orient and Millwall as a consultant and died in London on 8th November 1993.

| 1908 | Wolverhampton Wanderers | H | Second Division | 3-0 |

Tottenham Hotspur played their first ever Football League match, a home fixture with FA Cup holders Wolverhampton Wanderers (whose path seems to have constantly crossed with Spurs in the ensuing decades). Three of the Spurs team – Hewitson, McFarlane and Bob Steel – were making their debuts, although Spurs were strengthened by the presence of Vivian Woodward, who would normally have been playing cricket at this time of the year. The game was played on a Thursday, the weather was poor but the historical nature of the match attracted a crowd of 20,000. It took only six minutes for Spurs to take the lead; Walton took a free-kick just outside the Wolves penalty area and fired in a terrific shot which Lunn in the goal blocked but could not hold, the ball falling for the ideally placed Vivian Woodward to tap home from six yards for Spurs' first-ever Football League goal. Although Spurs continued to press for the rest of the first half and had the ball in the net on two further occasions, both were adjudged offside and the score remained 1-0 at the changeover. Early in the second half Vivian Woodward finally got a goal that counted and shortly before the end Tom Morris scored with a 30-yard shot to register a 3-0 win for Spurs.

| 1909 | Sunderland | A | First Division | 1-3 |

One year to the day since making their Football League debut (for many years the Football League programme started on September 1st, almost regardless of what day of the week it fell) Spurs made their debut in the First Division. It was a long trek up to Sunderland and no doubt an even longer journey back after they had lost 3-1 in front of a 10,000 crowd.

1910	Everton	A	First Division	0-2
1913	Sheffield United	A	First Division	4-1
1917	Crystal Palace	A	London Combination	4-2
1919	Leicester City	H	Second Division	4-0
1923	Preston North End	A	First Division	2-2
1928	Southampton	A	Second Division	1-1
1930	Burnley	H	Second Division	8-1

Spurs began the 1930-31 season in cavalier fashion, following their 7-1 win over Reading with this victory over Burnley. Billy Cook helped himself to a hat-trick, Taffy O'Callaghan and Ted Harper scored two apiece and Willie Davies completed the scoring. Despite the fine start, Spurs finished the season in 3rd place in the Second Division and thus missed out on promotion back to the top flight.

1934	Huddersfield Town	A	First Division	0-0
1945	Wolverhampton Wanderers	A	Football League South	2-4
1947	Bury	H	Second Division	2-2
1951	Newcastle United	A	First Division	2-7

Newcastle exacted revenge for their beating of the previous season (Spurs won 7-0 on their way to lifting the First Division title) with a hammering of Spurs in front of over 52,000 passionate Geordies. The rout took only four minutes to set in motion, Mitchell beating Alf Ramsey and then dribbling in along the goal line before scoring from close in. Spurs settled into the game for a while before Walker added a second on quarter of an hour and three minutes later Robledo scored a third despite Ted Ditchburn getting his hands to the shot. If Newcastle were having the most luck in front of goal then Spurs were certainly doing more than their fair share of the attacking and Simpson in the Newcastle goal was kept busy. Mitchell scored his second of the game to make the score 4-0 in Newcastle's favour before Jimmy Scarth at last brought Spurs back into the game with a goal right on half-time. Les Bennett further reduced the deficit ten minutes into the second half and Spurs' hopes soared, but an immediate reply from Robledo, the same player completing his hat-trick and a final goal from Taylor gave Newcastle a 7-2 win. The defence had an off day, with the full-backs being repeatedly beaten by Newcastle's fast and lively wingers, Mitchell and Walker, whilst Ted Ditchburn was not as commanding as he could be, despite making some good saves. On the same evening the reserves met Southampton Reserves at White Hart Lane, with the floodlights switched on for the first time in a competitive match.

1952	Manchester City	H	First Division	3-3
1956	Bolton Wanderers	A	First Division	0-1
1962	Manchester City	H	First Division	4-2
1965	Leicester City	A	First Division	2-2
1970	Huddersfield Town	A	First Division	1-1
1971	AC Torino	A	Anglo-Italian League Cup -Winners' Cup 1st Leg	1-0

When Swindon Town won the League Cup in 1969 they were not eligible for entrance into the Inter-Cities Fairs Cup. To compensate, the Football League and the Italian League put together a two-legged tie between the League Cup winners of their respective countries (even though Italy does not have a League Cup competition, so they were represented by the Italian FA Cup winners!). Spurs, of course, were eligible for European competition (the renamed UEFA Cup) but still found themselves committed to two matches with AC Torino. On the positive side, these matches did give them an opportunity to acclimatise themselves to European competition (having been absent since 1967-68) before the competition-proper started, and in the Stadium Communale in Turin were worth a little bit more than a 1-0 lead, which Martin Chivers provided on the hour. If the competition lacked stature, then the Italian public didn't know about it; a healthy crowd of 28,000 saw this Spurs win.

1973	Leeds United	H	First Division	0-3
1979	Manchester City	H	First Division	2-1
1984	Norwich City	H	First Division	3-1
1987	Oxford United	H	First Division	3-0
1990	Arsenal	A	First Division	0-0

Ever since he shed tears following England's World Cup semi-final defeat, the media spotlight had shone on Paul Gascoigne. Too brightly, as it turned out, for only three games into the season he was mentally and physically shattered. Over 40,000 crammed into Highbury to see the most talked-about man in the British game; he was little more than an onlooker himself. Shortly before the end of this goalless draw manager Terry Venables withdrew him from the action. Gascoigne would make an altogether more important contribution to Spurs in the coming months; right now he had little to offer.

1993	Chelsea	H	FA Premier League	1-1

Matches between Spurs and Chelsea are generally close, tight affairs, but this one was surrounded by considerable controversy after the game, all of it centred on Spurs' equaliser. Tony Cascarino had put Chelsea ahead in the first half, a lead they held on to until well into injury time. Many Spurs fans were convinced their team was going to lose and were already heading for the exits when Spurs mounted one last furious attack. As the ball entered the penalty area, Teddy Sheringham controlled it and stroked it past a defender, intending to retrieve the ball the other side. Before he was able to do so he was knocked to the ground, innocently claimed the Chelsea defenders, unfairly claimed Spurs. The referee sided with Spurs and awarded a penalty, a decision that was bitterly contested by Chelsea, most notably by their captain Dennis Wise. Sheringham ignored the furore and Wise's attempts to put him off and stroked home a late equaliser. After the game Chelsea continued their protests, claiming Sheringham had possibly dived and certainly made a meal of the challenge in order to win the penalty in the first place.

SEPTEMBER 2ND

1897	Glossop North End	H	Friendly	3-2
1899	Millwall Athletic	A	Southern League	3-1

Spurs spent 12 seasons in the Southern League, winning the title but once, in 1899-1900. Player-manager John Cameron had already assembled most of the team that was to astonish English football the following season, but it was ostensibly the winning of the Southern League which provided the launching pad. Spurs won the first six games of the season, starting with today's 3-1 win at Millwall Athletic, where Copeland and Kirwan (two) grabbed the goals.

1905	Reading	A	Southern League	1-1
1907	Queens Park Rangers	A	Southern League	3-3
1911	Everton	A	First Division	2-2
1912	Everton	H	First Division	0-2
1914	Everton	H	First Division	1-3

Since the end of one League season in April and the commencement of the next in September, the world had been plunged into war. There were few during the summer of 1914 who believed that the war would be anything more than a couple of months long and confined to the regular armies of the combatants. That, along with a desire to maintain public morale, encouraged the decision to continue with a normal League programme during the 1914-15 season. Of course, this was the season Spurs were to finish at the bottom of the First Division pile. It began with a defeat at home to Everton, the first win (out of only eight achieved all season) not coming until the end of the month.

1916	Chelsea	H	London Combination	0-2

A few days after this London Combination match, White Hart Lane was requisitioned by the Ministry of Munitions for the duration of the First World War.

1922	Cardiff City	A	First Division	3-2
1929	Millwall	A	Second Division	5-2
1933	Aston Villa	H	First Division	3-2
1935	Hull City	H	Second Division	3-1
1939	West Bromwich Albion	A	Second Division	4-3

Less than 24 hours after Spurs had maintained their unbeaten start to the season (with a win and two draws out of three matches) the British Government, having heard nothing from the German Government following the latter's invasion of Poland, announced the two countries at war – the Second World War had begun. The Football League was immediately suspended and the results expunged from the records. Ever since arguments have raged over whether Spurs would have gone on to earn promotion back into the top flight, for there are those convinced Peter McWilliam was going to work the miracle once again. Certainly, his arrival the previous year had seen the promotion of many of the juniors being developed in the club's Northfleet nursery (in particular Bill Nicholson), but by the time the Second World War had come to an end McWilliam considered himself too old for the job of guiding Spurs. Of the 11 players who played their part in collecting both points at the Hawthorns this day, only four would be in the Spurs line-up when the Football League resumed in 1946.

1944	Arsenal	H	Football League South	4-0
1950	Charlton Athletic	A	First Division	1-1
1959	West Bromwich Albion	A	First Division	2-1
1961	Cardiff City	H	First Division	3-2
1964	Burnley	H	First Division	4-1
1967	Burnley	A	First Division	1-5
1972	Ipswich Town	A	First Division	1-1
1978	Liverpool	A	First Division	0-7

As inspired and exciting the purchases of Ossie Ardiles and Ricky Villa undoubtedly were, there were those who believed Keith Burkinshaw bought both players 'blind' – that is to say, with little idea as to how either would fit into his game plan (there again, given Burkinshaw's propensity for having the team play off the cuff, one could ask whether he actually had a game plan?). The Spurs side of the previous season had achieved a fine balance between skill and muscle in its midfield, with players moving up and down the field as required. South American midfield players were superb when moving up but not so keen on coming back again. Such inter-continental differences were crudely exposed this day, with Spurs suffering the first seven-goal defeat of their entire League career and it could have been worse had Liverpool taken full advantage of the midfield supremacy they held. It would take Spurs another two years to get the midfield balance finely tuned once again.

| 1981 | West Ham United | H | First Division | 0-4 |

Spurs, the FA Cup holders, had begun the new season with supreme confidence. The League champions, Aston Villa, had been held 2-2 at Wembley in the FA Charity Shield, and Middlesbrough had been beaten at Ayrsome Park the previous Saturday. It was back down to earth with bump on the Wednesday, with West Ham running away with both points and handing out a 4-0 battering. All of the goals were scored by David Cross; it was not until 1988 that an opposition player would score as many as even three goals in one match against Spurs.

| 1986 | Southampton | A | First Division | 0-2 |
| 1992 | Sheffield United | H | FA Premier League | 2-0 |

SEPTEMBER 3RD

| 1896 | Rossendale | H | Friendly | 7-0 |
| 1898 | Thames Ironworks | H | Thames & Medway League | 3-0 |

This was the first and only season in which the first team competed in the Thames & Medway League, finally finishing the season in third place. However, as the first team were also on duty in the Southern League and United League, the demands being made on the players was considerable. In September of this year alone the club played seven matches, and this in an age before floodlights! This game also saw Sandy Hall, more normally at half-back, play in goal!

1900	Bristol Rovers	A	Friendly	0-1
1904	Fulham	H	Southern League	0-1
1906	Plymouth Argyle	H	Western League	0-0
1910	Sheffield Wednesday	H	First Division	3-1
1920				

Les Medley born in Edmonton. After playing for local school sides and Tottenham Juniors, Les joined Spurs as an amateur in 1935 and then the professional ranks in February 1939. Although he played for Spurs in a friendly against Arsenal in April the same year, he had to wait a considerable time to make his League debut – the outbreak of the Second World War put paid to that! He joined the Royal Air Force and was posted to Canada, where he met his future wife and on the cessation of hostilities returned to Spurs. He made his full debut in the cup-tie against Brentford in 1946, although once again he had to wait for his League debut – his wife was homesick for Canada and in November 1946 the Medleys sailed across the Atlantic to begin a new life. After less than two years Les announced he was homesick and the Medleys came home again! Les took time to re-adjust to English football and it was not until April 1949 he was able to firmly establish himself in the team. Of course, this was just prior to the 'push-and-run' side that was to dominate domestic football for two or three seasons and Les Medley certainly played a vital role. Operating from the wing he was both creator and taker of goals and in November 1950 was awarded the first of his six full England caps, against Wales. At the end of the 1952-53 season he announced his retirement, having made 150 League appearances and scored 45 goals. Once again the Medleys emigrated to Canada, although Les did have a spell coaching in South Africa from 1958 to 1961.

1921	Cardiff City	H	First Division	4-1
1923	Chelsea	H	First Division	0-1
1924	Birmingham	A	First Division	2-0
1925	Real Madrid	H	Friendly	4-0

Strange as it may seem, in 1925 Real Madrid were not considered 'first-class opposition' and Spurs put out a reserve side to face the touring Spaniards. With Spurs recording a 4-0 win perhaps the decision was vindicated, but in years to come Real Madrid would assume the mantle of the most famous club side in the world. For the time being, this match was not considered as a first-team game.

1927	Newcastle United	A	First Division	1-4
1932	Stoke City	A	Second Division	0-2
1934	Preston North End	A	First Division	0-1
1938	Coventry City	H	Second Division	2-1
1949	Cardiff City	A	Second Division	1-0
1951	Burnley	A	First Division	1-1

1953	Charlton Athletic	A	First Division	1-0
1955	Charlton Athletic	H	First Division	2-3
1956	Blackpool	A	First Division	1-4
1958	Chelsea	H	First Division	4-0
1960	Manchester United	H	First Division	4-1

Spurs' fifth successive victory of the season was described in one newspaper as being 'Spurs at their peak, and there is no finer team in Britain when they are in this mood.' How prophetic those words turned out to be! They took the lead after only five minutes, Bobby Smith scoring easily from John White's pass. Spurs kept up considerable pressure and added a second after 19 minutes, this time Les Allen benefiting from White's passing ability. Although United pulled one back Spurs pulled away again in the second half, with both Smith and Allen netting.

1966	Arsenal	H	First Division	3-1
1969	Wolverhampton Wanderers	A	League Cup 2nd Round	0-1
1977	Cardiff City	A	Second Division	0-0
1980	Orient	H	League Cup 2nd Round 2nd Leg	3-1
1983	West Ham United	H	First Division	0-2
1988	Newcastle United	A	First Division	2-2

With White Hart Lane having been deemed unfit to host the League match against Coventry City the previous week, this turned out to be Spurs' first match of the 1988-89 season. This also meant that Paul Gascoigne made his League debut for Spurs back at his old stamping ground of St James's Park! A full house of over 32,000, most of whom were following the home side, were quick to show their displeasure at the former hero, taunting him with chants of 'Judas, Judas' as he disembarked from the Spurs coach. The reception when he ran out on to the field was much the same – a barrage of Mars bars (a particular favourite of the sweet-toothed Gascoigne) were thrown whenever he or fellow Geordie Chris Waddle went anywhere near the crowd. Whether the antics of the crowd had a detrimental effect on the Spurs players is open to debate, but the first half was little short of a disaster, with Newcastle powering into a 2-0 lead thanks to identical defensive lapses. Spurs came out for the second half determined to do better and scored straight from the kick-off, Waddle stroking home before Newcastle's defence could react. Then Terry Fenwick equalised, appearing unmarked at the far post for a corner and heading home. Whilst that may have been the end of the scoring it was not the end of the drama, for with some considerable time still left on the clock, Terry Venables decided Gascoigne had suffered enough and replaced him with Paul Moran. With Spurs next match the visit of Arsenal, Gascoigne could be said to have had a baptism of fire.

SEPTEMBER 4TH

1897	Sheppey United	A	Southern League	1-1
1899	Notts County	H	Friendly	4-1

Following incidents at the home match with Woolwich Arsenal on April 29th, the Spurs directors looked around for a new site for a football ground. Not far from where the club was formed lay the neglected Beckwith's Nursery, which was owned by Charrington's Brewery and adjacent to the White Hart public house, upon which the brewery were thinking of building terraced houses to provide custom for the pub. Charles Roberts and Bobby Buckle approached the landlord to see whether he had any objections to them attempting to secure a lease on the property. As he had previously been landlord of a pub close to Millwall's ground and seen the resulting increase in trade, he encouraged them to talk to Charringtons. Negotiations with Charringtons proved a relatively simple matter – Charringtons requested guarantees that 1,000 spectators attend first-team matches, 500 reserve games and received an assurance from the club that this would be achieved. Having obtained a lease, Spurs moved the stands that had stood at Northumberland Park and were ready for an official opening with a friendly against Notts County of the First Division (although a number of trial matches had already been played at the ground). A crowd of 5,000 paying gate receipts of £115 18s 3d, of which £57 17s 9d was paid to the visitors, saw Spurs win. It was not until after the First World War that the ground became universally known as White Hart Lane; prior to the war it was known simply as 'The High Road Ground', since the club's offices were situated at 748 High Road. Whilst the club were known to have preferred calling the ground Percy Park (after Sir Henry Percy, otherwise known as Harry Hotspur) the now-accepted moniker was bestowed by the patrons. White Hart Lane, as a ground as well as a name proved extremely successful, with Spurs buying the freehold of the property from Charringtons for £8,900 in 1901, as well as other land and houses at the northern end (then known as the Edmonton goal) for £2,600.

1905	Reading	H	Western League	5-1
1909	Everton	A	First Division	2-4
1911	Sheffield Wednesday	H	First Division	3-1
1915	Arsenal	A	London Combination [1st competition]	0-2

At the end of the 1914-15 season the Football League announced that League football was shutting down for the duration of the First World War. The Government still wanted organised football to remain in one form or another as a morale booster, but in order to preserve vital materials insisted travelling should be restricted to an absolute minimum. Henry Norris (chairman of Arsenal), having received encouragement form the London FA, set out to form the London Combination, but this was not achieved without one or two setbacks along the way. There was a threat from the Football League to expel any club taking part in a war-time match not organised by the Football League, and it was not until the intervention of the Football Association that the London Combination got off the drawing board.

1920	Blackburn Rovers	A	First Division	1-1
1922	Everton	H	First Division	2-0
1926	Blackburn Rovers	A	First Division	0-1
1933	Wolverhampton Wanderers	A	First Division	0-1
1937	Nottingham Forest	A	Second Division	1-3

On the same day Les Allen born in Dagenham, Essex. After impressing for Briggs Sports (who reached the FA Amateur Cup semi-final in 1954) Les was signed by Chelsea in September 1954 and scored 11 goals in 44 League appearances for the club. These appearances took five years to amass for Les was more often than not stuck in the reserves. According to Bill Nicholson, Chelsea manager Ted Drake approached Spurs with a view to signing the popular Johnny Brooks in an attempt to stave off relegation. Nicholson took a look at Chelsea's reserve team and selected Les Allen, with the pair swapping clubs in a £20,000 deal. It has to be said that Spurs did far better out of this particular deal, for Les proved the perfect foil for Bobby Smith and weighed in with vital goals over the next two or three seasons. An ever present when Spurs won the 'double' in 1960-61 he scored 27 goals in both competitions and then saw his place come under threat when Jimmy Greaves arrived at the club. In fact, for a while Greaves and Allen played in tandem with Smith on the outside looking in until Bobby Smith recovered the centre-forward berth. Les' Spurs career was effectively ended with the arrival of Alan Gilzean and in 1965 he joined Third Division Queens Park Rangers for £21,000. There his experience was allied to the up-and-coming talents of Rodney Marsh *et al* and QPR won the Third Division championship and the League Cup in 1966-67. When Tommy Docherty left the club in 1968 Les took over as player-manager, holding the reigns until 1971 when he left to take over at Woodford Town. He returned to League management with Swindon and then had a spell in Greece before returning to England and working in the car industry. Of course, Les is one part of the exceptional Allen clan, which has seen Les, his son Clive and nephew Paul all play for Spurs, his brother Dennis play for Charlton, Reading and Bournemouth, and his two other sons Martin and Bradley turn out for QPR and West Ham and QPR respectively.

1943	Queens Park Rangers	A	Football League South	1-1
1948	Chesterfield	H	Second Division	4-0
1954	Arsenal	A	First Division	0-2
1957	Portsmouth	H	First Division	3-5
1961	Sheffield United	A	First Division	1-1
1963	Wolverhampton Wanderers	H	First Division	4-3
1965	Fulham	A	First Division	2-0
1968	Aston Villa	A	League Cup 2nd Round	4-1
1971	Liverpool	H	First Division	2-0
1976	Manchester United	A	First Division	3-2
1982	Everton	A	First Division	1-3
1984	Sunderland	A	First Division	0-1
1985	Chelsea	H	First Division	4-1
1991	Sparkasse Stockerau	H	European Cup-Winners' Cup Preliminary Round 2nd Leg	1-0

Having already won the first leg 1-0 in Vienna, Spurs were widely expected to canter home in the second leg against their Austrian Second Division opponents. Not for the last time reality was way off the mark, for although Spurs were seldom troubled at the back, up front they failed to find the net more than once, and even then it needed the skipper Gary Mabbutt to save the blushes.

| 1996 | Wimbledon | A | FA Premier League | 0-1 |

SEPTEMBER 5TH

1882   The closest the club has to an official formation date, for it was today that subscriptions for the new Hotspur Football Club were due from members of the Hotspur Cricket Club. Subscriptions were received from J Anderson; the sum of 5s (which we assume to be a transfer from the Hotspur Cricket Club), H Casey, E Beavon and F Dexter, each of whom paid 6d. The club's first expenditure, recorded by treasurer L Casey, was 2s 6d for goal posts, (according to other Spurs histories, the first goal posts were provided by Casey's father and painted blue and white, but despite the romantic nature of this story it would now appear that the materials were provided by the club and Mr Casey provided the expertise) 1s for flag posts [corner flags] and 6d for flags. Although we do not know the exact date that the cricket club was formed, evidence would suggest it to be the Spring of 1880.

| 1896 | Sheppey United | A | Southern League | 3-3 |

Having been unsuccessful during the summer with an application to join the Football League, Spurs turned their attentions to the Southern League and were immediately accepted into the First Division. This was the first match Spurs played in the Southern League, with a crowd of 2,000 turning out at Sheppey to see the game. The honour of scoring Spurs first goal in the Southern League fell to Harry Crump.

1898	Luton Town	H	United League	1-0
1903	Fulham	A	Southern League	0-0
1906	Watford	A	Southern League	1-1
1908	Leeds City	A	Second Division	0-1

1912   Ronnie Dix born in Bristol. Signed by Spurs in 1939 having previously played for Bristol Rovers, Blackburn Rovers, Aston Villa and Derby County, he played in the three League matches of that year before football was suspended owing to the Second World War. Although Ronnie was a regular in the side in the first season after the war, he was then past his best and transferred to Reading, subsequently retiring in June 1949.

| 1914 | Chelsea | H | First Division | 1-1 |
| 1921 | Bolton Wanderers | A | First Division | 0-1 |

1924   William Walters born in Edmonton. Known universally as Sonny, Walters signed as an amateur with Spurs in 1938 after being spotted by Billy Sage. After being farmed out to the club's nursery outfits Walthamstow Avenue and Finchley he made his debut appearance for the first team in a war-time match in 1943. His full League debut did not come until 1947, when he was selected against West Bromwich Albion and it took a further two years before he permanently dislodged Freddie Cox from the outside-right position. This put him in the right place at the right time – he scored 14 goals when the club won the Second Division championship in 1950 and the following year was top goalscorer with 15 as the First Division title was lifted for the first time. His worth to Spurs was not adequately reflected in representative honours, with Sonny collecting only an England B cap during his illustrious career, but it must be remembered that the two players ahead of him in the England line-up were none other than Stanley Matthews and Tom Finney. In 1957 Sonny left Spurs to play for Aldershot for a couple of years. He died in November 1970, with Walthamstow Avenue staging a memorial match in his honour shortly after.

1925	Manchester City	H	First Division	1-0
1931	Bradford Park Avenue	H	Second Division	3-3
1932	Nottingham Forest	H	Second Division	0-0
1936	Norwich City	H	Second Division	2-3
1937	Burnley	A	Second Division	1-2
1942	Queens Park Rangers	A	Football League South	1-0
1949	Sheffield Wednesday	H	Second Division	1-0
1953	West Bromwich Albion	A	First Division	0-3
1955	Sheffield United	A	First Division	0-2
1959	Arsenal	A	First Division	1-1
1964	Birmingham City	H	First Division	4-1
1970	Arsenal	A	First Division	0-2
1973	Burnley	H	First Division	2-3
1979	Manchester United	A	League Cup 2nd Round 2nd Leg	1-3
1981	Aston Villa	H	First Division	1-3
1987	Everton	A	First Division	0-0
1992	Everton	H	FA Premier League	2-1

Spurs' winning goal was scored by Andy Turner who became the FA Premier League's youngest scorer at the age of 17 years and 166 days.

SEPTEMBER 6TH

1882   Subscriptions were received from J Thompson, R Buckle and D Davis. This latter 'player' has appeared in most Tottenham history books (although with his name mis-spelt) as one of a half dozen players who joined the club later in the year and paid double subscriptions (we assume that the subscriptions for the football club were 6d, new members having to pay 1s in order to become members of both the football and cricket clubs). This latter part is certainly correct, for thanks to the entries made by L Casey, we know who paid what and when, and D Davis certainly paid 1s for the privilege of joining, but he was the only new member of the club in 1882. As we can find no subsequent mention of his name in a team line-up or photograph, his involvement with Hotspur FC is therefore brief.

1902	Queens Park Rangers	H	Southern League	0-0
1913	Chelsea	A	First Division	3-1
1919	Coventry City	H	Second Division	4-1
1920	Derby County	H	First Division	2-0

1922 Charlie Withers born in Edmonton. Taken on as an amateur in 1938, Charlie did not sign full professional forms with the club until October 1947 following his demobilisation from the services. He made his Spurs debut in March 1948 against Barnsley and was an established member of the first team as they romped away with the Second Division title in 1949-50. The following season Arthur Willis pushed Charlie out of the full-back position and he missed out as the team recorded their first First Division title. Although Willis subsequently moved on, there was a succession of rivals for the vacancy and Charlie finally left Spurs in 1956 for non-League football, having made 153 League appearances for Spurs.

1924	Notts County	A	First Division	0-0
1926	Leicester City	H	First Division	2-2
1930	Wolverhampton Wanderers	A	Second Division	1-3
1941	Aldershot	A	London War League	2-3
1947	Cardiff City	A	Second Division	3-0
1950	Liverpool	A	First Division	1-2
1952	Cardiff City	H	First Division	2-1
1958	Newcastle United	H	First Division	1-3
1966	Sheffield United	A	First Division	1-2
1967	Wolverhampton Wanderers	H	First Division	2-1
1969	West Ham United	A	First Division	1-0
1972	Huddersfield Town	H	League Cup 2nd Round	2-1
1975	Manchester United	A	First Division	2-3
1978	Swansea City	H	League Cup 2nd Round Replay	1-3
1980	Manchester United	H	First Division	0-0
1986	Arsenal	A	First Division	0-0
1988	Swansea City	A	Friendly	3-0

This match was a benefit for Michael Hughes with Spurs' goals being scored by Paul Gascoigne, David Howells and Phil Gray.

SEPTEMBER 7TH

| 1895 | Royal Engineers | A | Friendly | 3-0 |
| 1901 | Millwall Athletic | H | Southern League | 2-0 |

As this was Spurs' first League match since winning the FA Cup the previous season, a crowd of over 27,000 turned up at White Hart Lane for this fixture hoping to catch a glimpse of the famous trophy.

1903	Reading	H	Western League	3-1
1904	Reading	A	Western League	1-0
1907	West Ham United	A	Southern League	1-1
1912	Sheffield Wednesday	H	First Division	2-4
1918	Fulham	A	London Combination	2-2
1925	Sheffield United	H	First Division	3-2
1929	Barnsley	H	Second Division	2-1
1931	Southampton	A	Second Division	1-2
1940	West Ham United	A	Football League South	4-1

Aside from the anticipated problems of players being away on active duty, the Second World War brought unforeseen problems in its wake; after 80 minutes of this match, with Spurs leading 4-1, an air raid warning in the area necessitated an abandonment although the result was allowed to stand. Although this was not the last match to be so abandoned, it is no coincidence that all the other examples (of which there were four in total) took place during this season, when the Battle of Britain was at its height.

1946	West Bromwich Albion	A	Second Division	2-3
1953	Burnley	A	First Division	2-4
1957	Burnley	H	First Division	3-1
1960	Bolton Wanderers	A	First Division	2-1

Victory number six of the double season was perhaps Spurs' sternest test to date. When Bolton grabbed an early lead after three minutes it appeared as though the run might be coming to an end sooner than one might have wished or expected, but Bolton had the misfortune to lose their full-back Banks through a torn right thigh. Reprieved, Spurs fought back, with Les Allen grabbing an equaliser and ten minutes from time Danny Blanchflower chipping over a tantalising centre which John White, so often goalmaker, converted to become goal taker.

1963	Blackburn Rovers	A	First Division	2-7
1968	Burnley	H	First Division	7-0
1974	Liverpool	A	First Division	2-5
1983	West Bromwich Albion	A	First Division	1-1
1985	Newcastle United	H	First Division	5-1
1991	Aston Villa	A	First Division	0-0
1996	Newcastle United	H	FA Premier League	1-2

SEPTEMBER 8TH

| 1900 | Southampton | A | Friendly | 3-1 |
| 1902 | West Ham United | N | Southern Charity Cup Final | 2-1 |

This match was the final held over from the previous season. Goals from Bob Houston and John Kirwan gave Spurs victory in front of a 6,000 at Upton Park.

1906	Bristol Rovers	A	Southern League	3-2
1913	Sheffield United	H	First Division	2-1
1917	Chelsea	H-Highbury		
			London Combination	0-4
1923	Middlesbrough	H	First Division	2-1
1924	West Bromwich Albion	A	First Division	0-2
1928	Wolverhampton Wanderers	H	Second Division	3-2
1930	Preston North End	A	Second Division	1-2
1934	Wolverhampton Wanderers	H	First Division	3-1
1945	West Ham United	A	Football League South	1-1
1947	West Ham United	A	Second Division	1-1
1948	Leeds United	A	Second Division	0-0
1951	Bolton Wanderers	H	First Division	2-1
1954	Manchester United	H	First Division	0-2
1956	Wolverhampton Wanderers	H	First Division	4-1
1962	Blackpool	A	First Division	2-1
1965	Leeds United	H	First Division	3-2
1971	West Bromwich Albion	A	League Cup 2nd Round	1-0
1973	West Ham United	A	First Division	1-0
1979	Brighton & Hove Albion	H	First Division	2-1
1982	Southampton	H	First Division	6-0

Soon after helping Spurs gain a 1-0 lead, Glenn Hoddle was the victim of a late challenge and stretchered off the field and out of the game for the next eight weeks. The loss of the midfield playmaker against a side that are always guaranteed to work hard might have proved too big an obstacle for Spurs to overcome, but the rest of the team responded magnificently to the challenge and tore at Southampton, hitting a further five goals.

| 1984 | Sheffield Wednesday | A | First Division | 1-2 |
| 1990 | Derby County | H | First Division | 3-0 |

SEPTEMBER 9TH

| 1897 | Royal Scots Fusilliers | H | Friendly | 12-0 |
| 1899 | Queens Park Rangers | H | Southern League | 1-0 |

White Hart Lane hosted its first competitive match with an 11,000 crowd paying receipts of £329 4s 3d to see Spurs win 1-0. Season tickets for the first season at White Hart Lane cost 15s for all home matches!

1901	Reading	H	Western League	4-0
1905	Watford	H	Southern League	1-0
1907	Bristol Rovers	H	Western League	10-0

Spurs' opening game of the Western League in 1907-08 saw them reach double figures for the only time in the competition. Spurs' goals were scored by Tom Morris, Joe Walton, Jimmy Pass (four), Willie McNair and Jimmy Reid (three), although the crowd was a disappointing one of only 500 souls.

1911	West Bromwich Albion	H	First Division	1-0
1916	Arsenal	A	London Combination	1-1
1922	Burnley	H	First Division	1-3
1933	Leicester City	A	First Division	3-1
1944	Reading	A	Football League South	0-0
1946	Southampton	H	Second Division	2-1
1950	Manchester United	H	First Division	1-0
1959	West Ham United	H	First Division	2-2

1961	Manchester United	A	First Division	0-1
1964	Stoke City	A	First Division	0-2
1967	Sheffield Wednesday	H	First Division	2-1

This match was Spurs' 2000th League match (not including abandoned games) and goals from Alan Gilzean and Frank Saul were enough to give them victory over Sheffield Wednesday.

1970	Swansea City	H	League Cup 2nd Round	3-0
1972	Crystal Palace	H	First Division	2-1
1975	Watford	A	League Cup 2nd Round	1-0
1978	Bristol City	H	First Division	1-0
1989	Aston Villa	A	First Division	0-2
1995	Leeds United	H	FA Premier League	2-1

SEPTEMBER 10TH

1896	London Caledonians	H	Friendly	3-3
1898	Bedminster	H	Southern League	1-1
1900	Reading	H	Friendly	3-3
1904	Watford	A	Southern League	1-0
1906	Southampton	H	Western League	2-3
1910	Bristol City	A	First Division	2-0
1921	Middlesbrough	H	First Division	2-4
1927	Huddersfield Town	H	First Division	2-2
1932	Manchester United	H	Second Division	6-1
1938	Nottingham Forest	A	Second Division	1-2
1949	Leeds United	H	Second Division	2-0
1952	Liverpool	A	First Division	1-2
1954	Arsenal	H	First Division	3-1
1958	Nottingham Forest	A	First Division	1-1
1960	Arsenal	A	First Division	3-2

Victory at Highbury was more than just victory over Arsenal – Spurs set a new First Division record by winning their first seven games of the season. Frank Saul was again deputising for Bobby Smith and made his presence felt after only 12 minutes, netting the opening goal. Terry Dyson made it 2-0 11 minutes later and that appeared to be the end of Arsenal. Midway through the second half the Gunners pulled one back and then, incredibly, equalised four minutes later. Just when it seemed Arsenal might cause a further upset, Les Allen lobbed Kelsey and settled the game.

1966	Manchester United	H	First Division	2-1
1977	Fulham	H	Second Division	1-0
1983	Leicester City	A	First Division	3-0
1985	Fareham Town	A	Friendly	6-3
1988	Arsenal	H	First Division	2-3

With the match against Coventry City having been postponed at the last minute the North London clash with Arsenal turned out to be Spurs' first home game of the season and the first appearance at White Hart Lane for Paul Gascoigne. Despite Arsenal's win, Spurs fans did get to see the kind of impact Gascoigne was to have over the coming years – he scored, despite losing a boot midway through his run and stroked the ball home with a stockinged foot.

SEPTEMBER 11TH

1897	Chorley	H	Friendly	3-1
1905	Queens Park Rangers	A	Western League	1-1
1909	Manchester United	H	First Division	2-2

Both of Spurs' goals were scored by Bobby Steel from the penalty spot, the first penalties Spurs had been awarded since joining the Football League in 1908.

1915	Brentford	H	London Combination [1st competition]	1-1
1919	Leicester City	A	Second Division	4-2
1920	Aston Villa	A	First Division	2-4
1922	Corinthians	A	Friendly	2-1
1926	Huddersfield Town	H	First Division	3-3
1937	Newcastle United	H	Second Division	2-2
1943	Charlton Athletic	H	Football League South	4-2
1948	West Bromwich Albion	A	Second Division	1-1
1954	Sheffield Wednesday	A	First Division	2-2
1956	Racing Club de Paris	H	Friendly	2-0
1957	Birmingham City	A	First Division	0-0

1965	Arsenal	H	First Division	2-2

Spurs had begun the season in good form and were top of the table prior to the start of the match, whilst Arsenal were languishing in mid-table. But form counted for nothing on the day, with Arsenal powering into a two-goal lead thanks to a Laurie Brown own goal and Joe Baker. Frank Saul reduced the deficit ten minutes before half-time, although there was a suspicion that the ball had already crossed the line before Derek Possee crossed for Alan Gilzean, but the officials ruled the goal good. Possee was later injured and had to leave the field, giving Roy Low his place in history; he became Spurs' first ever substitute. Fifteen minutes from the end Spurs got the equaliser, Alan Gilzean scoring with a lobbed header that looped over Jim Furnell. Spurs might have won the game, creating a couple of other chances that went begging, but a draw was probably a fair result in the end.

1971	Sheffield United	A	First Division	2-2
1973	Burnley	A	First Division	2-2
1974	Middlesbrough	H	League Cup 2nd Round	0-4

Manager Bill Nicholson bowed out of White Hart Lane, an inglorious end to a career that had taken the club to heights previously undreamed off. He was later brought back to the club by manager Keith Burkinshaw as consultant and has remained with Spurs ever since.

1976	Leeds United	H	First Division	1-0
1982	Manchester City	H	First Division	1-2

Spurs gave a debut to the 16-year-old Alistair Dick, who had yet to sign professional forms with the club. However, Ally did become the youngest ever player to represent Spurs and was later substituted by Graham Roberts in the 2-1 home defeat by Manchester City.

1993	Sheffield United	A	FA Premier League	2-2

SEPTEMBER 12TH

1896	Wolverton	A	Southern League	0-1
1898	Surrey Wanderers	H	Friendly	5-0
1903	Millwall	H	Southern League	0-1
1904	Brighton & Hove Albion	H	Friendly	3-1
1908	Barnsley	H	Second Division	4-0
1914	Bradford City	A	First Division	2-2
1921	West Ham United	A	London Professional Football Charity Fund	0-1
1925	Everton	A	First Division	1-1
1927	Middlesbrough	H	First Division	4-2
1931	Manchester United	A	Second Division	1-1
1936	Newcastle United	A	Second Division	1-0
1938	Sheffield United	H	Second Division	2-2
1942	Charlton Athletic	H	Football League South	6-1
1945	Leicester City	H	Football League South	6-2
1953	Liverpool	H	First Division	2-1
1959	Manchester United	A	First Division	5-1

One of Spurs' best ever performances at Old Trafford, not just in terms of the result but in the style of play too which resulted in a standing ovation from the home crowd at the end of the game. Spurs effectively won the game in a ten minute spell in the first half, scoring three goals between the 18th and 28th minutes through Dave Dunmore, Bobby Smith and Tommy Harmer. United reduced the deficit two minutes before half-time and were handed the initiative immediately after the break when Spurs were reduced to ten men following Smith's non-appearance owing to a facial injury, (although he later managed to return). Spurs defended well during the opening period despite being pegged back in their own half for much of the 45 minutes. Then, with three minutes to go a counter-attack saw Bobby Smith score his second of the game and a minute later Dave Mackay scored his first goal for the club to complete a remarkable score line.

1962	Wolverhampton Wanderers	H	First Division	1-2
1964	West Ham United	A	First Division	2-3
1970	Blackpool	H	First Division	3-0
1981	Wolverhampton Wanderers	A	First Division	1-0
1984	Real Madrid	A	Friendly	0-1

This match was a testimonial for Real Madrid's Benito.

1987	Southampton	H	First Division	2-1
1994	Southampton	H	FA Premier League	1-2

SEPTEMBER 13TH

1899	Richmond	A	Friendly	3-1
1902	Southampton	A	Western League	1-1

1904   John Jones died in Edmonton. After impressing as an inside-forward with Small Heath and Bristol Rovers (where his tally of 50 goals in one season earned him the reputation of 'The deadliest forward in the South') he was signed by Spurs in the summer of 1902 and given the nickname 'Bristol' to distinguish him from the Spurs captain John L Jones. He made his Spurs debut in the Southern League match at home to Queens Park Rangers in September 1902 and in the space of two months became an integral part of the team until injury in November that year put him out for the rest of the season. He returned the following season and became the regular inside-right, scoring a total of 19 goals in just 32 Southern League appearances with Spurs. He reported back for training shortly before the beginning of the current season but was sent home with what was believed to be influenza. In fact it turned out to be typhoid and he died two months later at the age of only 29. A benefit match was later staged for his dependants.

1906	London Caledonians	H	Friendly	6-4
1913	Derby County	H	First Division	1-1
1919	South Shields	H	Second Division	2-0
1924	Everton	H	First Division	0-0
1926	Leicester City	A	First Division	2-2
1930	Bradford Park Avenue	H	Second Division	3-2
1941	Millwall	H	London War League	3-0
1947	Bradford Park Avenue	H	Second Division	3-1
1948	Leeds United	H	Second Division	2-2
1952	Sheffield Wednesday	A	First Division	0-2
1958	Arsenal	A	First Division	1-3
1961	Gornik Zabrze	A	European Cup Preliminary Round 1st Leg	2-4

The first ever match played by the club in European competition and after an hour there were those who thought it might well be the last. The entire trip to Poland had been an 'experience' – Bill Nicholson was unhappy with the hotel that had been laid on for the team (although it was the best hotel in the area) and the team played the first hour in a state of almost total lethargy. Late goals from Cliff Jones and Terry Dyson gave the scoreline a respectability it did not really deserve, but the important aspect was that it did at least give Spurs hope for the second leg in one week's time.

1969	Manchester City	H	First Division	0-3
1972	Lyn Oslo	A	UEFA Cup 1st Round 1st Leg	6-3

1974   With intense media speculation surrounding the appointment of the new manager of Spurs to replace Bill Nicholson, the Spurs board announced today they had got their man – Terry Neill! It would not be far off the mark to suggest his appointment was viewed in complete amazement by fans and media alike – among the media it was well known that the outgoing Bill Nicholson had already spoken to both Danny Blanchflower and Johnny Giles with a view to them taking over the role in tandem. Among the fans, Terry Neill was known for having been an Arsenal player. Neill was previously player-manager at Hull City and had also spoken to Bill Nicholson (although he was not interviewed by Nicholson for the position) and had applied on his advice. The Spurs board were later to admit that they had appointed Terry Neill because he was undoubtedly the best of the applicants. Neill arrived at a time the club were bottom of the First Division after their worst start to a League season in 62 years and having been just knocked out of the League Cup 4-0 at home to Middlesbrough.

1975	Derby County	H	First Division	2-3
1980	Leeds United	A	First Division	0-0
1986	Chelsea	H	First Division	1-3
1997	Leicester City	A	FA Premier League	0-3

SEPTEMBER 14TH

1895	1st Royal Scots Greys	H	Friendly	3-2
1901	Queens Park Rangers	H	Southern League	2-0
1903	Brentford	A	Southern League	0-0
1907	Queens Park Rangers	H	Southern League	3-2
1912	Blackburn Rovers	A	First Division	1-6
1918	Brentford	H-Homerton		
			London Combination	1-1
1925	Cardiff City	H	First Division	1-2
1929	Blackpool	A	Second Division	2-3
1931	Southampton	H	Second Division	5-2
1935	Sheffield United	A	Second Division	1-1
1936	Leicester City	H	Second Division	4-2
1940	Chelsea	H	Football League South	3-2

After 15 minutes of play the game was halted owing to an air raid warning. After the all-clear siren had sounded some 80 minutes later, play resumed and Spurs went on to win.

1946	Newcastle United	H	Second Division	1-1
1957	Preston North End	A	First Division	1-3
1959	West Ham United	A	First Division	2-1
1960	Bolton Wanderers	H	First Division	3-1

Spurs' second clash with Bolton inside a week was as fierce a contest as the first encounter and once again Bolton had the misfortune to score first and still lose. This time the match was won and lost on a dubious penalty decision; Spurs didn't appeal for it, but the referee saw something wrong with a challenge on Terry Dyson and, after spending a few moments contemplating his decision, gave a penalty. This came either side of goals from Bobby Smith. Spurs were now one win short of equalling Hull City's League record of nine wins in a row.

1963	Blackpool	H	First Division	6-1
1966	West Ham United	A	League Cup 2nd Round	0-1

The Football League Cup came into being in 1960-61, and yet this was the first occasion that Spurs took part. Entry to the competition was not yet compulsory for League members, and Spurs had previously taken the view that their fixture list was already busy and could not accommodate another cup competition. In the years when the club was involved in European competition such an argument would stand up, but as Spurs had not qualified for Europe since 1963-64, they entered the League Cup in 1966. Their involvement was as brief as it could be; defeat by West Ham in the 2nd round (Spurs were exempt from the 1st round). Interestingly enough, when Spurs won the FA Cup at the end of the season and again qualified for Europe, they refused to enter the following year's League Cup!

1968	West Ham United	A	First Division	2-2
1971	Keflavik	A	UEFA Cup 1st Round 1st Leg	6-1

This was Spurs' first European match since the European Cup-Winners' Cup ties of 1967-68 and mindful of the experience gave their Icelandic opponents little opportunity to cause an upset. Alan Gilzean netted a hat-trick, Alan Mullery collected a brace and Ralph Coates completed the scoring and made the second leg little more than a formality. In light of events in subsequent years, the most telling moment of the match came in the 74th minute when Spurs captain Alan Mullery was substituted by Graeme Souness, the latter's only appearance for Spurs. It was his frustration at not being able to get a first-team place that led him to walk out on the club at one stage and demand a transfer. Eventually, but reluctantly, Bill Nicholson agreed and sold him to Middlesbrough for £32,000 in January 1973. He was subsequently transferred on to Liverpool and became one of the most dominant midfield players in the domestic game, winning countless honours and medals before trying his luck on the continent and then returning to Britain as player-manager with Rangers.

1974	West Ham United	H	First Division	2-1

Terry Neill's first game in charge saw Spurs win for the second time this season; a 2-1 home win over West Ham United. Although this was not enough to lift the club off the bottom of the League table it instilled a bit of confidence, something that was sadly lacking in the previous seven games.

1983	Drogheda	A	UEFA Cup 1st Round 1st Leg	6-0
1985	Nottingham Forest	A	First Division	1-0
1991	Queens Park Rangers	H	First Division	2-0
1992	Coventry City	A	FA Premier League	0-1
1996	Southampton	A	FA Premier League	1-0

SEPTEMBER 15TH

1894	Uxbridge	A	Friendly	0-2
1900	Chatham	H	Southern League	5-0

Chatham resigned from the Southern League on December 20th 1900 and the result of this match was expunged from the records.

1902	Millwall Athletic	H	Western League	4-3
1906	Swindon Town	A	Southern League	0-0
1917	Brentford	A	London Combination	2-5
1923	Middlesbrough	A	First Division	1-0
1925	Brentford	H	London FA Charity Cup 1st Round	1-2
1928	Notts County	A	Second Division	0-2
1930	Preston North End	H	Second Division	0-0
1934	Chelsea	A	First Division	3-1
1945	West Ham United	H	Football League South	2-3
1947	West Ham United	H	Second Division	2-2
1951	Stoke City	A	First Division	6-1

Stoke were bottom of the table, having picked up only two points from their opening eight games and it was easy to pinpoint their problems – their defence had conceded more goals than anyone else in the First Division. Spurs too were not without their problems, for the League champions had recently been on the wrong end of a 7-2 hammering by Newcastle. Manager Arthur Rowe kept faith with the team that had beaten Bolton during the week, which meant Tommy Harmer retained his place at inside-left and Sid McClellan occupied the centre-forward berth in place of Len Duquemin. Both players were to play a prominent part in the afternoon's proceedings, with McClellan opening the scoring early on and Harmer being involved in most of Spurs' fine play. After 25 minutes Spurs went 2-0 up, Les Bennett the scorer. Shortly after Stoke were given an opportunity of getting back into the match, Colin Brittan fouling McIntosh in the area and giving away a penalty. Sadly for Stoke, Oscroft blazed the shot well wide and the team rarely troubled Spurs again. Spurs scored their third goal shortly before half-time, Alf Ramsey showing Oscroft how to take a penalty after McClellan had been fouled in the area. Spurs added a further three goals in the second half, Sonny Walters shooting into the roof of the net, McClellan netting twice (although one was disallowed for offside) and Les Medley hitting home the sixth. Oscroft managed a minor consolation effort for Stoke some ten minutes before the end, but by then Stoke had been soundly beaten. This result was Spurs' best away performance for many a year and would not be equalled until the 1962-63 season, when they recorded a similar victory at Upton Park against West Ham.

1954	Manchester United	A	First Division	1-2
1956	Aston Villa	A	First Division	4-2
1962	Blackburn Rovers	H	First Division	4-1
1965	Leeds United	A	First Division	0-2
1973	Sheffield United	H	First Division	1-2
1979	Southampton	A	First Division	2-5
1982	Coleraine	A	European Cup-Winners' Cup 1st Round 1st Leg	3-0
1984	Queens Park Rangers	H	First Division	5-0

Despite two defeats in a week, at Sunderland and Sheffield Wednesday, Spurs were still in the top half of the table, nicely poised within striking distance of the leaders. By 5 p.m. they were top – their 5-0 win over Queens Park Rangers improved their goal difference sufficiently to carry them to the summit. The goals that mattered were scored by Mark Falco and Clive Allen, who scored two apiece, and Micky Hazard. Although this was an exceptional team performance, manager Peter Shreeves was especially pleased with the way Falco and Allen were beginning to gel up front – Falco had proved to be a consistent goalscorer ever since he first broke into the first team and of sufficient quality that Spurs could afford to sell Steve Archibald and later Garth Crooks, and Clive Allen was justifying the fee that had brought him to White Hart Lane in the first place. Indeed, the story of the 1984-85 season might have turned out much more in Spurs' favour had Allen not been injured in December and forced to miss the rest of the season – although the goals didn't exactly dry up it left Mark Falco with an awful lot of work to do.

| 1990 | Leeds United | A | First Division | 2-0 |

This was the first meeting between the two sides since the 1981-82 season, when Leeds were relegated to the Second Division. They had begun the season in fine form, but so too had Spurs – unbeaten in the first four matches and with only one goal conceded, that being scored by Manchester City on the opening day. Despite the hostile nature of the Elland Road crowd, Spurs were soon into their stride, knocking the ball around well and giving Leeds a lesson in controlled football. David Howells opened the scoring for Spurs, finishing off a fine move. Leeds might have equalised, indeed they forced the ball into the net only for the referee to disallow the goal for, presumably, offside. Whilst Leeds remonstrated with the referee over the decision, Spurs quickly played the ball down to the other end of the field and Gary Lineker added a second Spurs goal. For the rest of the match it was Spurs who seemed the likeliest to add to the scoring and should have netted a third when Howells squared the ball for an unmarked Paul Gascoigne. Despite having a gaping goal and the keeper nowhere in sight, Gascoigne sliced his kick wide to accompanying groans from the travelling fans. As Gascoigne ran back to assume his position he gestured to the Spurs fans, acknowledging that he had missed an easy chance but that the team were still 2-0 ahead.

SEPTEMBER 16TH

1893	Enfield	A	Friendly	1-5
1897	Kettering Town	H	United League	1-1
1899	Chatham	A	Southern League	3-2
1901	Woolwich Arsenal	A	London League	2-0
1905	Brighton & Hove Albion	A	Southern League	0-2
1907	Bristol Rovers	A	Western League	1-2
1911	Sunderland	A	First Division	1-1
1916	Luton Town	H-Highbury		
			London Combination	2-3

Soon after playing Chelsea at White Hart Lane on 2nd September, the Ministry of Munitions commandeered the ground and turned it into a gas mask factory (by the time the Armistice was signed in 1918, 11 million gas masks had been produced under the stands and in temporary buildings constructed on the terraces). This left Spurs with no ground on which to play their home matches, but both Arsenal (at Highbury) and Clapton Orient (at Homerton) were quick to offer assistance, with the result that Spurs home matches until the beginning of the 1919-20 season were played at either of these grounds. Today's game, therefore, was played at Highbury – in unfamiliar surroundings Spurs lost 2-3.

1922	Burnley	A	First Division	1-0
1933	Arsenal	H	First Division	1-1
1935	Barnsley	H	Second Division	3-0
1937	Sheffield Wednesday	A	Second Division	3-0
1944	Portsmouth	H	Football League South	1-1
1950	Wolverhampton Wanderers	A	First Division	1-2
1953	Burnley	H	First Division	2-3
1961	Wolverhampton Wanderers	H	First Division	1-0
1964	Stoke City	H	First Division	2-1
1967	Arsenal	A	First Division	0-4

Terry Venables of Spurs and George Graham of Arsenal had first formed a friendship while both were players at Chelsea. On the morning of the North London derby Graham got married, with Terry as his best man. In the afternoon, Graham scored one of Arsenal's goals in their 4-0 win.

1969	Arsenal	A	First Division	3-2
1970	Dunfermline Athletic	H	Texaco Cup 1st Round 1st Leg	4-0

In previous seasons the Texaco Cup had been a curtain-raiser for the new domestic season and had featured English clubs exclusively. The new format followed lines similar to that of European competition – ties settled over home and away legs in what was an English and Scottish cup. Spurs' campaign in this competition got off to a flying start with a 4-0 home victory over Dunfermline, the goals coming from Mike England and a Martin Chivers hat-trick. The additional bonus for Spurs was an acceptance from the support – over 16,000 turned out.

1972	Manchester City	A	First Division	1-2
1978	Leeds United	A	First Division	2-1
1981	Ajax Amsterdam	A	European Cup-Winners' Cup 1st Round 1st Leg	3-1

As soon as the draw for the first round of the European Cup-Winners' Cup was made this was the one tie that raised fears and expectations – fears, because Spurs' last appearance in European competition had been in Holland and had ended with their supporters rioting in Rotterdam, expectations because Spurs and Ajax were two of Europe's premier names. Whilst there was a heavy police presence to chaperone Spurs fans to and from the stadium there was little trouble reported. Instead, the plaudits were earned by the team who gave a masterly display of attacking football and fully justified their 3-1 lead. Goals from Ricky Villa and a brace from Mark Falco made the second leg almost a formality – certainly the stream of Ajax fans filing out of the ground well before the final whistle seemed to think so.

1989	Chelsea	H	First Division	1-4
1995	Sheffield Wednesday	A	FA Premier League	3-1

SEPTEMBER 17TH

1892	Paddington	H	Friendly	10-0
1896	Casuals	H	Friendly	4-0
1898	Sheppey United	H	Southern League	3-2
1900	Millwall Athletic	A	Friendly	2-1
1904	Plymouth Argyle	H	Southern League	2-0

This match was also staged as a joint benefit for Ted Hughes and Tom Morris with a crowd of 25,000 seeing goals from Harry Stansfield and Vivian Woodward securing victory.

1906	Ilford	H	Friendly	4-4
1910	Newcastle United	H	First Division	1-2
1921	Middlesbrough	A	First Division	0-0
1927	Portsmouth	A	First Division	0-3
1932	Bury	A	Second Division	0-1
1938	Newcastle United	H	Second Division	1-0
1949	Bury	H	Second Division	3-1
1955	Everton	A	First Division	1-2
1956	Hibernian	A	Anglo-Scottish Floodlit Tournament	5-1
1958	Nottingham Forest	H	First Division	1-0
1960	Leicester City	A	First Division	2-1

1966	Burnley	A	First Division	2-2
1968	Coventry City	A	First Division	2-1
1977	Blackpool	A	Second Division	2-0
1983	Everton	H	First Division	1-2
1988	Liverpool	A	First Division	1-1
1991	Hajduk Split	A	European Cup-Winners' Cup 1st Round 1st Leg	0-1

With the former Yugoslavian republic tearing itself apart with civil war, it was a surprise that UEFA accepted an entry into the European Cup-Winners' Cup from the troubled state. There were stipulations; as UEFA had little or no wish to see rival political factions use the match as an excuse for demonstrations, Hajduk were instructed to play their 'home' leg well away from Yugoslavia. Thus Spurs travelled again to Austria (having met and beat Sparkasse in the previous round), journeying to the remote town of Linz for this tie. Hajduk had neither trained or played for many weeks prior to the game but turned in a performance that relied heavily on memory. They were worth their 1-0 win, but few gave them much hope for the return leg at White Hart Lane.

1994	Leicester City	A	FA Premier League	0-3
1996	Preston North End	A	Coca-Cola Cup 2nd Round 1st Leg	1-1
1997	Carlisle United	H	Coca-Cola Cup 2nd Round 1st Leg	3-2

SEPTEMBER 18TH

1897	Southampton	H	Southern League	2-0
1899	Portsmouth	H	Southern District Combination	2-0
1909	Bradford City	A	First Division	1-5
1911	Brentford	A	London FA Charity Cup 1st Round	1-4
1915	West Ham United	A	London Combination [1st competition]	1-1
1920	Aston Villa	H	First Division	1-2
1926	Sunderland	A	First Division	2-3
1937	Luton Town	A	Second Division	4-2
1943	West Ham United	A	Football League South	3-3
1950	Lovells Athletic	H	Friendly	8-0
1954	Portsmouth	H	First Division	1-1
1957	Birmingham City	H	First Division	7-1

Alfie Stokes equalled Ted Harper's record of most goals in a League match, crashing in five in this hammering of Birmingham City. Spurs' other goals were scored by Tommy Harmer from the penalty spot and Terry Dyson.

1965	Liverpool	H	First Division	2-1
1971	Crystal Palace	H	First Division	3-0
1974				

Sol Campbell born in Newham. Signed by Spurs as a trainee in 1992 one of his key strengths is his ability to slot into any position and perform as though he was made for the role. Indeed, he made his debut in a match against Chelsea, coming on as a substitute and playing up front, scoring one of Spurs' goals. He then became a regular in the side playing at full-back, but subsequent injuries to other players has seen him in midfield and back up front! He is at his happiest playing in central defence, and it is in this position that he has forced his way into the full England side. He gave particularly commanding performances in the 2-0 win over Georgia and the goalless draw in Italy that confirmed England's presence in the World Cup finals. His influence on Spurs is such that he has been made captain.

1976	Liverpool	A	First Division	0-2
1982	Sunderland	A	First Division	1-0
1993	Oldham Athletic	H	FA Premier League	5-0

Anyone arriving late because they were parking their car would have missed half of the action in this game – Spurs scored three times in a two-and-a-half minute spell between the fifth and eighth minutes! Teddy Sheringham continued his rich vein of goalscoring with a brace, and there were single strikes from Steve Sedgley, Gordon Durie and Jason Dozell.

SEPTEMBER 19TH

1896	Millwall Athletic	A	United League	5-6
1898	Luton Town	A	United League	4-3
1903	Queens Park Rangers	A	Southern League	0-2
1904	Queens Park Rangers	H	Western League	4-1
1908	Bolton Wanderers	H	Second Division	2-1
1910	Clapton Orient	H	London FA Charity Cup 1st Round	1-0
1914	Burnley	H	First Division	1-3
1921	Partick Thistle	A	Friendly	1-3

1925	Huddersfield Town	H	First Division	5-5
1931	Barnsley	H	Second Division	4-2
1936	Bradford Park Avenue	H	Second Division	5-1
1942	West Ham United	A	Football League South	1-3
1946	Newport County	A	Second Division	4-2
1953	Newcastle United	A	First Division	3-1
1959	Preston North End	H	First Division	5-1
1962	Wolverhampton Wanderers	A	First Division	2-2
1964	West Bromwich Albion	H	First Division	1-0
1970	Crystal Palace	A	First Division	3-0
1973	Grasshopper Zurich	A	UEFA Cup 1st Round 1st Leg	5-1

The final scoreline to this match owed almost everything to the superb goalkeeping skills of Pat Jennings! Spurs started brightly enough, taking the lead after only five minutes thanks to Martin Chivers' header. Thereafter, Grasshoppers piled on attack after attack, marching through the Spurs defence at will but finding Jennings an almost impenetrable wall. Ray Evans eased the pressure with a second Spurs goal in the 31st minute but Grasshoppers finally found a way through two minutes before half-time, Adolf Noventa scoring from the penalty spot after Jimmy Neighbour had handled. Jennings made four superb saves in the second half to stop Grasshoppers getting level, and Martin Chivers and Alan Gilzean with two completed the scoring for Spurs. After the game Spurs manager Bill Nicholson said 'It could have been a much different story but for Pat Jennings. He played a blinder. Grasshoppers were brilliant at times and could have been 3-1 up at one stage.'

1978	Aldershot	A	Friendly	1-1

This was a testimonial match for John Anderson and Spurs' goal was scored by Ricky Villa, his first for the club.

1981	Everton	H	First Division	3-0
1984	SC Braga	A	UEFA Cup 1st Round 1st Leg	3-0

This was Spurs' first defence of a trophy won in exciting circumstances the previous May. In the quiet town of Braga the only noise to be heard during the opening exchanges was the Portuguese crowd whistling at Spurs as the visitors took their time, trying to take the sting out of the game. Spurs' hero was Mark Falco, who had three strikes at goal and scored twice, the first on half an hour following a fine overlapping run by Chris Hughton and the second, with a suspicion of offside, in the 43rd minute. Tony Galvin netted a third for Spurs seconds before half-time and although Braga hit the bar twice in the second half, Spurs held on.

1987	West Ham United	A	First Division	1-0
1992	Manchester United	H	FA Premier League	1-1

SEPTEMBER 20TH

1902	Wellingborough	H	Southern League	6-1
1909	Nunhead	A	London FA Charity Cup	9-0
1913	Oldham Athletic	A	First Division	0-3
1919	South Shields	A	Second Division	3-0
1924	Sunderland	A	First Division	1-4
1930	Stoke City	A	Second Division	1-2
1941	Arsenal	A	London War League	0-4
1946				

Although he had yet to break into the first team on a regular basis, Len Duquemin was already a popular man at White Hart Lane among players and supporters alike. This day, on the eve of a Football Combination match at home to Birmingham City, it was reported that his brother Francis had been swept overboard from a Channel steamer by a tidal wave that broke over the ship and had died. The people of Guernsey sent a message of condolence to the club, together with a request that Duquemin should do his duty to his club and not drop out of the side for the game against Birmingham. Despite the bizarre nature of the tragedy, Len did indeed take part in the match and was heartily cheered throughout by the 8,000 crowd.

1947	Nottingham Forest	A	Second Division	0-1
1948	Chelmsford City	A	Fred Sargent Memorial	5-1

Fred Sargent played for Spurs before the Second World War having developed through the club's Northfleet nursery and made his debut for the club in 1934. An outstanding attacking winger he made 97 appearances in the League, scoring 25 goals and might have scored considerably more had not the war ended his career, at least as far Spurs were concerned. In May 1946 his Spurs contract was cancelled by mutual consent and he moved to non-League football with Chelmsford City, managed by former Spur Arthur Rowe. Sadly, Sargent died at the premature age of 36 in August 1948, and this match was staged as a benefit for his dependants.

| 1949 | | | | |

Ray Evans born in Edmonton. Ray joined Spurs in 1965, a time when the club were renowned more for their big money purchases than the home grown talent breaking into the side and Ray spent ten years with Spurs constantly battling to establish a regular spot in the team, usually against Joe Kinnear. It often seemed as though no sooner had Ray secured a spot in the side then a big match would loom on the horizon and the manager would require a little bit more experience than Ray had to offer. Therefore, although Roy was with the club whilst they won the League Cup twice and UEFA Cup once and Ray made appearances in all three runs, he missed out on the big occasion. He did, however, appear in the losing UEFA Cup final team of 1974. In 1975, having made 137 appearances for the League side (including four substitute appearances) he was transferred to Millwall for £35,000. After two years he moved to Fulham, and after spells in the United States finished his playing career in England with Stoke City.

1952	Arsenal	H	First Division	1-3
1958	Manchester United	A	First Division	2-2
1961	Gornik Zabrze	H	European Cup Preliminary Round 2nd Leg	8-1

Those fortunate enough to have lived through the era and attend this match still talk about the night the Poles were taken apart. The very phrase Glory Glory Nights is really about this one match. Everyone in Tottenham was convinced the team could score enough goals to overhaul Gornik, that is why so many of them descended upon White Hart Lane early before the match. The stadium was a cauldron of noise, with all the crowd singing as one voice to get behind the team. The players responded magnificently, charging at the Poles from the first minute to the last. The first goal came after nine minutes, Danny Blanchflower scoring from the penalty spot. Cliff Jones levelled the aggregate score on 19 minutes with a header then put Spurs ahead overall with his second of the night five minutes later. Although Spurs were pegged by Pohl's 25-yard volley, the pendulum had swung too far in Tottenham's favour; Jones completed his hat-trick on 35 minutes and Bobby Smith headed his first to send the teams in at half-time with Spurs leading 5-1. After a brief respite early in the second half, the onslaught continued in the 72nd minute – Bobby Smith headed home from close range, Terry Dyson latched on to Blanchflower's pass to slam in number seven a minute later and John White completed the scoring eight minutes from the end. At the end of the evening, Spurs had turned a 4-2 deficit into a 10-5 victory.

1967	Hajduk Split	A	European Cup-Winners' Cup 1st Round 1st Leg	2-0
1969	Derby County	A	First Division	0-5
1975	Leeds United	A	First Division	1-1
1980	Sunderland	H	First Division	0-0
1982	Barnet	A	Friendly	1-2

This match was a testimonial for Steve Brinkman with Spurs' goal being scored by Micky Hazard.

1986	Leicester City	A	First Division	2-1
1989	Southend United	H	Littlewoods Cup 2nd Round 1st Leg	1-0

Spurs defender Terry Fenwick had been the subject of barracking from the crowd in recent games; when he scored the only goal of the game he ran immediately to the front of the East Stand to acknowledge the cheers that greeted his strike. The East Stand, of course, was closed for building work and had little more than five workmen stationed there.

1995	Chester City	H	Coca-Cola Cup 2nd Round 1st Leg	4-0
1997	Blackburn Rovers	H	FA Premier League	0-0

SEPTEMBER 21ST

1889	Royal Arsenal	A	Friendly	1-10
1895	Casuals	H	Friendly	3-2
1901	Reading	A	Southern League	1-1
1903	Fulham	H	London League	2-1
1907	New Brompton	H	Southern League	2-1
1912	Derby County	H	First Division	1-2
1914	Nunhead	A	London FA Charity Cup 1st Round	2-1
1918	West Ham United	A	London Combination	1-0
1925	Cardiff City	A	First Division	1-0
1929	Bury	H	Second Division	2-2
1935	Manchester United	A	Second Division	0-0
1936	Blackpool	H	Second Division	1-2
1940	Chelsea	A	Football League South	1-4
1946	Swansea Town	A	Second Division	2-0

Spurs' second match in Wales inside three days saw a further two points collected. After the 4-2 win at Newport on Thursday Spurs made their headquarters at Porthcawl 'where they were able to inhale deep breaths of ozone that were brought along by the Atlantic gale', according to the next home programme. Whatever the players did certainly had an invigorating effect at Swansea; Spurs withstood all that Swansea could throw at them and scored twice through Les Bennett, who accepted a gift from the Town goalkeeper for his first goal and powered home from 15 yards for his second.

1953	Hibernian	A	Friendly	1-0
1957	Sheffield Wednesday	H	First Division	4-2
1963	Chelsea	A	First Division	3-0
1968	Nottingham Forest	H	First Division	2-1
1974	Wolverhampton Wanderers	A	First Division	3-2
1985	Sheffield Wednesday	H	First Division	5-1
1991	Wimbledon	A	First Division	5-3

If the final scoreline was somewhat close then it does not tell the true story of this match, for having piled up a 5-1 lead Spurs eased off the pressure and allowed Wimbledon to grab two late consolation goals. Star of the match was Gary Lineker, who weighed in with four goals, including one from the penalty spot.

| 1992 | Brentford | H | Coca-Cola Cup 2nd Round 1st Leg | 3-1 |
| 1994 | Watford | A | Coca-Cola Cup 2nd Round 1st Leg | 6-3 |

SEPTEMBER 22ND

1888	Royal Arsenal	A	Friendly	1-0
1894	Casuals	H	Friendly	3-1
1900	Bristol City	A	Southern League	1-1
1902	Queens Park Rangers	A	Western League	2-0
1906	Norwich City	H	Southern League	2-2
1913	Metrogas	H	London FA Charity Cup 1st Round	11-2
1917	Arsenal	H-Highbury		
			London Combination	1-2
1919	Millwall	H	London FA Charity Cup 1st Round	6-0
1921	Inverness Caledonians	A	Friendly	3-6
1923	Bolton Wanderers	H	First Division	0-0
1924	West Bromwich Albion	H	First Division	0-1
1927	Leicester City	H	First Division	2-1
1928	Millwall	H	Second Division	2-1
1934	Aston Villa	H	First Division	0-2
1945	West Bromwich Albion	A	Football League South	0-5
1951	Manchester United	H	First Division	2-0

The visit of Manchester United was enough to ensure the largest ever League attendance at White Hart Lane, with a crowd of 70,882 filling the ground. Although Spurs won 2-0 thanks to goals from Bennett and Medley, by the end of the season United would take over Spurs' mantle as champions, with Spurs sliding into second place in the table.

1956	Luton Town	H	First Division	5-0
1962	Sheffield United	A	First Division	1-3
1965	Walton & Hersham United	A	Friendly	8-1
1971	AC Torino	H	Anglo-Italian League Cup-Winners' Cup 2nd Leg	2-0

Having already won the first leg in Turin Spurs completed the job with a 2-0 victory over AC Torino in the second leg of the Anglo-Italian League Cup-Winners' Cup. The goals were scored by Martin Chivers and Alan Gilzean. Despite the fact that this was not a serious European competition over 34,000 attended to see Spurs lift their first trophy of the season.

1973	Liverpool	A	First Division	2-3
1976	Wrexham	H	League Cup 3rd Round	2-3
1979	West Bromwich Albion	H	First Division	1-1
1981	Swansea City	A	First Division	1-2
1984	Aston Villa	A	First Division	1-0
1990	Crystal Palace	H	First Division	1-1
1993	Burnley	A	Coca-Cola Cup 2nd Round 1st Leg	0-0
1996	Leicester City	H	FA Premier League	1-2

SEPTEMBER 23RD

1893	Romford	H	Friendly	2-2
1897	2nd Scots Guards	H	Friendly	4-1
1899	Reading	H	Southern League	2-1
1901	Sheffield United	A	Friendly	1-3
1903	New Brompton	A	Friendly	0-3
1905	West Ham United	H	Southern League	2-0

1907	Millwall	A	Western League	0-2
1911	Blackburn Rovers	H	First Division	0-2
1912	Bromley	H	London FA Charity Cup 1st Round	3-0
1916	Reading	A	London Combination	4-2
1922	Arsenal	H	First Division	1-2

The rivalry between Spurs and Arsenal, keen prior to 1919 (despite Arsenal's arrival at Highbury) but practically hostile since, exploded during this game between the two North London clubs. The referee, Mr C Austin, did well to get through the game without having to send anyone off, although even in the final minutes tempers were still frayed, and a consolation goal from Alex Lindsay for Spurs seemed to be the signal for a swarm of players to converge on the official. Arsenal claimed the goal to have been offside, although at that stage in the game it did not really matter to the outcome. But, as a result of the melée, the referee was duty bound to make reference to it in his report, which in turn had consequences for both clubs.

1929	Millwall	H	Second Division	1-1
1933	Liverpool	H	First Division	0-3
1939	Chelmsford City	A	Friendly	2-4
1944	Southampton	A	Football League South	3-1
1950	Sunderland	H	First Division	1-1
1961	Nottingham Forest	A	First Division	0-2
1964	Copenhagen Select XI	A	Friendly	1-2
1967	Manchester United	A	First Division	1-3
1972	West Ham United	H	First Division	1-0
1978	Manchester City	A	First Division	0-2
1985	Orient	A	Milk Cup 2nd Round 1st Leg	0-2
1986	Barnsley	A	Littlewoods Cup 2nd Round 1st Leg	3-2
1987	Torquay United	A	Littlewoods Cup 2nd Round 1st Leg	0-1
1989	Norwich City	A	First Division	2-2
1992	SS Lazio	A	Capital Cup 1st Leg	0-3

Part of the deal that took Paul Gascoigne to Rome and SS Lazio was the provision of two friendly matches between the two clubs. As neither was involved in European competition a trophy, the Capital Cup, was put up by the sponsors. SS Lazio completely dominated the match, with Paul Gascoigne waltzing around players who a few months previously had been team-mates.

1997	Bolton Wanderers	A	FA Premier League	1-1

SEPTEMBER 24TH

1892	Polytechnic	A	Southern Alliance	2-1

Spurs played their first ever League match having recently joined the Southern Alliance. They won 2-1 away at Polytechnic with goals from Sykes and Brigden. At the end of the season Spurs had played 12 matches, won seven, drawn two and lost only three, scoring 29 goals and conceding 21. There must have been some considerable travelling involved in the Alliance, for other teams in the League included Slough and Windsor & Eton.

1896	Luton Town	H	Friendly	0-0

The game was abandoned after 75 minutes because of rain.

1898	Warmley	H	Southern League	7-1

As Warmley subsequently withdrew from the Southern League (on January 21st 1899) the points gained from this match (and the return fixture on December 24th) were not included in the final League table. This was Spurs' biggest win of the season as well!

1900	Richmond Association	H	Friendly	8-0
1904	West Ham United	A	Southern League	0-0
1906	Fulham	H	Southern League	5-1
1910	Oldham Athletic	A	First Division	0-2
1921	Aston Villa	H	First Division	3-1
1927	Manchester United	A	First Division	0-3
1932	Grimsby Town	A	Second Division	2-3
1938	West Bromwich Albion	A	Second Division	3-4
1949	Leicester City	A	Second Division	2-1
1951	Newcastle United	H	FA Charity Shield	2-1
1955	Newcastle United	H	First Division	3-1
1960	Aston Villa	H	First Division	6-2
1966	Nottingham Forest	H	First Division	2-1
1977	Luton Town	H	Second Division	2-0
1980	Crystal Palace	H	League Cup 3rd Round	0-0

1983	Watford	A	First Division	3-2

Striker Steve Archibald had been in disgrace with his manager since walking off the pitch towards the end of the match with Coventry, claiming he was injured and did not want to risk further injury. Manager Keith Burkinshaw had promptly dropped him from the side, although Archibald was back on the substitutes' bench for this day's game. Things did not start too well for Spurs, for they were soon a goal behind and struggling to come to terms with a lively Watford side. The match effectively swung on one incident; Glenn Hoddle collected an infield pass from Garry Brooke and back-flicked the ball through an opponent's legs. Hoddle quickly moved around the defender, looked up and spotted Steve Sherwood a couple of yards off his line. Hoddle then delicately chipped the ball over the keeper and into the far corner of the net for one of the finest goals seen by a Spurs player for many a year. Immediately Spurs grew in confidence and stature; Archibald climbed off the subs bench and on to the score sheet with a 20-yard shot and Chris Hughton wrapped up the points after some fine inter-play with Archibald. Watford grabbed a late goal but were never likely to get back on level terms.

1988	Middlesbrough	H	First Division	3-2
1994	Nottingham Forest	H	FA Premier League	1-4

SEPTEMBER 25TH

1897	Millwall Athletic	H	Southern League	7-0
1905	Bristol Rovers	H	Western League	0-1
1909	Sheffield Wednesday	H	First Division	3-0
1915	Chelsea	H	London Combination [1st competition]	1-3
1920	Manchester United	A	First Division	1-0
1926	West Bromwich Albion	H	First Division	3-0

1932   Terry Medwin born in Swansea. Shortly before Alf Ramsey made wingers obsolete, Spurs were blessed with three of the finest; Cliff Jones, Terry Dyson and Terry Medwin. Terry Medwin was perhaps the most versatile of the three, for he had previously played in all positions of the front line for Swansea, who he joined in 1949. He stayed with Swansea until the end of the 1955-56 season, by which time he had won three Welsh caps, when a £25,000 transfer took him to Spurs. He quickly became a regular in the team, earning a recall to the Welsh side and winning a total of 30 caps. He was unfortunate to lose his place in the Spurs team to Terry Dyson just as the 'double' ball got rolling, but still weighed in with 15 appearances in the League and cup that term as deputy to either Dyson or Jones. He received more than adequate compensation the following year when he was a member of the side that retained the FA Cup. In his last full season with Spurs, 1962-63, he made 26 League appearances but on the end-of-season tour of South Africa suffered a broken leg in the match with a NSAFL Invitation XI that ended his career. He continued to work in football in a variety of capacities until ill-health forced his retirement in 1983.

1937	Barnsley	H	Second Division	3-0
1943	Southampton	H	Football League South	2-2
1948	West Ham United	A	Second Division	0-1
1954	Blackpool	A	First Division	1-5
1955	Aarhus Gymnastikforening	A	Friendly	4-3
1965	Aston Villa	A	First Division	2-3
1968	Exeter City	H	League Cup 3rd Round	6-3
1971	Coventry City	A	First Division	0-1
1976	Norwich City	H	First Division	1-1
1982	Nottingham Forest	H	First Division	4-1
1991	Swansea City	A	Rumbelows Cup 2nd Round 1st Leg	0-1
1995	Queens Park Rangers	A	FA Premier League	3-2
1996	Preston North End	H	Coca-Cola Cup 2nd Round 2nd Leg	3-0

SEPTEMBER 26TH

1891	Hampstead	H	Friendly	6-2
1896	Casuals	A	Friendly	4-1
1903	Plymouth Argyle	H	Southern League	0-2
1904	Bristol Rovers	H	Western League	1-0
1908	Hull City	A	Second Division	0-1
1914	Manchester City	A	First Division	1-2
1925	Sunderland	A	First Division	0-3
1931	Nottingham Forest	H	Second Division	1-3
1936	Barnsley	A	Second Division	0-1
1942	Southampton	H	Football League South	1-1
1953	Manchester United	H	First Division	1-1

| 1956 | Partick Thistle | H | Anglo-Scottish Floodlit Tournament | 4-1 |

Although the FA and Football League were still reluctant to allow their clubs to enter European competition (Manchester United ignored advice not to enter the European Cup) the advent of floodlights meant it would be possible to play midweek on a regular basis. Although the tournament was not officially sanctioned, five teams took part – Spurs, Hibernian, Partick Thistle, Hearts and Newcastle United, with Spurs winning three and drawing one of their six games. This was their first home match in the tournament and a crowd of 26,210 saw goals from Terry Medwin, Bobby Smith and Alfie Stokes (two) ensure the two points. Despite the interest the competition generated, it was abandoned after only one season.

1959	Leicester City	A	First Division	1-1
1964	Manchester United	A	First Division	1-4
1970	Manchester City	H	First Division	2-0
1978	IFK Gothenburg	A	Friendly	0-1
1981	Manchester City	A	First Division	1-0
1984	Halifax Town	A	Milk Cup 2nd Round 1st Leg	5-1
1987	Manchester United	A	First Division	0-1
1990	Hartlepool United	H	Rumbelows Cup 2nd Round 1st Leg	5-0
1993	Ipswich Town	A	FA Premier League	2-2

SEPTEMBER 27TH

| 1884 | A Billy Harston XI took on Jack Jull's XI and won 5-4. | | | |
| 1890 | Hampstead | H | Friendly | 6-3 |

1895 Alex Hunter born in Renfrew. After impressing with Queens Park Alex was signed by Spurs as cover for first-team goalkeeper Bill Jacques, and when Jacques was injured in February 1921 performed so well that Jacques was unable to gain his place back. That meant Alex collected an FA Cup winners' medal at the end of the season, but his demise at Spurs was just as swift and in May 1922 he joined Wigan Borough.

1898	Sheppey United	A	Thames & Medway League	3-2
1899	Clapton	A	Friendly	4-1
1900	Notts County	A	Friendly	1-4
1902	Bristol Rovers	A	Southern League	2-3
1913	Manchester City	H	First Division	3-1
1919	Lincoln City	H	Second Division	6-1
1924	Cardiff City	H	First Division	1-1
1926	Millwall	A	London FA Charity Cup 1st Round	2-5
1930	Millwall	H	Second Division	4-1
1941	Queens Park Rangers	H	London War League	3-1
1947	Doncaster Rovers	H	Second Division	2-0
1952	Burnley	H	First Division	2-1

1956 Steve Archibald born in Glasgow. After helping Clyde win the Scottish Second Division title Steve was snapped up by Aberdeen for £25,000 in 1978. At Pittodrie the success continued, with Aberdeen winning the Scottish League in 1980 and reaching the League Cup final in two successive seasons. In May 1980 Spurs paid £800,000 to bring him to White Hart Lane where he linked up with the also newly arrived Garth Crooks. Despite their differing temperaments, Archibald and Crooks was a marriage made in heaven out on the pitch, with the pair plundering 36 League goals in their first full season. Of course, this was the season that culminated in success in the FA Cup, a trophy that was retained the following season. Although Steve did not find the net in either finals or replays, he did grab Spurs' goal in the 1982 League Cup final. In 1984 he fell out with manager Keith Burkinshaw, but this did not prevent him playing his part in the winning of the UEFA Cup that season. That summer he became Barcelona manager Terry Venables' first signing, moving to Spain for £1,250,00. He won a medal in his first season in Spain as Barcelona won the title and the following year helped the club to the European Cup final. The arrival of Mark Hughes and Gary Lineker at Barcelona restricted his first-team opportunities and he came back to England, turning out for Blackburn on loan until his Barcelona contract expired, at which point he signed for Hibernian back in Scotland. He then spent a brief time with Espanol (back in Spain!) before signing variously with St Mirren, Ayr United and Fulham.

| 1958 | Wolverhampton Wanderers | H | First Division | 2-1 |
| 1967 | Hajduk Split | H | European Cup-Winners' Cup 1st Round 2nd Leg | 4-3 |

Spurs sailed through to the next round 6-3 on aggregate and 4-3 on the night, but fell asleep in the final ten minutes, allowing the Yugoslavian side to score three times and give the score a semblance of respectability.

| 1969 | Sunderland | H | First Division | 0-1 |

1972	Lyn Oslo	H	UEFA Cup 1st Round 2nd Leg	6-0
1975	Arsenal	H	First Division	0-0
1980	Leicester City	A	First Division	1-2
1986	Everton	H	First Division	2-0
1988	Notts County	A	Littlewoods Cup 2nd Round 1st Leg	1-1
1992	Sheffield Wednesday	A	FA Premier League	0-2
1997	Wimbledon	H	FA Premier League	0-0

SEPTEMBER 28TH

1889	Westminster	H	Friendly	13-0
1895	Royal Ordnance	H	Friendly	2-0
1901	Southampton	H	Western League	5-0
1903	Millwall	A	Southern Charity Cup 1st Round	1-3
1907	Swindon Town	A	Southern League	0-1
1912	Sunderland	A	First Division	2-2
1914	West Bromwich Albion	H	First Division	2-0
1916	West Ham United	H-Highbury		
			London Combination	1-2
1918	Clapton Orient	H-Homerton		
			London Combination	2-0
1929	Chelsea	A	Second Division	0-3
1935	Port Vale	H	Second Division	5-2
1938	Charlton Athletic	H	Second Division	1-3
1946	Manchester City	H	Second Division	0-0
1957	Manchester City	A	First Division	1-5
1963	West Ham United	H	First Division	3-0
1964	Blackpool	A	First Division	1-1
1968	Newcastle United	A	First Division	2-2
1971	Keflavik	H	UEFA Cup 1st Round 2nd Leg	9-0

Despite the 9-0 win, manager Bill Nicholson was not entirely happy at the final whistle, feeling his team should have scored more (though quite what that would have done to the moral of the Keflavik team!) and equalled, if not beaten the British record aggregate score in Europe, 16 set by Leeds United. Martin Chivers set the ball rolling with his first strike in the 8th minute and a second on 19 minutes. Thereafter, goals by Steve Perryman (24 minutes), Ralph Coates (44 minutes), Chivers completing his hat-trick (on 58 minutes), Cyril Knowles (65 minutes), two from Alan Gilzean (77 and 78 minutes) and a final goal from Phil Holder on 86 minutes completed the rout.

| 1974 | Middlesbrough | H | First Division | 1-2 |
| 1982 | Coleraine | H | European Cup-Winners' Cup 1st Round 2nd Leg | 4-0 |

Having already won the first leg 3-0 Spurs finished easy 7-0 victors on aggregate and moved into the second round where they would meet Bayern Munich.

| 1983 | Drogheda | H | UEFA Cup 1st Round 2nd Leg | 8-0 |

Spurs' eight goals were scored by Chris Hughton, Graham Roberts (two), Steve Archibald, Mark Falco (two) and Alan Brazil (two), giving Spurs a 14-0 aggregate victory. They would meet old rivals Feyenoord in the second round.

| 1985 | Liverpool | A | First Division | 1-4 |
| 1991 | Manchester United | H | First Division | 1-2 |

SEPTEMBER 29TH

1894	London Caledonians	A	Friendly	1-3
1897	Loughborough	A	United League	2-1
1900	Swindon Town	H	Southern League	2-0
1902	Reading	H	Western League	2-1
1906	Luton Town	A	Southern League	2-0
1909	Reading	A	Friendly	3-2
1917	West Ham United	A	London Combination	0-1
1923	Bolton Wanderers	A	First Division	1-3
1928	Port Vale	A	Second Division	1-2
1934	Derby County	A	First Division	1-2
1945	West Bromwich Albion	H	Football League South	4-2
1951	Arsenal	A	First Division	1-1
1953	Racing Club de Paris	H	Friendly	5-3

This was the first time the floodlights had been switched on for a first-team match, a friendly against crack French club Racing Club de Paris. A crowd of some 28,000 saw goals from Ronnie Burgess, George Hutchinson, Les Bennett (two) and Len Duquemin win the match for Spurs.

1956	Sunderland	A	First Division	2-0
1962	Nottingham Forest	H	First Division	9-2
1970	Dunfermline Athletic	A	Texaco Cup 1st Round 2nd Leg	3-0

Having already won the first leg at home 4-0, Spurs completed the job with a 3-0 win at Dunfermline for a 7-0 aggregate win.

1973	Derby County	H	First Division	1-0
1975	Le Stade Rennais	A	Friendly	1-1
1979	Coventry City	A	First Division	1-1
1981	Ajax Amsterdam	H	European Cup-Winners' Cup 1st Round 2nd Leg	3-0

Although there was little doubt that Spurs were going to march on to the next round, they did not break through a concentrated Ajax defence until the 70th minute and then crashed in three in the space of 12 minutes from Tony Galvin, Mark Falco and Ossie Ardiles. Ardiles' was the pick of the bunch; a curling shot from the edge of the penalty area.

1984	Luton Town	H	First Division	4-2
1990	Aston Villa	H	First Division	2-1
1996	Manchester United	A	FA Premier League	0-2

SEPTEMBER 30TH

1882	Radicals	Unknown	Friendly	0-2

This was the very first match played by Hotspur FC, a 2-0 defeat by local rivals Radicals and which remained unknown until the club's accounts covering this period were discovered. Apart from the opponents and score, we know little about the game; why should a group of boys playing on a field somewhere in London suppose that over one hundred years later the wider world would be extremely interested in their activities? What we do know, courtesy of the accounts, is that the club bought their first ball on the morning of the match (which contradicts many published histories of the club, all of which claimed the first ball the club used was a gift from one of the older Casey brothers), paying 6s 6d! This would indicate that the match was played at home.

1893	Casuals	H	Friendly	0-1
1899	Southampton	A	Friendly	1-1
1901	Queens Park Rangers	A	Western League	3-1
1905	Fulham	A	Southern League	0-0
1907	Millwall	H	Southern Charity Cup 1st Round	1-1
1911	Sheffield Wednesday	A	First Division	0-4
1916	Millwall	H-Homerton		
			London Combination	1-4

As White Hart Lane had been requisitioned during the First World War, home games in the London Combination were played at either Highbury (the home of Arsenal) or at Homerton. This particular match was the first occasion the latter venue was used.

1922	Arsenal	A	First Division	2-0
1933	Chelsea	A	First Division	4-0
1939	Chelsea	A	Friendly	2-4
1944	Charlton Athletic	H	Football League South	2-0
1950	Aston Villa	A	First Division	3-2

1951   Barry Daines born in Witham, Essex. Having trained as a schoolboy with West Ham United Barry signed with Spurs in 1969; a time when Pat Jennings was not only the first choice goalkeeper at Spurs but one of the best in the world. Therefore, although Barry made his debut for Spurs against West Bromwich Albion in November 1971, his appearances thereafter were restricted to whenever Pat Jennings was injured, which was seldom. By the time Barry got anything like an extended run, in 1976-77, he had made only 13 appearances in five seasons. The situation looming was similar to that which had occurred at Spurs over Jimmy Seed and Taffy O'Callaghan – Barry Daines proved himself to be a more than capable deputy whilst Jennings recovered and at the end of the season, manager Keith Burkinshaw allowed Jennings to move and placed his faith in Daines. It has often been said that the sale of Pat Jennings (to Arsenal of all people!) was the worst piece of transfer business the club ever conducted, but had it not been for Barry Daines suffering from injury matters might have turned out different. As it was, Barry would fight his way back into the team only to suffer another setback, missing out when Spurs won the FA Cup in 1981 (ironically in Barry's testimonial season – his match, against West Ham, was played between the final and replay). With Spurs then signing Ray Clemence during the summer of 1981 Barry slipped further down the ranking and left the club for Hong Kong, re-appearing in England to play for Mansfield Town in 1983.

1961	Aston Villa	H	First Division	1-0

The aftermath of Spurs' first European home match, against Gornik, had brought criticism from the media about some of the tackles flying in and the vociferous support the team had received. As far as the tackling was concerned, the match had never become vicious; the tackles were flying only during the opening spell when both teams were struggling to impose their authority. Once Spurs had achieved the upper hand, they began to play masterful football. The club were particularly stung at the way their supporters had been criticised and used this day's programme to put the matter straight. 'Harking back to our match with Gornik, it was thrilling to hear the old-time "Tottenham Roar" at full blast, but though our supporters were obviously out to do their best to help the team "wipe the slate clean" as soon as possible, their vocal enthusiasm seems to have worried some members of the Press. "Hate" and "fanaticism" have been suggested as the reasons for such prolonged enthusiasm, but those who know the true Spurs supporters know fans who appreciate good football, as was witnessed by the spontaneous ovation given to Gornik when Pohl hit that tremendous goal. But what's the use of supporters if they do not support, the more so in such an important game when support is even more necessary? We, at any rate, were proud of our supporters, and of our players who made it such a memorable evening.'

1967	Sunderland	H	First Division	3-0
1972	Derby County	A	First Division	1-2
1978	Coventry City	H	First Division	1-1
1980	Crystal Palace	A	League Cup 3rd Round Replay	3-1 [aet]
1989	Queens Park Rangers	H	First Division	3-2

It took Gary Lineker six games to get on the score sheet for Spurs, finally heading home their second in last week's 2-2 draw at Norwich. This day he got his first goals at White Lane, netting a hat-trick in the 3-2 win over Queens Park Rangers. By the end of the season he had hit 24 League goals, including one more hat-trick against Norwich City.

| 1995 | Wimbledon | H | FA Premier League | 3-1 |
| 1997 | Carlisle United | A | Coca-Cola Cup 2nd Round 2nd Leg | 2-0 |

OCTOBER 1ST

1887	Buckhurst Hill	H	Friendly	6-1
1892	Royal Arsenal Athletic	H	Friendly	3-0
1896	1st Coldstream Guards	H	Friendly	4-0
1898	Burton Wanderers	H	Friendly	5-2
1904	Reading	H	Southern League	1-3
1910	Middlesbrough	A	First Division	0-2
1921	Aston Villa	A	First Division	1-2

Spurs were so much the better side in this game that one reporter was moved to ask 'Who has killed a black cat at Tottenham?' Although the defence performed admirably enough, especially Alex Hunter in goal, Spurs were unusually hesitant in front of goal, with Bert Bliss trying to place the ball into the net rather than attempting to blast it as previously. Frank Barson also did a good job of marshalling Charlie Wilson, so much so that Barson was able not only to break up Spurs' attacks but set Villa on the march themselves. More importantly, Spurs picked up a number of mysterious injuries, with four players finishing the game with stud marks down their chest.

1927	Everton	H	First Division	1-3
1932	Oldham Athletic	H	Second Division	1-1
1938	Norwich City	H	Second Division	4-1
1949	Bradford Park Avenue	H	Second Division	5-0
1955	Birmingham City	A	First Division	0-3
1960	Wolverhampton Wanderers	A	First Division	4-0
1962				

Nico Claesen born in Leut, Belgium. A string of impressive performances for Belgium during the 1986 World Cup finals in Mexico impressed a host of clubs and Spurs manager David Pleat swooped to sign him in October that year, paying £600,000 to Standard Liege for his services. Pleat originally intended linking Nico with Clive Allen, but the discovery of an effective unit that utilised five in midfield and a lone striker put paid to that combination. Indeed, it was Clive Allen's 49 goals in one season that effectively ended Nico's Spurs career before it even started, with Nico invariably left on the bench. When he then lost his place in the Belgian national side he asked for a transfer, finally signing for Antwerp for £550,000 in August 1988. His time at Spurs was not entirely wasted, for his 18 League goals in only 37 full appearances (and 13 as substitute) indicated a fine striker. He subsequently broke back into the Belgian side and was a member of their squad for the 1990 World Cup finals. On the same day Paul Walsh was born in Plumstead in South London. Paul began his professional career with Charlton Athletic in 1979 and moved on to Luton in 1982, despite a number of bigger clubs showing an interest. In May 1984 he was transferred to Liverpool, helping them reach the European Cup final in 1985 and the Littlewoods Cup in 1987 and win the double in 1986, but he was in and out of the side and rarely able to get an extended run. In February 1988 he was signed by Terry Venables for £500,000, and although he collected a winners' medal in the 1991 FA Cup he did not command a regular place in the side. In 1992 he was sold to Portsmouth for £500,000 as part of the deal that brought Darren Anderton to White Hart Lane, although Paul later played for Manchester City.

1966	Fulham	A	First Division	4-3
1977	Orient	A	Second Division	1-1
1988	Manchester United	H	First Division	2-2
1994	Wimbledon	A	FA Premier League	2-1

OCTOBER 2ND

1886	South Hackney	H	Friendly	13-1
1897	New Brompton	A	Southern League	0-1
1899	Gravesend United	H	Southern League	4-0
1905	Plymouth Argyle	H	Western League	0-2
1907	Reading	A	Western League	2-1

On the same day Alf Day was born in Ebbw Vale. Alf joined Spurs in May 1931 and was considered a promising half-back, so much so that he made his international debut for Wales before making his League debut! However, he was unable to fulfil his potential at Spurs and was transferred to Millwall in May 1936. He later played for Southampton, Tranmere and had just joined Swindon when the Second World War broke out. Although he guested for a number of clubs during the conflict, by the time League football resumed he was too old and retired from the game.

1909	Bristol City	A	First Division	0-0
1915	Crystal Palace	H	London Combination [1st competition]	2-4
1920	Manchester United	H	First Division	4-1
1922	West Ham United	H	London Professional Football Charity Fund	2-1
1926	Bury	A	First Division	0-0
1937	Stockport County	A	Second Division	2-3
1943	Aldershot	H	Football League South	5-2
1948	Blackburn Rovers	H	Second Division	4-0
1954	Charlton Athletic	H	First Division	1-4
1957	Wolverhampton Wanderers	A	First Division	0-4
1963	Birmingham City	H	First Division	6-1
1964				

Mitchell Thomas born in Luton. Mitchell joined Luton Town straight from school and graduated through the ranks to make his first-team debut in February 1983. He also got selected for England Under-21 on three occasions, and when Luton manager David Pleat took over at White Hart Lane was his first signing, costing Spurs £275,000. He continued his progress under Pleat, playing in the 1987 FA Cup final and getting selected for the full England squad, but following Pleat's subsequent departure, the arrival of Terry Venables appeared to limit his opportunities. He was therefore sold to West Ham United for £500,000 in August 1991 and later returned to Luton.

1971	Ipswich Town	H	First Division	2-1
1976	West Bromwich Albion	A	First Division	2-4
1982	Swansea City	A	First Division	0-2
1983	Nottingham Forest	H	First Division	2-1
1985	Southampton	H	Screen Sports Super Cup Group A	2-1
1991	Hajduk Split	H	European Cup-Winners' Cup 1st Round 2nd Leg	2-0

Having lost the first leg played in Linz, Austria, by 1-0 Spurs needed an early goal to get on level terms. It came too, but from a somewhat unlikely source, for if Hajduk spent most of their time worrying about Gary Lineker and Gordon Durie, then this allowed David Tuttle the opportunity of sneaking in to score his first goal for the club and on his European debut as well. A later goal from Durie ensured Spurs' passage into the next round by virtue of a 2-1 aggregate win.

OCTOBER 3RD

| 1885 | Silesia College | A | Friendly | 4-3 |

This is quite possibly the first match the club played as Tottenham Hotspur. Towards the end of the previous season secretary Sam Casey had reported that he had been receiving mail intended for London Hotspur, and so the Hotspurs decided to change their name to Tottenham Hotspur to distinguish themselves from the other side. London Hotspur soon disbanded anyway.

1891	Grange Park	H	Friendly	4-2
1896	Gravesend	A	Southern League	3-1
1898	Gravesend United	H	Thames & Medway League	3-1
1900	Reading	H	Friendly	1-1
1903	Reading	A	Southern League	2-2

Spurs opened the 1903-04 season in dreadful fashion, failing to score in their opening six games and collecting just two points. Although they again failed to win on this occasion, they did at least score and then went from strength to strength; at the season's end they finished second in the Southern League!

1904	Millwall	A	Western League	2-3
1906	Southampton	A	Western League	0-2
1908	Derby County	H	Second Division	0-0
1910	Chelsea	A	London Professional Football Charity Fund	3-0
1914	Newcastle United	A	First Division	0-4
1925	Blackburn Rovers	H	First Division	4-2
1931	Chesterfield	A	Second Division	2-4

1932 Alfie Stokes born in Hackney, London. Alfie joined Spurs as an amateur in June 1951 and became a professional in February 1953, making his League debut in April the same year. Unfortunately, Alfie spent most of his Spurs career competing with the likes of Dave Dunmore, Tommy Harmer. Johnny Brooks and Bobby Smith for one of the forward positions and managed only 65 appearances during his time with the club. In July 1959, with Bill Nicholson assembling the double side, Alfie was allowed to sign for Fulham for £10,000 and later had a brief spell with Watford.

1936	Sheffield United	H	Second Division	2-2
1942	Aldershot	H	Football League South	4-0
1953	Bolton Wanderers	A	First Division	0-2
1959	Burnley	H	First Division	1-1
1970	Derby County	A	First Division	1-1
1972	Middlesbrough	A	League Cup 3rd Round	1-1
1973	Grasshopper Zurich	H	UEFA Cup 1st Round 2nd Leg	4-1

If Spurs' first leg performance when they won 5-1 had been more than a touch fortunate, then the second leg more than made up for it. A final scoreline of 4-1, with goals from Mike England, Martin Peters (two) and a Lador own goal gave Spurs a 9-2 aggregate win.

1981	Nottingham Forest	H	First Division	3-0
1984	SC Braga	H	UEFA Cup 1st Round 2nd Leg	6-0

Garth Crooks helped himself to a hat-trick as Spurs finished 9-0 aggregate winners, their other goals being scored by Gary Stevens, Chris Hughton and Mark Falco.

1987	Sheffield Wednesday	H	First Division	2-0
1992	Queens Park Rangers	A	FA Premier League	1-4
1993	Everton	H	FA Premier League	3-2

OCTOBER 4TH

1884	Remington	H	Friendly	4-0

This was Spurs' first match of the 1884-85 season against opponents who had been their last of 1883-84. This time Spurs doubled their win, with Amos and Buckle both scoring twice.

1890	Grove House	H	Friendly	Score unknown
1902	Northampton Town	H	Southern League	2-0
1913	Manchester United	A	First Division	1-3
1919	Lincoln City	A	Second Division	1-1
1924	Preston North End	A	First Division	3-0
1930	Oldham Athletic	A	Second Division	2-1
1941	Reading	A	London War League	1-1
1947	Southampton	A	Second Division	1-1
1952	Preston North End	A	First Division	0-1
1958	Portsmouth	A	First Division	1-1
1969	Southampton	A	First Division	2-2
1975	Newcastle United	A	First Division	2-2
1977	Hull City	A	Second Division	0-2
1980	Stoke City	A	First Division	3-2
1986	Luton Town	H	First Division	0-0
1989	Southend United	A	Littlewoods Cup 2nd Round 2nd Leg	2-3 [aet]

Spurs came perilously close to being eliminated by lowly Southend United, finally advancing into the next round by virtue of away goals counting double.

1994	Watford	H	Coca-Cola Cup 2nd Round 2nd Leg	2-3

As adventurous and exciting as the team were on attack, their inability to defend ultimately cost them any chance of winning trophies and Ossie Ardiles his job. In the first round Spurs had scored six at Watford but conceded three, a figure that Watford were to repeat at White Hart Lane. Spurs managed two in reply to register an 8-6 aggregate victory, but the writing was already on the wall for all to see.

| 1995 | Chester City | A | Coca-Cola Cup 2nd Round 2nd Leg | 3-1 |
| 1997 | Newcastle United | A | FA Premier League | 0-1 |

OCTOBER 5TH

1889	Vulcan	H	Friendly	5-1
1895	Clapton	A	Friendly	4-5
1898	Brighton United	A	United League	2-1
1901	Bristol Rovers	A	Southern League	2-1
1903	Queens Park Rangers	H	Western League	3-0

This match was also played as a benefit game for Harry Erentz, a member of the successful cup-winning side of 1900-01, who had joined the club in 1898. Goals from Ollie Burton, John 'Bristol' jones and John L. Jones gave Spurs victory.

1907	Crystal Palace	H	Southern League	1-2
1908	Queens Park Rangers	H	London FA Charity Cup 1st Round	1-0
1912	Middlesbrough	A	First Division	1-1
1918	Chelsea	H-Highbury		
			London Combination	2-1

1922   An FA Commission of Inquiry was called following events at the recent Spurs and Arsenal North London derby at White Hart Lane. After listening to evidence and testimony from the players and officials of both clubs, Bert Smith of Spurs was found guilty of using 'filthy language' and was suspended for a month. Alex Graham of Arsenal was censured for retaliating instead of reporting matters to the referee and Stephen Dunn, Arsenal's goalkeeper was also censured for his conduct after Spurs' goal had been allowed to stand.

1929	Nottingham Forest	H	Second Division	1-1
1935	Fulham	A	Second Division	2-1
1940	Queens Park Rangers	A	Football League South	1-1
1946	Burnley	H	Second Division	1-1

1954   Ian Moores born in Newcastle-under-Lyme. Ian began his career with Stoke City and had scored 14 goals in 50 League appearances when Spurs swooped to sign him for £75,000 in August 1976. Despite a good start the team were relegated at the end of his first season, although he was part of the side that won promotion straight back into the First Division. Whilst Colin Lee gained most of the plaudits after scoring four goals on his debut against Bristol Rovers that season, Ian also scored three in the same game. In October 1978 he was sold to Orient for £55,000, remaining at Brisbane Road for four years when he joined Bolton. He later played in Cyprus and in September 1997 was admitted to hospital. He died on 12th January 1998.

1957	Nottingham Forest	H	First Division	3-4
1963	Sheffield United	A	First Division	3-3
1964	Fulham	H	First Division	3-0
1968	Leicester City	H	First Division	3-2
1974	Burnley	H	First Division	2-3

Spurs' goals were scored by John Pratt and Mike England. Unfortunately, both players also put through their own nets in the first half to set Burnley up for a 3-2 win.

1983	Lincoln City	H	Milk Cup 2nd Round 1st Leg	3-1
1985	West Bromwich Albion	A	First Division	1-1
1991	Everton	A	First Division	1-3

OCTOBER 6TH

| 1883 | Brownlow Marshes | H | Friendly | 9-0 |

The earliest known match played by Spurs for which a newspaper report exists – played on the Marshes against Brownlow Rovers, the match, reported in the *Tottenham Herald* 'resulted in an easy victory for the home team by 9 goals to nil. Messrs Harston, Casey, Jull and Buckle did good service for Hotspur.' This report is something of a mystery, for the team line-up (Leaman, Tyrell, Dexter, Casey, Lovis, Lomas, Cottrell, Watson, Fisher, Harston and Buckle) obviously makes no mention of Jack Jull!

1894	3rd Grenadier Guards	H	Friendly	1-1
1900	Watford	A	Southern League	1-2
1902	Brentford	A	London League	5-1
1906	Crystal Palace	H	Southern League	3-0
1917	Fulham	H-Highbury		
			London Combination	1-0
1919	Crystal Palace	A	London FA Charity Cup 2nd Round	2-3
1921	Corinthians	H	Friendly	2-1

1923	Notts County	A	First Division	0-0
1928	Hull City	H	Second Division	4-1
1934	Leicester City	H	First Division	2-2
1945	Birmingham City	A	Football League South	0-8
1951	Manchester City	H	First Division	1-2
1956	Chelsea	A	First Division	4-2
1962	Arsenal	H	First Division	4-4
1965	Sunderland	H	First Division	3-0
1971	Torquay United	A	League Cup 3rd Round	4-1
1973	Ipswich Town	A	First Division	0-0
1979	Crystal Palace	A	First Division	1-1
1982	Brighton & Hove Albion	H	Milk Cup 2nd Round 1st Leg	1-1

Spurs had been runners-up in the competition the previous season and there were high hopes that they might go one better this season. They began with a stuttering performance against Brighton, with Garry Brookes getting Spurs' goal from the penalty spot.

1984	Southampton	A	First Division	0-1
1990	Queens Park Rangers	A	First Division	0-0
1993	Burnley	H	Coca-Cola Cup 2nd Round 2nd Leg	3-1

OCTOBER 7TH

1893	City Ramblers	H	Friendly	2-0
1897	3rd Grenadier Guards	H	Friendly	4-0
1899	Brighton United	H	Southern League	6-1

Brighton United resigned from the Southern League on March 10th 1900 and the results of both this and the return fixture on February 10th were expunged from the records. This was also the match that Ted Hughes made his debut for Spurs, having joined the club from Everton. Born in Ruabon, Wales in 1876 he had signed with Everton in 1896 but could not gain an automatic slot in the Everton first team, even though he was capped for Wales in 1899. Transferred to Spurs Ted soon established himself as a regular half-back and replaced injured captain James McNaught in the FA Cup tie against Preston in 1901 so effectively that McNaught couldn't get back into the team and Hughes ended up the season with a winners' medal. He left Spurs in 1908 and joined Clyde although one month later he returned south to become a publican, emigrating to the USA at the end of the First World War.

1901	Millwall Athletic	H	Western League	3-1
1905	Queens Park Rangers	H	Southern League	2-1
1907	West Ham United	H	Western League	2-1

This game was also staged as a benefit match for John Watson, with a crowd of 5,000 in attendance, one of the largest known to have attended a Western League match this season.

1911	Bury	H	First Division	2-1
1916	Watford	A	London Combination	2-0
1922	Aston Villa	A	First Division	0-2
1933	Sunderland	H	First Division	3-1
1939	West Ham United	H	Friendly	0-2
1944	Crystal Palace	A	Football League South	3-1
1946	Newport County	H	Second Division	3-1
1950	Burnley	H	First Division	1-0
1967	Sheffield United	H	First Division	1-1
1969	Liverpool	A	First Division	0-0
1970	Sheffield United	H	League Cup 3rd Round	2-1
1972	Stoke City	H	First Division	4-3
1978	West Bromwich Albion	A	First Division	1-0
1981	Manchester United	H	League Cup 2nd Round 1st Leg	1-0
1987	Torquay United	H	Littlewoods Cup 2nd Round 2nd Leg	3-0

Spurs overcame a 1-0 deficit from the first leg to win 3-1 on aggregate thanks to goals from Nico Claesen (two) and an own goal from Cole.

1992	Brentford	A	Coca-Cola Cup 2nd Round 2nd Leg	4-2

OCTOBER 8TH

1887	Hendon	A	London Senior Cup 1st Round	0-6

This was Spurs' first match in the London Senior Cup although they failed to win a game until 1890 when they beat Queens Park Rangers in a replay.

1892	2nd Coldstream Guards	H	Friendly	6-0
1896	Royal Scots Greys	H	Friendly	5-0

1898	Chatham	H	Southern League	2-0
1900	Notts County	H	Friendly	1-1
1904	Bristol Rovers	A	Southern League	1-3
1906	West Ham United	A	Western League	0-5
1910	Preston North End	H	First Division	1-1
1921	Manchester United	H	First Division	2-2
1923	Clapton Orient	H	London Professional Football Charity Fund	1-3
1927	Cardiff City	A	First Division	1-2

1931   Bill Brown born in Arbroath. After playing for a number of junior clubs he was signed by Dundee in 1949 helping them to win the Scottish League Cup in 1952, and broke into the Scottish B side, finally earning his first full cap in 1958. A year later, in July 1959, Bill Nicholson signed him for Spurs for a fee of £16,500 as replacement for Ted Ditchburn and he soon established himself as the safe custodian of the Spurs goal. A member of the team that won the double in 1961, the FA Cup in 1962 and the European Cup-Winners' Cup in 1963, his position at Spurs didn't come under serious threat until the emergence of Pat Jennings. He was sold to Northampton Town in October 1966 and later moved to Canada to play for Toronto Falcon. When his career ended he went into the real estate business in Canada. Whilst with Spurs he won 24 caps, finishing his career with 28 full appearances for his country.

1932	Preston North End	A	Second Division	6-2
1938	Luton Town	A	Second Division	0-0
1949	Southampton	A	Second Division	1-1
1955	Bolton Wanderers	H	First Division	0-3

1958   With Jimmy Anderson having resigned owing to ill-health, the Spurs board interviewed first-team coach Bill Nicholson and offered him the job of manager of the club. It was later revealed that Bill had no thoughts of becoming a manager and would have been happier remaining as coach, but realising that if the club brought in a manager from outside the new man might want his own backroom staff around him, had decided to accept the offer. The announcement of his appointment was made shortly before the next home match, against Everton on October 11th.

1966	Manchester City	A	First Division	2-1
1973	Queens Park Rangers	A	League Cup 2nd Round	0-1
1975	Crewe Alexandra	A	League Cup 3rd Round	2-0
1977	Oldham Athletic	H	Second Division	5-1
1983	Vale Recreation	Guernsey	Friendly	7-2
1986	Barnsley	H	Littlewoods Cup 2nd Round 2nd Leg	5-3
1988	Charlton Athletic	A	First Division	2-2
1994	Queens Park Rangers	H	FA Premier League	1-1

OCTOBER 9TH

1886	Woodford Bridge	H	Friendly	2-0
1897	Gravesend United	H	Southern League	2-0
1899	Reading	A	Southern District Combination	1-2
1909	Bury	H	First Division	1-0
1915	Queens Park Rangers	A	London Combination [1st competition]	4-0
1920	Chelsea	H	First Division	5-0

This match was also staged as a joint benefit for Bert Bliss, Jimmy Cantrell and Jimmy Dimmock. A crowd of 47,000 saw Bliss help himself to a hat-trick, with the other goals coming from Charlie Wilson and Dimmock.

1926	Birmingham	H	First Division	6-1
1929	Stoke City	H	Second Division	3-1
1937	Manchester City	H	Second Division	0-1
1943	Brighton & Hove Albion	H	Football League South	2-0
1948	Cardiff City	A	Second Division	1-0
1954	West Bromwich Albion	H	First Division	3-1
1961	Bolton Wanderers	A	First Division	2-1
1965	Everton	A	First Division	1-3
1968	Manchester United	H	First Division	2-2
1971	Derby County	A	First Division	2-2
1976	Arsenal	A	Friendly	2-1

This match was a testimonial for Peter Simpson and a crowd of 19,456 were present at Highbury to see Spurs win thanks to goals from Alfie Conn and John Duncan, with Malcolm Macdonald scoring for Arsenal.

1978	Saudi Arabian XI	Jeddah	Friendly	4-2

1982	Coventry City	H	First Division	4-0
1984	Halifax Town	H	Milk Cup 2nd Round 2nd Leg	4-0
1990	Hartlepool United	A	Rumbelows Cup 2nd Round 2nd Leg	2-1

Paul Gascoigne had been the star of the show in the first leg, scoring four of Spurs' five goals. He was rested from the starting line up in the second leg, although his warm up routines along the touchline were enjoyed by both the home and away fans, with several of the former joining in with the exercises! Two goals from Paul Stewart won the game for the visitors, with Gascoigne making an appearance in the second half when he replaced John Moncur.

| 1991 | Swansea City | H | Rumbelows Cup 2nd Round 2nd Leg | 5-1 |

OCTOBER 10TH

1882   John Chaplin born in Dundee. John joined Spurs in May 1905 and made his debut in the Western League match against Plymouth in October the same year, finally making the Southern League side in April 1906. The following season he managed to displace John Watson as first choice right full-back. When Spurs joined the Football League in 1908 John surprised everyone by returning to Dundee, subsequently returning to England and signing for Manchester City in 1910, but after only 17 League appearances for the Hyde Road club switched to management and coaching. He took over from Cecil Potter at Huddersfield just as they were completing their hat-trick of League titles, and although they never scaled such heights again, John did guide them to the 1928 FA Cup final. He stepped down as manager in 1929 but remained on the coaching staff until 1939. He died in Doncaster on 15th April 1952.

1885	Grange Park	A	Friendly	0-3
1891	Caledonian Athletic	H	London Senior Cup 1st Round	4-3
1896	Chatham	H	Southern League	3-1
1898	Southampton	H	United League	4-0
1903	Wellingborough	H	Southern League	1-0
1904	Woolwich Arsenal	A	Southern Charity Cup 1st Round	3-1
1908	Blackpool	A	Second Division	1-1
1910	Chelsea	H	London FA Charity Cup 2nd Round	3-0
1914	Middlesbrough	H	First Division	3-3
1925	Bury	A	First Division	0-3
1931	Burnley	H	Second Division	1-1
1936	Burnley	A	Second Division	1-3
1942	Millwall	H	Football League South	2-1
1951	Copenhagen Combined XI	H	Friendly	2-1
1953	Arsenal	H	First Division	1-4

Spurs' biggest crowd of the season, 69,821, saw Arsenal race into a four goal lead by half-time and effectively end the game as a contest. George Robb's second-half strike was little more than a consolation effort, but Spurs were to gain their revenge in the return match in February.

1959	Wolverhampton Wanderers	H	First Division	5-1
1960	Manchester City	H	First Division	1-1
1964	Arsenal	H	First Division	3-1
1966	Dundee	A	Friendly	3-2
1970	Liverpool	H	First Division	1-0
1979	Norwich City	H	First Division	3-2
1981	Stoke City	H	First Division	2-0
1987	Norwich City	A	First Division	1-2

OCTOBER 11TH

1884	Abbey	H	Friendly	1-0
1890	Edmonton	A	Friendly	4-6
1897	Luton Town	A	United League	0-5

1898   Jimmy Skinner born in Beckenham. Jimmy was signed by Spurs in 1919 as reserve cover for half-backs Bert Smith and Arthur Grimsdell and as such was unable to break into the side on a regular basis until Arthur was out with a broken leg. Once Arthur was fit, however, Jimmy was sent back into the reserves. During the 1926-27 season he himself suffered a ligament injury and was expected to turn up at the club on a regular basis for treatment. Unfortunately, Jimmy did not always do this and was twice suspended by the club for 14-day spells. When this happened a third time in March 1927 the club cancelled his contract. Jimmy immediately appealed to the Football League and a hearing was set, but as Jimmy then failed to turn up to the hearing, the decision was upheld. He later became a greengrocer, ran a building company and a fruit farm and died in September 1984.

| 1902 | Watford | A | Southern League | 2-1 |

1905	Reading	A	Western League	0-0
1909	Croydon City	H	London FA Charity Cup	7-1
1913	Bradford City	H	First Division	0-0
1919	Clapton Orient	H	Second Division	2-1
1920	Barking	A	London FA Charity Cup 1st Round	4-1
1924	Burnley	H	First Division	1-1
1930	Nottingham Forest	H	Second Division	2-1
1941	Brighton & Hove Albion	H	London War League	1-2
1947	Barnsley	A	Second Division	1-2
1952	Derby County	A	First Division	0-0
1954	Queens Park Rangers	A	Friendly	1-2
1958	Everton	H	First Division	10-4

Shortly before the game the Spurs board announced the official appointment of Bill Nicholson as manager of the club, replacing the recently departed Jimmy Anderson. A former player at the club, Nicholson had joined the groundstaff when his playing career had finished, becoming first-team coach in 1955 following Anderson's elevation to manager in place of Arthur Rowe. His promotion to manager, therefore, enabled the club to maintain continuity. Although Bill Nicholson was not offered a contract (and indeed did not work with a contract for his entire 16 years in charge), he became the most successful manager in Spurs history and one of the finest in the history of the English game, guiding Spurs to numerous honours – the League and FA Cup double, two further FA Cups, two League Cups, the European Cup-Winners' Cup and the UEFA Cup. His managerial career got off to a flying start too, with a 10-4 win over Everton thanks to goals from Bobby Smith (four), Alfie Stokes (two), John Ryden, Terry Medwin, Tommy Harmer and George Robb.

1959	Paul Miller born in Stepney, London. Signed by Spurs as an apprentice in April 1976, Paul was upgraded to the professional ranks in May 1977 and subsequently loaned to Skeid of Oslo between March and October 1978. Upon his return he slowly established himself as a regular feature of the Spurs defence and won FA Cup medals in 1981 and 1982, as well as a UEFA Cup medal in 1984. Indeed, it was his headed goal in the first leg that set Spurs on the road to victory. Although Paul had managed to see off virtually every challenger to his position, the arrival of David Pleat as manager and the subsequent purchase of Richard Gough indicated that Paul's Spurs career was at an end and he was sold to Charlton in February 1987. Although he later played for Watford, AFC Bournemouth, Brentford and Swansea City his time at Spurs represented the pinnacle of his career.
1963	Ronnie Rosenthal born in Haifa, Israel. Ronnie's spell at White Hart Lane will forever be remembered for one game; in February 1995 he scored a hat-trick in the 6-2 FA Cup replay win over Southampton, rescuing a game that Southampton had seemingly won when they powered into a 2-0 lead, only for Ronnie single-handedly to undo all their hard work. Ronnie had first been introduced to English football by Liverpool, joining them in 1991 from Standard Liege. Although he was a renowned goalscorer he struggled to retain a regular place in the Liverpool side and was subsequently sold to Spurs for £250,000 in 1994. His performance against Southampton aside, Ronnie found the going at Spurs just as difficult and at the end of the 1996-97 season he was released on a free transfer, subsequently signing for Watford.

1969	Wolverhampton Wanderers	H	First Division	0-1
1972	Middlesbrough	H	League Cup 3rd Round Replay	0-0 [aet]
1975	Aston Villa	A	First Division	1-1
1980	Middlesbrough	H	First Division	3-2
1986	Liverpool	A	First Division	1-0
1988	Notts County	H	Littlewoods Cup 2nd Round 2nd Leg	2-1
1993	Brann	A	Friendly	0-2

OCTOBER 12TH

1889	Iona	H	Friendly	10-0
1895	Luton Town	A	FA Cup 1st Qualifying Round	2-1
1901	New Brompton	H	Southern League	3-1
1907	Luton Town	A	Southern League	1-3
1912	Notts County	H	First Division	1-3

The game was abandoned after 80 minutes owing to fog and replayed the following month. Spurs only goal was netted by centre-half Charlie Rance and was the only Football League goal he scored for the club. Of course, his strike was wiped off the records when the game was abandoned! On the same day Bill Whatley was born in Ebbw Vale. Bill signed professional forms with Spurs in March 1932 having been groomed through the club's nursery sides. He made his debut for the club when replacing the injured Cecil Poynton and effectively made the position his until war broke out, collecting his first cap for Wales in 1938. At the start of the 1939-40 season, which was subsequently abandoned after only three games, Bill Nicholson had taken Bill's place in the side, although Bill Whatley remained on Spurs' books until an ankle injury forced his retirement in 1947. He then became a scout for the club, being responsible for the discovery of Harry Clarke and Mel Hopkins among others until being released in April 1954. He died in London in December 1974.

1918	Arsenal	A	London Combination	0-3
1929	Oldham Athletic	A	Second Division	0-2
1935	Burnley	H	Second Division	5-1
1939	Arsenal	H	Football League South	2-3
1940	Arsenal	H	Football League South	2-3

After 60 minutes and with Arsenal leading 3-2, an air raid warning was announced and the match was abandoned although the score was allowed to stand.

1946	Barnsley	A	Second Division	3-1
1955	FC Vasas	H	Friendly	1-2
1957	Arsenal	H	First Division	3-1
1963				

Bobby Mimms born in York. After failing to make the grade at Halifax Town Bobby signed for Rotherham and soon came to the attention of bigger clubs, subsequently joining Everton in June 1985. The continued good form of Neville Southall restricted Bobby's chances of first-team football and he spent spells on loan to numerous clubs, finally signing for Spurs in February 1988 for £375,000. Although he arrived at White Hart Lane and was quickly first choice, a series of hesitant performances prompted a further splash into the transfer market and the arrival of Erik Thorstvedt. Bobby was subsequently sold to Blackburn Rovers in 1990 for a fee of £250,000.

1968	Manchester City	A	First Division	0-4
1974	Chelsea	A	First Division	0-1
1976	Napredac Krusevac	A	Friendly	0-4
1981	Luton Town	A	Paul Price Testimonial	2-2

Kenilworth Road provided the venue for Paul Price's testimonial with Spurs' goals being scored by Glenn Hoddle and Garth Crooks.

| 1984 | Liverpool | H | First Division | 1-0 |
| 1996 | Aston Villa | H | FA Premier League | 1-0 |

OCTOBER 13TH

| 1883 | Evelyn | H | Friendly | 6-1 |

In addition to the six goals that were credited, Spurs also scored one other goal that was disputed and therefore not included in the final score.

| 1888 | Old Etonians | H | London Senior Cup | 2-8 |

Spurs were drawn at home to Old Etonians in the 1st round of the London Senior Cup. Six years previously, just as Spurs were coming into being, their opponents were winning the FA Cup for the second time in their history in their sixth final. Today, the two sides met at Northumberland Park. Although Old Etonians won quite convincingly by 8-2 (although Spurs held them to 2-3 at the half-time interval) the match itself was proof that Spurs were undoubtedly on the up – who would have thought six years previously that they would one day play against a team that had won the FA Cup?

| 1894 | West Herts | H | FA Cup 1st Qualifying Round | 3-2 |

Spurs made their debut in the trophy with which they are indelibly linked, the FA Cup. They were drawn at home to West Herts (forerunners to the present-day Watford FC) in the 1st qualifying round and won 3-2 with goals from Hunter and Goodall (two). The line-up for this game was Monk, Jull, Welham, Shepherd, Briggs, Julian, Cubberly, Goodall, Hunter, Eccles and Payne. Spurs got as far as the fourth qualifying round before being put out by Luton Town 0-4 in a replay.

1900	Corinthians	H	Friendly	2-2
1902	Bristol Rovers	H	Western League	0-1
1906	Brentford	A	Southern League	2-2
1917	Queens Park Rangers	A	London Combination	3-2
1923	Notts County	H	First Division	1-3
1928	Bradford Park Avenue	A	Second Division	1-4
1930	Charlton Athletic	H	London FA Charity Cup 1st Round	6-0
1934	Sunderland	A	First Division	2-1
1945	Birmingham City	H	Football League South	0-1
1951	Derby County	A	First Division	2-4
1956	Cardiff City	H	First Division	5-0
1962	West Bromwich Albion	A	First Division	2-1
1973	Arsenal	H	First Division	2-0
1979	Derby County	H	First Division	1-0
1990	Arsenal	A	Friendly	5-2

This match was a testimonial for Graham Rix and attracted a crowd of 14,806 to Highbury. A hat-trick from Paul Stewart and single strikes from Vinny Samways and Paul Walsh won the game for Spurs.

OCTOBER 14TH

1893	London Welsh	H	Friendly	1-0

1896   Frank Osborne born in Wynberg, South Africa. When his family returned home to England (Frank's father had been a colonel in the Royal Army Medical Corps serving in South Africa) Frank signed for Bromley as an amateur before joining the professional ranks with Fulham in 1921. He was transferred to Spurs in January 1924, his £1,500 fee reflecting the fact he was already an England international player. Able to play almost anywhere in the Spurs forward line he remained at White Hart Lane until June 1931 when he was sold to Southampton for £450. He retired as a player in 1933 and was appointed a director at Fulham in 1935. In September 1948 he resigned from the board in order to take over as manager, a position he held until 1964 when he retired. He died in Epsom on 8th March 1988.

1899	Bedminster	A	Southern League	1-2
1901	West Ham United	H	Western League	2-1
1903	Reading	A	Western League	2-0
1905	Bristol Rovers	A	Southern League	2-0
1907	Reading	H	Western League	0-2
1911	Middlesbrough	A	First Division	0-2
1912	Fulham	A	London Professional Football Charity Fund	0-1
1913	Fulham	A	London FA Charity Cup 2nd Round	2-0
1916	Clapton Orient	H-Homerton		
			London Combination	4-2
1922	Aston Villa	H	First Division	1-2
1929	Clapton Orient	A	London FA Charity Cup 1st Round	1-2
1933	Portsmouth	A	First Division	1-0
1944	Chelsea	H	Football League South	1-5
1950	Chelsea	A	First Division	2-0
1957	Hibernian	A	Friendly	2-5
1958	Bela Vista	H	Friendly	3-1

Brazilian club Bela Vista's last match on their short tour drew a crowd of 15,576 to White Hart Lane. Alfie Stokes scored twice and George Robb once to win the game.

1961	Manchester City	H	First Division	2-0
1967	Coventry City	A	First Division	3-2

This was Spurs' first League meeting at Highfield Road since 1949-50 and two goals from Jimmy Greaves and one from Frank Saul were enough to give them the victory.

1972	Norwich City	A	First Division	1-2
1978	Birmingham City	H	First Division	1-0
1984	Malta National XI	A	Friendly	1-0
1985	Maidstone United	A	Friendly	2-1

This match was a testimonial for Brian Thompson and Spurs' goals were scored by Mark Falco and Tony Galvin.

1989	Charlton Athletic	A	First Division	3-1
1995	Nottingham Forest	H	FA Premier League	0-1

OCTOBER 15TH

1892	Old St Stephen's	A	Southern Alliance	3-0
1898	Bristol City	A	United League	1-0
1900	Millwall Athletic	H	James McNaught & Tom Smith Benefit	2-1
1904	Northampton Town	H	Southern League	0-1
1910	Notts County	A	First Division	0-1
1914	Chelsea	A	Friendly	1-1
1921	Manchester United	A	First Division	1-2
1927	Blackburn Rovers	H	First Division	1-1
1928	London Caledonians	H	London FA Charity Cup 1st Round	2-1
1932	Burnley	H	Second Division	4-1
1938	Fulham	H	Second Division	1-0
1949	Coventry City	H	Second Division	3-1
1955	Chelsea	A	First Division	0-2
1956	Heart of Midlothian	A	Anglo-Scottish Floodlit Tournament	2-3

1960	Nottingham Forest	A	First Division	4-0
1963	Arsenal	A	First Division	4-4

International calls had meant switching the North London clash from Saturday to Tuesday, but the wait proved worthwhile for the 67,857 crowd who were treated to a classic encounter. The gates were locked almost an hour before kick off and right from the off Spurs went on the attack, taking the lead after three minutes through Jimmy Greaves. Bobby Smith added to the tally on 20 minutes before Arsenal had got into their stride, but a penalty on the half-hour gave them a brief glimmer of hope. Dave Mackay then restored Spurs two goal advantage, although a fourth goal was disallowed for offside. George Eastham scored his second of the game to reduce the deficit again and Bobby Smith got his second of the day to leave the half-time score 4-2 in Spurs favour. Spurs held on to the lead until the final five minutes of the match, Joe Baker pulling Arsenal within one goal and then, with barely 20 seconds left, Geoff Strong equalised.

1966	Blackpool	H	First Division	1-3
1977	Charlton Athletic	A	Second Division	1-4
1983	Wolverhampton Wanderers	A	First Division	3-2
1994	Leeds United	A	FA Premier League	1-1
1997	Derby County	H	Coca-Cola Cup 3rd Round	1-2

OCTOBER 16TH

1886	Upton Park	A	London Association Cup 1st Round	0-6

1895 Bob Brown born in Southampton. Signed by Spurs in 1919 the full-back broke into the first team in October 1919 and remained there for the rest of the season, helping the team to the Second Division title. Loss of form and a number of injuries restricted his appearances thereafter, but he did not leave until transfer listed in April 1925. Although he received a number of offers from other clubs he chose to retire from playing and opened a butcher's shop in Southampton. He later became a publican on the Isle of Wight, where he died in 1980.

1897	Millwall Athletic	A	United League	1-0
1899	Millwall Athletic	H	Southern District Combination	1-2
1901	Rest of Southern League	H	Friendly	2-0
1905	Fulham	H	Western League	1-0
1909	Middlesbrough	H	First Division	1-3
1915	Fulham	H	London Combination [1st competition]	3-1
1920	Chelsea	A	First Division	4-0
1922	Llanelly	A	Friendly	1-2
1926	Sheffield United	H	First Division	3-1
1937	Fulham	A	Second Division	1-3
1943	Reading	A	Football League South	3-2
1948	Queens Park Rangers	H	Second Division	1-0
1954	Newcastle United	A	First Division	4-4
1965	Manchester United	H	First Division	5-1

The two League meetings between Spurs and Manchester United in 1965-66 have since entered folklore, not least because they both ended with a 5-1 win for the home side. Spurs' win at White Hart Lane saw goals from Neil Johnson, Eddie Clayton, Alan Gilzean, Jimmy Greaves and Jimmy Robertson, with Jimmy Greaves' effort the pick of the bunch.

1968	Peterborough United	H	League Cup 4th Round	1-0
1971	Wolverhampton Wanderers	H	First Division	4-1
1974	Carlisle United	H	First Division	1-1
1976	Derby County	A	First Division	2-8

Spurs' record League defeat is usually regarded as the 7-0 reverse at Anfield in 1978, but it could be argued that this 2-8 defeat at the Baseball Ground represents Spurs heaviest defeat. At half-time it seemed as though Spurs were still in the game; although Derby had taken a 2-0 lead Steve Perryman had reduced the deficit to 2-1 and Keith Osgood scored a penalty on 40 minutes to bring Spurs back into contention at 3-2. It was Derby's fourth goal, scored on the hour, that effectively finished Spurs, and a further four goals rattled past a shell-shocked defence.

1978	Wolverhampton Wanderers	A	Friendly	1-2

This was a testimonial match for John McAlle and Spurs' goal was scored by Chris Jones.

1982	Norwich City	A	First Division	0-0
1993	Manchester United	A	FA Premier League	1-2

OCTOBER 17TH

1885	St Albans	H	London Association Cup 1st Round	5-2

Spurs played their first competitive match (all previous games having been friendlies) with a visit from St Albans (a London-based business house) in the 1st round of the London Association Cup. The line-up on this momentous day included six of the club's founder members and was Bumberry, Jull, Tyrell, Bull, Lovis, Casey, Buckle, Harston, Amos and Cottrell. Spurs won the match, although the names of the scorers were not recorded.

| 1896 | Gravesend | H | Southern League | 4-0 |
| 1898 | New Brompton | H | Thames & Medway League | 2-1 |

Long before testimonials became the norm (which at Spurs was later than almost anywhere else), it was customary for clubs to give the proceeds from the gate to a particular player for his benefit. This match was therefore John 'Tiny' Joyce's benefit match with a crowd of 6,000 attending.

1903	Bristol Rovers	A	Southern League	0-1
1908	Chesterfield	H	Second Division	4-0
1914	Sheffield United	A	First Division	1-1
1921	London Caledonians	H	London FA Charity Cup 1st Round	5-0
1925	Manchester United	A	First Division	0-0
1927	Fulham	A	London FA Charity Cup 1st Round	2-6
1931	Notts County	A	Second Division	1-3
1936	Southampton	H	Second Division	4-0
1942	Reading	A	Football League South	6-2
1953	Cardiff City	A	First Division	0-1
1959	Sheffield Wednesday	A	First Division	1-2
1964	Leeds United	A	First Division	1-3
1970	West Ham United	A	First Division	2-2
1972	Feyenoord	H	Jimmy Greaves Testimonial	2-1

For many years it was the policy of the club not to grant testimonial matches to players, although they had frequently provided the opposition to other clubs'. That policy was finally rescinded in 1972, with the popular striker Jimmy Greaves being the first such recipient. Jimmy had left Spurs in 1970 for West Ham, although he had retired at the end of the 1970-71 season whilst still only 31 years old. That he had retired too soon was amply demonstrated in his own testimonial, for he scored a goal reminiscent of his heyday, prompting many to believe he might be tempted back into the game he had done much to enrich. Eventually he was, but it was non-League supporters who reaped the benefit. Spurs' other goal against Feyenoord was scored by Ray Evans, with a full house of 45,799 packed into White Hart Lane.

| 1981 | Sunderland | A | First Division | 2-0 |
| 1992 | Middlesbrough | H | FA Premier League | 2-2 |

OCTOBER 18TH

1884	Woodgrange	H	Friendly	4-5
1890	Luton Town	A	Friendly	1-4
1902	Brentford	H	Southern League	3-1
1913	Burnley	A	First Division	1-3
1919	Clapton Orient	A	Second Division	4-0
1924	Leeds United	A	First Division	0-1
1930	Bury	H	Second Division	3-1
1941	Brentford	A	London War League	4-1
1947	Plymouth Argyle	H	Second Division	2-0
1952	Blackpool	H	First Division	4-0
1954	Sportklub Wacker	H	Friendly	1-2

The visit of Austrian club Sportklub Wacker drew 22,303 to White Hart Lane, despite there being severe transport difficulties on the day of the game. Sportklub took a quick two goal lead early on in the second half before Tommy Harmer got Spurs' only goal of the game.

1958	Leicester City	A	First Division	4-3
1969	Newcastle United	H	First Division	2-1
1975	Manchester City	H	First Division	2-2
1980	Aston Villa	A	First Division	0-3
1986	Sheffield Wednesday	H	First Division	1-1
1987	Arsenal	H	First Division	1-2
1988	Home Farm	A	Friendly	4-0
1989	Arsenal	H	First Division	2-1

This was Spurs' first victory over Arsenal since 1985 and was achieved thanks to two set pieces, both following fouls by Tony Adams. The first free-kick was floated into the Arsenal area and only partly cleared as far as Vinny Samways, who buried a shot past John Lukic. Three minutes later came the second goal, with Paul Walsh on hand to put a glancing header past the Arsenal keeper. Spurs retained their advantage until the 53rd minute when Michael Thomas scored, but the better chances in the remaining half hour fell to Spurs, with Gary Lineker seeing a number of efforts saved.

OCTOBER 19TH

1889	Edmonton	A	Friendly	2-3
1895	Ilford	A	Friendly	2-0
1901	Northampton Town	A	Southern League	1-3
1903	New Brompton	H	South Eastern League	4-2

This league was normally competed for by the reserve team, but on this occasion (and the match against Brighton & Hove Albion on November 28th) the full first team turned out.

1904	Plymouth Argyle	A	Western League	0-5
1907	Brighton & Hove Albion	H	Southern League	1-1
1912	Manchester United	A	First Division	0-2
1914	Crystal Palace	A	London FA Charity Cup 2nd Round	1-3
1918	Crystal Palace	H-Highbury		
			London Combination	2-0
1929	Wolverhampton Wanderers	A	Second Division	0-3
1935	Bradford Park Avenue	H	Second Division	4-0
1939	Charlton Athletic	A	Football League South	0-4
1940	Charlton Athletic	A	Football League South	0-4
1946	West Ham United	A	Second Division	2-2
1953	Millwall	A	Friendly	2-0
1957	Bolton Wanderers	A	First Division	2-3
1963	Leicester City	H	First Division	1-1
1968	Liverpool	H	First Division	2-1
1974	Arsenal	H	First Division	2-0
1983	Feyenoord	H	UEFA Cup 2nd Round 1st Leg	4-2

Spurs and Feyenoord met in European competition for the third time with the previous encounters delicately balanced – one win each and two draws, although Feyenoord's victory had come in the infamous second leg of the 1974 UEFA Cup final. If Spurs were once again little more than competent at League level, they were always capable of raising their game the higher the stakes went. The match pitted Glenn Hoddle against the ageing yet still equally graceful Johan Cruyff – Cruyff, over-confident he could shackle his opponent and Hoddle, eager to stamp his authority on the game regardless of who else was present on the pitch. Glenn Hoddle won the battle and ultimately set up victory in the war – at half-time Spurs led 4-0, all four goals coming as a result of moves orchestrated by Hoddle. The breakthrough came after just eight minutes; Hoddle setting Hughton free and his cross being easily converted by Archibald. Ten minutes later a cross from Hoddle was headed in by Tony Galvin for his first of the night. Five minutes on and Hoddle again bewildered Feyenoord, setting Falco free. Although his shot was parried to relative safety, Gary Mabbutt chased the seeming lost cause and turned the ball back along the line for Steve Archibald to have the simplest of tap-ins. Spurs' final goal came five minutes before half-time – a forty yard pass from Hoddle (surely his trademark) found Tony Galvin galloping in to put Spurs into an unassailable lead. The second half was never going to be quite the same, not least because Feyenoord decided Johann Cruyff was not the player to man mark Glenn Hoddle, and whilst Spurs were denied quite as much freedom and space they had enjoyed in the first half, it was Feyenoord who clawed themselves back into the tie with two goals, Cruyff reducing the deficit on the 70th minute and Neilsen with nine minutes left on the clock. Whilst much of the talk before and after the game had centred on the battle between the old master (Cruyff) and the new (Hoddle), there was one other player on the pitch who would have been more than an interested observer. In time, he would assume the mantle occupied by these two – Rudd Gullit, who began his career with Feyenoord.

1991	Manchester City	H	First Division	0-1
1994	Hartlepool United	A	Cyril Knowles Tribute	3-1

This match was staged by Hartlepool, where Cyril Knowles had been manager before having to retire owing to a brain tumour, with Spurs' goals being scored by Steve Sedgley, Jason Dozzell and David Howells.

1996	Middlesbrough	A	FA Premier League	3-0
1997	Sheffield Wednesday	H	FA Premier League	3-2

OCTOBER 20TH

1883	Grange Park	H	Friendly	1-3

Owing to the late arrival of the visitors, the game was halted after an hour's play with Spurs behind, Buckle having scored their only goal.

1888	Clapton	H	Friendly	2-5
1894	Old Harrovians	H	FA Amateur Cup 1st Qualifying Round	7-0

A week after making their debut appearance in the FA Cup Spurs returned to action in the FA Amateur Cup and trounced Old Harrovians.

1897	Reading	H	Friendly	2-1
1900	Queens Park Rangers	A	Southern League	1-2
1902	West Ham United	A	London League	0-0
1906	Millwall	H	Western League	1-0
1917	Clapton Orient	H-Homerton		
			London Combination	2-1
1923	Sunderland	A	First Division	0-1
1928	Grimsby Town	H	Second Division	2-1
1934	Arsenal	A	First Division	1-5
1945	Swansea Town	A	Football League South	2-4
1951	Aston Villa	H	First Division	2-0
1956	Arsenal	A	First Division	1-3
1971	FC Nantes	A	UEFA Cup 2nd Round 1st Leg	0-0

After the match Bill Nicholson was furious with his team, feeling they had under-estimated their opponents and should have won, saving most of his fury for Martin Chivers, who he felt had not applied himself. Chivers had a frustrating game, earning a booking as he tried to make things happen up front, but in truth the whole of the Spurs side performed below par on the day.

1973	Norwich City	A	First Division	1-1
1976	Birmingham City	H	First Division	1-0
1979	Leeds United	A	First Division	2-1
1982	Bayern Munich	H	European Cup-Winners' Cup 2nd Round 1st Leg	1-1

Five first-team regulars were missing from the Spurs line-up; Steve Perryman, Glenn Hoddle, Graham Roberts, Chris Hughton and Tony Galvin, with a number of reserve and fringe players being brought in to the side. Despite the under strength nature of the Spurs side, they performed admirably, with Garry Brooke hitting the underside of the bar and going close with a number of long range strikes, whilst Garth Crooks and Steve Archibald ensured the Bayern keeper was kept busy. Spurs' only goal came from a header by Steve Archibald, with two penalty appeals also turned down, and on 53 minutes Bayern got the equaliser with a Breitner shot after Gary O'Reilly had sliced a clearance.

1984	Manchester United	A	First Division	0-1
1985	Coventry City	A	First Division	3-2
1987	West Ham United	H	Tony Galvin Testimonial	2-2
1990	Sheffield United	H	First Division	4-0
1992	SS Lazio	H	Capital Cup 2nd Leg	0-2

OCTOBER 21ST

1893	Old St Mark's	H	London Senior Cup 1st Round	0-0

The match which became known as 'The Affair of Payne's Boots' and which unwittingly launched Spurs on the road to professionalism. Spurs were playing at home to Old St Mark's in the first round of the London Senior Cup. They had selected Ernie Payne in their line-up, who had for most of the season been on the books of Fulham, although had not been given a game by the team from the Half Moon (where Fulham played at that time) and was therefore grateful of a game with anyone. Payne returned to Fulham the morning of the game in order to collect his kit but found it had mysteriously disappeared (it is believed disgruntled Fulham officials hid them) and so hurried back to Northumberland Park to inform Spurs that he had no kit. As none of the spare boots Spurs had fitted him, Payne was given ten shillings by the club and told to go and buy a pair, which he did and then played in the 0-0 draw with St Mark's (under the assumed name of Burton). After the game the Fulham directors got to hear about the circumstances surrounding Payne's appearance and complained to the London FA accusing Spurs of poaching and professionalism.

1899	Bristol Rovers	H	Southern League	1-0

Spurs were leading 1-0 after 55 minutes when fog enshrouded the pitch and left the referee with little option but to take both sides off the field. When the fog showed no sign of lifting the match was abandoned.

1901	Bristol Rovers	H	Western League	4-1
1905	New Brompton	H	Southern League	6-0

This game was also staged as Sandy Tait's benefit match and a crowd of 15,000 attended the match. Goals from Joe Walton (two), Herbert Chapman (two), Peter Kyle and Alex Glen gave Spurs victory.

1911	Notts County	H	First Division	2-2
1912	Crystal Palace	H	London FA Charity Cup 2nd Round	2-0

Although Spurs won 2-0 a replay was later ordered after it was discovered that Jimmy Cantrell, who'd scored one of Spurs' goals, was unregistered. This match ended all square at 3-3, and in the second replay Palace won 4-1.

1916	Fulham	A	London Combination	1-2
1922	West Bromwich Albion	H	First Division	3-1
1933	Everton	A	First Division	1-1
1939	Southend United	A	Football League South Group A	2-1
1944	Luton Town	A	Football League South	9-1
1950	Stoke City	H	First Division	6-1
1959	Reading	A	Friendly	5-2

This was a joint testimonial for Reading players Campbell, Meeson and Reeves and Spurs' goals were scored by Johnny Brooks, Bobby Smith and Cliff Jones (three).

1961	Ipswich Town	A	First Division	2-3
1970	Motherwell	H	Texaco Cup 2nd Round 1st Leg	3-2
1972	Chelsea	H	First Division	0-1
1978	Derby County	A	First Division	2-2
1981	Dundalk	A	European Cup-Winners' Cup 2nd Round 1st Leg	1-1
1989	Sheffield Wednesday	H	First Division	3-0

OCTOBER 22ND

1892	Coldstream Guards	H	Friendly	3-2
1898	Millwall Athletic	A	Southern League	2-4
1900	Luton Town	H	Friendly	1-3
1904	Portsmouth	A	Western League	0-1
1906	West Ham United	H	Southern Charity Cup 1st Round	2-0
1910	Manchester United	H	First Division	2-2
1921	Liverpool	H	First Division	0-1
1923	Crystal Palace	A	London FA Charity Cup 1st Round	1-1
1925	Norwich City	Bury St Edmunds		
			Friendly	2-3
1927	Sunderland	H	First Division	3-1
1932	Southampton	H	Second Division	5-0
1938	Blackburn Rovers	A	Second Division	1-3
1949	Luton Town	A	Second Division	1-1
1955	Sunderland	H	First Division	2-3

1960   Mark Falco born in Hackney, London. One of Spurs' unsung heroes, Mark joined the club as an apprentice in 1977, being upgraded to full professional in July 1978. He made his League debut in 1979, scoring in the match against Bolton, but the subsequent arrival of Steve Archibald and Garth Crooks threatened to limit his opportunities for first-team football. Whenever called upon, however, Mark seldom let anyone down, and he scored a number of crucial goals on the way to the club lifting the 1984 UEFA Cup. He was sold to Watford for £350,000 in 1986 and later played for Glasgow Rangers, Queens Park Rangers and Millwall before injury called a halt to his career.

1975	Arsenal	H	Cyril Knowles Testimonial	2-2
1977	Bristol Rovers	H	Second Division	9-0

Having suffered a 4-1 reverse at Charlton the week previously, Spurs were in need of a good result against Bristol Rovers. They gave a debut to Colin Lee, recently arrived from Torquay United for £60,000. He scored four times in a remarkable match and managed to overshadow fellow strike partner Ian Moores, who got a hat-trick. Spurs' other goals were scored by Glenn Hoddle and Peter Taylor to give a final score of 9-0, the first time Spurs had scored as many as nine in a League match since 1962-63 when they beat Nottingham Forest 9-2.

1980	Manchester City	A	First Division	1-3
1983	Birmingham City	H	First Division	1-0
1988	Norwich City	A	First Division	1-3
1994	Manchester City	A	FA Premier League	2-5
1995	Everton	A	FA Premier League	1-1

OCTOBER 23RD

1897	Southampton	A	Southern League	1-4
1899	Queens Park Rangers	A	Southern District Combination	3-1
1905	Millwall	H	Western League	5-0
1907	Crystal Palace	A	Western League	0-2
1909	Preston North End	A	First Division	0-0

A Football League match involving Spurs was abandoned for the first time – after 50 minutes of the match the continuing rainfall left the referee with little option but to abandon the match with the score still at 0-0. When the match was replayed on November 22nd, Spurs lost 4-1; had the original match continued to its conclusion and the score remained at 0-0, Spurs might not have gone into the final week of the season so desperate for points to stave off threatened relegation.

1911	Fulham	H	London Professional Football Charity Fund	3-0

1912   Jack Hall born in Failsworth, Lancashire. Jack began his professional career with Manchester United in 1932 and was surprisingly persuaded to join Spurs in 1936, even though United had just won promotion to the First Division whilst Spurs languished in the Second! However he went straight into Spurs' first team and made 67 appearances for the club before the outbreak of the Second World War. At the end of the war he was not retained and went into non-League football.

1915	Clapton Orient	A	London Combination [1st competition]	0-0

On the same day Vic Buckingham was born in South London. After signing amateur forms with Spurs in 1931 he became a professional in 1935, making his League debut in November of that year. The Second World War effectively cut across the best years of his career, although he did make over 300 appearances for the first team and switched to coaching in 1949. He later managed Bradford Park Avenue, West Bromwich Albion, Ajax of Amsterdam, Sheffield Wednesday and Fulham as well as a number of clubs in Greece and Spain, including Barcelona.

1920	Burnley	H	First Division	1-2
1922	Arsenal	A	London FA Charity Cup 1st Round	2-3
1926	Derby County	A	First Division	1-4
1937	Plymouth Argyle	H	Second Division	3-2

1938   Alan Gilzean born in Coupar Angus, Perthshire. He began his professional career with Dundee in 1957 and by the time he joined Spurs was a member of the Scottish first team. Indeed, it was whilst playing for a Scottish XI in the John White benefit match that he first caught the eye, and a month later he was signed for £72,500. He went on to give Spurs almost ten years sterling service, linking exceptionally well with Jimmy Greaves and then Martin Chivers. Whilst at Spurs he helped the club to win FA Cup, League Cup and UEFA Cup honours, weighing in with many vital goals in that time. He finished his playing career in South Africa but remains a popular part of the folklore at White Hart Lane.

1943	Luton Town	A	Football League South	2-4
1948	Luton Town	A	Second Division	1-1
1954	Preston North End	H	First Division	3-1
1957	Swiss National XI	Basel	Friendly	5-4
1965	Newcastle United	A	First Division	0-0
1971	Nottingham Forest	H	First Division	6-1
1976	Coventry City	H	First Division	0-1
1982	Notts County	H	First Division	4-2

1987   Following newspaper allegations regarding his private life, Spurs' manager David Pleat resigned after a little over one year in charge. He joined Spurs from Luton and had a considerable impact on the club's fortunes, taking them to third in the League, the semi-finals of the Littlewoods Cup and final of the FA Cup, where they were beaten by Coventry City. The team had begun this season by setting a new record number of consecutive home wins and looked to be building on the near-success of last season. However, allegations made during the summer and repeated just recently made Pleat's position untenable and he offered his resignation as Spurs manager, which was accepted by the board.

1991	FC Porto	H	European Cup-Winners' Cup 2nd Round 1st Leg	3-1
1993	Swindon Town	H	FA Premier League	1-1
1996	Sunderland	H	Coca-Cola Cup 3rd Round	2-1

OCTOBER 24TH

1885	Westminster Rovers	H	Friendly	3-1
1891	Clapton	H	Friendly	1-2
1896	Royal Ordnance	A	Southern League	2-1

Later in the season Royal Ordnance resigned from the Southern League and this result was expunged from the records.

1903	Brighton & Hove Albion	H	Southern League	2-2
1904	West Ham United	H	Western League	0-1
1908	Glossop North End	A	Second Division	1-1
1914	Aston Villa	H	First Division	0-2

1921   Ted Ditchburn born in Gillingham. Although Ted joined Spurs in 1939 he lost seven years of League football to the Second World War, although by the time he left in 1959, he held the record for the most League appearances for Spurs, having made 419 if one abandoned match is taken into account. A safe and reliable goalkeeper he was the foundation upon which Spurs built their promotion and title winning sides of the early 1950s. Unfortunately England was served by a plethora of quality goalkeepers during the same period and Ted made only six appearances for the full team. Having seen off almost all competition at Spurs until 1958, a back injury forced his retirement from first class football in April 1959, although he did continue to play non-League football until 1965.

1931	Plymouth Argyle	H	Second Division	0-1
1936	Swansea Town	A	Second Division	1-2
1942	Portsmouth	A	Football League South	0-1
1953	Manchester City	H	First Division	3-0
1955	Plymouth Argyle	A	Friendly	0-0
1959	Nottingham Forest	H	First Division	2-1
1960	Army XI	H	Friendly	3-5
1962	Manchester United	H	First Division	6-2
1964	Chelsea	H	First Division	1-1
1970	Stoke City	H	First Division	3-0
1973	Aberdeen	A	UEFA Cup 2nd Round 1st Leg	1-1
1981	Brighton & Hove Albion	H	First Division	0-1
1984	Club Brugge KV	A	UEFA Cup 2nd Round 1st Leg	1-2

In the weeks leading up to the game Spurs had been concerned over the security arrangements in place for the match and eventually decided to ask their fans not to travel, cancelling all their own excursions. Although Spurs lost 2-1, Clive Allen scoring a goal that could prove vital if the tie required away goals, the main talking point after the game was the dismissal of Glenn Hoddle following his second booking. The offending card came as Brugge had been awarded a free-kick and Hoddle played the ball, the referee interpreting this as either dissent or an attempt to waste time. According to Hoddle it was neither, he simply hadn't heard the whistle above the noise of the crowd.

1987	Nottingham Forest	A	First Division	0-3

OCTOBER 25TH

1884	Grange Park	H	Friendly	4-0

The game was halted after only 60 minutes.

1890	Northumberland Fusiliers	H	Friendly	1-0
1902	Millwall Athletic	A	Southern League	0-2
1913	Blackburn Rovers	H	First Division	3-3
1923	Norwich City	A	Friendly	3-2
1924	Arsenal	A	First Division	0-1

The only goal of the game was credited to Jimmy Brain, making his debut for Arsenal, although he knew little about it; a fierce shot from Jock Rutherford hit Brain full in the face and deflected into the net whilst Brain lay unconscious!

1930	Everton	A	Second Division	2-4
1941	Crystal Palace	H	London War League	1-1
1947	Luton Town	A	Second Division	0-0
1952	Chelsea	A	First Division	1-2
1958	Leeds United	H	First Division	2-3

1962 Steve Hodge born in Nottingham. Steve began his career with Nottingham Forest, signing as a professional in 1980, and switched to Aston Villa in August 1985. A little over a year later he joined Spurs, costing the club £650,000 and scoring on his debut against West Ham on Boxing Day 1986. By August 1988 he was homesick and was sold to Nottingham Forest, later helping the club win the Littlewoods and Simod Cups and reach the FA Cup final against Spurs in 1991. The emergence of Roy Keane prompted a further move to Leeds United and he later played for QPR.

1967	Nottingham Forest	H	First Division	1-1
1969	Stoke City	A	First Division	1-1
1972	Olympiakos Pireus	H	UEFA Cup 2nd Round 1st Leg	4-0
1975	Leicester City	A	First Division	3-2
1980	Coventry City	H	First Division	4-1
1986	Queens Park Rangers	A	First Division	0-2
1988	Southampton	H	First Division	1-2
1989	Manchester United	A	Littlewoods Cup 3rd Round	3-0
1992	Wimbledon	A	FA Premier League	1-1
1995	Coventry City	A	Coca-Cola Cup 3rd Round	2-3
1997	Southampton	A	FA Premier League	2-3

1895	Royal Artillery	H	Friendly	1-2
1898	Dartford	A	Thames & Medway League	3-2
1901	Watford	H	Southern League	8-1

This remained Spurs' biggest ever win in the Southern League until 1904 when they recorded an 8-0 win over Wellingborough. Spurs' goals were scored by John Cameron (two), Sandy Brown (three), David Copeland (two) and John Kirwan.

1907	Portsmouth	A	Southern League	2-1
1912	Aston Villa	H	First Division	3-3
1918	Millwall	A	London Combination	2-0
1929	Bradford City	H	Second Division	1-1
1935	Leicester City	A	Second Division	1-4
1939	Portsmouth	H	Football League South	1-2
1940	Portsmouth	H	Football League South	1-2
1946	Sheffield Wednesday	H	Second Division	2-0
1957	Leeds United	H	First Division	2-0
1963	Everton	A	First Division	0-1
1966	Chelsea	A	First Division	0-3
1968	Ipswich Town	A	First Division	1-0
1974	Luton Town	A	First Division	1-1
1977	Coventry City	H	League Cup 3rd Round	2-3
1982	Brighton & Hove Albion	A	Milk Cup 2nd Round 2nd Leg	1-0
1983	Lincoln City	A	Milk Cup 2nd Round 2nd Leg	1-2
1985	Leicester City	H	First Division	1-3
1991	West Ham United	A	First Division	1-2
1993	Derby County	A	Coca-Cola Cup 3rd Round	1-0
1994	Notts County	A	Coca-Cola Cup 3rd Round	0-3

The match that effectively ended Ossie Ardiles' spell as manager of Spurs, for with the club still banned from the FA Cup this season, the Coca-Cola Cup represented the only possible route to glory in 1994-95. Ardiles' brave philosophy of attack and be damned was found out by a side that were languishing at the bottom of the First Division and had not won at home for six months. To make matters even worse on the night, Ilie Dumitrscu was sent off for a second bookable offence whilst Spurs were already two behind and there was no coming back in the game. Although Ardiles remained in charge for the next League match, less than a week after the cup exit he was called to Alan Sugar's house and given the sack.

1996	Chelsea	A	FA Premier League	1-1

1883	Leyton Rovers	H	Friendly	1-0
1894	Crouch End	A	Friendly	2-2
1900	West Ham United	H	Southern League	0-0
1906	Leyton	A	Southern League	1-1
1913	Crystal Palace	H	London Professional Football Charity Fund	1-2
1917	Crystal Palace	H-Highbury		
			London Combination	1-0
1919	Port Vale	A	Second Division	1-0
1923	Sunderland	H	First Division	1-1
1924	Fulham	H	London FA Charity Cup 1st Round	5-1
1928	Stoke City	A	Second Division	0-2

Cecil Poynton was sent off for an alleged foul on City's Williams, although the referee had to consult with a linesman before ordering Poynton off the field of play. It would be another 35 years before another Spurs player was sent off – Jimmy Greaves in a European Cup-Winners' Cup match against OFK Belgrade.

1930	Chelsea	A	London FA Charity Cup 2nd Round	2-1
1934	Portsmouth	H	First Division	4-1
1945	Swansea Town	H	Football League South	3-1
1951	Sunderland	A	First Division	1-0
1952	Gloucester City	A	Friendly	1-2
1956	Burnley	H	First Division	2-0
1957				

Glenn Hoddle born in Hayes, Middlesex. One of the most naturally gifted players of his generation, he signed with Spurs as a youngster after a recommendation from Martin Chivers. He made his

League debut in 1975 and was an established first-team player by the end of the following year. He made his England debut in 1979 against Bulgaria at Wembley and marked the occasion by scoring. He remained with Spurs until 1987, during which time he won two FA Cup winners' medals and 44 England caps, although it was felt by some that his work-rate was insufficient and he was not capped as often as his talent dictated. He joined AS Monaco in 1987 and won a League-championship medal in his first season in France but was then troubled by injuries. Upon returning to England in 1990 he trained with Chelsea but then accepted an offer to become player-manager at Swindon, guiding them into the Premier Division in 1993. He then left to hold a similar position with Chelsea and was subsequently appointed England manager in 1996.

| 1962 | Leyton Orient | A | First Division | 5-1 |

1968   Vinny Samways born in Bethnal Green, London. Signed by Spurs as an apprentice in April 1985 he was upgraded to the professional ranks in November, although he had to wait until May 1987 before making his League debut. The departure during that summer of Glenn Hoddle and injuries sustained by Johnny Metgod left much of the creative responsibility in midfield on Vinny's shoulders, but this talented man was not found wanting. Although he suffered a number of niggling injuries himself and had to contend with the arrival of Paul Gascoigne, Vinny still managed to claim a place in the side that won the FA Cup in 1991; indeed, once Paul Gascoigne had been carried off, Vinny performed heroics to ensure Spurs were at their creative best. In the summer of 1994 he announced he wanted to try his luck elsewhere and was subsequently transferred to Everton, although this move has not worked out and his is currently playing abroad on loan.

1971	Preston North End	H	League Cup 4th Round	1-1
1973	Newcastle United	A	First Division	0-2
1975	Millwall	A	Friendly	1-3
1979	Nottingham Forest	H	First Division	1-0
1984	Stoke City	H	First Division	4-0

1987   Spurs chairman Irving Scholar announced from Florida that he had successfully completed negotiations to make Terry Venables the new manager of Tottenham Hotspur. Venables was a player at White Hart Lane between 1966 and 1969 later moved into coaching and finally management, assuming control at Crystal Palace in 1976. He returned to Loftus Road in October then accepted an offer to take over as coach of Barcelona in Spain. In his first season they won the Spanish Championship, their first title in ten years, and 12 months later they reached the European Cup final where they were beaten by Steau Bucharest on penalties. After a poor start to the current season, Venables was relieved of his position at Barcelona and flew to Florida for a holiday. At roughly the same time, David Pleat was clearing his desk at White Hart Lane and Irving Scholar wasted little time in approaching Venables to take over at Spurs. Owing to business commitments Venables would be unable to take over at White Hart Lane until December 1st and put Ossie Ardiles in temporary charge of team matters until his arrival.

| 1990 | Nottingham Forest | A | First Division | 2-1 |

OCTOBER 28TH

| 1893 | Old St Mark's | H | London Senior Cup 1st Round Replay | 1-6 |

The first match a week earlier had also been played at Northumberland Park and after that had finished in a goalless draw it was mutually decided to replay the tie at the same venue. Despite this advantage, Spurs slipped to defeat with Stanley Briggs scoring their only goal.

1899	Southampton	H	Friendly	4-3
1905	Portsmouth	A	Western League	0-0
1911	Preston North End	H	First Division	6-2
1912	Crystal Palace	H	London FA Charity Cup 2nd Round Replay	3-3
1914	Crystal Palace	A	London Professional Football Charity Fund	2-2
1916	Queens Park Rangers	H-Homerton	London Combination	4-5
1922	West Bromwich Albion	A	First Division	1-5
1933	Middlesbrough	H	First Division	2-0
1939	Millwall	H	Football League South Group A	3-0
1944	Brentford	H	Football League South	2-2
1950	West Bromwich Albion	A	First Division	2-1
1953	FC Austria	H	Friendly	3-2
1961	Burnley	H	First Division	4-2

1962   Erik Thorstvedt born in Stavanger, Norway. Erik began his career with his local club and came over to the UK in 1984 for a trial with Spurs. Although Spurs were impressed enough to want to sign him, they were unable to obtain a work permit and he subsequently signed for Borussia Moenchengladbach. Arsenal then tried to sign him in 1987, but again were refused a work permit, and

Erik this time moved on to IFK Gothenburg. By December 1988 he was acknowledged as one of the best goalkeepers in Europe, and this time Spurs were able to sign him for £400,000 and get clearance for him to play. He immediately replaced Bobby Mimms in the Spurs goal and went on to win an FA Cup winners' medal in 1991, but by the following season his position was under threat from Ian Walker. A subsequent back injury allowed Walker to gain the initiative and Erik was released by Spurs, subsequently joining Wolves but retiring before making an appearance for them.

1967	Stoke City	A	First Division	1-2
1970	West Bromwich Albion	H	League Cup 4th Round	5-0
1972	Manchester United	A	First Division	4-1

Martin Peters scored all four of Spurs' goals, the first time such a feat was achieved by a Spurs player in a senior competitive game since Taffy O'Callaghan scored four in the 5-2 win at Everton in February 1928.

1978	Bolton Wanderers	H	First Division	2-0
1981	Manchester United	A	League Cup 2nd Round 2nd Leg	1-0

Spurs had drawn Manchester United in the second round of the League Cup for the second time in three seasons, although this time they emerged triumphant with a 1-0 win in both legs. Spurs' goal at Old Trafford was scored by Micky Hazard.

1987	Aston Villa	A	Littlewoods Cup 3rd Round	1-2
1992	Manchester City	A	Coca-Cola Cup 3rd Round	1-0

OCTOBER 29TH

1892	2nd Scots Guards	H	Friendly	2-4
1896	Southampton St Mary's	H	Friendly	3-1
1898	Wolverton	H	FA Cup 1st Qualifying Round	4-0
1902	Reading	A	Western League	0-3
1904	Brentford	H	Southern League	1-1
1906	Fulham	A	Southern League	1-2
1910	Liverpool	A	First Division	2-1
1921	Liverpool	A	First Division	1-1
1923	Crystal Palace	H	London FA Charity Cup 1st Round Replay	2-1
1927	Derby County	A	First Division	1-1
1928	Queens Park Rangers	A	London FA Charity Cup 2nd Round	1-1
1932	Millwall	A	Second Division	4-1
1938	West Ham United	H	Second Division	2-1
1949	Barnsley	H	Second Division	2-0
1955	Portsmouth	A	First Division	1-4
1960	Newcastle United	A	First Division	4-3

A crowd of 51,369 packed into St James's Park, 17,000 more than had seen any of Newcastle's previous games that season. The home crowd sensed a shock might be on the cards when Len White opened the scoring just after half an hour, but Spurs took just two minutes to get on level terms when Maurice Norman headed home a cross from Dyson. Then there was an unusual slip by Norman, miskicking the ball straight to White whose attempt was helped over the line by Ron Henry. When the half-time whistle blew it was the first time Spurs had been behind at the break all season, but after words of encouragement from Bill Nicholson they raised their game in the second half and quick goals from John White and Cliff Jones put them ahead and in control. Then it was Bill Brown's turn to make an unforced error, misjudging a cross from Hughes which sailed into the net. With three minutes to go and with almost everyone settling for a draw, Bobby Smith fired home Les Allen's cross for the winner. Spurs had little time to celebrate their victory after the game, for the train back to London was leaving at promptly five o'clock; most of the team were only half changed when they boarded the train!

1966	Aston Villa	H	First Division	0-1
1977	Stoke City	A	Second Division	3-1
1983	Notts County	H	First Division	1-0
1986	Birmingham City	H	Littlewoods Cup 3rd Round	5-0
1988	Aston Villa	A	First Division	1-2
1989	Liverpool	A	First Division	0-1
1991	Grimsby Town	A	Rumbelows Cup 3rd Round	3-0
1994	West Ham United	H	FA Premier League	3-1

Ossie Ardiles was in charge at White Hart Lane for the last time, for two days after the game he was dismissed. His final match in charge saw Spurs win thanks to goals from Jurgen Klinsmann, Nicky Barmby and substitute Teddy Sheringham.

1995	Newcastle United	H	FA Premier League	1-1

1886	Old St Paul's	H	Friendly	1-1
1897	2nd Coldstream Guards	H	FA Cup 1st Qualifying Round	7-0

Spurs were originally drawn away in this fixture, but the venue was switched by mutual consent. A crowd of 4,000 saw Spurs win thanks to goals from Sandy Hall, Harry Crump, Tom Meade (two), Bill Joyce, Bob Stormont and David Black.

1899	Reading	H	Southern District Combination	3-0
1909	Notts County	H	First Division	1-3
1915	Watford	H	London Combination [1st competition]	3-0
1920	Burnley	A	First Division	0-2
1926	Bolton Wanderers	H	First Division	1-0
1937	Chesterfield	A	Second Division	2-2
1943	Chelsea	H	Football League South	5-1
1948	Bradford Park Avenue	H	Second Division	5-1
1954	Sheffield United	A	First Division	1-4
1965	West Bromwich Albion	H	First Division	2-1
1968	Southampton	H	League Cup 5th Round	1-0
1971	Stoke City	A	First Division	0-2
1972	Middlesbrough	H	League Cup 3rd Round 2nd Replay	2-1 [aet]

Spurs finally managed to get past Middlesbrough at the third time of asking, but not before extra time was needed once again. A goal from Alan Gilzean in the extra half-hour (Martin Peters having scored the earlier goal) took Spurs through to the next round and a home match with Millwall, scheduled for just 48 hours later!

1976	Everton	H	First Division	3-3
1982	Aston Villa	A	First Division	0-4
1985	Orient	H	Milk Cup 2nd Round 2nd Leg	4-0

The second leg was delayed by over two weeks following civil unrest in the Tottenham area. A 4-0 win in the second leg enabled Spurs to win 4-2 on aggregate, with the goals coming from Graham Roberts (two), Tony Galvin and Chris Waddle.

1990	Bradford City	H	Rumbelows Cup 3rd Round	2-1
1993	Blackburn Rovers	A	FA Premier League	0-1

1891	Hampstead	A	London Senior Cup 2nd Round	3-2
1896	Chatham	A	Southern League	2-1
1900	Queens Park Rangers	H	Friendly	7-0
1903	Portsmouth	A	Western League	3-0
1904	London FA	H	Friendly	4-1
1908	Stockport County	H	Second Division	0-0
1914	Liverpool	A	First Division	2-7
1921	Brentford	H	London FA Charity Cup 2nd Round	1-1
1925	Leicester City	A	First Division	3-5
1931	Bristol City	A	Second Division	1-1
1936	Bradford City	H	Second Division	5-1
1942	Chelsea	H	Football League South	1-1
1953	Sunderland	A	First Division	3-4
1956	Hibernian	H	Anglo-Scottish Floodlit Tournament	3-3
1959	Manchester City	A	First Division	2-1
1962	Rangers	H	European Cup-Winners' Cup 1st Round 1st Leg	5-2
1964	Leicester City	A	First Division	2-4
1970	Nottingham Forest	A	First Division	1-0
1971				

Ian Walker born in Watford. The son of former Watford goalkeeper and Norwich manager Mike Walker, there was little surprise when Ian also took up goalkeeping, signing with Spurs as a trainee in 1988 and being upgraded to professional level in October 1989. After loan spells with Oxford United, Gillingham and Ipswich Town he returned to Spurs as deputy for Erik Thorstvedt, initially replacing him when Erik was away on international duty and then when Erik was injured. The second time around Ian kept his place on merit, and by the mid-1990s was firmly established as Spurs' number-one choice, a member of the England set-up and widely regarded as a permanent fixture between the posts for the next ten years or so. However, an injury sustained midway through the 1997-98 season threatened not only his place within the England squad for the forthcoming World Cup but even his own club place as Espen Baardsen responded to the challenge.

1981	Southampton	A	First Division	2-1
1984	Liverpool	H	Milk Cup 3rd Round	1-0
1987	Wimbledon	H	First Division	0-3
1989	Caen	Cherbourg		
			Friendly	2-1

At face value, this was a meaningless mid-season friendly, subsequently won by Spurs. But there was much more behind this game than met the eye. English clubs had already suffered a four-year exile from European competition following the events at the Heysel Stadium in 1985. Spurs were one of the regular English entrants up until the ban and indeed would have competed in the UEFA Cup in 1985-86 but for the ban. Their fans had also gained notoriety, not always for the right reasons. Whilst discussions between the FA and UEFA were conducted behind the scenes to try to end the ban, it was decided to arrange a match between a French and English side and try to keep the arrangements so secret that no English fans would be able to travel. The scheme worked, for the players were not told their destination, other than be at Heathrow airport on the morning of the game with their passports. The opposition and destination were revealed once the flight was in the air. The subterfuge worked equally as well in France, for no more than a handful of fans were present in Strasbourg to see Paul Stewart and David Howells score the goals that won the match. More importantly, however, was the success of the operation and at the end of the season English clubs were re-admitted to European competition.

| 1992 | Liverpool | H | FA Premier League | 2-0 |
| 1994 | | | | |

Despite a 3-1 win at home to West Ham United on Saturday, manager Ossie Ardiles was summoned to chairman Alan Sugar's house and given the sack. With Spurs facing a six-point deduction from their League total at the end of the season and a ban from the FA Cup, the previous week's Coca-Cola Cup tie at Notts County represented their last tangible chance of achieving success this season. A 3-0 defeat left the season in tatters and it was for this reason that Alan Sugar decided to remove Ardiles after just 17 months in the hot seat. Sugar commented afterwards 'Over the past few days I have struggled. A lot of soul searching and deep thought has been applied. The difficulty has been compounded by the fact that he is such a delightful person and good man.' He added that he would 'recall forever [his] dignity and strength and [Ardiles] would always be loved and welcome at our club.' Assistant manager Steve Perryman was appointed caretaker manager, at least until the end of the season, with a brief of getting the club out of the relegation dogfight.

NOVEMBER 1ST

1884	Sekforde Rovers	A	Friendly	4-0
1890	Queens Park Rangers	A	London Senior Cup 2nd Preliminary Round	1-1
1893				

The Council of the London FA reported their findings in the complaint brought against Spurs by Fulham FC. On the charge of poaching, Spurs were found not guilty, having successfully argued that although Ernie Payne had indeed been signed to Fulham he had not been picked to play for that club for a considerable time. On the charge of alleged infringements of the amateur laws, the Council found: '[1] That the sum of ten shillings was given by the club to Payne to buy a pair of boots. [2] That it was a breach of Rule ten to give money to a player to buy boots. [3] That the ten shillings given to Payne to buy boots was an unfair inducement offered to him to play for Tottenham Hotspur FC. [4] That the Council are of the opinion that the club has been guilty of misconduct, and, therefore, acting under Rule 9, the Council hereby suspend Tottenham Hotspur for a fortnight from the date; also that Payne be suspended for one week.' The club immediately lodged an appeal, and although this was ultimately unsuccessful, the delay in implementing the suspension did allow Spurs to play one match in the FA Amateur Cup.

1902	West Ham United	H	Southern League	1-1
1909	Woolwich Arsenal	H	London Professional Football Charity Fund	3-0
1913	Preston North End	A	First Division	2-1
1919	Port Vale	H	Second Division	2-0
1920	Arsenal	H	London FA Charity Cup 2nd Round	3-1
1924	Aston Villa	H	First Division	0-3
1930	Charlton Athletic	H	Second Division	5-0
1941	Fulham	A	London War League	2-2
1947	Brentford	H	Second Division	4-0
1952	Manchester United	H	First Division	1-2
1958	Manchester City	A	First Division	1-5
1961	Feyenoord	A	European Cup 1st Round 1st Leg	3-1

Despite the rather flattering scoreline, the actual game was considerably closer than had been expected, and Feyenoord hit the bar twice in the last three minutes. Two of Spurs' goals were scored by Frank Saul, making his debut in European competition, with Terry Dyson scoring the other, but

Bill Nicholson's comments after the game were more directed at his defence. 'We muddled through. That's all you can say. Our mistake? There were so many, I don't know where to start.'

1969	Sheffield Wednesday	H	First Division	1-0
1972	Millwall	H	League Cup 4th Round	2-0
1975	Wolverhampton Wanderers	H	First Division	2-1
1980	Everton	A	First Division	2-2
1986	Wimbledon	H	First Division	1-2
1988	Blackburn Rovers	H	Littlewoods Cup 3rd Round	0-0
1997	Leeds United	H	FA Premier League	0-1

NOVEMBER 2ND

1889	Old St Mark's	A	London Senior Cup 2nd Round	0-4
1895	Vampires	A	FA Cup 2nd Qualifying Round	2-4

After the game Spurs complained that the pitch had been incorrectly marked out and that the result should be declared void and a replay held. The FA found in Spurs' favour and did indeed order a replay, which Spurs won 2-1! This of course was an era when complaints were regularly made after teams had suffered defeat in the FA Cup; clubs would often spend as much time investigating their opponents for irregularities as to playing styles. If they lost the match, they would complain, if they won they kept quiet. Eventually, the FA ordered that any such complaints should be made before the match.

1896	Rushden	A	United League	0-2
1897	Eastbourne	A	Friendly	2-0
1898	Royal Engineers	A	Thames & Medway League	6-2

1900 Tom Meade born in Grassmoor, Derbyshire. Tom began his professional career with Stockport County in 1923 and was signed by reigning champions Huddersfield Town in 1927, although they finished the season in second place, as they also did the following year. By then Tom had moved on to Reading and after seven months with the Berkshire club he was transferred to Spurs. Making his debut against Bradford Park Avenue in August 1929, Tom went on to amass 184 League appearances for Spurs, usually at half-back. He lost his place to Wally Alsford in 1934 and the following year joined Notts County. He died on 30th January 1983.

1901	West Ham United	A	Southern League	1-0
1903	Brentford	H	Western League	1-1
1904	Littlehampton	A	Friendly	7-0
1907	Bradford Park Avenue	H	Southern League	0-0
1908	Clapton Orient	H	London Professional Football Charity Fund	0-0
1912	Liverpool	A	First Division	1-4
1918	Fulham	H-Homerton	London Combination	1-0
1929	Swansea Town	A	Second Division	1-0
1935	Swansea Town	H	Second Division	7-2
1940	Luton Town	A	Football League South	1-1

After 60 minutes and with the match all-square at 1-1, an air raid warning was announced and the match was abandoned, although the score was allowed to stand.

1946	Fulham	A	Second Division	1-1
1954	Rot-Weiss Essen	H	Friendly	4-2
1957	Sunderland	A	First Division	1-1
1960	Cardiff City	H	First Division	3-2
1963	Fulham	H	First Division	1-0
1968	Stoke City	H	First Division	1-1
1971	FC Nantes	H	UEFA Cup 2nd Round 2nd Leg	1-0

Spurs created so many chances, especially during the first half, that the match should have been put well beyond the reach of Nantes, but at the end of the game the only goal had come through Martin Peters. There was confusion in the second half when the French tried to play for a spell with 12 men; Eo came on whilst Rampillon was receiving treatment on the touchline, although Rampillon was obviously not aware he had been replaced when he recovered, for he ran back on to the field!

1974	Stoke City	A	First Division	2-2
1983	Feyenoord	A	UEFA Cup 2nd Round 2nd Leg	2-0

Two second half goals from Feyenoord in the first leg had given them hope of catching Spurs in the second leg, but the visitors turned in a masterly performance, silencing the partisan crowd after 25 minutes with a goal from defender Chris Hughton that put the tie beyond Feyenoord's reach. Five minutes from time Tony Galvin added a second to complete a 6-2 aggregate victory.

1985	Southampton	A	First Division	0-1

| 1991 | Sheffield Wednesday | A | First Division | 0-0 |

This match was Spurs' 3000th in the League (not including abandoned games), and Spurs had met Sheffield Wednesday in their 2000th as a League club!

| 1996 | West Ham United | H | FA Premier League | 1-0 |

NOVEMBER 3RD

1894	Wolverton	H	FA Cup 2nd Qualifying Round	5-3
1900	Portsmouth	A	Friendly	3-1
1902	Queens Park Rangers	H	Western League	3-0
1906	Portsmouth	H	Southern League	1-1
1917	Chelsea	A	London Combination	0-0
1923	Nottingham Forest	A	First Division	0-0
1924	Clapton Orient	A	London Professional Football Charity Fund	1-2
				[aet]

With the score level at the end of 90 minutes at 1-1, Harry Hargreaves having scored Spurs' goal from the penalty spot, extra time was required to settle the game. After 20 minutes, with Orient having scored a second goal, bad light forced the abandonment of the game, although the score was allowed to stand.

1928	Clapton Orient	H	Second Division	2-1
1930	Crystal Palace	A	London Professional Football Charity Fund	2-2
1934	Manchester City	A	First Division	1-3
1945	Brentford	H	Football League South	1-0
1951	Wolverhampton Wanderers	H	First Division	4-2
1956	Portsmouth	A	First Division	3-2
1962	Leicester City	H	First Division	4-0
1970	Motherwell	A	Texaco Cup 2nd Round 2nd Leg	1-3
1973	Everton	A	First Division	1-1
1979	Middlesbrough	A	First Division	0-0
1982	Bayern Munich	A	European Cup-Winners' Cup 2nd Round 2nd Leg	1-4

Whilst there have been countless examples where matches involving Spurs have been postponed or called off owing to fog, this is the one game that got away. The conditions prior to the start of the game were poor and deteriorated throughout; fans behind either goal were unable to see the action much beyond the half-way line. One can assume that the only reason the referee insisted upon completing the match was under UEFA instructions, for under any other circumstances the game would surely have been abandoned. Indeed, at the airport after the game, Chris Hughton had to describe his goal to the Spurs' fans as no one had seen it!

| 1984 | West Bromwich Albion | H | First Division | 2-3 |

NOVEMBER 4TH

1893	1st Scots Guards	H	Friendly	1-2
1899	Thames Ironworks	H	Southern League	7-0
1901	Woolwich Arsenal	H	London League	5-0
1905	Swindon Town	H	Southern League	2-1
1907	West Ham United	A	Western League	3-1
1911	Manchester United	A	First Division	2-1
1912	Notts County	H	First Division	0-3
1916	West Ham United	A	London Combination	1-5
1922	Liverpool	H	First Division	2-4
1929	Crystal Palace	H	London Professional Football Charity Fund	5-1
1933	West Bromwich Albion	A	First Division	2-1
1939	West Ham United	A	Football League South Group A	1-2
1944	Aldershot	H	Football League South	7-0
1950	Portsmouth	H	First Division	5-1
1961	Everton	A	First Division	0-3
1967	Liverpool	H	First Division	1-1
1972	Birmingham City	A	First Division	0-0
1978	Norwich City	A	First Division	2-2
1980	Arsenal	H	League Cup 4th Round	1-0

The game had originally been scheduled for a week earlier until World Cup call-ups for both Chris Hughton and David O'Leary had forced a delay. By the time Spurs and Arsenal met the draw for the next round had already been made and West Ham were waiting for the winners. This was also only the second time Spurs had drawn their closest rivals in the competition, with Arsenal winning the

1969 semi-final clash 3-2 on aggregate. A single goal from Ossie Ardiles gave Spurs their revenge, but Barry Daines also performed well in goal to ensure the win.

| 1981 | Dundalk | H | European Cup-Winners' Cup 2nd Round 2nd Leg | 1-0 |

A second half goal from Garth Crooks took Spurs into the next round 2-1 on aggregate, but it was hardly a good performance from the side who struggled to get going all night. The longer the game went on without Spurs scoring, the more Dundalk's own confidence grew, and at the end they were perhaps unfortunate not to have equalised through Fairclough.

1986	SV Hamburg	H	Friendly	5-0
1987	Portsmouth	A	First Division	0-0
1989	Southampton	A	First Division	1-1
1990	Liverpool	H	First Division	1-3
1995	Coventry City	A	FA Premier League	3-2

NOVEMBER 5TH

1892	Windsor & Eton	A	Southern Alliance	2-1
1898	Reading	H	Southern League	3-0
1900	Cambridge University	H	Friendly	3-1
1904	Queens Park Rangers	A	Southern League	2-1
1910	Bury	H	First Division	5-0
1921	Newcastle United	H	First Division	4-0
1923	Clapton Orient	A	London FA Charity Cup 2nd Round	0-2
1927	West Ham United	H	First Division	5-3
1928	Queens Park Rangers	H	London FA Charity Cup 2nd Round Replay	3-1
1932	Port Vale	H	Second Division	4-0
1938	Manchester City	A	Second Division	0-2
1949	West Ham United	A	Second Division	1-0
1955	Cardiff City	H	First Division	1-1
1960	Fulham	H	First Division	5-1
1966	Blackpool	A	First Division	2-2

On the same day Mohammed Ali Amar born in Ceuta, Morocco. Known as Nayim he was signed by Barcelona and put on the books of their nursery club Barcelona Athletico. Terry Venables gave him his first break in the Barcelona side and Nayim quickly picked up national honours at youth and Under-21 level. With a change of manager at Barcelona, with Johan Cruyff replacing Venables, it became plain that Nayim did not fit into Barcelona's plans for the future. Terry Venables returned to his former club and persuaded Nayim to come to England, initially on a loan basis. His crowd-pleasing skills and deft touches soon had the club clamouring for the deal to be made permanent and Nayim was eventually signed as part of the same deal that brought Gary Lineker to White Hart Lane. In 1991 he was brought on as substitute when Paul Gascoigne was injured in the early moments of the FA Cup final and gave a flawless performance as Spurs won the cup. In 1993 he announced he wished to return home to Spain in order to enhance his international chances and Spurs reluctantly agreed to transfer him to Real Zaragoza. However, he did later further endear himself to Spurs fans when he scored the winning goal in the last minute of extra time in the European Cup-Winners' Cup final against Arsenal with a lob of some 50 yards – the chants of 'Nayim from the halfway line' have greeted Spurs-Arsenal clashes ever since!

1977	Burnley	H	Second Division	3-0
1983	Stoke City	A	First Division	1-1
1988	Derby County	H	First Division	1-3
1994	Blackburn Rovers	A	FA Premier League	0-2

Steve Perryman took charge for the first and last time following the departure of Ossie Ardiles, acting as caretaker manager whilst Alan Sugar sought a more permanent replacement. It was not to be a winning spell either, for the champions won 2-0 against a side that looked totally demoralised by the events of the previous few weeks.

NOVEMBER 6TH

| 1897 | Reading | A | Southern League | 3-3 |
| 1899 | Chatham | H | Southern District Combination | 8-0 |

Goalkeeper Charlie Ambler made his last appearance for the club. Born in 1868 with the surname Toby, he had signed with Royal Arsenal in 1891 as an amateur, been upgraded to the professional ranks and subsequently reinstated as an amateur in 1892, enabling him also to turn out for Clapton. He joined Spurs in October 1894, although as the club were not members of any League he continued to appear for a number of other clubs, and indeed signed Football League forms for Woolwich Arsenal in 1895, appearing for both Spurs and Arsenal in the same season. Although he was established as first-team goalkeeper until 1897, he remained with the club until the summer of 1900 and when released signed with Gravesend. He died in 1952.

1904 Walter Bellamy born in Tottenham. After impressing for a number of local amateur clubs Walter signed with Spurs as an amateur and made his debut in September 1926 in the London FA Charity Cup and his League debut the following year. He signed as a professional in February 1927, but the continued form of Jimmy Dimmock and then Willie Evans restricted first-team opportunities for Walter. He was released in May 1935 and signed for Brighton and Hove Albion for one season, later playing in the Gibraltar League whilst serving there during the Second World War. He died in Hadley Wood on 19th October 1978.

1905	West Ham United	A	Western League	1-4
1909	Newcastle United	A	First Division	0-1
1915	Millwall	A	London Combination [1st competition]	2-3
1920	Oldham Athletic	H	First Division	5-1
1926	Aston Villa	A	First Division	3-2
1937	Swansea Town	H	Second Division	2-0
1943	Brentford	A	Football League South	2-0
1948	Southampton	A	Second Division	1-3
1954	Cardiff City	H	First Division	0-2
1957	Bristol City	A	Friendly	3-4
1965	Nottingham Forest	A	First Division	0-1
1971	Everton	H	First Division	3-0
1976	West Ham United	A	First Division	3-5
1979	Widad	Morocco	Friendly	4-2
1982	Watford	H	First Division	0-1
1985	Wimbledon	H	Milk Cup 3rd Round	2-0
1989	Leicester City	A	Friendly	5-2

This was a testimonial match for Paul Ramsey with Spurs' goals being scored by Paul Gascoigne (two), Paul Stewart (two) and Steve Sedgley.

| 1993 | Southampton | A | FA Premier League | 0-1 |

NOVEMBER 7TH

1885	Casuals	A	London Association Cup 2nd Round	0-8
1891	Coldstream Guards	H	Luton Charity Cup 1st Round	3-3
1895	Luton Town	H	Friendly	0-2
1896	Sheppey United	H	Southern League	3-2
1903	Northampton Town	H	Southern League	2-1
1904	Reading	H	Western League	2-2
1906	Portsmouth	a	Western League	0-1
1908	West Bromwich Albion	A	Second Division	0-3
1910	Millwall	N	London FA Charity Cup Semi-Final	2-2
1914	Bradford Park Avenue	H	First Division	3-0
1921	Brentford	A	London FA Charity Cup 2nd Round Replay	3-2
1925	West Ham United	H	First Division	4-2

Three of Spurs' goals were scored by Frank Osborne, the third consecutive match in which he had scored a hat-trick and a new Spurs record. Spurs' other goal in the 4-2 win was scored by Jack Elkes.

1927	Clapton Orient	H	London Professional Football Charity Fund	4-3
1931	Swansea Town	H	Second Division	6-2
1934	Corinthians	H	Dewar Shield	7-2

Goalkeeper Percy Hooper made his debut in a Spurs shirt in this win over Corinthians. On the same day Mel Hopkins was born in Ystrad Rhondda. After impressing with the local boys club Mel was signed by Spurs in May 1951 as an amateur, being upgraded to the professional ranks a year later. He made his debut in October 1952 and quickly became a regular for both Spurs and Wales, winning 34 caps. A broken nose sustained whilst playing for Wales in 1959 allowed Ron Henry to establish himself at full-back, and although Mel remained a regular for Wales his Spurs appearances became more sporadic. He joined Brighton in October 1964 and later played for Bradford Park Avenue and a number of non-League sides before retiring from the game.

1936	Aston Villa	A	Second Division	1-1
1942	Arsenal	H	Football League South	1-0
1953	Chelsea	H	First Division	2-1
1959	Bolton Wanderers	A	First Division	0-2
1964	Sunderland	H	First Division	3-0
1970	Burnley	H	First Division	4-0

1973	Aberdeen	H	UEFA Cup 2nd Round 2nd Leg	4-1
1981	West Bromwich Albion	H	First Division	1-2
1984	Club Brugge KV	H	UEFA Cup 2nd Round 2nd Leg	3-0

It took Spurs only five minutes to wipe out Brugges' aggregate lead, Micky Hazard scoring with a delightful clipped shot. That would have been enough to put Spurs through on away goals, but they continued pressing for an outright victory and, having created considerably more chances than their opponents over the two legs, got their just rewards with further goals from Clive Allen and Graham Roberts.

| 1991 | FC Porto | A | European Cup-Winners' Cup 2nd Round 2nd Leg | 0-0 |
| 1992 | Blackburn Rovers | A | FA Premier League | 2-0 |

NOVEMBER 8TH

| 1884 | Marlborough Rovers | H | Friendly | 1-0 |
| 1890 | Queens Park Rangers | H | London Senior Cup 2nd Preliminary Round Replay | 2-1 |

1896 Alex Lindsay born in Dundee. Having begun his career with Raith, Alex made a number of guest appearances for Spurs during the First World War and when the hostilities ended was transferred permanently to White Hart Lane. Over the next 11 years Alex proved an extremely useful player to have at the club, being equally at home as a half-back or forward. He made over 200 League appearances for Spurs, scoring 42 goals, and when released in April 1930 joined Thames, returning home to Scotland and Dundee when Thames gave him a free transfer. He died in Dundee on 9th December 1971.

1902	Portsmouth	H	Western League	0-0
1905	Queens Park Rangers	H	Southern Charity Cup 1st Round	2-0
1909	Queens Park Rangers	N	London FA Charity Cup Semi-Final	0-0
1913	Sunderland	H	First Division	1-4
1919	Bury	A	Second Division	1-2
1924	Huddersfield Town	A	First Division	2-1
1926	Clapton Orient	A	London Professional Football Charity Fund	3-1
1930	Bradford City	A	Second Division	0-2
1941	Clapton Orient	H	London War League	2-0

1943 Martin Peters born in Plaistow. Signed by West Ham as an apprentice in 1959 he became a professional in November 1960 and made his debut for the club in April 1962. A member of the side that won the European Cup-Winners' Cup in 1965, Martin won his first cap for England May 1966, just in time to be considered for the squad for the forthcoming World Cup finals. In fact, he was rather more than just a squad member, for West Ham supplied the winning captain in Bobby Moore and both of England's goalscorers in the final; Martin Peters and Geoff Hurst with a hat-trick. The exploits of both Moore and Hurst tended to overshadow Martin's own achievements, and coupled with the Alf Ramsey comment that he was 'ten years ahead of his time' led to him becoming unsettled with West Ham. He was transferred to Spurs in 1970 for a then British record fee of £200,000, with Jimmy Greaves making the opposite journey. Whilst at White Hart Lane Martin showed just why Sir Alf Ramsey had made his famous statement; his ability to ghost into positions few other players would have contemplated, his all round skill and vision meant he was a player who would have fitted into any era. Whilst with Spurs he helped the club win the League Cup in 1971 and 1973 (for which he was captain) and the UEFA Cup in 1972. He was surprisingly sold to Norwich City in March 1975 for £60,000 and after five years at Carrow Road joined Sheffield United as player-coach, later becoming player-manager and retiring in June 1981 following his dismissal after Sheffield United had been relegated. He joined the Spurs board of directors in 1998.

1947	Leicester City	A	Second Division	3-0
1952	Portsmouth	A	First Division	1-2
1958	Bolton Wanderers	H	First Division	1-1
1969	Nottingham Forest	A	First Division	2-2
1971	Preston North End	A	League Cup 4th Round Replay	2-1 [aet]
1972	Olympiakos Pireus	A	UEFA Cup 2nd Round 2nd Leg	0-1
1975	Queens Park Rangers	A	First Division	0-0
1980	Wolverhampton Wanderers	H	First Division	2-2
1986	Norwich City	A	First Division	1-2
1997	Liverpool	A	FA Premier League	0-4

NOVEMBER 9TH

1889	Clapton	H	Friendly	5-3
1895	London Westminsters	H	London Charity Cup 1st Round	2-1
1896	Woolwich Arsenal	A	United League	1-2

1897	New Brompton	H	Friendly	3-0
1898	Reading	A	United League	0-1
1901	Wellingborough	A	Southern League	1-0
1903	Queens Park Rangers	A	Western League	0-2
1907	Millwall	A	Southern League	2-1
1912	Bolton Wanderers	H	First Division	0-1
1918	Brentford	A	London Combination	1-7
1929	Cardiff City	H	Second Division	1-2
1935	West Ham United	A	Second Division	2-2
1946	Bury	H	Second Division	2-1
1957	Everton	H	First Division	3-1
1963	Manchester United	A	First Division	1-4
1968	Leeds United	A	First Division	0-0
1974	Everton	H	First Division	1-1
1982	Gillingham	A	Milk Cup 3rd Round	4-2
1983	Arsenal	H	Milk Cup 3rd Round	1-2

The absence of Gary Mabbutt for the first time in the season proved to be Spurs' undoing, for their midfield lacked industry, with Arsenal being allowed far too much room throughout. They swept into a two goal lead before Spurs managed to awake from their slumbers, Glenn Hoddle firing home a penalty after a handball in the penalty area. Although there was still considerable time left for Spurs to force an equaliser, it was Arsenal who looked the most likely to score and Spurs slipped out of the competition. If there was to be any consolation for Spurs it came in the next round; Arsenal lost at home to Walsall.

| 1985 | Luton Town | H | First Division | 1-3 |
| 1988 | Blackburn Rovers | A | Littlewoods Cup 3rd Round Replay | 2-1 [aet] |

Spurs showed considerable resilience and character eventually to overcome Blackburn in the replay. Having drawn the first match and lost four straight League games, Spurs' confidence had taken a battering, but Mitchell Thomas put Spurs ahead to settle the nerves. A late equaliser forced extra time, but Paul Stewart scored his second goal in consecutive games to win the tie for Spurs.

NOVEMBER 10TH

| 1883 | Brownlow Rovers | A | Friendly | 1-0 |

After 55 minutes the ball burst and as neither side had a replacement, the game was abandoned with Spurs leading thanks to Jack Jull's goal.

1894	City Ramblers	H	FA Amateur Cup 2nd Qualifying Round	6-1
1900	New Brompton	A	Southern League	2-1
1902	Cambridge University	H	Friendly	2-1
1906	New Brompton	A	Southern League	1-0
1913	Woolwich Arsenal	N	London FA Charity Cup Semi-Final	2-1
1917	Brentford	H-Highbury		
			London Combination	6-1
1923	Nottingham Forest	H	First Division	3-0
1924	Manchester City	H	First Division	1-1
1928	Swansea Town	A	Second Division	0-4
1934	Middlesbrough	H	First Division	3-1
1945	Brentford	A	Football League South	3-1
1951	Huddersfield Town	A	First Division	1-1
1956	Newcastle United	H	First Division	3-1
1958	Hibernian	H	Friendly	5-2
1962	Fulham	A	First Division	2-0
1973	Manchester United	H	First Division	2-1
1976				

Stefan Iversen born in Oslo, Norway. Stefan began his career with Astor before signing as a professional with Rosenborg BK in 1993. A series of impressive displays, particularly in European competition, alerted the bigger clubs across Europe and Spurs signed him for a fee of £2.7 million in December 1996. Although he has been in and out of the side owing to injury since, he has shown more than enough ability to mark him as having amazing potential in the years to come for both club and country.

1979	Bolton Wanderers	H	First Division	2-0
1984	Nottingham Forest	A	First Division	2-1
1987	St Albans City	A	Friendly	6-0
1990	Wimbledon	H	First Division	4-2
1991	Spurs 1981 v Spurs 1991	H	Cyril Knowles Memorial	2-2

Prior to the main match of the day, Spurs' 1971 League Cup-winning side took on their Arsenal double-winning counterparts of the same year. The result, a goalless draw, owed more to the age of the players (Cliff Jones, although he had not played in the 1971 side, played at the age of 56 years) than Arsenal's traditional defensive qualities!

1992   Swansea City   A   Friendly   3-3
This match was a testimonial for Harold Woolacott with Spurs' goals being scored by Jason Cundy, Teddy Sheringham and an own goal.

NOVEMBER 11TH

1893	Vampires	H	FA Amateur Cup 1st Qualifying Round	3-1

Spurs played their first match in the FA Amateur Cup and beat Vampires 3-1 at home. Despite this win, Spurs took no further part in the competition this season, for they were subsequently suspended for two weeks by the London FA for paying inducements to Ernie Payne and were therefore unable to play their second round match.

1899	Ilkeston Town	H	Friendly	7-0
1901	Swindon Town	H	Western League	6-0
1905	Millwall	A	Southern League	1-2
1911	Liverpool	H	First Division	2-0
1912	Crystal Palace	A	London FA Charity Cup 2nd Round 2nd Replay	1-4
1916	Southampton	A	London Combination	0-1
1922	Liverpool	A	First Division	0-0
1933	Newcastle United	H	First Division	4-0
1939	Watford	H	Football League South Group A	8-2
1944	Millwall	A	Football League South	4-3
1950	Everton	A	First Division	2-1

1953   Jimmy Holmes born in Dublin. Jimmy began his career with Coventry City, signing with them as a professional in November 1970. He joined Spurs in March 1977 for £100,000 shortly before the club was relegated into the Second Division, although he quickly established himself as a regular in the side. A broken leg sustained whilst on international duty for Eire in May 1979 deprived Spurs of his services for 11 months and by the time he recovered Chris Hughton had established himself as the regular left-back. Jimmy subsequently joined Vancouver Whitecaps and later played for Leicester City, Brentford, Torquay and Peterborough before turning to management in non-League circles.

1957	Vfb Stuttgart	H	Friendly	3-2
1961	Fulham	H	First Division	4-2
1964	Scotland XI	H	John White Memorial	2-6

The memorial match was originally scheduled for 24 hours earlier but was postponed due to fog. Spurs' side included a guest appearance from John's brother Tommy (he was a centre-forward with Hearts, Aberdeen, Crystal Palace, Blackpool, Bury and Crewe during his career) and he scored one of Spurs' goals on the night, the other being netted by Tony Marchi. A crowd of over 29,000 turned out to pay their respects to one of the finest midfield players ever to wear the Spurs colours.

1967	Southampton	A	First Division	2-1
1972	West Bromwich Albion	H	First Division	1-1
1978	Nottingham Forest	H	First Division	1-3
1981	Wrexham	H	League Cup 3rd Round	2-0
1989	Wimbledon	H	First Division	0-1
1994	Reading	A	Friendly	1-1

With the Premier League programme having been called off owing to England's match against Nigeria the following week, Spurs agreed to provide the opposition for a friendly at Reading. The match was hastily arranged – Reading informed their stewards of the game in the local paper on the day – and Spurs turned up after the scheduled kick-off. The game finally got under way at 8.15 p.m., with Steven Slade making his Spurs debut leading the attack. After 70 minutes, with Spurs 1-0 behind, he was replaced by Martin Nash, a Canadian on trial at the club. He scored with his first touch of the ball, earning Spurs a draw.

NOVEMBER 12TH

1887	Nondescripts	H	Friendly	6-1
1892	Clapton	H	Friendly	1-2
1898	Bristol City	H	United League	2-1
1900	Luton Town	A	Friendly	0-1
1904	Millwall	H	Southern League	1-0
1906	Cambridge University	H	Friendly	4-2
1910	Sheffield United	A	First Division	0-3

1921	Newcastle United	A	First Division	2-0
1927	Aston Villa	A	First Division	2-1
1932	Lincoln City	A	Second Division	2-2
1938	Bradford Park Avenue	H	Second Division	2-2
1949	Sheffield United	H	Second Division	7-0

With still only one League defeat all season Spurs really hit their stride with a seven goal hammering of Sheffield United at White Hart Lane. Spurs' goals came from Sonny Walters (three), Len Duquemin (two) and Les Medley (two) in front of over 54,000.

1955	Manchester City	A	First Division	2-1
1956	Heart of Midlothian	H	Anglo-Scottish Floodlit Tournament	4-2
1960	Sheffield Wednesday	A	First Division	1-2

1961 Danny Thomas born in Worksop. After failing trials with Sheffield United and Leeds United, Danny was signed by Coventry City in 1978 and soon developed into a full-back with the potential to break into the full England side, which he achieved during the England tour of Australia in 1983. Upon returning from international duty he was transferred to Spurs for £250,000 and earned a UEFA Cup winners' medal at the end of his first season with the club. In March 1987 he suffered a knee injury so serious it forced him to retire from the game, a decision he announced in January 1988. Although he was offered a position on the Spurs staff, he chose to pursue a career in physiotherapy and later linked with Ossie Ardiles at West Bromwich Albion in that position.

1966	West Ham United	H	First Division	3-4
1975	West Ham United	H	League Cup 4th Round	0-0
1977	Crystal Palace	A	Second Division	2-1
1980	Crystal Palace	H	First Division	4-2
1983	Liverpool	H	First Division	2-2
1988	Wimbledon	H	First Division	3-2
1990	West Ham United	A	Friendly	3-4

This match was a testimonial for Billy Bonds (the second time Spurs had provided the opposition for Billy Bonds' testimonial) with Spurs' goals being scored by Paul Stewart (two) and Scott Houghton.

NOVEMBER 13TH

1886	Silesia College	A	Friendly	2-3
1897	Bristol City	H	Southern League	2-2
1901	West Norwood	A	Friendly	3-1
1905	Brentford	H	Western League	2-3
1909	Liverpool	H	First Division	1-0
1915	Arsenal	H	London Combination [1st competition]	3-3
1920	Oldham Athletic	A	First Division	5-2
1926	Cardiff City	H	First Division	4-1

1934 Dave Mackay born in Musselburgh. Dave began his career with Hearts, signing professional forms in April 1952 and was widely regarded as a solid and reliable half-back, winning his first cap for Scotland in 1957. Whilst with Hearts he helped the club win the Scottish League and League and FA Cups, and there was considerable speculation that he might be on his way south as any number of clubs were keen to sign him. Although Bill Nicholson was known to be interested in acquiring him, he had insufficient funds to buy both Dave Mackay and Mel Charles, his initial target. It was when Mel turned Spurs down that Bill Nicholson swooped to take Dave to White Hart Lane, paying a fee of £30,000 in March 1959. Given the inspirational service Dave gave the club over the next nine years, Mel Charles turning Spurs down was a blessing in disguise, for Dave quickly formed a partnership with Danny Blanchflower that was the envy of football. A member of the side that won the double in 1961 and retained the cup the following year, Dave was sadly suffering from a stomach injury that caused him to miss the European Cup-Winners' Cup final in 1963. In December 1963 in the same competition he broke his leg against Manchester United, and it was whilst reuring to full fitness that he broke the same leg in a reserve match against Shrewsbury. However, Dave recovered once again and was captain when Spurs lifted the FA Cup in 1967. The following year he was allowed to move to Derby for a nominal fee of £5,000 and helped his new club to the Second Division title, and was jointly named Footballer of the Year with Manchester City's Tony Book. He then became player-manager at Swindon before taking over the reigns at first Nottingham Forest and then Derby County, following the departure of Brian Clough. Although most of the club wanted Clough to return, Dave helped steady the ship and took them to the League title in 1974-75. After a spell at Walsall as manager he then went abroad, coaching in Kuwait. Upon returning to England he managed Doncaster Rovers and Birmingham City, resigning from the latter in 1990.

1937	Norwich City	A	Second Division	1-2
1943	Clapton Orient	A	Football League South	4-0
1948	Barnsley	H	Second Division	4-1

| 1954 | Chelsea | A | First Division | 1-2 |

1961 Clive Wilson born in Manchester. Clive began his career with Manchester City in 1979 and made his League debut in 1981. After a loan spell with Chester City he was transferred to Chelsea for £250,000 in 1987 and three years later moved to QPR for £450,000. Released on a free transfer in June 1996, he linked up with former QPR manager Gerry Francis at Spurs, and although first-team opportunities have been limited since, he has seldom disappointed when selected.

1965	Sheffield Wednesday	H	First Division	2-3
1971	Manchester United	A	First Division	1-3
1976	Bristol City	H	First Division	0-1
1982	Manchester United	A	First Division	0-1
1984	Sutton United	A	Friendly	5-3

This match was a testimonial for Larry Pritchard with Spurs' goals being scored by Garth Crooks (three), Ian Crook and Mark Falco.

NOVEMBER 14TH

1885	Rutland	A	Friendly	0-3
1891	Coldstream Guards	H	Luton Charity Cup 1st Round Replay	7-2
1896	Swindon Town	H	Southern League	2-1
1903	Woolwich Arsenal	A	London League	1-1
1904	Fulham	A	Western League	0-0
1906	Corinthians	A	Friendly	1-6
1908	Birmingham	H	Second Division	4-0
1914	Oldham Athletic	A	First Division	1-4
1921	Arsenal	N	London FA Charity Cup Semi-Final	0-0 [aet]

The game, played at Stamford Bridge, was abandoned only five minutes into extra time and replayed at Homerton a week later, with Arsenal winning 2-1 after extra time.

1925	Newcastle United	A	First Division	1-3
1931	Bury	A	Second Division	1-1
1936	Chesterfield	H	Second Division	5-1
1942	Luton Town	A	Football League South	3-3

1946 Roger Morgan born in Walthamstow. Both Roger and his twin brother Ian were snapped up by QPR as youngsters and broke into the first team at roughly the same time, although only Roger was a member of the side that won the League Cup in 1967. Both, however, were important members of the team that won the Third Division title the same year and then won promotion into the First Division. In February 1969 Spurs paid £110,000 to take Roger, considered by many to be the better of the two wingers, to White Hart Lane, and he enjoyed a bright and promising start to his career with Spurs. Unfortunately he was injured early on in the 1970-71 season and struggled thereafter to make a comeback, finally admitting defeat and retiring from the game in the summer of 1973.

1953	Blackpool	A	First Division	0-1
1955	Partick Thistle	H	Friendly	0-1
1959	Luton Town	A	First Division	0-1
1960	Dinamo Tbilisi	H	Friendly	5-2
1962	Zamalek Sporting Club	Cairo	Friendly	7-3
1964	Wolverhampton Wanderers	A	First Division	1-3
1970	Chelsea	A	First Division	2-0
1981	Israel Select XI	A	Friendly	3-2
1987	Queens Park Rangers	H	First Division	1-1

NOVEMBER 15TH

| 1884 | Latymer | A | Friendly | 2-1 |

Latymer played with 12 men during the first half, a ploy they also tried in a reserve match soon after. As a result of the growing ill-feeling between the two sides, it was decided to drop the fixture.

1890	City Ramblers	H	Friendly	1-0
1899	Bristol City	A	Southern District Combination	3-3
1902	Corinthians	A	Friendly	3-1
1909	Queens Park Rangers	N	London FA Charity Cup Semi-Final Replay	4-1
1913	Newcastle United	A	First Division	0-2
1919	Bury	H	Second Division	2-1
1924	Blackburn Rovers	H	First Division	5-0
1930	Swansea Town	H	Second Division	1-1
1941	Portsmouth	A	London War League	2-1
1947	Leeds United	H	Second Division	3-1

1950	Jimmy Neighbour born in Chingford, Essex. Signed as an apprentice in April 1966 Jimmy was upgraded to the professional ranks in November 1968, but he did not make his debut until October 1970. Although he was in competition with first Jimmy Pearce and then Ralph Coates for the wing position, Jimmy did win a League Cup winners' medal in 1971 and got an extended run in the team following the appointment of Terry Neill as manager. In September 1976 he was sold to Norwich City for £75,000, and returned to the capital with West Ham in September 1979. He later played for AFC Bournemouth on loan before retiring and coaching Enfield.			
1952	Bolton Wanderers	H	First Division	1-1
1954	Finchley	H	Friendly	2-1
1958	Luton Town	A	First Division	2-1
1961	Feyenoord	H	European Cup 1st Round 2nd Leg	1-1
1969	West Bromwich Albion	H	First Division	2-0
1975	Stoke City	H	First Division	1-1
1980	Nottingham Forest	A	First Division	3-0
1986	Coventry City	H	First Division	1-0
1994	Gerry Francis, the former Queens Park Rangers manager, was confirmed as the new manager at White Hart Lane, replacing Ossie Ardiles, who left the club on October 31st. Since his departure there had been intense media speculation on the new appointment, ranging from David Pleat, who was interviewed for the post of director of football, which he subsequently turned down, and Graeme Souness, out of football since his sacking at Liverpool in January. Gerry Francis did not enter the fray until recently, when he resigned as manager at QPR on a point of principle – the QPR board wished to appoint Rodney Marsh as chief executive but omitted to tell Francis of their intentions. Francis resigned immediately, although it was not accepted for a week. With David Pleat ruling himself out of a return to Spurs, club chairman Alan Sugar held talks with Francis and confirmed his appointment at a press conference this day. Gerry Francis was a former England captain and had established a growing reputation as a tracksuit manager, first with Bristol Rovers, where he operated on strict financial guidelines, and more recently at QPR. It was hoped he would bring in some stability to White Hart Lane, where he was the third manager in two years. He was also bringing in his own coaching staff, which meant Steve Perryman would be leaving Spurs.			

NOVEMBER 16TH

1889	Finchley	A	Friendly	1-1
1895	Vampires	H	FA Cup 2nd Qualifying Round Replay	2-1
1896	Luton Town	A	Friendly	0-3
1901	Portsmouth	A	Western League	1-3
1903	Brentford	A	London League	2-0
1907	Brentford	H	Southern League	1-0
1912	Sheffield United	A	First Division	0-4
1918	West Ham United	H-Homerton		
			London Combination	1-4
1925	Queens Park Rangers	H	London Professional Football Charity Fund	1-0
1929	Preston North End	A	Second Division	0-4
1935	Bury	H	Second Division	4-3
1938	Spurs' Willie Hall scored a hat-trick in just three and a half minutes whilst playing for England against Ireland in Manchester. Hall grabbed a further two goals in the 7-0 win to become only the fourth England player to score as many as five goals in an international.			
1940	Arsenal	A	Football League South	1-1
1946	Luton Town	A	Second Division	2-3
1957	Aston Villa	A	First Division	1-1
1959	Torpedo Moscow	H	Friendly	3-2
1963	Burnley	H	First Division	3-2
1968	Sunderland	H	First Division	5-1
	Jimmy Greaves had already scored two hat-tricks during the season and had registered 15 goals in the 18 League games already played. This day he went one better, netting four times in the rout of Sunderland, with Mike England scoring Spurs' other goal.			
1974	Leicester City	A	First Division	2-1
1985	Manchester United	A	First Division	0-0
1991	Luton Town	H	First Division	4-1
	The floodlights failed midway through the second half with Luton leading 1-0. After a 15-minute delay whilst full power was restored, Spurs fought back to win thanks to two goals apiece from Gary Lineker and substitute Scott Houghton..			
1996	Sunderland	H	FA Premier League	2-0

NOVEMBER 17TH

1888	Millwall Rovers	H	Friendly	1-1
1894	Highland Light Infantry	H	Friendly	1-1
1900	Portsmouth	H	Western League	8-1

Spurs' opening game in the Western League saw them also register their biggest win in the League with this hammering of Portsmouth. Spurs' goals were scored by James McNaught (two), Arthur Jones, Tom Morris, Sandy Brown (two), James Cameron and John Kirwan.

1902	Woolwich Arsenal	A	London League	1-2
1906	Plymouth Argyle	H	Southern League	4-2
1917	Arsenal	H-Homerton		
			London Combination	1-0
1923	Arsenal	A	First Division	1-1
1924	Kingstonians	H	London FA Charity Cup 2nd Round	5-0
1928	Nottingham Forest	H	Second Division	2-1
1930	Ilford	N	London FA Charity Cup Semi-Final	8-1
1934	West Bromwich Albion	A	First Division	0-4
1945	Chelsea	A	Football League South	2-1
1951	Chelsea	H	First Division	3-2
1956	Sheffield Wednesday	A	First Division	1-4

1959 Terry Fenwick born in Camden, County Durham. He began his career with Crystal Palace, signing for the club when Terry Venables was manager and thus beginning a relationship that has remained strong ever since. He made his League debut for Palace against Spurs in 1977 and later followed Venables to QPR, where he became the first defender to score an FA Cup-final goal from open play, against Spurs! When Venables became manager of Spurs in 1987 Terry soon followed, joining the club in December 1987. Initially used as a central defender, his versatility saw him play in a number of other positions and he appeared to have settled as a right-back when he broke his leg in October 1989. When he recovered he forced his way back into the side but then broke his ankle warming up for a cup tie at Portsmouth. He left the club in 1993 and later became manager of Portsmouth (where Terry Venables was on the board) although was sacked in 1998.

1962	Sheffield Wednesday	H	First Division	1-1
1971	Blackpool	H	League Cup 5th Round	2-0
1973	Southampton	A	First Division	1-1
1979	Liverpool	A	First Division	1-2
1980	Weymouth	A	Friendly	6-1
1984	Ipswich Town	A	First Division	3-0

NOVEMBER 18TH

1893	London Welsh	H	Friendly	2-1
1899	Bolton Wanderers	H	Friendly	4-0
1901	Bristol Rovers	A	Western League	4-0
1905	Luton Town	H	Southern League	2-0
1911	Aston Villa	A	First Division	2-2
1916	Crystal Palace	H-Highbury		
			London Combination	3-1
1922	Newcastle United	H	First Division	0-1
1933	Leeds United	A	First Division	0-0
1939	Arsenal	A	Football League South Group A	1-2
1944	Clapton Orient	A	Football League South	2-0
1950	Newcastle United	H	First Division	7-0

This was Spurs' eighth consecutive win in the First Division, a run that had taken them towards the top of the table after a hesitant start to life in the top flight. The goals were scored by Alf Ramsey (penalty), Sonny Walters, Les Bennett, Eddie Baily and Les Medley (three) in front of a crowd of 70,336, the biggest crowd to watch Spurs home and away all season.

| 1961 | Sheffield Wednesday | A | First Division | 0-0 |
| 1965 | Hungarian Select XI | H | Friendly | 4-0 |

Maurice Norman broke his leg in five places during the game, an injury that eventually forced him to retire despite a two-year battle to recover full fitness. Spurs' goals were scored by Dave Mackay from the penalty spot and a hat-trick from Alan Gilzean.

1967	Chelsea	H	First Division	2-0
1970	Coventry City	H	League Cup 5th Round	4-1
1972	Leicester City	A	First Division	1-0

1978	Chelsea	A	First Division	3-1
1989	Crystal Palace	A	First Division	3-2
1990	Everton	A	First Division	1-1
1995	Arsenal	H	FA Premier League	2-1

The disappearance of all three of Spurs' foreign captures the previous season – Klinsmann, Popescu and Dumitrescu – had prompted a number of new arrivals, including Chris Armstrong and Ruel Fox, both of whom made their North London derby debuts. Arsenal had also brought in new faces, including Dennis Bergkamp, who cost £7.5 million. He too was making his first appearance in the big clash and scored the first goal; collecting the ball from Paul Merson he twisted and shot in one move that left Ian Walker bemused in the Spurs goal. It was Fox, however, who became the key man in the game, constantly running at Arsenal's defence and setting up an increasing number of chances for Spurs' strike force of Teddy Sheringham and Chris Armstrong. Sheringham brought Spurs level, converting Fox's cross at close range and then set up the winner, slotting through a pass for Armstrong that he in turn shot past Seaman before the Arsenal defence could react.

NOVEMBER 19TH

| 1887 | Woolwich Arsenal | H | Friendly | 2-1 |

Spurs met Arsenal for the first time: played at the Marshes (one of Spurs' last games at this venue) the match kicked off late following the late appearance of the Arsenal team and was therefore abandoned with 15 minutes still to play. The line-ups and scorers of this match do not survive.

| 1892 | Erith | H | Southern Alliance | 3-2 |

On the same day Tommy Clay was born in Leicester. After two years with Leicester Fosse Tommy joined Spurs in January 1914 after impressing manager Peter McWilliam with his performances in a cup tie between the two sides. Not only was Tommy Clay one of the finest full-backs of his day he is also rightly regarded as one of the best players to have turned out for Spurs. Captain of the team when they won the Second Division title in 1919-20 he handed over the captaincy the following season to Arthur Grimsdell but still turned in exceptional performances as Spurs lifted the FA Cup at Stamford Bridge. After 15 years with Spurs he was allowed to leave in 1929 and became player-coach at Northfleet, Spurs nursery side. He became a publican in St Albans, as well as joining the local non-League club as trainer and coach and later returned to his initial trade of bricklayer. He won five England caps whilst with Spurs and died in Southend in 1949.

1896	Gravesend	H	Wellingborough Charity Cup	3-2
1898	Clapton	A	FA Cup 2nd Qualifying Round	1-1
1904	Brighton & Hove Albion	A	Southern League	1-1
1906	Oxford University	H	Friendly	2-1
1907	Millwall	A	Southern Charity Cup 1st Round Replay	1-2
1910	Aston Villa	H	First Division	1-2
1921	Burnley	H	First Division	1-1
1927	Sheffield United	H	First Division	2-2
1932	Chesterfield	H	Second Division	4-1
1938	Swansea Town	A	Second Division	1-1
1949	Grimsby Town	A	Second Division	3-2
1955	Wolverhampton Wanderers	H	First Division	2-1
1960	Birmingham City	H	First Division	6-0
1966	Sheffield Wednesday	A	First Division	0-1
1977	Brighton & Hove Albion	H	Second Division	0-0
1983	Luton Town	A	First Division	4-2
1994	Aston Villa	H	FA Premier League	3-4
1997				

Christian Gross was appointed first-team coach following the recent resignation of Gerry Francis. Born in Switzerland, Gross had been a player for Grasshoppers, Lausanne, Neuchatel Xamax, Bochurn, St Gallen and Lugano, subsequently becoming coach with Swiss Fourth Division club FC Wil. After guiding them into the Second Division he took over at Grasshoppers in 1993 and took them to two League championships and the Swiss Cup.

NOVEMBER 20TH

1897	Luton Town	H	FA Cup 2nd Qualifying Round	3-4
1899	Queens Park Rangers	H	Southern District Combination	3-1
1905	Fulham	A	Western League	3-0
1909	Aston Villa	A	First Division	2-3
1915	Brentford	A	London Combination [1st competition]	1-1
1920	Preston North End	H	First Division	1-2
1926	Burnley	A	First Division	0-5

Despite the result Spurs did a good job in keeping the score down to five, for they lost three players before the end of the match and one or two of the others were little more than passengers. Both Poynton and Lindsay failed to return after half-time, Poynton through injury and Lindsay suffering the effects of flu, and Blair joined them in the dressing-room some 15 minutes before the end. In fact, Spurs finished the game with Bert Smith at full-back and Jimmy Seed and Jimmy Dimmock playing at half-back.

1929 Billy Minter resigned as manager of Spurs, a run of bad results having brought on stress and anxiety and with Minter therefore suffering from ill-health. Minter did not leave the club, however, switching to assistant-secretary, whilst Spurs subsequently appointed Bury manager Percy Smith to the vacant manager's position at White Hart Lane. Smith enjoyed some success during his early days at Spurs, guiding them to promotion back into the First Division in 1932-33 and third position in the top flight the following season, but thereafter it all began to go wrong. The club were relegated back to the Second Division at the end of 1934-35, and in April of that year Smith tendered his resignation, citing interference from the board as being behind his reason. The board strenuously denied the allegation.

1937	West Ham United	H	Second Division	2-0
1943	Watford	H	Football League South	4-2
1948	Grimsby Town	A	Second Division	1-1
1954	Leicester City	H	First Division	5-1
1965	Northampton Town	A	First Division	2-0
1968	Arsenal	A	League Cup Semi-Final 1st Leg	0-1

This was only the second time Spurs and Arsenal had met in senior cup football following their FA Cup pairing in 1949 and the first time they had met in the League Cup. The game was settled in injury time; an attempted header back to his own goalkeeper by Joe Kinnear did not have sufficient strength to carry it into the arms of Pat Jennings and John Radford pounced on the loose ball to fire home into the roof of the net.

1971	West Bromwich Albion	H	First Division	3-2
1976	Sunderland	A	First Division	1-2
1982	West Ham United	H	First Division	2-1
1985	Portsmouth	H	Milk Cup 4th Round	0-0
1988	Sheffield Wednesday	A	First Division	2-0
1993	Leeds United	H	FA Premier League	1-1

NOVEMBER 21ST

1885	South Hackney	A	Friendly	3-1
1891	City Ramblers	A	London Senior Cup 3rd Round	1-4
1896	Blackpool	H	Friendly	0-2
1903	West Ham United	H	Southern League	2-1
1904	Plymouth Argyle	H	Western League	2-0
1908	Gainsborough Trinity	A	Second Division	2-0

The only time Spurs visited Gainsborough Trinity for a League game saw goals from Bobby Steel and Bert Middlemiss settle the game. Spurs drew 1-1 at home later in the season, and by the time Spurs were back in the Second Division, Gainsborough had been voted out of the League.

1910	Millwall	N	London FA Charity Cup Semi-Final Replay	2-0
1914	Manchester United	H	First Division	2-0
1921	Arsenal	N	London FA Charity Cup Semi-Final Replay	1-2 [aet]
1924	West Ham United	A	First Division	1-1
1925	Bolton Wanderers	H	First Division	2-3
1931	Port Vale	H	Second Division	9-3

The first of only three occasions in which Spurs have scored nine goals in a League match (the other occasions being against Nottingham Forest in 1962 and Bristol Rovers in 1977) with the goals being scored by Bert Lyons (penalty), Davie Colquhoun, Willie Davies (three), Jimmy Brain (two) and George Hunt (two).

1942	Watford	H	Football League South	6-0
1953	Huddersfield Town	H	First Division	1-0
1959	Everton	H	First Division	3-0
1964	Aston Villa	H	First Division	4-0
1970	Newcastle United	H	First Division	1-2
1981	Manchester United	H	First Division	3-1
1984	Sunderland	A	Milk Cup 4th Round	0-0
1987	Luton Town	A	First Division	0-2
1992	Aston Villa	H	FA Premier League	0-0
1995	Middlesbrough	A	FA Premier League	1-0

Spurs first visit to Middlebrough's new Riverside Stadium saw them become the first visitors to register a win thanks to Chris Armstrong's goal.

NOVEMBER 22ND

1884	St Peter's 2nd XI	H	Friendly	3-2
1890	Barking	H	London Senior Cup Preliminary Round	2-0
1902	Swindon Town	H	Southern League	2-0
1909	Preston North End	A	First Division	1-4
1913	Everton	H	First Division	4-1
1919	Nottingham Forest	A	Second Division	1-1
1930	West Bromwich Albion	A	Second Division	2-0
1941	Chelsea	A	London War League	1-1
1947	Fulham	A	Second Division	2-0
1952	Aston Villa	A	First Division	3-0
1958	Birmingham City	H	First Division	0-4
1969	Manchester United	A	First Division	1-3
1975	Manchester City	A	First Division	1-2
1977	Arsenal	A	Friendly	3-1

This was a testimonial match for Pat Rice and Spurs' goals were scored by Thomas Heffernan, Ralph Coates and John Duncan.

1978	Liverpool	H	First Division	0-0
1980	Birmingham City	A	First Division	1-2
1986	Oxford United	A	First Division	4-2

This match is generally regarded as the first in which Spurs played a midfield of five players, all of whom were expected to support Clive Allen, the lone striker. Certainly Allen's form already during the season had seen him fire home 12 League goals before the visit to Oxford, where he struck twice more to take his tally to 14. Spurs' other goals were both scored by Chris Waddle, his first in the League that season.

1989	Tranmere Rovers	A	Littlewoods Cup 4th Round	2-2

NOVEMBER 23RD

1889	Hampstead	H	Friendly	1-0
1895	Ilford	A	FA Cup 3rd Qualifying Round	5-1
1898	Clapton	H	FA Cup 2nd Qualifying Round Replay	2-1
1901	Swindon Town	A	Southern League	3-1
1903	Millwall	H	London League	2-3
1907	Bristol Rovers	A	Southern League	0-0
1912	Newcastle United	H	First Division	1-0
1918	Clapton Orient	A	London Combination	3-0
1929	Bristol City	H	Second Division	2-1
1935	Southampton	A	Second Division	0-2
1940	Luton Town	H	Football League South	2-1

1941 Alan Mullery born in Notting Hill, London. Signed by Fulham as a professional at the age of 17, he was quickly drafted into the first team and soon established himself alongside such stars as Johnny Haynes and George Cohen. In March 1964, with Spurs looking for replacements for Danny Blanchflower and Dave Mackay, he was transferred for a fee of £72,500. Although he took time to settle at White Hart Lane he gradually became an integral part of the midfield and when Dave Mackay left in 1968 became club captain. He won an FA Cup medal in 1967, the League Cup in 1971 and the UEFA Cup the following year. That European success was made all the sweeter by coming at the end of a season that had seen Alan, struggling with a pelvic strain, loaned to Fulham in an attempt to recover. He was recalled on the morning of the semi-final first leg against AC Milan, scored in the second leg and then got the goal that ensured Spurs won the cup against Wolves. In the summer of 1972 he was transferred back to Fulham permanently and along with Bobby Moore guided them to the 1975 FA Cup, although they were beaten by West Ham at the last hurdle. He retired as a player in May 1976 and then went into management, taking over the reigns at Brighton, Charlton, Crystal Palace, QPR and a second spell with Brighton. He won 35 caps for England whilst with Spurs and was later awarded the MBE.

1946	Plymouth Argyle	H	Second Division	2-1
1957	Luton Town	H	First Division	3-1
1963	Ipswich Town	A	First Division	3-2
1966	Polish Select XI	H	Friendly	2-1
1968	Southampton	A	First Division	1-2

1974	Birmingham City	H	First Division	0-0
1976	Arsenal	H	Pat Jennings Testimonial	3-2

Pat Jennings' first testimonial, playing for Spurs against Arsenal, saw Spurs win 3-2 thanks to goals from Peter Taylor and two from Jimmy Greaves, who came out of retirement in order to play. Greaves later appeared for Spurs in the testimonials for John Pratt and Steve Perryman.

1983	Bayern Munich	A	UEFA Cup 3rd Round 1st Leg	0-1

Spurs' visit to the Olympic Stadium in Munich the previous year had seen fog engulf the stadium, leaving the spectators with little view of the proceedings on the pitch. In this game they were similarly inconvenienced, for although the fog stayed away, the temperature seldom rose above five degrees below zero! The only goal of the game was scored five minutes from time by Karl Heinz Rummenigge, but Spurs' overall defensive display had been good enough to give them hope of overcoming the deficit in the second leg.

1985	Queens Park Rangers	H	First Division	1-1
1988	Coventry City	H	First Division	1-1
1991	Sheffield United	H	First Division	0-1
1994	Chelsea	H	FA Premier League	0-0

NOVEMBER 24TH

1883	Sekforde Rovers	A	Friendly	2-0
1888	Plaistow	H	Friendly	4-0
1894	Clapton	A	FA Cup 3rd Qualifying Round	4-0
1900	Reading	A	Southern League	1-3
1902	Reading	H	Southern Charity Cup 1st Round	1-1
1906	Brighton & Hove Albion	A	Southern League	0-2
1917	West Ham United	H-Highbury		
			London Combination	2-0
1923	Arsenal	H	First Division	3-0
1924	Clapton Orient	N	London FA Charity Cup Semi-Final	1-2
1928	Bristol City	A	Second Division	1-2

1931 John L Jones died in Sunderland. Born in Rhuddlan in 1866, John had begun his career with his local club before moving into League circles with Grimsby Town. A subsequent move to Sheffield United resulted in him winning his first cap for Wales, and his next move to Spurs in 1897 was considered a highly valuable capture by the club. He was Spurs' centre-half and captain when they won the Southern League and FA Cup in consecutive seasons, and John further earned his place in Spurs' history books by becoming the first player to be capped whilst playing for the club, a feat he achieved in February 1898. In 1904 he was transferred to Watford, but after only one season left to join Worcester City. He was later a cricket coach and groundsman and at the time of his death was employed as a pattern maker, falling down a flight of stairs at work and sustaining a fatal head injury.

1934	Sheffield Wednesday	H	First Division	3-2
1945	Chelsea	H	Football League South	3-2
1951	Portsmouth	A	First Division	0-2
1956	Manchester United	H	First Division	2-2

1960 Garry Brooke born in Bethnal Green, London. If there is ever a debate for a Spurs 'super-sub' then Garry Brooke will be a definite candidate, for as well as making 84 appearances for the first team he was also brought on as substitute on 45 occasions! First linking with Spurs in June 1977 he worked his way through the ranks to make his League debut (as substitute, what else!) in November 1980 against West Bromwich Albion. At the end of the season he won an FA Cup winners' medal, coming on as substitute in the first match (in place of Ricky Villa) and remaining on the bench for the replay. He won a second medal the following year, coming on for Micky Hazard in both games! In February 1983 he suffered serious injuries in a car crash that effectively ended his Spurs career, for although he recovered he was transferred to Norwich for £50,000 in 1985. After that Garry played for numerous clubs both here and abroad, trying to recapture the form that made him a brief but firm Spurs favourite – a devilish midfielder with a thundering shot, exemplified by the hat-trick he scored against Coventry in October 1982.

1962	Burnley	A	First Division	1-2
1971	Arsenal	H	First Division	1-1
1973	Wolverhampton Wanderers	H	First Division	1-3
1975	West Ham United	A	League Cup 4th Round Replay	2-0 [aet]

Extra time goals from Willie Young and John Duncan finally took Spurs past West Ham in the League Cup and on to a home match against Doncaster Rovers in the next round.

1979	Everton	A	First Division	1-1
1984	Chelsea	H	First Division	1-1

1990	Norwich City	H	First Division	2-1
1993	Wimbledon	H	FA Premier League	1-1
1996	Arsenal	A	FA Premier League	1-1
1997	Crystal Palace	H	FA Premier League	0-1

NOVEMBER 25TH

1899	Corinthians	H	Friendly	5-1
1901	Cambridge University	H	Friendly	3-1
1907	Millwall	H	Western League	0-3
1911	Newcastle United	H	First Division	1-2
1916	Chelsea	A	London Combination	4-2
1922	Newcastle United	A	First Division	1-1
1933	Derby County	H	First Division	1-2
1939	Charlton Athletic	H	Football League South Group A	4-2
1944	Fulham	H	Football League South	2-1
1950	Huddersfield Town	A	First Division	2-3

1951 Willie Young born in Heriot. After failing a trial with Falkirk Willie was later snapped up by Aberdeen, signing professional forms in 1969. His 6' 3" frame made him an ideal man for the role of centre-half, and over the next six years he established himself as a commanding player for both club and country. In September 1975 he was signed by Spurs for £120,000 and instantly became a cult figure at White Hart Lane and an imposing sight for any attacker. In March 1977, with Spurs all but relegated from the First Division, Willie linked up again with Terry Neill at Arsenal for £80,000. He played in three consecutive FA Cup finals whilst at Highbury, then moved on to Nottingham Forest and effectively finished his career with Norwich City, although he later appeared as a non-contract player with Darlington.

1961	Leicester City	H	First Division	1-2
1967	West Bromwich Albion	A	First Division	0-2
1972	Liverpool	H	First Division	1-2
1978	Wolverhampton Wanderers	H	First Division	1-0
1989	Derby County	H	First Division	1-2
1995	Chelsea	A	FA Premier League	0-0

NOVEMBER 26TH

1876 Tom Smith born in Maryport, Cumberland. Tom joined Spurs in May 1898 from Preston North End and slotted into the team straight away at outside-right. He was an important member of the team that won the Southern League in 1899-1900 and the FA Cup the following year. Indeed, Tom scored Spurs' second goal in the replay, although he also created a considerable number of the 15 that Sandy Brown plundered in the same competition. Although Tom was highly prized at Spurs and equally coveted by other London clubs, he did not win any international honours whilst at Spurs. At the end of the 1901-02 season Tom announced he was retiring and returned to Cumberland, a move which totally shocked Spurs. Preston North End coaxed him out of retirement in March 1904 and he played in the final eight games of the season to help them to win the Second Division title. He later played for Carlisle United and made one final appearance for Spurs, playing for the 1901 cup-winning side in a benefit game for Sam Mountford in April 1907.

1892	Caledonian Athletic	H	Friendly	5-0
1898	Royal Artillery	A	Southern League	3-2
1900	Bristol City	H	Western League	4-1
1904	Luton Town	A	Southern League	0-1
1906	Portsmouth	H	Western League	4-2
1910	Sunderland	A	First Division	0-4
1921	Burnley	A	First Division	0-1
1928	Charlton Athletic	N	London FA Charity Cup Semi-Final	5-3
1932	Bradford City	A	Second Division	1-0
1938	Chesterfield	H	Second Division	2-2
1949	Queens Park Rangers	H	Second Division	3-0
1955	Aston Villa	A	First Division	2-0
1956	Partick Thistle	A	Anglo-Scottish Floodlit Tournament	0-2
1960	West Bromwich Albion	A	First Division	3-1
1966	Southampton	H	First Division	5-3
1977	Bolton Wanderers	A	Second Division	0-1

The Second Division's game of the day saw League leaders Bolton entertain second placed Spurs at Burnden Park in front of a crowd of 32,266. Bolton took both points with the only goal of the game being scored in the very last minute of the match through Roy Greaves, although Spurs had earlier had a goal by Neil McNab disallowed. This win enabled Bolton to open a four point gap at the top.

1983	Queens Park Rangers	H	First Division	3-2
1986	Cambridge United	A	Littlewoods Cup 4th Round	3-1
1988	Queens Park Rangers	H	First Division	2-2
1994	Liverpool	A	FA Premier League	1-1

NOVEMBER 27TH

1886	Fillebrook	A	Friendly	1-4
1897	Bristol City	A	Southern League	1-3
1899	The Kaffirs	H	Friendly	6-4
1905	Cambridge University	H	Friendly	2-1
1909	Sheffield United	H	First Division	2-1
1915	West Ham United	H	London Combination [1st competition]	3-0
1920	Preston North End	A	First Division	1-4
1926	Newcastle United	H	First Division	1-3
1937	Bradford Park Avenue	A	Second Division	1-3
1943	Crystal Palace	A	Football League South	0-3

1947   Jimmy Pearce born in Tottenham. Jimmy had been connected with the club whilst still at school and was signed as an apprentice in 1963, joining the professional ranks in May 1965. Although he is perhaps best known as a winger, he never really managed to make any one position his, with the result he was often brought on as a substitute, filling in wherever he could. He was however a member of the side that won the League Cup in 1973, although soon after it was revealed that he was suffering from a rare bone complaint and in 1974 he was forced to retire.

| 1948 | Nottingham Forest | H | Second Division | 0-0 |

The game was abandoned after only 17 minutes owing to fog and replayed on 12th February with Spurs winning 2-0.

1954	Burnley	A	First Division	2-1
1965	Stoke City	H	First Division	2-2
1971	Chelsea	A	First Division	0-1
1974	Red Star Belgrade	H	Alan Gilzean Testimonial	2-0
1976	Stoke City	H	First Division	2-0
1982	Liverpool	A	First Division	0-3
1985	Portsmouth	A	Milk Cup 4th Round Replay	0-0 [aet]
1990	Sheffield United	A	Rumbelows Cup 4th Round	2-0
1993	Queens Park Rangers	A	FA Premier League	1-1
1996	Bolton Wanderers	A	Coca-Cola Cup 4th Round	1-6

The match was a total disaster from Spurs' point of view, especially a woeful second-half performance. John McGinlay had given Bolton the lead after six minutes, but Teddy Sheringham equalised with a free-kick just before the 20 minute mark. McGinlay restored Bolton's lead on 37 minutes, but Spurs had matched their opponents for much of the half and returned after the break looking for a second equaliser. It didn't come, for a third goal by Bolton on the hour seemed to signal a Spurs collapse – three further goals were recorded and one denied after a shot hit the post and ran along the goal-line.

NOVEMBER 28TH

1885	Dalston Rovers	H	Friendly	3-0
1891	Old St Stephen's	H	Friendly	0-0
1896	Millwall Athletic	H	Southern League	1-3
1903	Brighton & Hove Albion	H	South Eastern League	7-0
1904	Cambridge University	H	Friendly	2-2

1907   Tom Evans born in Ton Pentre, Glamorgan. Signed by Spurs as an amateur in May 1927 he did not become a professional until 1931, by which time he had already made his debut for the club, being pressed into service on Boxing Day 1929. Thereafter he struggled to hold a regular place in the side, making just 94 League appearances before he was released in 1937. He then joined West Bromwich Albion although did not make an appearance for their first team.

1908	Grimsby Town	H	Second Division	2-0
1914	Bolton Wanderers	A	First Division	2-4
1925	Notts County	A	First Division	2-4
1931	Millwall	A	Second Division	2-1
1936	Plymouth Argyle	H	Second Division	1-3
1942	Crystal Palace	A	Football League South	0-0
1953	Sheffield United	A	First Division	2-5

1959	Blackpool	A	First Division	2-2
1964	Liverpool	A	First Division	1-1
1970	Everton	A	First Division	0-0
1973	Dinamo Tbilisi	A	UEFA Cup 3rd Round 1st Leg	1-1
1981	Notts County	A	First Division	2-2
1984	Bohemians Prague	H	UEFA Cup 3rd Round 1st Leg	2-0

The final score-line was flattering to Spurs to say the least, for Bohemians were undoubtedly the more creative and better side on the night, forcing their way through the Spurs defence all night yet not being able to finish. Even Spurs' first goal had an element of luck about it; a cross from John Chiedozie was sliced into the Bohemians net by one of their own players! Even with this kind of luck, Spurs still spent more time trying to prevent their opponents from scoring than creating chances of their own, although Gary Stevens scored a crucial second goal in the last minute to give them hope that they might be able to survive the second leg.

| 1987 | Liverpool | H | First Division | 0-2 |
| 1992 | Manchester City | A | FA Premier League | 1-0 |

NOVEMBER 29TH

1884	Hadley	H	Friendly	0-1
1902	Portsmouth	A	Western League	2-2
1913	Liverpool	A	First Division	1-2
1919	Nottingham Forest	H	Second Division	5-2
1924	Sheffield United	H	First Division	4-1
1930	Port Vale	H	Second Division	5-0

1934 Terry Dyson born in Malton, Yorkshire. Terry joined Spurs in December 1954 as an amateur, signing full professional forms in April 1955, by which time he had made his League debut. Although initially understudy to George Robb and Terry Medwin, Terry Dyson made sporadic appearances until the signing of Cliff Jones prompted him to ask Bill Nicholson for a transfer. Nicholson refused, and Terry thus became an important part of the team that won the double. Indeed, he scored the crucial second goal against Leicester with a header, even though he was barely 5' 3" tall. Although he lost his place in the side that retained the cup the following year, he did play in the 1963 European Cup-Winners' Cup final scoring two goals as Spurs overwhelmed Athletico Madrid 5-1. In 1965 he was given a cut price transfer to Fulham for £5,000, remaining at Craven Cottage for three years before finishing his League career with Colchester United.

| 1941 | Charlton Athletic | A | London War League | 1-2 |
| 1947 | Coventry City | H | Second Division | 2-1 |

1948 Peter Collins born in Chelmsford, Essex. Signed by Spurs in January 1968 for a fee of £5,500 from Chelmsford City (with a further £4,000 being payable once he had made ten first-team appearances), the high point of his career at Spurs was undoubtedly an appearance in the 1971 League Cup final, replacing the injured Mike England. When England recovered Peter went back into the reserves, but a serious ankle injury eventually led to him retiring in 1974 at the age of 26 years.

| 1952 | Sunderland | H | First Division | 2-2 |
| 1954 | Accrington Stanley | A | Friendly | 0-0 |

The only time Spurs met the romantically named Accrington Stanley at Peel Park came to an abrupt end when the referee abandoned the match after 52 minutes owing to heavy rainfall.

| 1958 | West Bromwich Albion | A | First Division | 3-4 |
| 1967 | Olympique Lyonnais | A | European Cup-Winners' Cup 2nd Round 2nd Leg | 0-1 |

Spurs had been involved in a few battles during their European campaigns, but nothing quite as bad as this. The problem initially seemed to stem from the kind of tackling Spurs put in, the type of tackle that would be seen on any English League ground on any Saturday but which was alien to the French. The French then seemed intent to get their retaliation in first, with Spurs players being kicked and punched while the ball was elsewhere. The game finally exploded on 33 minutes following an Alan Mullery tackle on Guy, both men falling to the ground. As they struggled to their feet, Guy aimed a kick at Mullery's face and knocked him unconscious, with Spurs players running over to protect their fallen team-mate. As they ran, the French players were aiming kicks and punches at all and sundry, also helped by scores of spectators from the crowd who poured on to the pitch. When order was eventually restored, Mullery and Guy were sent off, although that didn't stop Guy from trying to attack Alan Gilzean at half-time! After the game Bill Nicholson, who was also struck, said 'Some of their tackling was a disgrace, they were body-checking from the start. I can only assume Mullery was sent off for retaliating in that scuffle.' The only goal of the match came in the 75th minute, a further injustice for Spurs to contend with.

| 1972 | Red Star Belgrade | H | UEFA Cup 3rd Round 1st Leg | 2-0 |
| 1975 | Burnley | H | First Division | 2-1 |

1980	West Bromwich Albion	H	First Division	2-3
1986	Nottingham Forest	H	First Division	2-3
1988	Southampton	A	Littlewoods Cup 4th Round	1-2
1989	Tranmere Rovers	H	Littlewoods Cup 4th Round Replay	4-0
1997	Everton	A	FA Premier League	2-0

NOVEMBER 30TH

1889	Foxes	H	Friendly	1-0
1895	London Welsh	H	Friendly	3-2
1903	Bristol Rovers	H	Western League	2-1
1907	Leyton	H	Southern League	1-0
1908	West Ham United	A	London FA Charity Cup 2nd Round	2-0
1912	Oldham Athletic	A	First Division	1-4
1918	Chelsea	A	London Combination	1-3
1929	Notts County	A	Second Division	1-0
1935	Blackpool	H	Second Division	3-1
1940	Southend United	A	Football League South	2-3

1944   George Graham born in Bargeddie, North Lanarkshire. He began his playing career on the books of Aston Villa, signing professional forms in 1961. He went on to play for Chelsea, Arsenal, Manchester United, Portsmouth, Crystal Palace and had a brief spell in America in 1978. At Chelsea, he linked especially well with Terry Venables, although the pairing was broken up out by Terry being sold to Spurs and George going to Arsenal. Whilst at Highbury he helped Arsenal win the Inter-Cities Fairs Cup in 1970 and the domestic double of League title and FA Cup the following season, and subsequently went on to collect 12 caps for Scotland. He retired as a player in 1980 and coached at Queens Park Rangers before taking over as manager of Millwall in 1982. Having returned the club to the Second Division he was lured back to Arsenal in 1986, guiding the club to two League titles, two League Cups and the FA Cup and European Cup-Winners' Cup during his nine years in charge. In February 1995 he was forced to resign following allegations of financial improprieties, subsequently being handed a year's ban by the FA for misconduct. He returned in September 1996 as manager of Leeds United, steering the club into Europe. Two years later he agreed to take over as manager of Spurs in place of Christian Gross. While there was much media speculation that the fans at White Hart Lane would find it difficult to accept as manager a man who had such connections with Highbury, George Graham possesses the experience and ability to restore Spurs to former glories.

1946	Leicester City	A	Second Division	1-1
1957	Manchester United	A	First Division	4-3

Manchester United were the reigning League champions and were beginning to return to top form, sitting in third place in the League. Spurs, by comparison, had a slow start and had yet to win an away match during the season, a fact that was pointed out by United's manager Matt Busby in his programme notes! Bobby Smith scored a hat-trick and Spurs' other goal was scored by a name Spurs fans would have been familiar with; Blanchflower, although it was a Jackie own goal rather than an effort from his brother Danny. Sadly, this was to be the last time United's great side came into direct competition against Spurs, for in February 1958 they were decimated by the air crash at Munich.

1960   Gary Lineker born in Leicester. He joined the local club as an apprentice and after being upgraded to the professional ranks made his League debut in 1979. He won a Second Division championship medal with Leicester and in 1985 was transferred to Everton for £800,000. He spent just one season with the Merseysiders, scoring 40 goals but missing out on both the League and FA Cup honours to Liverpool, although he did win Footballer of the Year award from both the writers and players associations. He then went to Mexico with the England squad and won the 'Golden Boot' for finishing the competition's top goalscorer, which alerted Europe's top clubs as to his talents. A £2,750,000 deal took him to Barcelona where he won domestic and European honours, the latter in the European Cup-Winners' Cup. He moved back to Britain in 1989, linking up with former Barcelona manager Terry Venables at Spurs and two years later won his first major honour in the domestic game, an FA Cup-winners' medal (despite becoming only the second player to miss a penalty in an FA Cup final at Wembley). He won his first England cap in 1984 and finished his England career with 80 caps and 48 goals, one goal agonisingly short of Bobby Charlton's record, which he might have equalled but for an uncharacteristic penalty miss against Brazil. At the end of the 1991-92 season he moved on from Spurs to Japan to help launch the Japanese League, although a niggling injury later forced him to retire from playing. A superb ambassador for both the game, where he was never booked, and his country, being awarded the OBE in 1992. He is now a television presenter for the BBC.

1963	Sheffield Wednesday	H	First Division	1-1
1974	Sheffield United	A	First Division	1-0
1985	Aston Villa	A	First Division	2-1

DECEMBER 1ST

1883	Sekforde Rovers	A	Friendly	1-0
1888	Old St Mark's	H	Friendly	5-1
1894	Romford	A	FA Amateur Cup 3rd Qualifying Round	8-0
1897	Gravesend United	A	Friendly	0-3
1900	Kettering Town	H	Southern League	1-0
1902	Woolwich Arsenal	H	London League	1-0
1906	Reading	H	Southern League	2-0

1913 Arthur Hitchens born in Devonport. Arthur signed as a professional with Spurs in January 1935 having previously turned out for Lea Bridge Gasworks. Originally a full-back he was converted to half-back by the time he made his Spurs debut and looked set for a glittering career and a possible England call up when the Second World War broke out. Although he played in the first three seasons of war football, a shoulder injury sustained in January 1942 forced him to call a halt to his career and he retired from the game. He died on 10th October 1975.

1917	Fulham	A	London Combination	3-4
1923	West Bromwich Albion	H	First Division	0-0
1928	Barnsley	H	Second Division	2-0
1934	Birmingham City	A	First Division	1-2

1937 White Hart Lane played host to the England v Czechoslovakia international, with England winning 5-4. Three of England's goals were scored by Stanley Matthews, the only hat-trick of his career.

1945	Millwall	H	Football League South	5-1
1951	Liverpool	H	First Division	2-3
1956	Birmingham City	A	First Division	0-0
1962	Everton	H	First Division	0-0
1973	Leicester City	A	First Division	0-3
1979	Manchester United	H	First Division	1-2
1982	Luton Town	H	Milk Cup 4th Round	1-0
1984	Coventry City	A	First Division	1-1
1990	Chelsea	A	First Division	2-3

Spurs were subsequently fined by the Football League for being late in handing in their team sheet to the referee. The reason was simple enough; the team coach was clamped and later towed away from outside the hotel where the team were having lunch prior to journeying to Stamford Bridge! The kit was also on the coach at the time!

| 1991 | Arsenal | A | First Division | 0-2 |
| 1993 | Blackburn Rovers | H | Coca-Cola Cup 4th Round | 1-0 |

DECEMBER 2ND

1899	Swindon Town	A	Southern League	2-0
1901	Army Association	H	Friendly	2-1
1905	Brentford	A	Southern League	3-0
1907	Crystal Palace	H	Western League	1-0
1911	Sheffield United	A	First Division	2-1
1916	Arsenal	H-Highbury		
			London Combination	4-1
1922	Nottingham Forest	H	First Division	2-1
1933	Manchester City	A	First Division	0-2
1939	Clapton Orient	A	Football League South Group A	1-2

1941 Mike England born in Greenfield, North Wales. Originally signed by Blackburn Rovers as an inside-forward when aged 16, Mike was later tried at a number of other positions before settling into central defence, so much so that he was capped by Wales and considered one of the best prospects in the country. Signed by Spurs in 1966 as a replacement for Maurice Norman, he cost £95,000, then a record for a defender, but his performances over the next nine years confirmed he was well worth every penny of the fee. Whilst with Spurs he won the FA Cup, UEFA Cup and League Cup, although he missed the 1971 League Cup success through injury. After announcing his retirement in 1975 he later turned out for Cardiff and played in America before becoming manager of Wales in 1980, remaining in charge until 1988. He was awarded the MBE in 1984.

1944	West Ham United	A	Football League South	1-0
1950	Middlesbrough	H	First Division	3-3
1961	West Bromwich Albion	A	First Division	4-2
1967	Newcastle United	H	First Division	1-1
1972	Southampton	A	First Division	1-1

1980	West Ham United	A	League Cup 5th Round	0-1
1981	Fulham	H	League Cup 4th Round	1-0
1989	Luton Town	A	First Division	0-0
1995	Everton	H	FA Premier League	0-0
1996	Liverpool	H	FA Premier League	0-2

DECEMBER 3RD

1880   Percy Humphreys born in Cambridge. Percy was a renowned centre-forward for QPR, Notts County, Leicester Fosse and Chelsea before signing for Spurs in December 1909, having lost his place at Stamford Bridge to Vivian Woodward. Although Percy made only 45 appearances in the League for Spurs and scored 24 goals, none were as vital as the one he scored in the game against Chelsea in the final match of 1909-10 season, for it ensured Chelsea were relegated instead of Spurs into the Second Division. Thereafter he struggled to command a regular place in the side and was transferred back to Leicester in October 1911, later playing for Norwich City. He died in London on 13th April 1959.

1887	Luton Town	A	Friendly	2-1
1892	Polytechnic	A	London Senior Cup 3rd Round	3-3
1904	Swindon Town	H	Southern League	6-3
1910	Woolwich Arsenal	H	First Division	3-1
1921	Sheffield United	H	First Division	2-1
1927	Burnley	H	First Division	5-0
1928	Clapton Orient	A	London Professional Football Charity Fund	4-2
1932	Swansea Town	H	Second Division	7-0

Spurs' final goal was scored by Willie Evans from penalty spot, although his first attempt was saved by the Swansea keeper Ferguson. The referee ordered the kick retaken following an infringement by a Swansea player, and as Evans ran up to take the penalty again he was tripped! After a hold-up whilst the referee sought to regain control of the game Evans was allowed to take the kick and scored. As the players made their way back to the half-way line another altercation took place, with the referee consulting with his linesman before sending Swansea's Miller off the field.

1938	Tranmere Rovers	A	Second Division	2-0
1949	Preston North End	A	Second Division	3-1
1955	Blackpool	H	First Division	1-1
1956	Red Banner	H	Friendly	7-1
1960	Burnley	H	First Division	4-4
1963	Manchester United	H	European Cup-Winners' Cup 2nd Round 1st Leg	2-0

Thanks to Spurs' victory in the European Cup-Winners' Cup in 1963 England had two entrants for the following season's competition, and they were paired together in the second round! Despite a certain familiarity with their opponents, Spurs set about the match as they would with those from overseas, looking to build up a good lead to take into the second leg. But for the much of the game, it seemed as though the only reward they would have was a one-goal lead established by Dave Mackay just after the hour. Then, three minutes from time, Terry Dyson pounced on a moment of hesitancy by Tony Dunne to add a second goal.

1966	Sunderland	A	First Division	1-0
1973	Bayern Munich	H	Phil Beal Testimonial	2-2
1975	Doncaster Rovers	H	League Cup 5th Round	7-2
1977	Southampton	H	Second Division	0-0
1983	Norwich City	A	First Division	1-2
1985	Liverpool	A	Screen Sports Super Cup Group A	0-2
1988	Everton	A	First Division	0-1
1994	Newcastle United	H	FA Premier League	4-2

On the same day that Teddy Sheringham scored a hat-trick to help bury Newcastle United, the draw for the FA Cup 3rd round was held. Although Spurs were still bannned from the competition, the FA were mindful that there was an appeal pending and therefore allowed Spurs' name to enter the draw. When the respective ball was drawn from the bag, the announcement was made: 'Spurs or bye will play Altrincham.'

DECEMBER 4TH

1886	Iona	A	Friendly	5-0
1897	Wellingborough	H	United League	5-0
1899	Chatham	A	Southern District Combination	1-0
1909	Woolwich Arsenal	A	First Division	0-1
1915	Chelsea	A	London Combination [1st competition]	1-8
1920	Sheffield United	H	First Division	4-1

1926	Leeds United	A	First Division	1-1
1937	Aston Villa	H	Second Division	2-1
1943	Queens Park Rangers	H	Football League South	2-2
1948	Fulham	A	Second Division	1-1
1954	Everton	H	First Division	1-3
1965	Burnley	A	First Division	1-1

Frank Saul became the first Spurs player to be sent off in a League match since 1928 when he was dismissed, one of the longest runs for fair play since the League was formed.

1968	Arsenal	H	League Cup Semi-Final 2nd Leg	1-1

With Arsenal one goal ahead from the first leg it was imperative Spurs got back on level terms quickly, but Arsenal's defence were equally concentrated on holding them out. Spurs' goal finally came on 68 minutes through Jimmy Greaves, but other than three long range efforts by Terry Venables they seldom looked like breaching Arsenal before or after. Three minutes from time, with extra time looking certain, John Radford headed home the aggregate winner to take Arsenal on to their date with destiny and Swindon Town.

1971	Southampton	H	First Division	1-0
1972	Liverpool	A	League Cup 5th Round	1-1
1974	Leeds United	A	First Division	1-2
1978	West Ham United	A	Friendly	2-4

This match was a testimonial for Billy Bonds with Spurs' goals being scored by Jimmy Holmes and John Pratt.

1982	West Bromwich Albion	H	First Division	1-1
1991	Coventry City	A	Rumbelows Cup 4th Round	2-1
1992	Nottingham Forest	A	Coca-Cola Cup 4th Round	0-2
1993	Newcastle United	H	FA Premier League	1-2

DECEMBER 5TH

1891	Minerva	A	Middlesex Senior Cup 2nd Round	0-2
1896	Reading	A	Southern League	1-2
1898	Kettering Town	H	United League	3-0
1900	Swindon Town	A	Western League	1-0

On the same day the first team were winning at Swindon, Jimmy Dimmock was born in Edmonton. He is perhaps best known for having scored the goal that won the 1921 FA Cup final, but over the course of 15 years associated with Spurs, he did much more to make his name. Signed as an amateur in 1916, he was promoted to the professional ranks in May 1919, signing for Spurs in the face of competition from Clapton (for whom he had guested during the First World War) and Arsenal. Seizing his place in the side following an injury to Jimmy Chipperfield, Jimmy Dimmock made the left-wing berth his own and helped the side win the Second Division title at the end of his first season. The following year saw the FA Cup return to the White Hart Lane boardroom, placed there thanks to Jimmy's match-winning goal against Wolves at Stamford Bridge. He weighed in with a considerable number of goals for Spurs during his career, finishing with 100 in 400 League appearances. In 1931 he was allowed to leave the club, signing with Thames and switching to Clapton Orient when Thames folded at the end of the 1931-32 season. He finished his playing career with non-League Ashford and died on 23rd December 1972. Whilst with Spurs he won three England caps, a figure considerably lower than his skills dictated he should have had.

1903	Luton Town	A	Southern League	2-3
1908	Fulham	A	Second Division	3-2
1910	Fulham	N	London FA Charity Cup Final	2-1
1914	Blackburn Rovers	H	First Division	0-4
1925	Aston Villa	H	First Division	2-2
1931	Bradford City	H	Second Division	1-5
1936	Coventry City	A	Second Division	0-1
1942	Queens Park Rangers	H	Football League South	6-0

1948	Terry Naylor born in Islington. Terry was linked with both Arsenal and Millwall as a youngster but chose to sign for Spurs as an amateur and gave up his job as a porter at Smithfield Market when offered professional forms in July 1969. Originally used midfield, a surplus of players in this position prompted a switch to defence and after making his debut in 1970 he went on to make 237 appearances in the League side. The subsequent emergence of Chris Hughton limited Terry's first-team opportunities and he was allowed to leave for Charlton in November 1980, retiring after a sustaining a broken leg in a friendly against West Ham in 1982. He later played non-League football and then became a reporter for a national newspaper.

1953	Wolverhampton Wanderers	H	First Division	2-3

1959	Blackburn Rovers	H	First Division	2-1
1964	Sheffield Wednesday	H	First Division	3-2
1970	Manchester United	H	First Division	2-2
1981	Coventry City	H	First Division	1-2
1984	Sunderland	H	Milk Cup 4th Round Replay	1-2

Having drawn away at struggling Sunderland in the first match Spurs were confidently expected to finish the task in the replay at White Hart Lane. They got off to a good start as well, with Graham Roberts opening the scoring from the penalty spot, but rather than build on that they lost their way, allowing Sunderland back into the game. Sunderland would eventually go on to Wembley, where they lost to Norwich City, the first time both finalists in the competition had been relegated from the First Division.

1987	Brentford	A	Friendly	0-0
1992	Chelsea	H	FA Premier League	1-2

DECEMBER 6TH

1884	Tottenham	H	Friendly	4-0
1890	Unity	A	Friendly	1-1
1902	Luton Town	H	Southern League	1-1
1909	Fulham	N	London FA Charity Cup Final	1-4
1913	West Bromwich Albion	H	First Division	3-0
1919	Fulham	A	Second Division	4-1
1924	Newcastle United	A	First Division	1-1
1930	Plymouth Argyle	A	Second Division	0-2
1941	West Ham United	H	London War League	1-1
1947	Newcastle United	A	Second Division	0-1
1952	Wolverhampton Wanderers	A	First Division	0-0
1955	Swansea Town	H	Friendly	4-1
1958	Preston North End	H	First Division	1-2

1965 Gordon Durie born in Paisley. After impressing with Hibernian Gordon was signed by Chelsea in 1986, proving a first-rate striker and collecting 12 caps whilst at Stamford Bridge. By 1991 it was claimed he was homesick and he was promptly signed by Spurs for £2 million! Although he made a scoring debut, he never really settled at White Hart Lane and later moved on to Glasgow Rangers to rediscover his goalscoring form.

1969	Coventry City	A	First Division	2-3
1972	Liverpool	H	League Cup 5th Round Replay	3-1

The match was effectively settled in a 20-minute spell when Spurs scored three times to put themselves in an unassailable lead thanks to John Pratt and Martin Chivers, who scored twice. It was not just the goals that finished off Liverpool either, for Spurs' style of play also earned plaudits.

1975	Sheffield United	A	First Division	2-1
1980	Liverpool	A	First Division	1-2
1993	Arsenal	A	FA Premier League	1-1
1997	Chelsea	H	FA Premier League	1-6

At half-time the general consensus was that a draw was a fair reflection of what had occurred during the opening 45 minutes. Indeed, when Chelsea took the lead after 39 minutes through Flo it was seen as being against the run of play, with David Ginola having been denied on two occasions by reflex saves. Ramon Vega got the equaliser with a header five minutes later, and it was no more than Spurs deserved. But the second half was little short of a disaster, with Chelsea restoring their lead after two minutes and then piling on more agony for Spurs with a further four goals, capitalising on defensive slips as demoralised Spurs fell apart.

DECEMBER 7TH

1895	London Caledonians	H	Friendly	0-3
1901	Kettering Town	A	Southern League	2-0
1903	Burnley	H	Friendly	4-0
1907	Reading	A	Southern League	1-3
1912	Chelsea	H	First Division	1-0
1918	Arsenal	H-Highbury		
			London Combination	1-0
1929	Reading	H	Second Division	0-0
1935	Nottingham Forest	A	Second Division	1-4
1940	Queens Park Rangers	H	Football League South	2-3
1946	Chesterfield	H	Second Division	3-4

1957	Leicester City	H	First Division	1-4
1963	Bolton Wanderers	A	First Division	3-1
1968	Wolverhampton Wanderers	A	First Division	0-2
1974	Newcastle United	H	First Division	3-0
1983	Bayern Munich	H	UEFA Cup 3rd Round 2nd Leg	2-0

Last season Spurs were taught a thing or two in the European Cup-Winners' Cup against Bayern Munich; tonight they were the ones delivering the lesson. Firstly, a lesson in patience – although Spurs were a goal behind from the first leg there was little point in charging away in search of an equaliser only to leave huge gaps in defence which the Germans, though a mere shadow of the side of 12 months ago, would knowingly exploit. Secondly, in resilience – as time ticked away Spurs kept working at creating the openings. Thirdly, in shutting up shop – having seized the initiative and mindful of the fact that a lone German strike would send them out on away goals, the defence worked over time to protect the lead. Glenn Hoddle was the prompter of most of Spurs' attacks, freeing Cooke and Dick on the wing, creating openings for Falco and Archibald in the middle. Spurs finally drew level five minutes into the second half; a Hoddle free-kick being headed down by Graham Roberts to the waiting Steve Archibald almost to run into the net. Although Bayern fought back through the two Rummenigge brothers, Hoddle again worked the miracle with just four minutes to go. A delicate chip sent Mark Falco on a diagonal run across the penalty area and his shot rolled across goalkeeper Pfaff's body, hit the far post and then nestled in the net. Bayern threw everything they had at Spurs in the closing minutes, but the defence stood firm and Spurs progressed to the quarter-finals.

1985	Oxford United	H	First Division	5-1
1986	Manchester United	A	First Division	3-3

In the end a draw was a fair result, but not before one of the most exciting and open games in the history of United and Spurs fixtures. Although Spurs started brightly, hitting the post in the first minute, it was United who opened the scoring, going ahead after 12 minutes and then extending it some nine minutes before half-time. Spurs came out for the second half determined to get back into the game and were soon on their way when Gary Mabbutt dived to head home the first. A Glenn Hoddle chip was heading towards goal when a United defender hammered it into his own net, and then Clive Allen headed bravely to put Spurs into the lead, sustaining a broken nose in the process. Spurs held that lead until the last minute when Danny Thomas was adjudged to have fouled Bryan Robson and Davenport equalised from the penalty spot.

1991	Notts County	H	First Division	2-1
1996	Coventry City	A	FA Premier League	2-1

DECEMBER 8TH

1883	Leyton Rovers	A	Friendly	1-3

Spurs were only able to field ten men in this match and were defeated, Robert Buckle having scored for Spurs.

1888	Upton Excelsior	H	Friendly	3-3
1894	Crusaders	H	London Charity Cup 1st Round	4-2
1900	Millwall Athletic	A	Western League	1-1
1902	London FA	H	Friendly	2-2
1906	Corinthians	H	Friendly	5-0
1913	Crystal Palace	N	London FA Charity Cup Final	1-2
1917	Queens Park Rangers	H-Homerton		
			London Combination	0-1
1923	West Bromwich Albion	A	First Division	1-4
1928	Chelsea	A	Second Division	1-1
1930	West Ham United	A	Friendly	2-1
1934	Stoke City	H	First Division	3-2
1945	Millwall	A	Football League South	2-3
1950	Blackpool	A	First Division	0-1
1956	West Bromwich Albion	H	First Division	2-2
1958	Bucharest Select XI	H	Friendly	4-2
1962	Bolton Wanderers	A	First Division	0-1
1964	Leytonstone	A	Friendly	5-0
1966				

Les Ferdinand born in London. After impressing in the non-League for Hayes, Les was signed by QPR for £15,000 in 1987, later being loaned to Turkish side Besiktas, for whom he won a Turkish Cup medal in 1989. In 1995 he was sold to Newcastle United for £6 million and continued a rich vein of goalscoring form. After two years on Tyneside he was sold to Spurs for £6 million, although a series of injuries have restricted his first-team appearances at White Hart Lane. A full England international, he is the cousin of West Ham's Rio Ferdinand.

| 1971 | Rapid Bucharest | H | UEFA Cup 3rd Round 1st Leg | 3-0 |

Spurs took the lead after only 20 seconds through Martin Peters and created an abundance of chances throughout the game but finished with only three goals to their credit, the other two both scored by Martin Chivers. As far as the Rumanians were concerned, Spurs' second goal should have been disallowed for a foul by Jimmy Neighbour on a defender, but the referee signalled the goal. This prompted the Rumanians, including their manager, to complain vociferously, with the goalkeeper looking at one stage as though he would walk off the field in protest!

1973	Stoke City	H	First Division	2-1
1979	Bristol City	A	First Division	3-1
1984	Newcastle United	H	First Division	3-1
1990	Sunderland	H	First Division	3-3

DECEMBER 9TH

1893	Crusaders	H	London Charity Cup	2-5
1899	Bristol City	H	Southern League	2-2
1901	Queens Park Rangers	H	Western League	3-2
1905	Corinthians	H	Friendly	3-1
1907	Luton Town	A	Western League	5-1
1911	Oldham Athletic	H	First Division	4-0
1916	Luton Town	A	London Combination	3-1
1922	Nottingham Forest	A	First Division	1-0
1933	Birmingham City	H	First Division	3-2
1939	Crystal Palace	H	Football League South Group A	1-3
1944	Arsenal	A	Football League South	3-2
1950	Sheffield Wednesday	A	First Division	1-1
1961	Birmingham City	H	First Division	3-1
1967	Manchester City	A	First Division	1-4
1972	Arsenal	H	First Division	1-2
1978	Ipswich Town	H	First Division	1-0
1989	Everton	H	First Division	2-1

1994 The arbitration tribunal into the penalties imposed by the FA against Spurs earlier in the year found in favour of the club. The points deduction, originally 12 but reduced to six on appeal, was withdrawn. The ban from the FA Cup was overturned, although the £1.5 million fine was allowed to remain. In the view of the arbitration tribunal, the FA's charges against Spurs were 'misconceived, bad in law and should not have been proceeded with . . . and it was irrational to impose any penalty other than a fine.' The forthcoming FA Cup tie with Altrincham would therefore take place.

| 1995 | Queens Park Rangers | H | FA Premier League | 1-0 |

DECEMBER 10TH

1887	Priory	A	Friendly	3-0
1892	Hampstead	H	Friendly	1-1
1898	Luton Town	H	FA Cup 3rd Qualifying Round	1-1
1900	Bristol Rovers	H	Western League	6-0
1902	West Norwood	A	Friendly	9-0
1904	New Brompton	A	Southern League	1-1
1910	Bradford City	A	First Division	0-3
1921	Sheffield United	A	First Division	0-1
1927	Bury	A	First Division	2-1

1931 Peter Baker born in Hampstead. As the only member of Spurs' 'double' winning side not to gain international honours, it would be easy to overlook the role played by Peter Baker in the Spurs side. However he and full-back partner Ron Henry were a rock-solid combination and the perfect foundation for all that flowed in front of them. First spotted by Spurs whilst playing for Enfield he signed amateur forms in June 1949 and was upgraded to professional forms in October 1952. He made his debut in April 1953 away at Sunderland, but was ostensibly understudy to Alf Ramsey. Peter Baker seemed to slip down the priority list following the signing of Maurice Norman from Norwich, but when Maurice was injured Peter slotted into the role so well that Norman was forced to convert to centre-half in order to get back into the side. Peter was a member of the sides that won the double in 1960-61, retained the FA Cup the following year and then lifted the European Cup-Winners' Cup in 1963. A major factor in that success was the fact that manager Bill Nicholson was able to fill in the names 'Brown, Baker, Henry' week in and week out and get consistent displays back in return. Peter was unfortunate that Jimmy Armfield was such a solid performer on the international scene, but his domestic honours must have provided adequate compensation. His contract at Spurs was cancelled by mutual consent in May 1965 after he had played 299 League games and he left England to join Durban United in South Africa, eventually settling in the country.

1932	Fulham	A	Second Division	2-2
1938	Millwall	H	Second Division	4-0
1949	Swansea Town	H	Second Division	3-1
1955	Huddersfield Town	A	First Division	0-1
1960	Preston North End	A	First Division	1-0
1963	Manchester United	A	European Cup-Winners' Cup 2nd Round 2nd Leg	1-4

Spurs arrived at Old Trafford confident of protecting a 2-0 lead secured in the first leg. The plan all but fell apart in a little over 60 seconds of action – David Sadler netted United's first goal after only six minutes to set the temperature for the evening. Spurs' hopes were dashed a minute later when Dave Mackay came out of a challenge with Noel Cantwell with a broken leg. He was stretchered off the field and Spurs' hopes seemingly went with him, but the ten men put up a sterling performance to try and retain their hold on the trophy won so magnificently the previous season. They defended well until the 53rd minute when David Herd put United level on the evening. Jimmy Greaves pulled a goal back almost immediately and Spurs were ahead overall for the last time. Bobby Charlton levelled the aggregate scores with a shot that went in off the post on 78 minutes and, with minds beginning to wander to the prospect of extra time, hit the winner with less than two minutes left on the clock. Spurs therefore went out at the first hurdle but were widely praised for their at times heroic performance.

1966	Leicester City	H	First Division	2-0
1975	Everton	H	First Division	2-2
1977	Sunderland	A	Second Division	2-1
1983	Southampton	H	First Division	0-0
1985	Portsmouth	A	Milk Cup 4th Round 2nd Replay	0-1
1988	Millwall	H	First Division	2-0
1994	Sheffield Wednesday	H	FA Premier League	3-1

DECEMBER 11TH

1897	Kettering	H	Friendly	1-0
1899	Players of the South	H	John Jones & Bob Stormont Benefit	4-1
1909	Bolton Wanderers	H	First Division	1-1
1915	Crystal Palace	A	London Combination [1st competition]	2-4
1920	Sheffield United	A	First Division	1-1
1926	Liverpool	H	First Division	1-2
1937	Southampton	A	Second Division	1-2
1943	Charlton Athletic	A	Football League South	2-2
1948	Plymouth Argyle	H	Second Division	3-0
1954	Manchester City	A	First Division	0-0
1958				

Chris Hughton born in Forest Gate. Chris was signed to the club on a part-time basis in 1977, preferring to completing his apprenticeship as a lift engineer before committing himself full-time to football. He subsequently signed full forms with Spurs in June 1979 and took over as full-back following an injury to Jimmy Holmes. He made the spot his own for the next 11 years or so, collecting winners' medals in the FA Cup in 1981 and 1982 and the UEFA Cup in 1984 and runners-up medals in the League Cup in 1982 and FA Cup in 1987. Qualifying for Eire on his mother's side of the family he went on to make 50 appearances for the country. He was given a free transfer in 1990 and joined West Ham and later Brentford, returning to Spurs on the coaching side when his playing career ended. He is currently assistant to Christian Gross.

| 1962 | Rangers | A | European Cup-Winners' Cup 1st Round 2nd Leg | 3-2 |

Spurs followed their 5-2 home win with a 3-2 win at Ibrox in the second leg thanks to goals from Jimmy Greaves and Bobby Smith (two) that silenced an 80,000 crowd.

1965	Chelsea	H	First Division	4-2
1971	Leicester City	A	First Division	1-0
1976	Manchester City	H	First Division	2-2
1982	Stoke City	A	First Division	0-2
1993	Manchester City	A	FA Premier League	2-0

DECEMBER 12TH

| 1891 | Forest Swifts | H | Friendly | 1-1 |

The game was abandoned after an hour owing to bad light.

1896	Old St Stephen's	H	FA Cup 1st Qualifying Round	4-0
1903	Corinthians	H	Friendly	5-1
1906	Plymouth Argyle	A	Western League	2-2

1908	Burnley	H	Second Division	4-2
1914	Notts County	A	First Division	2-1
1925	Burnley	A	First Division	2-1
1931	Leeds United	A	Second Division	0-1
1936	Doncaster Rovers	H	Second Division	2-0
1942	Charlton Athletic	A	Football League South	3-0
1953	Aston Villa	A	First Division	2-1
1959	Fulham	A	First Division	1-1
1963	Sheffield United	A	First Division	3-3
1970	West Bromwich Albion	A	First Division	1-3
1973	Dinamo Tbilisi	H	UEFA Cup 3rd Round 2nd Leg	5-1

Two goals apiece from Martin Chivers and Martin Peters, together with a single strike from Chris McGrath were sufficient to take Spurs into the next round 6-2 on aggregate. During the first leg Spurs had shown they were capable of absorbing pressure from opponents and hitting them on the counter attack, a tactic they also used at home to devastating effect.

| 1981 | Leeds United | A | First Division | 0-0 |
| 1984 | Bohemians Prague | A | UEFA Cup 3rd Round 2nd Leg | 1-1 |

Peter Shreeves prepared for the second leg tie with Bohemians by listening to the European grapevine; numerous managers had warned him about the Czech club's almost schizophrenic style of play – open, adventurous and attacking away from home (which Shreeves had already discovered) and little more than butchers and thugs at home. At the final whistle, Graham Roberts and Glenn Hoddle would verify for the second aspect! The Czechs were undoubtedly a talented side; their performance at White Hart Lane testified to that, but the longer the second leg went on without Bohemians scoring, the worse the tackles became. Mark Falco scored a priceless away goal after only seven minutes and that effectively ended the contest. There was still plenty of time for Bohemians to make their mark – Glenn Hoddle was caught late and high by Jakubec Sloup and stretchered off with a thigh injury and head wound that required four stitches, Graham Roberts had a cut head and most of the other Spurs players were nursing injuries of one kind or another. Although Bohemians levelled the score on the evening in the 50th minute with a header from captain Prokes, they needed to score three more to go through and never looked like getting them.

| 1992 | Arsenal | H | FA Premier League | 1-0 |

DECEMBER 13TH

| 1884 | Woodgrange | A | Friendly | 0-0 |

The game lasted only 40 minutes before bad light forced an end to play.

1902	Corinthians	H	Friendly	2-2
1913	Aston Villa	A	First Division	3-3
1919	Fulham	H	Second Division	4-0
1924	Liverpool	H	First Division	1-1
1930	Bristol City	H	Second Division	4-1
1941	Watford	A	London War League	2-1
1947	Birmingham City	H	Second Division	1-2
1948				

Tony Want born in Hackney. Signed by Spurs as an apprentice in November 1963 he was upgraded to professional in December 1965. Unfortunately, the continued good form of both Joe Kinnear and Cyril Knowles, coupled with the emergence of Ray Evans, restricted Tony's first-team opportunities whilst at White Hart Lane, even though Tony never let anyone down when he did get a chance. The club appreciated his need for regular first-team football and sold him to Birmingham City in June 1972 for £50,000, where he remained for six years. He then finished his playing career in America.

1952	Charlton Athletic	H	First Division	2-0
1958	Burnley	A	First Division	1-3
1967	Olympique Lyonnais	H	European Cup-Winners' Cup 2nd Round 2nd Leg	4-3

Although Spurs attackers did all of and more than what was expected of them, a series of mishaps in defence eventually put them out of the competition against a side considered the worst Spurs had ever faced in Europe. Spurs were two goals ahead at half-time thanks to Jimmy Greaves, who slotted home a drive and penalty to put the home side in the driving seat. They took their foot off the pedal in the second half, allowing the French to score in the 54th minute and thus level the aggregate score but take an advantage on away goals. And the goals kept coming in similar fashion; Spurs would restore their advantage up front, only for the defence to let them down as the score went through 3-1, 3-2, 4-2 and finally 4-3. Spurs other goals were scored by Cliff Jones and Jimmy Robertson, but at the end of the night they went out of the cup.

| 1969 | Manchester City | A | First Division | 1-1 |
| 1972 | Red Star Belgrade | A | UEFA Cup 3rd Round 2nd Leg | 0-1 |

Protecting a two goal lead from the first leg it was imperative Spurs were at their best to repel a concerted attempt by the Yugoslavians to recover the tie, even though they were without Alan Gilzean and Martin Chivers played although still suffering from flu. In the end it was the defence that earned all the plaudits, holding out against all but one of the attacks the Yugoslavians threw against them, a goal in the 48th minute from Lazarevic. Spurs also had their moments in front of goal, with John Pratt having an attempt in the 34th minute that was subsequently disallowed for a foul on the goalkeeper.

1975	Liverpool	H	First Division	0-4
1980	Manchester City	H	First Division	2-1
1986	Watford	H	First Division	2-1
1987	Charlton Athletic	H	First Division	0-1
1997	Coventry City	A	FA Premier League	0-4

DECEMBER 14TH

1895	Old St Stephen's	H	FA Cup 4th Qualifying Round	2-1
1898	Luton Town	A	FA Cup 3rd Qualifying Round Replay	1-1
1901	Corinthians	A	Friendly	0-3
1903	West Ham United	H	Western League	4-0
1907	Watford	H	Southern League	5-0
1912	Woolwich Arsenal	A	First Division	3-0
1918	Crystal Palace	A	London Combination	3-6
1929	Charlton Athletic	A	Second Division	0-1
1935	Norwich City	H	Second Division	2-1
1946	Millwall	A	Second Division	3-0
1957	Blackpool	A	First Division	2-0

1960 Chris Waddle born in Gateshead, Tyneside. Having had various trials before signing with non-League Tow Law Town, a professional career as a footballer seemed to have passed Chris Waddle by. In July 1980 he was given one last try and this time managed to impress Newcastle United, who signed him almost immediately and gave him his League debut in October that year. Guided by manager Arthur Cox and with the experience of Kevin Keegan and Peter Beardsley alongside, Chris soon developed into a winger of considerable talent. After representing England at Under-21 level he was selected for the full England side in March 1985. He joined Spurs for £650,000 in July 1985 and immediately formed a partnership with Glenn Hoddle both on the pitch for Spurs and England and off it too, the pair hitting the UK Top 20 with 'Diamond Lights'. That year also saw Spurs reach the FA Cup final, but they lost out to Coventry. Following Glenn's departure for Monaco Chris became the main creative player within the side and was given very much a free role. As such he developed into one of the most complete players in the country and a prized asset, and in July 1989 Olympique Marseille offered £4.5 million to take him to France. There he helped the club win successive League titles and reach the final of the European Cup. He returned home in 1992 with Sheffield Wednesday. He later played for Bradford City and Sunderland (the club he supported as a boy) before taking the position of player-manager at Burnley in 1997. He left the club in 1998 looking to resume his playing career.

1963	Stoke City	H	First Division	2-1
1968	Manchester City	H	First Division	1-1
1974	Ipswich Town	A	First Division	0-4
1985	Watford	A	First Division	0-1
1991	Leeds United	A	First Division	1-1
1996	Leeds United	A	FA Premier League	0-0

DECEMBER 15TH

1883	Claremont	H	Friendly	2-0

The game was halted after 60 minutes.

1888	Plaistow	A	Friendly	2-1
1894	Luton Town	H	FA Cup 4th Qualifying Round	2-2
1900	Millwall Athletic	A	Southern League	2-1
1902	West Ham United	H	London League	4-0
1904	George Robey's XI	H	John 'Bristol' Jones Dependants Benefit	2-1
1906	Northampton Town	H	Southern League	6-0
1917	Clapton Orient	A	London Combination	4-2
1919	Corinthians	H	Friendly	4-1
1923	Blackburn Rovers	H	First Division	2-1
1928	Blackpool	H	Second Division	1-2
1934	Liverpool	A	First Division	1-4

1935 Jim Iley born in Kirkby, Yorkshire. Jim began his career with Sheffield United, although when he initially signed for the club he was also working at the Frickley Colliery. After more than 100 appearances for the Blades he was signed by Spurs as replacement for the Italy-bound Tony Marchi, costing the club £16,000. He found it difficult to settle at White Hart Lane at first, a situation not helped by the fact that he continued to live in Sheffield and therefore had to travel down by train for matches. By 1958 however he was established as the first choice left-half, and it was only the subsequent arrival of Dave Mackay that put his position under threat. He left Spurs in July 1959 and joined Nottingham Forest, later playing for Newcastle United and Peterborough United, becoming player-manager at the latter club. Later still he was manager of Barnsley, Blackburn Rovers, Bury and Exeter City and coach at Charlton Athletic.

1945	Southampton	A	Football League South	2-3
1951	Middlesbrough	H	First Division	3-1
1956	Preston North End	H	First Division	1-1
1962	Birmingham City	A	First Division	2-0

1967   David Howells born in Guildford, Surrey. David signed with Spurs as a professional in January 1985, making his debut the following February when he scored against Sheffield Wednesday. Initially played as a striker he was later successfully converted to midfield, where his ability to read the game has proved beneficial for Spurs. He was a member of the side that won the 1991 FA Cup and was given a free transfer at the end of the 1997-98 season, subsequently joining Southampton.

1970	Bristol City	A	League Cup Semi-Final 1st Leg	1-1
1971	Rapid Bucharest	A	UEFA Cup 3rd Round 2nd Leg	2-0

Although Spurs were three goals ahead after the first leg, the Rumanians tore at them in the first half in a desperate attempt to reduce the deficit. The Spurs goal survived three lucky escapes during the first period, with Pat Jennings again performing heroics in goal to keep the opposition at bay. After half-time, however, the nature of the game changed. An early goal from Martin Chivers forced the realisation that time and the tie were slipping away from Rapid and their style changed with it. They protested so vehemently that Chivers had been offside when scoring that two of their number were booked. Jimmy Pearce and Pop were sent off for fighting, although not before Pearce had added a second Spurs goal, and thereafter the Rumanians kicked anything in a Spurs shirt, prompting Bill Nicholson after the game to describe Rapid as the dirtiest side Spurs had ever played.

1973	Manchester City	H	First Division	0-2
1979	Aston Villa	H	First Division	1-2
1984	Watford	A	First Division	2-1
1990	Manchester City	A	First Division	1-2

1995   Both Spurs and Wimbledon were banned from European competition for one year, effective for the next five years, following the under-strength teams both sides fielded during the summer's Inter-Toto Cup competition. Both successfully appealed, with Spurs chairman Alan Sugar claiming that the club was in possession of written documentation from the FA and the Premier League that allowed them to field a weakened side.

DECEMBER 16TH

1893	Erith	H	Friendly	0-1

1895   A meeting of the club was held at The Eagle. The club's president, Mr J Oliver chaired the meeting and after discussing other business moved on to the proposal put forward by Mr Buckle, that the club should adopt professionalism. Mr Buckle informed the meeting that a committee meeting held last Tuesday had considered the subject and was of the opinion that the club should adopt professionalism immediately. Others were not so sure, including a Mr Roynan, who was most vociferous in his objections to both the plan and the manner in which it had been sprung on them.

1899	Cowes	A	Southern League	6-1

Cowes resigned from the Southern League on December 18th 1899 and so the result of this match was expunged from the records.

1901	West Ham United	A	London League	1-3
1905	Plymouth Argyle	A	Southern League	1-2
1907	Luton Town	H	Western League	2-0
1911	Bolton Wanderers	A	First Division	0-1
1916	Portsmouth	H-Highbury		
			London Combination	1-0

Spurs had taken an early lead through Jimmy Banks when fog descended on Highbury with only 15 minutes having been played. When this showed no sign of lifting, the referee abandoned the game.

1922	Chelsea	A	First Division	0-0
1933	Sheffield Wednesday	A	First Division	1-2
1939	Norwich City	A	Football League South Group A	2-5
1944	Reading	H	Football League South	3-2

1950	Blackpool	A	First Division	1-0
1960	Pat Van Den Hauwe born in Dendermode, Belgium. Pat was brought up in London and began his			

1960 Pat Van Den Hauwe born in Dendermode, Belgium. Pat was brought up in London and began his League career with Birmingham City, signing as an apprentice in July 1976 and being upgraded in August 1978. Initially he was used as either a full-back or in midfield, but by 1983 he had firmly established himself as first choice left-back and was subsequently signed by Everton in September 1984. Whilst at Goodison he helped the club win two League titles and the European Cup-Winners' Cup and reach three FA Cup finals, and in August 1989 was signed by Spurs for £575,000. In 1991 he finally added an FA Cup winners' medal to go with his three runners-up ones, helping Spurs beat Nottingham Forest in the final. Despite his surname and birthplace, he opted out of National Service and became ineligible to play for Belgium and subsequently represented Wales. In the mid-1990s he was released by Spurs and joined Millwall.

1961	Blackpool	H	First Division	5-2
1967	Leicester City	H	First Division	0-1
1972	Everton	A	First Division	1-3
1978	Manchester United	A	First Division	0-2
1983	Manchester United	A	First Division	2-4
1986	Bermuda National XI	A	Friendly	3-1
1989	Manchester United	A	First Division	1-0
1995	Wimbledon	A	FA Premier League	1-0

DECEMBER 17TH

1892	Polytechnic	H	London Senior Cup 3rd Round Replay	3-0
1898	Sheppey United	A	Southern League	2-3
1900	Preston North End	H	Friendly	1-1
1904	Wellingborough	H	Southern League	8-0
1910	Blackburn Rovers	H	First Division	2-2

1914 Percy Hooper born in Lambeth, London. Although Percy had been associated with Spurs as an amateur he did not sign for the club until January 1935 after impressing in a game when Spurs reserve goalkeeper was injured. After making his League debut in April 1935 he eventually became first choice goalkeeper and would have made considerably more than the 101 appearances he did but for the Second World War. Although Percy was a regular in the side during the war, the eventual emergence of Ted Ditchburn limited his appearances when League football resumed and he was sold to Swansea Town in March 1947 before finishing his career in the non-League game.

1921	Chelsea	H	First Division	0-0
1927	Liverpool	H	First Division	3-1
1932	West Ham United	H	Second Division	2-2
1938	Bury	A	Second Division	1-3

1944 Jimmy Robertson born in Cardonald, Glasgow. After brief spells with Middlesbrough and Celtic Jimmy signed with Cowdenbeath as an amateur and made the first team by the time he was 16. He signed as a professional with St Mirren in 1962 and continued his progress, winning an Under-23 cap in January 1964 and was snapped up by Spurs for £25,000 three months later. Playing on the right wing he was expected to keep Jimmy Greaves and Alan Gilzean supplied with crosses, as well as weighing in with vital goals himself, none more so than in the 1967 FA Cup final against Chelsea. In October 1968 he was swapped with Arsenal's David Jenkins, a surprising move that baffled Spurs fans in particular. In truth, the move didn't work out for either player, since Jimmy later moved on to Ipswich Town and Stoke City before finishing his career with Walsall and Crewe.

1949	Brentford	H	Second Division	1-1
1955	Burnley	A	First Division	0-2
1960	Everton	A	First Division	3-1
1966	Leeds United	A	First Division	2-3
1969	Everton	H	First Division	0-0

This game was to have been played on 29th November but was postponed owing to a heavy fall of snow on the day of the match. A re-arrangement was hastily sought, bearing in mind that the season had to end relatively early owing to the World Cup due to take place in Mexico, but Spurs and Everton had no better luck in the re-arranged game – a fault at a power sub-station plunged the ground into total darkness after 29 minutes! As it was impossible to get the floodlights working again the game was subsequently abandoned. On the night of the match it was announced that tickets would be valid for the re-arranged game (which was subsequently arranged for 7th January but postponed owing to Spurs' involvement in a cup replay and finally played on 11th March) but this was rescinded and everyone had to pay again.

1977	Crystal Palace	H	Second Division	2-2
1980	Ipswich Town	H	First Division	5-3

1985	Southampton	A	Screen Sports Super Cup Group A	3-1
1988	West Ham United	A	First Division	2-0
1994	Everton	A	FA Premier League	0-0

DECEMBER 18TH

1886	Phoenix	H	East End Cup 1st Round	6-0
1897	Wolverton	A	Southern League	2-1
1899	HR Burkes XI	H	Friendly	12-2
1909	Chelsea	A	First Division	1-2
1915	Queens Park Rangers	H	London Combination [1st competition]	2-1
1920	Bolton Wanderers	H	First Division	5-2
1926	Arsenal	A	First Division	4-2
1937	Blackburn Rovers	H	Second Division	3-1
1943	Arsenal	H	Football League South	2-1
1948	Sheffield Wednesday	A	Second Division	1-3
1954	Aston Villa	H	First Division	1-1
1965	Manchester United	A	First Division	1-5

United gained ample revenge for a 5-1 battering at White Hart Lane by reversing the score at Old Trafford. Spurs' consolation goal was scored by Cliff Jones.

1969   Justin Edinburgh born in Brentwood, Essex. After graduating through the ranks at Southend United he signed professional forms at Roots Hall in 1988 and quickly established himself in the side at full-back. Spotted by Spurs he was invited to White Hart Lane in January 1990 on loan for three months and then returned to Southend to help them win the Fourth Division title. At the end of the season he was transferred to Spurs for £150,000, ostensibly as cover for Pat Van Den Hauwe. He got his chance sooner than expected and retained his place for the 1991 Cup final win over Nottingham Forest. With the subsequent managerial comings and goings at White Hart Lane, Justin has struggled to hold on to his place in the team, but can always be relied upon when called.

1971	Liverpool	A	First Division	0-0
1976	Leicester City	A	First Division	1-2
1978	El Nasar	A	Friendly	7-0
1982	Birmingham City	H	First Division	2-1
1991	Liverpool	H	First Division	1-2
1993	Liverpool	H	FA Premier League	3-3

DECEMBER 19TH

1891	1st Battalion Scots Guards	A	Luton Charity Cup 2nd Round	0-4
1893	Friars	H	Friendly	2-1
1894	Luton Town	A	FA Cup 4th Qualifying Round Replay	0-4
1896	Clapton	A	Friendly	2-1
1898	Luton Town	N	FA Cup 3rd Qualifying Round 2nd Replay	2-0

The second replay against Luton was played at Tufnell Park where a crowd of 8,000 saw goals from James Cameron and Tom Bradshaw take Spurs into the first round proper to face Newton Heath (forerunners of Manchester United).

1903	Kettering Town	A	Southern League	3-3
1908	Bradford Park Avenue	A	Second Division	2-0
1914	Sunderland	H	First Division	0-6

The 1914-15 season was little short of a disaster for Spurs, who finished bottom of the table having won only eight games all season and suffered some heavy defeats throughout. They included this reverse at home to Sunderland, Spurs' record defeat at home until equalled by a 6-0 win for Arsenal in 1935. Spurs also lost at Roker Park 5-0 in the last game of the season.

1925	Leeds United	H	First Division	3-2
1931	Oldham Athletic	A	Second Division	3-2
1936	Fulham	A	Second Division	3-3

This match was Spurs' 1000th in the League (not including matches which had been abandoned) and goals from Ralph Ward (penalty), Johnny Morrison and Les Miller earned them a point at Craven Cottage.

1942	West Ham United	H	Football League South	2-0
1953	Sheffield Wednesday	H	First Division	3-1
1959	Newcastle United	H	First Division	4-0

Spurs moved to the top of the table with this demolition of Newcastle, although the game attracted Spurs' smallest home crowd of the season this far. Goals from Danny Blanchflower, Maurice Norman, John White and Cliff Jones secured the points that lifted them above Preston North End.

1964	Everton	H	First Division	2-2
1970	Wolverhampton Wanderers	H	First Division	0-0
1992	Oldham Athletic	A	FA Premier League	1-2

DECEMBER 20TH

1884	Sekforde Rovers	H	Friendly	5-0
1902	Queens Park Rangers	A	Southern League	4-0
1913	Sheffield Wednesday	H	First Division	1-1
1919	Barnsley	A	Second Division	0-3
1924	Nottingham Forest	A	First Division	0-1
1930	Barnsley	A	Second Division	1-0
1941	Aldershot	H	London War League	1-1
1947	West Bromwich Albion	H	Second Division	1-1
1952	West Bromwich Albion	A	First Division	1-2
1958	Blackpool	A	First Division	0-0
1969	West Ham United	H	First Division	0-2
1972	Wolverhampton Wanderers	A	League Cup Semi-Final 1st Leg	2-1

Just as they had done the previous season in the UEFA Cup against Wolves, Spurs gained the upper hand with a win at Molineux in the first leg. It took Martin Peters only three minutes to open the scoring, taking a pass from Jimmy Pearce and driving home his 17th goal of the season. By 15 minutes Spurs were two ahead, John Pratt shooting from 25 yards and watching the ball swerve in flight past Phil Parkes. Alan Gilzean might have added to the lead, hitting the crossbar in the 39th minute, but shortly before half-time Wolves were put back in the game with a penalty by Kenny Hibbitt after Cyril Knowles was adjudged to have fouled Alan Sunderland. That goal gave Wolves extra fight for the second half, but Spurs defence held firm to ensure a one goal lead to take into the second leg.

1975	Middlesbrough	A	First Division	0-1
1980	Middlesbrough	A	First Division	1-4
1982	Borussia Monchengladbach	Tel Aviv	Friendly	0-2
1986	Chelsea	A	First Division	2-0
1987	Derby County	A	First Division	2-1
1997	Barnsley	H	FA Premier League	3-0

With Barnsley occupying the bottom position in the Premier League and Spurs only two places ahead, the match was rightly billed as a vital one for both clubs' Premiership aspirations. Spurs grabbed three goals in the opening 17 minutes to finish off the game as a contest, although they missed the chance to improve their goal difference with a later series of near misses. Allan Neilsen opened the scoring in the fifth minute before David Ginola took over with two goals, the second coming from a very rare header. Neilsen later hit the post and Spurs were denied two seemingly legitimate penalty appeals, but the 3-0 win eased some of the gloom around the ground.

DECEMBER 21ST

| 1895 | Casuals | H | Friendly | 3-1 |

Spurs played their first match as a professional club with a friendly against The Casuals and won 3-1. The opposition is something of a surprise, for as strict adherents to the amateur principle, it is unlikely the Casuals would have countenanced a match against a professional side. Perhaps they were kept in the dark until after the match had been played!

1898	Surrey Wanderers	A	Friendly	1-1
1901	Millwall Athletic	A	Southern League	1-1
1907	Norwich City	A	Southern League	1-2
1912	Bradford City	H	First Division	2-1

For four years the team had been selected officially by the board of directors, although in fact it was invariably secretary Arthur Turner who had been responsible. By December 1912 the club realised that if real progress was to be made, then a full-time manager was needed. They chose Peter McWilliam, the former Newcastle United half-back who had been a member of the side that had won three League championships and the FA Cup. The announcement that he was to join Spurs on January 1st 1913 was made before the start of this match against Bradford City, one of the last occasions Arthur Turner would select the team – they did him proud with a 2-1 win.

1918	Millwall	H-Homerton		
			London Combination	0-3
1929	Hull City	H	Second Division	2-2
1935	Doncaster Rovers	A	Second Division	1-2
1940	Clapton Orient	H	Football League South	9-0

1946	Bradford Park Avenue	H	Second Division	3-3

1951 Steve Perryman born in Ealing. Having represented London and England Schools as a youngster Steve had the pick of the clubs to join, finally choosing Spurs and joining as an apprentice in July 1967. He was upgraded to the professional ranks in January 1969 and made his League debut in September the same year, appearing in the game against Sunderland. Once in the side he proved impossible to dislodge, for his energetic performances and ability to win the ball in midfield, then allowing the likes of Alan Mullery and later Martin Peters to use their creative skills to fire Spurs up at the turn of the decade. Of course, there was more to Steve's game than just ball-winning, for he was creative in his own right and his ability to cover the area between both penalty areas meant he could be found one minute stopping a certain goal, as he did in the League Cup final of 1971, and the next scoring a vital one of his own, as he did on two occasions in the UEFA Cup semi-final against AC Milan. When Alan Mullery and Martin Peters called it a day as far as playing was concerned, Steve took over the captaincy at Spurs and proved to be an inspiration. Switched into the back four he guided the club to promotion from the Second Division and then led the club to their FA Cup triumphs of 1981 and 1982. He was unlucky to miss only one game of the 1984 UEFA Cup run – the second leg of the final, for which he was suspended, a rather harsh booking in the first leg putting paid to his tournament. He still ended up with a medal however, for Ossie Ardiles insisted that Steve should have his. He also collected winners' medals from the League Cup in 1971 and 1973 and the UEFA Cup in 1972, was named Footballer of the Year in 1982 by the writers' association and was capped by England the same year. That he won only one cap during a long and illustrious career was something of a travesty, but he perhaps sacrificed his own development as a player in order to benefit the team overall, the ultimate sacrifice. He was awarded the MBE in 1986, the same year he finally left Spurs as a player. By this time he had amassed 656 League appearances, a club record. Not surprisingly, he has also made more appearances than any other Spurs player in the FA Cup, League Cup and Europe. After leaving Spurs he joined Oxford and in November 1986 joined Brentford as a player, later becoming player-manager. In 1990 he resigned, later becoming manager of Watford, but when Ossie Ardiles took over at White Hart Lane in 1993 Steve came with him as his assistant. When the pair were dismissed he became a manager in Japan.

1957	Chelsea	A	First Division	4-2
1963	Nottingham Forest	A	First Division	2-1
1968	Liverpool	A	First Division	0-1
1974	Queens Park Rangers	H	First Division	1-2
1985	Ipswich Town	H	First Division	2-0
1996	Sheffield Wednesday	H	FA Premier League	1-1

DECEMBER 22ND

1883	Latymer	H	Friendly	2-0

Latymer had only five players on the field when the game kicked off, although two arrived later. The final score could not be agreed at the end of the game either, with Spurs claiming a 2-0 win and the local paper, the *Tottenham Weekly Herald* refusing to print the score as it was under dispute, although they did mention the fact that Latymer had been the subject of considerable verbal abuse from the spectators!

1888	Bowes Park	A	Friendly	4-0
1894	London Welsh	H	FA Amateur Cup Divisional Final	1-1
1900	Southampton	H	Western League	2-0
1905	Queens Park Rangers	A	Southern League	1-3
1917	Crystal Palace	A	London Combination	3-2

1920 Jack Jull died at the age of 53. Whatever his accomplishments as a player, however stylish a performer, Jack Jull will be guaranteed his eternal place in Spurs' history for the simple fact that he was one of the club's founding fathers. That coupled with the great service he gave the club as a player during its fledgling years and later as president of the club make him as important a character of his age as Bill Nicholson was to become in a later era. Jack played for Spurs until 1897, a period which therefore covered the first match (against Radicals in 1882), the first cup-tie (against St Albans in October 1885), the first FA Amateur cup-tie (against Vampires in November 1893), the first FA Cup tie (against West Herts in October 1894) and even the first League match of any kind (the Southern Alliance game against Polytechnic in September 1892). Two years before his retirement as a player Jack was made president of the club in recognition of the service he had provided. His brother Tommy also played for the club on a number of occasions.

1923	Blackburn Rovers	A	First Division	1-0
1928	West Bromwich Albion	A	Second Division	2-3
1934	Leeds United	H	First Division	1-1
1945	Southampton	H	Football League South	4-3
1951	West Bromwich Albion	A	First Division	1-3

| 1962 | West Ham United | H | First Division | 4-4 |
| 1971 | Chelsea | A | League Cup Semi-Final 1st Leg | 2-3 |

Given what was at stake this match was never likely to be a classic in footballing terms, but both sides played their part in ensuring an exciting and eventful game. By the 74th minute Spurs were 2-1 ahead and looking good to take a priceless lead back to White Hart Lane. Chelsea had taken the lead in the 39th minute through Peter Osgood, but Terry Naylor scored his first goal for the club five minutes after the break to level the scores. Two minutes later Martin Chivers put Spurs ahead, but the match turned once again in the final 15 minutes. Chris Garland equalised in the 74th minute and then Terry Naylor was unluckily adjudged to have handled inside the area and John Hollins scored the winner from the penalty spot.

1973	Derby County	A	First Division	0-2
1981	Plymouth Argyle	A	Friendly	1-1
1982	Israel Select XI	Tel Aviv	Friendly	2-2
1984	Norwich City	A	First Division	2-1
1990	Luton Town	H	First Division	2-1

The match that was the making of Paul Stewart – Spurs were a goal down and had lost two players (Nayim, sent off for comments made to the referee, and Pat Van Den Hauwe for a late challenge), requiring a tactical and positional reshuffle. Stewart dropped back into midfield and played the game of his life, scoring both goals as Spurs overcame Luton.

| 1991 | Crystal Palace | A | First Division | 2-1 |

DECEMBER 23RD

1893	Wolverton	H	Friendly	2-2
1905	Southampton	H	Western League	5-0
1911	Bradford City	H	First Division	2-3
1916	Millwall	A	London Combination	3-3
1922	Chelsea	H	First Division	3-1
1931				

Johnny Brooks born in Reading. After signing for his local club Johnny was transferred to Spurs for a fee of £3,000 in February 1953, with Dennis Uphill and Harry Robshaw making the opposite journey as part of the deal. Johnny's career at Spurs covered the transitional period between the 'push-and-run' side of the early 1950s and the great double side of the early 1960s, but Johnny was a highly creative player and came into his own following the departure of Eddie Baily in 1956. The subsequent emergence of Alfie Stokes put Brooks's position under threat and he was subsequently swapped with Chelsea's Les Allen, finishing his career with Brentford and then Crystal Palace. Whilst with Spurs he won three England caps, but despite scoring in two of those games, could not dovetail with Johnny Haynes and was not selected again.

| 1939 | Southend United | H | Football League South Group A | 3-4 |

After 60 minutes and with Southend leading 4-3, the match was abandoned owing to fog.

1944	Queens Park Rangers	A	Football League South	0-0
1950	Arsenal	H	First Division	1-0
1961	Arsenal	A	First Division	1-2
1962				

Terry Gibson born in Walthamstow. Signed by Spurs as an apprentice in April 1979 he was upgraded to the professional ranks in January 1980 having already made his League debut. Unable to claim a regular place in the Spurs side he was allowed to sign for Coventry in 1983 for £100,000. He was later sold to Manchester United, although struggled there to find his earlier form and returned to London with Wimbledon, playing in the FA Cup success in 1988.

| 1967 | West Ham United | A | First Division | 1-2 |
| 1970 | Bristol City | H | League Cup Semi-Final 2nd Leg | 2-0 [aet] |

Spurs gave their fans an early Christmas present by booking their place in the League Cup final at Wembley, where they would face Aston Villa. Spirited defence by Bristol City had made the job at hand difficult for Spurs, but goals from Martin Chivers and Jimmy Pearce in extra time ensured there would be no upset on the day.

1972	Sheffield United	H	First Division	2-0
1978	Arsenal	H	First Division	0-5
1995	Bolton Wanderers	H	FA Premier League	2-2

DECEMBER 24TH

1887	Balmoral	H	Friendly	1-1
1892	Coldstream Guards	H	Friendly	Score unknown
1898	Warmley	A	Southern League	5-1

Warmley subsequently withdrew from the Southern League and this match, together with the first encounter on September 24th, was expunged from the records.

1904	Southampton	H	Western League	2-1

Torrential rain during the first half forced the referee to abandon the game at half-time with Spurs leading 2-1 thanks to goals from Sandy Tait from the penalty spot and Charlie O'Hagan. The match was subsequently replayed on 29th March and finished 1-1.

1910	Nottingham Forest	A	First Division	2-1
1921	Chelsea	A	First Division	2-1
1927	Leicester City	A	First Division	1-6
1932	Notts County	A	Second Division	0-3
1938	Southampton	H	Second Division	1-1
1949	Blackburn Rovers	A	Second Division	2-1
1955	Luton Town	H	First Division	2-1

Two successive away defeats had left Spurs second from bottom in the First Division and looking for a vital win to keep in touch with the sides above them. Goals from Johnny Brooks and Len Duquemin were enough to win the game for Spurs, but the attack had also been suitably bolstered by the arrival of Bobby Smith from Chelsea who made his debut in our colours.

1960	West Ham United	H	First Division	2-0

DECEMBER 25TH

1894	Sheffield & District League	H	Friendly	7-1
1895	Millwall Athletic	A	Friendly	3-5

On the same day Bill Hinton was born in Swindon. Bill started his career with Swindon before signing with Bolton in 1920. After making only 36 appearances in four years he was signed by Spurs in June 1924, making his debut in the Spurs goal in the first game of the season, against Bolton! Early into the 1925-26 season he was struck by a mystery illness and was later given a free transfer, returning to Swindon in 1928. He died in Poole on 8th March 1976.

1896	Millwall Athletic	A	Southern League	4-0
1897	Woolwich Arsenal	A	United League	3-2
1899	Portsmouth	H	Southern League	3-0
1900	Portsmouth	H	Southern League	4-1
1901	Portsmouth	H	Southern League	1-2
1902	Portsmouth	H	Southern League	2-2
1903	Portsmouth	H	Southern League	1-1
1905	Portsmouth	H	Southern League	3-1
1906	Millwall	H	Southern League	3-1
1907	Northampton Town	H	Southern League	2-0
1908	Oldham Athletic	A	Second Division	0-1
1909	Nottingham Forest	H	First Division	2-2
1911	Woolwich Arsenal	H	First Division	5-0
1912	Manchester City	A	First Division	2-2
1914	Sheffield Wednesday	A	First Division	2-3
1915	Croydon City	H	London Combination [1st competition]	3-0
1916	Brentford	A	London Combination	5-1
1917	Millwall	A	London Combination	6-0
1918	Queens Park Rangers	A	London Combination	1-1
1919	Hull City	H	Second Division	4-0
1920	Newcastle United	A	First Division	1-1
1922	Sheffield United	H	First Division	2-1
1923	Huddersfield Town	H	First Division	1-0
1924	Bury	H	First Division	1-1
1925	Birmingham	A	First Division	1-3
1926	Manchester United	H	First Division	1-1
1928	Reading	H	Second Division	2-2
1929	Southampton	H	Second Division	3-2
1930	Southampton	H	Second Division	1-3
1931	Charlton Athletic	H	Second Division	0-1
1933	Huddersfield Town	H	First Division	1-3
1934	Grimsby Town	A	First Division	0-3
1935	Plymouth Argyle	H	Second Division	1-2
1936	Blackburn Rovers	A	Second Division	4-0
1937	Bury	A	Second Division	2-1
1939	Millwall	A	Football League South Group A	1-5
1940	Millwall	H	Football League South	3-3

1941	Millwall	A	London War League	2-1
1942	Brentford	H	Football League South	1-1
1943	Fulham	H	Football League South	2-0
1944	Queens Park Rangers	H	Football League South	4-2
1945	Derby County	H	Football League South	2-5
1946	Coventry City	A	Second Division	1-3
1947	Chesterfield	H	Second Division	3-0
1948	Leicester City	A	Second Division	2-1
1950	Derby County	A	First Division	1-1
1951	Charlton Athletic	A	First Division	3-0
1952	Middlesbrough	H	First Division	7-1

Spurs' biggest Christmas Day win was achieved almost by accident. Les Bennett had given Spurs the lead after 12 minutes, only for Norris to equalise on the 20 minute mark. An injury to Bennett then forced him to move to the wing and much of Spurs' threat up front was blunted, but after the interval Bennett was restored to the centre, despite his injury, and the two usual wingers set about exploiting their respective full-backs. A succession of crosses and passes in the second half found Les Bennett who scored a hat-trick to take his tally to four in the match, and Len Duquemin, who scored twice. Spurs' other goal was netted by Eddie Baily.

1953	Portsmouth	H	First Division	1-1
1954	Bolton Wanderers	A	First Division	2-1
1956	Everton	H	First Division	6-0
1958	West Ham United	A	First Division	1-2

The last time Spurs played a match on Christmas Day saw them go down 2-1 at Upton Park against West Ham. West Ham did much of the attacking throughout the first half, although John Hollowbread did well to keep them at bay. The home side took the lead straight after the restart through Dick and soon after extended their advantage with a mis-hit shot from Keeble that eluded the goalkeeper. That prompted something of a Spurs fight back, although all they had to show for their efforts was a single goal by Bobby Smith.

DECEMBER 26TH

1884	Grove	H	Friendly	Score unknown

Boxing Day football has long been a highlight of the football season, and this match was the first match Spurs played on the day after Christmas. However, neither the score nor the line-up is known for this game.

1885	Edmonton Independent	A	Friendly	2-1
1888	Orion Gymnasium	H	Friendly	Score unknown

This is believed to be the first match for which a charge was made for admission to the ground at Northumberland Park. As the usual charge was 3d and the match produced receipts of 17s, the paying crowd was 68!

1892	Edmonton	H	Friendly	Score unknown
1893	Southampton St Mary's	A	Friendly	0-1

Curious to see the club which had recently caused the London FA so much trouble, over 6,000 turned out to see Spurs play against Southampton St Mary's (forerunners to the current Southampton FC) in a friendly at Southampton.

1894	West Liverpool	H	Friendly	3-0
1895	Accrington	H	Friendly	3-0
1896	3rd Grenadier Guards	H	Friendly	2-3
1896	Vampires	H	Friendly	4-0
1898	Southampton	A	Southern League	1-1
1899	Southampton	A	Southern League	1-3
1900	Southampton	A	Southern League	1-3
1901	Southampton	A	Southern League	0-1
1902	Southampton	A	Southern League	1-0
1903	Southampton	A	Southern League	0-1
1904	Southampton	A	Southern League	1-1
1905	Southampton	A	Southern League	0-1
1906	Southampton	A	Southern League	1-2
1907	Southampton	A	Southern League	1-1
1908	Oldham Athletic	H	Second Division	3-0
1909	Nottingham Forest	A	First Division	2-2
1910	Nottingham Forest	H	First Division	1-4
1911	Woolwich Arsenal	A	First Division	1-3

1912	Manchester City	H	First Division	4-0
1913	Middlesbrough	H	First Division	0-1
1914	Sheffield Wednesday	H	First Division	6-1
1916	Brentford	H-Homerton		
			London Combination	5-2
1917	Millwall	H-Homerton		
			London Combination	0-1
1918	Queens Park Rangers	H-Homerton		
			London Combination	0-0
1919	Hull City	A	Second Division	3-1
1921	Bradford City	H	First Division	1-0
1922	Sheffield United	A	First Division	0-2
1923	Huddersfield Town	A	First Division	1-2
1925	Birmingham	H	First Division	2-1
1927	Bolton Wanderers	A	First Division	1-4
1928	Reading	A	Second Division	3-4
1929	Southampton	A	Second Division	0-1
1930	Southampton	A	Second Division	3-0
1931	Charlton Athletic	A	Second Division	5-2
1932	Bradford Park Avenue	A	Second Division	3-3
1933	Huddersfield Town	A	First Division	0-2
1934	Grimsby Town	H	First Division	2-1
1935	Plymouth Argyle	A	Second Division	1-2
1936	West Ham United	H	Second Division	2-3
1938	Burnley	A	Second Division	0-1
1939	West Ham United	H	Football League South Group A	0-1
1942	Brentford	A	Football League South	1-2
1945	Derby County	A	Football League South	0-2
1946	Coventry City	H	Second Division	0-0
1949	Chesterfield	H	Second Division	1-0
1950	Derby County	H	First Division	2-1
1951	Charlton Athletic	H	First Division	2-3
1953	Portsmouth	A	First Division	1-1
1954	Bolton Wanderers	H	First Division	2-0
1955	West Bromwich Albion	H	First Division	4-1
1956	Everton	A	First Division	1-1
1957	Wolverhampton Wanderers	H	First Division	1-0
1958	West Ham United	H	First Division	1-4
1959	Leeds United	A	First Division	4-2
1960	West Ham United	A	First Division	3-0
1961	Chelsea	A	First Division	2-0
1962	Ipswich Town	H	First Division	5-0

Although Ipswich Town were League Champions Bill Nicholson had been the first manager to work out how to combat effectively the Suffolk side, inflicting a 5-1 defeat at Portman Road in the FA Charity Shield at the beginning of the season. Spurs followed this up with a hammering in the League at White Hart Lane thanks to goals from Bobby Smith, Cliff Jones and a Jimmy Greaves hat-trick.

1963	West Bromwich Albion	A	First Division	4-4
1964	Nottingham Forest	A	First Division	2-1
1966	West Bromwich Albion	A	First Division	0-3
1967	Fulham	H	First Division	2-2
1969	Crystal Palace	H	First Division	2-0
1972	West Ham United	A	First Division	2-2
1973	Queens Park Rangers	H	First Division	0-0
1974	West Ham United	A	First Division	1-1
1975	Birmingham City	H	First Division	1-3
1977	Millwall	A	Second Division	3-1
1978	Queens Park Rangers	A	First Division	2-2
1979	Arsenal	A	First Division	0-1
1980	Southampton	H	First Division	4-4
1983	Arsenal	H	First Division	2-4

The previous Boxing Day clash between Spurs and Arsenal took place at White Hart Lane and saw the visitors emerge victorious. They had recently parted company with manager Terry Neill, with coach Don Howe stepping up to become caretaker-manager and later appointed to the post full-time. Among his early decisions was to pull Charlie Nicholas into a deeper position, a move that paid dividends in this game as Nicholas scored twice, Raphael Meade also grabbing two goals for Arsenal. Spurs' goals came from Graham Roberts and Steve Archibald, although Spurs' eyes were already being focused on the UEFA Cup, following their recent victory over Bayern Munich.

1984	West Ham United	H	First Division	2-2
1985	West Ham United	H	First Division	1-0
1986	West Ham United	H	First Division	4-0
1987	Southampton	A	First Division	1-2
1988	Luton Town	H	First Division	0-0
1989	Millwall	H	First Division	3-1
1990	Coventry City	A	First Division	0-2
1991	Nottingham Forest	H	First Division	1-2
1992	Norwich City	A	FA Premier League	0-0
1994	Norwich City	A	FA Premier League	2-0
1995	Southampton	A	FA Premier League	0-0
1996	Southampton	H	FA Premier League	3-1
1997	Aston Villa	A	FA Premier League	1-4

DECEMBER 27TH

1874 Willie Newbigging born in Larkhall, Strathclyde. Having begun his career with Lanark County Willie was signed by Spurs in 1896 and made ten appearances in the Southern League during the 1896-97 season, although he had more joy in front of goal in the various friendlies the team played that season. At the end of the season he was released and later played for Folkestone. He died on 16th October 1954.

1884	Enfield	H	Friendly	3-0
1886	Dreadnought	H	Friendly	6-0
1897	Ilkeston Town	H	Friendly	4-2
1898	Ilkeston Town	A	Friendly	1-0
1902	Southampton	H	Western League	0-0
1904	Portsmouth	H	Southern League	1-1
1913	Chelsea	H	First Division	1-2
1915	Croydon City	A	London Combination [1st competition]	0-0
1919	Barnsley	H	Second Division	4-0
1920	Newcastle United	H	First Division	2-0

The gates were locked over an hour before kick off with 54,500 inside the ground and mounted police preventing those unfortunate not to have gained admittance from breaking down the iron gates. Whilst the game was not a particularly good one from a purist's point of view, it was a triumph for Spurs' winger Jimmy Dimmock, who was mobbed at the end of the game by excited fans, having scored one goal and made the other for Bert Bliss. Indeed, his performance was generally reckoned to have been worthy of a cup final – four months later he would do just that!

1921	Bradford City	A	First Division	4-0
1924	Bolton Wanderers	A	First Division	0-3
1926	Manchester United	A	First Division	1-2
1930	Reading	A	Second Division	2-1
1932	Bradford Park Avenue	H	Second Division	2-0
1937	Bury	H	Second Division	1-3
1938	Burnley	H	Second Division	1-0
1941	Arsenal	H	London War League	1-2
1943	Fulham	A	Football League South	2-0
1947	Chesterfield	A	Second Division	1-3

On the same day Joe Kinnear was born in Dublin. After representing Watford and Hertfordshire schools as a youth, he joined St Albans City and was soon spotted by Spurs. He signed as an amateur at White Hart Lane in August 1963, upgrading to full professional in February 1965. After making his debut in April 1966 he got his real chance the following February, winning his first cap for Eire and then seeing regular full-back Phil Beal break his arm. That enabled Joe to establish himself in the side, retaining his place for the FA Cup final against Chelsea. Indeed, Joe's performances had been so solid that when Phil Beal recovered he could not dislodge Joe and another position had to be found for him. Joe suffered a broken leg in 1969 and saw Ray Evans threaten his place, but Joe later helped Spurs win the League Cup in 1971 and 1973 and the UEFA Cup in 1972, and was released to join Brighton in August 1975. When he retired as a player he moved on to coaching and management, and took over at Wimbledon as manager in January 1992. Whilst with Spurs he won 24 caps for Eire.

1948	Leicester City	H	Second Division	1-1
1949	Chesterfield	A	Second Division	1-1
1952	Middlesbrough	A	First Division	4-0

Forty-eight hours after handing out a 7-1 battering at White Hart Lane, Spurs journeyed to Ayresome Park and won thanks to goals from Sonny Walters, Les Bennett, Len Duquemin and an own goal.

1955	West Bromwich Albion	A	First Division	0-1
1965	Sheffield United	H	First Division	1-0
1966	West Bromwich Albion	H	First Division	0-0
1969	Ipswich Town	A	First Division	0-2
1971	West Ham United	H	First Division	0-1
1976	Arsenal	H	First Division	2-2
1977	Mansfield Town	H	Second Division	1-1
1980	Norwich City	A	First Division	2-2
1982	Arsenal	A	First Division	0-2
1983	Aston Villa	A	First Division	0-0
1986	Coventry City	A	First Division	3-4
1993	Norwich City	H	FA Premier League	1-3
1994	Crystal Palace	H	FA Premier League	0-0

DECEMBER 28TH

1895	Freemantle	H	Friendly	2-2
1897	Stockton	H	Friendly	3-0
1901	Queens Park Rangers	A	Southern League	3-0
1903	Southampton	H	Western League	1-0
1907	Northampton Town	A	Southern League	1-2
1908	Wolverhampton Wanderers	A	Second Division	0-1
1912	Sheffield Wednesday	A	First Division	1-2
1918	Fulham	A	London Combination	1-3
1926	Sheffield Wednesday	A	First Division	1-3
1929	Bradford Park Avenue	H	Second Division	1-1
1935	Bradford City	H	Second Division	4-0
1936	Blackburn Rovers	H	Second Division	5-1
1940	Clapton Orient	A	Football League South	7-0

Both Billy and Jimmy Sperrin scored for Spurs in this win; Spurs' other goals came from Jack Gibbons (three), Taffy O'Callaghan and George Ludford. The Sperrin brothers were both on Spurs' books prior to the Second World War and made their debuts in regional football, although the war effectively ruined both players' careers. Billy Sperrin later played for Brentford for six seasons.

1957	Newcastle United	H	First Division	3-3
1959	Leeds United	H	First Division	1-4
1963	West Bromwich Albion	H	First Division	0-2
1964	Nottingham Forest	H	First Division	4-0
1965	Sheffield United	A	First Division	3-1
1974	Coventry City	H	First Division	1-1
1982	Brighton & Hove Albion	H	First Division	2-0
1985	Chelsea	A	First Division	0-2
1987	West Ham United	H	First Division	2-1
1991	Norwich City	H	First Division	3-0
1992	Nottingham Forest	H	FA Premier League	2-1
1993	West Ham United	A	FA Premier League	3-1
1996	Newcastle United	A	FA Premier League	1-7

Newcastle handed out Spurs' biggest defeat since their 7-0 defeat at Liverpool in 1978 with a breathtaking display of attacking football. But for the heroics of Ian Walker in the Spurs goal, the final score might well have reached double figures, and Allan Neilsen's late strike in response was not any consolation at all. It was later claimed that the sight of Gerry Francis looking devastated at the final whistle was enough to prompt Newcastle manager Kevin Keegan to hand in his shock resignation, but this was later disproved.

| 1997 | Arsenal | H | FA Premier League | 1-1 |

DECEMBER 29TH

1894	Vampires	H	Friendly	4-1
1896	Northfleet	H	Friendly	4-0
1900	Newark	H	Friendly	3-0

1906	West Ham United	A	Southern League	2-4
1917	Chelsea	H-Highbury		
			London Combination	2-0
1923	Birmingham	H	First Division	1-1
1928	Oldham Athletic	A	Second Division	1-3
1934	Everton	A	First Division	2-5
1945	Leicester City	A	Football League South	0-4
1951	Newcastle United	H	First Division	2-1
1956	Bolton Wanderers	H	First Division	4-0

Manchester United were two points clear at the top of the table and had a game in hand, so a win for Spurs was vital if they were to keep in touch with the leaders. A fine first-half performance ensured this was the case, with goals from Terry Dyson, Bobby Smith and George Robb, but Spurs lost their way a little in the second half and had only Tommy Harmer's penalty conversion to show for their efforts.

1973	West Ham United	H	First Division	2-0
1979	Stoke City	H	First Division	1-0
1981	Sporting Lisbon	A	Friendly	2-3
1984	Sunderland	H	First Division	2-0

Since their 2-3 defeat at home to West Bromwich Albion on 3rd November, Spurs had been unbeaten and had taken over at the top of the table by virtue of their win at Norwich a week previously. Although Sunderland put up a spirited defence, goals from Glenn Hoddle and Garth Crooks ensured full points to Spurs and their continued presence at the top of the table.

| 1990 | Southampton | A | First Division | 0-3 |

DECEMBER 30TH

1893	Uxbridge	A	Friendly	0-1
1899	Millwall Athletic	H	Southern League	2-1
1905	Reading	H	Southern League	1-0
1911	Everton	H	First Division	0-1
1916	Watford	H-Highbury		
			London Combination	3-0
1922	Middlesbrough	A	First Division	0-2
1933	Sheffield United	H	First Division	4-1
1939	Watford	A	Football League South Group A	1-6
1944	Portsmouth	A	Football League South	0-0
1950	Charlton Athletic	H	First Division	1-0
1961	Chelsea	H	First Division	5-2
1967	Fulham	A	First Division	2-1
1972	Wolverhampton Wanderers	H	League Cup Semi-Final 2nd Leg	2-2 [aet]

Spurs booked a Wembley appearance against Norwich City in the final of the League Cup, but not before Wolves had almost overcome the odds and won at White Hart Lane. Spurs and Wolves had originally been due to meet in the League on this day, with the League Cup semi-final provisionally scheduled for the following Monday, but it was subsequently decided to play the League Cup semi-final on the Saturday and the League match later in the season. On the morning of the game Graeme Souness was sold to Middlesbrough for £30,000, but by three o'clock all thoughts were on the job at hand. It took Wolves only a minute to wipe out Spurs' one-goal advantage, Terry Naylor turning in an own goal, and goals from Martin Peters for Spurs and John Richards for Wolves ensured an extra half-hour to separate the two teams. Martin Chivers scored the goal that took the club to Wembley for the second time in three seasons.

1978	Everton	A	First Division	1-1
1989	Nottingham Forest	H	First Division	2-3
1994				

Barely five months after he arrived at Spurs, Ilie Dumitrescu was sent on loan to Seville of the Spanish League until the end of the season. Although Ilie had been an immediate hit with the fans, the arrival of Gerry Francis and change in formation had left him out in the cold and it was felt his career would be better served playing in Spain.

| 1995 | Blackburn Rovers | A | FA Premier League | 1-2 |

DECEMBER 31ST

| 1887 | St Martin's | H | Friendly | 3-0 |
| 1894 | | | | |

Jack Elkes born in Snedshill. After playing for a number of amateur clubs Jack became a professional with Birmingham and then moved to Southampton in 1922, impressing Spurs enough for them to pay £1,000 for his services in May 1923. During his six years at Spurs he was unlucky not to have won any international honours, although he did play in four trial games. Equally at home as an inside-forward or centre-half, he was allowed to leave the club in 1929 and subsequently joined Middlesbrough and later Watford before finishing his career in non-League circles. He died in Essex on 22nd January 1972.

1897	Swindon Town	A	Southern League	3-4
1904	Fulham	A	Southern League	0-1
1910	Sheffield Wednesday	A	First Division	1-2
1921	Preston North End	H	First Division	5-0

Spurs were to finish the season in second place in the First Division, the highest placing achieved to date by a London club. They also reached the FA Cup semi-finals, where they were beaten by Preston, the side Spurs had beaten at the same stage the previous year. For the League match, however, Spurs made home advantage count thanks to goals from Jimmy Seed, Charlie Wilson (two), Andy Thompson and Jimmy Dimmock.

1927	Birmingham	A	First Division	2-3
1932	Charlton Athletic	A	Second Division	3-0
1938	Coventry City	A	Second Division	0-4
1949	Cardiff City	H	Second Division	2-0
1955	Charlton Athletic	A	First Division	2-1
1960	Blackburn Rovers	H	First Division	5-2
1966	Newcastle United	H	First Division	4-0
1977	Blackburn Rovers	H	Second Division	4-0
1983	West Ham United	A	First Division	1-4
1988	Newcastle United	H	First Division	2-0
1994	Coventry City	A	FA Premier League	4-0

Spurs signed off the year with this convincing victory at Highfield Road. Coventry spent much of their time worrying about the threat posed by Jurgen Klinsmann, to such an extent that gaps were created that others were only too happy to exploit. After the gift of an own goal, strikes by Teddy Sheringham, Nick Barmby and Darren Anderton gave Spurs their biggest away win of the season.